THE
NEW TESTAMENT

The New King James Version

THOMAS NELSON PUBLISHERS
Nashville

Reasons To Believe created the helps that are part of this book. The editor for these pages is Hugh Ross. Contributing editors are Ray Albrektson, Janet Kobobel, Kathy Ross, Alan Scholes, and Gary Stanley.

Reasons To Believe, located in Pasadena, California, is an international, interdenominational ministry established to communicate the uniquely factual basis for belief in the Bible as the wholly true Word of God and for personal faith in Jesus Christ.

Contents

Books of the New Testament v

Introduction

    Should You Trust a Book That Claims to Be
        the "Word of God"? vii

    What's So Special About Christianity? ix

    How Can I Get the Most Out of My Bible? x

What Was the Christmas Star? 3

Is the Devil Real? 5

How Accurate Is the Bible's Forecast of Future Events? 43

Are Some Sins Unforgivable? 49

Did Jesus Ever Say He Was God? 58

Is the End Near? 69

Who Can Be Possessed by a Demon? 83

What if God Has Let Me Down? 89

If I Give Myself to God, Won't He Make My Life Miserable? 100

What Does It Mean to "Believe"? 123

Why Can't God Just Accept Me the Way I Am? 135

What Sin? What Judgment? 149

How Does Your Life Change When You Believe? 163

What Can a Person Who Has Never Read the Bible Know About God? .. 173

Can We Prove That God Is Personal and Caring? 185

Who Needs God? 204

Isn't "Just Believing" Too Simple? 207

Was There Death Before Adam Sinned? 210

Why Are So Many Different "Laws" Mentioned in Romans? 213

Why Does the Environment Have to Suffer and Decay? 215

Do We Have Any Choice? 217

Why Are Some People Called Blameless
    When They Obviously Aren't? 227

Will My Sins Keep Me from God? 232

Did Jesus Rise from the Dead? 243

What Is a Cult? 258

Am I Really Responsible for the Consequences of My Actions? 263

Don't Christians Actually Have Three Gods? 266

How Do You Get Rid of Bitterness? 270

Is Astrology a Reliable Way to Learn Who I Am and
    What the Future Holds?..278
Do I Have to Take Christianity on Blind Faith? 284
What Does God Have Against Women?..289
What's So Amazing About Grace?..294
Can't a Person Just Pick Out the Best from Each Religion?..........296
But Who Created God? 298
Has God Changed His Mind About How He Relates to Us?.........302
What Is Jesus Like?...305
Why Does God Allow Evil and Suffering?...................................315
What if I've Tried Religion, and It Doesn't Work for Me? 321
Can You *Know* What Your Eternal Destiny Will Be?...................335
Why Doesn't Revelation Reveal? 339
What in the World Is God Up To? 343
What's So Terrible About the End-Times?...................................346
How Can I Get to Heaven? 362
What Do These Biblical Terms Mean?...363
About the New King James Version 367

Books of the New Testament

Matthew...1
Mark 45
Luke 75
John 122
Acts 157
Romans...202
1 Corinthians...226
2 Corinthians...246
Galatians...257
Ephesians..264
Philippians...272
Colossians 276
1 Thessalonians 280
2 Thessalonians 285
1 Timothy 287
2 Timothy 292
Titus...297
Philemon 300
Hebrews..301
James..318
1 Peter...323
2 Peter...327
1 John..330
2 John..336
3 John..336
Jude..337
Revelation 338

Should You Trust a Book That Claims to Be the "Word of God"?

Just because a book claims divine authority does not make it so. A handful of sacred writings, including the Bible, claim divine authorship. But each of these books presents a very different view of reality (see "Can't a Person Just Pick Out the Best from Each Religion?" page 296). They cannot all be right.

Before we can confidently claim something is true "because it's in the Bible," we must confirm that whatever is in the Bible is there because it is true.

The label "Word of God" raises certain expectations in any reader who takes the claim seriously. What would God's Word look like? What characteristics would separate it from the writings of fallible humans? Are there any ways to test the validity of such a label?

We might begin by asking if the Bible exhibits any supernatural qualities. The average Bible does not glow in the dark or defy gravity. So it seems that any reportedly divine qualities would have to reside in the words and thoughts of the Bible rather than in its paper, ink, and glue.

Surely a book of divine origin would never contradict itself or anything else that is known to be true. Such a book would predict future events and scientific discoveries with 100 percent accuracy. And since its author is God, the message it contains should have a profound influence on its readers.

These are just the sorts of expectations the Bible welcomes.

■ **The Bible has amazing internal agreement amidst great diversity.** The Bible addresses dozens of controversial topics while maintaining such consistency, harmony, and continuity that it is thought of as a single story of God's restoration of humanity. Yet the Bible was written over 1,500 years of diverse history by nearly forty human writers from various backgrounds and countries. It is not reasonable to expect this kind of unity apart from divine intervention.

■ **The Bible is an excellent history book.** While historical accuracy does not "prove" the Bible's spiritual authority, it does enhance its credibility in nonhistoric areas. The spiritual truths of the Bible are often played out within historical events. For example, Jesus' claim that He is God is strongly supported by the historical evidence that He actually rose from the dead (see "Did Jesus Rise from the Dead?" page 243). Dr. William F. Albright, a world-class archaeologist, wrote that every archaeological discovery establishes more firmly that the Bible is historically accurate.

■ **The Bible accurately predicts future events and scientific discoveries.** The Bible is accurate not only in recording, but also in predicting events that later came true, even scientific discoveries. Here are just three examples:

1. More than eight hundred years before Jesus' crucifixion, the prophet Isaiah described it with such accuracy that it sounds like an eyewitness account (Isaiah 53).
2. The prophet Ezekiel described in detail the total destruction of the city of Tyre 250 years before Alexander the Great made it happen in 332 B.C. (Ezekiel 26).
3. The apostle Paul declared that time has a beginning. Astrophysicists announced their discovery of this fact in 1970 (2 Timothy 2; Titus 1).

The Bible has proven to be accurate in its predictions—just what one would expect from the Word of God. (For further discussion, see "How Accurate Is the Bible's Forecast of Future Events?" page 43.)

■ The Bible's message has profoundly influenced generations of its readers.

Untold millions throughout history have embraced the new life promised in the Bible and have attested to its reality. They often report inner peace, freedom from guilt, a higher purpose, and a new source of strength and direction for their lives.

Where the Bible has been honored, whole societies have prospered. Slavery was abolished in England through the efforts of men like William Wilberforce who found their motivation in the Bible. Some of the modern-day Maasai tribes of Kenya have ceased to banish their own people due to the biblical teachings they now embrace. And in America, most of the hospitals and universities founded during its first 150 years were formed in response to biblical mandates.

■ Is the Bible the Word of God?

Those who take the question of the Bible's authority seriously, gather the available evidence, and examine the difficulties will discover they have more than enough compelling reasons to confidently embrace the Bible for what it claims to be— God's Word.

What's So Special About Christianity?

Christianity is distinct from philosophy, religion, and other worldviews not only in what it claims (see "Can't a Person Just Pick Out the Best from Each Religion?" page 296) but also in how it arrives at its conclusions. Christianity draws evenly from all four traditional ways of knowing—reason, personal experience, authority, and history, giving it firm footing in the marketplace of ideas.

■ **Reason.** Jesus challenged people to use their minds (Matthew 22:42–46). The apostle Peter wrote, "Always *be* ready to *give* . . . a reason for the hope that is in you" (1 Peter 3:15).

Today people want to know if a worldview squares with science. Scripture is consistent with the record of nature. For example, the Bible is unique among all holy books in describing how the universe was created (see "But Who Created God?" page 298).

■ **Personal experience.** Christianity at its heart is a personal relationship with Jesus. The Bible is filled with appeals to personal experience as a proof of Christ's presence within the believer (for example, 1 John 3:16–24).

■ **Authority and history.** Christianity's appeal to authority is closely linked to its appeal to history. The truths of the Bible are not divine revelations isolated from the realities and experiences of human history (as is the case in most religions). The Bible is not the work of one person in one lifetime but encompasses 1,500 years and nearly forty authors. The Bible's spiritual truths are woven together with earthly events, and history is frequently called on to supply evidences of God's divine intervention.

Christianity is grounded in a verifiable historical record. Nowhere is this more evident than in the resurrection of Jesus Christ (see "Did Jesus Rise from the Dead?" page 243). The historical evidence for Jesus' resurrection supports His claim to be the only way to God (John 14:6)—a claim made by no other religion.

If we limit our knowledge to reason and personal experience, then Christianity and philosophy are on the same footing. If we limit our knowledge to authority and personal experience, then Christianity could be viewed as just another religion. One authority cancels out the other, and the appeal to personal experience throws the whole matter into the foggy realm of subjectivism (see "Do I Have to Take Christianity on Blind Faith?" page 284).

However, if we hold that knowledge and truth are built on (at least) a fourfold structure of practical reason, experience, authority, and history, then Christianity occupies a uniquely secure and trustworthy place in the marketplace of beliefs.

How Can I Get the Most Out of My Bible?

Learning about the Bible is a bit like playing the guitar. It's easy to learn three chords and strum along with most songs, but it takes a lifetime to master the instrument. The Bible holds a wealth of answers to life's most probing questions. However, the maturity and wisdom to be gleaned from the Bible are not the product of a moment but the pursuit of a lifetime.

The New Testament is a library of twenty-seven books, written by nine authors over a fifty-year period beginning around A.D. 45. It has five historical books, followed by twenty-one letters, and one book of prophecy.

In the thirteenth century, chapter divisions were added; and three hundred years later verse notations were introduced. Taken together, the book's name, chapter number, and verse number make up the address of each passage. For example:

(book)   (chapter)   (verse)

John 3:16

■ Where do I begin?

1. Explore major sections of the Bible at one sitting. Few things are as confusing or frustrating as reading bits and pieces of a story. Catching the context is important to understanding a portion of Scripture.

Many New Testament books are less than a dozen pages long. Even the lengthy books are divided into readable sections. So before digging into a single passage, try to discern its overall flow by reading at least the surrounding chapters.

2. Read purposefully and expectantly. Take notes, write out questions that come to mind, and underline verses that hold special meaning to you. In other words, engage your mind and heart as you read. The Bible promises patience, comfort, and hope to those who do (Romans 15:4).

3. Look for the general principles revealed in the action and advice of the various books. The accounts and letters of the Bible are not there primarily for our entertainment or as information concerning bygone days. The Bible was given for our instruction so that we can prosper in our relationship with God and our fellow human beings.

The Bible offers the rare opportunity of talking to the divine Author about what you're reading. Prayer (talking to God) is a profitable way to begin, continue, and close your study time in the Bible.

4. Read the Bible aloud. It may surprise you to learn that the Bible was written for the ear rather than the eye. When it was first written, few

folks had personal copies of the Bible so most heard rather than read it. You will hear things you might never see!

5. Be cautious in forming opinions about the various teachings of the Bible. God did not collect all of His instructions on any given topic in a single place. The best way to avoid a lopsided view of the Bible is to collect all of the teaching on a given subject before drawing your conclusions. Remember, the best commentary on a biblical passage is another biblical passage.

6. Give preference to the ordinary sense of a word or phrase when reading the Bible. The Bible's stories are not myths or fables but historic accounts, and the Bible seldom makes use of allegory.

However, Jesus often spoke in parables (Matthew 13:3). Luke was fond of poetry (Luke 1:46-55). Paul sometimes employed irony to drive home his point (1 Corinthians 4:10). John used idioms, such as being "under the fig tree," which probably refers to Nathanael's prayer time (John 1:48). And much of the Book of Revelation is cloaked in imagery and symbolism. About the only kind of literature you will not find in the Bible is fiction.

7. Start with a simple book and build a basic understanding of major events and doctrines before tackling the more challenging books. The Gospel of John has been a favorite starting place for those new to the Bible or to faith in Christ. In this gospel you are introduced to the Son of God in a simple yet compelling fashion. Another book that especially rewards first-time readers is 2 Timothy. In this letter, you can look over Paul's shoulder in the weeks before his death as he encourages Timothy to live out his Christian walk.

8. Check out some of the basic aids to Bible study. A small dictionary defining terms is located at the back of this New Testament. Also, a handful of books can greatly enhance your understanding of the Bible.

Concordances list all of the verses in the Bible according to key words so that you can find passages addressing similar subjects or a particular verse you only partially remember.

Bible dictionaries not only define and explain biblical words but also give a brief history of the people and places encountered.

Commentaries seek to clarify the meaning and intent of each major passage by pointing out common themes, explaining key words, and drawing out principles.

■ Special instructions for the Gospels and Acts

Knowing the purpose of each book can give you a running start. "The Gospels" refers to the first four books of the New Testament. They were written by Jesus' followers and contain the "good news" (that's what *gospel* means) about the Messiah. Matthew draws on His Jewish background and concentrates on Jesus' teachings. Mark addresses a secular audience and offers a *Reader's Digest* version of Jesus' life. Luke's gospel is the most literary of the four and highlights stories of special interest. John portrays Jesus with broad, simple strokes of the pen and focuses on Jesus' deity and His final instructions to His disciples. Acts is a continuation of Luke's gospel and recounts the history of the first-century church.

■ Special instructions for the letters

The twenty-one letters of the New Testament are written to various churches or Christian leaders. They can sometimes read like a telephone conversation in which you hear only one person's part of the discussion. Watch for clues concerning the specific situation that prompted each letter to be written. These are real letters addressed to real people. Nearly all of them follow the same two-part pattern: The writer usually first develops a theological foundation (the "why") and then explains the practical application to his readers (the "how").

■ Special instructions for Revelation

John's Revelation is the only prophetic book in the New Testament (however, several other books do include prophecies). Revelation 1:19 gives the outline for the book—it's about the past, present, and future (see "Why Doesn't Revelation Reveal?" page 339).

Above everything else, remember that the Bible is also addressed to you, and it never goes out of date. It is "profitable for doctrine, for reproof, for correction, for instruction in righteousness, that the man [or woman] of God may be complete, thoroughly equipped for every good work" (2 Timothy 3:16, 17).

THE
NEW TESTAMENT

of

OUR LORD AND SAVIOR
JESUS CHRIST

THE GOSPEL ACCORDING TO
MATTHEW

THE book of the genealogy of Jesus Christ, the Son of David, the Son of Abraham:

2 Abraham begot Isaac, Isaac begot Jacob, and Jacob begot Judah and his brothers.

3 Judah begot Perez and Zerah by Tamar, Perez begot Hezron, and Hezron begot Ram.

4 Ram begot Amminadab, Amminadab begot Nahshon, and Nahshon begot Salmon.

5 Salmon begot Boaz by Rahab, Boaz begot Obed by Ruth, Obed begot Jesse,

6 and Jesse begot David the king.

David the king begot Solomon by her *who had been the wife of Uriah.*

7 Solomon begot Rehoboam, Rehoboam begot Abijah, and Abijah begot Asa.

8 Asa begot Jehoshaphat, Jehoshaphat begot Joram, and Joram begot Uzziah.

9 Uzziah begot Jotham, Jotham begot Ahaz, and Ahaz begot Hezekiah.

10 Hezekiah begot Manasseh, Manasseh begot Amon, and Amon begot Josiah.

11 Josiah begot Jeconiah and his brothers about the time they were carried away to Babylon.

12 And after they were brought to Babylon, Jeconiah begot Shealtiel, and Shealtiel begot Zerubbabel.

13 Zerubbabel begot Abiud, Abiud begot Eliakim, and Eliakim begot Azor.

14 Azor begot Zadok, Zadok begot Achim, and Achim begot Eliud.

15 Eliud begot Eleazar, Eleazar begot Matthan, and Matthan begot Jacob.

16 And Jacob begot Joseph the husband of Mary, of whom was born Jesus who is called Christ.

17 So all the generations from Abraham to David *are* fourteen generations, from David until the captivity in Babylon *are* fourteen generations, and from the captivity in Babylon until the Christ *are* fourteen generations.

18 Now the birth of Jesus Christ was as follows: After His mother Mary was betrothed to Joseph, before they came together, she was found with child of the Holy Spirit.

19 Then Joseph her husband, being a just *man,* and not wanting to make her a public example, was minded to put her away secretly.

20 But while he thought about these things, behold, an angel of the Lord appeared to him in a dream, saying, "Joseph, son of David, do not be afraid to take to you Mary your wife, for that which is conceived in her is of the Holy Spirit.

21 "And she will bring forth a Son, and you shall call His name JESUS, for He will save His people from their sins."

22 Now all this was done that it might be fulfilled which was spoken by the Lord through the prophet, saying:

23 *"Behold, a virgin shall be with child, and bear a Son, and they shall call His name Immanuel,"* which is translated, "God with us."

24 Then Joseph, being aroused from sleep, did as the angel of the Lord commanded him and took to him his wife,

25 and did not know her till she had brought forth her firstborn Son. And he called His name JESUS.

2 Now after Jesus was born in Bethlehem of Judea in the days of Herod the king, behold, wise men from the East came to Jerusalem,

2 saying, "Where is He who has been born King of the Jews? For

The Flight into Egypt

we have seen His star in the East and have come to worship Him."

3 When Herod the king heard *these things*, he was troubled, and all Jerusalem with him.

4 And when he had gathered all the chief priests and scribes of the people together, he inquired of them where the Christ was to be born.

5 So they said to him, "In Bethlehem of Judea, for thus it is written by the prophet:

6 'But you, Bethlehem, in the
   land of Judah,
  Are not the least among the
   rulers of Judah;
  For out of you shall come a
   Ruler
  Who will shepherd My people
   Israel.'"

7 Then Herod, when he had secretly called the wise men, determined from them what time the star appeared.

8 And he sent them to Bethlehem and said, "Go and search diligently for the young Child, and when you have found *Him*, bring back word to me, that I may come and worship Him also."

9 When they heard the king, they departed; and behold, the star which they had seen in the East went before them, till it came and stood over where the young Child was.

10 When they saw the star, they rejoiced with exceedingly great joy.

11 And when they had come into the house, they saw the young Child with Mary His mother, and fell down and worshiped Him. And when they had opened their treasures, they presented gifts to Him: gold, frankincense, and myrrh.

12 Then, being divinely warned in a dream that they should not return to Herod, they departed for their own country another way.

13 Now when they had departed, behold, an angel of the Lord appeared to Joseph in a dream, saying, "Arise, take the young Child and His mother, flee to Egypt, and stay there until I bring you word; for Herod will seek the young Child to destroy Him."

14 When he arose, he took the young Child and His mother by night and departed for Egypt,

15 and was there until the death of Herod, that it might be fulfilled which was spoken by the Lord through the prophet, saying, *"Out of Egypt I called My Son."*

16 Then Herod, when he saw that he was deceived by the wise men, was exceedingly angry; and he sent forth and put to death all the male children who were in Bethlehem and in all its districts, from two years old and under, according to the time which he had determined from the wise men.

17 Then was fulfilled what was spoken by Jeremiah the prophet, saying:

18 *"A voice was heard in Ramah,
  Lamentation, weeping,
   and great mourning,
  Rachel weeping for her
   children,
  Refusing to be comforted,
   because they were no more."*

19 But when Herod was dead, behold, an angel of the Lord appeared in a dream to Joseph in Egypt,

20 saying, "Arise, take the young Child and His mother, and go to the land of Israel, for those who sought the young Child's life are dead."

21 Then he arose, took the young Child and His mother, and came into the land of Israel.

22 But when he heard that Archelaus was reigning over Judea instead of his father Herod, he was afraid to go there. And being

What Was the Christmas Star?

Although the word *star* is used in our English translation, in the original text, the word selected could have described a star, a planet, a comet, an asteroid, a meteor, or an exploding star (called a nova or supernova). The celestial object that guided the wise men may have been entirely supernatural, but let's consider the most likely natural possibilities

■ **Comet**—A comet could have been observed by the wise men. Like Halley's Comet as viewed in 1986, it might have been faint at first sighting, appearing to disappear as it moved toward the sun and then becoming more spectacular after it rounded the sun and returned on a path closer to earth. However, comets are fairly common, and no records mention a spectacular one during the appropriate time frame.

■ **Conjunction**—Two or more planets lining up in one part of the sky could occur briefly, then they could move apart and line up again a year or two later, which fits Matthew's writings. But planetary conjunctions of this type are common, and none were close enough during the time of Jesus' birth to be acknowledged as a single star.

■ **Recurring Nova**—When a star explodes, or becomes a nova, it usually dims permanently after the initial flare-up. But a tiny fraction of novæ have the capacity to undergo multiple explosions separated by months or years. This repeat occurrence seems necessary to fit Matthew's description of a star that appeared, disappeared, and then reappeared and disappeared sometime later. So the recurring nova is a distinct possibility that would match what Matthew wrote.

■ Were the wise men astrologers?

Some scholars believe the wise men who saw Christ's star were astrologers. The word translated "wise men" in the original Greek text is *magi.* That same word often refers to "scholars," "counselors," or "advisors," none of which necessarily would connect them with astrology.

"Wise man" in the English translation is also the word used to describe the Jewish prophet Daniel, who was not an astrologer. He lived five centuries before the Christmas star and experienced a vision that predicted the approximate date and approximate location for the coming of the Messiah (Daniel 9:24–26). Because of Daniel's prominence among Babylonian and Persian intellectuals, his successors knew about the vision. This may explain why the wise men of Matthew's gospel understood what the unusual star meant.

warned by God in a dream, he turned aside into the region of Galilee.

23 And he came and dwelt in a city called Nazareth, that it might be fulfilled which was spoken by the prophets, "He shall be called a Nazarene."

3 In those days John the Baptist came preaching in the wilderness of Judea,

2 and saying, "Repent, for the kingdom of heaven is at hand!"

3 For this is he who was spoken of by the prophet Isaiah, saying:

"The voice of one crying
in the wilderness:
'Prepare the way of the LORD,
Make His paths straight.' "

4 And John himself was clothed in camel's hair, with a leather belt around his waist; and his food was locusts and wild honey.

5 Then Jerusalem, all Judea, and all the region around the Jordan went out to him

6 and were baptized by him in the Jordan, confessing their sins.

7 But when he saw many of the Pharisees and Sadducees coming to his baptism, he said to them, "Brood of vipers! Who has warned you to flee from the wrath to come?

8 "Therefore bear fruits worthy of repentance,

9 "and do not think to say to yourselves, 'We have Abraham as *our* father.' For I say to you that God is able to raise up children to Abraham from these stones.

10 "And even now the ax is laid to the root of the trees. Therefore every tree which does not bear good fruit is cut down and thrown into the fire.

11 "I indeed baptize you with water unto repentance, but He who is coming after me is mightier than I, whose sandals I am not worthy to carry. He will baptize you with the Holy Spirit and fire.

12 "His winnowing fan *is* in His hand, and He will thoroughly purge His threshing floor, and gather His wheat into the barn; but He will burn up the chaff with unquenchable fire."

13 Then Jesus came from Galilee to John at the Jordan to be baptized by him.

14 And John *tried to* prevent Him, saying, "I have need to be baptized by You, and are You coming to me?"

15 But Jesus answered and said to him, "Permit *it to be so* now, for thus it is fitting for us to fulfill all righteousness." Then he allowed Him.

16 Then Jesus, when He had been baptized, came up immediately from the water; and behold, the heavens were opened to Him, and He saw the Spirit of God descending like a dove and alighting upon Him.

17 And suddenly a voice *came* from heaven, saying, "This is My beloved Son, in whom I am well pleased."

4 Then Jesus was led up by the Spirit into the wilderness to be tempted by the devil.

2 And when He had fasted forty days and forty nights, afterward He was hungry.

3 Now when the tempter came to Him, he said, "If You are the Son of God, command that these stones become bread."

4 But He answered and said, "It is written, *'Man shall not live by bread alone, but by every word that proceeds from the mouth of God.' "*

5 Then the devil took Him up into the holy city, set Him on the pinnacle of the temple,

6 and said to Him, "If You are the Son of God, throw Yourself down. For it is written:

4

Is the Devil Real?

Most people believe God exists, but many have difficulty with the idea of the Devil, or Satan. How are we to understand stories in the Bible like Matthew 4 in which Jesus is tempted by the Devil? Is this a tale, like a Greek or Roman myth? Is it a symbolic story representing all human temptation? Or could Jesus have met a real being called Satan?

The Bible portrays Satan as a real, personal being.

The caricature of the devil as a red imp with horns and a tail did not originate in the Bible. Intead, the Bible portrays Satan as an angelic being—the highest, most intelligent, and most beautiful of all God's creations (Ezekiel 28:12–15). Originally called Lucifer, he became proud and discontented and tried to overthrow God (Isaiah 14:12–14). In this fall into sin, Lucifer became Satan (which means "Adversary"), God's enemy.

Satan has retained much of his intelligence and power and can still appear as a beautiful "angel of light" (2 Corinthians 11:14). However, his true nature is revealed in his names. Jesus called him "the thief" (John 10:10) and the father of lies (John 8:44), and in Revelation he is identified as the accuser (Revelation 12:10).

Jesus had a real encounter with him.

For those who see Jesus as the perfect Son of God or even those who consider Him a prophet and great moral teacher, it's hard to discount His firsthand encounter with the Devil. He clearly accepted without question Satan's reality. How can His followers believe less?

Common questions about Satan.

Are there any limits to his power? Yes. Satan is a finite, created being. Even though he is more powerful and intelligent than humans, he does not know everything, cannot be everywhere at once, and his power is limited. Only God possesses unlimited knowledge and power.

Do we need to be afraid of the Devil? No, but we should have a healthy respect for any being as clever and powerful as Satan. Many have been drawn into his circle of influence. (See "Who Can Be Possessed by a Demon?" page 83). Our greatest protection is to place our lives in Christ's hands. Believers don't need to fear Satan because God protects all who trust Him and appeal to Him for help (Job 1:10).

'He shall give His angels charge
concerning you,'

and,

'In their hands they shall bear
you up,
Lest you dash your foot
against a stone.'"

7 Jesus said to him, "It is written again, *'You shall not tempt the LORD your God.'"*

8 Again, the devil took Him up on an exceedingly high mountain, and showed Him all the kingdoms of the world and their glory.

9 And he said to Him, "All these things I will give You if You will fall down and worship me."

10 Then Jesus said to him, "Away with you, Satan! For it is written, *'You shall worship the LORD your God, and Him only you shall serve.'"*

11 Then the devil left Him, and behold, angels came and ministered to Him.

12 Now when Jesus heard that John had been put in prison, He departed to Galilee.

13 And leaving Nazareth, He came and dwelt in Capernaum, which is by the sea, in the regions of Zebulun and Naphtali,

14 that it might be fulfilled which was spoken by Isaiah the prophet, saying:

15 "The land of Zebulun and the
land of Naphtali,
The way of the sea, beyond the
Jordan,
Galilee of the Gentiles:

16 The people who sat in darkness
saw a great light,
And upon those who sat in the
region and shadow of death
Light has dawned."

17 From that time Jesus began to preach and to say, "Repent, for the kingdom of heaven is at hand."

18 Now Jesus, walking by the Sea of Galilee, saw two brothers, Simon called Peter, and Andrew his brother, casting a net into the sea; for they were fishermen.

19 And He said to them, "Follow Me, and I will make you fishers of men."

20 Then they immediately left *their* nets and followed Him.

21 And going on from there, He saw two other brothers, James *the son* of Zebedee, and John his brother, in the boat with Zebedee their father, mending their nets. And He called them,

22 and immediately they left the boat and their father, and followed Him.

23 Now Jesus went about all Galilee, teaching in their synagogues, preaching the gospel of the kingdom, and healing all kinds of sickness and all kinds of disease among the people.

24 Then His fame went throughout all Syria; and they brought to Him all sick people who were afflicted with various diseases and torments, and those who were demon-possessed, epileptics, and paralytics; and He healed them.

25 And great multitudes followed Him—from Galilee, and *from* Decapolis, Jerusalem, Judea, and beyond the Jordan.

5 And seeing the multitudes, He went up on a mountain, and when He was seated His disciples came to Him.

2 Then He opened His mouth and taught them, saying:

3 "Blessed *are* the poor in spirit,
For theirs is the kingdom of
heaven.

4 Blessed *are* those who mourn,
For they shall be comforted.

5 Blessed *are* the meek,
For they shall inherit the
earth.

6 Blessed *are* those who hunger
and thirst for righteousness,
For they shall be filled.

7 Blessed *are* the merciful,
  For they shall obtain mercy.
8 Blessed *are* the pure in heart,
  For they shall see God.
9 Blessed *are* the peacemakers,
  For they shall be called sons
    of God.
10 Blessed are those who are
    persecuted for righ-
    teousness' sake,
  For theirs is the kingdom of
    heaven.

11 "Blessed are you when they revile and persecute you, and say all
kinds of evil against you falsely for
My sake.
12 "Rejoice and be exceedingly
glad, for great *is* your reward in
heaven, for so they persecuted the
prophets who were before you.
13 "You are the salt of the earth;
but if the salt loses its flavor, how
shall it be seasoned? It is then good
for nothing but to be thrown out
and trampled under foot by men.
14 "You are the light of the world.
A city that is set on a hill cannot
be hidden.
15 "Nor do they light a lamp and
put it under a basket, but on a
lampstand, and it gives light to all
who *are* in the house.
16 "Let your light so shine before
men, that they may see your good
works and glorify your Father in
heaven.
17 "Do not think that I came to
destroy the Law or the Prophets. I
did not come to destroy but to
fulfill.
18 "For assuredly, I say to you, till
heaven and earth pass away, one
jot or one tittle will by no means
pass from the law uill all is fulfilled.
19 "Whoever therefore breaks one
of the least of these commandments, and teaches men so, shall
be called least in the kingdom of
heaven; but whoever does and
teaches *them*, he shall be called
great in the kingdom of heaven.
20 "For I say to you, that unless

your righteousness exceeds *the
righteousness* of the scribes and
Pharisees, you will by no means
enter the kingdom of heaven.
21 "You have heard that it was
said to those of old, *'You shall not
murder,'* and whoever murders
will be in danger of the judgment.
22 "But I say to you that whoever
is angry with his brother without a
cause shall be in danger of the
judgment. And whoever says to his
brother, 'Raca!' shall be in danger
of the council. But whoever says,
'You fool!' shall be in danger of hell
fire.
23 "Therefore if you bring your gift
to the altar, and there remember
that your brother has something
against you,
24 "leave your gift there before the
altar, and go your way. First be
reconciled to your brother, and
then come and offer your gift.
25 "Agree with your adversary
quickly, while you are on the way
with him, lest your adversary deliver you to the judge, the judge
hand you over to the officer, and
you be thrown into prison.
26 "Assuredly, I say to you, you
will by no means get out of there
till you have paid the last penny.
27 "You have heard that it was
said to those of old, *'You shall not
commit adultery.'*
28 "But I say to you that whoever
looks at a woman to lust for her
has already committed adultery
with her in his heart.
29 "And if your right eye causes
you to sin, pluck it out and cast *it*
from you; for it is more profitable
for you that one of your members
perish, than for your whole body
to be cast into hell.
30 "And if your right hand causes
you to sin, cut it off and cast *it*
from you; for it is more profitable
for you that one of your members
perish, than for your whole body
to be cast into hell.
31 "Furthermore it has been said,

'Whoever divorces his wife, let him give her a certificate of divorce.'

32 "But I say to you that whoever divorces his wife for any reason except sexual immorality causes her to commit adultery; and whoever marries a woman who is divorced commits adultery.

33 "Again you have heard that it was said to those of old, 'You shall not swear falsely, but shall perform your oaths to the Lord.'

34 "But I say to you, do not swear at all: neither by heaven, for it is God's throne;

35 "nor by the earth, for it is His footstool; nor by Jerusalem, for it is the city of the great King.

36 "Nor shall you swear by your head, because you cannot make one hair white or black.

37 "But let your 'Yes' be 'Yes,' and your 'No,' 'No.' For whatever is more than these is from the evil one.

38 "You have heard that it was said, *'An eye for an eye and a tooth for a tooth.'*

39 "But I tell you not to resist an evil person. But whoever slaps you on your right cheek, turn the other to him also.

40 "If anyone wants to sue you and take away your tunic, let him have *your* cloak also.

41 "And whoever compels you to go one mile, go with him two.

42 "Give to him who asks you, and from him who wants to borrow from you do not turn away.

43 "You have heard that it was said, 'You shall love your neighbor and hate your enemy.'

44 "But I say to you, love your enemies, bless those who curse you, do good to those who hate you, and pray for those who spitefully use you and persecute you,

45 "that you may be sons of your Father in heaven; for He makes His sun rise on the evil and on the good, and sends rain on the just and on the unjust.

46 "For if you love those who love you, what reward have you? Do not even the tax collectors do the same?

47 "And if you greet your brethren only, what do you do more *than others?* Do not even the tax collectors do so?

48 "Therefore you shall be perfect, just as your Father in heaven is perfect.

6 "Take heed that you do not do your charitable deeds before men, to be seen by them. Otherwise you have no reward from your Father in heaven.

2 "Therefore, when you do a charitable deed, do not sound a trumpet before you as the hypocrites do in the synagogues and in the streets, that they may have glory from men. Assuredly, I say to you, they have their reward.

3 "But when you do a charitable deed, do not let your left hand know what your right hand is doing,

4 "that your charitable deed may be in secret; and your Father who sees in secret will Himself reward you openly.

5 "And when you pray, you shall not be like the hypocrites. For they love to pray standing in the synagogues and on the corners of the streets, that they may be seen by men. Assuredly, I say to you, they have their reward.

6 "But you, when you pray, go into your room, and when you have shut your door, pray to your Father who *is* in the secret *place;* and your Father who sees in secret will reward you openly.

7 "But when you pray, do not use vain repetitions as the heathen *do.* For they think that they will be heard for their many words.

8 "Therefore do not be like them. For your Father knows the things you have need of before you ask Him.

9 "In this manner, therefore, pray:

Our Father in heaven,
Hallowed be Your name.
10 Your kingdom come.
Your will be done
On earth as *it is* in heaven.
11 Give us this day our daily
bread.
12 And forgive us our debts,
As we forgive our debtors.
13 And do not lead us into
temptation,
But deliver us from the evil
one.
For Yours is the kingdom and
the power and the glory
forever. Amen.

14 "For if you forgive men their
trespasses, your heavenly Father
will also forgive you.
15 "But if you do not forgive men
their trespasses, neither will your
Father forgive your trespasses.
16 "Moreover, when you fast, do
not be like the hypocrites, with a
sad countenance. For they disfig-
ure their faces that they may appear to men to be fasting. Assuredly, I say to you, they have
their reward.
17 "But you, when you fast, anoint
your head and wash your face,
18 "so that you do not appear to
men to be fasting, but to your Father who *is* in the secret *place;* and
your Father who sees in secret will
reward you openly.
19 "Do not lay up for yourselves
treasures on earth, where moth
and rust destroy and where thieves
break in and steal;
20 "but lay up for yourselves treasures in heaven, where neither
moth nor rust destroys and where
thieves do not break in and steal.
21 "For where your treasure is,
there your heart will be also.
22 "The lamp of the body is the
eye. If therefore your eye is good,
your whole body will be full of
light.
23 "But if your eye is bad, your

whole body will be full of darkness.
If therefore the light that is in you
is darkness, how great *is* that darkness!
24 "No one can serve two masters;
for either he will hate the one and
love the other, or else he will be
loyal to the one and despise the
other. You cannot serve God and
mammon.
25 "Therefore I say to you, do not
worry about your life, what you
will eat or what you will drink; nor
about your body, what you will put
on. Is not life more than food and
the body more than clothing?
26 "Look at the birds of the air, for
they neither sow nor reap nor
gather into barns; yet your heavenly Father feeds them. Are you
not of more value than they?
27 "Which of you by worrying can
add one cubit to his stature?
28 "So why do you worry about
clothing? Consider the lilies of the
field, how they grow: they neither
toil nor spin;
29 "and yet I say to you that even
Solomon in all his glory was not
arrayed like one of these.
30 "Now if God so clothes the
grass of the field, which today is,
and tomorrow is thrown into the
oven, *will He* not much more
clothe you, O you of little faith?
31 "Therefore do not worry, saying, 'What shall we eat?' or 'What
shall we drink?' or 'What shall we
wear?'
32 "For after all these things the
Gentiles seek. For your heavenly
Father knows that you need all
these things.
33 "But seek first the kingdom of
God and His righteousness, and all
these things shall be added to you.
34 "Therefore do not worry about
tomorrow, for tomorrow will
worry about its own things. Sufficient for the day *is* its own trouble.

7 "Judge not, that you be not
judged.
2 "For with what judgment you

judge, you will be judged; and with the *same* measure you use, it will be measured back to you.

3 "And why do you look at the speck in your brother's eye, but do not consider the plank in your own eye?

4 "Or how can you say to your brother, 'Let me remove the speck out of your eye'; and look, a plank *is* in your own eye?

5 "Hypocrite! First remove the plank from your own eye, and then you will see clearly to remove the speck out of your brother's eye.

6 "Do not give what is holy to the dogs; nor cast your pearls before swine, lest they trample them under their feet, and turn and tear you in pieces.

7 "Ask, and it will be given to you; seek, and you will find; knock, and it will be opened to you.

8 "For everyone who asks receives, and he who seeks finds, and to him who knocks it will be opened.

9 "Or what man is there among you who, if his son asks for bread, will give him a stone?

10 "Or if he asks for a fish, will he give him a serpent?

11 "If you then, being evil, know how to give good gifts to your children, how much more will your Father who is in heaven give good things to those who ask Him!

12 "Therefore, whatever you want men to do to you, do also to them, for this is the Law and the Prophets.

13 "Enter by the narrow gate; for wide *is* the gate and broad *is* the way that leads to destruction, and there are many who go in by it.

14 "Because narrow *is* the gate and difficult *is* the way which leads to life, and there are few who find it.

15 "Beware of false prophets, who come to you in sheep's clothing, but inwardly they are ravenous wolves.

16 "You will know them by their fruits. Do men gather grapes from thornbushes or figs from thistles?

17 "Even so, every good tree bears good fruit, but a bad tree bears bad fruit.

18 "A good tree cannot bear bad fruit, nor *can* a bad tree bear good fruit.

19 "Every tree that does not bear good fruit is cut down and thrown into the fire.

20 "Therefore by their fruits you will know them.

21 "Not everyone who says to Me, 'Lord, Lord,' shall enter the kingdom of heaven, but he who does the will of My Father in heaven.

22 "Many will say to Me in that day, 'Lord, Lord, have we not prophesied in Your name, cast out demons in Your name, and done many wonders in Your name?'

23 "And then I will declare to them, 'I never knew you; depart from Me, you who practice lawlessness!'

24 "Therefore whoever hears these sayings of Mine, and does them, I will liken him to a wise man who built his house on the rock:

25 "and the rain descended, the floods came, and the winds blew and beat on that house; and it did not fall, for it was founded on the rock.

26 "Now everyone who hears these sayings of Mine, and does not do them, will be like a foolish man who built his house on the sand:

27 "and the rain descended, the floods came, and the winds blew and beat on that house; and it fell. And great was its fall."

28 And so it was, when Jesus had ended these sayings, that the people were astonished at His teaching,

29 for He taught them as one having authority, and not as the scribes.

8 When He had come down from the mountain, great multitudes followed Him.

10

2 And behold, a leper came and worshiped Him, saying, "Lord, if You are willing, You can make me clean."

3 Then Jesus put out *His* hand and touched him, saying, "I am willing; be cleansed." And immediately his leprosy was cleansed.

4 And Jesus said to him, "See that you tell no one; but go your way, show yourself to the priest, and offer the gift that Moses commanded, as a testimony to them."

5 Now when Jesus had entered Capernaum, a centurion came to Him, pleading with Him,

6 saying, "Lord, my servant is lying at home paralyzed, dreadfully tormented."

7 And Jesus said to him, "I will come and heal him."

8 The centurion answered and said, "Lord, I am not worthy that You should come under my roof. But only speak a word, and my servant will be healed.

9 "For I also am a man under authority, having soldiers under me. And I say to this *one*, 'Go,' and he goes; and to another, 'Come,' and he comes; and to my servant, 'Do this,' and he does *it*."

10 When Jesus heard *it*, He marveled, and said to those who followed, "Assuredly, I say to you, I have not found such great faith, not even in Israel!

11 "And I say to you that many will come from east and west, and sit down with Abraham, Isaac, and Jacob in the kingdom of heaven.

12 "But the sons of the kingdom will be cast out into outer darkness. There will be weeping and gnashing of teeth."

13 Then Jesus said to the centurion, "Go your way; and as you have believed, *so* let it be done for you." And his servant was healed that same hour.

14 Now when Jesus had come into Peter's house, He saw his wife's mother lying sick with a fever.

15 And He touched her hand, and the fever left her. Then she arose and served them.

16 When evening had come, they brought to Him many who were demon-possessed. And He cast out the spirits with a word, and healed all who were sick,

17 that it might be fulfilled which was spoken by Isaiah the prophet, saying:

> *"He Himself took our infirmities*
> *And bore our sicknesses."*

18 Now when Jesus saw great multitudes about Him, He gave a command to depart to the other side.

19 Then a certain scribe came and said to Him, "Teacher, I will follow You wherever You go."

20 And Jesus said to him, "Foxes have holes and birds of the air *have* nests, but the Son of Man has nowhere to lay *His* head."

21 Then another of His disciples said to Him, "Lord, let me first go and bury my father."

22 But Jesus said to him, "Follow Me, and let the dead bury their own dead."

23 Now when He got into a boat, His disciples followed Him.

24 And suddenly a great tempest arose on the sea, so that the boat was covered with the waves. But He was asleep.

25 Then His disciples came to *Him* and awoke Him, saying, "Lord, save us! We are perishing!"

26 But He said to them, "Why are you fearful, O you of little faith?" Then He arose and rebuked the winds and the sea. And there was a great calm.

27 And the men marveled, saying, "Who can this be, that even the winds and the sea obey Him?"

28 When He had come to the other side, to the country of the Gergesenes, there met Him two demon-possessed *men*, coming out of the tombs, exceedingly fierce, so that no one could pass that way.

11

suddenly they cried out, "What have we to do with Jesus, You Son of God? Have You come here to torment us before the time?"

30 Now a good way off from them there was a herd of many swine feeding.

31 So the demons begged Him, saying, "If You cast us out, permit us to go away into the herd of swine."

32 And He said to them, "Go." So when they had come out, they went into the herd of swine. And suddenly the whole herd of swine ran violently down the steep place into the sea, and perished in the water.

33 Then those who kept *them* fled; and they went away into the city and told everything, including what *had happened* to the demon-possessed *men*.

34 And behold, the whole city came out to meet Jesus. And when they saw Him, they begged *Him* to depart from their region.

9 So He got into a boat, crossed over, and came to His own city.

2 And behold, they brought to Him a paralytic lying on a bed. And Jesus, seeing their faith, said to the paralytic, "Son, be of good cheer; your sins are forgiven you."

3 And at once some of the scribes said within themselves, "This *Man* blasphemes!"

4 But Jesus, knowing their thoughts, said, "Why do you think evil in your hearts?

5 "For which is easier, to say, 'Your sins are forgiven you,' or to say, 'Arise and walk'?

6 "But that you may know that the Son of Man has power on earth to forgive sins"—then He said to the paralytic, "Arise, take up your bed, and go to your house."

7 And he arose and departed to his house.

8 Now when the multitudes saw *it*, they marveled and glorified

God, who had given such power to men.

9 Then as Jesus passed on from there, He saw a man named Matthew sitting at the tax office. And He said to him, "Follow Me." And he arose and followed Him.

10 And so it was, as Jesus sat at the table in the house, *that* behold, many tax collectors and sinners came and sat down with Him and His disciples.

11 And when the Pharisees saw *it*, they said to His disciples, "Why does your Teacher eat with tax collectors and sinners?"

12 But when Jesus heard *that*, He said to them, "Those who are well have no need of a physician, but those who are sick.

13 "But go and learn what *this* means: *'I desire mercy and not sacrifice.'* For I did not come to call the righteous, but sinners, to repentance."

14 Then the disciples of John came to Him, saying, "Why do we and the Pharisees fast often, but Your disciples do not fast?"

15 And Jesus said to them, "Can the friends of the bridegroom mourn as long as the bridegroom is with them? But the days will come when the bridegroom will be taken away from them, and then they will fast.

16 "No one puts a piece of unshrunk cloth on an old garment; for the patch pulls away from the garment, and the tear is made worse.

17 "Nor do *people* put new wine into old wineskins, or else the wineskins break, the wine is spilled, and the wineskins are ruined. But they put new wine into new wineskins, and both are preserved."

18 While He spoke these things to them, behold, a ruler came and worshiped Him, saying, "My daughter has just died, but come

and lay Your hand on her and she will live."

19 So Jesus arose and followed him, and so *did* His disciples.

20 And suddenly, a woman who had a flow of blood for twelve years came from behind and touched the hem of His garment;

21 for she said to herself, "If only I may touch His garment, I shall be made well."

22 But Jesus turned around, and when He saw her He said, "Be of good cheer, daughter; your faith has made you well." And the woman was made well from that hour.

23 And when Jesus came into the ruler's house, and saw the flute players and the noisy crowd wailing,

24 He said to them, "Make room, for the girl is not dead, but sleeping." And they laughed Him to scorn.

25 But when the crowd was put outside, He went in and took her by the hand, and the girl arose.

26 And the report of this went out into all that land.

27 When Jesus departed from there, two blind men followed Him, crying out and saying, "Son of David, have mercy on us!"

28 And when He had come into the house, the blind men came to Him. And Jesus said to them, "Do you believe that I am able to do this?" They said to Him, "Yes, Lord."

29 Then He touched their eyes, saying, "According to your faith let it be to you."

30 And their eyes were opened. And Jesus sternly warned them, saying, "See *that* no one knows *it.*"

31 But when they had departed, they spread the news about Him in all that country.

32 As they went out, behold, they brought to Him a man, mute and demon-possessed.

33 And when the demon was cast out, the mute spoke. And the mul-titudes marveled, saying, "It was never seen like this in Israel!"

34 But the Pharisees said, "He casts out demons by the ruler of the demons."

35 And Jesus went about all the cities and villages, teaching in their synagogues, preaching the gospel of the kingdom, and healing every sickness and every disease among the people.

36 But when He saw the multitudes, He was moved with compassion for them, because they were weary and scattered, like sheep having no shepherd.

37 Then He said to His disciples, "The harvest truly *is* plentiful, but the laborers *are* few.

38 "Therefore pray the Lord of the harvest to send out laborers into His harvest."

10 And when He had called His twelve disciples to *Him,* He gave them power *over* unclean spirits, to cast them out, and to heal all kinds of sickness and all kinds of disease.

2 Now the names of the twelve apostles are these: first, Simon, who is called Peter, and Andrew his brother; James the *son* of Zebedee, and John his brother;

3 Philip and Bartholomew; Thomas and Matthew the tax collector; James the *son* of Alphaeus, and Lebbaeus, whose surname was Thaddaeus;

4 Simon the Canaanite, and Judas Iscariot, who also betrayed Him.

5 These twelve Jesus sent out and commanded them, saying: "Do not go into the way of the Gentiles, and do not enter a city of the Samaritans.

6 "But go rather to the lost sheep of the house of Israel.

7 "And as you go, preach, saying, 'The kingdom of heaven is at hand.'

8 "Heal the sick, cleanse the lepers, raise the dead, cast out de-

mons. Freely you have received, freely give.

9 "Provide neither gold nor silver nor copper in your moneybelts,

10 "nor bag for *your* journey, nor two tunics, nor sandals, nor staffs; for a worker is worthy of his food.

11 "Now whatever city or town you enter, inquire who in it is worthy, and stay there till you go out.

12 "And when you go into a household, greet it.

13 "If the household is worthy, let your peace come upon it. But if it is not worthy, let your peace return to you.

14 "And whoever will not receive you nor hear your words, when you depart from that house or city, shake off the dust from your feet.

15 "Assuredly, I say to you, it will be more tolerable for the land of Sodom and Gomorrah in the day of judgment than for that city!

16 "Behold, I send you out as sheep in the midst of wolves. Therefore be wise as serpents and harmless as doves.

17 "But beware of men, for they will deliver you up to councils and scourge you in their synagogues.

18 "And you will be brought before governors and kings for My sake, as a testimony to them and to the Gentiles.

19 "But when they deliver you up, do not worry about how or what you should speak. For it will be given to you in that hour what you should speak;

20 "for it is not you who speak, but the Spirit of your Father who speaks in you.

21 "Now brother will deliver up brother to death, and a father *his* child; and children will rise up against parents and cause them to be put to death.

22 "And you will be hated by all for My name's sake. But he who endures to the end will be saved.

23 "But when they persecute you in this city, flee to another. For

assuredly, I say to you, you will not have gone through the cities of Israel before the Son of Man comes.

24 "A disciple is not above *his* teacher, nor a servant above his master.

25 "It is enough for a disciple that he be like his teacher, and a servant like his master. If they have called the master of the house Beelzebub, how much more *will they call* those of his household!

26 "Therefore do not fear them. For there is nothing covered that will not be revealed, and hidden that will not be known.

27 "Whatever I tell you in the dark, speak in the light; and what you hear in the ear, preach on the housetops.

28 "And do not fear those who kill the body but cannot kill the soul. But rather fear Him who is able to destroy both soul and body in hell.

29 "Are not two sparrows sold for a copper coin? And not one of them falls to the ground apart from your Father's will.

30 "But the very hairs of your head are all numbered.

31 "Do not fear therefore; you are of more value than many sparrows.

32 "Therefore whoever confesses Me before men, him I will also confess before My Father who is in heaven.

33 "But whoever denies Me before men, him I will also deny before My Father who is in heaven.

34 "Do not think that I came to bring peace on earth. I did not come to bring peace but a sword.

35 "For I have come to *'set a man against his father, a daughter against her mother, and a daughter-in-law against her mother-in-law.'*

36 "And *'a man's foes will be those of his own household.'*

37 "He who loves father or mother more than Me is not worthy of Me.

14

And he who loves son or daughter more than Me is not worthy of Me.
38 "And he who does not take his cross and follow after Me is not worthy of Me.
39 "He who finds his life will lose it, and he who loses his life for My sake will find it.
40 "He who receives you receives Me, and he who receives Me receives Him who sent Me.
41 "He who receives a prophet in the name of a prophet shall receive a prophet's reward. And he who receives a righteous man in the name of a righteous man shall receive a righteous man's reward.
42 "And whoever gives one of these little ones only a cup of cold *water* in the name of a disciple, assuredly, I say to you, he shall by no means lose his reward."

11 Now it came to pass, when Jesus finished commanding His twelve disciples, that He departed from there to teach and to preach in their cities.
2 And when John had heard in prison about the works of Christ, he sent two of his disciples
3 and said to Him, "Are You the Coming One, or do we look for another?"
4 Jesus answered and said to them, "Go and tell John the things which you hear and see:
5 "*The* blind receive their sight and *the* lame walk; *the* lepers are cleansed and *the* deaf hear; *the* dead are raised up and *the* poor have the gospel preached to them.
6 "And blessed is he who is not offended because of Me."
7 As they departed, Jesus began to say to the multitudes concerning John: "What did you go out into the wilderness to see? A reed shaken by the wind?
8 "But what did you go out to see? A man clothed in soft garments? Indeed, those who wear soft *clothing* are in kings' houses.
9 "But what did you go out to see? A prophet? Yes, I say to you, and more than a prophet.
10 "For this is *he* of whom it is written:

'Behold, I send My messenger
before Your face,
Who will prepare Your way
before You.'

11 "Assuredly, I say to you, among those born of women there has not risen one greater than John the Baptist; but he who is least in the kingdom of heaven is greater than he.
12 "And from the days of John the Baptist until now the kingdom of heaven suffers violence, and the violent take it by force.
13 "For all the prophets and the law prophesied until John.
14 "And if you are willing to receive *it*, he is Elijah who is to come.
15 "He who has ears to hear, let him hear!
16 "But to what shall I liken this generation? It is like children sitting in the marketplaces and calling to their companions,
17 "and saying:

'We played the flute for you,
And you did not dance;
We mourned to you,
And you did not lament.'

18 "For John came neither eating nor drinking, and they say, 'He has a demon.'
19 "The Son of Man came eating and drinking, and they say, 'Look, a gluttonous man and a winebibber, a friend of tax collectors and sinners!' But wisdom is justified by her children."
20 Then He began to upbraid the cities in which most of His mighty works had been done, because they did not repent:
21 "Woe to you, Chorazin! Woe to

15

you, Bethsaida! For if the mighty works which were done in you had been done in Tyre and Sidon, they would have repented long ago in sackcloth and ashes.

22 "But I say to you, it will be more tolerable for Tyre and Sidon in the day of judgment than for you.

23 "And you, Capernaum, who are exalted to heaven, will be brought down to Hades; for if the mighty works which were done in you had been done in Sodom, it would have remained until this day.

24 "But I say to you that it shall be more tolerable for the land of Sodom in the day of judgment than for you."

25 At that time Jesus answered and said, "I thank You, Father, Lord of heaven and earth, because You have hidden these things from the wise and prudent and have revealed them to babes.

26 "Even so, Father, for so it seemed good in Your sight.

27 "All things have been delivered to Me by My Father, and no one knows the Son except the Father. Nor does anyone know the Father except the Son, and *he* to whom the Son wills to reveal *Him.*

28 "Come to Me, all *you* who labor and are heavy laden, and I will give you rest.

29 "Take My yoke upon you and learn from Me, for I am gentle and lowly in heart, and you will find rest for your souls.

30 "For My yoke *is* easy and My burden is light."

12 At that time Jesus went through the grainfields on the Sabbath. And His disciples were hungry, and began to pluck heads of grain and to eat.

2 But when the Pharisees saw *it,* they said to Him, "Look, Your disciples are doing what is not lawful to do on the Sabbath!"

3 Then He said to them, "Have you not read what David did when he was hungry, he and those who were with him:

4 "how he entered the house of God and ate the showbread which was not lawful for him to eat, nor for those who were with him, but only for the priests?

5 "Or have you not read in the law that on the Sabbath the priests in the temple profane the Sabbath, and are blameless?

6 "But I say to you that in this place there is *One* greater than the temple.

7 "But if you had known what *this* means, *'I desire mercy and not sacrifice,'* you would not have condemned the guiltless.

8 "For the Son of Man is Lord even of the Sabbath."

9 Now when He had departed from there, He went into their synagogue.

10 And behold, there was a man who had a withered hand. And they asked Him, saying, "Is it lawful to heal on the Sabbath?"—that they might accuse Him.

11 Then He said to them, "What man is there among you who has one sheep, and if it falls into a pit on the Sabbath, will not lay hold of it and lift *it* out?

12 "Of how much more value then is a man than a sheep? Therefore it is lawful to do good on the Sabbath."

13 Then He said to the man, "Stretch out your hand." And he stretched *it* out, and it was restored as whole as the other.

14 Then the Pharisees went out and took counsel against Him, how they might destroy Him.

15 But when Jesus knew *it,* He withdrew from there; and great multitudes followed Him, and He healed them all.

16 And He warned them not to make Him known,

17 that it might be fulfilled which was spoken by Isaiah the prophet, saying:

18 *"Behold, My Servant whom I have chosen,*
My Beloved in whom My soul is well pleased;
I will put My Spirit upon Him, And He will declare justice to the Gentiles.

19 *He will not quarrel nor cry out, Nor will anyone hear His voice in the streets.*

20 *A bruised reed He will not break,*
And smoking flax He will not quench,
Till He sends forth justice to victory.

21 *And in His name Gentiles will trust."*

22 Then one was brought to Him who was demon-possessed, blind and mute; and He healed him, so that the blind and mute man both spoke and saw.

23 And all the multitudes were amazed and said, "Could this be the Son of David?"

24 But when the Pharisees heard *it* they said, "This *fellow* does not cast out demons except by Beelzebub, the ruler of the demons."

25 But Jesus knew their thoughts, and said to them: "Every kingdom divided against itself is brought to desolation, and every city or house divided against itself will not stand.

26 "And if Satan casts out Satan, he is divided against himself. How then will his kingdom stand?

27 "And if I cast out demons by Beelzebub, by whom do your sons cast *them* out? Therefore they shall be your judges.

28 "But if I cast out demons by the Spirit of God, surely the kingdom of God has come upon you.

29 "Or *else* how can one enter a strong man's house and plunder his goods, unless he first binds the strong man? And then he will plunder his house.

30 "He who is not with Me is against Me, and he who does not gather with Me scatters abroad.

31 "Therefore I say to you, every sin and blasphemy will be forgiven men, but the blasphemy *against* the Spirit will not be forgiven men.

32 "Anyone who speaks a word against the Son of Man, it will be forgiven him; but whoever speaks against the Holy Spirit, it will not be forgiven him, either in this age or in the *age* to come.

33 "Either make the tree good and its fruit good, or else make the tree bad and its fruit bad; for a tree is known by *its* fruit.

34 "Brood of vipers! How can you, being evil, speak good things? For out of the abundance of the heart the mouth speaks.

35 "A good man out of the good treasure of his heart brings forth good things, and an evil man out of the evil treasure brings forth evil things.

36 "But I say to you that for every idle word men may speak, they will give account of it in the day of judgment.

37 "For by your words you will be justified, and by your words you will be condemned."

38 Then some of the scribes and Pharisees answered, saying, "Teacher, we want to see a sign from You."

39 But He answered and said to them, "An evil and adulterous generation seeks after a sign, and no sign will be given to it except the sign of the prophet Jonah.

40 "For as Jonah was three days and three nights in the belly of the great fish, so will the Son of Man be three days and three nights in the heart of the earth.

41 "The men of Nineveh will rise in the judgment with this generation and condemn it, because they repented at the preaching of Jonah; and indeed a greater than Jonah *is* here.

42 "The queen of the South will

rise up in the judgment with this generation and condemn it, for she came from the ends of the earth to hear the wisdom of Solomon; and indeed a greater than Solomon *is* here.

43 "When an unclean spirit goes out of a man, he goes through dry places, seeking rest, and finds none.

44 "Then he says, 'I will return to my house from which I came.' And when he comes, he finds it empty, swept, and put in order.

45 "Then he goes and takes with him seven other spirits more wicked than himself, and they enter and dwell there; and the last *state* of that man is worse than the first. So shall it also be with this wicked generation."

46 While He was still talking to the multitudes, behold, His mother and brothers stood outside, seeking to speak with Him.

47 Then one said to Him, "Look, Your mother and Your brothers are standing outside, seeking to speak with You."

48 But He answered and said to the one who told Him, "Who is My mother and who are My brothers?"

49 And He stretched out His hand toward His disciples and said, "Here are My mother and My brothers!

50 "For whoever does the will of My Father in heaven is My brother and sister and mother."

13 On the same day Jesus went out of the house and sat by the sea.

2 And great multitudes were gathered together to Him, so that He got into a boat and sat; and the whole multitude stood on the shore.

3 Then He spoke many things to them in parables, saying: "Behold, a sower went out to sow.

4 "And as he sowed, some *seed* fell by the wayside; and the birds came and devoured them.

5 "Some fell on stony places, where they did not have much earth; and they immediately sprang up because they had no depth of earth.

6 "But when the sun was up they were scorched, and because they had no root they withered away.

7 "And some fell among thorns, and the thorns sprang up and choked them.

8 "But others fell on good ground and yielded a crop: some a hundredfold, some sixty, some thirty.

9 "He who has ears to hear, let him hear!"

10 And the disciples came and said to Him, "Why do You speak to them in parables?"

11 He answered and said to them, "Because it has been given to you to know the mysteries of the kingdom of heaven, but to them it has not been given.

12 "For whoever has, to him more will be given, and he will have abundance; but whoever does not have, even what he has will be taken away from him.

13 "Therefore I speak to them in parables, because seeing they do not see, and hearing they do not hear, nor do they understand.

14 "And in them the prophecy of Isaiah is fulfilled, which says:

'Hearing you will hear
  and shall not understand,
And seeing you will see
  and not perceive;
15 For the heart of this people
  has grown dull.
Their ears are hard of hearing,
  And their eyes they have
  closed,
Lest they should see with their
  eyes and hear with their ears,
Lest they should understand
  with their heart and turn,
So that I should heal them.'

16 "But blessed *are* your eyes for

they see, and your ears for they hear;

17 "for assuredly, I say to you that many prophets and righteous *men* desired to see what you see, and did not see *it*, and to hear what you hear, and did not hear *it*.

18 "Therefore hear the parable of the sower:

19 "When anyone hears the word of the kingdom, and does not understand *it*, then the wicked *one* comes and snatches away what was sown in his heart. This is he who received seed by the wayside.

20 "But he who received the seed on stony places, this is he who hears the word and immediately receives it with joy;

21 "yet he has no root in himself, but endures only for a while. For when tribulation or persecution arises because of the word, immediately he stumbles.

22 "Now he who received seed among the thorns is he who hears the word, and the cares of this world and the deceitfulness of riches choke the word, and he becomes unfruitful.

23 "But he who received seed on the good ground is he who hears the word and understands *it*, who indeed bears fruit and produces: some a hundredfold, some sixty, some thirty."

24 Another parable He put forth to them, saying: "The kingdom of heaven is like a man who sowed good seed in his field;

25 "but while men slept, his enemy came and sowed tares among the wheat and went his way.

26 "But when the grain had sprouted and produced a crop, then the tares also appeared.

27 "So the servants of the owner came and said to him, 'Sir, did you not sow good seed in your field? How does it have tares?'

28 "He said to them, 'An enemy has done this.' The servants said to

him, 'Do you want us then to go and gather them up?'

29 "But he said, 'No, lest while you gather up the tares you also uproot the wheat with them.

30 'Let both grow together until the harvest, and at the time of harvest I will say to the reapers, "First gather together the tares and bind them in bundles to burn them, but gather the wheat into my barn." ' "

31 Another parable He put forth to them, saying: "The kingdom of heaven is like a mustard seed, which a man took and sowed in his field,

32 "which indeed is the least of all the seeds; but when it is grown it is greater than the herbs and becomes a tree, so that the birds of the air come and nest in its branches."

33 Another parable He spoke to them: "The kingdom of heaven is like leaven, which a woman took and hid in three measures of meal till it was all leavened."

34 All these things Jesus spoke to the multitude in parables; and without a parable He did not speak to them,

35 that it might be fulfilled which was spoken by the prophet, saying:

> *"I will open My mouth in parables;*
> *I will utter things which have been kept secret from the foundation of the world."*

36 Then Jesus sent the multitude away and went into the house. And His disciples came to Him, saying, "Explain to us the parable of the tares of the field."

37 He answered and said to them: "He who sows the good seed is the Son of Man.

38 "The field is the world, the good seeds are the sons of the kingdom, but the tares are the sons of the wicked *one*.

39 "The enemy who sowed them is the devil, the harvest is the end of the age, and the reapers are the angels.

40 "Therefore as the tares are gathered and burned in the fire, so it will be at the end of this age.

41 "The Son of Man will send out His angels, and they will gather out of His kingdom all things that offend, and those who practice lawlessness,

42 "and will cast them into the furnace of fire. There will be wailing and gnashing of teeth.

43 "Then the righteous will shine forth as the sun in the kingdom of their Father. He who has ears to hear, let him hear!

44 "Again, the kingdom of heaven is like treasure hidden in a field, which a man found and hid; and for joy over it he goes and sells all that he has and buys that field.

45 "Again, the kingdom of heaven is like a merchant seeking beautiful pearls,

46 "who, when he had found one pearl of great price, went and sold all that he had and bought it.

47 "Again, the kingdom of heaven is like a dragnet that was cast into the sea and gathered some of every kind,

48 "which, when it was full, they drew to shore; and they sat down and gathered the good into vessels, but threw the bad away.

49 "So it will be at the end of the age. The angels will come forth, separate the wicked from among the just,

50 "and cast them into the furnace of fire. There will be wailing and gnashing of teeth."

51 Jesus said to them, "Have you understood all these things?" They said to Him, "Yes, Lord."

52 Then He said to them, "Therefore every scribe instructed concerning the kingdom of heaven is like a householder who brings out of his treasure *things* new and old."

53 Now it came to pass, when Jesus had finished these parables, that He departed from there.

54 And when He had come to His own country, He taught them in their synagogue, so that they were astonished and said, "Where did this *Man* get this wisdom and *these* mighty works?

55 "Is this not the carpenter's son? Is not His mother called Mary? And His brothers James, Joses, Simon, and Judas?

56 "And His sisters, are they not all with us? Where then did this *Man* get all these things?"

57 So they were offended at Him. But Jesus said to them, "A prophet is not without honor except in his own country and in his own house."

58 And He did not do many mighty works there because of their unbelief.

14 At that time Herod the tetrarch heard the report about Jesus

2 and said to his servants, "This is John the Baptist; he is risen from the dead, and therefore these powers are at work in him."

3 For Herod had laid hold of John and bound him, and put *him* in prison for the sake of Herodias, his brother Philip's wife.

4 For John had said to him, "It is not lawful for you to have her."

5 And although he wanted to put him to death, he feared the multitude, because they counted him as a prophet.

6 But when Herod's birthday was celebrated, the daughter of Herodias danced before them and pleased Herod.

7 Therefore he promised with an oath to give her whatever she might ask.

8 So she, having been prompted by her mother, said, "Give me

20

John the Baptist's head here on a platter."

9 And the king was sorry; nevertheless, because of the oaths and because of those who sat with him at the table, he commanded *it* to be given to her.

10 So he sent and had John beheaded in prison.

11 And his head was brought on a platter and given to the girl, and she brought *it* to her mother.

12 Then his disciples came and took away the body and buried it, and went and told Jesus.

13 When Jesus heard *it,* He departed from there by boat to a deserted place by Himself. But when the multitudes heard it, they followed Him on foot from the cities.

14 And when Jesus went out He saw a great multitude; and He was moved with compassion for them, and healed their sick.

15 When it was evening, His disciples came to Him, saying, "This is a deserted place, and the hour is already late. Send the multitudes away, that they may go into the villages and buy themselves food."

16 But Jesus said to them, "They do not need to go away. You give them something to eat."

17 And they said to Him, "We have here only five loaves and two fish."

18 He said, "Bring them here to Me."

19 Then He commanded the multitudes to sit down on the grass. And He took the five loaves and the two fish, and looking up to heaven, He blessed and broke and gave the loaves to the disciples; and the disciples gave to the multitudes.

20 So they all ate and were filled, and they took up twelve baskets full of the fragments that remained.

21 Now those who had eaten were about five thousand men, besides women and children.

22 Immediately Jesus made His disciples get into the boat and go before Him to the other side, while He sent the multitudes away.

23 And when He had sent the multitudes away, He went up on a mountain by Himself to pray. And when evening had come, He was alone there.

24 But the boat was now in the middle of the sea, tossed by the waves, for the wind was contrary.

25 Now in the fourth watch of the night Jesus went to them, walking on the sea.

26 And when the disciples saw Him walking on the sea, they were troubled, saying, "It is a ghost!" And they cried out for fear.

27 But immediately Jesus spoke to them, saying, "Be of good cheer! It is I; do not be afraid."

28 And Peter answered Him and said, "Lord, if it is You, command me to come to You on the water."

29 So He said, "Come." And when Peter had come down out of the boat, he walked on the water to go to Jesus.

30 But when he saw that the wind *was* boisterous, he was afraid; and beginning to sink he cried out, saying, "Lord, save me!"

31 And immediately Jesus stretched out *His* hand and caught him, and said to him, "O you of little faith, why did you doubt?"

32 And when they got into the boat, the wind ceased.

33 Then those who were in the boat came and worshiped Him, saying, "Truly You are the Son of God."

34 When they had crossed over, they came to the land of Gennesaret.

35 And when the men of that place recognized Him, they sent out into all that surrounding region, brought to Him all who were sick,

36 and begged Him that they might only touch the hem of His garment. And as many as touched it were made perfectly well.

15 Then the scribes and Pharisees who were from Jerusalem came to Jesus, saying,

2 "Why do Your disciples transgress the tradition of the elders? For they do not wash their hands when they eat bread."

3 But He answered and said to them, "Why do you also transgress the commandment of God because of your tradition?

4 "For God commanded, saying, '*Honor your father and your mother*'; and, '*He who curses father or mother, let him be put to death.*'

5 "But you say, 'Whoever says to *his* father or mother, "Whatever profit you might have received from me has been dedicated *to the temple*'—

6 '*is released from* honoring his father or mother.' Thus you have made the commandment of God of no effect by your tradition.

7 "Hypocrites! Well did Isaiah prophesy about you, saying:

8 '*These people draw near to Me
with their mouth,
And honor Me with their lips,
But their heart is far from Me.*

9 *And in vain they worship Me,
Teaching as doctrines the
commandments of men.*'"

10 Then He called the multitude and said to them, "Hear and understand:

11 "Not what goes into the mouth defiles a man; but what comes out of the mouth, this defiles a man."

12 Then His disciples came and said to Him, "Do You know that the Pharisees were offended when they heard this saying?"

13 But He answered and said, "Every plant which My heavenly Father has not planted will be uprooted.

14 "Let them alone. They are blind leaders of the blind. And if the blind leads the blind, both will fall into a ditch."

15 Then Peter answered and said to Him, "Explain this parable to us."

16 So Jesus said, "Are you also still without understanding?

17 "Do you not yet understand that whatever enters the mouth goes into the stomach and is eliminated?

18 "But those things which proceed out of the mouth come from the heart, and they defile a man.

19 "For out of the heart proceed evil thoughts, murders, adulteries, fornications, thefts, false witness, blasphemies.

20 "These are *the* things which defile a man, but to eat with unwashed hands does not defile a man."

21 Then Jesus went out from there and departed to the region of Tyre and Sidon.

22 And behold, a woman of Canaan came from that region and cried out to Him, saying, "Have mercy on me, O Lord, Son of David! My daughter is severely demon-possessed."

23 But He answered her not a word. And His disciples came and urged Him, saying, "Send her away, for she cries out after us."

24 But He answered and said, "I was not sent except to the lost sheep of the house of Israel."

25 Then she came and worshiped Him, saying, "Lord, help me!"

26 But He answered and said, "It is not good to take the children's bread and throw *it* to the little dogs."

27 And she said, "True, Lord, yet even the little dogs eat the crumbs which fall from their masters' table."

28 Then Jesus answered and said to her, "O woman, great *is* your faith! Let it be to you as you desire." And her daughter was healed from that very hour.

29 And Jesus departed from there, skirted the Sea of Galilee, and went up on the mountain and sat down there.

30 Then great multitudes came to Him, having with them *those who were* lame, blind, mute, maimed, and many others; and they laid them down at Jesus' feet, and He healed them.

31 So the multitude marveled when they saw *the* mute speaking, *the* maimed made whole, *the* lame walking, and *the* blind seeing; and they glorified the God of Israel.

32 Then Jesus called His disciples *to Him* and said, "I have compassion on the multitude, because they have now continued with Me three days and have nothing to eat. And I do not want to send them away hungry, lest they faint on the way."

33 Then His disciples said to Him, "Where could we get enough bread in the wilderness to fill such a great multitude?"

34 Jesus said to them, "How many loaves do you have?" And they said, "Seven, and a few little fish."

35 And He commanded the multitude to sit down on the ground.

36 And He took the seven loaves and the fish and gave thanks, broke *them* and gave *them* to His disciples; and the disciples *gave* to the multitude.

37 So they all ate and were filled, and they took up seven large baskets full of the fragments that were left.

38 Now those who ate were four thousand men, besides women and children.

39 And He sent away the multitude, got into the boat, and came to the region of Magdala.

16 Then the Pharisees and Sadducees came, and testing Him asked that He would show them a sign from heaven.

2 He answered and said to them, "When it is evening you say, '*It will be* fair weather, for the sky is red';

3 "and in the morning, '*It will be* foul weather today, for the sky is red and threatening.' Hypocrites! You know how to discern the face of the sky, but you cannot *discern* the signs of the times.

4 "A wicked and adulterous generation seeks after a sign, and no sign shall be given to it except the sign of the prophet Jonah." And He left them and departed.

5 And when His disciples had come to the other side, they had forgotten to take bread.

6 Then Jesus said to them, "Take heed and beware of the leaven of the Pharisees and the Sadducees."

7 And they reasoned among themselves, saying, "*It is* because we have taken no bread."

8 But when Jesus perceived it, He said to them, "O you of little faith, why do you reason among yourselves because you have brought no bread?

9 "Do you not yet understand, or remember the five loaves of the five thousand and how many baskets you took up?

10 "Nor the seven loaves of the four thousand and how many large baskets you took up?

11 "How is it you do not understand that I did not speak to you concerning bread?—*but* you should beware of the leaven of the Pharisees and Sadducees."

12 Then they understood that He did not tell *them* to beware of the leaven of bread, but of the doctrine of the Pharisees and Sadducees.

13 When Jesus came into the region of Caesarea Philippi, He asked His disciples, saying, "Who do men say that I, the Son of Man, am?"

14 So they said, "Some *say* John the Baptist, some Elijah, and others Jeremiah or one of the prophets."

15 He said to them, "But who do you say that I am?"

16 And Simon Peter answered and said, "You are the Christ, the Son of the living God."

17 Jesus answered and said to him, "Blessed are you, Simon Bar-Jonah, for flesh and blood has not revealed *this* to you, but My Father who is in heaven.

18 "And I also say to you that you are Peter, and on this rock I will build My church, and the gates of Hades shall not prevail against it.

19 "And I will give you the keys of the kingdom of heaven, and whatever you bind on earth will be bound in heaven, and whatever you loose on earth will be loosed in heaven."

20 Then He commanded His disciples that they should tell no one that He was Jesus the Christ.

21 From that time Jesus began to show to His disciples that He must go to Jerusalem, and suffer many things from the elders and chief priests and scribes, and be killed, and be raised again the third day.

22 Then Peter took Him aside and began to rebuke Him, saying, "Far be it from You, Lord; this shall not happen to You!"

23 But He turned and said to Peter, "Get behind Me, Satan! You are an offense to Me, for you are not mindful of the things of God, but the things of men."

24 Then Jesus said to His disciples, "If anyone desires to come after Me, let him deny himself, and take up his cross, and follow Me.

25 "For whoever desires to save his life will lose it, and whoever loses his life for My sake will find it.

26 "For what is a man profited if he gains the whole world, and loses his own soul? Or what will a man give in exchange for his soul?

27 "For the Son of Man will come in the glory of His Father with His angels, and then He will reward each according to his works.

28 "Assuredly, I say to you, there are some standing here who shall not taste death till they see the Son of Man coming in His kingdom."

17 Now after six days Jesus took Peter, James, and John his brother, brought them up on a high mountain by themselves,

2 and was transfigured before them. His face shone like the sun, and His clothes became as white as the light.

3 And behold, Moses and Elijah appeared to them, talking with Him.

4 Then Peter answered and said to Jesus, "Lord, it is good for us to be here; if You wish, let us make here three tabernacles: one for You, one for Moses, and one for Elijah."

5 While he was still speaking, behold, a bright cloud overshadowed them; and suddenly a voice came out of the cloud, saying, "This is My beloved Son, in whom I am well pleased. Hear Him!"

6 And when the disciples heard *it*, they fell on their faces and were greatly afraid.

7 But Jesus came and touched them and said, "Arise, and do not be afraid."

8 And when they had lifted up their eyes, they saw no one but Jesus only.

9 Now as they came down from the mountain, Jesus commanded them, saying, "Tell the vision to no one until the Son of Man is risen from the dead."

10 And His disciples asked Him, saying, "Why then do the scribes say that Elijah must come first?"

11 Then Jesus answered and said to them, "Elijah truly is coming first and will restore all things.

12 "But I say to you that Elijah has come already, and they did not know him but did to him whatever they wished. Likewise the Son of

24

Man is also about to suffer at their hands."

13 Then the disciples understood that He spoke to them of John the Baptist.

14 And when they had come to the multitude, a man came to Him, kneeling down to Him and saying, 15 "Lord, have mercy on my son, for he is an epileptic and suffers severely; for he often falls into the fire and often into the water.

16 "So I brought him to Your disciples, but they could not cure him."

17 Then Jesus answered and said, "O faithless and perverse generation, how long shall I be with you? How long shall I bear with you? Bring him here to Me."

18 And Jesus rebuked the demon, and he came out of him; and the child was cured from that very hour.

19 Then the disciples came to Jesus privately and said, "Why could we not cast him out?"

20 So Jesus said to them, "Because of your unbelief; for assuredly, I say to you, if you have faith as a mustard seed, you will say to this mountain, 'Move from here to there,' and it will move; and nothing will be impossible for you.

21 "However, this kind does not go out except by prayer and fasting."

22 Now while they were staying in Galilee, Jesus said to them, "The Son of Man is about to be betrayed into the hands of men,

23 "and they will kill Him, and the third day He will be raised up." And they were exceedingly sorrowful.

24 And when they had come to Capernaum, those who received the *temple* tax came to Peter and said, "Does your Teacher not pay the *temple* tax?"

25 He said, "Yes." And when he had come into the house, Jesus anticipated him, saying, "What do you think, Simon? From whom do the kings of the earth take cus-toms or taxes, from their *own* sons or from strangers?"

26 Peter said to Him, "From strangers." Jesus said to him, "Then the sons are free.

27 "Nevertheless, lest we offend them, go to the sea, cast in a hook, and take the fish that comes up first. And when you have opened its mouth, you will find a piece of money; take that and give it to them for Me and you."

18

At that time the disciples came to Jesus, saying, "Who then is greatest in the kingdom of heaven?"

2 And Jesus called a little child to Him, set him in the midst of them, 3 and said, "Assuredly, I say to you, unless you are converted and become as little children, you will by no means enter the kingdom of heaven.

4 "Therefore whoever humbles himself as this little child is the greatest in the kingdom of heaven.

5 "And whoever receives one little child like this in My name receives Me.

6 "But whoever causes one of these little ones who believe in Me to sin, it would be better for him if a millstone were hung around his neck, and he were drowned in the depth of the sea.

7 "Woe to the world because of offenses! For offenses must come, but woe to that man by whom the offense comes!

8 "And if your hand or foot causes you to sin, cut it off and cast *it* from you. It is better for you to enter into life lame or maimed, rather than having two hands or two feet, to be cast into the everlasting fire.

9 "And if your eye causes you to sin, pluck it out and cast *it* from you. It is better for you to enter into life with one eye, rather than having two eyes, to be cast into hell fire.

10 "Take heed that you do not de-

spise one of these little ones, for I say to you that in heaven their angels always see the face of My Father who is in heaven.

11 "For the Son of Man has come to save that which was lost.

12 "What do you think? If a man has a hundred sheep, and one of them goes astray, does he not leave the ninety-nine and go to the mountains to seek the one that is straying?

13 "And if he should find it, assuredly, I say to you, he rejoices more over that *sheep* than over the ninety-nine that did not go astray.

14 "Even so it is not the will of your Father who is in heaven that one of these little ones should perish.

15 "Moreover if your brother sins against you, go and tell him his fault between you and him alone. If he hears you, you have gained your brother.

16 "But if he will not hear *you*, take with you one or two more, that *'by the mouth of two or three witnesses every word may be established.'*

17 "And if he refuses to hear them, tell *it* to the church. But if he refuses even to hear the church, let him be to you like a heathen and a tax collector.

18 "Assuredly, I say to you, whatever you bind on earth will be bound in heaven, and whatever you loose on earth will be loosed in heaven.

19 "Again I say to you that if two of you agree on earth concerning anything that they ask, it will·be done for them by My Father in heaven.

20 "For where two or three are gathered together in My name, I am there in the midst of them."

21 Then Peter came to Him and said, "Lord, how often shall my brother sin against me, and I forgive him? Up to seven times?"

22 Jesus said to him, "I do not say to you, up to seven times, but up to seventy times seven.

23 "Therefore the kingdom of heaven is like a certain king who wanted to settle accounts with his servants.

24 "And when he had begun to settle accounts, one was brought to him who owed him ten thousand talents.

25 "But as he was not able to pay, his master commanded that he be sold, and all that he had, and that payment be made.

26 "The servant therefore fell down before him, saying, 'Master, have patience with me, and I will pay you all.'

27 "Then the master of that servant was moved with compassion, released him, and forgave him the debt.

28 "But that servant went out and found one of his fellow servants who owed him a hundred denarii; and he laid hands on him and took *him* by the throat, saying, 'Pay me what you owe!'

29 "So his fellow servant fell down at his feet and begged him, saying, 'Have patience with me, and I will pay you all.'

30 "And he would not, but went and threw him into prison till he should pay the debt.

31 "So when his fellow servants saw what had been done, they were very grieved, and came and told their master all that had been done.

32 "Then his master, after he had called him, said to him, 'You wicked servant! I forgave you all that debt because you begged me.

33 'Should you not also have had compassion on your fellow servant, just as I had pity on you?'

34 "And his master was angry, and delivered him to the torturers until he should pay all that was due to him.

35 "So My heavenly Father also will do to you if each of you, from his heart, does not forgive his brother his trespasses."

19 Now it came to pass, when Jesus had finished these sayings, *that* He departed from Galilee and came to the region of Judea beyond the Jordan.

2 And great multitudes followed Him, and He healed them there.

3 The Pharisees also came to Him, testing Him, and saying to Him, "Is it lawful for a man to divorce his wife for *just* any reason?"

4 And He answered and said to them, "Have you not read that He who made *them* at the beginning *'made them male and female,'*

5 "and said, *'For this reason a man shall leave his father and mother and be joined to his wife, and the two shall become one flesh'*?

6 "So then, they are no longer two but one flesh. Therefore what God has joined together, let not man separate."

7 They said to Him, "Why then did Moses command to give a certificate of divorce, and to put her away?"

8 He said to them, "Moses, because of the hardness of your hearts, permitted you to divorce your wives, but from the beginning it was not so.

9 "And I say to you, whoever divorces his wife, except for sexual immorality, and marries another, commits adultery; and whoever marries her who is divorced commits adultery."

10 His disciples said to Him, "If such is the case of the man with *his* wife, it is better not to marry."

11 But He said to them, "All cannot accept this saying, but only *those* to whom it has been given:

12 "For there are eunuchs who were born thus from *their* mother's womb, and there are eunuchs who were made eunuchs by men, and

there are eunuchs who have made themselves eunuchs for the kingdom of heaven's sake. He who is able to accept *it,* let him accept *it.*"

13 Then little children were brought to Him that He might put *His* hands on them and pray, but the disciples rebuked them.

14 But Jesus said, "Let the little children come to Me, and do not forbid them; for of such is the kingdom of heaven."

15 And He laid *His* hands on them and departed from there.

16 Now behold, one came and said to Him, "Good Teacher, what good thing shall I do that I may have eternal life?"

17 So He said to him, "Why do you call Me good? No one *is* good but One, *that is,* God. But if you want to enter into life, keep the commandments."

18 He said to Him, "Which ones?" Jesus said, "'You shall not murder,' 'You shall not commit adultery,' 'You shall not steal,' 'You shall not bear false witness,'

19 'Honor your father and your mother,' and, 'You shall love your neighbor as yourself.'"

20 The young man said to Him, "All these things I have kept from my youth. What do I still lack?"

21 Jesus said to him, "If you want to be perfect, go, sell what you have and give to the poor, and you will have treasure in heaven; and come, follow Me."

22 But when the young man heard that saying, he went away sorrowful, for he had great possessions.

23 Then Jesus said to His disciples, "Assuredly, I say to you that it is hard for a rich man to enter the kingdom of heaven.

24 "And again I say to you, it is easier for a camel to go through the eye of a needle than for a rich man to enter the kingdom of God."

25 When His disciples heard *it,* they were exceedingly amazed, saying, "Who then can be saved?"

26 But Jesus looked at *them* and said to them, "With men this is impossible, but with God all things are possible."

27 Then Peter answered and said to Him, "See, we have left all and followed You. Therefore what shall we have?"

28 So Jesus said to them, "Assuredly I say to you, that in the regeneration, when the Son of Man sits on the throne of His glory, you who have followed Me will also sit on twelve thrones, judging the twelve tribes of Israel.

29 "And everyone who has left houses or brothers or sisters or father or mother or wife or children or lands, for My name's sake, shall receive a hundredfold, and inherit everlasting life.

30 "But many *who are* first will be last, and the last first.

20 "For the kingdom of heaven is like a landowner who went out early in the morning to hire laborers for his vineyard.

2 "Now when he had agreed with the laborers for a denarius a day, he sent them into his vineyard.

3 "And he went out about the third hour and saw others standing idle in the marketplace.

4 "and said to them, 'You also go into the vineyard, and whatever is right I will give you.' And they went.

5 "Again he went out about the sixth and the ninth hour, and did likewise.

6 "And about the eleventh hour he went out and found others standing idle, and said to them, 'Why have you been standing here idle all day?'

7 "They said to him, 'Because no one hired us.' He said to them, 'You also go into the vineyard, and whatever is right you will receive.'

8 "So when evening had come, the owner of the vineyard said to his steward, 'Call the laborers and give them *their* wages, beginning with the last to the first.'

9 "And when those came who *were hired* about the eleventh hour, they each received a denarius.

10 "But when the first came, they supposed that they would receive more; and they likewise received each a denarius.

11 "And when they had received *it*, they murmured against the landowner,

12 "saying, 'These last *men* have worked *only* one hour, and you made them equal to us who have borne the burden and the heat of the day.'

13 "But he answered one of them and said, 'Friend, I am doing you no wrong. Did you not agree with me for a denarius?

14 'Take *what is* yours and go your way. I wish to give to this last man *the same* as to you.

15 'Is it not lawful for me to do what I wish with my own things? Or is your eye evil because I am good?'

16 "So the last will be first, and the first last. For many are called, but few chosen."

17 Then Jesus, going up to Jerusalem, took the twelve disciples aside on the road and said to them,

18 "Behold, we are going up to Jerusalem, and the Son of Man will be betrayed to the chief priests and to the scribes; and they will condemn Him to death,

19 "and deliver Him to the Gentiles to mock and to scourge and to crucify. And the third day He will rise again."

20 Then the mother of Zebedee's sons came to Him with her sons, kneeling down and asking something from Him.

21 And He said to her, "What do you wish?" She said to Him, "Grant that these two sons of mine may sit, one on Your right hand

and the other on the left, in Your kingdom."

22 But Jesus answered and said, "You do not know what you ask. Are you able to drink the cup that I am about to drink, and be baptized with the baptism that I am baptized with?" They said to Him, "We are able."

23 So He said to them, "You will indeed drink My cup, and be baptized with the baptism that I am baptized with; but to sit on My right hand and on My left is not Mine to give, but *it is for those* for whom it is prepared by My Father."

24 And when the ten heard *it,* they were moved with indignation against the two brothers.

25 But Jesus called them *to Himself* and said, "You know that the rulers of the Gentiles lord it over them, and those who are great exercise authority over them.

26 "Yet it shall not be so among you; but whoever desires to become great among you, let him be your servant.

27 "And whoever desires to be first among you, let him be your slave—

28 "just as the Son of Man did not come to be served, but to serve, and to give His life a ransom for many."

29 Now as they departed from Jericho, a great multitude followed Him.

30 And behold, two blind men sitting by the road, when they heard that Jesus was passing by, cried out, saying, "Have mercy on us, O Lord, Son of David!"

31 Then the multitude warned them that they should be quiet; but they cried out all the more, saying, "Have mercy on us, O Lord, Son of David!"

32 So Jesus stood still and called them, and said, "What do you want Me to do for you?"

33 They said to Him, "Lord, that our eyes may be opened."

34 So Jesus had compassion and touched their eyes. And immediately their eyes received sight, and they followed Him.

21 Now when they drew near to Jerusalem, and came to Bethphage, at the Mount of Olives, then Jesus sent two disciples,

2 saying to them, "Go into the village opposite you, and immediately you will find a donkey tied, and a colt with her. Loose *them* and bring *them* to Me.

3 "And if anyone says anything to you, you shall say, 'The Lord has need of them,' and immediately he will send them."

4 All this was done that it might be fulfilled which was spoken by the prophet, saying:

5 "Tell the daughter of Zion,
  'Behold, your King is coming to you,
  Lowly, and sitting on a donkey,
  A colt, the foal of a donkey.'"

6 So the disciples went and did as Jesus commanded them.

7 They brought the donkey and the colt, laid their clothes on them, and set *Him* on them.

8 And a very great multitude spread their garments on the road; others cut down branches from the trees and spread *them* on the road.

9 Then the multitudes who went before and those who followed cried out, saying:

"Hosanna to the Son of David!
'Blessed is He who comes
  in the name of the LORD!'
Hosanna in the highest!"

10 And when He had come into Jerusalem, all the city was moved, saying, "Who is this?"

11 So the multitudes said, "This is Jesus, the prophet from Nazareth of Galilee."

12 Then Jesus went into the temple of God and drove out all those who bought and sold in the temple, and overturned the tables of the moneychangers and the seats of those who sold doves.

13 And He said to them, "It is written, *'My house shall be called a house of prayer,'* but you have made it a *'den of thieves.'"*

14 Then *the* blind and *the* lame came to Him in the temple, and He healed them.

15 But when the chief priests and scribes saw the wonderful things that He did, and the children crying out in the temple and saying, "Hosanna to the Son of David!" they were indignant

16 and said to Him, "Do You hear what these are saying?" And Jesus said to them, "Yes. Have you never read, *'Out of the mouth of babes and nursing infants You have perfected praise'* ? "

17 Then He left them and went out of the city to Bethany, and He lodged there.

18 Now in the morning, as He returned to the city, He was hungry.

19 And seeing a fig tree by the road, He came to it and found nothing on it but leaves, and said to it, "Let no fruit grow on you ever again." And immediately the fig tree withered away.

20 Now when the disciples saw *it*, they marveled, saying, "How did the fig tree wither away so soon?"

21 So Jesus answered and said to them, "Assuredly, I say to you, if you have faith and do not doubt, you will not only do what was done to the fig tree, but also if you say to this mountain, 'Be removed and be cast into the sea,' it will be done.

22 "And all things, whatever you ask in prayer, believing, you will receive."

23 Now when He came into the temple, the chief priests and the elders of the people confronted Him as He was teaching, and said, "By what authority are You doing these things? And who gave You this authority?"

24 But Jesus answered and said to them, "I also will ask you one thing, which if you tell Me, I likewise will tell you by what authority I do these things:

25 "The baptism of John, where was it from? From heaven or from men?" And they reasoned among themselves, saying, "If we say, 'From heaven,' He will say to us, 'Why then did you not believe him?'

26 "But if we say, 'From men,' we fear the multitude, for all count John as a prophet."

27 So they answered Jesus and said, "We do not know." And He said to them, "Neither will I tell you by what authority I do these things.

28 "But what do you think? A man had two sons, and he came to the first and said, 'Son, go, work today in my vineyard.'

29 "He answered and said, 'I will not,' but afterward he regretted it and went.

30 "Then he came to the second and said likewise. And he answered and said, 'I go, sir,' but he did not go.

31 "Which of the two did the will of *his* father?" They said to Him, "The first." Jesus said to them, "Assuredly, I say to you that tax collectors and harlots enter the kingdom of God before you.

32 "For John came to you in the way of righteousness, and you did not believe him; but tax collectors and harlots believed him; and when you saw *it*, you did not afterward relent and believe him.

33 "Hear another parable: There was a certain landowner who planted a vineyard and set a hedge around it, dug a winepress in it and built a tower. And he leased it to vinedressers and went into a far country.

34 "Now when vintage-time drew near, he sent his servants to the vinedressers, that they might receive its fruit.

35 "And the vinedressers took his servants, beat one, killed one, and stoned another.

36 "Again he sent other servants, more than the first, and they did likewise to them.

37 "Then last of all he sent his son to them, saying, 'They will respect my son.'

38 "But when the vinedressers saw the son, they said among themselves, 'This is the heir. Come, let us kill him and seize his inheritance.'

39 "And they caught him, and cast *him* out of the vineyard, and killed *him.*

40 "Therefore, when the owner of the vineyard comes, what will he do to those vinedressers?"

41 They said to Him, "He will destroy those wicked men miserably, and lease *his* vineyard to other vinedressers who will render to him the fruits in their seasons."

42 Jesus said to them, "Did you never read in the Scriptures:

'The stone which the builders
　　rejected
Has become the chief
　　cornerstone.
This was the LORD's doing,
And it is marvelous in our
　　eyes'?

43 "Therefore I say to you, the kingdom of God will be taken from you and given to a nation bearing the fruits of it.

44 "And whoever falls on this stone will be broken; but on whomever it falls, it will grind him to powder."

45 Now when the chief priests and Pharisees heard His parables, they perceived that He was speaking of them.

46 But when they sought to lay hands on Him, they feared the multitudes, because they took Him for a prophet.

22 And Jesus answered and spoke to them again by parables and said:

2 "The kingdom of heaven is like a certain king who arranged a marriage for his son,

3 "and sent out his servants to call those who were invited to the wedding; and they were not willing to come.

4 "Again, he sent out other servants, saying, 'Tell those who are invited, "See, I have prepared my dinner; my oxen and fatted cattle *are* killed, and all things *are* ready. Come to the wedding." '

5 "But they made light of it and went their ways, one to his own farm, another to his business.

6 "And the rest seized his servants, treated *them* spitefully, and killed *them.*

7 "But when the king heard *about it,* he was furious. And he sent out his armies, destroyed those murderers, and burned up their city.

8 "Then he said to his servants, 'The wedding is ready, but those who were invited were not worthy.

9 'Therefore go into the highways, and as many as you find, invite to the wedding.'

10 "So those servants went out into the highways and gathered together all whom they found, both bad and good. And the wedding *hall* was filled with guests.

11 "But when the king came in to see the guests, he saw a man there who did not have on a wedding garment.

12 "So he said to him, 'Friend, how did you come in here without a wedding garment?' And he was speechless.

13 "Then the king said to the servants, 'Bind him hand and foot,

31

take him away, and cast *him* into outer darkness; there will be weeping and gnashing of teeth.'

14 "For many are called, but few *are* chosen."

15 Then the Pharisees went and plotted how they might entangle Him in *His* talk.

16 And they sent to Him their disciples with the Herodians, saying, "Teacher, we know that You are true, and teach the way of God in truth; nor do You care about anyone, for You do not regard the person of men.

17 "Tell us, therefore, what do You think? Is it lawful to pay taxes to Caesar, or not?"

18 But Jesus perceived their wickedness, and said, "Why do you test Me, *you* hypocrites?

19 "Show Me the tax money." So they brought Him a denarius.

20 And He said to them, "Whose image and inscription *is* this?"

21 They said to Him, "Caesar's." And He said to them, "Render therefore to Caesar the things that are Caesar's, and to God the things that are God's."

22 When they had heard *these* words, they marveled, and left Him and went their way.

23 The same day the Sadducees, who say there is no resurrection, came to Him and asked Him,

24 saying: "Teacher, Moses said that if a man dies, having no children, his brother shall marry his wife and raise up offspring for his brother.

25 "Now there were with us seven brothers. The first died after he had married, and having no offspring, left his wife to his brother.

26 "Likewise the second also, and the third, even to the seventh.

27 "And last of all the woman died also.

28 "Therefore, in the resurrection, whose wife of the seven will she be? For they all had her."

29 Jesus answered and said to them, "You are mistaken, not knowing the Scriptures nor the power of God.

30 "For in the resurrection they neither marry nor are given in marriage, but are like angels of God in heaven.

31 "But concerning the resurrection of the dead, have you not read what was spoken to you by God, saying,

32 *'I am the God of Abraham, the God of Isaac, and the God of Jacob'*? God is not the God of the dead, but of the living."

33 And when the multitudes heard *this*, they were astonished at His teaching.

34 But when the Pharisees heard that He had silenced the Sadducees, they gathered together.

35 Then one of them, a lawyer, asked *Him a question*, testing Him, and saying,

36 "Teacher, which *is* the great commandment in the law?"

37 Jesus said to him, "'*You shall love the* LORD *your God with all your heart, with all your soul, and with all your mind.*

38 "This is *the* first and great commandment.

39 "And *the* second *is* like it: '*You shall love your neighbor as yourself.*'

40 "On these two commandments hang all the Law and the Prophets."

41 While the Pharisees were gathered together, Jesus asked them,

42 saying, "What do you think about the Christ? Whose Son is He?" They said to Him, "The Son of David."

43 He said to them, "How then does David in the Spirit call Him '*Lord*', saying:

44 *'The* LORD *said to my Lord,*
    "*Sit at My right hand,*
    Till I make Your enemies
        Your footstool"'?

32

45 "If David then calls Him *'Lord'*, how is He his Son?"

46 And no one was able to answer Him a word, nor from that day on did anyone dare question Him anymore.

23 Then Jesus spoke to the multitudes and to His disciples,

2 saying: "The scribes and the Pharisees sit in Moses' seat.

3 "Therefore whatever they tell you to observe, *that* observe and do, but do not do according to their works; for they say, and do not do.

4 "For they bind heavy burdens, hard to bear, and lay *them* on men's shoulders; but they *themselves* will not move them with one of their fingers.

5 "But all their works they do to be seen by men. They make their phylacteries broad and enlarge the borders of their garments.

6 "They love the best places at feasts, the best seats in the synagogues,

7 "greetings in the marketplaces, and to be called by men, 'Rabbi, Rabbi.'

8 "But you, do not be called 'Rabbi'; for One is your Teacher, the Christ, and you are all brethren.

9 "Do not call anyone on earth your father; for One is your Father, He who is in heaven.

10 "And do not be called teachers; for One is your Teacher, the Christ.

11 "But he who is greatest among you shall be your servant.

12 "And whoever exalts himself will be abased, and he who humbles himself will be exalted.

13 "But woe to you, scribes and Pharisees, hypocrites! For you shut up the kingdom of heaven against men; for you neither go in *yourselves*, nor do you allow those who are entering to go in.

14 "Woe to you, scribes and Pharisees, hypocrites! For you devour widows' houses, and for a pretense make long prayers. Therefore you will receive greater condemnation.

15 "Woe to you, scribes and Pharisees, hypocrites! For you travel land and sea to win one proselyte, and when he is won, you make him twice as much a son of hell as yourselves.

16 "Woe to you, blind guides, who say, 'Whoever swears by the temple, it is nothing; but whoever swears by the gold of the temple, he is obliged *to perform it.*'

17 "Fools and blind! For which is greater, the gold or the temple that sanctifies the gold?

18 "And, 'Whoever swears by the altar, it is nothing; but whoever swears by the gift that is on it, he is obliged *to perform it.*'

19 "Fools and blind! For which is greater, the gift or the altar that sanctifies the gift?

20 "Therefore he who swears by the altar, swears by it and by all things on it.

21 "He who swears by the temple, swears by it and by Him who dwells in it.

22 "And he who swears by heaven, swears by the throne of God and by Him who sits on it.

23 "Woe to you, scribes and Pharisees, hypocrites! For you pay tithe of mint and anise and cummin, and have neglected the weightier *matters* of the law: justice and mercy and faith. These you ought to have done, without leaving the others undone.

24 "Blind guides, who strain out a gnat and swallow a camel!

25 "Woe to you, scribes and Pharisees, hypocrites! For you cleanse the outside of the cup and dish, but inside they are full of extortion and self-indulgence.

26 "Blind Pharisee, first cleanse the inside of the cup and dish, that the outside of them may be clean also.

27 "Woe to you, scribes and Pharisees, hypocrites! For you are like

whitewashed tombs which indeed appear beautiful outwardly, but inside are full of dead *men's* bones and all uncleanness.

28 "Even so you also outwardly appear righteous to men, but inside you are full of hypocrisy and lawlessness.

29 "Woe to you, scribes and Pharisees, hypocrites! Because you build the tombs of the prophets and adorn the monuments of the righteous,

30 "and say, 'If we had lived in the days of our fathers, we would not have been partakers with them in the blood of the prophets.'

31 "Therefore you are witnesses against yourselves that you are sons of those who murdered the prophets.

32 "Fill up, then, the measure of your fathers' *guilt*.

33 "Serpents, brood of vipers! How can you escape the condemnation of hell?

34 "Therefore, indeed, I send you prophets, wise men, and scribes: *some* of them you will kill and crucify, and *some* of them you will scourge in your synagogues and persecute from city to city,

35 "that on you may come all the righteous blood shed on the earth, from the blood of righteous Abel to the blood of Zechariah, son of Berechiah, whom you murdered between the temple and the altar.

36 "Assuredly, I say to you, all these things will come upon this generation.

37 "O Jerusalem, Jerusalem, the one who kills the prophets and stones those who are sent to her! How often I wanted to gather your children together, as a hen gathers her chicks under *her* wings, but you were not willing!

38 "See! Your house is left to you desolate.

39 "for I say to you, you shall see Me no more till you say, 'Blessed is *He who comes in the name of the* LORD!' "

24 Then Jesus went out and departed from the temple, and His disciples came to *Him* to show Him the buildings of the temple.

2 And Jesus said to them, "Do you not see all these things? Assuredly, I say to you, not one stone shall be left here upon another, that shall not be thrown down."

3 Now as He sat on the Mount of Olives, the disciples came to Him privately, saying, "Tell us, when will these things be? And what *will be* the sign of Your coming, and of the end of the age?"

4 And Jesus answered and said to them: "Take heed that no one deceives you.

5 "For many will come in My name, saying, 'I am the Christ,' and will deceive many.

6 "And you will hear of wars and rumors of wars. See that you are not troubled; for all *these things* must come to pass, but the end is not yet.

7 "For nation will rise against nation, and kingdom against kingdom. And there will be famines, pestilences, and earthquakes in various places.

8 "All these *are* the beginning of sorrows.

9 "Then they will deliver you up to tribulation and kill you, and you will be hated by all nations for My name's sake.

10 "And then many will be offended, will betray one another, and will hate one another.

11 "Then many false prophets will rise up and deceive many.

12 "And because lawlessness will abound, the love of many will grow cold.

13 "But he who endures to the end shall be saved.

14 "And this gospel of the kingdom will be preached in all the world as a witness to all the nations, and then the end will come.

15 "Therefore when you see the 'abomination of desolation,' spoken of by Daniel the prophet, standing in the holy place" (whoever reads, let him understand),

16 "then let those who are in Judea flee to the mountains.

17 "Let him who is on the housetop not come down to take anything out of his house.

18 "And let him who is in the field not go back to get his clothes.

19 "But woe to those who are pregnant and to those with nursing babies in those days!

20 "And pray that your flight may not be in winter or on the Sabbath.

21 "For then there will be great tribulation, such as has not been since the beginning of the world until this time, no, nor ever shall be.

22 "And unless those days were shortened, no flesh would be saved; but for the elect's sake those days will be shortened.

23 "Then if anyone says to you, 'Look, here *is* the Christ!' or 'There!' do not believe *it*.

24 "For false christs and false prophets will arise and show great signs and wonders, so as to deceive, if possible, even the elect.

25 "See, I have told you beforehand.

26 "Therefore if they say to you, 'Look, He is in the desert!' do not go out; *or* 'Look, *He is* in the inner rooms!' do not believe *it*.

27 "For as the lightning comes from the east and flashes to the west, so also will the coming of the Son of Man be.

28 "For wherever the carcass is, there the eagles will be gathered together.

29 "Immediately after the tribulation of those days the sun will be darkened, and the moon will not give its light; and the stars will fall from heaven, and the powers of the heavens will be shaken.

30 "Then the sign of the Son of Man will appear in heaven, and then all the tribes of the earth will mourn, and they will see the Son of Man coming on the clouds of heaven with power and great glory.

31 "And He will send His angels with a great sound of a trumpet, and they will gather together His elect from the four winds, from one end of heaven to the other.

32 "Now learn this parable from the fig tree: When its branch has already become tender and puts forth leaves, you know that summer *is* near.

33 "So you also, when you see all these things, know that it is near, at the *very* doors.

34 "Assuredly, I say to you, this generation will by no means pass away till all these things are fulfilled.

35 "Heaven and earth will pass away, but My words will by no means pass away.

36 "But of that day and hour no one knows, no, not even the angels of heaven, but My Father only.

37 "But as the days of Noah *were*, so also will the coming of the Son of Man be.

38 "For as in the days before the flood, they were eating and drinking, marrying and giving in marriage, until the day that Noah entered the ark,

39 "and did not know until the flood came and took them all away, so also will the coming of the Son of Man be.

40 "Then two *men* will be in the field: one will be taken and the other left.

41 "Two *women will be* grinding at the mill: one will be taken and the other left.

42 "Watch therefore, for you do not know what hour your Lord is coming.

43 "But know this, that if the master of the house had known what hour the thief would come, he would have watched and not allowed his house to be broken into.

44 "Therefore you also be ready, for the Son of Man is coming at an hour when you do not expect *Him.*

45 "Who then is a faithful and wise servant, whom his master made ruler over his household, to give them food in due season?

46 "Blessed *is* that servant whom his master, when he comes, will find so doing.

47 "Assuredly, I say to you that he will make him ruler over all his goods.

48 "But if that evil servant says in his heart, 'My master is delaying his coming,'

49 "and begins to beat *his* fellow servants, and to eat and drink with the drunkards,

50 "the master of that servant will come on a day when he is not looking for *him* and at an hour that he is not aware of,

51 "and will cut him in two and appoint *him* his portion with the hypocrites. There shall be weeping and gnashing of teeth.

25 "Then the kingdom of heaven shall be likened to ten virgins who took their lamps and went out to meet the bridegroom.

2 "Now five of them were wise, and five *were* foolish.

3 "Those who *were* foolish took their lamps and took no oil with them,

4 "but the wise took oil in their vessels with their lamps.

5 "But while the bridegroom delayed, they all slumbered and slept.

6 "And at midnight a cry was *heard:* 'Behold, the bridegroom is coming; go out to meet him!'

7 "Then all those virgins arose and trimmed their lamps.

8 "And the foolish said to the wise, 'Give us *some* of your oil, for our lamps are going out.'

9 "But the wise answered, saying,

'*No,* lest there should not be enough for us and you; but go rather to those who sell, and buy for yourselves.'

10 "And while they went to buy, the bridegroom came, and those who were ready went in with him to the wedding; and the door was shut.

11 "Afterward the other virgins came also, saying, 'Lord, Lord, open to us!'

12 "But he answered and said, 'Assuredly, I say to you, I do not know you.'

13 "Watch therefore, for you know neither the day nor the hour in which the Son of Man is coming.

14 "For *the kingdom of heaven is* like a man traveling to a far country, *who* called his own servants and delivered his goods to them.

15 "And to one he gave five talents, to another two, and to another one, to each according to his own ability; and immediately he went on a journey.

16 "Then he who had received the five talents went and traded with them, and made another five talents.

17 "And likewise he who *had received* two gained two more also.

18 "But he who had received one went and dug in the ground, and hid his lord's money.

19 "After a long time the lord of those servants came and settled accounts with them.

20 "So he who had received five talents came and brought five other talents, saying, 'Lord, you delivered to me five talents; look, I have gained five more talents besides them.'

21 "His lord said to him, 'Well done, good and faithful servant; you were faithful over a few things, I will make you ruler over many things. Enter into the joy of your lord.'

22 "He also who had received two talents came and said, 'Lord, you

delivered to me two talents; look, I have gained two more talents besides them.'

23 "His lord said to him, 'Well *done*, good and faithful servant; you have been faithful over a few things, I will make you ruler over many things. Enter into the joy of your lord.'

24 "Then he who had received the one talent came and said, 'Lord, I knew you to be a hard man, reaping where you have not sown, and gathering where you have not scattered seed.

25 'And I was afraid, and went and hid your talent in the ground. Look, *there* you have *what is* yours.'

26 "But his lord answered and said to him, 'You wicked and lazy servant, you knew that I reap where I have not sown, and gather where I have not scattered seed.

27 'Therefore you ought to have deposited my money with the bankers, and at my coming I would have received back my own with interest.

28 'Therefore take the talent from him, and give *it* to him who has ten talents.

29 'For to everyone who has, more will be given, and he will have abundance; but from him who does not have, even what he has will be taken away.

30 'And cast the unprofitable servant into the outer darkness. There will be weeping and gnashing of teeth.'

31 "When the Son of Man comes in His glory, and all the holy angels with Him, then He will sit on the throne of His glory.

32 "All the nations will be gathered before Him, and He will separate them one from another, as a shepherd divides *his* sheep from the goats.

33 "And He will set the sheep on His right hand, but the goats on the left.

34 "Then the King will say to those on His right hand, 'Come, you blessed of My Father, inherit the kingdom prepared for you from the foundation of the world:

35 'for I was hungry and you gave Me food; I was thirsty and you gave Me drink; I was a stranger and you took Me in;

36 'I *was* naked and you clothed Me; I was sick and you visited Me; I was in prison and you came to Me.'

37 "Then the righteous will answer Him, saying, 'Lord, when did we see You hungry and feed *You*, or thirsty and give *You* drink?

38 'When did we see You a stranger and take *You* in, or naked and clothe *You*?

39 'Or when did we see You sick, or in prison, and come to You?'

40 "And the King will answer and say to them, 'Assuredly, I say to you, inasmuch as you did *it* to one of the least of these My brethren, you did *it* to Me.'

41 "Then He will also say to those on the left hand, 'Depart from Me, you cursed, into the everlasting fire prepared for the devil and his angels:

42 'for I was hungry and you gave Me no food; I was thirsty and you gave Me no drink;

43 'I was a stranger and you did not take Me in, naked and you did not clothe Me, sick and in prison and you did not visit Me.'

44 "Then they also will answer Him, saying, 'Lord, when did we see You hungry or thirsty or a stranger or naked or sick or in prison, and did not minister to You?'

45 "Then He will answer them, saying, 'Assuredly, I say to you, inasmuch as you did not do *it* to one of the least of these, you did not do *it* to Me.'

46 "And these will go away into everlasting punishment, but the righteous into eternal life."

26 Now it came to pass, when Jesus had finished all these sayings, *that* He said to His disciples,

2 "You know that after two days is the Passover, and the Son of Man will be delivered up to be crucified."

3 Then the chief priests, the scribes, and the elders of the people assembled at the palace of the high priest, who was called Caiaphas,

4 and plotted to take Jesus by trickery and kill *Him.*

5 But they said, "Not during the feast, lest there be an uproar among the people."

6 And when Jesus was in Bethany at the house of Simon the leper,

7 a woman came to Him having an alabaster flask of very costly fragrant oil, and she poured it on His head as He sat *at the table.*

8 But when His disciples saw *it,* they were indignant, saying, "To what purpose *is* this waste?

9 "For this fragrant oil might have been sold for much and given to *the* poor."

10 But when Jesus was aware of *it,* He said to them, "Why do you trouble the woman? For she has done a good work for Me.

11 "For you have the poor with you always, but Me you do not have always.

12 "For in pouring this fragrant oil on My body, she did *it* for My burial.

13 "Assuredly, I say to you, wherever this gospel is preached in the whole world, what this woman has done will also be told as a memorial to her."

14 Then one of the twelve, called Judas Iscariot, went to the chief priests

15 and said, "What are you willing to give me if I deliver Him to you?" And they counted out to him thirty pieces of silver.

16 So from that time he sought opportunity to betray Him.

17 Now on the first *day* of the *Feast* of the Unleavened Bread the disciples came to Jesus, saying to Him, "Where do You want us to prepare for You to eat the Passover?"

18 And He said, "Go into the city to a certain man, and say to him, 'The Teacher says, "My time is at hand; I will keep the Passover at your house with My disciples." ' "

19 So the disciples did as Jesus had directed them; and they prepared the Passover.

20 Now when evening had come, He sat down with the twelve.

21 Now as they were eating, He said, "Assuredly, I say to you, one of you will betray Me."

22 And they were exceedingly sorrowful, and each of them began to say to Him, "Lord, is it I?"

23 Then He answered and said, "He who dipped *his* hand with Me in the dish will betray Me.

24 "The Son of Man goes as it is written of Him, but woe to that man by whom the Son of Man is betrayed! It would have been good for that man if he had not been born."

25 Then Judas, who was betraying Him, answered and said, "Rabbi, is it I?" He said to him, "You have said it."

26 And as they were eating, Jesus took bread, blessed *it* and broke *it,* and gave *it* to the disciples and said, "Take, eat; this is My body."

27 Then He took the cup, and gave thanks, and gave *it* to them, saying, "Drink from it, all of you.

28 "For this is My blood of the new covenant, which is shed for many for the remission of sins.

29 "But I say to you, I will not drink of this fruit of the vine from now on until that day when I drink it new with you in My Father's kingdom."

30 And when they had sung a

hymn, they went out to the Mount of Olives.

31 Then Jesus said to them, "All of you will be made to stumble because of Me this night, for it is written:

'I will strike the Shepherd,
And the sheep of the flock
will be scattered.'

32 "But after I have been raised, I will go before you to Galilee."

33 Peter answered and said to Him, "Even if all are made to stumble because of You, I will never be made to stumble."

34 Jesus said to him, "Assuredly, I say to you that this night, before the rooster crows, you will deny Me three times."

35 Peter said to Him, "Even if I have to die with You, I will not deny You!" And so said all the disciples.

36 Then Jesus came with them to a place called Gethsemane, and said to the disciples, "Sit here while I go and pray over there."

37 And He took with Him Peter and the two sons of Zebedee, and He began to be sorrowful and deeply distressed.

38 Then He said to them, "My soul is exceedingly sorrowful, even to death. Stay here and watch with Me."

39 He went a little farther and fell on His face, and prayed, saying, "O My Father, if it is possible, let this cup pass from Me; nevertheless, not as I will, but as You *will*."

40 Then He came to the disciples and found them asleep, and said to Peter, "What, could you not watch with Me one hour?

41 "Watch and pray, lest you enter into temptation. The spirit indeed *is* willing, but the flesh *is* weak."

42 He went away again a second time and prayed, saying, "O My Father, if this cup cannot pass away from Me unless I drink it, Your will be done."

43 And He came and found them asleep again, for their eyes were heavy.

44 So He left them, went away again, and prayed the third time, saying the same words.

45 Then He came to His disciples and said to them, "Are *you* still sleeping and resting? Behold, the hour is at hand, and the Son of Man is being betrayed into the hands of sinners.

46 "Rise, let us be going. See, he who betrays Me is at hand."

47 And while He was still speaking, behold, Judas, one of the twelve, with a great multitude with swords and clubs, came from the chief priests and elders of the people.

48 Now His betrayer had given them a sign, saying, "Whomever I kiss, He is the One; seize Him."

49 Then immediately he went up to Jesus and said, "Greetings, Rabbi!" and kissed Him.

50 And Jesus said to him, "Friend, why have you come?" Then they came and laid hands on Jesus and took Him.

51 And suddenly, one of those *who were* with Jesus stretched out *his* hand and drew his sword, struck the servant of the high priest, and cut off his ear.

52 Then Jesus said to him, "Put your sword in its place, for all who take the sword will perish by the sword.

53 "Or do you think that I cannot now pray to My Father, and He will provide Me with more than twelve legions of angels?

54 "How then could the Scriptures be fulfilled, that it must happen thus?"

55 In that hour Jesus said to the multitudes, "Have you come out, as against a robber, with swords and clubs to take Me? I sat daily with you, teaching in the temple, and you did not seize Me.

56 "But all this was done that the Scriptures of the prophets might be fulfilled." Then all the disciples forsook Him and fled.

57 And those who had laid hold of Jesus led *Him* away to Caiaphas the high priest, where the scribes and the elders were assembled.

58 But Peter followed Him at a distance to the high priest's courtyard. And he went in and sat with the servants to see the end.

59 Now the chief priests, the elders, and all the council sought false testimony against Jesus to put Him to death,

60 but found none. Even though many false witnesses came forward, they found none. But at last two false witnesses came forward

61 and said, "This *fellow* said, 'I am able to destroy the temple of God and to build it in three days.'"

62 And the high priest arose and said to Him, "Do You answer nothing? What *is it that* these men testify against You?"

63 But Jesus kept silent. And the high priest answered and said to Him, "I adjure You by the living God that You tell us if You are the Christ, the Son of God."

64 Jesus said to him, "*It is as you* said. Nevertheless, I say to you, hereafter you will see the Son of Man sitting at the right hand of the Power, and coming on the clouds of heaven."

65 Then the high priest tore his clothes, saying, "He has spoken blasphemy! What further need do we have of witnesses? Look, now you have heard His blasphemy!

66 "What do you think?" They answered and said, "He is deserving of death."

67 Then they spat in His face and beat Him; and others struck *Him* with the palms of their hands,

68 saying, "Prophesy to us, Christ! Who is the one who struck You?"

69 Now Peter sat outside in the courtyard. And a servant girl came to him, saying, "You also were with Jesus of Galilee."

70 But he denied it before *them* all, saying, "I do not know what you are saying."

71 And when he had gone out to the gateway, another *girl* saw him and said to those *who were* there, "This *fellow* also was with Jesus of Nazareth."

72 But again he denied with an oath, "I do not know the Man!"

73 And after a while those who stood by came to *him* and said to Peter, "Surely you also are *one* of them, because your speech betrays you."

74 Then he began to curse and swear, *saying*, "I do not know the Man!" And immediately a rooster crowed.

75 And Peter remembered the word of Jesus who had said to him, "Before the rooster crows, you will deny Me three times." Then he went out and wept bitterly.

27 When morning came, all the chief priests and elders of the people took counsel against Jesus to put Him to death.

2 And when they had bound Him, they led Him away and delivered Him to Pontius Pilate the governor.

3 Then Judas, His betrayer, seeing that He had been condemned, was remorseful and brought back the thirty pieces of silver to the chief priests and elders,

4 saying, "I have sinned by betraying innocent blood." And they said, "What *is that* to us? You see *to it!*"

5 Then he threw down the pieces of silver in the temple and departed, and went and hanged himself.

6 But the chief priests took the silver pieces and said, "It is not lawful to put them into the treasury, because they are the price of blood."

7 And they took counsel and

40

bought with them the potter's field, to bury strangers in.

8 Therefore that field has been called the Field of Blood to this day.

9 Then was fulfilled what was spoken by Jeremiah the prophet, saying, *"And they took the thirty pieces of silver, the value of Him who was priced,* whom they of the children of Israel priced,

10 *"and gave them for the potter's field, as the* LORD *directed me."*

11 Now Jesus stood before the governor. And the governor asked Him, saying, "Are You the King of the Jews?" So Jesus said to him, *"It is as* you say."

12 And while He was being accused by the chief priests and elders, He answered nothing.

13 Then Pilate said to Him, "Do You not hear how many things they testify against You?"

14 And He answered not one word, so that the governor marveled greatly.

15 Now at the feast the governor was accustomed to releasing to the multitude one prisoner whom they wished.

16 And they had then a notorious prisoner called Barabbas.

17 Therefore, when they had gathered together, Pilate said to them, "Whom do you want me to release to you? Barabbas, or Jesus who is called Christ?"

18 For he knew that because of envy they had delivered Him.

19 While he was sitting on the judgment seat, his wife sent to him, saying, "Have nothing to do with that just Man, for I have suffered many things today in a dream because of Him."

20 But the chief priests and elders persuaded the multitudes that they should ask for Barabbas and destroy Jesus.

21 The governor answered and said to them, "Which of the two do you want me to release to you?" They said, "Barabbas!"

22 Pilate said to them, "What then shall I do with Jesus who is called Christ?" *They* all said to him, "Let Him be crucified!"

23 Then the governor said, "Why, what evil has He done?" But they cried out all the more, saying, "Let Him be crucified!"

24 When Pilate saw that he could not prevail at all, but rather *that a* tumult was rising, he took water and washed *his* hands before the multitude, saying, "I am innocent of the blood of this just Person. You see *to it."*

25 And all the people answered and said, "His blood *be* on us and on our children."

26 Then he released Barabbas to them; and when he had scourged Jesus, he delivered *Him* to be crucified.

27 Then the soldiers of the governor took Jesus into the Praetorium and gathered the whole garrison around Him.

28 And they stripped Him and put a scarlet robe on Him.

29 When they had twisted a crown of thorns, they put *it* on His head, and a reed in His right hand. And they bowed the knee before Him and mocked Him, saying, "Hail, King of the Jews!"

30 Then they spat on Him, and took the reed and struck Him on the head.

31 Then when they had mocked Him, they took the robe off Him, put His *own* clothes on Him, and led Him away to be crucified.

32 Now as they came out, they found a man of Cyrene, Simon by name. Him they compelled to bear His cross.

33 And when they had come to a place called Golgotha, that is to say, Place of a Skull,

34 they gave Him sour wine mingled with gall to drink. But when

He had tasted *it*, He would not drink.

35 Then they crucified Him, and divided His garments, casting lots, that it might be fulfilled which was spoken by the prophet:

*"They divided My garments among them,
And for My clothing they cast lots."*

36 Sitting down, they kept watch over Him there.

37 And they put up over His head the accusation written against Him:

THIS IS JESUS
THE KING OF THE JEWS.

38 Then two robbers were crucified with Him, one on the right and another on the left.

39 And those who passed by blasphemed Him, wagging their heads

40 and saying, "You who destroy the temple and build *it* in three days, save Yourself! If You are the Son of God, come down from the cross."

41 Likewise the chief priests, also mocking with the scribes and elders, said,

42 "He saved others; Himself He cannot save. If He is the King of Israel, let Him now come down from the cross, and we will believe Him.

43 "He trusted in God; let Him deliver Him now if He will have Him; for He said, 'I am the Son of God.'"

44 Even the robbers who were crucified with Him reviled Him with the same thing.

45 Now from the sixth hour until the ninth hour there was darkness over all the land.

46 And about the ninth hour Jesus cried out with a loud voice, saying, "Eli, Eli, lama sabachthani?" that is, *"My God, My God, why have You forsaken Me?"*

47 Some of those who stood there, when they heard *that*, said, "This *Man* is calling for Elijah!"

48 Immediately one of them ran and took a sponge, filled *it* with sour wine and put *it* on a reed, and gave it to Him to drink.

49 The rest said, "Let Him alone; let us see if Elijah will come to save Him."

50 Jesus, when He had cried out again with a loud voice, yielded up His spirit.

51 And behold, the veil of the temple was torn in two from top to bottom; and the earth quaked, and the rocks were split,

52 and the graves were opened; and many bodies of the saints who had fallen asleep were raised;

53 and coming out of the graves after His resurrection, they went into the holy city and appeared to many.

54 Now when the centurion and those with him, who were guarding Jesus, saw the earthquake and the things that had happened, they feared greatly, saying, "Truly this was the Son of God!"

55 And many women who followed Jesus from Galilee, ministering to Him, were there looking on from afar,

56 among whom were Mary Magdalene, Mary the mother of James and Joses, and the mother of Zebedee's sons.

57 Now when evening had come, there came a rich man from Arimathea, named Joseph, who himself had also become a disciple of Jesus.

58 This man went to Pilate and asked for the body of Jesus. Then Pilate commanded the body to be given to him.

59 And when Joseph had taken the body, he wrapped it in a clean linen cloth,

60 and laid it in his new tomb which he had hewn out of the

How Accurate Is the Bible's Forecast of Future Events?

The Bible forecasts thousands of specific events—in detail—often centuries before they occurred. Just how accurate are those predictions?

Several hundred of the prophecies recorded in the Old Testament point toward the coming Savior. A sampling is listed below along with an estimate of the odds that each prediction could be fulfilled by chance.

To be born in Bethlehem.
Seven hundred years before Jesus' birth, the prophet Micah (in Micah 5:2) predicted that the tiny village of Bethlehem would be the birthplace of Israel's Messiah. If there were a thousand villages in Israel, the rough estimate of the chances of being born in Bethlehem would be a thousand to one. To keep track of the large numbers, let's express the probability of being born in Bethlehem rather than somewhere else as 1 in 10^3 (the number 1 followed by three zeros, or 1,000).

Would be betrayed for thirty pieces of silver. In the
fifth century B.C., the prophet Zechariah predicted that the Messiah would be betrayed for the price of a slave and that the money would be used to buy a burial ground for poor foreigners. See fulfillment in Matthew 27:3–10. Probability of chance fulfillment: a million to one (1 in 10^6).

Would be crucified. Some
four hundred years before crucifixion became a standard form of execution, the Messiah's death was predicted in words that vividly portray crucifixion (Psalm 22; 34:20; Zechariah 12:10). His quick death eliminated the usual breaking of leg bones. Probability of chance fulfillment: one in a million (1 to 10^6).

Soldiers would gamble for His clothing. Psalm 22:18
predicted this division of Jesus' clothes a thousand years before the prophecy was fulfilled (Matthew 27:35). Probability of chance fulfillment: one in a thousand (1 in 10^3).

The combined odds of just these four predictions occurring in an individual's life is 1 in 10^{18}.

The odds are inconceivably tiny. If the Superdome were completely filled with sand, the odds of selecting a single specific grain by chance would be only ten thousand times greater than these four predictions coming true.

rock; and he rolled a large stone against the door of the tomb, and departed.

61 And Mary Magdalene was there, and the other Mary, sitting opposite the tomb.

62 On the next day, which followed the Day of Preparation, the chief priests and Pharisees gathered together to Pilate,

63 saying, "Sir, we remember, while He was still alive, how that deceiver said, 'After three days I will rise.'

64 "Therefore command that the tomb be made secure until the third day, lest His disciples come by night and steal Him *away*, and say to the people, 'He has risen from the dead.' So the last deception will be worse than the first."

65 Pilate said to them, "You have a guard; go your way, make *it* as secure as you know how."

66 So they went and made the tomb secure, sealing the stone and setting the guard.

28 Now after the Sabbath, as the first *day* of the week began to dawn, Mary Magdalene and the other Mary came to see the tomb.

2 And behold, there was a great earthquake; for an angel of the Lord descended from heaven, and came and rolled back the stone from the door, and sat on it.

3 His countenance was like lightning, and his clothing as white as snow.

4 And the guards shook for fear of him, and became like dead *men*.

5 But the angel answered and said to the women, "Do not be afraid, for I know that you seek Jesus who was crucified.

6 "He is not here; for He is risen, as He said. Come, see the place where the Lord lay.

7 "And go quickly and tell His disciples that He is risen from the dead, and indeed He is going before you into Galilee; there you will see Him. Behold, I have told you."

8 So they departed quickly from the tomb with fear and great joy, and ran to bring His disciples word.

9 And as they went to tell His disciples, behold, Jesus met them, saying, "Rejoice!" And they came and held Him by the feet and worshiped Him.

10 Then Jesus said to them, "Do not be afraid. Go *and* tell My brethren to go to Galilee, and there they will see Me."

11 Now while they were going, behold, some of the guard came into the city and reported to the chief priests all the things that had happened.

12 When they had assembled with the elders and taken counsel, they gave a large sum of money to the soldiers,

13 saying, "Tell them, 'His disciples came at night and stole Him *away* while we slept.'

14 "And if this comes to the governor's ears, we will appease him and make you secure."

15 So they took the money and did as they were instructed; and this saying is commonly reported among the Jews until this day.

16 Then the eleven disciples went away into Galilee, to the mountain which Jesus had appointed for them.

17 And when they saw Him, they worshiped Him; but some doubted.

18 Then Jesus came and spoke to them, saying, "All authority has been given to Me in heaven and on earth.

19 "Go therefore and make disciples of all the nations, baptizing them in the name of the Father and of the Son and of the Holy Spirit,

20 "teaching them to observe all things that I have commanded you; and lo, I am with you always, *even* to the end of the age." Amen.

THE GOSPEL ACCORDING TO

MARK

THE beginning of the gospel of Jesus Christ, the Son of God.

2 As it is written in the Prophets:

"Behold, I send My messenger
before Your face,
Who will prepare Your way
before You."

3 *"The voice of one crying in the*
wilderness:
'Prepare the way of the LORD,
Make His paths straight.'"

4 John came baptizing in the wilderness and preaching a baptism of repentance for the remission of sins.

5 And all the land of Judea, and those from Jerusalem, went out to him and were all baptized by him in the Jordan River, confessing their sins.

6 Now John was clothed with camel's hair and with a leather belt around his waist, and he ate locusts and wild honey.

7 And he preached, saying, "There comes One after me who is mightier than I, whose sandal strap I am not worthy to stoop down and loose.

8 "I indeed baptized you with water, but He will baptize you with the Holy Spirit."

9 It came to pass in those days *that* Jesus came from Nazareth of Galilee, and was baptized by John in the Jordan.

10 And immediately, coming up from the water, He saw the heavens parting and the Spirit descending upon Him like a dove.

11 Then a voice came from heaven, "You are My beloved Son, in whom I am well pleased."

12 And immediately the Spirit drove Him into the wilderness.

13 And He was there in the wilderness forty days, tempted by Satan, and was with the wild beasts; and the angels ministered to Him.

14 Now after John was put in prison, Jesus came to Galilee, preaching the gospel of the kingdom of God,

15 and saying, "The time is fulfilled, and the kingdom of God is at hand. Repent, and believe in the gospel."

16 And as He walked by the Sea of Galilee, He saw Simon and Andrew his brother casting a net into the sea; for they were fishermen.

17 Then Jesus said to them, "Come after Me, and I will make you become fishers of men."

18 And immediately they left their nets and followed Him.

19 When He had gone a little farther from there, He saw James the *son* of Zebedee, and John his brother, who also *were* in the boat mending their nets.

20 And immediately He called them, and they left their father Zebedee in the boat with the hired servants, and went after Him.

21 Then they went into Capernaum, and immediately on the Sabbath He entered the synagogue and taught.

22 And they were astonished at His teaching, for He taught them as one having authority, and not as the scribes.

23 Now there was a man in their synagogue with an unclean spirit. And he cried out,

24 saying, "Let *us* alone! What have we to do with You, Jesus of Nazareth? Did You come to destroy us? I know who You are—the Holy One of God!"

25 But Jesus rebuked him, saying, "Be quiet, and come out of him!"

26 And when the unclean spirit had convulsed him and cried out with a loud voice, he came out of him.

27 Then they were all amazed, so that they questioned among themselves, saying, "What is this? What new doctrine *is* this? For with authority He commands even the unclean spirits, and they obey Him."

28 And immediately His fame spread throughout all the region around Galilee.

29 Now as soon as they had come out of the synagogue, they entered the house of Simon and Andrew, with James and John.

30 But Simon's wife's mother lay sick with a fever, and they told Him about her at once.

31 So He came and took her by the hand and lifted her up, and immediately the fever left her. And she served them.

32 Now at evening, when the sun had set, they brought to Him all who were sick and those who were demon-possessed.

33 And the whole city was gathered together at the door.

34 Then He healed many who were sick with various diseases, and cast out many demons; and He did not allow the demons to speak, because they knew Him.

35 Now in the morning, having risen a long while before daylight, He went out and departed to a solitary place; and there He prayed.

36 And Simon and those *who were* with Him searched for Him.

37 When they found Him, they said to Him, "Everyone is looking for You."

38 But He said to them, "Let us go into the next towns, that I may preach there also, because for this purpose I have come forth."

39 And He was preaching in their synagogues throughout all Galilee, and casting out demons.

40 Then a leper came to Him, imploring Him, kneeling down to Him and saying to Him, "If You

are willing, You can make me clean."

41 And Jesus, moved with compassion, put out *His* hand and touched him, and said to him, "I am willing; be cleansed."

42 As soon as He had spoken, immediately the leprosy left him, and he was cleansed.

43 And He strictly warned him and sent him away at once.

44 And He said to him, "See that you say nothing to anyone; but go your way, show yourself to the priest, and offer for your cleansing those things which Moses commanded, as a testimony to them."

45 But he went out and began to proclaim *it* freely, and to spread the matter, so that Jesus could no longer openly enter the city, but was outside in deserted places; and they came to Him from every quarter.

2 And again He entered Capernaum after *some* days, and it was heard that He was in the house.

2 Immediately many gathered together, so that there was no longer room to receive *them*, not even near the door. And He preached the word to them.

3 Then they came to Him, bringing a paralytic who was carried by four *men*.

4 And when they could not come near Him because of the crowd, they uncovered the roof where He was. And when they had broken through, they let down the bed on which the paralytic was lying.

5 When Jesus saw their faith, He said to the paralytic, "Son, your sins are forgiven you."

6 But some of the scribes were sitting there and reasoning in their hearts,

7 "Why does this *Man* speak blasphemies like this? Who can forgive sins but God alone?"

8 And immediately, when Jesus perceived in His spirit that they

reasoned thus within themselves, He said to them, "Why do you reason about these things in your hearts?

9 "Which is easier, to say to the paralytic, 'Your sins are forgiven you,' or to say, 'Arise, take up your bed and walk?'

10 "But that you may know that the Son of Man has power on earth to forgive sins"—He said to the paralytic,

11 "I say to you, arise, take up your bed, and go your way to your house."

12 And immediately he arose, took up the bed, and went out in the presence of them all, so that all were amazed and glorified God, saying, "We never saw *anything* like this!"

13 Then He went out again by the sea; and all the multitude came to Him, and He taught them.

14 And as He passed by, He saw Levi the *son* of Alphaeus sitting at the tax office, and said to him, "Follow Me." And he arose and followed Him.

15 Now it happened, as He was dining in *Levi's* house, that many tax collectors and sinners also sat together with Jesus and His disciples; for there were many, and they followed Him.

16 And when the scribes and Pharisees saw Him eating with the tax collectors and sinners, they said to His disciples, "How *is it* that He eats and drinks with tax collectors and sinners?"

17 When Jesus heard *it*, He said to them, "Those who are well have no need of a physician, but those who are sick. I did not come to call *the* righteous, but sinners, to repentance."

18 And the disciples of John and of the Pharisees were fasting. And they came and said to Him, "Why do the disciples of John and of the Pharisees fast, but Your disciples do not fast?"

19 So Jesus said to them, "Can the friends of the bridegroom fast while the bridegroom is with them? As long as they have the bridegroom with them they cannot fast.

20 "But the days will come when the bridegroom will be taken away from them, and then they will fast in those days.

21 "No one sews a piece of unshrunk cloth on an old garment; or else the new piece pulls away from the old, and the tear is made worse.

22 "And no one puts new wine into old wineskins; or else the new wine bursts the wineskins, the wine is spilled, and the wineskins are ruined. But new wine must be put into new wineskins."

23 Now it happened that He went through the grainfields on the Sabbath; and as they went His disciples began to pluck the heads of grain.

24 And the Pharisees said to Him, "Look, why do they do what is not lawful on the Sabbath?"

25 But He said to them, "Have you never read what David did when he was in need and hungry, he and those with him:

26 "how he went into the house of God *in the days* of Abiathar the high priest, and ate the showbread, which is not lawful to eat, except for the priests, and also gave some to those who were with him?"

27 And He said to them, "The Sabbath was made for man, and not man for the Sabbath.

28 "Therefore the Son of Man is also Lord of the Sabbath."

3 And He entered the synagogue again, and a man was there who had a withered hand.

2 And they watched Him closely, whether He would heal him on the Sabbath, so that they might accuse Him.

3 Then He said to the man who

47

had the withered hand, "Step forward."

4 And He said to them, "Is it lawful on the Sabbath to do good or to do evil, to save life or to kill?" But they kept silent.

5 So when He had looked around at them with anger, being grieved by the hardness of their hearts, He said to the man, "Stretch out your hand." And he stretched *it* out, and his hand was restored as whole as the other.

6 Then the Pharisees went out and immediately plotted with the Herodians against Him, how they might destroy Him.

7 But Jesus withdrew with His disciples to the sea. And a great multitude from Galilee followed Him, and from Judea

8 and Jerusalem and Idumea and beyond the Jordan; and those from Tyre and Sidon, a great multitude, when they heard how many things He was doing, came to Him.

9 And He told His disciples that a small boat should be kept ready for Him because of the multitude, lest they should crush Him.

10 For He healed many, so that as many as had afflictions pressed about Him to touch Him.

11 And the unclean spirits, whenever they saw Him, fell down before Him and cried out, saying, "You are the Son of God."

12 But He sternly warned them that they should not make Him known.

13 And He went up on the mountain and called *to Him* those He Himself wanted. And they came to Him.

14 Then He appointed twelve, that they might be with Him and that He might send them out to preach,

15 and to have power to heal sicknesses and to cast out demons:

16 Simon, to whom He gave the name Peter;

17 James the *son* of Zebedee and John the brother of James, to whom He gave the name Boanerges, that is, "Sons of Thunder";

18 Andrew, Philip, Bartholomew, Matthew, Thomas, James the *son* of Alphaeus, Thaddaeus, Simon the Canaanite;

19 and Judas Iscariot, who also betrayed Him. And they went into a house.

20 And the multitude came together again, so that they could not so much as eat bread.

21 But when His own people heard *about this,* they went out to lay hold of Him, for they said, "He is out of His mind."

22 And the scribes who came down from Jerusalem said, "He has Beelzebub," and, "By the ruler of the demons He casts out demons."

23 So He called them *to Him* and said to them in parables: "How can Satan cast out Satan?

24 "If a kingdom is divided against itself, that kingdom cannot stand.

25 "And if a house is divided against itself, that house cannot stand.

26 "And if Satan has risen up against himself, and is divided, he cannot stand, but has an end.

27 "No one can enter a strong man's house and plunder his goods, unless he first binds the strong man, and then he will plunder his house.

28 "Assuredly, I say to you, all sins will be forgiven the sons of men, and whatever blasphemies they may utter;

29 "but he who blasphemes against the Holy Spirit never has forgiveness, but is subject to eternal condemnation"—

30 because they said, "He has an unclean spirit."

31 Then His brothers and His mother came, and standing outside they sent to Him, calling Him.

32 And a multitude was sitting around Him; and they said to Him, "Look, Your mother and Your brothers are outside seeking You."

Are Some Sins Unforgivable?

Christianity (unlike all other world religions) offers a genuine solution for sin. Because Jesus died on the cross, every sin can be forgiven—except one. The highlighted passage in Mark 3 refers to this sin as blaspheming against the Holy Spirit. How can we know if we have committed this unpardonable sin?

Before answering the question, let's examine the situation in which the statement came up. Jesus' enemies had just leveled a serious charge against Him. In verse 22, they said, "He has Beelzebub" (a name that at the time was synonymous with the Devil), and "by the ruler of demons, He casts out demons." Note that they didn't deny His miracle, His goodness, or His compassion. They acknowledged His power and righteousness but said these attributes came from an evil source.

Jesus briefly refuted their charge by pointing out their twisted logic. Why would Satan work to defeat himself? But Jesus was chiefly concerned with what the accusation told Him about His enemies' attitude.

Recognizing the hand of God and choosing to call it evil is blasphemy against the Holy Spirit.

Blasphemers against the Holy Spirit are described in Romans 1, Hebrews 6 and 10, 2 Peter 2, Jude, and in many other passages. They are people who are convinced of God's existence, know the Bible is true, have no doubts about the offer of salvation through Christ, and recognize the benefits of walking with Christ here on earth and of eternal life in heaven. Yet in understanding all this, they are utterly committed to rebellion and wickedness. They openly and knowingly mock God, ascribe evil to Him and His followers, delight in encouraging others to join them in their rebellion, mock humility and righteous living, call good evil and evil good, ignore judgment, and reject their need of redemption. Their consciences are seared, their hearts completely hardened. Because they are incapable of repenting, of giving or receiving love and forgiveness, it is impossible for them to ever receive salvation. For these reasons, anyone worried about having committed the unpardonable sin is definitely *not* a blasphemer.

33 But He answered them, saying, "Who is My mother, or My brothers?"

34 And He looked around in a circle at those who sat about Him, and said, "Here are My mother and My brothers!

35 "For whoever does the will of God is My brother and My sister and mother."

4 And again He began to teach by the sea. And a great multitude was gathered to Him, so that He got into a boat and sat *in it* on the sea; and the whole multitude was on the land facing the sea.

2 Then He taught them many things by parables, and said to them in His teaching:

3 "Listen! Behold, a sower went out to sow.

4 "And it happened, as he sowed, *that* some *seed* fell by the wayside; and the birds of the air came and devoured it.

5 "Some fell on stony ground, where it did not have much earth; and immediately it sprang up because it had no depth of earth.

6 "But when the sun was up it was scorched, and because it had no root it withered away.

7 "And some *seed* fell among thorns; and the thorns grew up and choked it, and it yielded no crop.

8 "But other *seed* fell on good ground and yielded a crop that sprang up, increased and produced: some thirtyfold, some sixty, and some a hundred."

9 And He said to them, "He who has ears to hear, let him hear!"

10 But when He was alone, those around Him with the twelve asked Him about the parable.

11 And He said to them, "To you it has been given to know the mystery of the kingdom of God; but to those who are outside, all things come in parables,

12 "so that

'Seeing they may see and not perceive,
And hearing they may hear and not understand;
Lest they should turn,
And their sins be forgiven them.' "

13 And He said to them, "Do you not understand this parable? How then will you understand all the parables?

14 "The sower sows the word.

15 "And these are the ones by the wayside where the word is sown. And when they hear, Satan comes immediately and takes away the word that was sown in their hearts.

16 "These likewise are the ones sown on stony ground who, when they hear the word, immediately receive it with gladness;

17 "and they have no root in themselves, and so endure only for a time. Afterward, when tribulation or persecution arises for the word's sake, immediately they stumble.

18 "Now these are the ones sown among thorns; *they are* the ones who hear the word,

19 "and the cares of this world, the deceitfulness of riches, and the desires for other things entering in choke the word, and it becomes unfruitful.

20 "But these are the ones sown on good ground, those who hear the word, accept *it,* and bear fruit: some thirtyfold, some sixty, and some a hundred."

21 And He said to them, "Is a lamp brought to be put under a basket or under a bed? Is it not to be set on a lampstand?

22 "For there is nothing hidden which will not be revealed, nor has anything been kept secret but that it should come to light.

23 "If anyone has ears to hear, let him hear."

24 And He said to them, "Take heed what you hear. With the

same measure you use, it will be measured to you; and to you who hear, more will be given.

25 "For whoever has, to him more will be given; but whoever does not have, even what he has will be taken away from him."

26 And He said, "The kingdom of God is as if a man should scatter seed on the ground,

27 "and should sleep by night and rise by day, and the seed should sprout and grow, he himself does not know how.

28 "For the earth yields crops by itself: first the blade, then the head, after that the full grain in the head.

29 "But when the grain ripens, immediately he puts in the sickle, because the harvest has come."

30 And He said, "To what shall we liken the kingdom of God? Or with what parable shall we picture it?

31 "*It is* like a mustard seed which, when it is sown on the ground, is smaller than all the seeds on earth;

32 "but when it is sown, it grows up and becomes greater than all herbs, and shoots out large branches, so that the birds of the air may nest under its shade."

33 And with many such parables He spoke the word to them as they were able to hear *it*.

34 But without a parable He did not speak to them. And when they were alone, He explained all things to His disciples.

35 On the same day, when evening had come, He said to them, "Let us cross over to the other side."

36 Now when they had left the multitude, they took Him along in the boat as He was. And other little boats were also with Him.

37 And a great windstorm arose, and the waves beat into the boat, so that it was already filling.

38 But He was in the stern, asleep on a pillow. And they awoke Him and said to Him, "Teacher, do You not care that we are perishing?"

39 Then He arose and rebuked the wind, and said to the sea, "Peace, be still!" And the wind ceased and there was a great calm.

40 But He said to them, "Why are you so fearful? How *is it* that you have no faith?"

41 And they feared exceedingly, and said to one another, "Who can this be, that even the wind and the sea obey Him!"

5 Then they came to the other side of the sea, to the country of the Gadarenes.

2 And when He had come out of the boat, immediately there met Him out of the tombs a man with an unclean spirit,

3 who had *his* dwelling among the tombs; and no one could bind him, not even with chains,

4 because he had often been bound with shackles and chains. And the chains had been pulled apart by him, and the shackles broken in pieces; neither could anyone tame him.

5 And always, night and day, he was in the mountains and in the tombs, crying out and cutting himself with stones.

6 But when he saw Jesus from afar, he ran and worshiped Him.

7 And he cried out with a loud voice and said, "What have I to do with You, Jesus, Son of the Most High God? I implore You by God that You do not torment me."

8 For He said to him, "Come out of the man, unclean spirit!"

9 Then He asked him, "What *is* your name?" And he answered, saying, "My name *is* Legion; for we are many."

10 And he begged Him earnestly that He would not send them out of the country.

11 Now a large herd of swine was feeding there near the mountains.

12 And all the demons begged Him, saying, "Send us to the swine, that we may enter them."

13 And at once Jesus gave them permission. Then the unclean spir-

its went out and entered the swine (there were about two thousand); and the herd ran violently down the steep place into the sea, and drowned in the sea.

14 Now those who fed the swine fled, and they told *it* in the city and in the country. And they went out to see what it was that had happened.

15 Then they came to Jesus, and saw the one *who had been* demon-possessed and had the legion, sitting and clothed and in his right mind. And they were afraid.

16 And those who saw it told them how it happened to him *who had been* demon-possessed, and about the swine.

17 Then they began to plead with Him to depart from their region.

18 And when He got into the boat, he who had been demon-possessed begged Him that he might be with Him.

19 However, Jesus did not permit him, but said to him, "Go home to your friends, and tell them what great things the Lord has done for you, and how He has had compassion on you."

20 And he departed and began to proclaim in Decapolis all that Jesus had done for him; and all marveled.

21 Now when Jesus had crossed over again by boat to the other side, a great multitude gathered to Him; and He was by the sea.

22 And behold, one of the rulers of the synagogue came, Jairus by name. And when he saw Him, he fell at His feet

23 and begged Him earnestly, saying, "My little daughter lies at the point of death. Come and lay Your hands on her, that she may be healed, and she will live."

24 So *Jesus* went with him, and a great multitude followed Him and thronged Him.

25 Now a certain woman had a flow of blood for twelve years,

26 and had suffered many things from many physicians. She had spent all that she had and was no better, but rather grew worse.

27 When she heard about Jesus, she came behind *Him* in the crowd and touched His garment;

28 for she said, "If only I may touch His clothes, I shall be made well."

29 Immediately the fountain of her blood was dried up, and she felt in *her* body that she was healed of the affliction.

30 And Jesus, immediately knowing in Himself that power had gone out of Him, turned around in the crowd and said, "Who touched My clothes?"

31 But His disciples said to Him, "You see the multitude thronging You, and You say, 'Who touched Me?' "

32 And He looked around to see her who had done this thing.

33 But the woman, fearing and trembling, knowing what had happened to her, came and fell down before Him and told Him the whole truth.

34 And He said to her, "Daughter, your faith has made you well. Go in peace, and be healed of your affliction."

35 While He was still speaking, *some* came from the ruler of the synagogue's *house* who said, "Your daughter is dead. Why trouble the Teacher any further?"

36 As soon as Jesus heard the word that was spoken, He said to the ruler of the synagogue, "Do not be afraid; only believe."

37 And He permitted no one to follow Him except Peter, James, and John the brother of James.

38 Then He came to the house of the ruler of the synagogue, and saw a tumult and those who wept and wailed loudly.

39 When He came in, He said to them, "Why make this commotion

and weep? The child is not dead, but sleeping."

40 And they laughed Him to scorn. But when He had put them all out, He took the father and the mother of the child, and those *who were* with Him, and entered where the child was lying.

41 Then He took the child by the hand, and said to her, "Talitha, cumi," which is translated, "Little girl, I say to you, arise."

42 Immediately the girl arose and walked, for she was twelve years *of age*. And they were overcome with great amazement.

43 But He commanded them strictly that no one should know it, and said that *something* should be given her to eat.

6 Then He went out from there and came to His own country, and His disciples followed Him.

2 And when the Sabbath had come, He began to teach in the synagogue. And many hearing *Him* were astonished, saying, "Where *did* this *Man* get these things? And what wisdom *is* this which is given to Him, that such mighty works are performed by His hands!

3 "Is this not the carpenter, the Son of Mary, and brother of James, Joses, Judas, and Simon? And are not His sisters here with us?" And they were offended at Him.

4 But Jesus said to them, "A prophet is not without honor except in his own country, among his own relatives, and in his own house."

5 Now He could do no mighty work there, except that He laid His hands on a few sick people and healed *them*.

6 And He marveled because of their unbelief. Then He went about the villages in a circuit, teaching.

7 And He called the twelve *to* Him, and began to send them out two *by* two, and gave them power over unclean spirits.

8 He commanded them to take nothing for the journey except a staff—no bag, no bread, no copper in *their* money belts—

9 but to wear sandals, and not to put on two tunics.

10 Also He said to them, "In whatever place you enter a house, stay there till you depart from that place.

11 "And whoever will not receive you nor hear you, when you depart from there, shake off the dust under your feet as a testimony against them. Assuredly, I say to you, it will be more tolerable for Sodom and Gomorrah in the day of judgment than for that city!"

12 So they went out and preached that *people* should repent.

13 And they cast out many demons, and anointed with oil many who were sick, and healed *them*.

14 Now King Herod heard *of Him*, for His name had become well known. And he said, "John the Baptist is risen from the dead, and therefore these powers are at work in him."

15 Others said, "It is Elijah." And others said, "It is the Prophet, or like one of the prophets."

16 But when Herod heard, he said, "This is John, whom I beheaded; he has been raised from the dead!"

17 For Herod himself had sent and laid hold of John, and bound him in prison for the sake of Herodias, his brother Philip's wife; for he had married her.

18 For John had said to Herod, "It is not lawful for you to have your brother's wife."

19 Therefore Herodias held it against him and wanted to kill him, but she could not;

20 for Herod feared John, knowing that he *was* a just and holy man, and he protected him. And when he heard him, he did many things, and heard him gladly.

21 Then an opportune day came when Herod on his birthday gave a

feast for his nobles, the high officers, and the chief *men* of Galilee.

22 And when Herodias' daughter herself came in and danced, and pleased Herod and those who sat with him, the king said to the girl, "Ask me whatever you want, and I will give *it* to you."

23 He also swore to her, "Whatever you ask me, I will give you, up to half of my kingdom."

24 So she went out and said to her mother, "What shall I ask?" And she said, "The head of John the Baptist!"

25 Immediately she came in with haste to the king and asked, saying, "I want you to give me at once the head of John the Baptist on a platter."

26 And the king was exceedingly sorry; *yet*, because of the oaths and because of those who sat with him, he did not want to refuse her.

27 And immediately the king sent an executioner and commanded his head to be brought. And he went and beheaded him in prison,

28 brought his head on a platter, and gave it to the girl; and the girl gave it to her mother.

29 And when his disciples heard *of it*, they came and took away his corpse and laid it in a tomb.

30 Then the apostles gathered to Jesus and told Him all things, both what they had done and what they had taught.

31 And He said to them, "Come aside by yourselves to a deserted place and rest a while." For there were many coming and going, and they did not even have time to eat.

32 So they departed to a deserted place in the boat by themselves.

33 But the multitudes saw them departing, and many knew Him and ran there on foot from all the cities. They arrived before them and came together to Him.

34 And Jesus, when He came out, saw a great multitude and was moved with compassion for them,

because they were like sheep not having a shepherd. So He began to teach them many things.

35 And when the day was now far spent, His disciples came to Him and said, "This is a deserted place, and already the hour is late.

36 "Send them away, that they may go into the surrounding country and villages and buy themselves bread; for they have nothing to eat."

37 But He answered and said to them, "You give them something to eat." And they said to Him, "Shall we go and buy two hundred denarii worth of bread and give them *something* to eat?"

38 But He said to them, "How many loaves do you have? Go and see." And when they found out they said, "Five, and two fish."

39 Then He commanded them to make them all sit down in groups on the green grass.

40 So they sat down in ranks, in hundreds and in fifties.

41 And when He had taken the five loaves and the two fish, He looked up to heaven, blessed and broke the loaves, and gave *them* to His disciples to set before them; and the two fish He divided among *them* all.

42 So they all ate and were filled.

43 And they took up twelve baskets full of fragments and of the fish.

44 Now those who had eaten the loaves were about five thousand men.

45 Immediately He made His disciples get into the boat and go before Him to the other side, to Bethsaida, while He sent the multitude away.

46 And when He had sent them away, He departed to the mountain to pray.

47 Now when evening came, the boat was in the middle of the sea; and He *was* alone on the land.

48 Then He saw them straining at rowing, for the wind was against

54

them. And about the fourth watch of the night He came to them, walking on the sea, and would have passed them by.

49 But when they saw Him walking on the sea, they supposed it was a ghost, and cried out;

50 for they all saw Him and were troubled. And immediately He talked with them and said to them, "Be of good cheer! It is I; do not be afraid."

51 Then He went up into the boat to them, and the wind ceased. And they were greatly amazed in themselves beyond measure, and marveled.

52 For they had not understood about the loaves, because their heart was hardened.

53 When they had crossed over, they came to the land of Gennesaret and anchored there.

54 And when they came out of the boat, immediately the people recognized Him,

55 ran through that whole surrounding region, and began to carry about on beds those who were sick to wherever they heard He was.

56 Wherever He entered, into villages, cities, or the country, they laid the sick in the marketplaces, and begged Him that they might just touch the border of His garment. And as many as touched Him were made well.

7 Then the Pharisees and some of the scribes came together to Him, having come from Jerusalem.

2 Now when they saw some of His disciples eat bread with defiled, that is, with unwashed hands, they found fault.

3 For the Pharisees and all the Jews do not eat unless they wash *their* hands in a special way, holding the tradition of the elders.

4 *When they come* from the marketplace, they do not eat unless they wash. And there are many other things which they have received and hold, *like* the washing of cups, pitchers, copper vessels, and couches.

5 Then the Pharisees and scribes asked Him, "Why do Your disciples not walk according to the tradition of the elders, but eat bread with unwashed hands?"

6 He answered and said to them, "Well did Isaiah prophesy of you hypocrites, as it is written:

'This people honors Me with
their lips,
But their heart is far from Me.
7 And in vain they worship Me,
Teaching as doctrines the
commandments of men.'

8 "For laying aside the commandment of God, you hold the tradition of men—the washing of pitchers and cups, and many other such things you do."

9 And He said to them, "*All too* well you reject the commandment of God, that you may keep your tradition.

10 "For Moses said, '*Honor your father and your mother*'; and, '*He who curses father or mother, let him be put to death.*'

11 "But you say, 'If a man says to his father or mother, "Whatever profit you might have received from me *is* Corban"—'" (that is, dedicated *to the temple*);

12 "and you no longer let him do anything for his father or his mother,

13 "making the word of God of no effect through your tradition which you have handed down. And many such things you do."

14 And when He had called all the multitude *to Him*, He said to them, "Hear Me, everyone, and understand:

15 "There is nothing that enters a man from outside which can defile him; but the things which come out of him, those are the things that defile a man.

16 "If anyone has ears to hear, let him hear!"

17 And when He had entered a house away from the crowd, His disciples asked Him concerning the parable.

18 So He said to them, "Are you thus without understanding also? Do you not perceive that whatever enters a man from outside cannot defile him,

19 "because it does not enter his heart but his stomach, and is eliminated, *thus* purifying all foods?"

20 And He said, "What comes out of a man, that defiles a man.

21 "For from within, out of the heart of men, proceed evil thoughts, adulteries, fornications, murders,

22 "thefts, covetousness, wickedness, deceit, licentiousness, an evil eye, blasphemy, pride, foolishness.

23 "All these evil things come from within and defile a man."

24 And from there He arose and went to the region of Tyre and Sidon. And He entered a house and wanted no one to know *it*, but He could not be hidden.

25 For a woman whose young daughter had an unclean spirit heard about Him, and she came and fell at His feet.

26 The woman was a Greek, a Syro-Phoenician by birth, and she kept asking Him to cast the demon out of her daughter.

27 But Jesus said to her, "Let the children be filled first, for it is not good to take the children's bread and throw *it* to the little dogs."

28 And she answered and said to Him, "Yes, Lord, yet even the little dogs under the table eat from the children's crumbs."

29 Then He said to her, "For this saying go your way; the demon has gone out of your daughter."

30 And when she had come to her house, she found the demon gone out, and her daughter lying on the bed.

31 And again, departing from the region of Tyre and Sidon, He came through the midst of the region of Decapolis to the Sea of Galilee.

32 Then they brought to Him one who was deaf and had an impediment in his speech, and they begged Him to put His hand on him.

33 And He took him aside from the multitude, and put His fingers in his ears, and He spat and touched his tongue.

34 Then, looking up to heaven, He sighed, and said to him, "Ephphatha," that is, "Be opened."

35 Immediately his ears were opened, and the impediment in his tongue was loosed, and he spoke plainly.

36 Then He commanded them that they should tell no one; but the more He commanded them, the more widely they proclaimed *it*.

37 And they were astonished beyond measure, saying, "He has done all things well. He makes both the deaf to hear and the mute to speak."

8 In those days, the multitude being very great and having nothing to eat, Jesus called His disciples *to Him* and said to them,

2 "I have compassion on the multitude, because they have now been with Me three days and have nothing to eat.

3 "And if I send them away hungry to their own houses, they will faint on the way; for some of them have come from afar."

4 Then His disciples answered Him, "How can one satisfy these people with bread here in the wilderness?"

5 He asked them, "How many loaves do you have?" And they said, "Seven."

6 And He commanded the multitude to sit down on the ground. And He took the seven loaves and gave thanks, broke *them* and gave *them* to His disciples to set before

56

them; and they set *them* before the multitude.

7 And they had a few small fish; and having blessed them, He said to set them also before *them.*

8 So they ate and were filled, and they took up seven large baskets of leftover fragments.

9 Now those who had eaten were about four thousand. And He sent them away.

10 And immediately He got into the boat with His disciples and came to the region of Dalmanutha.

11 And the Pharisees came out and began to dispute with Him, seeking from Him a sign from heaven, testing Him.

12 But He sighed deeply in His spirit, and said, "Why does this generation seek a sign? Assuredly, I say to you, no sign shall be given to this generation."

13 And He left them, and getting into the boat again, departed to the other side.

14 Now the disciples had forgotten to take bread, and they did not have more than one loaf with them in the boat.

15 Then He charged them, saying, "Take heed, beware of the leaven of the Pharisees and the leaven of Herod."

16 So they reasoned among themselves, saying, "*It is* because we have no bread."

17 And Jesus, being aware of *it,* said to them, "Why do you reason because you have no bread? Do you not yet perceive nor understand? Is your heart still hardened?

18 "Having eyes, do you not see? And having ears, do you not hear? And do you not remember?

19 "When I broke the five loaves for the five thousand, how many baskets full of fragments did you take up?" They said to Him, "Twelve."

20 "And when I broke the seven for the four thousand, how many large baskets full of fragments did

you take up?" And they said, "Seven."

21 So He said to them, "How *is it* you do not understand?"

22 Then He came to Bethsaida; and they brought a blind man to Him, and begged Him to touch him.

23 So He took the blind man by the hand and led him out of the town. And when He had spit on his eyes and put His hands on him, He asked him if he saw anything.

24 And he looked up and said, "I see men like trees, walking."

25 Then He put *His* hands on his eyes again and made him look up. And he was restored and saw everyone clearly.

26 And He sent him away to his house, saying, "Neither go into the town, nor tell anyone in the town."

27 Now Jesus and His disciples went out to the towns of Caesarea Philippi; and on the road He asked His disciples, saying to them, "Who do men say that I am?"

28 And they answered, "John the Baptist; but some *say,* Elijah; and others, one of the prophets."

29 He said to them, "But who do you say that I am?" And Peter answered and said to Him, "You are the Christ."

30 Then He charged them that they should tell no one about Him.

31 And He began to teach them that the Son of Man must suffer many things, and be rejected by the elders and chief priests and scribes, and be killed, and after three days rise again.

32 He spoke this word openly. And Peter took Him aside and began to rebuke Him.

33 But when He had turned around and looked at His disciples, He rebuked Peter, saying, "Get behind Me, Satan! For you are not mindful of the things of God, but the things of men."

34 And when He had called the people *to* Him, with His disciples

Did Jesus Ever Say He Was God?

People who encountered Jesus knew He was extraordinary. But they puzzled over who He was. Was He a long-dead prophet come back to life? Was He God?

What did Jesus have to say about Himself? He claimed He

◆ **Came from heaven.** "No one has ascended to heaven but He who came down from heaven, *that is,* the Son of Man who is in heaven" (John 3:13).

◆ **Was the Christ or Messiah.** "I who speak to you am *He* [that is, the Christ]" (John 4:26).

◆ **Had the right to judge humankind.** "For the Father judges no one, but has committed all judgment to the Son" (John 5:22).

◆ **Deserved the same degree of honor as God.** "That all should honor the Son just as they honor the Father. He who does not honor the Son does not honor the Father who sent Him" (John 5:23).

◆ **Was the Anointed One** predicted by ancient prophets,

including Moses. "For if you believed Moses, you would believe Me; for he wrote about Me" (John 5:46).

◆ **Had the right to forgive sins committed against God,** something only God could do. "When Jesus saw their faith, He said to the paralytic, 'Son, your sins are forgiven you'" (Mark 2:5).

◆ **Had the power to raise Himself from the dead.** "In three days I will raise it up [His own body]" (John 2:19).

◆ **Had the power to raise others from the dead.** "And this is the will of Him who sent Me, that everyone who sees the Son and believes in Him may have everlasting life; and I will raise him up at the last day" (John 6:40).

◆ **Never committed a sin.** "I always do those things that please Him [God]" (John 8:29b). "Which of you convicts Me of sin?" (John 8:46).

◆ **Has existed forever.** "Most assuredly, I say to you, before Abraham was, I AM" (John 8:58).

His listeners understood His words as a claim to be God.

The preceding verses provide the evidence: Jesus did, in fact, claim to be God. Like His listeners, we are faced with two choices: Was He demented? If so, ignore Him. Was He telling the truth? If so, worship Him as Lord.

also, He said to them, "Whoever desires to come after Me, let him deny himself, and take up his cross, and follow Me.

35 "For whoever desires to save his life will lose it, but whoever loses his life for My sake and the gospel's will save it.

36 "For what will it profit a man if he gains the whole world, and loses his own soul?

37 "Or what will a man give in exchange for his soul?

38 "For whoever is ashamed of Me and My words in this adulterous and sinful generation, of him the Son of Man also will be ashamed when He comes in the glory of His Father with the holy angels."

9 And He said to them, "Assuredly, I say to you that there are some standing here who will not taste death till they see the kingdom of God present with power."

2 Now after six days Jesus took Peter, James, and John, and led them up on a high mountain apart by themselves; and He was transfigured before them.

3 His clothes became shining, exceedingly white, like snow, such as no launderer on earth can whiten them.

4 And Elijah appeared to them with Moses, and they were talking with Jesus.

5 Then Peter answered and said to Jesus, "Rabbi, it is good for us to be here; and let us make three tabernacles: one for You, one for Moses, and one for Elijah"—

6 because he did not know what to say, for they were greatly afraid.

7 And a cloud came and overshadowed them; and a voice came out of the cloud, saying, "This is My beloved Son. Hear Him!"

8 Suddenly, when they had looked around, they saw no one anymore, but only Jesus with themselves.

9 Now as they came down from the mountain, He commanded them that they should tell no one the things they had seen, till the Son of Man had risen from the dead.

10 So they kept this word to themselves, questioning what the rising from the dead meant.

11 And they asked Him, saying, "Why do the scribes say that Elijah must come first?"

12 Then He answered and told them, "Elijah does come first, and restores all things. And how is it written concerning the Son of Man, that He must suffer many things and be treated with contempt?

13 "But I say to you that Elijah has also come, and they did to him whatever they wished, as it is written of him."

14 And when He came to the disciples, He saw a great multitude around them, and scribes disputing with them.

15 Immediately, when they saw Him, all the people were greatly amazed, and running to *Him*, greeted Him.

16 And He asked the scribes, "What are you discussing with them?"

17 Then one from the multitude answered and said, "Teacher, I brought You my son, who has a mute spirit.

18 "And wherever he seizes him, he throws him down; he foams at the mouth, gnashes his teeth, and becomes rigid. So I spoke to Your disciples, that they should cast him out, but they could not."

19 He answered him and said, "O faithless generation, how long shall I be with you? How long shall I bear with you? Bring him to Me."

20 Then they brought him to Him. And when he saw Him, immediately the spirit convulsed him, and he fell on the ground and wallowed, foaming at the mouth.

21 So He asked his father, "How

long has this been happening to him?" And he said, "From childhood.

22 "And often he has thrown him both into the fire and into the water to destroy him. But if You can do anything, have compassion on us and help us."

23 Jesus said to him, "If you can believe, all things *are* possible to him who believes."

24 Immediately the father of the child cried out and said with tears, "Lord, I believe; help my unbelief!"

25 When Jesus saw that the people came running together, He rebuked the unclean spirit, saying to him, "You deaf and dumb spirit, I command you, come out of him, and enter him no more!"

26 Then *the* spirit cried out, convulsed him greatly, and came out of him. And he became as one dead, so that many said, "He is dead."

27 But Jesus took him by the hand and lifted him up, and he arose.

28 And when He had come into the house, His disciples asked Him privately, "Why could we not cast him out?"

29 So He said to them, "This kind can come out by nothing but prayer and fasting."

30 Then they departed from there and passed through Galilee, and He did not want anyone to know *it.*

31 For He taught His disciples and said to them, "The Son of Man is being delivered into the hands of men, and they will kill Him. And after He is killed, He will rise the third day."

32 But they did not understand this saying, and were afraid to ask Him.

33 Then He came to Capernaum. And when He was in the house He asked them, "What was it you disputed among yourselves on the road?"

34 But they kept silent, for on the road they had disputed among themselves who *would be the* greatest.

35 And He sat down, called the twelve, and said to them, "If anyone desires to be first, he shall be last of all and servant of all."

36 Then He took a little child and set him in the midst of them. And when He had taken him in His arms, He said to them,

37 "Whoever receives one of these little children in My name receives Me; and whoever receives Me, receives not Me but Him who sent Me."

38 Now John answered Him, saying, "Teacher, we saw someone who does not follow us casting out demons in Your name, and we forbade him because he does not follow us."

39 But Jesus said, "Do not forbid him, for no one who works a miracle in My name can soon afterward speak evil of Me.

40 "For he who is not against us is on our side.

41 "For whoever gives you a cup of water to drink in My name, because you belong to Christ, assuredly, I say to you, he will by no means lose his reward.

42 "And whoever causes one of these little ones who believe in Me to stumble, it would be better for him if a millstone were hung around his neck, and he were thrown into the sea.

43 "And if your hand makes you sin, cut it off. It is better for you to enter life maimed, than having two hands, to go to hell, into the fire that shall never be quenched—

44 "where *'their worm does not die and the fire is not quenched.'*

45 "And if your foot makes you sin, cut it off. It is better for you to enter life lame, than having two feet, to be cast into hell, into the fire that shall never be quenched—

Marriage and Divorce

46 "where *'their worm does not die and the fire is not quenched.'*

47 "And if your eye makes you sin, pluck it out. It is better for you to enter the kingdom of God with one eye, than having two eyes, to be cast into hell fire—

48 "where *'their worm does not die and the fire is not quenched.'*

49 "For everyone will be seasoned with fire, and every sacrifice will be seasoned with salt.

50 "Salt *is* good, but if the salt loses its flavor, how will you season it? Have salt in yourselves, and have peace with one another."

10 Then He arose from there and came to the region of Judea by the other side of the Jordan. And the people gathered to Him again, and as He was accustomed, He taught them again.

2 The Pharisees came and asked Him, "Is it lawful for a man to divorce *his* wife?" testing Him.

3 And He answered and said to them, "What did Moses command you?"

4 They said, "Moses permitted *a man* to write a certificate of divorce, and to dismiss *her.*"

5 And Jesus answered and said to them, "Because of the hardness of your heart he wrote you this precept.

6 "But from the beginning of the creation, God *'made them male and female.'*

7 *'For this reason a man shall leave his father and mother and be joined to his wife,*

8 *'and the two shall become one flesh';* so then they are no longer two, but one flesh.

9 "Therefore what God has joined together, let not man separate."

10 And in the house His disciples asked Him again about the same *matter.*

11 So He said to them, "Whoever divorces his wife and marries another commits adultery against her.

12 "And if a woman divorces her husband and marries another, she commits adultery."

13 Then they brought young children to Him, that He might touch them; but the disciples rebuked those who brought *them.*

14 But when Jesus saw *it,* He was greatly displeased and said to them, "Let the little children come to Me, and do not forbid them; for of such is the kingdom of God.

15 "Assuredly, I say to you, whoever does not receive the kingdom of God as a little child will by no means enter it."

16 And He took them up in His arms, put *His* hands on them, and blessed them.

17 Now as He was going out on the road, one came running, knelt before Him, and asked Him, "Good Teacher, what shall I do that I may inherit eternal life?"

18 So Jesus said to him, "Why do you call Me good? No one *is* good but One, *that is,* God.

19 "You know the commandments: *'Do not commit adultery,' 'Do not murder,' 'Do not steal,' 'Do not bear false witness,' 'Do not defraud,' 'Honor your father and your mother.'*"

20 And he answered and said to Him, "Teacher, all these I have observed from my youth."

21 Then Jesus, looking at him, loved him, and said to him, "One thing you lack: Go your way, sell whatever you have and give to the poor, and you will have treasure in heaven; and come, take up the cross, and follow Me."

22 But he was sad at this word, and went away grieved, for he had great possessions.

23 Then Jesus looked around and said to His disciples, "How hard it is for those who have riches to enter the kingdom of God!"

24 And the disciples were astonished at His words. But Jesus answered again and said to them,

"Children, how hard it is for those who trust in riches to enter the kingdom of God!

25 "It is easier for a camel to go through the eye of a needle than for a rich man to enter the kingdom of God."

26 And they were astonished beyond measure, saying among themselves, "Who then can be saved?"

27 But looking at them, Jesus said, "With men *it is* impossible, but not with God; for with God all things are possible."

28 Then Peter began to say to Him, "See, we have left all and followed You."

29 So Jesus answered and said, "Assuredly, I say to you, there is no one who has left house or brothers or sisters or father or mother or wife or children or lands, for My sake and the gospel's,

30 "who shall not receive a hundredfold now in this time—houses and brothers and sisters and mothers and children and lands, with persecutions—and in the age to come, eternal life.

31 "But many *who are* first will be last, and the last first."

32 Now they were on the road, going up to Jerusalem, and Jesus was going before them; and they were amazed. And as they followed they were afraid. Then He took the twelve aside again and began to tell them the things that would happen to Him:

33 "Behold, we are going up to Jerusalem, and the Son of Man will be delivered to the chief priests and to the scribes, and they will condemn Him to death and deliver Him to the Gentiles;

34 "and they will mock Him, and scourge Him, and spit on Him, and kill Him. And the third day He will rise again."

35 Then James and John, the sons of Zebedee, came to Him, saying,

"Teacher, we want You to do for us whatever we ask."

36 And He said to them, "What do you want Me to do for you?"

37 They said to Him, "Grant us that we may sit, one on Your right hand and the other on Your left, in Your glory."

38 But Jesus said to them, "You do not know what you ask. Can you drink the cup that I drink, and be baptized with the baptism that I am baptized with?"

39 And they said to Him, "We can." And Jesus said to them, "You will indeed drink the cup that I drink, and with the baptism I am baptized with you will be baptized;

40 "but to sit on My right hand and on My left is not Mine to give, but *it is for those* for whom it is prepared."

41 And when the ten heard *it*, they began to be greatly displeased with James and John.

42 But Jesus called them to *Himself* and said to them, "You know that those who are considered rulers over the Gentiles lord it over them, and their great ones exercise authority over them.

43 "Yet it shall not be so among you; but whoever desires to become great among you shall be your servant.

44 "And whoever of you desires to be first shall be slave of all.

45 "For even the Son of Man did not come to be served, but to serve, and to give His life a ransom for many."

46 Then they came to Jericho. And as He went out of Jericho with His disciples and a great multitude, blind Bartimaeus, the son of Timaeus, sat by the road begging.

47 And when he heard that it was Jesus of Nazareth, he began to cry out and say, "Jesus, Son of David, have mercy on me!"

48 Then many warned him to be quiet; but he cried out all the more,

"Son of David, have mercy on me!"

49 So Jesus stood still and commanded him to be called. Then they called the blind man, saying to him, "Be of good cheer. Rise, He is calling you."

50 And throwing aside his garment, he rose and came to Jesus.

51 And Jesus answered and said to him, "What do you want Me to do for you?" The blind man said to Him, "Rabboni, that I may receive my sight."

52 Then Jesus said to him, "Go your way; your faith has made you well." And immediately he received his sight and followed Jesus on the road.

11 Now when they came near Jerusalem, to Bethphage and Bethany, at the Mount of Olives, He sent out two of His disciples;

2 and He said to them, "Go into the village opposite you; and as soon as you have entered it you will find a colt tied, on which no one has sat. Loose it and bring it.

3 "And if anyone says to you, 'Why are you doing this?' say, 'The Lord has need of it,' and immediately he will send it here."

4 So they went their way, and found the colt tied by the door outside on the street, and they loosed it.

5 And some of those who stood there said to them, "What are you doing, loosing the colt?"

6 So they spoke to them just as Jesus had commanded. And they let them go.

7 Then they brought the colt to Jesus and threw their garments on it, and He sat on it.

8 And many spread their garments on the road, and others cut down leafy branches from the trees and spread *them* on the road.

9 Then those who went before and those who followed cried out, saying:

"Hosanna!
'Blessed is He who comes in the name of the Lord!'

10 Blessed *is* the kingdom of our father David
That comes in the name of the Lord!
Hosanna in the highest!"

11 And Jesus went into Jerusalem and into the temple. So when He had looked around at all things, as the hour was already late, He went out to Bethany with the twelve.

12 Now the next day, when they had come out from Bethany, He was hungry.

13 And seeing from afar a fig tree having leaves, He went to see if perhaps He would find something on it. And when He came to it, He found nothing but leaves, for it was not the season for figs.

14 In response Jesus said to it, "Let no one eat fruit from you ever again." And His disciples heard *it*.

15 So they came to Jerusalem. And Jesus went into the temple and began to drive out those who bought and sold in the temple, and overturned the tables of the moneychangers and the seats of those who sold doves.

16 And He would not allow anyone to carry wares through the temple.

17 Then He taught, saying to them, "Is it not written, *'My house shall be called a house of prayer for all nations'?* But you have made it a *'den of thieves.'*

18 And the scribes and chief priests heard it and sought how they might destroy Him; for they feared Him, because all the people were astonished at His teaching.

19 And when evening had come, He went out of the city.

20 Now in the morning, as they passed by, they saw the fig tree dried up from the roots.

21 And Peter, remembering, said to Him, "Rabbi, look! The fig tree

which You cursed has withered away."

22 So Jesus answered and said to them, "Have faith in God.

23 "For assuredly, I say to you, whoever says to this mountain, 'Be removed and be cast into the sea,' and does not doubt in his heart, but believes that those things he says will come to pass, he will have whatever he says.

24 "Therefore I say to you, whatever things you ask when you pray, believe that you receive *them*, and you will have *them*.

25 "And whenever you stand praying, if you have anything against anyone, forgive him, that your Father in heaven may also forgive you your trespasses.

26 "But if you do not forgive, neither will your Father in heaven forgive your trespasses."

27 Then they came again to Jerusalem. And as He was walking in the temple, the chief priests, the scribes, and the elders came to Him.

28 And they said to Him, "By what authority are You doing these things? And who gave You this authority to do these things?"

29 But Jesus answered and said to them, "I will also ask you one question; then answer Me, and I will tell you by what authority I do these things:

30 "The baptism of John—was it from heaven or from men? Answer Me."

31 And they reasoned among themselves, saying, "If we say, 'From heaven,' He will say, 'Why then did you not believe him?'

32 "But if we say, 'From men' "— they feared the people, for all counted John to have been a prophet indeed.

33 So they answered and said to Jesus, "We do not know." And Jesus answered and said to them, "Neither will I tell you by what authority I do these things."

12 Then He began to speak to them in parables: "A man planted a vineyard and set a hedge around *it*, dug *a place for* the wine vat and built a tower. And he leased it to vinedressers and went into a far country.

2 "Now at vintage-time he sent a servant to the vinedressers, that he might receive some of the fruit of the vineyard from the vinedressers.

3 "And they took *him* and beat him and sent *him* away empty-handed.

4 "Again he sent them another servant, and at him they threw stones, wounded *him* in the head, and sent *him* away shamefully treated.

5 "And again he sent another, and him they killed; and many others, beating some and killing some.

6 "Therefore still having one son, his beloved, he also sent him to them last, saying, 'They will respect my son.'

7 "But those vinedressers said among themselves, 'This is the heir. Come, let us kill him, and the inheritance will be ours.'

8 "And they took him and killed *him* and cast *him* out of the vineyard.

9 "Therefore what will the owner of the vineyard do? He will come and destroy the vinedressers, and give the vineyard to others.

10 "Have you not read this Scripture:

*'The stone which the builders
    rejected
Has become the chief
    cornerstone.*
11 *This was the LORD's doing,
And it is marvelous in our
    eyes'?"*

12 And they sought to lay hold of Him, but feared the multitude, for they knew He had spoken the parable against them. So they left Him and went away.

13 Then they sent to Him some of the Pharisees and the Herodians, to catch Him in *His* words.

14 When they had come, they said to Him, "Teacher, we know that You are true, and care about no one; for You do not regard the person of men, but teach the way of God in truth. Is it lawful to pay taxes to Caesar, or not?

15 "Shall we pay, or shall we not pay?" But He, knowing their hypocrisy, said to them, "Why do you test Me? Bring Me a denarius that I may see *it.*"

16 So they brought *it.* And He said to them, "Whose image and inscription *is* this?" And they said to Him, "Caesar's."

17 And Jesus answered and said to them, "Render to Caesar the things that are Caesar's, and to God the things that are God's." And they marveled at Him.

18 Then *some* Sadducees, who say there is no resurrection, came to Him; and they asked Him, saying:

19 "Teacher, Moses wrote to us that if a man's brother dies, and leaves *his* wife behind, and leaves no children, his brother should take his wife and raise up offspring for his brother.

20 "Now there were seven brothers. The first took a wife; and dying, he left no offspring.

21 "And the second took her, and he died; nor did he leave any offspring. And the third likewise.

22 "So the seven had her and left no offspring. Last of all the woman died also.

23 "Therefore, in the resurrection, when they rise, whose wife will she be? For all seven had her as wife."

24 Jesus answered and said to them, "Are you not therefore mistaken, because you do not know the Scriptures nor the power of God?

25 "For when they rise from the dead, they neither marry nor are given in marriage, but are like angels in heaven.

26 "But concerning the dead, that they rise, have you not read in the book of Moses, in the *burning bush passage,* how God spoke to him, saying, '*I am the God of Abraham, the God of Isaac, and the God of Jacob*'?

27 "He is not the God of the dead, but the God of the living. You are therefore greatly mistaken."

28 Then one of the scribes came, and having heard them reasoning together, perceiving that He had answered them well, asked Him, "Which is the first commandment of all?"

29 Jesus answered him, "The first of all the commandments *is:* '*Hear, O Israel, the* LORD *our God, the* LORD *is one.*

30 '*And you shall love the* LORD *your God with all your heart, with all your soul, with all your mind, and with all your strength.*' This is the first commandment.

31 "And the second, like *it, is* this: '*You shall love your neighbor as yourself.*' There is no other commandment greater than these."

32 So the scribe said to Him, "Well said, Teacher. You have spoken the truth, for there is one God, and there is no other but He.

33 "And to love Him with all the heart, with all the understanding, with all the soul, and with all the strength, and to love one's neighbor as oneself, is more than all the whole burnt offerings and sacrifices."

34 So when Jesus saw that he answered wisely, He said to him, "You are not far from the kingdom of God." And after that no one dared question Him.

35 Then Jesus answered and said, while He taught in the temple, "How *is it* that the scribes say that the Christ is the Son of David?

36 "For David himself said by the Holy Spirit:

'The LORD said to my Lord,
"Sit at My right hand,
Till I make Your enemies
    Your footstool." '

37 "Therefore David himself calls Him *'Lord'*; how is He *then* his Son?" And the common people heard Him gladly.

38 Then He said to them in His teaching, "Beware of the scribes, who desire to go around in long robes, *love* greetings in the marketplaces,

39 "the best seats in the synagogues, and the best places at feasts,

40 "who devour widows' houses, and for a pretense make long prayers. These will receive greater condemnation."

41 Now Jesus sat opposite the treasury and saw how the people put money into the treasury. And many *who were* rich put in much.

42 Then one poor widow came and threw in two mites, which make a quadrans.

43 So He called His disciples *to Him* and said to them, "Assuredly, I say to you that this poor widow has put in more than all those who have given to the treasury;

44 "for they all put in out of their abundance, but she out of her poverty put in all that she had, her whole livelihood."

13 Then as He went out of the temple, one of His disciples said to Him, "Teacher, see what manner of stones and what buildings *are here!*"

2 And Jesus answered and said to him, "Do you see these great buildings? Not *one* stone shall be left upon another, that shall not be thrown down."

3 Now as He sat on the Mount of Olives opposite the temple, Peter, James, John, and Andrew asked Him privately,

4 "Tell us, when will these things be? And what *will be* the sign

when all these things will be fulfilled?"

5 And Jesus, answering them, began to say: "Take heed that no one deceives you.

6 "For many will come in My name, saying, 'I am *He*,' and will deceive many.

7 "And when you hear of wars and rumors of wars, do not be troubled; for *such things* must happen, but the end is not yet.

8 "For nation will rise against nation, and kingdom against kingdom. And there will be earthquakes in various places, and there will be famines and troubles. These *are* the beginnings of sorrows.

9 "But watch out for yourselves, for they will deliver you up to councils, and you will be beaten in the synagogues. And you will be brought before rulers and kings for My sake, for a testimony to them.

10 "And the gospel must first be preached to all the nations.

11 "But when they arrest *you* and deliver you up, do not worry beforehand, or premeditate what you will speak. But whatever is given you in that hour, speak that; for it is not you who speak, but the Holy Spirit.

12 "Now brother will betray brother to death, and a father *his* child; and children will rise up against parents and cause them to be put to death.

13 "And you will be hated by all *men* for My name's sake. But he who endures to the end shall be saved.

14 "But when you see the *'abomination of desolation,'* spoken of by Daniel the prophet, standing where it ought not" (let the reader understand), "then let those who are in Judea flee to the mountains.

15 "And let him who is on the housetop not go down into the house, nor enter to take anything out of his house.

16 "And let him who is in the field not go back to get his garment.

17 "But woe to those who are pregnant and to those with nursing babies in those days!

18 "And pray that your flight may not be in winter.

19 "For *in* those days there will be tribulation, such as has not been from the beginning of creation which God created until this time, nor ever shall be.

20 "And unless the Lord had shortened those days, no flesh would be saved; but for the elect's sake, whom He chose, He shortened the days.

21 "Then if anyone says to you, 'Look, here *is* the Christ!' or, 'Look, He *is* there!' do not believe it.

22 "For false christs and false prophets will rise and show signs and wonders to deceive, if possible, even the elect.

23 "But take heed; see, I have told you all things beforehand.

24 "But in those days, after that tribulation, the sun will be darkened, and the moon will not give its light;

25 "the stars of heaven will fall, and the powers in heaven will be shaken.

26 "Then they will see the Son of Man coming in the clouds with great power and glory.

27 "And then He will send His angels, and gather together His elect from the four winds, from the farthest part of earth to the farthest part of heaven.

28 "Now learn this parable from the fig tree: When its branch has already become tender, and puts forth leaves, you know that summer is near.

29 "So you also, when you see these things happening, know that it is near, at the very doors.

30 "Assuredly, I say to you, this generation will by no means pass away till all these things take place.

31 "Heaven and earth will pass away, but My words will by no means pass away.

32 "But of that day and hour no one knows, neither the angels in heaven, nor the Son, but only the Father.

33 "Take heed, watch and pray; for you do not know when the time is.

34 "*It is* like a man going to a far country, who left his house and gave authority to his servants, and to each his work, and commanded the doorkeeper to watch.

35 "Watch therefore, for you do not know when the master of the house is coming—in the evening, at midnight, at the crowing of the rooster, or in the morning—

36 "lest, coming suddenly, he find you sleeping.

37 "And what I say to you, I say to all: Watch!"

14 After two days it was the Passover and *the Feast* of Unleavened Bread. And the chief priests and the scribes sought how they might take Him by trickery and put *Him* to death.

2 But they said, "Not during the feast, lest there be an uproar of the people."

3 And being in Bethany at the house of Simon the leper, as He sat at the table, a woman came having an alabaster flask of very costly oil of spikenard. And she broke the flask and poured *it* on His head.

4 But there were some who were indignant among themselves, and said, "Why was this fragrant oil wasted?

5 "For it might have been sold for more than three hundred denarii and given to the poor." And they criticized her sharply.

6 But Jesus said, "Let her alone. Why do you trouble her? She has done a good work for Me.

7 "For you have the poor with you always, and whenever you wish you may do them good; but Me you do not have always.

Is the End Near?

Doomsayers have been around for so long we tend to ignore them. Yet there are nagging questions: Will the world come to an end? Is Jesus coming back again? If so, when?

Scripture says the answer to all of the above is yes. When Jesus' disciples questioned Him about His return to earth and the end of this present age, He replied with a list of twenty-three indicators. Then He concluded: "Assuredly, I say to you, this generation will by no means pass away till all these things take place" (Mark 13:30). So at least some people who see "all these things" will also witness earth's devastation and Christ's second coming. What are "these things"? Do we see indications they are true for our generation?

The appearance of many false Christs (Mark 13:6, 21) and the rise of cults (Mark 13:22).

The post-World War II era has seen an unprecedented spread of cults, new religious movements, and leaders claiming to be the Messiah.

Numerous and intense wars (Mark 13:7).

Since World War II, far more people have died in war than in all the previous wars combined.

Great earthquakes in various places (Mark 13:8).

Geophysicists have recorded more severe earthquakes in the last two decades than at any period in history. Not all of this increase is due to improved methods of detecting and recording earthquakes.

Great famines in various places (Mark 13:8).

Africa and Southeast Asia have undergone devastating famines in recent decades. Even in good harvest years millions die from starvation.

Widespread hatred and persecution of Christians (Mark 13:9, 13).

The fascist and communist movements, among others, have persecuted more Christians than any other anti-Christian movements or groups in history.

Spread of the gospel to all nations (Mark 13:10).

Even as opposition to Christianity has increased, an exponential increase worldwide has taken place in the numbers of people responding to the Christian gospel.

Conclusion: Does this mean we are approaching the end? At no other time in history have all these signs occurred together or with such intensity. While Jesus said no one could know the exact "day or hour" of His return, He did call us to be alert to the time and to be ready spiritually.

8 "She has done what she could. She has come beforehand to anoint My body for burial.

9 "Assuredly, I say to you, wherever this gospel is preached throughout the whole world, what this woman did will also be spoken of as a memorial to her."

10 Then Judas Iscariot, one of the twelve, went to the chief priests to betray Him to them.

11 So when they heard *it*, they were glad, and promised to give him money. So he sought how he might conveniently betray Him.

12 Now on the first day of Unleavened Bread, when they killed the Passover *lamb*, His disciples said to Him, "Where do You want us to go and prepare, that You may eat the Passover?"

13 So He sent out two of His disciples and said to them, "Go into the city, and a man will meet you carrying a pitcher of water; follow him.

14 "And wherever he goes in, say to the master of the house, 'The Teacher says, "Where is the guest room in which I may eat the Passover with My disciples?"'

15 "Then he will show you a large upper room, furnished *and* prepared; there make ready for us."

16 And His disciples went out, and came into the city, and found it just as He had said to them; and they prepared the Passover.

17 In the evening He came with the twelve.

18 Now as they sat and ate, Jesus said, "Assuredly, I say to you, one of you who eats with Me will betray Me."

19 And they began to be sorrowful, and to say to Him one by one, "Is it I?" And another *said*, "Is it I?"

20 Then He answered and said to them, "*It is* one of the twelve, who dips with Me in the dish.

21 "The Son of Man indeed goes just as it is written of Him, but woe to that man by whom the Son of Man is betrayed! It would have been good for that man if he had never been born."

22 And as they were eating, Jesus took bread, blessed *it* and broke *it*, and gave *it* to them and said, "Take, eat; this is My body."

23 Then He took the cup, and when He had given thanks He gave *it* to them, and they all drank from it.

24 And He said to them, "This is My blood of the new covenant, which is shed for many.

25 "Assuredly, I say to you, I will no longer drink of the fruit of the vine until that day when I drink it new in the kingdom of God."

26 And when they had sung a hymn, they went out to the Mount of Olives.

27 Then Jesus said to them, "All of you will be made to stumble because of Me this night, for it is written:

> '*I will strike the Shepherd,*
> *And the sheep will be*
> *scattered.*'

28 "But after I have been raised, I will go before you to Galilee."

29 But Peter said to Him, "Even if all are made to stumble, yet I *will* not *be*."

30 And Jesus said to him, "Assuredly, I say to you that today, *even* this night, before the rooster crows twice, you will deny Me three times."

31 But he spoke more vehemently, "If I have to die with You, I will not deny You!" And they all said likewise.

32 Then they came to a place which was named Gethsemane; and He said to His disciples, "Sit here while I pray."

33 And He took Peter, James, and John with Him, and He began to be troubled and deeply distressed.

34 Then He said to them, "My soul is exceedingly sorrowful, *even* to death. Stay here and watch."

35 He went a little farther, and fell on the ground, and prayed that if it were possible, the hour might pass from Him.

36 And He said, "Abba, Father, all things *are* possible for You. Take this cup away from Me; nevertheless, not what I will, but what You will."

37 Then He came and found them sleeping, and said to Peter, "Simon, are you sleeping? Could you not watch one hour?

38 "Watch and pray, lest you enter into temptation. The spirit truly *is* ready, but the flesh *is* weak."

39 Again He went away and prayed, and spoke the same words.

40 And when He returned, He found them asleep again, for their eyes were heavy; and they did not know what to answer Him.

41 Then He came the third time and said to them, "Are you still sleeping and resting? It is enough! The hour has come; behold, the Son of Man is being betrayed into the hands of sinners.

42 "Rise up, let us go. See, My betrayer is at hand."

43 And immediately, while He was still speaking, Judas, one of the twelve, with a great multitude with swords and clubs, came from the chief priests and the scribes and the elders.

44 Now His betrayer had given them a signal, saying, "Whomever I kiss, He is the One; take Him and lead *Him* away safely."

45 And as soon as He had come, immediately he went up to Him and said to Him, "Rabbi, Rabbi!" and kissed Him.

46 Then they laid their hands on Him and took Him.

47 And one of those who stood by drew his sword and struck the servant of the high priest, and cut off his ear.

48 Then Jesus answered and said to them, "Have you come out, as against a robber, with swords and clubs to take Me?

49 "I was daily with you in the temple teaching, and you did not take Me. But the Scriptures must be fulfilled."

50 Then they all forsook Him and fled.

51 Now a certain young man followed Him, having a linen cloth thrown around *his* naked *body*. And the young men laid hold of him,

52 and he left the linen cloth and fled from them naked.

53 And they led Jesus away to the high priest; and with him were assembled all the chief priests, the elders, and the scribes.

54 But Peter followed Him at a distance, right into the courtyard of the high priest. And he sat with the servants and warmed himself at the fire.

55 And the chief priests and all the council sought testimony against Jesus to put Him to death, and found none.

56 For many bore false witness against Him, but their testimonies did not agree.

57 And some rose up and bore false witness against Him, saying,

58 "We heard Him say, 'I will destroy this temple that *is* made with hands, and within three days I will build another made without hands.' "

59 But not even then did their testimony agree.

60 And the high priest stood up in the midst and asked Jesus, saying, "Do You answer nothing? What *is it* these men testify against You?"

61 But He kept silent and answered nothing. Again the high priest asked Him, saying to Him, "Are You the Christ, the Son of the Blessed?"

62 And Jesus said, "I am. And you will see the Son of Man sitting at the right hand of the Power, and coming with the clouds of heaven."

63 Then the high priest tore his

clothes and said, "What further need do we have of witnesses?

64 "You have heard the blasphemy! What do you think?" And they all condemned Him to be worthy of death.

65 Then some began to spit on Him, and to blindfold Him, and to beat Him, and to say to Him, "Prophesy!" And the officers struck Him with the palms of their hands.

66 Now as Peter was below in the courtyard, one of the servant girls of the high priest came.

67 And when she saw Peter warming himself, she looked at him and said, "You also were with Jesus of Nazareth."

68 But he denied it, saying, "I neither know nor understand what you are saying." And he went out on the porch, and a rooster crowed.

69 And the servant girl saw him again, and began to say to those who stood by, "This is one of them."

70 But he denied it again. And a little later those who stood by said to Peter again, "Surely you are *one* of them; for you are a Galilean, and your speech shows *it.*"

71 But he began to curse and swear, "I do not know this Man of whom you speak!"

72 And a second time *the* rooster crowed. And Peter called to mind the word that Jesus had said to him, "Before the rooster crows twice, you will deny Me three times." And when he thought about it, he wept.

15 Immediately, in the morning, the chief priests held a consultation with the elders and scribes and the whole council; and they bound Jesus, led *Him* away, and delivered *Him* to Pilate.

2 Then Pilate asked Him, "Are You the King of the Jews?" And He answered and said to him, "*It is as* you say."

3 And the chief priests accused Him of many things, but He answered nothing.

4 Then Pilate asked Him again, saying, "Do You answer nothing? See how many things they testify against You!"

5 But Jesus still answered nothing, so that Pilate marveled.

6 Now at the feast he was accustomed to releasing one prisoner to them, whomever they requested.

7 And there was one named Barabbas, *who was* chained with his fellow insurrectionists; they had committed murder in the insurrection.

8 Then the multitude, crying aloud, began to ask *him to do* just as he had always done for them.

9 But Pilate answered them, saying, "Do you want me to release to you the King of the Jews?"

10 For he knew that the chief priests had handed Him over because of envy.

11 But the chief priests stirred up the crowd, so that he should rather release Barabbas to them.

12 And Pilate answered and said to them again, "What then do you want me to do *with Him* whom you call the King of the Jews?"

13 So they cried out again, "Crucify Him!"

14 Then Pilate said to them, "Why, what evil has He done?" And they cried out more exceedingly, "Crucify Him!"

15 So Pilate, wanting to gratify the crowd, released Barabbas to them; and he delivered Jesus, after he had scourged *Him,* to be crucified.

16 Then the soldiers led Him away into the hall called Praetorium; and they called together the whole garrison.

17 And they clothed Him with purple; and they twisted a crown of thorns, put it on His *head,*

18 and began to salute Him, "Hail, King of the Jews!"

19 Then they struck Him on the head with a reed and spat on Him;

and bowing the knee, they worshiped Him.

20 And when they had mocked Him, they took the purple off Him, put His own clothes on Him, and led Him out to crucify Him.

21 Now they compelled a certain man, Simon a Cyrenian, the father of Alexander and Rufus, as he was coming out of the country and passing by, to bear His cross.

22 And they brought Him to the place Golgotha, which is translated, Place of a Skull.

23 Then they gave Him wine mingled with myrrh to drink, but He did not take *it*.

24 And when they crucified Him, they divided His garments, casting lots for them to determine what every man should take.

25 Now it was the third hour, and they crucified Him.

26 And the inscription of His accusation was written above:

THE KING OF THE JEWS.

27 With Him they also crucified two robbers, one on His right and the other on His left.

28 So the Scripture was fulfilled which says, *"And He was numbered with the transgressors."*

29 And those who passed by blasphemed Him, wagging their heads and saying, "Aha! *You* who destroy the temple and build *it* in three days,

30 "save Yourself, and come down from the cross!"

31 Likewise the chief priests also, together with the scribes, mocked and said among themselves, "He saved others; Himself He cannot save.

32 "Let the Christ, the King of Israel, descend now from the cross, that we may see and believe." And those who were crucified with Him reviled Him.

33 Now when the sixth hour had come, there was darkness over the whole land until the ninth hour.

34 And at the ninth hour Jesus cried out with a loud voice, saying, "Eloi, Eloi, lama sabachthani?" which is translated, *"My God, My God, why have You forsaken Me?"*

35 Some of those who stood by, when they heard *it*, said, "Look, He is calling for Elijah!"

36 Then someone ran and filled a sponge full of sour wine, put *it* on a reed, and offered *it* to Him to drink, saying, "Let Him alone; let us see if Elijah will come to take Him down."

37 And Jesus cried out with a loud voice, and breathed His last.

38 Then the veil of the temple was torn in two from top to bottom.

39 Now when the centurion, who stood opposite Him, saw that He cried out like this and breathed His last, he said, "Truly this Man was the Son of God!"

40 There were also women looking on from afar, among whom were Mary Magdalene, Mary the mother of James the Less and of Joses, and Salome,

41 who also followed Him and ministered to Him when He was in Galilee; and many other women who came up with Him to Jerusalem.

42 Now when evening had come, because it was the Preparation Day, that is, the day before the Sabbath,

43 Joseph of Arimathea, a prominent council member, who was himself waiting for the kingdom of God, coming and taking courage, went in to Pilate and asked for the body of Jesus.

44 Pilate marveled that He was already dead; and summoning the centurion, he asked him if He had been dead for some time.

45 And when he found out from the centurion, he granted the body to Joseph.

46 Then he bought fine linen, took Him down, and wrapped Him in the linen. And he laid Him in a

tomb which had been hewn out of the rock, and rolled a stone against the door of the tomb.

47 And Mary Magdalene and Mary *the mother* of Joses observed where He was laid.

16 Now when the Sabbath was past, Mary Magdalene, Mary *the mother* of James, and Salome bought spices, that they might come and anoint Him.

2 Very early in the morning, on the first *day* of the week, they came to the tomb when the sun had risen.

3 And they said among themselves, "Who will roll away the stone from the door of the tomb for us?"

4 But when they looked up, they saw that the stone had been rolled away—for it was very large.

5 And entering the tomb, they saw a young man clothed in a long white robe sitting on the right side; and they were alarmed.

6 But he said to them, "Do not be alarmed. You seek Jesus of Nazareth, who was crucified. He is risen! He is not here. See the place where they laid Him.

7 "But go *and* tell His disciples—and Peter—that He is going before you into Galilee; there you will see Him, as He said to you."

8 And they went out quickly and fled from the tomb, for they trembled and were amazed. And they said nothing to anyone, for they were afraid.

9 Now when *He* rose early on the first *day* of the week, He appeared first to Mary Magdalene, out of whom He had cast seven demons.

10 She went and told those who had been with Him, as they mourned and wept.

11 And when they heard that He was alive and had been seen by her, they did not believe.

12 After that, He appeared in another form to two of them as they walked and went into the country.

13 And they went and told *it* to the rest, *but* they did not believe them either.

14 Afterward He appeared to the eleven as they sat at the table; and He rebuked their unbelief and hardness of heart, because they did not believe those who had seen Him after He had risen.

15 And He said to them, "Go into all the world and preach the gospel to every creature.

16 "He who believes and is baptized will be saved; but he who does not believe will be condemned.

17 "And these signs will follow those who believe: In My name they will cast out demons; they will speak with new tongues;

18 "they will take up serpents; and if they drink anything deadly, it will by no means hurt them; they will lay hands on the sick, and they will recover."

19 So then, after the Lord had spoken to them, He was received up into heaven, and sat down at the right hand of God.

20 And they went out and preached everywhere, the Lord working with *them* and confirming the word through the accompanying signs. Amen.

THE GOSPEL ACCORDING TO
LUKE

INASMUCH as many have taken in hand to set in order a narrative of those things which are most surely believed among us,

2 just as those who from the beginning were eyewitnesses and ministers of the word delivered them to us,

3 it seemed good to me also, having had perfect understanding of all things from the very first, to write to you an orderly account, most excellent Theophilus,

4 that you may know the certainty of those things in which you were instructed.

5 There was in the days of Herod, the king of Judea, a certain priest named Zacharias, of the division of Abijah. His wife *was* of the daughters of Aaron, and her name *was* Elizabeth.

6 And they were both righteous before God, walking in all the commandments and ordinances of the Lord blameless.

7 But they had no child, because Elizabeth was barren, and they were both well advanced in years.

8 So it was, that while he was serving as priest before God in the order of his division,

9 according to the custom of the priesthood, his lot fell to burn incense when he went into the temple of the Lord.

10 And the whole multitude of the people was praying outside at the hour of incense.

11 Then an angel of the Lord appeared to him, standing on the right side of the altar of incense.

12 And when Zacharias saw *him*, he was troubled, and fear fell upon him.

13 But the angel said to him, "Do not be afraid, Zacharias, for your prayer is heard; and your wife Elizabeth will bear you a son, and you shall call his name John.

14 "And you will have joy and gladness, and many will rejoice at his birth.

15 "For he will be great in the sight of the Lord, and shall drink neither wine nor strong drink. He will also be filled with the Holy Spirit, even from his mother's womb.

16 "And he will turn many of the children of Israel to the Lord their God.

17 "He will also go before Him in the spirit and power of Elijah, 'to turn the hearts of the fathers to the children,' and the disobedient to the wisdom of the just, to make ready a people prepared for the Lord."

18 And Zacharias said to the angel, "How shall I know this? For I am an old man, and my wife is well advanced in years."

19 And the angel answered and said to him, "I am Gabriel, who stands in the presence of God, and was sent to speak to you and bring you these glad tidings.

20 "But behold, you will be mute and not able to speak until the day these things take place, because you did not believe my words which will be fulfilled in their own time."

21 And the people waited for Zacharias, and marveled that he lingered so long in the temple.

22 But when he came out, he could not speak to them; and they perceived that he had seen a vision in the temple, for he beckoned to them and remained speechless.

23 And so it was, as soon as the days of his service were completed, that he departed to his own house.

24 Now after those days his wife Elizabeth conceived; and she hid herself five months, saying,

25 "Thus the Lord has dealt with me, in the days when He looked on

me, to take away my reproach among men."

26 Now in the sixth month the angel Gabriel was sent by God to a city of Galilee named Nazareth.

27 to a virgin betrothed to a man whose name was Joseph, of the house of David. The virgin's name *was* Mary.

28 And having come in, the angel said to her, "Rejoice, highly favored *one*, the Lord *is* with you; blessed *are* you among women!"

29 But when she saw *him*, she was troubled at his saying, and considered what manner of greeting this was.

30 Then the angel said to her, "Do not be afraid, Mary, for you have found favor with God.

31 "And behold, you will conceive in your womb and bring forth a Son, and shall call His name JESUS.

32 "He will be great, and will be called the Son of the Highest; and the Lord God will give Him the throne of His father David.

33 "And He will reign over the house of Jacob forever, and of His kingdom there will be no end."

34 Then Mary said to the angel, "How can this be, since I do not know a man?"

35 And the angel answered and said to her, "*The* Holy Spirit will come upon you, and the power of the Highest will overshadow you; therefore, also, that Holy One who is to be born will be called the Son of God.

36 "Now indeed, Elizabeth your relative has also conceived a son in her old age; and this is now the sixth month for her who was called barren.

37 "For with God nothing will be impossible."

38 Then Mary said, "Behold the maidservant of the Lord! Let it be to me according to your word." And the angel departed from her.

39 Now Mary arose in those days

and went into the hill country with haste, to a city of Judah,

40 and entered the house of Zacharias and greeted Elizabeth.

41 And it happened, when Elizabeth heard the greeting of Mary, that the babe leaped in her womb; and Elizabeth was filled with the Holy Spirit.

42 Then she spoke out with a loud voice and said, "Blessed *are* you among women, and blessed *is* the fruit of your womb!

43 "But why *is* this *granted* to me, that the mother of my Lord should come to me?

44 "For indeed, as soon as the voice of your greeting sounded in my ears, the babe leaped in my womb for joy.

45 "Blessed *is* she who believed, for there will be a fulfillment of those things which were told her from the Lord."

46 And Mary said:

"My soul magnifies the Lord,
47 And my spirit has rejoiced
    in God my Savior.
48 For He has regarded the lowly
    state of His maidservant;
    For behold, henceforth all
    generations will call me
    blessed.
49 For He who is mighty has done
    great things for me,
    And holy *is* His name.
50 And His mercy *is* on those
    who fear Him
    From generation to generation.
51 He has shown strength with
    His arm;
    He has scattered *the* proud in
    the imagination of their
    hearts.
52 He has put down the mighty
    from *their* thrones,
    And exalted the lowly.
53 He has filled *the* hungry
    with good things,
    And *the* rich He has sent away
    empty.

76

54 He has helped His servant
Israel,
In remembrance of *His* mercy,
55 As He spoke to our fathers,
To Abraham and to his seed
forever."

56 And Mary remained with her about three months, and returned to her house.
57 Now Elizabeth's full time came for her to be delivered, and she brought forth a son.
58 When her neighbors and relatives heard how the Lord had shown great mercy to her, they rejoiced with her.
59 Now so it was, on the eighth day, that they came to circumcise the child; and they would have called him by the name of his father, Zacharias.
60 And his mother answered and said, "No; he shall be called John."
61 But they said to her, "There is no one among your relatives who is called by this name."
62 So they made signs to his father—what he would have him called.
63 And he asked for a writing tablet, and wrote, saying, "His name is John." And they all marveled.
64 Immediately his mouth was opened and his tongue *loosed*, and he spoke, praising God.
65 Then fear came on all who dwelt around them; and all these sayings were discussed throughout all the hill country of Judea.
66 And all those who heard *them* kept *them* in their hearts, saying, "What kind of child will this be?" And the hand of the Lord was with him.
67 Now his father Zacharias was filled with the Holy Spirit, and prophesied, saying:

68"Blessed *is* the Lord God of
Israel,
For He has visited and
redeemed His people,

69 And has raised up a horn of
salvation for us
In the house of His servant
David,
70 As He spoke by the mouth of
His holy prophets,
Who *have been* since the world
began,
71 That we should be saved from
our enemies
And from the hand of all who
hate us,
72 To perform the mercy
promised to our fathers
And to remember His holy
covenant,
73 The oath which He swore to
our father Abraham:
74 To grant us that we,
Being delivered from the hand
of our enemies,
Might serve Him without fear,
75 In holiness and righteousness
before Him all the days of
our life.
76 And you, child, will be called
the prophet of the Highest;
For you will go before the face
of the Lord to prepare His
ways,
77 To give knowledge of salvation
to His people
By the remission of their sins,
78 Through the tender mercy of
our God,
With which the Dayspring
from on high has visited us;
79 To give light to those who sit
in darkness and the shadow
of death,
To guide our feet into the way
of peace."

80 So the child grew and became strong in spirit, and was in the deserts till the day of his manifestation to Israel.

2 And it came to pass in those days *that* a decree went out from Caesar Augustus that all the world should be registered.
2 This census first took place while Quirinius was governing Syria.

77

3 So all went to be registered, everyone to his own city.

4 And Joseph also went up from Galilee, out of the city of Nazareth, into Judea, to the city of David, which is called Bethlehem, because he was of the house and lineage of David,

5 to be registered with Mary, his betrothed wife, who was with child.

6 So it was, that while they were there, the days were completed for her to be delivered.

7 And she brought forth her firstborn Son, and wrapped Him in swaddling cloths, and laid Him in a manger, because there was no room for them in the inn.

8 Now there were in the same country shepherds living out in the fields, keeping watch over their flock by night.

9 And behold, an angel of the Lord stood before them, and the glory of the Lord shone around them, and they were greatly afraid.

10 Then the angel said to them, "Do not be afraid, for behold, I bring you good tidings of great joy which will be to all people.

11 "For there is born to you this day in the city of David a Savior, who is Christ the Lord.

12 "And this *will be* the sign to you: You will find a Babe wrapped in swaddling cloths, lying in a manger."

13 And suddenly there was with the angel a multitude of the heavenly host praising God and saying:

14"Glory to God in the highest,
    And on earth peace,
      good will toward men!"

15 So it was, when the angels had gone away from them into heaven, that the shepherds said to one another, "Let us now go to Bethlehem and see this thing that has come to pass, which the Lord has made known to us."

16 And they came with haste and found Mary and Joseph, and the Babe lying in a manger.

17 Now when they had seen *Him*, they made widely known the saying which was told them concerning this Child.

18 And all those who heard *it* marveled at those things which were told them by the shepherds.

19 But Mary kept all these things and pondered *them* in her heart.

20 Then the shepherds returned, glorifying and praising God for all the things that they had heard and seen, as it was told them.

21 And when eight days were completed for the circumcision of the Child, His name was called JESUS, the name given by the angel before He was conceived in the womb.

22 Now when the days of her purification according to the law of Moses were completed, they brought Him to Jerusalem to present *Him* to the Lord

23 (as it is written in the law of the Lord, *"Every male who opens the womb shall be called holy to the LORD"*),

24 and to offer a sacrifice according to what is said in the law of the Lord, *"A pair of turtledoves or two young pigeons."*

25 And behold, there was a man in Jerusalem whose name was Simeon, and this man was just and devout, waiting for the Consolation of Israel, and the Holy Spirit was upon him.

26 And it had been revealed to him by the Holy Spirit that he would not see death before he had seen the Lord's Christ.

27 So he came by the Spirit into the temple. And when the parents brought in the Child Jesus, to do for Him according to the custom of the law,

28 he took Him up in his arms and blessed God and said:

29"Lord, now You are letting Your
      servant depart in peace,
        According to Your word;

78

30 For my eyes have seen Your salvation
31 Which You have prepared before the face of all peoples,
32 A light to *bring* revelation to the Gentiles,
And the glory of Your people Israel."

33 And Joseph and His mother marveled at those things which were spoken of Him.
34 Then Simeon blessed them, and said to Mary His mother, "Behold, this *Child* is destined for the fall and rising of many in Israel, and for a sign which will be spoken against
35 (yes, a sword will pierce through your own soul also), that the thoughts of many hearts may be revealed."
36 Now there was one, Anna, a prophetess, the daughter of Phanuel, of the tribe of Asher. She was of a great age, and had lived with a husband seven years from her virginity;
37 and this woman *was* a widow of about eighty-four years, who did not depart from the temple, but served God with fastings and prayers night and day.
38 And coming in that instant she gave thanks to the Lord, and spoke of Him to all those who looked for redemption in Jerusalem.
39 So when they had performed all things according to the law of the Lord, they returned to Galilee, to their *own* city, Nazareth.
40 And the Child grew and became strong in spirit, filled with wisdom; and the grace of God was upon Him.
41 His parents went to Jerusalem every year at the Feast of the Passover.
42 And when He was twelve years old, they went up to Jerusalem according to the custom of the feast.
43 When they had finished the

days, as they returned, the Boy Jesus lingered behind in Jerusalem. And Joseph and His mother did not know *it;*
44 but supposing Him to have been in the company, they went a day's journey, and sought Him among *their* relatives and acquaintances.
45 So when they did not find Him, they returned to Jerusalem, seeking Him.
46 Now so it was that after three days they found Him in the temple, sitting in the midst of the teachers, both listening to them and asking them questions.
47 And all who heard Him were astonished at His understanding and answers.
48 So when they saw Him, they were amazed; and His mother said to Him, "Son, why have You done this to us? Look, Your father and I have sought You anxiously."
49 And He said to them, "Why *is it* that you sought Me? Did you not know that I must be about My Father's business?"
50 But they did not understand the statement which He spoke to them.
51 Then He went down with them and came to Nazareth, and was subject to them, but His mother kept all these things in her heart.
52 And Jesus increased in wisdom and stature, and in favor with God and men.
3 Now in the fifteenth year of the reign of Tiberius Caesar, Pontius Pilate being governor of Judea, Herod being tetrarch of Galilee, his brother Philip tetrarch of Iturea and the region of Trachonitis, and Lysanias tetrarch of Abilene,
2 Annas and Caiaphas being high priests, the word of God came to John the son of Zacharias in the wilderness.
3 And he went into all the region around the Jordan, preaching a baptism of repentance for the remission of sins,

4 as it is written in the book of the words of Isaiah the prophet, saying:

> *"The voice of one crying in the wilderness:*
> *'Prepare the way of the LORD,*
> *Make His paths straight.*
> 5 *Every valley shall be filled*
> *And every mountain and hill brought low;*
> *And the crooked places shall be made straight*
> *And the rough ways made smooth;*
> 6 *And all flesh shall see the salvation of God.' "*

7 Then he said to the multitudes that came out to be baptized by him, "Brood of vipers! Who warned you to flee from the wrath to come?

8 "Therefore bear fruits worthy of repentance, and do not begin to say to yourselves, 'We have Abraham as *our* father.' For I say to you that God is able to raise up children to Abraham from these stones.

9 "And even now the ax is laid to the root of the trees. Therefore every tree which does not bear good fruit is cut down and thrown into the fire."

10 So the people asked him, saying, "What shall we do then?"

11 He answered and said to them, "He who has two tunics, let him give to him who has none; and he who has food, let him do likewise."

12 Then tax collectors also came to be baptized, and said to him, "Teacher, what shall we do?"

13 And he said to them, "Collect no more than what is appointed for you."

14 Likewise the soldiers asked him, saying, "And what shall we do?" So he said to them, "Do not intimidate anyone or accuse falsely, and be content with your wages."

15 Now as the people were in expectation, and all reasoned in their hearts about John, whether he was the Christ *or* not,

16 John answered, saying to *them* all, "I indeed baptize you with water; but One mightier than I is coming, whose sandal strap I am not worthy to loose. He will baptize you with the Holy Spirit and with fire.

17 "His winnowing fan *is* in His hand, and He will thoroughly purge His threshing floor, and gather the wheat into His barn; but the chaff He will burn with unquenchable fire."

18 And with many other exhortations he preached to the people.

19 But Herod the tetrarch, being rebuked by him concerning Herodias, his brother Philip's wife, and for all the evils which Herod had done,

20 also added this, above all, that he shut John up in prison.

21 Now when all the people were baptized, it came to pass that Jesus also was baptized; and while He prayed, the heaven was opened.

22 And the Holy Spirit descended in bodily form like a dove upon Him, and a voice came from heaven which said, "You are My beloved Son; in You I am well pleased."

23 Now Jesus Himself began *His* ministry *at* about thirty years of age, being (as was supposed) *the* son of Joseph, *the son* of Heli,

24 *the son* of Matthat, *the son* of Levi, *the son* of Melchi, *the son* of Janna, *the son* of Joseph,

25 *the son* of Mattathiah, *the son* of Amos, *the son* of Nahum, *the son* of Esli, *the son* of Naggai,

26 *the son* of Maath, *the son* of Mattathiah, *the son* of Semei, *the son* of Joseph, *the son* of Judah,

27 *the son* of Joannas, *the son* of Rhesa, *the son* of Zerubbabel, *the son* of Shealtiel, *the son* of Neri,

28 *the son* of Melchi, *the son* of Addi, *the son* of Cosam, *the son* of Elmodam, *the son* of Er,

29 *the son* of Jose, *the son* of Elie-
zer, *the son* of Jorim, *the son* of
Matthat, *the son* of Levi,
30 *the son* of Simeon, *the son* of
Judah, *the son* of Joseph, *the son*
of Jonan, *the son* of Eliakim,
31 *the son* of Melea, *the son* of
Menan, *the son* of Mattathah, *the
son* of Nathan, *the son* of David,
32 *the son* of Jesse, *the son* of
Obed, *the son* of Boaz, *the son* of
Salmon, *the son* of Nahshon,
33 *the son* of Amminadab, *the son*
of Ram, *the son* of Hezron, *the son*
of Perez, *the son* of Judah,
34 *the son* of Jacob, *the son* of
Isaac, *the son* of Abraham, *the son*
of Terah, *the son* of Nahor,
35 *the son* of Serug, *the son* of Reu,
the son of Peleg, *the son* of Eber,
the son of Shelah,
36 *the son* of Cainan, *the son* of
Arphaxad, *the son* of Shem, *the
son* of Noah, *the son* of Lamech,
37 *the son* of Methuselah, *the son*
of Enoch, *the son* of Jared, *the son*
of Mahalalel, *the son* of Cainan,
38 *the son* of Enos, *the son* of Seth,
the son of Adam, *the son* of God.

4 Then Jesus, being filled with the
Holy Spirit, returned from the
Jordan and was led by the Spirit
into the wilderness,
2 being tempted for forty days by
the devil. And in those days He ate
nothing, and afterward, when they
had ended, He was hungry.
3 And the devil said to Him, "If
You are the Son of God, command
this stone to become bread."
4 But Jesus answered him, saying,
"It is written, *'Man shall not live
by bread alone, but by every word
of God.'"*
5 Then the devil, taking Him up
on a high mountain, showed Him
all the kingdoms of the world in a
moment of time.
6 And the devil said to Him, "All
this authority I will give You, and
their glory; for *this* has been delivered to me, and I give it to whomever I wish.

7 "Therefore, if You will worship
before me, all will be Yours."
8 And Jesus answered and said to
him, "Get behind Me, Satan! For it
is written, *'You shall worship the
LORD your God, and Him only you
shall serve.'"*
9 Then he brought Him to Jerusalem, set Him on the pinnacle of the
temple, and said to Him, "If You
are the Son of God, throw Yourself
down from here.
10 "For it is written:

'He shall give His angels charge
over you,
To keep you,'

11 "and,

'In their hands they shall bear
you up,
Lest you dash your foot
against a stone.'"

12 And Jesus answered and said to
him, "It has been said, *'You shall
not tempt the LORD your God.'"*
13 Now when the devil had ended
every temptation, he departed
from Him until an opportune time.
14 Then Jesus returned in the
power of the Spirit to Galilee, and
news of Him went out through all
the surrounding region.
15 And He taught in their synagogues, being glorified by all.
16 So He came to Nazareth, where
He had been brought up. And as
His custom was, He went into the
synagogue on the Sabbath day,
and stood up to read.
17 And He was handed the book of
the prophet Isaiah. And when He
had opened the book, He found the
place where it was written:

18 "The Spirit of the LORD is upon
Me,
Because He has anointed Me to
preach the gospel to the poor.
He has sent Me to heal the
brokenhearted,

*To preach deliverance to the
   captives
And recovery of sight to the
   blind,
To set at liberty those who are
   oppressed,*
19 *To preach the acceptable year
   of the* LORD."

20 Then He closed the book, and gave *it* back to the attendant and sat down. And the eyes of all who were in the synagogue were fixed on Him.

21 And He began to say to them, "Today this Scripture is fulfilled in your hearing."

22 So all bore witness to Him, and marveled at the gracious words which proceeded out of His mouth. And they said, "Is this not Joseph's son?"

23 And He said to them, "You will surely say this proverb to Me, 'Physician, heal yourself! Whatever we have heard done in Capernaum, do also here in Your country.'"

24 Then He said, "Assuredly, I say to you, no prophet is accepted in his own country.

25 "But I tell you truly, many widows were in Israel in the days of Elijah, when the heaven was shut up three years and six months, and there was a great famine throughout all the land;

26 "but to none of them was Elijah sent except to Zarephath, *in the region* of Sidon, to a woman *who was* a widow.

27 "And many lepers were in Israel in the time of Elisha the prophet, and none of them was cleansed except Naaman the Syrian."

28 Then all those in the synagogue, when they heard these things, were filled with wrath,

29 and rose up and thrust Him out of the city; and they led Him to the brow of the hill on which their city was built, that they might throw Him down over the cliff.

30 Then passing through the midst of them, He went His way.

31 Then He went down to Capernaum, a city of Galilee, and was teaching them on the Sabbaths.

32 And they were astonished at His teaching, for His word was with authority.

33 Now in the synagogue there was a man who had a spirit of an unclean demon. And he cried out with a loud voice,

34 saying, "Let *us* alone! What have we to do with You, Jesus of Nazareth? Did You come to destroy us? I know You, who You are—the Holy One of God!"

35 But Jesus rebuked him, saying, "Be quiet, and come out of him!" And when the demon had thrown him in *their* midst, it came out of him and did not hurt him.

36 So they were all amazed and spoke among themselves, saying, "What a word this *is!* For with authority and power He commands the unclean spirits, and they come out."

37 And the report about Him went out into every place in the surrounding region.

38 Now He arose from the synagogue and entered Simon's house. But Simon's wife's mother was sick with a high fever, and they made request of Him concerning her.

39 So He stood over her and rebuked the fever, and it left her. And immediately she arose and served them.

40 Now when the sun was setting, all those who had anyone sick with various diseases brought them to Him; and He laid His hands on every one of them and healed them.

41 And demons also came out of many, crying out and saying, "You are the Christ, the Son of God!" And He, rebuking *them,* did not allow them to speak, for they knew that He was the Christ.

Who Can Be Possessed by a Demon?

The Bible uses the terms "demon" or "evil spirit" to describe angelic beings who joined Satan in his rebellion against God in the kingdom of heaven. (See "Is the Devil Real?" page 5.) While many people today don't acknowledge the reality of demons, Jesus recognized demons' existence and gave no indication they were limited to a certain era.

How do demons get involved with humans?

Activities such as séances, fortune-telling, drug use, astrology, witchcraft, and other occult practices encourage demonic influence. When power becomes more important than truth, a person opens the door for one or more evil spirits actually to inhabit his or her body, taking control of it at will and expressing words and activities through that body.

Case studies of demonic possession

Jesus encountered two demon-possessed men living along the shores of the Sea of Galilee (Luke 8:27–30). Some of the characteristics they displayed include abnormal fear and anxiety; abnormal reclusiveness (living among tombs); violent and reckless behavior; outbursts of rage and hatred (expressed against the villagers); supernatural strength (breaking chains); intense, highly disturbed reaction to Jesus' presence or the mention of His name; lack of self-restraint.

The apostle Paul encountered a demon-possessed woman in Philippi who could predict the future. Possession of supernatural or occultic powers (including the ability to levitate tables, to travel outside the body, and so on) is also a sign of demonic activity.

How to close the door to demonic activity

1. Acknowledge to God the action(s) that opened the door (for example, use of drugs or participation in séances), agreeing with Him that these actions were wrong.

2. Demonstrate your commitment to turn away from such actions. Two expressions of your decision could be:
   a. Releasing God and others from any resentments and grudges you may hold.
   b. Repudiating and renouncing all occultic involvement; destroying all books and other objects connected with it.

3. Turn your life over to Jesus Christ. (See page 362 for a prayer you could pray.)

A Word of Caution: Some symptoms that might indicate demonic activity could result from years of unresolved hurt, anger, and bitterness or from mental illness. On the other hand, sometimes demon possession is misdiagnosed as mental illness. When in doubt, seek out a mature Christian with experience in dealing with demons.

42 Now when it was day, He departed and went into a deserted place. And the crowd sought Him and came to Him, and tried to keep Him from leaving them;

43 but He said to them, "I must preach the kingdom of God to the other cities also, because for this purpose I have been sent."

44 And He was preaching in the synagogues of Galilee.

5 Now so it was, as the multitude pressed about Him to hear the word of God, that He stood by the Lake of Gennesaret,

2 and saw two boats standing by the lake; but the fishermen had gone from them and were washing *their* nets.

3 Then He got into one of the boats, which was Simon's, and asked him to put out a little from the land. And He sat down and taught the multitudes from the boat.

4 Now when He had stopped speaking, He said to Simon, "Launch out into the deep and let down your nets for a catch."

5 But Simon answered and said to Him, "Master, we have toiled all night and caught nothing; nevertheless at Your word I will let down the net."

6 And when they had done this, they caught a great number of fish, and their net was breaking.

7 So they signaled to *their* partners in the other boat to come and help them. And they came and filled both the boats, so that they began to sink.

8 When Simon Peter saw *it*, he fell down at Jesus' knees, saying, "Depart from me, for I am a sinful man, O Lord!"

9 For he and all who were with him were astonished at the catch of fish which they had taken;

10 and so also *were* James and John, the sons of Zebedee, who were partners with Simon. And Jesus said to Simon, "Do not be afraid. From now on you will catc[h] men."

11 So when they had brought the[ir] boats to land, they forsook all an[d] followed Him.

12 And it happened when He wa[s] in a certain city, that behold, [a] man who was full of leprosy sa[w] Jesus; and he fell on *his* face an[d] implored Him, saying, "Lord, [if] You are willing, You can make m[e] clean."

13 Then He put out *His* hand an[d] touched him, saying, "I am willin[g;] be cleansed." And immediately th[e] leprosy left him.

14 And He charged him to tell n[o] one, "But go and show yourself [to] the priest, and make an offerin[g] for your cleansing, as a testimon[y] to them, just as Moses com[-] manded."

15 Then the report went aroun[d] concerning Him all the more; an[d] great multitudes came together t[o] hear, and to be healed by Him o[f] their infirmities.

16 So He Himself *often* withdre[w] into the wilderness and prayed.

17 Now it happened on a certai[n] day, as He was teaching, that ther[e] were Pharisees and teachers of th[e] law sitting by, who had come o[ut] of every town of Galilee, Jude[a,] and Jerusalem. And the power [of] the Lord was *present* to heal the[m.]

18 Then behold, men brought on [a] bed a man who was paralyze[d.] And they sought to bring him i[n] and lay *him* before Him.

19 And when they could not fin[d] how they might bring him in, be[-] cause of the crowd, they went u[p] on the housetop and let him dow[n] with *his* bed through the tiling int[o] the midst before Jesus.

20 So when He saw their faith, H[e] said to him, "Man, your sins a[re] forgiven you."

21 And the scribes and the Phar[i-] sees began to reason, sayin[g,] "Who is this who speaks blasph[-] mies? Who can forgive sins but God alone?"

22 But when Jesus perceived their thoughts, He answered and said to them, "Why are you reasoning in your hearts?

23 "Which is easier, to say, 'Your sins are forgiven you,' or to say, 'Rise up and walk'?

24 "But that you may know that the Son of Man has power on earth to forgive sins"—He said to the man who was paralyzed, "I say to you, arise, take up your bed, and go to your house."

25 Immediately he rose up before them, took up what he had been lying on, and departed to his own house, glorifying God.

26 And they were all amazed, and they glorified God and were filled with fear, saying, "We have seen strange things today!"

27 After these things He went out and saw a tax collector named Levi, sitting at the tax office. And He said to him, "Follow Me."

28 And he left all, rose up, and followed Him.

29 Then Levi gave Him a great feast in his own house. And there were a great number of tax collectors and others who sat down with them.

30 But their scribes and the Pharisees murmured against His disciples, saying, "Why do You eat and drink with tax collectors and sinners?"

31 And Jesus answered and said to them, "Those who are well do not need a physician, but those who are sick.

32 "I have not come to call *the* righteous, but sinners, to repentance."

33 Then they said to Him, "Why do the disciples of John fast often and make prayers, and likewise those of the Pharisees, but Yours eat and drink?"

34 And He said to them, "Can you make the friends of the bride-groom fast while the bridegroom is with them?

35 "But the days will come when the bridegroom will be taken away from them; then they will fast in those days."

36 Then He spoke a parable to them: "No one puts a piece from a new garment on an old one; otherwise the new makes a tear, and also the piece that was *taken* out of the new does not match the old.

37 "And no one puts new wine into old wineskins; or else the new wine will burst the wineskins and be spilled, and the wineskins will be ruined.

38 "But new wine must be put into new wineskins, and both are preserved.

39 "And no one, having drunk old *wine,* immediately desires new; for he says, 'The old is better.' "

6 Now it happened on the second Sabbath after the first that He went through the grainfields. And His disciples plucked the heads of grain and ate *them,* rubbing *them* in *their* hands.

2 And some of the Pharisees said to them, "Why are you doing what is not lawful to do on the Sabbath?"

3 But Jesus answering them said, "Have you not even read this, what David did when he was hungry, he and those who were with him:

4 "how he went into the house of God, took and ate the showbread, and also gave some to those *who were* with him, which is not lawful for any but the priests to eat?"

5 And He said to them, "The Son of Man is also Lord of the Sabbath."

6 Now it happened on another Sabbath, also, that He entered the synagogue and taught. And a man was there whose right hand was withered.

7 And the scribes and Pharisees watched Him closely, whether He

would heal on the Sabbath, that they might find an accusation against Him.

8 But He knew their thoughts, and said to the man who had the withered hand, "Arise and stand here." And he arose and stood.

9 Then Jesus said to them, "I will ask you one thing: Is it lawful on the Sabbath to do good or to do evil, to save life or to destroy *it?*"

10 And looking around at them all, He said to the man, "Stretch out your hand." And he did so, and his hand was restored as whole as the other.

11 But they were filled with rage, and discussed with one another what they might do to Jesus.

12 Now it came to pass in those days that He went out to the mountain to pray, and continued all night in prayer to God.

13 And when it was day, He called His disciples *to Him;* and from them He chose twelve whom He also named apostles:

14 Simon, whom He also named Peter, and Andrew his brother; James and John; Philip and Bartholomew;

15 Matthew and Thomas; James the *son* of Alphaeus, and Simon called the Zealot;

16 Judas *the son* of James, and Judas Iscariot who also became a traitor.

17 And He came down with them and stood on a level place with a crowd of His disciples and a great multitude of people from all Judea and Jerusalem, and from the seacoast of Tyre and Sidon, who came to hear Him and be healed of their diseases;

18 as well as those who were tormented with unclean spirits. And they were healed.

19 And the whole multitude sought to touch Him, for power went out from Him and healed *them* all.

20 Then He lifted up His eyes toward His disciples, and said:

"Blessed *are you* poor,
  For yours is the kingdom of God.
21 Blessed *are you* who hunger now,
  For you shall be filled.
Blessed *are you* who weep now,
  For you shall laugh.
22 Blessed are you when men hate you,
  And when they exclude you,
  And revile *you,* and cast out your name as evil,
  For the Son of Man's sake.
23 Rejoice in that day and leap for joy!
  For indeed your reward *is* great in heaven,
  For in like manner their fathers did to the prophets.

24 "But woe to you who are rich,
  For you have received your consolation.
25 Woe to you who are full,
  For you shall hunger.
Woe to you who laugh now,
  For you shall mourn and weep.
26 Woe to you when all men speak well of you,
  For so did their fathers to the false prophets.

27 "But I say to you who hear: Love your enemies, do good to those who hate you,

28 "bless those who curse you, and pray for those who spitefully use you.

29 "To him who strikes you on the *one* cheek, offer the other also. And from him who takes away your cloak, do not withhold *your* tunic either.

30 "Give to everyone who asks of you. And from him who takes away your goods do not ask *them* back.

31 "And just as you want men to

do to you, you also do to them likewise.

32 "But if you love those who love you, what credit is that to you? For even sinners love those who love them.

33 "And if you do good to those who do good to you, what credit is that to you? For even sinners do the same.

34 "And if you lend *to those* from whom you hope to receive back, what credit is that to you? For even sinners lend to sinners to receive as much back.

35 "But love your enemies, and do good, and lend, hoping for nothing in return; and your reward will be great, and you will be sons of the Highest. For He is kind to the unthankful and evil.

36 "Therefore be merciful, just as your Father also is merciful.

37 "Judge not, and you shall not be judged. Condemn not, and you shall not be condemned. Forgive, and you will be forgiven.

38 "Give, and it will be given to you: good measure, pressed down, shaken together, and running over will be put into your bosom. For with the same measure that you use, it will be measured back to you."

39 And He spoke a parable to them: "Can the blind lead the blind? Will they not both fall into the ditch?

40 "A disciple is not above his teacher, but everyone who is perfectly trained will be like his teacher.

41 "And why do you look at the speck in your brother's eye, but do not perceive the plank in your own eye?

42 "Or how can you say to your brother, 'Brother, let me remove the speck that *is* in your eye,' when you yourself do not see the plank that *is* in your own eye? Hypocrite! First remove the plank from your own eye, and then you

will see clearly to remove the speck that is in your brother's eye.

43 "For a good tree does not bear bad fruit, nor does a bad tree bear good fruit.

44 "For every tree is known by its own fruit. For *men* do not gather figs from thorns, nor do they gather grapes from a bramble bush.

45 "A good man out of the good treasure of his heart brings forth good; and an evil man out of the evil treasure of his heart brings forth evil. For out of the abundance of the heart his mouth speaks.

46 "But why do you call Me 'Lord, Lord,' and do not do the things which I say?

47 "Whoever comes to Me, and hears My sayings and does them, I will show you whom he is like:

48 "He is like a man building a house, who dug deep and laid the foundation on the rock. And when the flood arose, the stream beat vehemently against that house, and could not shake it, for it was founded on the rock.

49 "But he who heard and did nothing is like a man who built a house on the earth without a foundation, against which the stream beat vehemently; and immediately it fell. And the ruin of that house was great."

7 Now when He concluded all His sayings in the hearing of the people, He entered Capernaum.

2 And a certain centurion's servant, who was dear to him, was sick and ready to die.

3 So when he heard about Jesus, he sent elders of the Jews to Him, pleading with Him to come and heal his servant.

4 And when they came to Jesus, they begged Him earnestly, saying that the one for whom He should do this was worthy,

5 "for he loves our nation, and has built us a synagogue."

6 Then Jesus went with them. And when He was already not far from the house, the centurion sent friends to Him, saying to Him, "Lord, do not trouble Yourself, for I am not worthy that You should enter under my roof.

7 "Therefore I did not even think myself worthy to come to You. But say the word, and my servant will be healed.

8 "For I also am a man placed under authority, having soldiers under me. And I say to one, 'Go,' and he goes; and to another, 'Come,' and he comes; and to my servant, 'Do this,' and he does it."

9 When Jesus heard these things, He marveled at him, and turned around and said to the crowd that followed Him, "I say to you, I have not found such great faith, not even in Israel!"

10 And those who were sent, returning to the house, found the servant well who had been sick.

11 Now it happened, the day after, that He went into a city called Nain; and many of His disciples went with Him, and a large crowd.

12 And when He came near the gate of the city, behold, a dead man was being carried out, the only son of his mother; and she was a widow. And a large crowd from the city was with her.

13 When the Lord saw her, He had compassion on her and said to her, "Do not weep."

14 Then He came and touched the open coffin, and those who carried *him* stood still. And He said, "Young man, I say to you, arise."

15 And he who was dead sat up and began to speak. And He presented him to his mother.

16 Then fear came upon all, and they glorified God, saying, "A great prophet has risen up among us"; and, "God has visited His people."

17 And this report about Him went throughout all Judea and all the surrounding region.

18 Then the disciples of John reported to him concerning all these things.

19 And John, calling two of his disciples to *him*, sent *them* to Jesus, saying, "Are You the Coming One, or do we look for another?"

20 When the men had come to Him, they said, "John the Baptist has sent us to You, saying, 'Are You the Coming One, or do we look for another?' "

21 And that very hour He cured many *people* of *their* infirmities, afflictions, and evil spirits; and to many *who were* blind He gave sight.

22 Then Jesus answered and said to them, "Go and tell John the things you have seen and heard: that *the* blind see, *the* lame walk, *the* lepers are cleansed, *the* deaf hear, *the* dead are raised, *the* poor have the gospel preached to them.

23 "And blessed is *he* who is not offended because of Me."

24 When the messengers of John had departed, He began to speak to the multitudes concerning John: "What did you go out into the wilderness to see? A reed shaken by the wind?

25 "But what did you go out to see? A man clothed in soft garments? Indeed those who are gorgeously appareled and live in luxury are in kings' courts.

26 "But what did you go out to see? A prophet? Yes, I say to you, and more than a prophet.

27 "This is *he* of whom it is written:

> *'Behold, I send My messenger*
> *   before Your face,*
> *Who will prepare Your way*
> *   before You.'*

28 "For I say to you, among those born of women there is not a

What if God Has Let Me Down?

Few things in life are so troublesome as unmet expectations. We expect our cars to start, our work to be appreciated, and life to run a predictable course. When life doesn't go as anticipated, we end up frustrated and disappointed. This is doubly true when it is *God* who doesn't meet our expectations. That's where John the Baptist was—on the edge of doubt and despair, driven there by his unmet expectations. "Are You [Jesus] the Coming One, or do we look for another?" he asks.

John was starting to wonder if Jesus was the promised Savior. After all, John had believed with fervor and fulfilled his calling, but now he sat in prison. This wasn't how he thought it would be.

You've probably been in a similar situation. You expected God to do something, to make things right. Instead, the child died; the divorce went through; all your work went for naught. It's easy in this moment of confusion and frustration to miss one of life's great opportunities. John didn't miss his. And at the moment of John's greatest doubt, Jesus paid him His greatest compliment: "For I say to you, among those born of women there is not a greater prophet than John" (Luke 7:28).

What happened? How did John's unmet expectation turn into praise from Jesus? John took his doubt, confusion, and frustration to Jesus.

Unmet expectations either drive us away from God or draw us to Him. We either reach our own conclusions as to why things didn't go as anticipated, or we seek an answer from the One who loves an honest question almost as much as the questioner.

By the way, Jesus did solve John's puzzle. He reminded John the prophet of something he had forgotten, an 800-year-old prophecy about the Promised One (Isaiah 61:1). Jesus knew John would recognize the fulfillment of each and every aspect of it.

"Go and tell John the things you have seen and heard," answered Jesus, "that *the* blind see, *the* lame walk, *the* lepers are cleansed, *the* deaf hear, *the* dead are raised, *the* poor have the gospel preached to them" (Luke 7:22).

What should you do with your unmet expectations about God? Perhaps you need God's perspective, or better yet, His peace on whatever is troubling you. You can expect one thing for sure: He'll be very glad you came. (See also "What if I've Tried Religion, and It Doesn't Work for Me?" page 321.)

greater prophet than John the Baptist; but he who is least in the kingdom of God is greater than he."

29 And when all the people heard *Him*, even the tax collectors justified God, having been baptized with the baptism of John.

30 But the Pharisees and lawyers rejected the counsel of God for themselves, not having been baptized by him.

31 And the Lord said, "To what then shall I liken the men of this generation, and what are they like?

32 "They are like children sitting in the marketplace and calling to one another, saying:

'We played the flute for you,
    And you did not dance;
We mourned to you,
    And you did not weep.'

33 "For John the Baptist came neither eating bread nor drinking wine, and you say, 'He has a demon.'

34 "The Son of Man has come eating and drinking, and you say, 'Look, a glutton and a winebibber, a friend of tax collectors and sinners!'

35 "But wisdom is justified by all her children."

36 Then one of the Pharisees asked Him to eat with him. And He went to the Pharisee's house, and sat down to eat.

37 And behold, a woman in the city who was a sinner, when she knew that *Jesus* sat at the table in the Pharisee's house, brought an alabaster flask of fragrant oil,

38 and stood at His feet behind *Him* weeping; and she began to wash His feet with her tears, and wiped *them* with the hair of her head; and she kissed His feet and anointed *them* with the fragrant oil.

39 Now when the Pharisee who

had invited Him saw *this*, he spoke to himself, saying, "This man, if He were a prophet, would know who and what manner of woman *this is* who is touching Him, for she is a sinner."

40 And Jesus answered and said to him, "Simon, I have something to say to you." And he said, "Teacher, say it."

41 "There was a certain creditor who had two debtors. One owed five hundred denarii, and the other fifty.

42 "And when they had nothing with which to repay, he freely forgave them both. Tell Me, therefore, which of them will love him more?"

43 Simon answered and said, "I suppose the *one* whom he forgave more." And He said to him, "You have rightly judged."

44 Then He turned to the woman and said to Simon, "Do you see this woman? I entered your house; you gave Me no water for My feet, but she has washed My feet with her tears and wiped *them* with the hair of her head.

45 "You gave Me no kiss, but this woman has not ceased to kiss My feet since the time I came in.

46 "You did not anoint My head with oil, but this woman has anointed My feet with fragrant oil.

47 "Therefore I say to you, her sins, *which are* many, are forgiven, for she loved much. But to whom little is forgiven, *the same* loves little."

48 And He said to her, "Your sins are forgiven."

49 And those who sat at the table with Him began to say to themselves, "Who is this who even forgives sins?"

50 Then He said to the woman, "Your faith has saved you. Go in peace."

8 Now it came to pass, afterward, that He went through every city and village, preaching and

bringing the glad tidings of the kingdom of God. And the twelve *were* with Him,

2 and certain women who had been healed of evil spirits and infirmities—Mary called Magdalene, out of whom had come seven demons,

3 and Joanna the wife of Chuza, Herod's steward, and Susanna, and many others who provided for Him from their substance.

4 And when a great multitude had gathered, and *others* had come to Him from every city, He spoke by a parable:

5 "A sower went out to sow his seed. And as he sowed, some fell by the wayside; and it was trampled down, and the birds of the air devoured it.

6 "Some fell on rock; and as soon as it sprang up, it withered away because it lacked moisture.

7 "And some fell among thorns, and the thorns sprang up with it and choked it.

8 "But others fell on good ground, sprang up, and yielded a crop a hundredfold." When He had said these things He cried, "He who has ears to hear, let him hear!"

9 Then His disciples asked Him, saying, "What does this parable mean?"

10 And He said, "To you it has been given to know the mysteries of the kingdom of God, but to the rest *it is given* in parables, that

> '*Seeing they may not see,
> And hearing they may not
> understand.*'

11 "Now the parable is this: The seed is the word of God.

12 "Those by the wayside are the ones who hear; then the devil comes and takes away the word out of their hearts, lest they should believe and be saved.

13 "But the ones on the rock *are those* who, when they hear, re-

ceive the word with joy; and these have no root, who believe for a while and in time of temptation fall away.

14 "And the ones *that* fell among thorns are those who, when they have heard, go out and are choked with cares, riches, and pleasures of life, and bring no fruit to maturity.

15 "But the ones *that* fell on the good ground are those who, having heard the word with a noble and good heart, keep *it* and bear fruit with patience.

16 "No one, when he has lit a lamp, covers it with a vessel or puts *it* under a bed, but sets *it* on a lampstand, that those who enter may see the light.

17 "For nothing is secret that will not be revealed, nor *anything* hidden that will not be known and come to light.

18 "Therefore take heed how you hear. For whoever has, to him *more* will be given; and whoever does not have, even what he seems to have will be taken from him."

19 Then His mother and brothers came to Him, and could not approach Him because of the crowd.

20 And it was told Him *by some,* who said, "Your mother and Your brothers are standing outside, desiring to see You."

21 But He answered and said to them, "My mother and My brothers are these who hear the word of God and do it."

22 Now it happened, on a certain day, that He got into a boat with His disciples. And He said to them, "Let us go over to the other side of the lake." And they launched out.

23 But as they sailed He fell asleep. And a windstorm came down on the lake, and they were filling *with water,* and were in jeopardy.

24 And they came to Him and awoke Him, saying, "Master, Master, we are perishing!" Then He arose and rebuked the wind and

the raging of the water. And they ceased, and there was a calm.

25 But He said to them, "Where is your faith?" And they were afraid, and marveled, saying to one another, "Who can this be? For He commands even the winds and water, and they obey Him!"

26 Then they sailed to the country of the Gadarenes, which is opposite Galilee.

27 And when He stepped out on the land, there met Him a certain man from the city who had demons for a long time. And he wore no clothes, nor did he live in a house but in the tombs.

28 When he saw Jesus, he cried out, fell down before Him, and with a loud voice said, "What have I to do with You, Jesus, Son of the Most High God? I beg You, do not torment me!"

29 For He had commanded the unclean spirit to come out of the man. For it had often seized him, and he was kept under guard, bound with chains and shackles; and he broke the bonds and was driven by the demon into the wilderness.

30 Jesus asked him, saying, "What is your name?" And he said, "Legion," because many demons had entered him.

31 And they begged Him that He would not command them to go out into the abyss.

32 Now a herd of many swine was feeding there on the mountain. And they begged Him that He would permit them to enter them. And He permitted them.

33 Then the demons went out of the man and entered the swine, and the herd ran violently down the steep place into the lake and drowned.

34 When those who fed *them* saw what had happened, they fled and told *it* in the city and in the country.

35 Then they went out to see what had happened, and came to Jesus, and found the man from whom the demons had departed, sitting at the feet of Jesus, clothed and in his right mind. And they were afraid.

36 They also who had seen *it* told them by what means he who had been demon-possessed was healed.

37 Then the whole multitude of the surrounding region of the Gadarenes asked Him to depart from them, for they were seized with great fear. And He got into the boat and returned.

38 Now the man from whom the demons had departed begged Him that he might be with Him. But Jesus sent him away, saying,

39 "Return to your own house, and tell what great things God has done for you." And he went his way and proclaimed throughout the whole city what great things Jesus had done for him.

40 So it was, when Jesus returned, that the multitude welcomed Him, for they were all waiting for Him.

41 And behold, there came a man named Jairus, and he was a ruler of the synagogue. And he fell down at Jesus' feet and begged Him to come to his house,

42 for he had an only daughter about twelve years of age, and she was dying. But as He went, the multitudes thronged Him.

43 Now a woman, having a flow of blood for twelve years, who had spent all her livelihood on physicians and could not be healed by any,

44 came from behind and touched the border of His garment. And immediately her flow of blood stopped.

45 And Jesus said, "Who touched Me?" When all denied it, Peter and those with him said, "Master, the multitudes throng You and press *You*, and You say, 'Who touched Me?' "

46 But Jesus said, "Somebody

touched Me, for I perceived power going out from Me."

47 Now when the woman saw that she was not hidden, she came trembling; and falling down before Him, she declared to Him in the presence of all the people the reason she had touched Him and how she was healed immediately.

48 And He said to her, "Daughter, be of good cheer; your faith has made you well. Go in peace."

49 While He was still speaking, someone came from the ruler of the synagogue's *house,* saying to him, "Your daughter is dead. Do not trouble the Teacher."

50 But when Jesus heard *it,* He answered him, saying, "Do not be afraid; only believe, and she will be made well."

51 When He came into the house, He permitted no one to go in except Peter, James, and John, and the father and mother of the girl.

52 Now all wept and mourned for her; but He said, "Do not weep; she is not dead, but sleeping."

53 And they laughed Him to scorn, knowing that she was dead.

54 But He put them all out, took her by the hand and called, saying, "Little girl, arise."

55 Then her spirit returned, and she arose immediately. And He commanded that she be given *something* to eat.

56 And her parents were astonished, but He charged them to tell no one what had happened.

9 Then He called His twelve disciples together and gave them power and authority over all demons, and to cure diseases.

2 He sent them to preach the kingdom of God and to heal the sick.

3 And He said to them, "Take nothing for the journey, neither staffs nor bag nor bread nor money; and do not have two tunics apiece.

4 "Whatever house you enter,

stay there, and from there depart.

5 "And whoever will not receive you, when you go out of that city, shake off the very dust from your feet as a testimony against them."

6 So they departed and went through the towns, preaching the gospel and healing everywhere.

7 Now Herod the tetrarch heard of all that was done by Him; and he was perplexed, because it was said by some that John had risen from the dead,

8 and by some that Elijah had appeared, and by others that one of the old prophets had risen again.

9 And Herod said, "John I have beheaded, but who is this of whom I hear such things?" And he sought to see Him.

10 And the apostles, when they had returned, told Him all that they had done. And He took them and went aside privately into a deserted place belonging to the city called Bethsaida.

11 But when the multitudes knew *it,* they followed Him; and He received them and spoke to them about the kingdom of God, and healed those who had need of healing.

12 When the day began to wear away, the twelve came and said to Him, "Send the multitude away, that they may go into the surrounding towns and country, and lodge and get provisions; for we are in a deserted place here."

13 But He said to them, "You give them something to eat." And they said, "We have no more than five loaves and two fish, unless we go and buy food for all these people."

14 For there were about five thousand men. And He said to His disciples, "Make them sit down in groups of fifty."

15 And they did so, and made them all sit down.

16 Then He took the five loaves and the two fish, and looking up to heaven, He blessed and broke

them, and gave *them* to the disciples to set before the multitude.

17 So they all ate and were filled, and twelve baskets of the leftover fragments were taken up by them.

18 And it happened, as He was alone praying, *that* His disciples joined Him, and He asked them, saying, "Who do the crowds say that I am?"

19 So they answered and said, "John the Baptist, but some *say* Elijah; and others *say* that one of the old prophets has risen again."

20 He said to them, "But who do you say that I am?" Peter answered and said, "The Christ of God."

21 And He strictly warned and commanded them to tell this to no one,

22 saying, "The Son of Man must suffer many things, and be rejected by the elders and chief priests and scribes, and be killed, and be raised the third day."

23 Then He said to *them* all, "If anyone desires to come after Me, let him deny himself, and take up his cross daily, and follow Me.

24 "For whoever desires to save his life will lose it, but whoever loses his life for My sake will save it.

25 "For what advantage is it to a man if he gains the whole world, and is himself destroyed or lost?

26 "For whoever is ashamed of Me and My words, of him the Son of Man will be ashamed when He comes in His *own* glory, and *in* His Father's, and of the holy angels.

27 "But I tell you truly, there are some standing here who shall not taste death till they see the kingdom of God."

28 And it came to pass, about eight days after these sayings, that He took Peter, John, and James, and went up on the mountain to pray.

29 And as He prayed, the appearance of His face was altered, and His robe *became* white *and* glistening.

30 Then behold, two men talked with Him, who were Moses and Elijah,

31 who appeared in glory and spoke of His decease which He was about to accomplish at Jerusalem.

32 But Peter and those with him were heavy with sleep; and when they were fully awake, they saw His glory and the two men who stood with Him.

33 And it happened, as they were parting from Him, *that* Peter said to Jesus, "Master, it is good for us to be here; and let us make three tabernacles: one for You, one for Moses, and one for Elijah"—not knowing what he said.

34 While he was saying this, a cloud came and overshadowed them; and they were fearful as they entered the cloud.

35 Then a voice came out of the cloud, saying, "This is My beloved Son. Hear Him!"

36 And when the voice had ceased, Jesus was found alone. But they kept quiet, and told no one in those days any of the things they had seen.

37 Now it happened on the next day, when they had come down from the mountain, that a great multitude met Him.

38 Suddenly a man from the multitude cried out, saying, "Teacher, I implore You, look on my son, for he is my only child.

39 "And behold, a spirit seizes him, and he suddenly cries out; it convulses him so that he foams *at the mouth*, and bruising him, it departs from him with great difficulty.

40 "So I implored Your disciples to cast it out, but they could not."

41 Then Jesus answered and said, "O faithless and perverse generation, how long shall I be with you and bear with you? Bring your son here."

42 And as he was still coming, the demon threw him down and convulsed *him*. Then Jesus rebuked

the unclean spirit, healed the child, and gave him back to his father.

43 And they were all amazed at the majesty of God. But while everyone marveled at all the things which Jesus did, He said to His disciples,

44 "Let these words sink down into your ears, for the Son of Man is about to be delivered into the hands of men."

45 But they did not understand this saying, and it was hidden from them so that they did not perceive it; and they were afraid to ask Him about this saying.

46 Then a dispute arose among them as to which of them would be greatest.

47 And Jesus, perceiving the thought of their heart, took a little child and set him by Him,

48 and said to them, "Whoever receives this little child in My name receives Me; and whoever receives Me receives Him who sent Me. For he who is least among you all will be great."

49 Then John answered and said, "Master, we saw someone casting out demons in Your name, and we forbade him because he does not follow with us."

50 But Jesus said to him, "Do not forbid *him*, for he who is not against us is for us."

51 Now it came to pass, when the time had come for Him to be received up, that He steadfastly set His face to go to Jerusalem,

52 and sent messengers before His face. And as they went, they entered a village of the Samaritans, to prepare for Him.

53 But they did not receive Him, because His face was *set* for the journey to Jerusalem.

54 And when His disciples James and John saw *this,* they said, "Lord, do You want us to command fire to come down from heaven and consume them, just as Elijah did?"

55 But He turned and rebuked them, and said, "You do not know what manner of spirit you are of.

56 "For the Son of Man did not come to destroy men's lives but to save *them.*" And they went to another village.

57 Now it happened as they journeyed on the road, *that* someone said to Him, "Lord, I will follow You wherever You go."

58 And Jesus said to him, "Foxes have holes and birds of the air *have* nests, but the Son of Man has nowhere to lay *His* head."

59 Then He said to another, "Follow Me." But he said, "Lord, let me first go and bury my father."

60 Jesus said to him, "Let the dead bury their own dead, but you go and preach the kingdom of God."

61 And another also said, "Lord, I will follow You, but let me first go *and* bid them farewell who are at my house."

62 But Jesus said to him, "No one, having put his hand to the plow, and looking back, is fit for the kingdom of God."

10 After these things the Lord appointed seventy others also, and sent them two by two before His face into every city and place where He Himself was about to go.

2 Then He said to them, "The harvest truly *is* great, but the laborers *are* few; therefore pray the Lord of the harvest to send out laborers into His harvest.

3 "Go your way; behold, I send you out as lambs among wolves.

4 "Carry neither money bag, sack, nor sandals; and greet no one along the road.

5 "But whatever house you enter, first say, 'Peace to this house.'

6 "And if a son of peace is there, your peace will rest on it; if not, it will return to you.

7 "And remain in the same house, eating and drinking such things as they give, for the laborer is worthy of his wages. Do not go from house to house.

8 "Whatever city you enter, and they receive you, eat such things as are set before you.

9 "And heal the sick *who are* there, and say to them, 'The kingdom of God has come near to you.'

10 "But whatever city you enter, and they do not receive you, go out into its streets and say,

11 'The very dust of your city which clings to us we wipe off against you. Nevertheless know this, that the kingdom of God has come near you.'

12 "But I say to you that it will be more tolerable in that Day for Sodom than for that city.

13 "Woe to you, Chorazin! Woe to you, Bethsaida! For if the mighty works which were done in you had been done in Tyre and Sidon, they would have repented a great while ago, sitting in sackcloth and ashes.

14 "But it will be more tolerable for Tyre and Sidon at the judgment than for you.

15 "And you, Capernaum, who are exalted to heaven, will be thrust down to Hades.

16 "He who hears you hears Me, he who rejects you rejects Me, and he who rejects Me rejects Him who sent Me."

17 Then the seventy returned with joy, saying, "Lord, even the demons are subject to us in Your name."

18 And He said to them, "I saw Satan fall like lightning from heaven.

19 "Behold, I give you the authority to trample on serpents and scorpions, and over all the power of the enemy, and nothing shall by any means hurt you.

20 "Nevertheless do not rejoice in this, that the spirits are subject to you, but rather rejoice because your names are written in heaven."

21 In that hour Jesus rejoiced in the Spirit and said, "I praise You, Father, Lord of heaven and earth, that You have hidden these things from *the* wise and prudent and revealed them to babes. Even so, Father, for so it seemed good in Your sight.

22 "All things have been delivered to Me by My Father, and no one knows who the Son is but the Father, and who the Father is but the Son, and *the one* to whom the Son wills to reveal *Him*."

23 And He turned to *His* disciples and said privately, "Blessed *are* the eyes which see the things you see;

24 "for I tell you that many prophets and kings have desired to see what you see, and have not seen *it*, and to hear what you hear, and have not heard *it*."

25 And behold, a certain lawyer stood up and tested Him, saying, "Teacher, what shall I do to inherit eternal life?"

26 He said to him, "What is written in the law? What is your reading of *it*?"

27 So he answered and said, " '*You shall love the* LORD *your God with all your heart, with all your soul, with all your strength, and with all your mind,*' and '*your neighbor as yourself.*' "

28 And He said to him, "You have answered rightly; do this and you will live."

29 But he, wanting to justify himself, said to Jesus, "And who is my neighbor?"

30 Then Jesus answered and said: "A certain *man* went down from Jerusalem to Jericho, and fell among thieves, who stripped him of his clothing, wounded *him*, and departed, leaving *him* half dead.

31 "Now by chance a certain priest came down that road. And when he saw him, he passed by on the other side.

32 "Likewise a Levite, when he arrived at the place, came and

looked, and passed by on the other side.

33 "But a certain Samaritan, as he journeyed, came where he was. And when he saw him, he had compassion *on him,*

34 "and went to *him* and bandaged his wounds, pouring on oil and wine; and he set him on his own animal, brought him to an inn, and took care of him.

35 "On the next day, when he departed, he took out two denarii, gave *them* to the innkeeper, and said to him, 'Take care of him; and whatever more you spend, when I come again, I will repay you.'

36 "So which of these three do you think was neighbor to him who fell among the thieves?"

37 And he said, "He who showed mercy on him." Then Jesus said to him, "Go and do likewise."

38 Now it happened as they went that He entered a certain village; and a certain woman named Martha welcomed Him into her house.

39 And she had a sister called Mary, who also sat at Jesus' feet and heard His word.

40 But Martha was distracted with much serving, and she approached Him and said, "Lord, do You not care that my sister has left me to serve alone? Therefore tell her to help me."

41 And Jesus answered and said to her, "Martha, Martha, you are worried and troubled about many things.

42 "But one thing is needed, and Mary has chosen that good part, which will not be taken away from her."

11 And it came to pass, as He was praying in a certain place, when He ceased, *that* one of His disciples said to Him, "Lord, teach us to pray, as John also taught his disciples."

2 So He said to them, "When you pray, say:

Our Father in heaven,
Hallowed be Your name.
Your kingdom come.
Your will be done
On earth as *it is* in heaven.
3 Give us day by day our daily
        bread.
4 And forgive us our sins,
For we also forgive everyone
        who is indebted to us.
And do not lead us into
        temptation,
But deliver us from the evil
        one."

5 And He said to them, "Which of you shall have a friend, and go to him at midnight and say to him, 'Friend, lend me three loaves;

6 'for a friend of mine has come to me on his journey, and I have nothing to set before him';

7 "and he will answer from within and say, 'Do not trouble me; the door is now shut, and my children are with me in bed; I cannot rise and give to you'?

8 "I say to you, though he will not rise and give to him because he is his friend, yet because of his persistence he will rise and give him as many as he needs.

9 "And I say to you, ask, and it will be given to you; seek, and you will find; knock, and it will be opened to you.

10 "For everyone who asks receives, and he who seeks finds, and to him who knocks it will be opened.

11 "If a son asks for bread from any father among you, will he give him a stone? Or if *he asks* for a fish, will he give him a serpent instead of a fish?

12 "Or if he asks for an egg, will he offer him a scorpion?

13 "If you then, being evil, know how to give good gifts to your children, how much more will *your*

heavenly Father give the Holy Spirit to those who ask Him!"

14 And He was casting out a demon, and it was mute. So it was, when the demon had gone out, that the mute spoke; and the multitudes marveled.

15 But some of them said, "He casts out demons by Beelzebub, the ruler of the demons."

16 And others, testing *Him*, sought from Him a sign from heaven.

17 But He, knowing their thoughts, said to them: "Every kingdom divided against itself is brought to desolation, and a house *divided* against a house falls.

18 "If Satan also is divided against himself, how will his kingdom stand? Because you say I cast out demons by Beelzebub.

19 "And if I cast out demons by Beelzebub, by whom do your sons cast *them* out? Therefore they will be your judges.

20 "But if I cast out demons with the finger of God, surely the kingdom of God has come upon you.

21 "When a strong man, fully armed, guards his own palace, his goods are in peace.

22 "But when a stronger than he comes upon him and overcomes him, he takes from him all his armor in which he trusted, and divides his spoils.

23 "He who is not with Me is against Me, and he who does not gather with Me scatters.

24 "When an unclean spirit goes out of a man, he goes through dry places, seeking rest; and finding none, he says, 'I will return to my house from which I came.'

25 "And when he comes, he finds *it* swept and put in order.

26 "Then he goes and takes with *him* seven other spirits more wicked than himself, and they enter and dwell there; and the last *state* of that man is worse than the first."

27 And it happened, as He spoke these things, that a certain woman from the crowd raised her voice and said to Him, "Blessed *is* the womb that bore You, and *the* breasts which nursed You!"

28 But He said, "More than that, blessed *are* those who hear the word of God and keep it!"

29 And while the crowds were thickly gathered together, He began to say, "This is an evil generation. It seeks a sign, and no sign will be given to it except the sign of Jonah the prophet.

30 "For as Jonah became a sign to the Ninevites, so also the Son of Man will be to this generation.

31 "The queen of the South will rise up in the judgment with the men of this generation and condemn them, for she came from the ends of the earth to hear the wisdom of Solomon; and indeed a greater than Solomon *is* here.

32 "The men of Nineveh will rise up in the judgment with this generation and condemn it, for they repented at the preaching of Jonah; and indeed a greater than Jonah *is* here.

33 "No one, when he has lit a lamp, puts *it* in a secret place or under a basket, but on a lampstand, that those who come in may see the light.

34 "The lamp of the body is the eye. Therefore, when your eye is good, your whole body also is full of light. But when *your eye* is bad, your body also *is* full of darkness.

35 "Therefore take heed that the light which is in you is not darkness.

36 "If then your whole body is full of light, having no part dark, *the* whole *body* will be full of light, as when the bright shining of a lamp gives you light."

37 And as He spoke, a certain Pharisee asked Him to dine with him. So He went in and sat down to eat.

38 And when the Pharisee saw *it*,

he marveled that He had not first washed before dinner.

39 But the Lord said to him, "Now you Pharisees make the outside of the cup and dish clean, but your inward part is full of greed and wickedness.

40 "Foolish ones! Did not He who made the outside make the inside also?

41 "But rather give alms of such things as you have; then indeed all things are clean to you.

42 "But woe to you Pharisees! For you tithe mint and rue and all manner of herbs, and pass by justice and the love of God. These you ought to have done, without leaving the others undone.

43 "Woe to you Pharisees! For you love the best seats in the synagogues and greetings in the marketplaces.

44 "Woe to you, scribes and Pharisees, hypocrites! For you are like graves which are not seen, and the men who walk over *them* are not aware *of them*."

45 Then one of the lawyers answered and said to Him, "Teacher, by saying these things You reproach us also."

46 And He said, "Woe to you also, *you* lawyers! For you load men with burdens hard to bear, and you yourselves do not touch the burdens with one of your fingers.

47 "Woe to you! For you build the tombs of the prophets, and your fathers killed them.

48 "In fact, you bear witness that you approve the deeds of your fathers; for they indeed killed them, and you build their tombs.

49 "Therefore the wisdom of God also said, 'I will send them prophets and apostles, and *some* of them they will kill and persecute,'

50 "that the blood of all the prophets which was shed from the foundation of the world may be required of this generation,

51 "from the blood of Abel to the blood of Zechariah who perished between the altar and the temple. Yes, I say to you, it shall be required of this generation.

52 "Woe to you lawyers! For you have taken away the key of knowledge. You did not enter in yourselves, and those who were entering in you hindered."

53 And as He said these things to them, the scribes and the Pharisees began to assail *Him* vehemently, and to cross-examine Him about many things,

54 lying in wait for Him, and seeking to catch Him in something He might say, that they might accuse Him.

12 In the meantime, when an innumerable multitude of people had gathered together, so that they trampled one another, He began to say to His disciples first *of all*, "Beware of the leaven of the Pharisees, which is hypocrisy.

2 "For there is nothing covered that will not be revealed, nor hidden that will not be known.

3 "Therefore whatever you have spoken in the dark will be heard in the light, and what you have spoken in the ear in inner rooms will be proclaimed on the housetops.

4 "And I say to you, My friends, do not be afraid of those who kill the body, and after that have no more that they can do.

5 "But I will show you whom you should fear: Fear Him who, after He has killed, has power to cast into hell; yes, I say to you, fear Him!

6 "Are not five sparrows sold for two copper coins? And not one of them is forgotten before God.

7 "But the very hairs of your head are all numbered. Do not fear therefore; you are of more value than many sparrows.

8 "Also I say to you, whoever confesses Me before men, him the Son of Man also will confess before the angels of God.

If I Give Myself to God, Won't He Make My Life Miserable?

Have you ever harbored a suspicion that God didn't have your best interests at heart? or that following Him would be a good way to miss out on all the enjoyable things in life like sex, security, and status?

This fear has caused many to postpone any real brush with God until all the wild oats have been sown and taken root. Is it a justifiable fear? The most often repeated instruction in the Bible is "do not fear" the wrong things (Luke 12:7).

One test of maturity is what you do or do not fear. A child may be afraid of the dark but have no fear of playing in traffic. As the child grows in understanding, the fears are reversed. In the same way, as you grow in your understanding of what God is like, you will become less fearful of His intents for you. The apostle John says, "God is love," and "perfect love casts out fear" (1 John 4:8, 18). If you fear anything, let it be the possibility of missing out on what God holds in store for you.

We are often afraid to give ourselves to God because we think that what we desire is better than what He desires for us. We desire intimate and loving relationships, but we'll settle for a moment's pleasure. God says, "I know you perfectly, yet I'll love you now and forever." (See Romans 5:8.)

We desire the security of possessions but often mortgage our lives in the pursuit of real estate, health care, and retirement. God says, "I'll care for you now and ultimately take you home with Me." (See John 14:1–3.)

We desire the status of fame, position, and power but fret over how to get it. God says, "I, the Creator of the universe, will call you by name, and you will be known as My child." (See John 1:12.)

God's will brings about the greatest possible good in your life; His will is so acceptable you will feel you were created for it; and it is so perfect that, if you could see the whole picture, you wouldn't change a thing. (See Romans 12:1, 2.)

Will God make your life miserable if you entrust it to Him? Far from it. He wants to restore your life, not ruin it (John 3:16). (For more details on God's plan, see "What in the World Is God Up To?" page 343.)

9 "But he who denies Me before men will be denied before the angels of God.

10 "And anyone who speaks a word against the Son of Man, it will be forgiven him; but to him who blasphemes against the Holy Spirit, it will not be forgiven.

11 "Now when they bring you to the synagogues and magistrates and authorities, do not worry about how or what you should answer, or what you should say.

12 "For the Holy Spirit will teach you in that very hour what you ought to say."

13 Then one from the crowd said to Him, "Teacher, tell my brother to divide the inheritance with me."

14 But He said to him, "Man, who made Me a judge or an arbitrator over you?"

15 And He said to them, "Take heed and beware of covetousness, for one's life does not consist in the abundance of the things he possesses."

16 Then He spoke a parable to them, saying: "The ground of a certain rich man yielded plentifully.

17 "And he thought within himself, saying, 'What shall I do, since I have no room to store my crops?'

18 "So he said, 'I will do this: I will pull down my barns and build greater, and there I will store all my crops and my goods.

19 'And I will say to my soul, "Soul, you have many goods laid up for many years; take your ease; eat, drink, *and* be merry." '

20 "But God said to him, '*You* fool! This night your soul will be required of you; then whose will those things be which you have provided?'

21 "So *is* he who lays up treasure for himself, and is not rich toward God."

22 And He said to His disciples, "Therefore I say to you, do not worry about your life, what you will eat; nor about the body, what you will put on.

23 "Life is more than food, and the body *is more* than clothing.

24 "Consider the ravens, for they neither sow nor reap, which have neither storehouse nor barn; and God feeds them. Of how much more value are you than the birds?

25 "And which of you by worrying can add one cubit to his stature?

26 "If you then are not able to do *the* least, why are you anxious for the rest?

27 "Consider the lilies, how they grow: they neither toil nor spin; and yet I say to you, even Solomon in all his glory was not arrayed like one of these.

28 "If then God so clothes the grass, which today is in the field and tomorrow is thrown into the oven, how much more *will He clothe* you, O *you* of little faith?

29 "And do not seek what you should eat or what you should drink, nor have an anxious mind.

30 "For all these things the nations of the world seek after, and your Father knows that you need these things.

31 "But seek the kingdom of God, and all these things shall be added to you.

32 "Do not fear, little flock, for it is your Father's good pleasure to give you the kingdom.

33 "Sell what you have and give alms; provide yourselves money bags which do not grow old, a treasure in the heavens that does not fail, where no thief approaches nor moth destroys.

34 "For where your treasure is, there your heart will be also.

35 "Let your waist be girded and *your* lamps burning;

36 "and you yourselves be like men who wait for their master, when he will return from the wedding, that when he comes and knocks they may open to him immediately.

37 "Blessed *are* those servants

whom the master, when he comes, will find watching. Assuredly, I say to you that he will gird himself and have them sit down *to eat,* and will come and serve them.

38 "And if he should come in the second watch, or come in the third watch, and find *them* so, blessed are those servants.

39 "But know this, that if the master of the house had known what hour the thief would come, he would have watched and not allowed his house to be broken into.

40 "Therefore you also be ready, for the Son of Man is coming at an hour you do not expect."

41 Then Peter said to Him, "Lord, do You speak this parable *only* to us, or to all *people?*"

42 And the Lord said, "Who then is that faithful and wise steward, whom *his* master will make ruler over his household, to give *them their* portion of food in due season?

43 "Blessed *is* that servant whom his master will find so doing when he comes.

44 "Truly, I say to you that he will make him ruler over all that he has.

45 "But if that servant says in his heart, 'My master is delaying his coming,' and begins to beat the menservants and maidservants, and to eat and drink and be drunk,

46 "the master of that servant will come on a day when he is not looking for *him,* and at an hour when he is not aware, and will cut him in two and appoint *him* his portion with the unbelievers.

47 "And that servant who knew his master's will, and did not prepare *himself* or do according to his will, shall be beaten with many *stripes.*

48 "But he who did not know, yet committed things worthy of stripes, shall be beaten with few. For everyone to whom much is given, from him much will be required; and to whom much has

been committed, of him they will ask the more.

49 "I came to send fire on the earth, and how I wish it were already kindled!

50 "But I have a baptism to be baptized with, and how distressed I am till it is accomplished!

51 "Do *you* suppose that I came to give peace on earth? I tell you, not at all, but rather division.

52 "For from now on five in one house will be divided: three against two, and two against three.

53 "Father will be divided against son and son against father, mother against daughter and daughter against mother, mother-in-law against her daughter-in-law and daughter-in-law against her mother-in-law."

54 Then He also said to the multitudes, "When *you see* a cloud rising out of the west, immediately you say, 'A shower is coming'; and so it is.

55 "And when you see the south wind blow, you say, 'There will be hot weather'; and there is.

56 "Hypocrites! You can discern the face of the sky and of the earth, but how *is it* you do not discern this time?

57 "Yes, and why, even of yourselves, do you not judge what is right?

58 "When you go with your adversary to the magistrate, make every effort along the way to settle with him, lest he drag you to the judge, the judge deliver you to the officer, and the officer throw you into prison.

59 "I tell you, you shall not depart from there till you have paid the very last mite."

13 There were present at that season some who told Him about the Galileans whose blood Pilate had mingled with their sacrifices.

2 And Jesus answered and said to them, "Do you suppose that these

Galileans were worse sinners than all *other* Galileans, because they suffered such things?

3 "I tell you, no; but unless you repent you will all likewise perish.

4 "Or those eighteen on whom the tower in Siloam fell and killed them, do you think that they were worse sinners than all *other* men who dwelt in Jerusalem?

5 "I tell you, no; but unless you repent you will all likewise perish."

6 He also spoke this parable: "A certain *man* had a fig tree planted in his vineyard, and he came seeking fruit on it and found none.

7 "Then he said to the keeper of his vineyard, 'Look, for three years I have come seeking fruit on this fig tree and find none. Cut it down; why does it use up the ground?'

8 "But he answered and said to him, 'Sir, let it alone this year also, until I dig around it and fertilize *it*.

9 'And if it bears fruit, *well*. But if not, after that you can cut it down.' "

10 Now He was teaching in one of the synagogues on the Sabbath.

11 And behold, there was a woman who had a spirit of infirmity eighteen years, and was bent over and could in no way raise *herself* up.

12 But when Jesus saw her, He called *her* to Him and said to her, "Woman, you are loosed from your infirmity."

13 And He laid *His* hands on her, and immediately she was made straight, and glorified God.

14 But the ruler of the synagogue answered with indignation, because Jesus had healed on the Sabbath; and he said to the crowd, "There are six days on which men ought to work; therefore come and be healed on them, and not on the Sabbath day."

15 The Lord then answered him and said, "Hypocrite! Does not each one of you on the Sabbath loose his ox or *his* donkey from the stall, and lead *it* away to water it?

16 "So ought not this woman, being a daughter of Abraham, whom Satan has bound—think of it—for eighteen years, be loosed from this bond on the Sabbath?"

17 And when He said these things, all His adversaries were put to shame; and all the multitude rejoiced for all the glorious things that were done by Him.

18 Then He said, "What is the kingdom of God like? And to what shall I compare it?

19 "It is like a mustard seed, which a man took and put in his garden; and it grew and became a large tree, and the birds of the air nested in its branches."

20 And again He said, "To what shall I liken the kingdom of God?

21 "It is like leaven, which a woman took and hid in three measures of meal till it was all leavened."

22 And He went through the cities and villages, teaching, and journeying toward Jerusalem.

23 Then one said to Him, "Lord, are there few who are saved?" And He said to them,

24 "Strive to enter through the narrow gate, for many, I say to you, will seek to enter and will not be able.

25 "When once the Master of the house has risen up and shut the door, and you begin to stand outside and knock at the door, saying, 'Lord, Lord, open for us,' and He will answer and say to you, 'I do not know you, where you are from,'

26 "then you will begin to say, 'We ate and drank in Your presence, and You taught in our streets.'

27 "But He will say, 'I tell you I do not know you, where you are from. Depart from Me, all you workers of iniquity.'

28 "There will be weeping and gnashing of teeth, when you see Abraham and Isaac and Jacob and all the prophets in the kingdom of God, and yourselves thrust out.

29 "They will come from the east and the west, from the north and the south, and sit down in the kingdom of God.

30 "And indeed there are last who will be first, and there are first who will be last."

31 On that very day some Pharisees came, saying to Him, "Get out and depart from here, for Herod wants to kill You."

32 And He said to them, "Go, tell that fox, 'Behold, I cast out demons and perform cures today and tomorrow, and the third *day* I shall be perfected.'

33 "Nevertheless I must journey today, tomorrow, and the *day* following; for it cannot be that a prophet should perish outside of Jerusalem.

34 "O Jerusalem, Jerusalem, the one who kills the prophets and stones those who are sent to her! How often I wanted to gather your children together, as a hen *gathers* her brood under *her* wings, but you were not willing!

35 "See! Your house is left to you desolate; and assuredly, I say to you, you shall not see Me until the *time* comes when you say, *'Blessed is He who comes in the name of the* LORD!'"

14 Now it happened, as He went into the house of one of the rulers of the Pharisees to eat bread on the Sabbath, that they watched Him closely.

2 And behold, there was a certain man before Him who had dropsy.

3 And Jesus, answering, spoke to the lawyers and Pharisees, saying, "Is it lawful to heal on the Sabbath?"

4 But they kept silent. And He took *him* and healed him, and let him go.

5 Then He answered them, saying, "Which of you, having a donkey or an ox that has fallen into a pit, will not immediately pull him out on the Sabbath day?"

6 And they could not answer Him regarding these things.

7 So He told a parable to those who were invited, when He noted how they chose the best places, saying to them:

8 "When you are invited by anyone to a wedding feast, do not sit down in the best place, lest one more honorable than you be invited by him;

9 "and he who invited you and him come and say to you, 'Give place to this man,' and then you begin with shame to take the lowest place.

10 "But when you are invited, go and sit down in the lowest place, so that when he who invited you comes he may say to you, 'Friend, go up higher.' Then you will have glory in the presence of those who sit at the table with you.

11 "For whoever exalts himself will be abased, and he who humbles himself will be exalted."

12 Then He also said to him who invited Him, "When you give a dinner or a supper, do not ask your friends, your brothers, your relatives, nor your rich neighbors, lest they also invite you back, and you be repaid.

13 "But when you give a feast, invite *the* poor, *the* maimed, *the* lame, *the* blind.

14 "And you will be blessed, because they cannot repay you; for you shall be repaid at the resurrection of the just."

15 Now when one of those who sat at the table with Him heard these things, he said to Him, "Blessed is he who shall eat bread in the kingdom of God!"

16 Then He said to him, "A certain man gave a great supper and invited many,

17 "and sent his servant at supper time to say to those who were invited, 'Come, for all things are now ready.'

18 "But they all with one *accord*

began to make excuses. The first said to him, 'I have bought a piece of ground, and I must go and see it. I ask you to have me excused.'

19 "And another said, 'I have bought five yoke of oxen, and I am going to test them. I ask you to have me excused.'

20 "Still another said, 'I have married a wife, and therefore I cannot come.'

21 "So that servant came and reported these things to his master. Then the master of the house, being angry, said to his servant, 'Go out quickly into the streets and lanes of the city, and bring in here the poor and the maimed and the lame and the blind.'

22 "And the servant said, 'Master, it is done as you commanded, and still there is room.'

23 "Then the master said to the servant, 'Go out into the highways and hedges, and compel *them* to come in, that my house may be filled.

24 'For I say to you that none of those men who were invited shall taste my supper.' "

25 And great multitudes went with Him. And He turned and said to them,

26 "If anyone comes to Me and does not hate his father and mother, wife and children, brothers and sisters, yes, and his own life also, he cannot be My disciple.

27 "And whoever does not bear his cross and come after Me cannot be My disciple.

28 "For which of you, intending to build a tower, does not sit down first and count the cost, whether he has *enough* to finish *it*—

29 "lest, after he has laid the foundation, and is not able to finish *it*, all who see *it* begin to mock him,

30 "saying, 'This man began to build and was not able to finish.'

31 "Or what king, going to make war against another king, does not

sit down first and consider whether he is able with ten thousand to meet him who comes against him with twenty thousand?

32 "Or else, while the other is still a great way off, he sends a delegation and asks conditions of peace.

33 "So likewise, whoever of you does not forsake all that he has cannot be My disciple.

34 "Salt *is* good; but if the salt has lost its flavor, how shall it be seasoned?

35 "It is neither fit for the land nor for the dunghill, *but* men throw it out. He who has ears to hear, let him hear!"

15 Then all the tax collectors and the sinners drew near to Him to hear Him.

2 And the Pharisees and scribes murmured, saying, "This man receives sinners and eats with them."

3 So He spoke this parable to them, saying:

4 "What man of you, having a hundred sheep, if he loses one of them, does not leave the ninety-nine in the wilderness, and go after the one which is lost until he finds it?

5 "And when he has found *it*, he lays *it* on his shoulders, rejoicing.

6 "And when he comes home, he calls together *his* friends and neighbors, saying to them, 'Rejoice with me, for I have found my sheep which was lost!'

7 "I say to you that likewise there will be more joy in heaven over one sinner who repents than over ninety-nine just persons who need no repentance.

8 "Or what woman, having ten silver coins, if she loses one coin, does not light a lamp, sweep the house, and seek diligently until she finds *it*?

9 "And when she has found *it*, she calls *her* friends and neighbors together, saying, 'Rejoice with me,

for I have found the piece which I lost!'

10 "Likewise, I say to you, there is joy in the presence of the angels of God over one sinner who repents."

11 Then He said: "A certain man had two sons.

12 "And the younger of them said to *his* father, 'Father, give me the portion of goods that falls *to me.*' So he divided to them *his* livelihood.

13 "And not many days after, the younger son gathered all together, journeyed to a far country, and there wasted his possessions with prodigal living.

14 "But when he had spent all, there arose a severe famine in that land, and he began to be in want.

15 "Then he went and joined himself to a citizen of that country, and he sent him into his fields to feed swine.

16 "And he would gladly have filled his stomach with the pods that the swine ate, and no one gave him *anything.*

17 "But when he came to himself, he said, 'How many of my father's hired servants have bread enough and to spare, and I perish with hunger!

18 'I will arise and go to my father, and will say to him, "Father, I have sinned against heaven and before you,

19 and I am no longer worthy to be called your son. Make me like one of your hired servants." '

20 "And he arose and came to his father. But when he was still a great way off, his father saw him and had compassion, and ran and fell on his neck and kissed him.

21 "And the son said to him, 'Father, I have sinned against heaven and in your sight, and am no longer worthy to be called your son.'

22 "But the father said to his servants, 'Bring out the best robe and put *it* on him, and put a ring on his hand and sandals on *his* feet.

23 'And bring the fatted calf here and kill *it,* and let us eat and be merry;

24 'for this my son was dead and is alive again; he was lost and is found.' And they began to be merry.

25 "Now his older son was in the field. And as he came and drew near to the house, he heard music and dancing.

26 "So he called one of the servants and asked what these things meant.

27 "And he said to him, 'Your brother has come, and because he has received him safe and sound, your father has killed the fatted calf.'

28 "But he was angry and would not go in. Therefore his father came out and pleaded with him.

29 "So he answered and said to *his* father, 'Lo, these many years I have been serving you; I never transgressed your commandment at any time; and yet you never gave me a young goat, that I might make merry with my friends.

30 'But as soon as this son of yours came, who has devoured your livelihood with harlots, you killed the fatted calf for him.'

31 "And he said to him, 'Son, you are always with me, and all that I have is yours.

32 'It was right that we should make merry and be glad, for your brother was dead and is alive again, and was lost and is found.' "

16 And He also said to His disciples: "There was a certain rich man who had a steward, and an accusation was brought to him that this man was wasting his goods.

2 "So he called him and said to him, 'What is this I hear about you? Give an account of your stewardship, for you can no longer be steward.'

3 "Then the steward said within himself, 'What shall I do? For my

master is taking the stewardship away from me. I cannot dig; I am ashamed to beg.

4 'I have resolved what to do, that when I am put out of the stewardship, they may receive me into their houses.'

5 "So he called every one of his master's debtors to *him*, and said to the first, 'How much do you owe my master?'

6 "And he said, 'A hundred measures of oil.' So he said to him, 'Take your bill, and sit down quickly and write fifty.'

7 "Then he said to another, 'And how much do you owe?' So he said, 'A hundred measures of wheat.' And he said to him, 'Take your bill, and write eighty.'

8 "So the master commended the unjust steward because he had dealt shrewdly. For the sons of this world are more shrewd than the generation of light.

9 "And I say to you, make friends for yourselves by unrighteous mammon, that when you fail, they may receive you into everlasting habitations.

10 "He who *is* faithful in *what is* least is faithful also in much; and he who is unjust in *what is* least is unjust also in much.

11 "Therefore if you have not been faithful in the unrighteous mammon, who will commit to your trust the true *riches*?

12 "And if you have not been faithful in what is another man's, who will give you what is your own?

13 "No servant can serve two masters; for either he will hate the one and love the other, or else he will be loyal to the one and despise the other. You cannot serve God and mammon."

14 Now the Pharisees, who were lovers of money, also heard all these things, and they derided Him.

15 And He said to them, "You are those who justify yourselves before men, but God knows your hearts. For what is highly esteemed among men is an abomination in the sight of God.

16 "The law and the prophets *were* until John. Since that time the kingdom of God has been preached, and everyone is pressing into it.

17 "And it is easier for heaven and earth to pass away than for one tittle of the law to fail.

18 "Whoever divorces his wife and marries another commits adultery; and whoever marries her who is divorced from *her* husband commits adultery.

19 "There was a certain rich man who was clothed in purple and fine linen and fared sumptuously every day.

20 "But there was a certain beggar named Lazarus, full of sores, who was laid at his gate,

21 "desiring to be fed with the crumbs which fell from the rich man's table. Moreover the dogs came and licked his sores.

22 "So it was that the beggar died, and was carried by the angels to Abraham's bosom. The rich man also died and was buried.

23 "And being in torments in Hades, he lifted up his eyes and saw Abraham afar off, and Lazarus in his bosom.

24 "Then he cried and said, 'Father Abraham, have mercy on me, and send Lazarus that he may dip the tip of his finger in water and cool my tongue; for I am tormented in this flame.'

25 "But Abraham said, 'Son, remember that in your lifetime you received your good things, and likewise Lazarus evil things; but now he is comforted and you are tormented.

26 'And besides all this, between us and you there is a great gulf fixed, so that those who want to pass from here to you cannot, nor can those from there pass to us.'

27 "Then he said, 'I beg you therefore, father, that you would send him to my father's house,

28 'for I have five brothers, that he may testify to them, lest they also come to this place of torment.'

29 "Abraham said to him, 'They have Moses and the prophets; let them hear them.'

30 "And he said, 'No, father Abraham; but if one goes to them from the dead, they will repent.'

31 "But he said to him, 'If they do not hear Moses and the prophets, neither will they be persuaded though one rise from the dead.'"

17 Then He said to the disciples, "It is impossible that no offenses should come, but woe *to him* through whom they do come!

2 "It would be better for him if a millstone were hung around his neck, and he were thrown into the sea, than that he should offend one of these little ones.

3 "Take heed to yourselves. If your brother sins against you, rebuke him; and if he repents, forgive him.

4 "And if he sins against you seven times in a day, and seven times in a day returns to you, saying, 'I repent,' you shall forgive him."

5 And the apostles said to the Lord, "Increase our faith."

6 So the Lord said, "If you have faith as a mustard seed, you can say to this mulberry tree, 'Be pulled up by the roots and be planted in the sea,' and it would obey you.

7 "And which of you, having a servant plowing or tending sheep, will say to him when he has come in from the field, 'Come at once and sit down to eat'?

8 "But will he not rather say to him, 'Prepare something for my supper, and gird yourself and serve me till I have eaten and drunk, and afterward you will eat and drink'?

9 "Does he thank that servant because he did the things that were commanded him? I think not.

10 "So likewise you, when you have done all those things which you are commanded, say, 'We are unprofitable servants. We have done what was our duty to do.' "

11 Now it happened as He went to Jerusalem that He passed through the midst of Samaria and Galilee.

12 Then as He entered a certain village, there met Him ten men who were lepers, who stood afar off.

13 And they lifted up *their* voices and said, "Jesus, Master, have mercy on us!"

14 So when He saw *them*, He said to them, "Go, show yourselves to the priests." And so it was that as they went, they were cleansed.

15 Now one of them, when he saw that he was healed, returned, and with a loud voice glorified God,

16 and fell down on *his* face at His feet, giving Him thanks. And he was a Samaritan.

17 So Jesus answered and said, "Were there not ten cleansed? But where *are* the nine?

18 "Were there not any found who returned to give glory to God except this foreigner?"

19 And He said to him, "Arise, go your way. Your faith has made you well."

20 Now when He was asked by the Pharisees when the kingdom of God would come, He answered them and said, "The kingdom of God does not come with observation;

21 "nor will they say, 'See here!' or 'See there!' For indeed, the kingdom of God is within you."

22 Then He said to the disciples, "The days will come when you will desire to see one of the days of the Son of Man, and you will not see *it*.

23 "And they will say to you, 'Look here!' or 'Look there!' Do not go after *them* or follow *them*.

24 "For as the lightning that

flashes out of one *part* under heaven shines to the other *part* under heaven, so also the Son of Man will be in His day.

25 "But first He must suffer many things and be rejected by this generation.

26 "And as it was in the days of Noah, so it will be also in the days of the Son of Man:

27 "They ate, they drank, they married wives, they were given in marriage, until the day that Noah entered the ark, and the flood came and destroyed them all.

28 "Likewise as it was also in the days of Lot: They ate, they drank, they bought, they sold, they planted, they built;

29 "but on the day that Lot went out of Sodom it rained fire and brimstone from heaven and destroyed *them* all.

30 "Even so will it be in the day when the Son of Man is revealed.

31 "In that day, he who is on the housetop, and his goods *are* in the house, let him not come down to take them away. And likewise the one who is in the field, let him not turn back.

32 "Remember Lot's wife.

33 "Whoever seeks to save his life will lose it, and whoever loses his life will preserve it.

34 "I tell you, in that night there will be two *men* in one bed: the one will be taken and the other will be left.

35 "Two *women* will be grinding together: the one will be taken and the other left.

36 "Two *men* will be in the field: the one will be taken and the other left."

37 And they answered and said to Him, "Where, Lord?" So He said to them, "Wherever the body is, there the eagles will be gathered together."

18 Then He spoke a parable to them, that men always ought to pray and not lose heart,

2 saying: "There was in a certain city a judge who did not fear God nor regard man.

3 "Now there was a widow in that city; and she came to him, saying, 'Avenge me of my adversary.'

4 "And he would not for a while; but afterward he said within himself, 'Though I do not fear God nor regard man,

5 'yet because this widow troubles me I will avenge her, lest by her continual coming she weary me.' "

6 Then the Lord said, "Hear what the unjust judge said.

7 "And shall God not avenge His own elect who cry out day and night to Him, though He bears long with them?

8 "I tell you that He will avenge them speedily. Nevertheless, when the Son of Man comes, will He really find faith on the earth?"

9 Also He spoke this parable to some who trusted in themselves that they were righteous, and despised others:

10 "Two men went up to the temple to pray, one a Pharisee and the other a tax collector.

11 "The Pharisee stood and prayed thus with himself, 'God, I thank You that I am not like other men—extortioners, unjust, adulterers, or even as this tax collector.

12 'I fast twice a week; I give tithes of all that I possess.'

13 "And the tax collector, standing afar off, would not so much as raise *his* eyes to heaven, but beat his breast, saying, 'God be merciful to me a sinner!'

14 "I tell you, this man went down to his house justified *rather* than the other; for everyone who exalts himself will be abased, and he who humbles himself will be exalted."

15 Then they also brought infants to Him that He might touch them; but when *His* disciples saw *it*, they rebuked them.

16 But Jesus called them to Him

and said, "Let the little children come to Me, and do not forbid them; for of such is the kingdom of God.

17 "Assuredly, I say to you, whoever does not receive the kingdom of God as a little child will by no means enter it."

18 Now a certain ruler asked Him, saying, "Good Teacher, what shall I do to inherit eternal life?"

19 So Jesus said to him, "Why do you call Me good? No one *is* good but One, *that is,* God.

20 "You know the commandments: *'Do not commit adultery,' 'Do not murder,' 'Do not steal,' 'Do not bear false witness,' 'Honor your father and your mother.'*"

21 And he said, "All these I have kept from my youth."

22 So when Jesus heard these things, He said to him, "You still lack one thing. Sell all that you have and distribute to the poor, and you will have treasure in heaven; and come, follow Me."

23 But when he heard this, he became very sorrowful, for he was very rich.

24 And when Jesus saw that he became very sorrowful, He said, "How hard it is for those who have riches to enter the kingdom of God!

25 "For it is easier for a camel to go through a needle's eye than for a rich man to enter the kingdom of God."

26 And those who heard it said, "Who then can be saved?"

27 But He said, "The things which are impossible with men are possible with God."

28 Then Peter said, "See, we have left all and followed You."

29 So He said to them, "Assuredly, I say to you, there is no one who has left house or parents or brothers or wife or children, for the sake of the kingdom of God,

30 "who shall not receive many times more in this present time,

and in the age to come everlasting life."

31 Then He took the twelve aside and said to them, "Behold, we are going up to Jerusalem, and all things that are written by the prophets concerning the Son of Man will be accomplished.

32 "For He will be delivered to the Gentiles and will be mocked and insulted and spit upon.

33 "And they will scourge *Him* and put Him to death. And the third day He will rise again."

34 But they understood none of these things; this saying was hidden from them, and they did not know the things which were spoken.

35 Then it happened, that as He was coming near Jericho, that a certain blind man sat by the road begging.

36 And hearing a multitude passing by, he asked what it meant.

37 So they told him that Jesus of Nazareth was passing by.

38 And he cried out, saying, "Jesus, Son of David, have mercy on me!"

39 Then those who went before warned him that he should be quiet; but he cried out all the more, "Son of David, have mercy on me!"

40 So Jesus stood still and commanded him to be brought to Him. And when he had come near, He asked him,

41 saying, "What do you want Me to do for you?" And he said, "Lord, that I may receive my sight."

42 Then Jesus said to him, "Receive your sight; your faith has saved you."

43 And immediately he received his sight, and followed Him, glorifying God. And all the people, when they saw *it,* gave praise to God.

19 Then *Jesus* entered and passed through Jericho.

2 Now behold, *there was* a man

110

named Zacchaeus who was a chief tax collector, and he was rich.

3 And he sought to see who Jesus was, but could not because of the crowd, for he was of short stature.

4 So he ran ahead and climbed up into a sycamore tree to see Him, for He was going to pass that *way*.

5 And when Jesus came to the place, He looked up and saw him, and said to him, "Zacchaeus, make haste and come down, for today I must stay at your house."

6 So he made haste and came down, and received Him joyfully.

7 But when they saw *it*, they all murmured, saying, "He has gone to be a guest with a man who is a sinner."

8 Then Zacchaeus stood and said to the Lord, "Look, Lord, I give half of my goods to the poor; and if I have taken anything from anyone by false accusation, I restore fourfold."

9 And Jesus said to him, "Today salvation has come to this house, because he also is a son of Abraham;

10 "for the Son of Man has come to seek and to save that which was lost."

11 Now as they heard these things, He spoke another parable, because He was near Jerusalem and because they thought the kingdom of God would appear immediately.

12 Therefore He said: "A certain nobleman went into a far country to receive for himself a kingdom and to return.

13 "So he called ten of his servants, delivered to them ten minas, and said to them, 'Do business till I come.'

14 "But his citizens hated him, and sent a delegation after him, saying, 'We will not have this *man* to reign over us.'

15 "And so it was that when he returned, having received the kingdom, he then commanded these servants, to whom he had given the money, to be called to

him, that he might know how much every man had gained by trading.

16 "Then came the first, saying, 'Master, your mina has earned ten minas.'

17 "And he said to him, 'Well *done*, good servant; because you were faithful in a very little, have authority over ten cities.'

18 "And the second came, saying, 'Master, your mina has earned five minas.'

19 "Likewise he said to him, 'You also be over five cities.'

20 "And another came, saying, 'Master, here is your mina, which I have kept put away in a handkerchief.

21 'For I feared you, because you are an austere man. You collect what you did not deposit, and reap what you did not sow.'

22 "And he said to him, 'Out of your own mouth I will judge you, *you* wicked servant. You knew that I was an austere man, collecting what I did not deposit and reaping what I did not sow.

23 'Why then did you not put my money in the bank, that at my coming I might have collected it with interest?'

24 "And he said to those who stood by, 'Take the mina from him, and give *it* to him who has ten minas.'

25 ("But they said to him, 'Master, he has ten minas.')

26 'For I say to you, that to everyone who has will be given; and from him who does not have, even what he has will be taken away from him.

27 'But bring here those enemies of mine, who did not want me to reign over them, and slay *them* before me.'"

28 When He had said this, He went on ahead, going up to Jerusalem.

29 And it came to pass, when He came near to Bethphage and Bethany, at the mountain called Olivet, *that* He sent two of His disciples,

30 saying, "Go into the village op-

posite *you,* where as you enter you will find a colt tied, on which no one has ever sat. Loose him and bring *him here.*

31 "And if anyone asks you, 'Why are you loosing *him?'* thus you shall say to him, 'Because the Lord has need of him.' "

32 So those who were sent departed and found *it* just as He had said to them.

33 But as they were loosing the colt, the owners of it said to them, "Why are you loosing the colt?"

34 And they said, "The Lord has need of him."

35 Then they brought him to Jesus. And they threw their own garments on the colt, and they set Jesus on him.

36 And as He went, they spread their clothes on the road.

37 Then, as He was now drawing near the descent of the Mount of Olives, the whole multitude of the disciples began to rejoice and praise God with a loud voice for all the mighty works they had seen,

38 saying:

" 'Blessed is the King who comes
    in the name of the LORD!'
Peace in heaven and glory in
    the highest!"

39 And some of the Pharisees called to Him from the crowd, "Teacher, rebuke Your disciples."

40 But He answered and said to them, "I tell you that if these should keep silent, the stones would immediately cry out."

41 Now as He drew near, He saw the city and wept over it,

42 saying, "If you had known, even you, especially in this your day, the things *that make* for your peace! But now they are hidden from your eyes.

43 "For *the* days will come upon you when your enemies will build an embankment around you, sur-

round you and close you in on every side,

44 "and level you, and your children within you, to the ground; and they will not leave in you one stone upon another, because you did not know the time of your visitation."

45 Then He went into the temple and began to drive out those who bought and sold in it,

46 saying to them, "It is written, *'My house is a house of prayer,'* but you have made it a *'den of thieves.'"*

47 And He was teaching daily in the temple. But the chief priests, the scribes, and the leaders of the people sought to destroy Him,

48 and were unable to do anything; for all the people were very attentive to hear Him.

20 Now it happened on one of those days, as He taught the people in the temple and preached the gospel, *that* the chief priests and the scribes, together with the elders, confronted *Him*

2 and spoke to Him, saying, "Tell us, by what authority are You doing these things? Or who is he who gave You this authority?"

3 But He answered and said to them, "I will also ask you one thing, and answer Me:

4 "The baptism of John—was it from heaven or from men?"

5 And they reasoned among themselves, saying, "If we say, 'From heaven,' He will say, 'Why then did you not believe him?'

6 "But if we say, 'From men,' all the people will stone us, for they are persuaded that John was a prophet."

7 So they answered that they did not know where *it was* from.

8 And Jesus said to them, "Neither will I tell you by what authority I do these things."

9 Then He began to tell the people this parable: "A certain man planted a vineyard, leased it to

vinedressers, and went into a far country for a long time.

10 "Now at vintage-time he sent a servant to the vinedressers, that they might give him some of the fruit of the vineyard. But the vinedressers beat him and sent *him* away empty-handed.

11 "Again he sent another servant; and they beat him also, treated *him* shamefully, and sent *him* away empty-handed.

12 "And again he sent a third; and they wounded him also and cast *him* out.

13 "Then the owner of the vineyard said, 'What shall I do? I will send my beloved son. Probably they will respect *him* when they see him.'

14 "But when the vinedressers saw him, they reasoned among themselves, saying, 'This is the heir. Come, let us kill him, that the inheritance may be ours.'

15 "So they cast him out of the vineyard and killed *him.* Therefore what will the owner of the vineyard do to them?

16 "He will come and destroy those vinedressers and give the vineyard to others." And when they heard *it* they said, "Certainly not!"

17 And He looked at them and said, "What then is this that is written:

'The stone which the builders
    rejected
Has become the chief
    cornerstone'?

18 "Whoever falls on that stone will be broken; but on whomever it falls, it will grind him to powder."

19 And the chief priests and the scribes that very hour sought to lay hands on Him, but they feared the people—for they knew that He had spoken this parable against them.

20 So they watched *Him,* and sent spies who pretended to be righteous, that they might seize on His words, in order to deliver Him to the power and the authority of the governor.

21 And they asked Him, saying, "Teacher, we know that You say and teach rightly, and You do not show personal favoritism, but teach the way of God truly:

22 "Is it lawful for us to pay taxes to Caesar or not?"

23 But He perceived their craftiness, and said to them, "Why do you test Me?

24 "Show Me a denarius. Whose image and inscription does it have?" They answered and said, "Caesar's."

25 And He said to them, "Render therefore to Caesar the things that are Caesar's, and to God the things that are God's."

26 But they could not catch Him in His words in the presence of the people. And they marveled at His answer and kept silent.

27 Then some of the Sadducees, who deny that there is a resurrection, came to *Him* and asked Him,

28 saying: "Teacher, Moses wrote to us *that* if a man's brother dies, having a wife, and he dies without children, his brother should take his wife and raise up offspring for his brother.

29 "Now there were seven brothers. And the first took a wife, and died without children.

30 "And the second took her as wife, and he died childless.

31 "Then the third took her, and in like manner the seven also; and they left no children, and died.

32 "Last of all the woman died also.

33 "Therefore, in the resurrection, whose wife does she become? For all seven had her as wife."

34 And Jesus answered and said to them, "The sons of this age marry and are given in marriage.

35 "But those who are counted worthy to attain that age, and the

113

resurrection from the dead, neither marry nor are given in marriage;
36 "nor can they die anymore, for they are equal to the angels and are sons of God, being sons of the resurrection.
37 "Now even Moses showed in the *burning* bush *passage* that the dead are raised, when he called the Lord *'the God of Abraham, the God of Isaac, and the God of Jacob.'*
38 "For He is not the God of the dead but of the living, for all live to Him."
39 Then some of the scribes answered and said, "Teacher, You have spoken well."
40 But after that they dared not question Him anymore.
41 And He said to them, "How can they say that the Christ is David's Son?
42 "Now David himself said in the Book of Psalms,

'The LORD said to my Lord,
"Sit at My right hand,
43 Till I make Your enemies
Your footstool." '

44 "David therefore calls Him *'Lord'*; how is He then his Son?"
45 Then, in the hearing of all the people, He said to His disciples,
46 "Beware of the scribes, who desire to walk in long robes, love greetings in the marketplaces, the best seats in the synagogues, and the best places at feasts,
47 "who devour widows' houses, and for a pretense make long prayers. These will receive greater condemnation."

21 Then He looked up and saw the rich putting their gifts into the treasury.
2 And He saw also a certain poor widow putting in two mites.
3 So He said, "Truly I say to you that this poor widow has put in more than all;
4 "for all these out of their abun-

dance have put in offerings for God, but she out of her poverty has put in all the livelihood that she had."
5 Then, as some spoke of the temple, how it was adorned with beautiful stones and donations, He said,
6 "*As for* these things which you see, the days will come in which not one stone shall be left upon another that shall not be thrown down."
7 And they asked Him, saying, "Teacher, but when will these things be? And what sign *will there be* when these things are about to take place?"
8 And He said: "Take heed that you not be deceived. For many will come in My name, saying, 'I am He,' and, 'The time has drawn near.' Therefore do not go after them.
9 "But when you hear of wars and commotions, do not be terrified; for these things must come to pass first, but the end *will not come* immediately."
10 Then He said to them, "Nation will rise against nation, and kingdom against kingdom.
11 "And there will be great earthquakes in various places, and famines and pestilences; and there will be fearful sights and great signs from heaven.
12 "But before all these things, they will lay their hands on you and persecute *you*, delivering *you* up to the synagogues and prisons, and you will be brought before kings and rulers for My name's sake.
13 "But it will turn out for you as an occasion for testimony.
14 "Therefore settle *it* in your hearts not to meditate beforehand on what you will answer;
15 "for I will give you a mouth and wisdom which all your adversaries will not be able to contradict or resist.

16 "You will be betrayed even by parents and brothers, relatives and friends; and they will send *some* of you to *your* death.

17 "And you will be hated by all for My name's sake.

18 "But not a hair of your head shall be lost.

19 "In your patience possess your souls.

20 "But when you see Jerusalem surrounded by armies, then know that its desolation is near.

21 "Then let those in Judea flee to the mountains, let those who are in the midst of her depart, and let not those who are in the country enter her.

22 "For these are the days of vengeance, that all things which are written may be fulfilled.

23 "But woe to those who are pregnant and to those who are nursing babies in those days! For there will be great distress in the land and wrath upon this people.

24 "And they will fall by the edge of the sword, and be led away captive into all nations. And Jerusalem will be trampled by Gentiles until the times of the Gentiles are fulfilled.

25 "And there will be signs in the sun, in the moon, and in the stars; and on the earth distress of nations, with perplexity, the sea and the waves roaring;

26 "men's hearts failing them from fear and the expectation of those things which are coming on the earth, for the powers of heaven will be shaken.

27 "Then they will see the Son of Man coming in a cloud with power and great glory.

28 "Now when these things begin to happen, look up and lift up your heads, because your redemption draws near."

29 And He spoke to them a parable: "Look at the fig tree, and all the trees.

30 "When they are already bud-

ding, you see and know for yourselves that summer is now near.

31 "So you, likewise, when you see these things happening, know that the kingdom of God is near.

32 "Assuredly, I say to you, this generation will by no means pass away till all things are fulfilled.

33 "Heaven and earth will pass away, but My words will by no means pass away.

34 "But take heed to yourselves, lest your hearts be weighed down with carousing, drunkenness, and cares of this life, and that Day come on you unexpectedly.

35 "For it will come as a snare on all those who dwell on the face of the whole earth.

36 "Watch therefore, and pray always that you may be counted worthy to escape all these things that will come to pass, and to stand before the Son of Man."

37 And in the daytime He was teaching in the temple, but at night He went out and stayed on the mountain called Olivet.

38 Then early in the morning all the people came to Him in the temple to hear Him.

22 Now the Feast of Unleavened Bread drew near, which is called Passover.

2 And the chief priests and the scribes sought how they might kill Him, for they feared the people.

3 Then Satan entered Judas, surnamed Iscariot, who was numbered among the twelve.

4 So he went his way and conferred with the chief priests and captains, how he might betray Him to them.

5 And they were glad, and agreed to give him money.

6 Then he promised and sought opportunity to betray Him to them in the absence of the multitude.

7 Then came the Day of Unleavened Bread, when the Passover must be killed.

8 And He sent Peter and John,

115

saying, "Go and prepare the Passover for us, that we may eat."

9 So they said to Him, "Where do You want us to prepare?"

10 And He said to them, "Behold, when you have entered the city, a man will meet you carrying a pitcher of water; follow him into the house which he enters.

11 "Then you shall say to the master of the house, 'The Teacher says to you, "Where is the guest room in which I may eat the Passover with My disciples?"'

12 "Then he will show you a large, furnished upper room; there make ready."

13 So they went and found it as He had said to them, and they prepared the Passover.

14 And when the hour had come, He sat down, and the twelve apostles with Him.

15 Then He said to them, "With *fervent* desire I have desired to eat this Passover with you before I suffer;

16 "for I say to you, I will no longer eat of it until it is fulfilled in the kingdom of God."

17 Then He took the cup, and gave thanks, and said, "Take this and divide *it* among yourselves;

18 "for I say to you, I will not drink of the fruit of the vine until the kingdom of God comes."

19 And He took bread, gave thanks and broke *it*, and gave *it* to them, saying, "This is My body which is given for you; do this in remembrance of Me."

20 Likewise He also took *the* cup after supper, saying, "This cup is the new covenant in My blood, which is shed for you.

21 "But behold, the hand of My betrayer *is* with Me on the table.

22 "And truly the Son of Man goes as it has been determined, but woe to that man by whom He is betrayed!"

23 Then they began to question

among themselves, which of them it was who would do this thing.

24 But there was also rivalry among them, as to which of them should be considered the greatest.

25 And He said to them, "The kings of the Gentiles exercise lordship over them, and those who exercise authority over them are called 'benefactors.'

26 "But not so *among* you; on the contrary, he who is greatest among you, let him be as the younger, and he who governs as he who serves.

27 "For who *is* greater, he who sits at the table, or he who serves? *Is* it not he who sits at the table? Yet I am among you as the One who serves.

28 "But you are those who have continued with Me in My trials.

29 "And I bestow upon you a kingdom, just as My Father bestowed *one* upon Me,

30 "that you may eat and drink at My table in My kingdom, and sit on thrones judging the twelve tribes of Israel."

31 And the Lord said, "Simon, Simon! Indeed, Satan has asked for you, that he may sift *you* as wheat.

32 "But I have prayed for you, that your faith should not fail; and when you have returned to *Me*, strengthen your brethren."

33 But he said to Him, "Lord, I am ready to go with You, both to prison and to death."

34 Then He said, "I tell you, Peter, the rooster will not crow this day before you will deny three times that you know Me."

35 And He said to them, "When I sent you without money bag, sack, and sandals, did you lack anything?" So they said, "Nothing."

36 Then He said to them, "But now, he who has a money bag, let him take *it*, and likewise a sack; and he who has no sword, let him sell his garment and buy one.

37 "For I say to you that this

which is written must still be accomplished in Me: *'And He was numbered with the transgressors.'* For the things concerning Me have an end."

38 Then they said, "Lord, look, here *are* two swords." And He said to them, "It is enough."

39 And coming out, He went to the Mount of Olives, as He was accustomed, and His disciples also followed Him.

40 When He came to the place, He said to them, "Pray that you may not enter into temptation."

41 And He was withdrawn from them about a stone's throw, and He knelt down and prayed,

42 saying, "Father, if it is Your will, remove this cup from Me; nevertheless not My will, but Yours, be done."

43 Then an angel appeared to Him from heaven, strengthening Him.

44 And being in agony, He prayed more earnestly. And His sweat became like great drops of blood falling down to the ground.

45 When He rose up from prayer, and had come to His disciples, He found them sleeping from sorrow.

46 Then He said to them, "Why do you sleep? Rise and pray, lest you enter into temptation."

47 And while He was still speaking, behold, a multitude; and he who was called Judas, one of the twelve, went before them and drew near to Jesus to kiss Him.

48 But Jesus said to him, "Judas, are you betraying the Son of Man with a kiss?"

49 When those around Him saw what was going to happen, they said to Him, "Lord, shall we strike with the sword?"

50 And one of them struck the servant of the high priest and cut off his right ear.

51 But Jesus answered and said, "Permit even this." And He touched his ear and healed him.

52 Then Jesus said to the chief priests, captains of the temple, and the elders who had come to Him, "Have you come out, as against a robber, with swords and clubs?

53 "When I was with you daily in the temple, you did not try to seize Me. But this is your hour, and the power of darkness."

54 Then, having arrested Him, they led *Him* and brought Him into the high priest's house. And Peter followed at a distance.

55 Now when they had kindled a fire in the midst of the courtyard and sat down together, Peter sat among them.

56 And a certain servant girl, seeing him as he sat by the fire, looked intently at him and said, "This man was also with Him."

57 But he denied Him, saying, "Woman, I do not know Him."

58 And after a little while another saw him and said, "You also are of them." But Peter said, "Man, I am not!"

59 Then after about an hour had passed, another confidently affirmed, saying, "Surely this *fellow* also was with Him, for he is a Galilean."

60 But Peter said, "Man, I do not know what you are saying!" And immediately, while he was still speaking, the rooster crowed.

61 And the Lord turned and looked at Peter. And Peter remembered the word of the Lord, how He had said to him, "Before the rooster crows, you will deny Me three times."

62 Then Peter went out and wept bitterly.

63 Now the men who held Jesus mocked Him and beat Him.

64 And having blindfolded Him, they struck Him on the face and asked Him, saying, "Prophesy! Who is it that struck You?"

65 And many other things they blasphemously spoke against Him.

66 As soon as it was day, the elders of the people, both chief priests and scribes, came together and led Him into their council, saying,

67 "If You are the Christ, tell us." But He said to them, "If I tell you, you will by no means believe.

68 "And if I also ask *you*, you will by no means answer Me or let *Me* go.

69 "Hereafter the Son of Man will sit on the right hand of the power of God."

70 Then they all said, "Are You then the Son of God?" And He said to them, "You *rightly* say that I am."

71 And they said, "What further testimony do we need? For we have heard it ourselves from His own mouth."

23 Then the whole multitude of them arose and led Him to Pilate.

2 And they began to accuse Him, saying, "We found this *fellow* perverting the nation, and forbidding to pay taxes to Caesar, saying that He Himself is Christ, a King."

3 So Pilate asked Him, saying, "Are You the King of the Jews?" And He answered him and said, "*It is as* you say."

4 Then Pilate said to the chief priests and the crowd, "I find no fault in this Man."

5 But they were the more fierce, saying, "He stirs up the people, teaching throughout all Judea, beginning from Galilee to this place."

6 When Pilate heard of Galilee, he asked if the Man were a Galilean.

7 And as soon as he knew that He belonged to Herod's jurisdiction, he sent Him to Herod, who was also in Jerusalem at that time.

8 Now when Herod saw Jesus, he was exceedingly glad; for he had desired for a long *time* to see Him, because he had heard many things about Him, and he hoped to see some miracle done by Him.

9 Then he questioned Him with many words, but He answered him nothing.

10 And the chief priests and scribes stood and vehemently accused Him.

11 Then Herod, with his men of war, treated Him with contempt and mocked *Him*, arrayed Him in a gorgeous robe, and sent Him back to Pilate.

12 That very day Pilate and Herod became friends with each other, for before *that* they had been at enmity with each other.

13 Then Pilate, when he had called together the chief priests, the rulers, and the people,

14 said to them, "You have brought this Man to me, as one who misleads the people. And indeed, having examined *Him* in your presence, I have found no fault in this Man concerning those things of which you accuse Him;

15 "no, neither did Herod, for I sent you back to him; and indeed nothing worthy of death has been done by Him.

16 "I will therefore chastise Him and release *Him*"

17 (for it was necessary for him to release one to them at the feast).

18 And they all cried out at once, saying, "Away with this *Man*, and release to us Barabbas"—

19 who had been thrown into prison for a certain insurrection made in the city, and for murder.

20 Pilate, therefore, wishing to release Jesus, again called out to them.

21 But they shouted, saying, "Crucify *Him*, crucify Him!"

22 Then he said to them the third time, "Why, what evil has He done? I have found no reason for death in Him. I will therefore chastise Him and let *Him* go."

23 But they were insistent, demanding with loud voices that He be crucified. And the voices of these men and of the chief priests prevailed.

24 So Pilate gave sentence that it should be as they requested.

25 And he released to them the one they requested, who for insurrection and murder had been thrown into prison; but he delivered Jesus to their will.

26 Now as they led Him away, they laid hold of a certain man, Simon a Cyrenian, who was coming from the country, and on him they laid the cross that he might bear *it* after Jesus.

27 And a great multitude of the people followed Him, and women who also mourned and lamented Him.

28 But Jesus, turning to them, said, "Daughters of Jerusalem, do not weep for Me, but weep for yourselves and for your children.

29 "For indeed the days are coming in which they will say, 'Blessed *are* the barren, *the* wombs that never bore, and *the* breasts which never nursed!'

30 "Then they will begin *'to say to the mountains, "Fall on us!" and to the hills, "Cover us!"'*

31 "For if they do these things in the green wood, what will be done in the dry?"

32 There were also two others, criminals, led with Him to be put to death.

33 And when they had come to the place called Calvary, there they crucified Him, and the criminals, one on the right hand and the other on the left.

34 Then Jesus said, "Father, forgive them, for they do not know what they do." And they divided His garments and cast lots.

35 And the people stood looking on. But even the rulers with them sneered, saying, "He saved others; let Him save Himself if He is the Christ, the chosen of God."

36 And the soldiers also mocked Him, coming and offering Him sour wine,

37 and saying, "If You are the King of the Jews, save Yourself."

38 And an inscription also was written over Him in letters of Greek, Latin, and Hebrew:

THIS IS
THE KING OF THE JEWS.

39 Then one of the criminals who were hanged blasphemed Him, saying, "If You are the Christ, save Yourself and us."

40 But the other, answering, rebuked him, saying, "Do you not even fear God, seeing you are under the same condemnation?

41 "And we indeed justly, for we receive the due reward of our deeds; but this Man has done nothing wrong."

42 Then he said to Jesus, "Lord, remember me when You come into Your kingdom."

43 And Jesus said to him, "Assuredly, I say to you, today you will be with Me in Paradise."

44 And it was about the sixth hour, and there was darkness over all the earth until the ninth hour.

45 Then the sun was darkened, and the veil of the temple was torn in two.

46 And when Jesus had cried out with a loud voice, He said, "Father, *'into Your hands I commend My spirit.'*" And having said this, He breathed His last.

47 Now when the centurion saw what had happened, he glorified God, saying, "Certainly this was a righteous Man!"

48 And the whole crowd who came together to that sight, seeing what had been done, beat their breasts and returned.

49 But all His acquaintances, and the women who followed Him from Galilee, stood at a distance, watching these things.

50 And behold, *there was* a man named Joseph, a council member, a good and just man.

51 He had not consented to their counsel and deed. *He was* from Arimathea, a city of the Jews, who himself was also waiting for the kingdom of God.

52 This *man* went to Pilate and asked for the body of Jesus.

53 Then he took it down, wrapped it in linen, and laid it in a tomb *that was* hewn out of the rock, where no one had ever lain before.

54 That day was the Preparation, and the Sabbath drew near.

55 And the women who had come with Him from Galilee followed after, and they observed the tomb and how His body was laid.

56 Then they returned and prepared spices and fragrant oils. And they rested on the Sabbath according to the commandment.

24 Now on the first *day* of the week, very early in the morning, they, and certain *other women* with them, came to the tomb bringing the spices which they had prepared.

2 But they found the stone rolled away from the tomb.

3 Then they went in and did not find the body of the Lord Jesus.

4 And it happened, as they were greatly perplexed about this, that behold, two men stood by them in shining garments.

5 Then, as they were afraid and bowed *their* faces to the earth, they said to them, "Why do you seek the living among the dead?

6 "He is not here, but is risen! Remember how He spoke to you when He was still in Galilee,

7 "saying, 'The Son of Man must be delivered into the hands of sinful men, and be crucified, and the third day rise again.' "

8 And they remembered His words.

9 Then they returned from the tomb and told all these things to the eleven and to all the rest.

10 It was Mary Magdalene, Joanna, Mary *the mother* of James, and the other *women* with them, who told these things to the apostles.

11 And their words seemed to them like idle tales, and they did not believe them.

12 But Peter arose and ran to the tomb; and stooping down, he saw the linen cloths lying by themselves; and he departed, marveling to himself at what had happened.

13 Now behold, two of them were traveling that same day to a village called Emmaus, which was *about* seven miles from Jerusalem.

14 And they talked together of all these things which had happened.

15 So it was, while they conversed and reasoned, that Jesus Himself drew near and went with them.

16 But their eyes were restrained, so that they did not know Him.

17 And He said to them, "What kind of conversation *is* this that you have with one another as you walk and are sad?"

18 Then the one whose name was Cleopas answered and said to Him, "Are You the only stranger in Jerusalem, and have You not known the things which happened there in these days?"

19 And He said to them, "What things?" And they said to Him, "The things concerning Jesus of Nazareth, who was a Prophet mighty in deed and word before God and all the people,

20 "and how the chief priests and our rulers delivered Him to be condemned to death, and crucified Him.

21 "But we were hoping that it was He who was going to redeem Israel. Indeed, besides all this, today is the third day since these things happened.

22 "Yes, and certain women of our company, who arrived at the tomb early, astonished us.

23 "When they did not find His body, they came saying that they had also seen a vision of angels who said He was alive.

24 "And certain of those *who were* with us went to the tomb and found *it* just as the women had said; but Him they did not see."

25 Then He said to them, "O fool-

ish ones, and slow of heart to believe in all that the prophets have spoken!

26 "Ought not the Christ to have suffered these things and to enter into His glory?"

27 And beginning at Moses and all the Prophets, He expounded to them in all the Scriptures the things concerning Himself.

28 Then they drew near to the village where they were going, and He indicated that He would have gone farther.

29 But they constrained Him, saying, "Abide with us, for it is toward evening, and the day is far spent." And He went in to stay with them.

30 Now it came to pass, as He sat at the table with them, that He took bread, blessed and broke *it*, and gave it to them.

31 Then their eyes were opened and they knew Him; and He vanished from their sight.

32 And they said to one another, "Did not our heart burn within us while He talked with us on the road, and while He opened the Scriptures to us?"

33 So they rose up that very hour and returned to Jerusalem, and found the eleven and those who *were* with them gathered together,

34 saying, "The Lord is risen indeed, and has appeared to Simon!"

35 And they told about the things *that had happened* on the road, and how He was known to them in the breaking of bread.

36 Now as they said these things, Jesus Himself stood in the midst of them, and said to them, "Peace to you."

37 But they were terrified and frightened, and supposed they had seen a spirit.

38 And He said to them, "Why are you troubled? And why do doubts arise in your hearts?

39 "Behold My hands and My feet, that it is I Myself. Handle Me and see, for a spirit does not have flesh and bones as you see I have."

40 When He had said this, He showed them His hands and His feet.

41 But while they still did not believe for joy, and marveled, He said to them, "Have you any food here?"

42 So they gave Him a piece of a broiled fish and some honeycomb.

43 And He took *it* and ate in their presence.

44 Then He said to them, "These *are* the words which I spoke to you while I was still with you, that all things must be fulfilled which were written in the Law of Moses and *the* Prophets and *the* Psalms concerning Me."

45 And He opened their understanding, that they might comprehend the Scriptures.

46 Then He said to them, "Thus it is written, and thus it was necessary for the Christ to suffer and to rise from the dead the third day,

47 "and that repentance and remission of sins should be preached in His name to all nations, beginning at Jerusalem.

48 "And you are witnesses of these things.

49 "Behold, I send the Promise of My Father upon you; but tarry in the city of Jerusalem until you are endued with power from on high."

50 And He led them out as far as Bethany, and He lifted up His hands and blessed them.

51 Now it came to pass, while He blessed them, that He was parted from them and carried up into heaven.

52 And they worshiped Him, and returned to Jerusalem with great joy,

53 and were continually in the temple praising and blessing God. Amen.

THE GOSPEL ACCORDING TO

JOHN

IN the beginning was the Word, and the Word was with God, and the Word was God.

2 He was in the beginning with God.

3 All things were made through Him, and without Him nothing was made that was made.

4 In Him was life, and the life was the light of men.

5 And the light shines in the darkness, and the darkness did not comprehend it.

6 There was a man sent from God, whose name *was* John.

7 This man came for a witness, to bear witness of the Light, that all through him might believe.

8 He was not that Light, but *was sent* to bear witness of that Light.

9 *That was* the true Light which gives light to every man who comes into the world.

10 He was in the world, and the world was made through Him, and the world did not know Him.

11 He came to His own, and His own did not receive Him.

12 But as many as received Him, to them He gave the right to become children of God, *even* to those who believe in His name:

13 who were born, not of blood, nor of the will of the flesh, nor of the will of man, but of God.

14 And the Word became flesh and dwelt among us, and we beheld His glory, the glory as of the only begotten of the Father, full of grace and truth.

15 John bore witness of Him and cried out, saying, "This was He of whom I said, 'He who comes after me is preferred before me, for He was before me.'"

16 And of His fullness we have all received, and grace for grace.

17 For the law was given through Moses, *but* grace and truth came through Jesus Christ.

18 No one has seen God at any time. The only begotten Son, who is in the bosom of the Father, He has declared *Him*.

19 Now this is the testimony of John, when the Jews sent priests and Levites from Jerusalem to ask him, "Who are you?"

20 He confessed, and did not deny, but confessed, "I am not the Christ."

21 And they asked him, "What then? Are you Elijah?" He said, "I am not." "Are you the Prophet?" And he answered, "No."

22 Then they said to him, "Who are you, that we may give an answer to those who sent us? What do you say about yourself?"

23 He said: "I am

'The voice of one crying in the wilderness:
"Make straight the way of the LORD," '

as the prophet Isaiah said."

24 Now those who were sent were from the Pharisees.

25 And they asked him, saying, "Why then do you baptize if you are not the Christ, nor Elijah, nor the Prophet?"

26 John answered them, saying, "I baptize with water, but there stands One among you whom you do not know.

27 "It is He who, coming after me, is preferred before me, whose sandal strap I am not worthy to loose."

28 These things were done in Bethabara beyond the Jordan, where John was baptizing.

29 The next day John saw Jesus coming toward him, and said, "Behold! The Lamb of God who takes away the sin of the world!

30 "This is He of whom I said, 'After me comes a Man who is pre-

What Does It Mean to "Believe"?

"Faith is trying to make yourself believe something you know isn't true," the skeptic said.

What does it mean to have faith or to believe in God? Some, like the skeptic, think Christian belief is an irrational decision to believe. Others think of faith as an inherited cultural tradition. Still others see religious faith as the result of some mystical experience.

You may find it surprising to discover that, in the Gospel of John, the object of belief is as important as the nature of the belief. See what you can learn about faith by observing in the verses listed below what people believed *in*.

Example: John 1:12 says that the right to become children of God was given to those who believe *in His name*. In Hebrew culture, a name was not just an arbitrary tag but represented a person's entire character and identity. For John, to believe in Jesus' name meant to

believe in who He is: God in human form, the Savior.

Note: All these verses are in the Book of John. (For a shorter study, look up only the references with asterisks.)

```
 2:22
*3:16–21
 4:42
 8:30–37
*10:37, 38
*11:25, 26
*11:41–43
*12:35–37
*14:1
 14:11
 16:30, 31
 17:20, 21
*20:29
*20:30, 31
```

Now that you have seen how John uses the word "believe," you may want to expand your understanding of faith by looking at how Luke (Acts 4:32) and Paul (Romans 4:2–5) developed the idea of belief.

ferred before me, for He was before me.'

31 "I did not know Him; but that He should be revealed to Israel, therefore I came baptizing with water."

32 And John bore witness, saying, "I saw the Spirit descending from heaven like a dove, and He remained upon Him.

33 "I did not know Him, but He who sent me to baptize with water said to me, 'Upon whom you see the Spirit descending, and remaining on Him, this is He who baptizes with the Holy Spirit.'

34 "And I have seen and testified that this is the Son of God."

35 Again, the next day, John stood with two of his disciples.

36 And looking at Jesus as He walked, he said, "Behold the Lamb of God!"

37 The two disciples heard him speak, and they followed Jesus.

38 Then Jesus turned, and seeing them following, said to them, "What do you seek?" They said to Him, "Rabbi" (which is to say, when translated, Teacher), "where are You staying?"

39 He said to them, "Come and see." They came and saw where He was staying, and remained with Him that day (now it was about the tenth hour).

40 One of the two who heard John speak, and followed Him, was Andrew, Simon Peter's brother.

41 He first found his own brother Simon, and said to him, "We have found the Messiah" (which is translated, the Christ).

42 And he brought him to Jesus. Now when Jesus looked at him, He said, "You are Simon the son of Jonah. You shall be called Cephas" (which is translated, A Stone).

43 The following day Jesus wanted to go to Galilee, and He found Philip and said to him, "Follow Me."

44 Now Philip was from Bethsaida, the city of Andrew and Peter.

45 Philip found Nathanael and said to him, "We have found Him of whom Moses in the law, and also the prophets, wrote—Jesus of Nazareth, the son of Joseph."

46 And Nathanael said to him, "Can anything good come out of Nazareth?" Philip said to him, "Come and see."

47 Jesus saw Nathanael coming toward Him, and said of him, "Behold, an Israelite indeed, in whom is no guile!"

48 Nathanael said to Him, "How do You know me?" Jesus answered and said to him, "Before Philip called you, when you were under the fig tree, I saw you."

49 Nathanael answered and said to Him, "Rabbi, You are the Son of God! You are the King of Israel!"

50 Jesus answered and said to him, "Because I said to you, 'I saw you under the fig tree,' do you believe? You will see greater things than these."

51 And He said to him, "Most assuredly, I say to you, hereafter you shall see heaven open, and the angels of God ascending and descending upon the Son of Man."

2 On the third day there was a wedding in Cana of Galilee, and the mother of Jesus was there.

2 Now both Jesus and His disciples were invited to the wedding.

3 And when they ran out of wine, the mother of Jesus said to Him, "They have no wine."

4 Jesus said to her, "Woman, what does your concern have to do with Me? My hour has not yet come."

5 His mother said to the servants, "Whatever He says to you, do *it*."

6 Now there were set there six waterpots of stone, according to the manner of purification of the Jews, containing twenty or thirty gallons apiece.

7 Jesus said to them, "Fill the waterpots with water." And they filled them up to the brim.

8 And He said to them, "Draw

some out now, and take *it* to the master of the feast." And they took *it.*

9 When the master of the feast had tasted the water that was made wine, and did not know where it came from (but the servants who had drawn the water knew), the master of the feast called the bridegroom.

10 And he said to him, "Every man at the beginning sets out the good wine, and when the *guests* have well drunk, then that *which is* inferior; *but* you have kept the good wine until now."

11 This beginning of signs Jesus did in Cana of Galilee, and manifested His glory; and His disciples believed in Him.

12 After this He went down to Capernau.n, He, His mother, His brothers, and His disciples; and they did not stay there many days.

13 Now the Passover of the Jews was at hand, and Jesus went up to Jerusalem.

14 And He found in the temple those who sold oxen and sheep and doves, and the moneychangers doing business.

15 When He had made a whip of cords, He drove them all out of the temple, with the sheep and the oxen, and poured out the changers' money and overturned the tables.

16 And He said to those who sold doves, "Take these things away! Do not make My Father's house a house of merchandise!"

17 Then His disciples remembered that it was written, *"Zeal for Your house has eaten Me up."*

18 So the Jews answered and said to Him, "What sign do You show to us, since You do these things?"

19 Jesus answered and said to them, "Destroy this temple, and in three days I will raise it up."

20 Then the Jews said, "It has taken forty-six years to build this temple, and will You raise it up in three days?"

21 But He was speaking of the temple of His body.

22 Therefore, when He had risen from the dead, His disciples remembered that He had said this to them; and they believed the Scripture and the word which Jesus had said.

23 Now when He was in Jerusalem at the Passover, during the feast, many believed in His name when they saw the signs which He did.

24 But Jesus did not commit Himself to them, because He knew all *men,*

25 and had no need that anyone should testify of man, for He knew what was in man.

3 There was a man of the Pharisees named Nicodemus, a ruler of the Jews.

2 This man came to Jesus by night and said to Him, "Rabbi, we know that You are a teacher come from God; for no one can do these signs that You do unless God is with him."

3 Jesus answered and said to him, "Most assuredly, I say to you, unless one is born again, he cannot see the kingdom of God."

4 Nicodemus said to Him, "How can a man be born when he is old? Can he enter a second time into his mother's womb and be born?"

5 Jesus answered, "Most assuredly, I say to you, unless one is born of water and the Spirit, he cannot enter the kingdom of God.

6 "That which is born of the flesh is flesh, and that which is born of the Spirit is spirit.

7 "Do not marvel that I said to you, 'You must be born again.'

8 "The wind blows where it wishes, and you hear the sound of it, but cannot tell where it comes from and where it goes. So is everyone who is born of the Spirit."

9 Nicodemus answered and said to Him, "How can these things be?"

10 Jesus answered and said to him,

"Are you the teacher of Israel, and do not know these things?

11 "Most assuredly, I say to you, We speak what We know and testify what We have seen, and you do not receive Our witness.

12 "If I have told you earthly things and you do not believe, how will you believe if I tell you heavenly things?

13 "No one has ascended to heaven but He who came down from heaven, *that is*, the Son of Man who is in heaven.

14 "And as Moses lifted up the serpent in the wilderness, even so must the Son of Man be lifted up,

15 "that whoever believes in Him should not perish but have eternal life.

16 "For God so loved the world that He gave His only begotten Son, that whoever believes in Him should not perish but have everlasting life.

17 "For God did not send His Son into the world to condemn the world, but that the world through Him might be saved.

18 "He who believes in Him is not condemned; but he who does not believe is condemned already, because he has not believed in the name of the only begotten Son of God.

19 "And this is the condemnation, that the light has come into the world, and men loved darkness rather than light, because their deeds were evil.

20 "For everyone practicing evil hates the light and does not come to the light, lest his deeds should be exposed.

21 "But he who does the truth comes to the light, that his deeds may be clearly seen, that they have been done in God."

22 After these things Jesus and His disciples came into the land of Judea, and there He remained with them and baptized.

23 Now John also was baptizing in Aenon near Salim, because there was much water there. And they came and were baptized.

24 For John had not yet been thrown into prison.

25 Then there arose a dispute between some of John's disciples and the Jews about purification.

26 And they came to John and said to him, "Rabbi, He who was with you beyond the Jordan, to whom you have testified—behold, He is baptizing, and all are coming to Him!"

27 John answered and said, "A man can receive nothing unless it has been given to him from heaven.

28 "You yourselves bear me witness, that I said, 'I am not the Christ,' but, 'I have been sent before Him.'

29 "He who has the bride is the bridegroom; but the friend of the bridegroom, who stands and hears him, rejoices greatly because of the bridegroom's voice. Therefore this joy of mine is fulfilled.

30 "He must increase, but I *must* decrease.

31 "He who comes from above is above all; he who is of the earth is earthly and speaks of the earth. He who comes from heaven is above all.

32 "And what He has seen and heard, that He testifies; and no one receives His testimony.

33 "He who has received His testimony has certified that God is true.

34 "For He whom God has sent speaks the words of God, for God does not give the Spirit by measure.

35 "The Father loves the Son, and has given all things into His hand.

36 "He who believes in the Son has everlasting life; and he who does not believe the Son shall not see life, but the wrath of God abides on him."

126

4 Therefore, when the Lord knew that the Pharisees had heard that Jesus made and baptized more disciples than John

2 (though Jesus Himself did not baptize, but His disciples),

3 He left Judea and departed again to Galilee.

4 But He needed to go through Samaria.

5 So He came to a city of Samaria which is called Sychar, near the plot of ground that Jacob gave to his son Joseph.

6 Now Jacob's well was there. Jesus therefore, being wearied from *His* journey, sat thus by the well. It was about the sixth hour.

7 A woman of Samaria came to draw water. Jesus said to her, "Give Me a drink."

8 For His disciples had gone away into the city to buy food.

9 Then the woman of Samaria said to Him, "How is it that You, being a Jew, ask a drink from me, a Samaritan woman?" For Jews have no dealings with Samaritans.

10 Jesus answered and said to her, "If you knew the gift of God, and who it is who says to you, 'Give Me a drink,' you would have asked Him, and He would have given you living water."

11 The woman said to Him, "Sir, You have nothing to draw with, and the well is deep. Where then do You get that living water?

12 "Are You greater than our father Jacob, who gave us the well, and drank from it himself, as well as his sons and his livestock?"

13 Jesus answered and said to her, "Whoever drinks of this water will thirst again,

14 "but whoever drinks of the water that I shall give him will never thirst. But the water that I shall give him will become in him a fountain of water springing up into everlasting life."

15 The woman said to Him, "Sir, give me this water, that I may not thirst, nor come here to draw."

16 Jesus said to her, "Go, call your husband, and come here."

17 The woman answered and said, "I have no husband." Jesus said to her, "You have well said, 'I have no husband,'

18 "for you have had five husbands, and the one whom you now have is not your husband; in that you spoke truly."

19 The woman said to Him, "Sir, I perceive that You are a prophet.

20 "Our fathers worshiped on this mountain, and you *Jews* say that in Jerusalem is the place where one ought to worship."

21 Jesus said to her, "Woman, believe Me, the hour is coming when you will neither on this mountain, nor in Jerusalem, worship the Father.

22 "You worship what you do not know; we know what we worship, for salvation is of the Jews.

23 "But the hour is coming, and now is, when the true worshipers will worship the Father in spirit and truth; for the Father is seeking such to worship Him.

24 "God *is* Spirit, and those who worship Him must worship in spirit and truth."

25 The woman said to Him, "I know that Messiah is coming" (who is called Christ). "When He comes, He will tell us all things."

26 Jesus said to her, "I who speak to you am *He.*"

27 And at this *point* His disciples came, and they marveled that He talked with a woman; yet no one said, "What do You seek?" or, "Why are You talking with her?"

28 The woman then left her waterpot, went her way into the city, and said to the men,

29 "Come, see a Man who told me all things that I ever did. Could this be the Christ?"

30 Then they went out of the city and came to Him.

31 In the meantime His disciples urged Him, saying, "Rabbi, eat."

32 But He said to them, "I have

food to eat of which you do not know."

33 Therefore the disciples said to one another, "Has anyone brought Him *anything* to eat?"

34 Jesus said to them, "My food is to do the will of Him who sent Me, and to finish His work.

35 "Do you not say, 'There are still four months and *then* comes the harvest'? Behold, I say to you, lift up your eyes and look at the fields, for they are already white for harvest!

36 "And he who reaps receives wages, and gathers fruit for eternal life, that both he who sows and he who reaps may rejoice together.

37 "For in this the saying is true: 'One sows and another reaps.'

38 "I sent you to reap that for which you have not labored; others have labored, and you have entered into their labors."

39 And many of the Samaritans of that city believed in Him because of the word of the woman who testified, "He told me all that I *ever* did."

40 So when the Samaritans had come to Him, they urged Him to stay with them; and He stayed there two days.

41 And many more believed because of His own word.

42 Then they said to the woman, "Now we believe, not because of what you said, for we have heard for ourselves and know that this is indeed the Christ, the Savior of the world."

43 Now after the two days He departed from there and went to Galilee.

44 For Jesus Himself testified that a prophet has no honor in his own country.

45 So when He came to Galilee, the Galileans received Him, having seen all the things He did in Jerusalem at the feast; for they also had gone to the feast.

46 So Jesus came again to Cana of Galilee where He had made the water wine. And there was a certain nobleman whose son was sick at Capernaum.

47 When he heard that Jesus had come out of Judea into Galilee, he went to Him and implored Him to come down and heal his son, for he was at the point of death.

48 Then Jesus said to him, "Unless you *people* see signs and wonders, you will by no means believe."

49 The nobleman said to Him, "Sir, come down before my child dies!"

50 Jesus said to him, "Go your way; your son lives." So the man believed the word that Jesus spoke to him, and he went his way.

51 And as he was now going down, his servants met him and told *him*, saying, "Your son lives!"

52 Then he inquired of them the hour when he got better. And they said to him, "Yesterday at the seventh hour the fever left him."

53 So the father knew that *it was* at the same hour in which Jesus said to him, "Your son lives." And he himself believed, and his whole household.

54 This again *is* the second sign *that* Jesus did when He had come out of Judea into Galilee.

5 After this there was a feast of the Jews, and Jesus went up to Jerusalem.

2 Now there is in Jerusalem by the Sheep *Gate* a pool, which is called in Hebrew, Bethesda, having five porches.

3 In these lay a great multitude of sick people, blind, lame, paralyzed, waiting for the moving of the water.

4 For an angel went down at a certain time into the pool and stirred up the water; then whoever stepped in first, after the stirring of the water, was made well of whatever disease he had.

5 Now a certain man was there who had an infirmity thirty-eight years.

6 When Jesus saw him lying there, and knew that he already had been *in that condition* a long time, He said to him, "Do you want to be made well?"

7 The sick man answered Him, "Sir, I have no man to put me into the pool when the water is stirred up; but while I am coming, another steps down before me."

8 Jesus said to him, "Rise, take up your bed and walk."

9 And immediately the man was made well, took up his bed, and walked. And that day was the Sabbath.

10 The Jews therefore said to him who was cured, "It is the Sabbath; it is not lawful for you to carry *your* bed."

11 He answered them, "He who made me well said to me, 'Take up your bed and walk.' "

12 Then they asked him, "Who is the Man who said to you, 'Take up your bed and walk'?"

13 But the one who was healed did not know who it was, for Jesus had withdrawn, a multitude being in *that* place.

14 Afterward Jesus found him in the temple, and said to him, "See, you have been made well. Sin no more, lest a worse thing come upon you."

15 The man departed and told the Jews that it was Jesus who had made him well.

16 For this reason the Jews persecuted Jesus, and sought to kill Him, because He had done these things on the Sabbath.

17 But Jesus answered them, "My Father has been working until now, and I have been working."

18 Therefore the Jews sought all the more to kill Him, because He not only broke the Sabbath, but also said that God was His Father, making Himself equal with God.

19 Then Jesus answered and said to them, "Most assuredly, I say to you, the Son can do nothing of Himself, but what He sees the Father do; for whatever He does, the Son also does in like manner.

20 "For the Father loves the Son, and shows Him all things that He Himself does; and He will show Him greater works than these, that you may marvel.

21 "For as the Father raises the dead and gives life to *them,* even so the Son gives life to whom He will.

22 "For the Father judges no one, but has committed all judgment to the Son,

23 "that all should honor the Son just as they honor the Father. He who does not honor the Son does not honor the Father who sent Him.

24 "Most assuredly, I say to you, he who hears My word and believes in Him who sent Me has everlasting life, and shall not come into judgment, but has passed from death into life.

25 "Most assuredly, I say to you, the hour is coming, and now is, when the dead will hear the voice of the Son of God; and those who hear will live.

26 "For as the Father has life in Himself, so He has granted the Son to have life in Himself,

27 "and has given Him authority to execute judgment also, because He is the Son of Man.

28 "Do not marvel at this; for the hour is coming in which all who are in the graves will hear His voice

29 "and come forth—those who have done good, to the resurrection of life, and those who have done evil, to the resurrection of condemnation.

30 "I can of Myself do nothing. As I hear, I judge; and My judgment is righteous, because I do not seek My own will but the will of the Father who sent Me.

31 "If I bear witness of Myself, My witness is not true.

32 "There is another who bears witness of Me, and I know that the witness which He witnesses of Me is true.

33 "You have sent to John, and he has borne witness to the truth.

34 "Yet I do not receive testimony from man, but I say these things that you may be saved.

35 "He was the burning and shining lamp, and you were willing for a time to rejoice in his light.

36 "But I have a greater witness than John's; for the works which the Father has given Me to finish—the very works that I do—bear witness of Me, that the Father has sent Me.

37 "And the Father Himself, who sent Me, has testified of Me. You have neither heard His voice at any time, nor seen His form.

38 "But you do not have His word abiding in you, because whom He sent, Him you do not believe.

39 "You search the Scriptures, for in them you think you have eternal life; and these are they which testify of Me.

40 "But you are not willing to come to Me that you may have life.

41 "I do not receive honor from men.

42 "But I know you, that you do not have the love of God in you.

43 "I have come in My Father's name, and you do not receive Me; if another comes in his own name, him you will receive.

44 "How can you believe, who receive honor from one another, and do not seek the honor that *comes* from the only God?

45 "Do not think that I shall accuse you to the Father; there is one who accuses you—Moses, in whom you trust.

46 "For if you believed Moses, you would believe Me; for he wrote about Me.

47 "But if you do not believe his writings, how will you believe My words?"

6 After these things Jesus went over the Sea of Galilee, which is *the Sea* of Tiberias.

2 Then a great multitude followed Him, because they saw His signs which He performed on those who were diseased.

3 And Jesus went up on a mountain, and there He sat with His disciples.

4 Now the Passover, a feast of the Jews, was near.

5 Then Jesus lifted up *His* eyes, and seeing a great multitude coming toward Him, He said to Philip, "Where shall we buy bread, that these may eat?"

6 But this He said to test him, for He Himself knew what He would do.

7 Philip answered Him, "Two hundred denarii worth of bread is not sufficient for them, that every one of them may have a little."

8 One of His disciples, Andrew, Simon Peter's brother, said to Him,

9 "There is a lad here who has five barley loaves and two small fish, but what are they among so many?"

10 Then Jesus said, "Make the people sit down." Now there was much grass in the place. So the men sat down, in number about five thousand.

11 And Jesus took the loaves, and when He had given thanks He distributed *them* to the disciples, and the disciples to those sitting down; and likewise of the fish, as much as they wanted.

12 So when they were filled, He said to His disciples, "Gather up the fragments that remain, so that nothing is lost."

13 Therefore they gathered *them* up, and filled twelve baskets with the fragments of the five barley loaves which were left over by those who had eaten.

14 Then those men, when they had seen the sign that Jesus did, said, "This is truly the Prophet who is to come into the world."

15 Therefore when Jesus perceived that they were about to come and take Him by force to make Him king, He departed again to a mountain by Himself alone.

16 And when evening came, His disciples went down to the sea,

17 got into the boat, and went over the sea toward Capernaum. And it was now dark, and Jesus had not come to them.

18 Then the sea arose because a great wind was blowing.

19 So when they had rowed about three or four miles, they saw Jesus walking on the sea and drawing near the boat; and they were afraid.

20 But He said to them, "It is I; do not be afraid."

21 Then they willingly received Him into the boat, and immediately the boat was at the land where they were going.

22 On the following day, when the people who were standing on the other side of the sea saw that there was no other boat there, except that one which His disciples had entered, and that Jesus had not entered the boat with His disciples, but His disciples had gone away alone—

23 however, other boats came from Tiberias, near the place where they ate bread after the Lord had given thanks—

24 when the people therefore saw that Jesus was not there, nor His disciples, they also got into boats and came to Capernaum, seeking Jesus.

25 And when they found Him on the other side of the sea, they said to Him, "Rabbi, when did You come here?"

26 Jesus answered them and said, "Most assuredly, I say to you, you seek Me, not because you saw the signs, but because you ate of the loaves and were filled.

27 "Do not labor for the food which perishes, but for the food which endures to everlasting life, which the Son of Man will give you, because God the Father has set His seal on Him."

28 Then they said to Him, "What shall we do, that we may work the works of God?"

29 Jesus answered and said to them, "This is the work of God, that you believe in Him whom He sent."

30 Therefore they said to Him, "What sign will You perform then, that we may see it and believe You? What work will You do?

31 "Our fathers ate the manna in the desert; as it is written, *'He gave them bread from heaven to eat.'"*

32 Then Jesus said to them, "Most assuredly, I say to you, Moses did not give you the bread from heaven, but My Father gives you the true bread from heaven.

33 "For the bread of God is He who comes down from heaven and gives life to the world."

34 Then they said to Him, "Lord, give us this bread always."

35 And Jesus said to them, "I am the bread of life. He who comes to Me shall never hunger, and he who believes in Me shall never thirst.

36 "But I said to you that you have seen Me and yet do not believe.

37 "All that the Father gives Me will come to Me, and the one who comes to Me I will by no means cast out.

38 "For I have come down from heaven, not to do My own will, but the will of Him who sent Me.

39 "This is the will of the Father who sent Me, that of all He has given Me I should lose nothing, but should raise it up at the last day.

40 "And this is the will of Him who sent Me, that everyone who sees the Son and believes in Him may have everlasting life; and I will raise him up at the last day."

41 The Jews then murmured against Him, because He said, "I am the bread which came down from heaven."

42 And they said, "Is not this Jesus, the son of Joseph, whose father and mother we know? How is it then that He says, 'I have come down from heaven'?"

43 Jesus therefore answered and said to them, "Do not murmur among yourselves.

44 "No one can come to Me unless the Father who sent Me draws him; and I will raise him up at the last day.

45 "It is written in the prophets, *'And they shall all be taught by God.'* Therefore everyone who has heard and learned from the Father comes to Me.

46 "Not that anyone has seen the Father, except He who is from God; He has seen the Father.

47 "Most assuredly, I say to you, he who believes in Me has everlasting life.

48 "I am the bread of life.

49 "Your fathers ate the manna in the wilderness, and are dead.

50 "This is the bread which comes down from heaven, that one may eat of it and not die.

51 "I am the living bread which came down from heaven. If anyone eats of this bread, he will live forever; and the bread that I shall give is My flesh, which I shall give for the life of the world."

52 The Jews therefore quarreled among themselves, saying, "How can this *Man* give us *His* flesh to eat?"

53 Then Jesus said to them, "Most assuredly, I say to you, unless you eat the flesh of the Son of Man and drink His blood, you have no life in you.

54 "Whoever eats My flesh and drinks My blood has eternal life, and I will raise him up at the last day.

55 "For My flesh is food indeed, and My blood is drink indeed.

56 "He who eats My flesh and drinks My blood abides in Me, and I in him.

57 "As the living Father sent Me, and I live because of the Father, so he who feeds on Me will live because of Me.

58 "This is the bread which came down from heaven—not as your fathers ate the manna, and are dead. He who eats this bread will live forever."

59 These things He said in the synagogue as He taught in Capernaum.

60 Therefore many of His disciples, when they heard *this*, said, "This is a hard saying; who can understand it?"

61 When Jesus knew in Himself that His disciples murmured about this, He said to them, "Does this offend you?

62 "*What* then if you should see the Son of Man ascend where He was before?

63 "It is the Spirit who gives life; the flesh profits nothing. The words that I speak to you are spirit, and *they* are life.

64 "But there are some of you who do not believe." For Jesus knew from the beginning who they were who did not believe, and who would betray Him.

65 And He said, "Therefore I have said to you that no one can come to Me unless it has been granted to him by My Father."

66 From that *time* many of His disciples went back and walked with Him no more.

67 Then Jesus said to the twelve, "Do you also want to go away?"

68 Then Simon Peter answered Him, "Lord, to whom shall we go? You have the words of eternal life.

69 "Also we have come to believe and know that You are the Christ, the Son of the living God."

70 Jesus answered them, "Did I not choose you, the twelve, and one of you is a devil?"

71 He spoke of Judas Iscariot, *the*

132

son of Simon, for it was he who would betray Him, being one of the twelve.

7 After these things Jesus walked in Galilee; for He did not want to walk in Judea, because the Jews sought to kill Him.

2 Now the Jews' Feast of Tabernacles was at hand.

3 His brothers therefore said to Him, "Depart from here and go into Judea, that Your disciples also may see the works that You are doing.

4 "For no one does anything in secret while he himself seeks to be known openly. If You do these things, show Yourself to the world."

5 For even His brothers did not believe in Him.

6 Then Jesus said to them, "My time has not yet come, but your time is always ready.

7 "The world cannot hate you, but it hates Me because I testify of it that its works are evil.

8 "You go up to this feast. I am not yet going up to this feast, for My time has not yet fully come."

9 When He had said these things to them, He remained in Galilee.

10 But when His brothers had gone up, then He also went up to the feast, not openly, but as it were in secret.

11 Then the Jews sought Him at the feast, and said, "Where is He?"

12 And there was much murmuring among the people concerning Him. Some said, "He is good"; others said, "No, on the contrary, He deceives the people."

13 However, no one spoke openly of Him for fear of the Jews.

14 Now about the middle of the feast Jesus went up into the temple and taught.

15 And the Jews marveled, saying, "How does this Man know letters, having never studied?"

16 Jesus answered them and said, "My doctrine is not Mine, but His who sent Me.

17 "If anyone wants to do His will, he shall know concerning the doctrine, whether it is from God or *whether* I speak on My own *authority*.

18 "He who speaks from himself seeks his own glory; but He who seeks the glory of the One who sent Him is true, and no unrighteousness is in Him.

19 "Did not Moses give you the law, and *yet* none of you keeps the law? Why do you seek to kill Me?"

20 The people answered and said, "You have a demon. Who is seeking to kill You?"

21 Jesus answered and said to them, "I did one work, and you all marvel.

22 "Moses therefore gave you circumcision (not that it is from Moses, but from the fathers), and you circumcise a man on the Sabbath.

23 "If a man receives circumcision on the Sabbath, so that the law of Moses should not be broken, are you angry with Me because I made a man completely well on the Sabbath?

24 "Do not judge according to appearance, but judge with righteous judgment."

25 Then some of them from Jerusalem said, "Is this not He whom they seek to kill?

26 "But look! He speaks boldly, and they say nothing to Him. Do the rulers know indeed that this is truly the Christ?

27 "However, we know where this Man is from; but when the Christ comes, no one knows where He is from."

28 Then Jesus cried out, as He taught in the temple, saying, "You both know Me, and you know where I am from; and I have not come of Myself, but He who sent Me is true, whom you do not know.

29 "But I know Him, for I am from Him, and He sent Me."

30 Then they sought to take Him; but no one laid a hand on Him,

because His hour had not yet come.

31 And many of the people believed in Him, and said, "When the Christ comes, will He do more signs than these which this *Man* has done?"

32 The Pharisees heard the crowd murmuring these things concerning Him, and the Pharisees and the chief priests sent officers to take Him.

33 Then Jesus said to them, "I shall be with you a little while longer, and *then* I go to Him who sent Me.

34 "You will seek Me and not find *Me*, and where I am you cannot come."

35 Then the Jews said among themselves, "Where does He intend to go that we shall not find Him? Does He intend to go to the Dispersion among the Greeks and teach the Greeks?

36 "What is this thing that He said, 'You will seek Me and not find Me, and where I am you cannot come'?"

37 On the last day, that great *day* of the feast, Jesus stood and cried out, saying, "If anyone thirsts, let him come to Me and drink.

38 "He who believes in Me, as the Scripture has said, out of his heart will flow rivers of living water."

39 But this He spoke concerning the Spirit, whom those believing in Him would receive; for the Holy Spirit was not yet *given*, because Jesus was not yet glorified.

40 Therefore many from the crowd, when they heard this saying, said, "Truly this is the Prophet."

41 Others said, "This is the Christ," but some said, "Will the Christ come out of Galilee?

42 "Has not the Scripture said that the Christ comes from the seed of David and from the town of Bethlehem, where David was?"

43 So there was a division among the people because of Him.

44 Now some of them wanted to take Him, but no one laid hands on Him.

45 Then the officers came to the chief priests and Pharisees, who said to them, "Why have you not brought Him?"

46 The officers answered, "No man ever spoke like this Man!"

47 Then the Pharisees answered them, "Are you also deceived?

48 "Have any of the rulers or the Pharisees believed in Him?

49 "But this crowd that does not know the law is accursed."

50 Nicodemus (he who came to Jesus by night, being one of them) said to them,

51 "Does our law judge a man before it hears him and knows what he is doing?"

52 They answered and said to him, "Are you also from Galilee? Search and look, for no prophet has arisen out of Galilee."

53 And everyone went to his *own* house.

8 But Jesus went to the Mount of Olives.

2 But early in the morning He came again into the temple, and all the people came to Him; and He sat down and taught them.

3 Then the scribes and Pharisees brought to Him a woman caught in adultery. And when they had set her in the midst,

4 they said to Him, "Teacher, this woman was caught in adultery, in the very act.

5 "Now Moses, in the law, commanded us that such should be stoned. But what do You say?"

6 This they said, testing Him, that they might have *something* of which to accuse Him. But Jesus stooped down and wrote on the ground with *His* finger, as though He did not hear.

7 So when they continued asking Him, He raised Himself up and said to them, "He who is without sin among you, let him throw a stone at her first."

Why Can't God Just Accept Me the Way I Am?

The world is divided into two groups, us and them. We tolerate "our" behavior reasonably well, but we're fairly intolerant of "their" behavior. Little middle ground seems to exist when we're forced to interact with each another; we either condone or condemn. Take the case of the woman caught in adultery (John 8:3–11).

The religious leaders of the day are all for stoning this woman, a decision open to them based on Jewish law. They want to know where Jesus stands. Is He the condemning sort or the condoning kind? Actually, He's neither. And by the time Jesus is finished, no one is feeling very judgmental about the woman or very charitable toward themselves. What happened?

A little three-letter word got in the way of business as usual. *Sin.* Not the woman's, but the religious leaders'. They started out to test God and ended up learning an important lesson—there's a difference between the sinner and the sin. Once the religious leaders see the reality of the point, throwing stones ceases to be an option.

And what is Jesus' response after the woman's accusers retreat? Does He accept her just the way she is? (That is certainly how she has come—a woman involved in sinning.)

The answer is not a simple yes or no. Jesus does something far better. He distinguishes the woman from her sin. And then He separates her from the sin. Notice how it was done:

> "Neither do I condemn you;
> go
> and sin no more."

The religious leaders leave the scene while the woman has a chance to leave her sin.

What remains after you have eliminated condemning and condoning? A third option, open only to God. He forgives her sin so that she can become who she was always meant to be, a godly woman.

Does God accept us the way we are? Yes and no. He loves us but not the sin that damages our lives.

What does He do with our sin? He casts it "into the depths of the sea" (Micah 7:19); He separates it from us "as far as the east is from the west" (Psalm 103:12); He nails it to the cross (2 Corinthians 5:21)—all so that He can embrace everyone who comes to Him.

8 And again He stooped down and wrote on the ground.

9 Then those who heard *it*, being convicted by *their* conscience, went out one by one, beginning with the oldest *even* to the last. And Jesus was left alone, and the woman standing in the midst.

10 When Jesus had raised Himself up and saw no one but the woman, He said to her, "Woman, where are those accusers of yours? Has no one condemned you?"

11 She said, "No one, Lord." And Jesus said to her, "Neither do I condemn you; go and sin no more."

12 Then Jesus spoke to them again, saying, "I am the light of the world. He who follows Me shall not walk in darkness, but have the light of life."

13 The Pharisees therefore said to Him, "You bear witness of Yourself; Your witness is not true."

14 Jesus answered and said to them, "Even if I bear witness of Myself, My witness is true, for I know where I came from and where I am going; but you do not know where I come from and where I am going.

15 "You judge according to the flesh; I judge no one.

16 "And yet if I do judge, My judgment is true; for I am not alone, but I *am* with the Father who sent Me.

17 "It is also written in your law that the testimony of two men is true.

18 "I am One who bears witness of Myself, and the Father who sent Me bears witness of Me."

19 Then they said to Him, "Where is Your Father?" Jesus answered, "You know neither Me nor My Father. If you had known Me, you would have known My Father also."

20 These words Jesus spoke in the treasury, as He taught in the temple; and no one laid hands on Him, for His hour had not yet come.

21 Then Jesus said to them again, "I am going away, and you will seek Me, and will die in your sin. Where I go you cannot come."

22 So the Jews said, "Will He kill Himself, because He says, 'Where I go you cannot come'?"

23 And He said to them, "You are from beneath; I am from above. You are of this world; I am not of this world.

24 "Therefore I said to you that you will die in your sins; for if you do not believe that I am *He*, you will die in your sins."

25 Then they said to Him, "Who are You?" And Jesus said to them, "Just what I have been saying to you from the beginning.

26 "I have many things to say and to judge concerning you, but He who sent Me is true; and I speak to the world those things which I heard from Him."

27 They did not understand that He spoke to them of the Father.

28 Then Jesus said to them, "When you lift up the Son of Man, then you will know that I am *He*, and *that* I do nothing of Myself; but as My Father taught Me, I speak these things.

29 "And He who sent Me is with Me. The Father has not left Me alone, for I always do those things that please Him."

30 As He spoke these words, many believed in Him.

31 Then Jesus said to those Jews who believed Him, "If you abide in My word, you are My disciples indeed.

32 "And you shall know the truth, and the truth shall make you free."

33 They answered Him, "We are Abraham's descendants, and have never been in bondage to anyone. How *can* you say, 'You will be made free'?"

34 Jesus answered them, "Most assuredly, I say to you, whoever commits sin is a slave of sin.

35 "And a slave does not abide in

the house forever, *but* a son abides forever.

36 "Therefore if the Son makes you free, you shall be free indeed.

37 "I know that you are Abraham's descendants, but you seek to kill Me, because My word has no place in you.

38 "I speak what I have seen with My Father, and you do what you have seen with your father."

39 They answered and said to Him, "Abraham is our father." Jesus said to them, "If you were Abraham's children, you would do the works of Abraham.

40 "But now you seek to kill Me, a Man who has told you the truth which I heard from God. Abraham did not do this.

41 "You do the deeds of your father." Then they said to Him, "We were not born of fornication; we have one Father—God."

42 Jesus said to them, "If God were your Father, you would love Me, for I proceeded forth and came from God; nor have I come of Myself, but He sent Me.

43 "Why do you not understand My speech? Because you are not able to listen to My word.

44 "You are of *your* father the devil, and the desires of your father you want to do. He was a murderer from the beginning, and *does not* stand in the truth, because there is no truth in him. When he speaks a lie, he speaks from his own *resources,* for he is a liar and the father of it.

45 "But because I tell the truth, you do not believe Me.

46 "Which of you convicts Me of sin? And if I tell the truth, why do you not believe Me?

47 "He who is of God hears God's words; therefore you do not hear, because you are not of God."

48 Then the Jews answered and said to Him, "Do we not say rightly that You are a Samaritan and have a demon?"

49 Jesus answered, "I do not have a demon; but I honor My Father, and you dishonor Me.

50 "And I do not seek My *own* glory; there is One who seeks and judges.

51 "Most assuredly, I say to you, if anyone keeps My word he shall never see death."

52 Then the Jews said to Him, "Now we know that You have a demon! Abraham is dead, and the prophets; and You say, 'If anyone keeps My word he shall never taste death.'

53 "Are You greater than our father Abraham, who is dead? And the prophets are dead. Who do You make Yourself out to be?"

54 Jesus answered, "If I honor Myself, My honor is nothing. It is My Father who honors Me, of whom you say that He is your God.

55 "Yet you have not known Him, but I know Him. And if I say, 'I do not know Him,' I shall be a liar like you; but I do know Him and keep His word.

56 "Your father Abraham rejoiced to see My day, and he saw *it* and was glad."

57 Then the Jews said to Him, "You are not yet fifty years old, and have You seen Abraham?"

58 Jesus said to them, "Most assuredly, I say to you, before Abraham was, I AM."

59 Then they took up stones to throw at Him; but Jesus hid Himself and went out of the temple, going through the midst of them, and so passed by.

9 Now as *Jesus* passed by, He saw a man who was blind from birth.

2 And His disciples asked Him, saying, "Rabbi, who sinned, this man or his parents, that he was born blind?"

3 Jesus answered, "Neither this man nor his parents sinned, but that the works of God should be revealed in him.

4 "I must work the works of Him who sent Me while it is day; *the* night is coming when no one can work.

5 "As long as I am in the world, I am the light of the world."

6 When He had said these things, He spat on the ground and made clay with the saliva; and He anointed the eyes of the blind man with the clay.

7 And He said to him, "Go, wash in the pool of Siloam" (which is translated, Sent). So he went and washed, and came back seeing.

8 Therefore the neighbors and those who previously had seen that he was blind said, "Is not this he who sat and begged?"

9 Some said, "This is he." Others *said*, "He is like him." He said, "I am *he*."

10 Therefore they said to him, "How were your eyes opened?"

11 He answered and said, "A Man called Jesus made clay and anointed my eyes and said to me, 'Go to the pool of Siloam and wash.' So I went and washed, and I received sight."

12 Then they said to him, "Where is He?" He said, "I do not know."

13 They brought him who formerly was blind to the Pharisees.

14 Now it was a Sabbath when Jesus made the clay and opened his eyes.

15 Then the Pharisees also asked him again how he had received his sight. He said to them, "He put clay on my eyes, and I washed, and I see."

16 Therefore some of the Pharisees said, "This Man is not from God, because He does not keep the Sabbath." Others said, "How can a man who is a sinner do such signs?" And there was a division among them.

17 They said to the blind man again, "What do you say about Him because He opened your eyes?" He said, "He is a prophet."

18 But the Jews did not believe concerning him, that he had been blind and received his sight, until they called the parents of him who had received his sight.

19 And they asked them, saying, "Is this your son, who you say was born blind? How then does he now see?"

20 His parents answered them and said, "We know that this is our son, and that he was born blind;

21 "but by what means he now sees we do not know, or who opened his eyes we do not know. He is of age; ask him. He will speak for himself."

22 His parents said these *things* because they feared the Jews; for the Jews had agreed already that if anyone confessed *that* He *was* Christ, he would be put out of the synagogue.

23 Therefore his parents said, "He is of age; ask him."

24 So they again called the man who was blind, and said to him, "Give God the glory! We know that this Man is a sinner."

25 He answered and said, "Whether He is a sinner *or not* I do not know. One thing I know: that though I was blind, now I see."

26 Then they said to him again, "What did He do to you? How did He open your eyes?"

27 He answered them, "I told you already, and you did not listen. Why do you want to hear *it* again? Do you also want to become His disciples?"

28 Then they reviled him and said, "You are His disciple, but we are Moses' disciples.

29 "We know that God spoke to Moses; *as for this fellow*, we do not know where He is from."

30 The man answered and said to them, "Why, this is a marvelous thing, that you do not know where He is from, and *yet* He has opened my eyes!

31 "Now we know that God does

not hear sinners; but if anyone is a worshiper of God and does His will, He hears him.

32 "Since the world began it has been unheard of that anyone opened the eyes of one who was born blind.

33 "If this Man were not from God, He could do nothing."

34 They answered and said to him, "You were completely born in sins, and are you teaching us?" And they cast him out.

35 Jesus heard that they had cast him out; and when He had found him, He said to him, "Do you believe in the Son of God?"

36 He answered and said, "Who is He, Lord, that I may believe in Him?"

37 And Jesus said to him, "You have both seen Him and it is He who is talking with you."

38 Then he said, "Lord, I believe!" And he worshiped Him.

39 And Jesus said, "For judgment I have come into this world, that those who do not see may see, and that those who see may be made blind."

40 Then *some* of the Pharisees who were with Him heard these words, and said to Him, "Are we blind also?"

41 Jesus said to them, "If you were blind, you would have no sin; but now you say, 'We see.' Therefore your sin remains.

10 "Most assuredly, I say to you, he who does not enter the sheepfold by the door, but climbs up some other way, the same is a thief and a robber.

2 "But he who enters by the door is the shepherd of the sheep.

3 "To him the doorkeeper opens, and the sheep hear his voice; and he calls his own sheep by name and leads them out.

4 "And when he brings out his own sheep, he goes before them; and the sheep follow him, for they know his voice.

5 "Yet they will by no means follow a stranger, but will flee from him, for they do not know the voice of strangers."

6 Jesus used this illustration, but they did not understand the things which He spoke to them.

7 Then Jesus said to them again, "Most assuredly, I say to you, I am the door of the sheep.

8 "All who *ever* came before Me are thieves and robbers, but the sheep did not hear them.

9 "I am the door. If anyone enters by Me, he will be saved, and will go in and out and find pasture.

10 "The thief does not come except to steal, and to kill, and to destroy. I have come that they may have life, and that they may have *it* more abundantly.

11 "I am the good shepherd. The good shepherd gives His life for the sheep.

12 "But *he who is* a hireling and not the shepherd, one who does not own the sheep, sees the wolf coming and leaves the sheep and flees; and the wolf catches the sheep and scatters them.

13 "The hireling flees because he is a hireling and does not care about the sheep.

14 "I am the good shepherd; and I know My *sheep*, and am known by My own.

15 "As the Father knows Me, even so I know the Father; and I lay down My life for the sheep.

16 "And other sheep I have which are not of this fold; them also I must bring, and they will hear My voice; and there will be one flock *and* one shepherd.

17 "Therefore My Father loves Me, because I lay down My life that I may take it again.

18 "No one takes it from Me, but I lay it down of Myself. I have power to lay it down, and I have power to take it again. This command I have received from My Father."

19 Therefore there was a division

again among the Jews because of these sayings.

20 And many of them said, "He has a demon and is mad. Why do you listen to Him?"

21 Others said, "These are not the words of one who has a demon. Can a demon open the eyes of the blind?"

22 Now it was the Feast of Dedication in Jerusalem, and it was winter.

23 And Jesus walked in the temple, in Solomon's porch.

24 Then the Jews surrounded Him and said to Him, "How long do You keep us in doubt? If You are the Christ, tell us plainly."

25 Jesus answered them, "I told you, and you do not believe. The works that I do in My Father's name, they bear witness of Me.

26 "But you do not believe, because you are not of My sheep, as I said to you.

27 "My sheep hear My voice, and I know them, and they follow Me.

28 "And I give them eternal life, and they shall never perish; neither shall anyone snatch them out of My hand.

29 "My Father, who has given *them* to Me, is greater than all; and no one is able to snatch *them* out of My Father's hand.

30 "I and *My* Father are one."

31 Then the Jews took up stones again to stone Him.

32 Jesus answered them, "Many good works I have shown you from My Father. For which of those works do you stone Me?"

33 The Jews answered Him, saying, "For a good work we do not stone You, but for blasphemy, and because You, being a Man, make Yourself God."

34 Jesus answered them, "Is it not written in your law, *'I said, "You are gods"'* ?

35 "If He called them gods, to whom the word of God came (and the Scripture cannot be broken),

36 "do you say of Him whom the Father sanctified and sent into the world, 'You are blaspheming,' because I said, 'I am the Son of God'?

37 "If I do not do the works of My Father, do not believe Me;

38 "but if I do, though you do not believe Me, believe the works, that you may know and believe that the Father *is* in Me, and I in Him."

39 Therefore they sought again to seize Him, but He escaped out of their hand.

40 And He went away again beyond the Jordan to the place where John was baptizing at first, and there He stayed.

41 Then many came to Him and said, "John performed no sign, but all the things that John spoke about this Man were true."

42 And many believed in Him there.

11 Now a certain *man* was sick, Lazarus of Bethany, the town of Mary and her sister Martha.

2 It was *that* Mary who anointed the Lord with fragrant oil and wiped His feet with her hair, whose brother Lazarus was sick.

3 Therefore the sisters sent to Him, saying, "Lord, behold, he whom You love is sick."

4 When Jesus heard *that*, He said, "This sickness is not unto death, but for the glory of God, that the Son of God may be glorified through it."

5 Now Jesus loved Martha and her sister and Lazarus.

6 So, when He heard that he was sick, He stayed two more days in the place where He was.

7 Then after this He said to *the* disciples, "Let us go to Judea again."

8 *The* disciples said to Him, "Rabbi, lately the Jews sought to stone You, and are You going there again?"

9 Jesus answered, "Are there not twelve hours in the day? If anyone

walks in the day, he does not stumble, because he sees the light of this world.

10 "But if one walks in the night, he stumbles, because the light is not in him."

11 These things He said, and after that He said to them, "Our friend Lazarus sleeps, but I go that I may wake him up."

12 Then His disciples said, "Lord, if he sleeps he will get well."

13 However, Jesus spoke of his death, but they thought that He was speaking about taking rest in sleep.

14 Then Jesus said to them plainly, "Lazarus is dead.

15 "And I am glad for your sakes that I was not there, that you may believe. Nevertheless let us go to him."

16 Then Thomas, who is called Didymus, said to his fellow disciples, "Let us also go, that we may die with Him."

17 So when Jesus came, He found that he had already been in the tomb four days.

18 Now Bethany was near Jerusalem, about two miles away.

19 And many of the Jews had joined the women around Martha and Mary, to comfort them concerning their brother.

20 Then Martha, as soon as she heard that Jesus was coming, went and met Him, but Mary was sitting in the house.

21 Then Martha said to Jesus, "Lord, if You had been here, my brother would not have died.

22 "But even now I know that whatever You ask of God, God will give You."

23 Jesus said to her, "Your brother will rise again."

24 Martha said to Him, "I know that he will rise again in the resurrection at the last day."

25 Jesus said to her, "I am the resurrection and the life. He who believes in Me, though he may die, he shall live.

26 "And whoever lives and believes in Me shall never die. Do you believe this?"

27 She said to Him, "Yes, Lord, I believe that You are the Christ, the Son of God, who is to come into the world."

28 And when she had said these things, she went her way and secretly called Mary her sister, saying, "The Teacher has come and is calling for you."

29 As soon as she heard *that*, she arose quickly and came to Him.

30 Now Jesus had not yet come into the town, but was in the place where Martha met Him.

31 Then the Jews who were with her in the house, and comforting her, when they saw that Mary rose up quickly and went out, followed her, saying, "She is going to the tomb to weep there."

32 Then, when Mary came where Jesus was, and saw Him, she fell down at His feet, saying to Him, "Lord, if You had been here, my brother would not have died."

33 Therefore, when Jesus saw her weeping, and the Jews who came with her weeping, He groaned in the spirit and was troubled.

34 And He said, "Where have you laid him?" They said to Him, "Lord, come and see."

35 Jesus wept.

36 Then the Jews said, "See how He loved him!"

37 And some of them said, "Could not this Man, who opened the eyes of the blind, also have kept this man from dying?"

38 Then Jesus, again groaning in Himself, came to the tomb. It was a cave, and a stone lay against it.

39 Jesus said, "Take away the stone." Martha, the sister of him who was dead, said to Him, "Lord, by this time there is a stench, for he has been *dead* four days."

40 Jesus said to her, "Did I not say to you that if you would believe you would see the glory of God?"

41 Then they took away the stone

from the place where the dead man was lying. And Jesus lifted up *His* eyes and said, "Father, I thank You that You have heard Me.

42 "And I know that You always hear Me, but because of the people who are standing by I said *this*, that they may believe that You sent Me."

43 Now when He had said these things, He cried with a loud voice, "Lazarus, come forth!"

44 And he who had died came out bound hand and foot with grave-clothes, and his face was wrapped with a cloth. Jesus said to them, "Loose him, and let him go."

45 Then many of the Jews who had come to Mary, and had seen the things Jesus did, believed in Him.

46 But some of them went away to the Pharisees and told them the things Jesus did.

47 Then the chief priests and the Pharisees gathered a council and said, "What shall we do? For this Man works many signs.

48 "If we let Him alone like this, everyone will believe in Him, and the Romans will come and take away both our place and nation."

49 And one of them, Caiaphas, being high priest that year, said to them, "You know nothing at all,

50 "nor do you consider that it is expedient for us that one man should die for the people, and not that the whole nation should perish."

51 Now this he did not say on his own *authority;* but being high priest that year he prophesied that Jesus would die for the nation,

52 and not for that nation only, but also that He would gather together in one the children of God who were scattered abroad.

53 Then from that day on they plotted to put Him to death.

54 Therefore Jesus no longer walked openly among the Jews, but went from there into the country near the wilderness, to a city called Ephraim, and there remained with His disciples.

55 And the Passover of the Jews was near, and many went from the country up to Jerusalem before the Passover, to purify themselves.

56 Then they sought Jesus, and spoke among themselves as they stood in the temple, "What do you think—that He will not come to the feast?"

57 Now both the chief priests and the Pharisees had given a command, that if anyone knew where He was, he should report *it*, that they might seize Him.

12 Then, six days before the Passover, Jesus came to Bethany, where Lazarus was who had been dead, whom He had raised from the dead.

2 There they made Him a supper; and Martha served, but Lazarus was one of those who sat at the table with Him.

3 Then Mary took a pound of very costly oil of spikenard, anointed the feet of Jesus, and wiped His feet with her hair. And the house was filled with the fragrance of the oil.

4 Then one of His disciples, Judas Iscariot, Simon's *son,* who would betray Him, said,

5 "Why was this fragrant oil not sold for three hundred denarii and given to the poor?"

6 This he said, not that he cared for the poor, but because he was a thief, and had the money box; and he used to take what was put in it.

7 Then Jesus said, "Let her alone; she has kept this for the day of My burial.

8 "For the poor you have with you always, but Me you do not have always."

9 Then a great many of the Jews knew that He was there; and they came, not for Jesus' sake only, but that they might also see Lazarus, whom He had raised from the dead.

10 But the chief priests took counsel that they might also put Lazarus to death,

11 because on account of him many of the Jews went away and believed in Jesus.

12 The next day a great multitude that had come to the feast, when they heard that Jesus was coming to Jerusalem,

13 took branches of palm trees and went out to meet Him, and cried out:

"Hosanna!
   *'Blessed is He who comes
      in the name of the LORD!'*
   The King of Israel!"

14 Then Jesus, when He had found a young donkey, sat on it; as it is written:

15 *"Fear not, daughter of Zion;
   Behold, your King is coming,
   Sitting on a donkey's colt."*

16 His disciples did not understand these things at first; but when Jesus was glorified, then they remembered that these things were written about Him and *that* they had done these things to Him.

17 Therefore the people, who were with Him when He called Lazarus out of his tomb and raised him from the dead, bore witness.

18 For this reason the people also met Him, because they heard that He had done this sign.

19 The Pharisees therefore said among themselves, "You see that you are accomplishing nothing. Look, the world has gone after Him!"

20 Now there were certain Greeks among those who came up to worship at the feast.

21 Then they came to Philip, who was from Bethsaida of Galilee, and asked him, saying, "Sir, we wish to see Jesus."

22 Philip came and told Andrew, and in turn Andrew and Philip told Jesus.

23 But Jesus answered them, saying, "The hour has come that the Son of Man should be glorified.

24 "Most assuredly, I say to you, unless a grain of wheat falls into the ground and dies, it remains alone; but if it dies, it produces much grain.

25 "He who loves his life will lose it, and he who hates his life in this world will keep it for eternal life.

26 "If anyone serves Me, let him follow Me; and where I am, there My servant will be also. If anyone serves Me, him *My* Father will honor.

27 "Now My soul is troubled, and what shall I say? 'Father, save Me from this hour'? But for this purpose I came to this hour.

28 "Father, glorify Your name." Then a voice came from heaven, *saying*, "I have both glorified *it* and will glorify *it* again."

29 Therefore the people who stood by and heard *it* said that it had thundered. Others said, "An angel has spoken to Him."

30 Jesus answered and said, "This voice did not come because of Me, but for your sake.

31 "Now is the judgment of this world; now the ruler of this world will be cast out.

32 "And I, if I am lifted up from the earth, will draw all *peoples* to Myself."

33 This He said, signifying by what death He would die.

34 The people answered Him, "We have heard from the law that the Christ remains forever; and how *can* You say, 'The Son of Man must be lifted up'? Who is this Son of Man?"

35 Then Jesus said to them, "A little while longer the light is with you. Walk while you have the light, lest darkness overtake you; he who walks in darkness does not know where he is going.

36 "While you have the light, believe in the light, that you may become sons of light." These things Jesus spoke, and departed, and was hidden from them.

37 But although He had done so many signs before them, they did not believe in Him,

38 that the word of Isaiah the prophet might be fulfilled, which he spoke:

> *"Lord, who has believed our*
>   *report?*
> *And to whom has the arm*
>   *of the LORD been revealed?"*

39 Therefore they could not believe, because Isaiah said again:

40 *"He has blinded their eyes and*
>   *hardened their heart,*
> *Lest they should see with*
>   *their eyes*
> *And understand with their*
>   *heart,*
> *Lest they should turn,*
>   *so that I should heal them."*

41 These things Isaiah said when he saw His glory and spoke of Him.
42 Nevertheless even among the rulers many believed in Him, but because of the Pharisees they did not confess *Him*, lest they should be put out of the synagogue;

43 for they loved the praise of men more than the praise of God.

44 Then Jesus cried out and said, "He who believes in Me, believes not in Me but in Him who sent Me.

45 "And he who sees Me sees Him who sent Me.

46 "I have come *as* a light into the world, that whoever believes in Me should not abide in darkness.

47 "And if anyone hears My words and does not believe, I do not judge him; for I did not come to judge the world but to save the world.

48 "He who rejects Me, and does not receive My words, has that which judges him—the word that I have spoken will judge him in the last day."

49 "For I have not spoken on My own *authority*; but the Father who sent Me gave Me a command, what I should say and what I should speak.

50 "And I know that His command is everlasting life. Therefore, whatever I speak, just as the Father has told Me, so I speak."

13 Now before the feast of the Passover, when Jesus knew that His hour had come that He should depart from this world to the Father, having loved His own who were in the world, He loved them to the end.

2 And supper being ended, the devil having already put it into the heart of Judas Iscariot, Simon's *son*, to betray Him,

3 Jesus, knowing that the Father had given all things into His hands, and that He had come from God and was going to God,

4 rose from supper and laid aside His garments, took a towel and girded Himself.

5 After that, He poured water into a basin and began to wash the disciples' feet, and to wipe *them* with the towel with which He was girded.

6 Then He came to Simon Peter. And *Peter* said to Him, "Lord, are You washing my feet?"

7 Jesus answered and said to him, "What I am doing you do not understand now, but you will know after this."

8 Peter said to Him, "You shall never wash my feet!" Jesus answered him, "If I do not wash you, you have no part with Me."

9 Simon Peter said to Him, "Lord, not my feet only, but also *my* hands and *my* head!"

10 Jesus said to him, "He who is bathed needs only to wash *his* feet, but is completely clean; and you are clean, but not all of you."

11 For He knew who would betray Him; therefore He said, "You are not all clean."

12 So when He had washed their feet, taken His garments, and sat down again, He said to them, "Do you know what I have done to you?

13 "You call Me Teacher and Lord, and you say well, for *so* I am.

14 "If I then, *your* Lord and Teacher, have washed your feet, you also ought to wash one another's feet.

15 "For I have given you an example, that you should do as I have done to you.

16 "Most assuredly, I say to you, a servant is not greater than his master; nor is he who is sent greater than he who sent him.

17 "If you know these things, happy are you if you do them.

18 "I do not speak concerning all of you. I know whom I have chosen; but that the Scripture may be fulfilled, *'He who eats bread with Me has lifted up his heel against Me.'*

19 "Now I tell you before it comes, that when it does come to pass, you may believe that I am He.

20 "Most assuredly, I say to you, he who receives whomever I send receives Me; and he who receives Me receives Him who sent Me."

21 When Jesus had said these things, He was troubled in spirit, and testified and said, "Most assuredly, I say to you, one of you will betray Me."

22 Then the disciples looked at one another, perplexed about whom He spoke.

23 Now there was leaning on Jesus' bosom one of His disciples, whom Jesus loved.

24 Simon Peter therefore motioned to him to ask who it was of whom He spoke.

25 Then, leaning back on Jesus' breast, he said to Him, "Lord, who is it?"

26 Jesus answered, "It is he to whom I shall give a piece of bread when I have dipped *it.*" And having dipped the bread, He gave *it* to Judas Iscariot, *the son* of Simon.

27 Now after the piece of bread, Satan entered him. Then Jesus said to him, "What you do, do quickly."

28 But no one at the table knew for what reason He said this to him.

29 For some thought, because Judas had the money box, that Jesus had said to him, "Buy *those things* we need for the feast," or that he should give something to the poor.

30 Having received the piece of bread, he then went out immediately. And it was night.

31 So, when he had gone out, Jesus said, "Now the Son of Man is glorified, and God is glorified in Him.

32 "If God is glorified in Him, God will also glorify Him in Himself, and glorify Him immediately.

33 "Little children, I shall be with you a little while longer. You will seek Me; and as I said to the Jews, 'Where I am going, you cannot come,' so now I say to you.

34 "A new commandment I give to you, that you love one another; as I have loved you, that you also love one another.

35 "By this all will know that you are My disciples, if you have love for one another."

36 Simon Peter said to Him, "Lord, where are You going?" Jesus answered him, "Where I am going you cannot follow Me now, but you shall follow Me afterward."

37 Peter said to Him, "Lord, why can I not follow You now? I will lay down my life for Your sake."

38 Jesus answered him, "Will you lay down your life for My sake? Most assuredly, I say to you, the rooster shall not crow till you have denied Me three times.

14 "Let not your heart be troubled; you believe in God, believe also in Me.

2 "In My Father's house are many

mansions; if *it were* not *so*, I would have told you. I go to prepare a place for you.

3 "And if I go and prepare a place for you, I will come again and receive you to Myself; that where I am, *there* you may be also.

4 "And where I go you know, and the way you know."

5 Thomas said to Him, "Lord, we do not know where You are going, and how can we know the way?"

6 Jesus said to him, "I am the way, the truth, and the life. No one comes to the Father except through Me.

7 "If you had known Me, you would have known My Father also; and from now on you know Him and have seen Him."

8 Philip said to Him, "Lord, show us the Father, and it is sufficient for us."

9 Jesus said to him, "Have I been with you so long, and yet you have not known Me, Philip? He who has seen Me has seen the Father; so how can you say, 'Show us the Father?'

10 "Do you not believe that I am in the Father, and the Father in Me? The words that I speak to you I do not speak on My own *authority;* but the Father who dwells in Me does the works.

11 "Believe Me that I *am* in the Father and the Father in Me, or else believe Me for the sake of the works themselves.

12 "Most assuredly, I say to you, he who believes in Me, the works that I do he will do also; and greater *works* than these he will do, because I go to My Father.

13 "And whatever you ask in My name, that I will do, that the Father may be glorified in the Son.

14 "If you ask anything in My name, I will do *it.*

15 "If you love Me, keep My commandments.

16 "And I will pray the Father, and He will give you another Helper, that He may abide with you forever,

17 "*even* the Spirit of truth, whom the world cannot receive, because it neither sees Him nor knows Him; but you know Him, for He dwells with you and will be in you.

18 "I will not leave you orphans; I will come to you.

19 "A little while longer and the world will see Me no more, but you will see Me. Because I live, you will live also.

20 "At that day you will know that I *am* in My Father, and you in Me, and I in you.

21 "He who has My commandments and keeps them, it is he who loves Me. And he who loves Me will be loved by My Father, and I will love him and manifest Myself to him."

22 Judas (not Iscariot) said to Him, "Lord, how is it that You will manifest Yourself to us, and not to the world?"

23 Jesus answered and said to him, "If anyone loves Me, he will keep My word; and My Father will love him, and We will come to him and make Our home with him.

24 "He who does not love Me does not keep My words; and the word which you hear is not Mine but the Father's who sent Me.

25 "These things I have spoken to you while being present with you.

26 "But the Helper, the Holy Spirit, whom the Father will send in My name, He will teach you all things, and bring to your remembrance all things that I said to you.

27 "Peace I leave with you, My peace I give to you; not as the world gives do I give to you. Let not your heart be troubled, neither let it be afraid.

28 "You have heard Me say to you, 'I am going away and coming *back* to you.' If you loved Me, you would rejoice because I said, 'I am going to the Father,' for My Father is greater than I.

29 "And now I have told you before it comes, that when it does come to pass, you may believe.

30 "I will no longer talk much with you, for the ruler of this world is coming, and he has nothing in Me.

31 "But that the world may know that I love the Father, and as the Father gave Me commandment, so I do. Arise, let us go from here.

15 "I am the true vine, and My Father is the vinedresser.

2 "Every branch in Me that does not bear fruit He takes away; and every *branch* that bears fruit He prunes, that it may bear more fruit.

3 "You are already clean because of the word which I have spoken to you.

4 "Abide in Me, and I in you. As the branch cannot bear fruit of itself, unless it abides in the vine, neither can you, unless you abide in Me.

5 "I am the vine, you *are* the branches. He who abides in Me, and I in him, bears much fruit; for without Me you can do nothing.

6 "If anyone does not abide in Me, he is cast out as a branch and is withered; and they gather them and throw *them* into the fire, and they are burned.

7 "If you abide in Me, and My words abide in you, you will ask what you desire, and it shall be done for you.

8 "By this My Father is glorified, that you bear much fruit; so you will be My disciples.

9 "As the Father loved Me, I also have loved you; abide in My love.

10 "If you keep My commandments, you will abide in My love, just as I have kept My Father's commandments and abide in His love.

11 "These things I have spoken to you, that My joy may remain in you, and *that* your joy may be full.

12 "This is My commandment, that you love one another as I have loved you.

13 "Greater love has no one than this, than to lay down one's life for his friends.

14 "You are My friends if you do whatever I command you.

15 "No longer do I call you servants, for a servant does not know what his master is doing; but I have called you friends, for all things that I heard from My Father I have made known to you.

16 "You did not choose Me, but I chose you and appointed you that you should go and bear fruit, and *that* your fruit should remain, that whatever you ask the Father in My name He may give you.

17 "These things I command you, that you love one another.

18 "If the world hates you, you know that it hated Me before *it hated* you.

19 "If you were of the world, the world would love its own. Yet because you are not of the world, but I chose you out of the world, therefore the world hates you.

20 "Remember the word that I said to you, 'A servant is not greater than his master.' If they persecuted Me, they will also persecute you. If they kept My word, they will keep yours also.

21 "But all these things they will do to you for My name's sake, because they do not know Him who sent Me.

22 "If I had not come and spoken to them, they would have no sin, but now they have no excuse for their sin.

23 "He who hates Me hates My Father also.

24 "If I had not done among them the works which no one else did, they would have no sin; but now they have seen and also hated both Me and My Father.

25 "But *this happened* that the word might be fulfilled which is written in their law, 'They hated Me without a cause.'

26 "But when the Helper comes,

whom I shall send to you from the Father, the Spirit of truth who proceeds from the Father, He will testify of Me.

27 "And you also will bear witness, because you have been with Me from the beginning.

16 "These things I have spoken to you, that you should not be made to stumble.

2 "They will put you out of the synagogues; yes, the time is coming that whoever kills you will think that he offers God service.

3 "And these things they will do to you because they have not known the Father nor Me.

4 "But these things I have told you, that when the time comes, you may remember that I told you of them. And these things I did not say to you at the beginning, because I was with you.

5 "But now I go away to Him who sent Me, and none of you asks Me, 'Where are You going?'

6 "But because I have said these things to you, sorrow has filled your heart.

7 "Nevertheless I tell you the truth. It is to your advantage that I go away; for if I do not go away, the Helper will not come to you; but if I depart, I will send Him to you.

8 "And when He has come, He will convict the world of sin, and of righteousness, and of judgment:

9 "of sin, because they do not believe in Me;

10 "of righteousness, because I go to My Father and you see Me no more;

11 "of judgment, because the ruler of this world is judged.

12 "I still have many things to say to you, but you cannot bear *them* now.

13 "However, when He, the Spirit of truth, has come, He will guide you into all truth; for He will not speak on His own *authority*, but whatever He hears He will speak;

and He will tell you things to come.

14 "He will glorify Me, for He will take of what is Mine and declare *it* to you.

15 "All things that the Father has are Mine. Therefore I said that He will take of Mine and declare *it* to you.

16 "A little while, and you will not see Me; and again a little while, and you will see Me, because I go to the Father."

17 Then *some* of His disciples said among themselves, "What is this that He says to us, 'A little while, and you will not see Me; and again a little while, and you will see Me'; and, 'because I go to the Father'?"

18 They said therefore, "What is this that He says, 'A little while'? We do not know what He is saying."

19 Now Jesus knew that they desired to ask Him, and He said to them, "Are you inquiring among yourselves about what I said, 'A little while, and you will not see Me; and again a little while, and you will see Me'?

20 "Most assuredly, I say to you that you will weep and lament, but the world will rejoice; and you will be sorrowful, but your sorrow will be turned to joy.

21 "A woman, when she is in labor, has sorrow because her hour has come; but as soon as she has given birth to the child, she no longer remembers the anguish, for joy that a human being has been born into the world.

22 "Therefore you now have sorrow; but I will see you again and your heart will rejoice, and your joy no one will take from you.

23 "And in that day you will ask Me nothing. Most assuredly, I say to you, whatever you ask the Father in My name He will give you.

24 "Until now you have asked nothing in My name. Ask, and you

What Sin? What Judgment?

Jesus tells us in John 16:7–11 that we need a supernatural eye-opener, the Holy Spirit, to show us we're sinful and to warn us of eventual judgment. We even need His help to understand what these words mean.

The Bible makes a distinction between sin and sins. Sin, the less familiar concept (see "Why Are So Many Different 'Laws' Mentioned in Romans?" page 213), is challenging God's right to rule us. It is our inner compulsion to follow our own inclinations rather than God's. It is allowing life to revolve around self, or around anything other than God. Sin ultimately results in eternal separation from God. Sins are the specific thoughts, words, and actions that sin produces.

Judgment refers to a courtroom decision. God convenes His court twice.

There is a judgment (actually an awards ceremony) for all who "turn themselves in" to God, acknowledge their guilt (sin), and accept their eternal pardon from the One who suffered the death penalty for them (1 Corinthians 3:12–15). Imagine. Not one of their offenses will be counted against them or even remembered. They will be judged, that is, assigned a reward in heaven, based only on what they've done in obedience to God.

When God's court convenes again (Revelation 20:11–15), He will sentence those who insist on appearing before Him on their own merit. Because of their arrogance, their "good works" will have to be discounted. (Works are not "good," after all, if they are done to bring honor to self or anyone other than God.) They will be judged, that is, assigned to a cell in the lake of fire (hell) as their rebellion and wickedness deserve.

John 16:8 proclaims that everyone knows he or she falls short of God's perfect standard and eventually must face God in judgment. But the same Holy Spirit who has communicated to everyone about sin and judgment has also revealed to us the truth, life, and love of God available through His Son.

will receive, that your joy may be full.

25 "These things I have spoken to you in figurative language; but the time is coming when I will no longer speak to you in figurative language, but I will tell you plainly about the Father.

26 "In that day you will ask in My name, and I do not say to you that I shall pray the Father for you;

27 "for the Father Himself loves you, because you have loved Me, and have believed that I came forth from God.

28 "I came forth from the Father and have come into the world. Again, I leave the world and go to the Father."

29 His disciples said to Him, "See, now You are speaking plainly, and using no figure of speech!

30 "Now we are sure that You know all things, and have no need that anyone should question You. By this we believe that You came forth from God."

31 Jesus answered them, "Do you now believe?

32 "Indeed the hour is coming, yes, has now come, that you will be scattered, each to his own, and will leave Me alone. And yet I am not alone, because the Father is with Me.

33 "These things I have spoken to you, that in Me you may have peace. In the world you will have tribulation; but be of good cheer, I have overcome the world."

17 Jesus spoke these words, lifted up His eyes to heaven, and said: "Father, the hour has come. Glorify Your Son, that Your Son also may glorify You,

2 "as You have given Him authority over all flesh, that He should give eternal life to as many as You have given Him.

3 "And this is eternal life, that they may know You, the only true God, and Jesus Christ whom You have sent.

4 "I have glorified You on the earth. I have finished the work which You have given Me to do.

5 "And now, O Father, glorify Me together with Yourself, with the glory which I had with You before the world was.

6 "I have manifested Your name to the men whom You have given Me out of the world. They were Yours, You gave them to Me, and they have kept Your word.

7 "Now they have known that all things which You have given Me are from You.

8 "For I have given to them the words which You have given Me and they have received *them*, and have known surely that I came forth from You; and they have believed that You sent Me.

9 "I pray for them. I do not pray for the world but for those whom You have given Me, for they are Yours.

10 "And all Mine are Yours, and Yours are Mine, and I am glorified in them.

11 "Now I am no longer in the world, but these are in the world and I come to You. Holy Father, keep through Your name those whom You have given Me, that they may be one as We *are*.

12 "While I was with them in the world, I kept them in Your name. Those whom You gave Me I have kept; and none of them is lost except the son of perdition, that the Scripture might be fulfilled.

13 "But now I come to You, and these things I speak in the world that they may have My joy fulfilled in themselves.

14 "I have given them Your word and the world has hated them because they are not of the world just as I am not of the world.

15 "I do not pray that You should take them out of the world, but that You should keep them from the evil *one*.

16 "They are not of the world, just as I am not of the world.

17 "Sanctify them by Your truth. Your word is truth.

18 "As You sent Me into the world, I also have sent them into the world.

19 "And for their sakes I sanctify Myself, that they also may be sanctified by the truth.

20 "I do not pray for these alone, but also for those who will believe in Me through their word;

21 "that they all may be one, as You, Father, *are* in Me, and I in You; that they also may be one in Us, that the world may believe that You sent Me.

22 "And the glory which You gave Me I have given them, that they may be one just as We are one:

23 "I in them, and You in Me; that they may be made perfect in one, and that the world may know that You have sent Me, and have loved them as You have loved Me.

24 "Father, I desire that they also whom You gave Me may be with Me where I am, that they may behold My glory which You have given Me; for You loved Me before the foundation of the world.

25 "O righteous Father! The world has not known You, but I have known You; and these have known that You sent Me.

26 "And I have declared to them Your name, and will declare *it*, that the love with which You loved Me may be in them, and I in them."

18 When Jesus had spoken these words, He went out with His disciples over the Brook Kidron, where there was a garden, which He and His disciples entered.

2 And Judas, who betrayed Him, also knew the place; for Jesus often met there with His disciples.

3 Then Judas, having received a detachment *of troops,* and officers from the chief priests and Pharisees, came there with lanterns, torches, and weapons.

4 Jesus therefore, knowing all things that would come upon Him, went forward and said to them, "Whom are you seeking?"

5 They answered Him, "Jesus of Nazareth." Jesus said to them, "I am *He.*" And Judas, who betrayed Him, also stood with them.

6 Then—when He said to them, "I am *He,*"—they drew back and fell to the ground.

7 Then He asked them again, "Whom are you seeking?" And they said, "Jesus of Nazareth."

8 Jesus answered, "I have told you that I am *He.* Therefore, if you seek Me, let these go their way,"

9 that the saying might be fulfilled which He spoke, "Of those whom You gave Me I have lost none."

10 Then Simon Peter, having a sword, drew it and struck the high priest's servant, and cut off his right ear. The servant's name was Malchus.

11 Then Jesus said to Peter, "Put your sword into the sheath. Shall I not drink the cup which My Father has given Me?"

12 Then the detachment *of troops* and the captain and the officers of the Jews arrested Jesus and bound Him.

13 And they led Him away to Annas first, for he was the father-in-law of Caiaphas who was high priest that year.

14 Now it was Caiaphas who gave counsel to the Jews that it was expedient that one man should die for the people.

15 And Simon Peter followed Jesus, and so *did* another disciple. Now that disciple was known to the high priest, and went with Jesus into the courtyard of the high priest.

16 But Peter stood at the door outside. Then the other disciple, who was known to the high priest, went out and spoke to her who kept the door, and brought Peter in.

17 Then the servant girl who kept the door said to Peter, "You are not also *one* of this Man's disciples, are you?" He said, "I am not."

18 And the servants and officers who had made a fire of coals stood there, for it was cold, and they warmed themselves. And Peter stood with them and warmed himself.

19 The high priest then asked Jesus about His disciples and His doctrine.

20 Jesus answered him, "I spoke openly to the world. I always taught in synagogues and in the temple, where the Jews always meet, and in secret I have said nothing.

21 "Why do you ask Me? Ask those who have heard Me what I said to them. Indeed they know what I said."

22 And when He had said these things, one of the officers who stood by struck Jesus with the palm of his hand, saying, "Do You answer the high priest like that?"

23 Jesus answered him, "If I have spoken evil, bear witness of the evil; but if well, why do you strike Me?"

24 Then Annas sent Him bound to Caiaphas the high priest.

25 Now Simon Peter stood and warmed himself. Therefore they said to him, "You are not also *one* of His disciples, are you?" He denied *it* and said, "I am not!"

26 One of the servants of the high priest, a relative *of him* whose ear Peter cut off, said, "Did I not see you in the garden with Him?"

27 Peter then denied again; and immediately a rooster crowed.

28 Then they led Jesus from Caiaphas to the Praetorium, and it was early morning. But they themselves did not go into the Praetorium, lest they should be defiled, but that they might eat the Passover.

29 Pilate then went out to them and said, "What accusation do you bring against this Man?"

30 They answered and said to him, "If He were not an evildoer, we would not have delivered Him up to you."

31 Then Pilate said to them, "You take Him and judge Him according to your law." Therefore the Jews said to him, "It is not lawful for us to put anyone to death,"

32 that the saying of Jesus might be fulfilled which He spoke, signifying by what death He would die.

33 Then Pilate entered the Praetorium again, called Jesus, and said to Him, "Are You the King of the Jews?"

34 Jesus answered him, "Are you speaking for yourself on this, or did others tell you this about Me?"

35 Pilate answered, "Am I a Jew? Your own nation and the chief priests have delivered You to me. What have You done?"

36 Jesus answered, "My kingdom is not of this world. If My kingdom were of this world, My servants would fight, so that I should not be delivered to the Jews; but now My kingdom is not from here."

37 Pilate therefore said to Him, "Are You a king then?" Jesus answered, "You say *rightly* that I am a king. For this cause I was born, and for this cause I have come into the world, that I should bear witness to the truth. Everyone who is of the truth hears My voice."

38 Pilate said to Him, "What is truth?" And when he had said this, he went out again to the Jews, and said to them, "I find no fault in Him *at all.*

39 "But you have a custom that I should release someone to you at the Passover. Do you therefore want me to release to you the King of the Jews?"

40 Then they all cried again, saying, "Not this Man, but Barabbas!" Now Barabbas was a robber.

19 So then Pilate took Jesus and scourged *Him.*

2 And the soldiers twisted a crown of thorns and put *it* on His head, and they put on Him a purple robe.

3 Then they said, "Hail, King of the Jews!" And they struck Him with their hands.

4 Pilate then went out again, and said to them, "Behold, I am bringing Him out to you, that you may know that I find no fault in Him."

5 Then Jesus came out, wearing the crown of thorns and the purple robe. And *Pilate* said to them, "Behold the Man!"

6 Therefore, when the chief priests and officers saw Him, they cried out, saying, "Crucify *Him,* crucify *Him!*" Pilate said to them, "You take Him and crucify *Him,* for I find no fault in Him."

7 The Jews answered him, "We have a law, and according to our law He ought to die, because He made Himself the Son of God."

8 Therefore, when Pilate heard that saying, he was the more afraid,

9 and went again into the Praetorium, and said to Jesus, "Where are You from?" But Jesus gave him no answer.

10 Then Pilate said to Him, "Are You not speaking to me? Do You not know that I have power to crucify You, and power to release You?"

11 Jesus answered, "You could have no power *at all* against Me unless it had been given you from above. Therefore the one who delivered Me to you has the greater sin."

12 From then on Pilate sought to release Him, but the Jews cried out, saying, "If you let this Man go, you are not Caesar's friend. Whoever makes himself a king speaks against Caesar."

13 When Pilate therefore heard that saying, he brought Jesus out and sat down in the judgment seat in a place that is called *The* Pavement, but in Hebrew, Gabbatha.

14 Now it was the Preparation Day of the Passover, and about the sixth hour. And he said to the Jews, "Behold your King!"

15 But they cried out, "Away with *Him,* away with *Him!* Crucify Him!" Pilate said to them, "Shall I crucify your King?" The chief priests answered, "We have no king but Caesar!"

16 So he delivered Him to them to be crucified. So they took Jesus and led *Him* away.

17 And He, bearing His cross, went out to a place called *the Place* of a Skull, which is called in Hebrew, Golgotha,

18 where they crucified Him, and two others with Him, one on either side, and Jesus in the center.

19 Now Pilate wrote a title and put *it* on the cross. And the writing was:

JESUS OF NAZARETH,
THE KING OF THE JEWS.

20 Then many of the Jews read this title, for the place where Jesus was crucified was near the city; and it was written in Hebrew, Greek, *and* Latin.

21 Then the chief priests of the Jews said to Pilate, "Do not write, 'The King of the Jews,' but, 'He said, "I am the King of the Jews." ' "

22 Pilate answered, "What I have written, I have written."

23 Then the soldiers, when they had crucified Jesus, took His garments and made four parts, to each soldier a part, and also the tunic. Now the tunic was without seam, woven from the top in one piece.

24 They said therefore among themselves, "Let us not tear it, but cast lots for it, whose it shall be," that the Scripture might be fulfilled which says:

*"They divided My garments
among them,
And for My clothing they cast
lots."*

Therefore the soldiers did these
things.

25 Now there stood by the cross of
Jesus His mother, and His mother's
sister, Mary the *wife* of Clopas,
and Mary Magdalene.

26 When Jesus therefore saw His
mother, and the disciple whom He
loved standing by, He said to His
mother, "Woman, behold your
son!"

27 Then He said to the disciple,
"Behold your mother!" And from
that hour that disciple took her to
his own *home.*

28 After this, Jesus, knowing that
all things were now accomplished,
that the Scripture might be fulfilled, said, "I thirst!"

29 Now a vessel full of sour wine
was sitting there; and they filled a
sponge with sour wine, put *it* on
hyssop, and put *it* to His mouth.

30 So when Jesus had received the
sour wine, He said, "It is finished!"
And bowing His head, He gave up
His spirit.

31 Therefore, because it was the
Preparation *Day,* that the bodies
should not remain on the cross on
the Sabbath (for that Sabbath was
a high day), the Jews asked Pilate
that their legs might be broken,
and *that* they might be taken
away.

32 Then the soldiers came and
broke the legs of the first and of
the other who was crucified with
Him.

33 But when they came to Jesus
and saw that He was already dead,
they did not break His legs.

34 But one of the soldiers pierced
His side with a spear, and immediately blood and water came out.

35 And he who has seen has testified, and his testimony is true; and
he knows that he is telling the
truth, so that you may believe.

36 For these things were done that
the Scripture should be fulfilled,
"Not one of His bones shall be
broken."

37 And again another Scripture
says, "They shall look on Him
whom they pierced."

38 After this, Joseph of Arimathea,
being a disciple of Jesus, but secretly, for fear of the Jews, asked
Pilate that he might take away the
body of Jesus; and Pilate gave *him*
permission. So he came and took
the body of Jesus.

39 And Nicodemus, who at first
came to Jesus by night, also came,
bringing a mixture of myrrh and
aloes, about a hundred pounds.

40 Then they took the body of
Jesus, and bound it in strips of
linen with the spices, as the custom of the Jews is to bury.

41 Now in the place where He was
crucified there was a garden, and
in the garden a new tomb in which
no one had yet been laid.

42 So there they laid Jesus, because of the Jews' Preparation
Day, for the tomb was nearby.

20 On the first *day* of the week
Mary Magdalene came to the
tomb early, while it was still dark,
and saw *that* the stone had been
taken away from the tomb.

2 Then she ran and came to Simon Peter, and to the other disciple, whom Jesus loved, and said to
them, "They have taken away the
Lord out of the tomb, and we do
not know where they have laid
Him."

3 Peter therefore went out, and
the other disciple, and were going
to the tomb.

4 So they both ran together, and
the other disciple outran Peter and
came to the tomb first.

5 And he, stooping down and
looking in, saw the linen cloths
lying *there;* yet he did not go in.

6 Then Simon Peter came, following him, and went into the tomb;
and he saw the linen cloths lying
there,

7 and the handkerchief that had been around His head, not lying with the linen cloths, but folded together in a place by itself.

8 Then the other disciple, who came to the tomb first, went in also; and he saw and believed.

9 For as yet they did not know the Scripture, that He must rise again from the dead.

10 Then the disciples went away again to their own homes.

11 But Mary stood outside by the tomb weeping, and as she wept she stooped down *and looked* into the tomb.

12 And she saw two angels in white sitting, one at the head and the other at the feet, where the body of Jesus had lain.

13 Then they said to her, "Woman, why are you weeping?" She said to them, "Because they have taken away my Lord, and I do not know where they have laid Him."

14 Now when she had said this, she turned around and saw Jesus standing *there,* and did not know that it was Jesus.

15 Jesus said to her, "Woman, why are you weeping? Whom are you seeking?" She, supposing Him to be the gardener, said to Him, "Sir, if You have carried Him away, tell me where You have laid Him, and I will take Him away."

16 Jesus said to her, "Mary!" She turned and said to Him, "Rabboni!" (which is to say, Teacher).

17 Jesus said to her, "Do not cling to Me, for I have not yet ascended to My Father; but go to My brethren and say to them, 'I am ascending to My Father and your Father, and *to* My God and your God.'"

18 Mary Magdalene came and told the disciples that she had seen the Lord, and *that* He had spoken these things to her.

19 Then, the same day at evening, being the first *day* of the week, when the doors were shut where the disciples were assembled, for fear of the Jews, Jesus came and stood in the midst, and said to them, "Peace *be* with you."

20 Now when He had said this, He showed them *His* hands and His side. Then the disciples were glad when they saw the Lord.

21 Then Jesus said to them again, "Peace to you! As the Father has sent Me, I also send you."

22 And when He had said this, He breathed on *them,* and said to them, "Receive the Holy Spirit.

23 "If you forgive the sins of any, they are forgiven them; if you retain the *sins* of any, they are retained."

24 But Thomas, called Didymus, one of the twelve, was not with them when Jesus came.

25 The other disciples therefore said to him, "We have seen the Lord." But he said to them, "Unless I see in His hands the print of the nails, and put my finger into the print of the nails, and put my hand into His side, I will not believe."

26 And after eight days His disciples were again inside, and Thomas with them. Jesus came, the doors being shut, and stood in the midst, and said, "Peace to you!"

27 Then He said to Thomas, "Reach your finger here, and look at My hands; and reach your hand *here,* and put *it* into My side. Do not be unbelieving, but believing."

28 And Thomas answered and said to Him, "My Lord and my God!"

29 Jesus said to him, "Thomas, because you have seen Me, you have believed. Blessed *are* those who have not seen and *yet* have believed."

30 And truly Jesus did many other signs in the presence of His disciples, which are not written in this book;

31 but these are written that you may believe that Jesus is the Christ, the Son of God, and that

believing you may have life in His name.

21 After these things Jesus showed Himself again to the disciples at the Sea of Tiberias, and in this way He showed *Himself:*

2 Simon Peter, Thomas called Didymus, Nathanael of Cana in Galilee, the *sons* of Zebedee, and two others of His disciples were together.

3 Simon Peter said to them, "I am going fishing." They said to him, "We are going with you also." They went out and immediately got into the boat, and that night they caught nothing.

4 But when the morning had now come, Jesus stood on the shore; yet the disciples did not know that it was Jesus.

5 Then Jesus said to them, "Children, have you any food?" They answered Him, "No."

6 And He said to them, "Cast the net on the right side of the boat, and you will find *some.*" So they cast, and now they were not able to draw it in because of the multitude of fish.

7 Therefore that disciple whom Jesus loved said to Peter, "It is the Lord!" Now when Simon Peter heard that it was the Lord, he put on *his* outer garment (for he had removed it), and plunged into the sea.

8 But the other disciples came in the little boat (for they were not far from land, but about two hundred cubits), dragging the net with fish.

9 Then, as soon as they had come to land, they saw a fire of coals there, and fish laid on it, and bread.

10 Jesus said to them, "Bring some of the fish which you have just caught."

11 Simon Peter went up and dragged the net to land, full of large fish, one hundred and fifty-three; and although there were so many, the net was not broken.

12 Jesus said to them, "Come *and* eat breakfast." Yet none of the disciples dared ask Him, "Who are You?"—knowing that it was the Lord.

13 Jesus then came and took the bread and gave it to them, and likewise the fish.

14 This *is* now the third time Jesus showed Himself to His disciples after He was raised from the dead.

15 So when they had eaten breakfast, Jesus said to Simon Peter, "Simon, *son* of Jonah, do you love Me more than these?" He said to Him, "Yes, Lord; You know that I love You." He said to him, "Feed My lambs."

16 He said to him again a second time, "Simon, *son* of Jonah, do you love Me?" He said to Him, "Yes, Lord; You know that I love You." He said to him, "Tend My sheep."

17 He said to him the third time, "Simon, *son* of Jonah, do you love Me?" Peter was grieved because He said to him the third time, "Do you love Me?" And he said to Him, "Lord, You know all things; You know that I love You." Jesus said to him, "Feed My sheep.

18 "Most assuredly, I say to you, when you were younger, you girded yourself and walked where you wished; but when you are old, you will stretch out your hands, and another will gird you and carry *you* where you do not wish."

19 This He spoke, signifying by what death he would glorify God. And when He had spoken this, He said to him, "Follow Me."

20 Then Peter, turning around, saw the disciple whom Jesus loved following, who also had leaned on His breast at the supper, and said, "Lord, who is the one who betrays You?"

21 Peter, seeing him, said to Jesus, "But Lord, what *about* this man?"

22 Jesus said to him, "If I will that he remain till I come, what *is that* to you? You follow Me."

23 Then this saying went out among the brethren that this disciple would not die. Yet Jesus did not say to him that he would not die, but, "If I will that he remain till I come, what *is that* to you?"

24 This is the disciple who testifies of these things, and wrote these things; and we know that his testimony is true.

25 And there are also many other things that Jesus did, which if they were written one by one, I suppose that even the world itself could not contain the books that would be written. Amen.

THE ACTS
OF THE APOSTLES

THE former account I made, O Theophilus, of all that Jesus began both to do and teach,

2 until the day in which He was taken up, after He through the Holy Spirit had given commandments to the apostles whom He had chosen,

3 to whom He also presented Himself alive after His suffering by many infallible proofs, being seen by them during forty days and speaking of the things pertaining to the kingdom of God.

4 And being assembled together with *them*, He commanded them not to depart from Jerusalem, but to wait for the Promise of the Father, "which," *He said*, "you have heard from Me;

5 "for John truly baptized with water, but you shall be baptized with the Holy Spirit not many days from now."

6 Therefore, when they had come together, they asked Him, saying, "Lord, will You at this time restore the kingdom to Israel?"

7 And He said to them, "It is not for you to know times or seasons which the Father has put in His own authority.

8 "But you shall receive power when the Holy Spirit has come upon you; and you shall be witnesses to Me in Jerusalem, and in all Judea and Samaria, and to the end of the earth."

9 Now when He had spoken these things, while they watched, He was taken up, and a cloud received Him out of their sight.

10 And while they looked steadfastly toward heaven as He went up, behold, two men stood by them in white apparel,

11 who also said, "Men of Galilee, why do you stand gazing up into heaven? This *same* Jesus, who was taken up from you into heaven, will so come in like manner as you saw Him go into heaven."

12 Then they returned to Jerusalem from the Mount called Olivet, which is near Jerusalem, a Sabbath day's journey.

13 And when they had entered, they went up into the upper room where they were staying: Peter, James, John, and Andrew; Philip and Thomas; Bartholomew and Matthew; James *the son* of Alphaeus and Simon the Zealot; and Judas *the son* of James.

14 These all continued with one accord in prayer and supplication, with the women and Mary the mother of Jesus, and with His brothers.

15 And in those days Peter stood up in the midst of the disciples (altogether the number of names

was about a hundred and twenty), and said,

16 "Men *and* brethren, this Scripture had to be fulfilled, which the Holy Spirit spoke before by the mouth of David concerning Judas, who became a guide to those who arrested Jesus;

17 "for he was numbered with us and obtained a part in this ministry."

18 (Now this man purchased a field with the wages of iniquity; and falling headlong, he burst open in the middle and all his entrails gushed out.

19 And it became known to all those dwelling in Jerusalem; so that field is called in their own language, Akel Dama, that is, Field of Blood.)

20 "For it is written in the book of Psalms:

> 'Let his habitation be desolate,
> And let no one live in it';

and,

> 'Let another take his office.'

21 "Therefore, of these men who have accompanied us all the time that the Lord Jesus went in and out among us,

22 "beginning from the baptism of John to that day when He was taken up from us, one of these must become a witness with us of His resurrection."

23 And they proposed two: Joseph called Barsabas, who was surnamed Justus, and Matthias.

24 And they prayed and said, "You, O Lord, who know the hearts of all, show which of these two You have chosen

25 "to take part in this ministry and apostleship from which Judas by transgression fell, that he might go to his own place."

26 And they cast their lots, and the lot fell on Matthias. And he was numbered with the eleven apostles.

2 Now when the Day of Pentecost had fully come, they were all with one accord in one place.

2 And suddenly there came a sound from heaven, as of a rushing mighty wind, and it filled the whole house where they were sitting.

3 Then there appeared to them divided tongues, as of fire, and *one* sat upon each of them.

4 And they were all filled with the Holy Spirit and began to speak with other tongues, as the Spirit gave them utterance.

5 Now there were dwelling in Jerusalem Jews, devout men, from every nation under heaven.

6 And when this sound occurred, the multitude came together, and were confused, because everyone heard them speak in his own language.

7 Then they were all amazed and marveled, saying to one another, "Look, are not all these who speak Galileans?

8 "And how *is it that* we hear, each in our own language in which we were born?

9 "Parthians and Medes and Elamites, those dwelling in Mesopotamia, Judea and Cappadocia, Pontus and Asia,

10 "Phrygia and Pamphylia, Egypt and the parts of Libya adjoining Cyrene, visitors from Rome, both Jews and proselytes,

11 "Cretans and Arabs—we hear them speaking in our own tongues the wonderful works of God."

12 So they were all amazed and perplexed, saying to one another, "Whatever could this mean?"

13 Others mocking said, "They are full of new wine."

14 But Peter, standing up with the eleven, raised his voice and said to them, "Men of Judea and all who dwell in Jerusalem, let this be known to you, and heed my words.

15 "For these are not drunk, as you

suppose, since it is only the third hour of the day.

16 "But this is what was spoken by the prophet Joel:

17 'And it shall come to pass in
    the last days, says God,
    That I will pour out of My
        Spirit on all flesh;
    Your sons and your daughters
        shall prophesy,
    Your young men shall see
        visions,
    Your old men shall dream
        dreams.
18 And on My menservants and
        on My maidservants
    I will pour out My Spirit in
        those days;
    And they shall prophesy.
19 I will show wonders in heaven
        above
    And signs in the earth beneath:
    Blood and fire and vapor of
        smoke.
20 The sun shall be turned into
        darkness,
    And the moon into blood,
    Before the coming of the great
        and notable day of the LORD.
21 And it shall come to pass that
    whoever calls on the name of
    the LORD shall be saved.'

22 "Men of Israel, hear these words: Jesus of Nazareth, a Man attested by God to you by miracles, wonders, and signs which God did through Him in your midst, as you yourselves also know—
23 "Him, being delivered by the determined counsel and foreknowledge of God, you have taken by lawless hands, have crucified, and put to death;
24 "whom God raised up, having loosed the pains of death, because it was not possible that He should be held by it.
25 "For David says concerning Him:

'I foresaw the LORD always
    before my face,
For He is at my right hand,
    that I may not be shaken;
26 Therefore my heart rejoiced,
    and my tongue was glad;
    Moreover my flesh will also
        rest in hope,
27 Because You will not leave
        my soul in Hades,
    Nor will You allow Your Holy
        One to see corruption.
28 You have made known to me
        the ways of life;
    You will make me full of joy
        in Your presence.'

29 "Men and brethren, let me speak freely to you of the patriarch David, that he is both dead and buried, and his tomb is with us to this day.
30 "Therefore, being a prophet, and knowing that God had sworn with an oath to him that of the fruit of his body, according to the flesh, He would raise up the Christ to sit on his throne,
31 "he, foreseeing this, spoke concerning the resurrection of the Christ, that His soul was not left in Hades, nor did His flesh see corruption.
32 "This Jesus God has raised up, of which we are all witnesses.
33 "Therefore being exalted to the right hand of God, and having received from the Father the promise of the Holy Spirit, He poured out this which you now see and hear.
34 "For David did not ascend into the heavens, but he says himself:

'The LORD said to my Lord,
"Sit at My right hand,
35 Till I make Your enemies Your
    footstool." '

36 "Therefore let all the house of Israel know assuredly that God has made this Jesus, whom you crucified, both Lord and Christ."

37 Now when they heard *this*, they were cut to the heart, and said to Peter and the rest of the apostles, "Men *and* brethren, what shall we do?"

38 Then Peter said to them, "Repent, and let every one of you be baptized in the name of Jesus Christ for the remission of sins; and you shall receive the gift of the Holy Spirit.

39 "For the promise is to you and to your children, and to all who are afar off, as many as the Lord our God will call."

40 And with many other words he testified and exhorted them, saying, "Be saved from this perverse generation."

41 Then those who gladly received his word were baptized; and that day about three thousand souls were added *to them.*

42 And they continued steadfastly in the apostles' doctrine and fellowship, in the breaking of bread, and in prayers.

43 Then fear came upon every soul, and many wonders and signs were done through the apostles.

44 Now all who believed were together, and had all things in common,

45 and sold their possessions and goods, and divided them among all, as anyone had need.

46 So continuing daily with one accord in the temple, and breaking bread from house to house, they ate their food with gladness and simplicity of heart,

47 praising God and having favor with all the people. And the Lord added to the church daily those who were being saved.

3 Now Peter and John went up together to the temple at the hour of prayer, the ninth *hour.*

2 And a certain man lame from his mother's womb was carried, whom they laid daily at the gate of the temple which is called Beautiful, to ask alms from those who entered the temple;

3 who, seeing Peter and John about to go into the temple, asked for alms.

4 And fixing his eyes on him, with John, Peter said, "Look at us."

5 So he gave them his attention, expecting to receive something from them.

6 Then Peter said, "Silver and gold I do not have, but what I do have I give you: In the name of Jesus Christ of Nazareth, rise up and walk."

7 And he took him by the right hand and lifted *him* up, and immediately his feet and ankle bones received strength.

8 So he, leaping up, stood and walked and entered the temple with them—walking, leaping, and praising God.

9 And all the people saw him walking and praising God.

10 Then they knew that it was he who sat begging alms at the Beautiful Gate of the temple; and they were filled with wonder and amazement at what had happened to him.

11 Now as the lame man who was healed held on to Peter and John, all the people ran together to them in the porch which is called Solomon's, greatly amazed.

12 So when Peter saw *it*, he responded to the people: "Men of Israel, why do you marvel at this? Or why look so intently at us, as though by our own power or godliness we had made this man walk?

13 "The God of Abraham, Isaac, and Jacob, the God of our fathers, glorified His Servant Jesus, whom you delivered up and denied in the presence of Pilate, when he was determined to let *Him* go.

14 "But you denied the Holy One and the Just, and asked for a murderer to be granted to you,

15 "and killed the Prince of life, whom God raised from the dead, of which we are witnesses.

16 "And His name, through faith in

His name, has made this man strong, whom you see and know. Yes, the faith which *comes* through Him has given him this perfect soundness in the presence of you all.

17 "Yet now, brethren, I know that you did *it* in ignorance, as *did* also your rulers.

18 "But those things which God foretold by the mouth of all His prophets, that the Christ would suffer, He has thus fulfilled.

19 "Repent therefore and be converted, that your sins may be blotted out, so that times of refreshing may come from the presence of the Lord,

20 "and that He may send Jesus Christ, who was preached to you before,

21 "whom heaven must receive until the times of restoration of all things, which God has spoken by the mouth of all His holy prophets since the world began.

22 "For Moses truly said to the fathers, *'The Lord your God will raise up for you a Prophet like me from your brethren. Him you shall hear in all things, whatever He says to you.*

23 *'And it shall come to pass that every soul who will not hear that Prophet shall be utterly destroyed from among the people.'*

24 "Yes, and all the prophets, from Samuel and those who follow, as many as have spoken, have also foretold these days.

25 "You are sons of the prophets, and of the covenant which God made with our fathers, saying to Abraham, *'And in your seed all the families of the earth shall be blessed.'*

26 "To you first, God, having raised up His Servant Jesus, sent Him to bless you, in turning away every one *of you* from your iniquities."

4 Now as they spoke to the people, the priests, the captain of the temple, and the Sadducees came upon them,

2 being greatly disturbed that they taught the people and preached in Jesus the resurrection from the dead.

3 And they laid hands on them, and put *them* in custody until the next day, for it was already evening.

4 However, many of those who heard the word believed; and the number of the men came to be about five thousand.

5 And it came to pass, on the next day, that their rulers, elders, and scribes,

6 as well as Annas the high priest, Caiaphas, John, and Alexander, and as many as were of the family of the high priest, were gathered together at Jerusalem.

7 And when they had set them in the midst, they asked, "By what power or by what name have you done this?"

8 Then Peter, filled with the Holy Spirit, said to them, "Rulers of the people and elders of Israel:

9 "If we this day are judged for a good deed *done* to *the* helpless man, by what means he has been made well,

10 "let it be known to you all, and to all the people of Israel, that by the name of Jesus Christ of Nazareth, whom you crucified, whom God raised from the dead, by Him this man stands here before you whole.

11 "This is the *'stone which was rejected by you builders, which has become the chief cornerstone.'*

12 "Nor is there salvation in any other, for there is no other name under heaven given among men by which we must be saved."

13 Now when they saw the boldness of Peter and John, and perceived that they were uneducated and untrained men, they marveled. And they realized that they had been with Jesus.

161

14 And seeing the man who had been healed standing with them, they could say nothing against it.
15 But when they had commanded them to go aside out of the council, they conferred among themselves,
16 saying, "What shall we do to these men? For, indeed, that a notable miracle has been done through them *is* evident to all who dwell in Jerusalem, and we cannot deny *it*.
17 "But so that it spreads no further among the people, let us severely threaten them, that from now on they speak to no man in this name."
18 And they called them and commanded them not to speak at all nor teach in the name of Jesus.
19 But Peter and John answered and said to them, "Whether it is right in the sight of God to listen to you more than to God, you judge.
20 "For we cannot but speak the things which we have seen and heard."
21 So when they had further threatened them, they let them go, finding no way of punishing them, because of the people, since they all glorified God for what had been done.
22 For the man was over forty years old on whom this miracle of healing had been performed.
23 And being let go, they went to their own *companions* and reported all that the chief priests and elders had said to them.
24 So when they heard that, they raised their voice to God with one accord and said: "Lord, You *are* God, who made heaven and earth and the sea, and all that is in them,
25 "who by the mouth of Your servant David have said:

'Why did the nations rage,
And the people plot vain
things?
26 The kings of the earth took
their stand,

And the rulers were gathered
together
Against the Lord and against
His Christ.'

27 "For truly against Your holy Servant Jesus, whom You anointed, both Herod and Pontius Pilate, with the Gentiles and the people of Israel, were gathered together
28 "to do whatever Your hand and Your purpose determined before to be done.
29 "Now, Lord, look on their threats, and grant to Your servants that with all boldness they may speak Your word,
30 "by stretching out Your hand to heal, and that signs and wonders may be done through the name of Your holy Servant Jesus."
31 And when they had prayed, the place where they were assembled together was shaken; and they were all filled with the Holy Spirit, and they spoke the word of God with boldness.
32 Now the multitude of those who believed were of one heart and one soul; neither did anyone say that any of the things he possessed was his own, but they had all things in common.
33 And with great power the apostles gave witness to the resurrection of the Lord Jesus. And great grace was upon them all.
34 Nor was there anyone among them who lacked; for all who were possessors of lands or houses sold them, and brought the proceeds of the things that were sold,
35 and laid *them* at the apostles' feet; and they distributed to each as anyone had need.
36 And Joses, who was also named Barnabas by the apostles (which is translated Son of Encouragement), a Levite of the country of Cyprus,
37 having land, sold *it*, and brought the money and laid *it* at the apostles' feet.

How Does Your Life Change When You Believe?

The Book of Acts depicts the birth and growth of the early Christian church. Acts includes many stories of people who came to believe in Jesus as the Son of God and Savior. To learn more about what it means to believe in Jesus, look up the following verses and take special note of the events and actions that accompanied or soon followed people's initial coming to believe.

Example: In Acts 4:32, most of the new believers had an immediate surge of generosity and care for the other Christians. Some think this was an early form of communism, but in truth, it was very different. Communism is a political and economic system imposed on individuals from the outside. What these believers were experiencing was a spontaneous outpouring of love that came from their new life within.

Note: All of these verses are found in Acts. For a shorter study, look up only the references with asterisks.

5:14–16
*8:36–38
*11:19–21
16:26–34
*19:18, 19

Marks of a True Christian

A person who establishes a relationship with God will manifest, to some degree, at least some of the following qualities that Scriptures say will be expressed by those who believe. For the one who has just begun this relationship, some of these indicators may not yet show up. However, in time, with the nurturing and encouragement of God's Spirit within, these characteristics will be evidenced to a greater and greater degree. The growing believer will come to experience

1. a hunger to read the Bible as he or she discovers the Scriptures now make much more sense when they are read.
2. a desire to talk to God through prayer.
3. a heightened sensitivity to right and wrong and the desire to live as Christ would.
4. new strength to withstand temptation.
5. genuine love for and desire to be with other believers.
6. the desire and courage to share Christ with others.
7. a firm belief that he or she has established a relationship with Jesus Christ. (See "Can You *Know* What Your Eternal Destiny Will Be?" page 335.)

If you have enjoyed this look at belief, you may wish to try two other studies found in Romans 4:2–5 and John 1:12.

5 But a certain man named Ananias, with Sapphira his wife, sold a possession.

2 And he kept back *part* of the proceeds, his wife also being aware of *it*, and brought a certain part and laid *it* at the apostles' feet.

3 But Peter said, "Ananias, why has Satan filled your heart to lie to the Holy Spirit and keep back *part* of the price of the land for yourself?

4 "While it remained, was it not your own? And after it was sold, was it not in your own control? Why have you conceived this thing in your heart? You have not lied to men but to God."

5 Then Ananias, hearing these words, fell down and breathed his last. So great fear came upon all those who heard these things.

6 And the young men arose and wrapped him up, carried *him* out, and buried *him*.

7 Now it was about three hours later when his wife came in, not knowing what had happened.

8 And Peter answered her, "Tell me whether you sold the land for so much?" And she said, "Yes, for so much."

9 Then Peter said to her, "How is it that you have agreed together to test the Spirit of the Lord? Look, the feet of those who have buried your husband *are* at the door, and they will carry you out."

10 Then immediately she fell down at his feet and breathed her last. And the young men came in and found her dead, and carrying *her* out, buried *her* by her husband.

11 So great fear came upon all the church and upon all who heard these things.

12 And through the hands of the apostles many signs and wonders were done among the people. And they were all with one accord in Solomon's Porch.

13 Yet none of the rest dared join them, but the people esteemed them highly.

14 And believers were increasingly added to the Lord, multitudes of both men and women,

15 so that they brought the sick out into the streets and laid *them* on beds and couches, that at least the shadow of Peter passing by might fall on some of them.

16 Also a multitude gathered from the surrounding cities to Jerusalem, bringing sick people and those who were tormented by unclean spirits, and they were all healed.

17 Then the high priest rose up, and all those who *were* with him (which is the sect of the Sadducees), and they were filled with indignation,

18 and laid their hands on the apostles and put them in the common prison.

19 But at night an angel of the Lord opened the prison doors and brought them out, and said,

20 "Go, stand in the temple and speak to the people all the words of this life."

21 And when they heard *that,* they entered the temple early in the morning and taught. But the high priest and those with him came and called the council together, with all the elders of the children of Israel, and sent to the prison to have them brought.

22 But when the officers came and did not find them in the prison, they returned and reported,

23 saying, "Indeed we found the prison shut securely, and the guards standing outside before the doors; but when we opened them, we found no one inside!"

24 Now when the high priest, the captain of the temple, and the chief priests heard these things, they wondered what the outcome would be.

25 Then one came and told them, saying, "Look, the men whom you put in prison are standing in the temple and teaching the people!"

26 Then the captain went with the officers and brought them without

violence, for they feared the people, lest they should be stoned.

27 And when they had brought them, they set *them* before the council. And the high priest asked them,

28 saying, "Did we not strictly command you not to teach in this name? And look, you have filled Jerusalem with your doctrine, and intend to bring this Man's blood on us!"

29 Then Peter and the *other* apostles answered and said: "We ought to obey God rather than men.

30 "The God of our fathers raised up Jesus whom you murdered by hanging on a tree.

31 "Him God has exalted to His right hand *to be* Prince and Savior, to give repentance to Israel and forgiveness of sins.

32 "And we are His witnesses to these things, and *so also is* the Holy Spirit whom God has given to those who obey Him."

33 When they heard *this*, they were furious and took counsel to kill them.

34 Then one in the council stood up, a Pharisee named Gamaliel, a teacher of the law held in respect by all the people, and commanded them to put the apostles outside for a little while.

35 And he said to them: "Men of Israel, take heed to yourselves what you intend to do regarding these men.

36 "For some time ago Theudas rose up, claiming to be somebody. A number of men, about four hundred, joined him. He was slain, and all who obeyed him were scattered and came to nothing.

37 "After this man, Judas of Galilee rose up in the days of the census, and drew away many people after him. He also perished, and all who obeyed him were dispersed.

38 "And now I say to you, keep away from these men and let them alone; for if this plan or this work is of men, it will come to nothing;

39 "but if it is of God, you cannot overthrow it—lest you even be found to fight against God."

40 And they agreed with him, and when they had called for the apostles and beaten *them*, they commanded that they should not speak in the name of Jesus, and let them go.

41 So they departed from the presence of the council, rejoicing that they were counted worthy to suffer shame for His name.

42 And daily in the temple, and in every house, they did not cease teaching and preaching Jesus *as* the Christ.

6 Now in those days, when *the number of* the disciples was multiplying, there arose a murmuring against the Hebrews by the Hellenists, because their widows were neglected in the daily distribution.

2 Then the twelve summoned the multitude of the disciples and said, "It is not desirable that we should leave the word of God and serve tables.

3 "Therefore, brethren, seek out from among you seven men of *good* reputation, full of the Holy Spirit and wisdom, whom we may appoint over this business;

4 "but we will give ourselves continually to prayer and to the ministry of the word."

5 And the saying pleased the whole multitude. And they chose Stephen, a man full of faith and the Holy Spirit, and Philip, Prochorus, Nicanor, Timon, Parmenas, and Nicolas, a proselyte from Antioch,

6 whom they set before the apostles; and when they had prayed, they laid hands on them.

7 And the word of God spread, and the number of the disciples multiplied greatly in Jerusalem, and a great many of the priests were obedient to the faith.

8 And Stephen, full of faith and

power, did great wonders and signs among the people.

9 Then there arose some from what is called the Synagogue of the Freedmen (Cyrenians, Alexandrians, and those from Cilicia and Asia), disputing with Stephen.

10 And they were not able to resist the wisdom and the Spirit by which he spoke.

11 Then they secretly induced men to say, "We have heard him speak blasphemous words against Moses and God."

12 And they stirred up the people, the elders, and the scribes; and they came upon *him*, seized him, and brought *him* to the council.

13 They also set up false witnesses who said, "This man does not cease to speak blasphemous words against this holy place and the law;

14 "for we have heard him say that this Jesus of Nazareth will destroy this place and change the customs which Moses delivered to us."

15 And all who sat in the council, looking steadfastly at him, saw his face as the face of an angel.

7 Then the high priest said, "Are these things so?"

2 And he said, "Men and brethren and fathers, listen: The God of glory appeared to our father Abraham when he was in Mesopotamia, before he dwelt in Haran,

3 "and said to him, 'Get out of your country and from your relatives, and come to a land that I will show you.'

4 "Then he came out of the land of the Chaldeans and dwelt in Haran. And from there, when his father was dead, He moved him to this land in which you now dwell.

5 "And *God* gave him no inheritance in it, not even *enough* to set his foot on. But even when *Abraham* had no child, He promised to give it to him for a possession, and to his descendants after him.

6 "But God spoke in this way: that his descendants would sojourn in a foreign land, and that

they would bring them into bondage and oppress *them* four hundred years.

7 '*And the nation to whom they will be in bondage I will judge,*' said God, '*and after that they shall come out and serve Me in this place.*'

8 "Then He gave him the covenant of circumcision; and so *Abraham* begot Isaac and circumcised him on the eighth day; and Isaac *begot* Jacob, and Jacob *begot* the twelve patriarchs.

9 "And the patriarchs, becoming envious, sold Joseph into Egypt. But God was with him

10 "and delivered him out of all his troubles, and gave him favor and wisdom in the presence of Pharaoh, king of Egypt; and he made him governor over Egypt and all his house.

11 "Now a famine and great trouble came over all the land of Egypt and Canaan, and our fathers found no sustenance.

12 "But when Jacob heard that there was grain in Egypt, he sent out our fathers first.

13 "And the second *time* Joseph was made known to his brothers, and Joseph's family became known to the Pharaoh.

14 "Then Joseph sent and called his father Jacob and all his relatives to *him*, seventy-five people.

15 "So Jacob went down to Egypt; and he died, he and our fathers.

16 "And they were carried back to Shechem and laid in the tomb that Abraham bought for a sum of money from the sons of Hamor, the *father of* Shechem.

17 "But when the time of the promise drew near which God had sworn to Abraham, the people grew and multiplied in Egypt

18 "till another king arose who did not know Joseph.

19 "This man dealt treacherously with our people, and oppressed our forefathers, making them expose

their babies, so that they might not live.

20 "At this time Moses was born, and was well pleasing to God; and he was brought up in his father's house for three months.

21 "But when he was set out, Pharaoh's daughter took him away and brought him up as her own son.

22 "And Moses was learned in all the wisdom of the Egyptians, and was mighty in words and deeds.

23 "But when he was forty years old, it came into his heart to visit his brethren, the children of Israel.

24 "And seeing one of *them* suffer wrong, he defended and avenged him who was oppressed, and struck down the Egyptian.

25 "For he supposed that his brethren would have understood that God would deliver them by his hand, but they did not understand.

26 "And the next day he appeared to two of them as they were fighting, and *tried* to reconcile them, saying, 'Men, you are brethren; why do you wrong one another?'

27 "But he who did his neighbor wrong pushed him away, saying, *'Who made you a ruler and a judge over us?*

28 *'Do you want to kill me as you did the Egyptian yesterday?'*

29 "Then, at this saying, Moses fled and became a sojourner in the land of Midian, where he had two sons.

30 "And when forty years had passed, an Angel of the Lord appeared to him in a flame of fire in a bush, in the wilderness of Mount Sinai.

31 "When Moses saw *it*, he marveled at the sight; and as he drew near to observe, the voice of the Lord came to him,

32 *"saying, 'I am the God of your fathers—the God of Abraham, the God of Isaac, and the God of Jacob.'* And Moses trembled and dared not look.

33 *'Then the LORD said to him, "Take your sandals off your feet,*

for the place where you stand is holy ground.

34 *"I have certainly seen the oppression of My people who are in Egypt; I have heard their groaning and have come down to deliver them. And now come, I will send you to Egypt." '*

35 "This Moses whom they rejected, saying, *'Who made you a ruler and a judge?'* is the one God sent *to be* a ruler and a deliverer by the hand of the Angel who appeared to him in the bush.

36 "He brought them out, after he had shown wonders and signs in the land of Egypt, and in the Red Sea, and in the wilderness forty years.

37 "This is that Moses who said to the children of Israel, *'The LORD your God will raise up for you a Prophet like me from your brethren. Him you shall hear.'*

38 "This is he who was in the congregation in the wilderness with the Angel who spoke to him on Mount Sinai, and *with* our fathers, the one who received the living oracles to give to us,

39 "whom our fathers would not obey, but rejected. And in their hearts they turned back to Egypt,

40 "saying to Aaron, *'Make us gods to go before us; as for this Moses who brought us out of the land of Egypt, we do not know what has become of him.'*

41 "And they made a calf in those days, offered sacrifices to the idol, and rejoiced in the works of their own hands.

42 "Then God turned and gave them up to worship the host of heaven, as it is written in the book of the Prophets:

'Did you offer Me slaughtered animals and sacrifices during forty years in the wilderness, O house of Israel?

43 *Yes, you took up the tabernacle of Moloch,*

*And the star of your god
    Remphan,
Images which you made to
    worship;
And I will carry you away
    beyond Babylon.'*

44 "Our fathers had the tabernacle of witness in the wilderness, as He appointed, instructing Moses to make it according to the pattern that he had seen,

45 "which our fathers, having received it in turn, also brought with Joshua into the land possessed by the Gentiles, whom God drove out before the face of our fathers until the days of David,

46 "who found favor before God and asked to find a dwelling for the God of Jacob.

47 "But Solomon built Him a house.

48 "However, the Most High does not dwell in temples made with hands, as the prophet says:

49 *'Heaven is My throne,
    And earth is My footstool.
What house will you build for
    Me? says the LORD,
Or what is the place of My
    rest?*

50 *Has My hand not made all
    these things?'*

51 "You stiff-necked and uncircumcised in heart and ears! You always resist the Holy Spirit; as your fathers did, so do you.

52 "Which of the prophets did your fathers not persecute? And they killed those who foretold the coming of the Just One, of whom you now have become the betrayers and murderers,

53 "who have received the law by the direction of angels and have not kept it."

54 When they heard these things they were cut to the heart, and they gnashed at him with *their* teeth.

55 But he, being full of the Holy Spirit, gazed into heaven and saw the glory of God, and Jesus standing at the right hand of God,

56 and said, "Look! I see the heavens opened and the Son of Man standing at the right hand of God!"

57 Then they cried out with a loud voice, stopped their ears, and ran at him with one accord;

58 and they cast *him* out of the city and stoned *him*. And the witnesses laid down their clothes at the feet of a young man named Saul.

59 And they stoned Stephen as he was calling on God and saying, "Lord Jesus, receive my spirit."

60 Then he knelt down and cried out with a loud voice, "Lord, do not charge them with this sin." And when he had said this, he fell asleep.

8 Now Saul was consenting to his death. At that time a great persecution arose against the church which was at Jerusalem; and they were all scattered throughout the regions of Judea and Samaria, except the apostles.

2 And devout men carried Stephen to *his* burial, and made great lamentation over him.

3 As for Saul, he made havoc of the church, entering every house, and dragging off men and women, committing *them* to prison.

4 Therefore those who were scattered went everywhere preaching the word.

5 Then Philip went down to the city of Samaria and preached Christ to them.

6 And the multitudes with one accord heeded the things spoken by Philip, hearing and seeing the miracles which he did.

7 For unclean spirits, crying with a loud voice, came out of many who were possessed; and many who were paralyzed and lame were healed.

8 And there was great joy in that city.

9 But there was a certain man called Simon, who previously practiced sorcery in the city and astonished the people of Samaria, claiming that he was someone great,

10 to whom they all gave heed, from the least to the greatest, saying, "This man is the great power of God."

11 And they heeded him because he had astonished them with his sorceries for a long time.

12 But when they believed Philip as he preached the things concerning the kingdom of God and the name of Jesus Christ, both men and women were baptized.

13 Then Simon himself also believed; and when he was baptized he continued with Philip, and was amazed, seeing the miracles and signs which were done.

14 Now when the apostles who were at Jerusalem heard that Samaria had received the word of God, they sent Peter and John to them,

15 who, when they had come down, prayed for them that they might receive the Holy Spirit.

16 For as yet He had fallen upon none of them. They had only been baptized in the name of the Lord Jesus.

17 Then they laid hands on them, and they received the Holy Spirit.

18 Now when Simon saw that through the laying on of the apostles' hands the Holy Spirit was given, he offered them money,

19 saying, "Give me this power also, that anyone on whom I lay hands may receive the Holy Spirit."

20 But Peter said to him, "Your money perish with you, because you thought that the gift of God could be purchased with money!

21 "You have neither part nor portion in this matter, for your heart is not right in the sight of God.

22 "Repent therefore of this your wickedness, and pray God if per-

haps the thought of your heart may be forgiven you.

23 "For I see that you are poisoned by bitterness and bound by iniquity."

24 Then Simon answered and said, "Pray to the Lord for me, that none of the things which you have spoken may come upon me."

25 So when they had testified and preached the word of the Lord, they returned to Jerusalem, preaching the gospel in many villages of the Samaritans.

26 Now an angel of the Lord spoke to Philip, saying, "Arise and go toward the south along the road which goes down from Jerusalem to Gaza." This is desert.

27 So he arose and went. And behold, a man of Ethiopia, a eunuch of great authority under Candace the queen of the Ethiopians, who had charge of all her treasury, and had come to Jerusalem to worship,

28 was returning. And sitting in his chariot, he was reading Isaiah the prophet.

29 Then the Spirit said to Philip, "Go near and overtake this chariot."

30 So Philip ran to him, and heard him reading the prophet Isaiah, and said, "Do you understand what you are reading?"

31 And he said, "How can I, unless someone guides me?" And he asked Philip to come up and sit with him.

32 The place in the Scripture which he read was this:

"He was led as a sheep to the
    slaughter;
And like a lamb silent before
    its shearer,
So He opened not His mouth.
33 In His humiliation His justice
    was taken away.
And who will declare His
    generation?
For His life is taken from the
    earth."

34 So the eunuch answered Philip and said, "I ask you, of whom does the prophet say this, of himself or of some other man?"

35 Then Philip opened his mouth, and beginning at this Scripture, preached Jesus to him.

36 Now as they went down the road, they came to some water. And the eunuch said, "See, *here is* water. What hinders me from being baptized?"

37 Then Philip said, "If you believe with all your heart, you may." And he answered and said, "I believe that Jesus Christ is the Son of God."

38 So he commanded the chariot to stand still. And both Philip and the eunuch went down into the water, and he baptized him.

39 Now when they came up out of the water, the Spirit of the Lord caught Philip away, so that the eunuch saw him no more; and he went on his way rejoicing.

40 But Philip was found at Azotus. And passing through, he preached in all the cities till he came to Caesarea.

9 Then Saul, still breathing threats and murder against the disciples of the Lord, went to the high priest

2 and asked letters from him to the synagogues of Damascus, so that if he found any who were of the Way, whether men or women, he might bring them bound to Jerusalem.

3 And as he journeyed he came near Damascus, and suddenly a light shone around him from heaven.

4 Then he fell to the ground, and heard a voice saying to him, "Saul, Saul, why are you persecuting Me?"

5 And he said, "Who are You, Lord?" And the Lord said, "I am Jesus, whom you are persecuting. *It is* hard for you to kick against the goads."

6 So he, trembling and astonished, said, "Lord, what do You want me to do?" And the Lord *said* to him, "Arise and go into the city, and you will be told what you must do."

7 And the men who journeyed with him stood speechless, hearing a voice but seeing no one.

8 Then Saul arose from the ground, and when his eyes were opened he saw no one. But they led him by the hand and brought *him* into Damascus.

9 And he was three days without sight, and neither ate nor drank.

10 Now there was a certain disciple at Damascus named Ananias; and to him the Lord said in a vision, "Ananias." And he said, "Here I am, Lord."

11 So the Lord *said* to him, "Arise and go to the street called Straight, and inquire at the house of Judas for *one* called Saul of Tarsus, for behold, he is praying.

12 "And in a vision he has seen a man named Ananias coming in and putting *his* hand on him, so that he might receive his sight."

13 Then Ananias answered, "Lord, I have heard from many about this man, how much harm he has done to Your saints in Jerusalem.

14 "And here he has authority from the chief priests to bind all who call on Your name."

15 But the Lord said to him, "Go, for he is a chosen vessel of Mine to bear My name before Gentiles, kings, and the children of Israel.

16 "For I will show him how many things he must suffer for My name's sake."

17 And Ananias went his way and entered the house; and laying his hands on him he said, "Brother Saul, the Lord Jesus, who appeared to you on the road as you came, has sent me that you may receive your sight and be filled with the Holy Spirit."

18 Immediately there fell from his eyes *something* like scales, and he

received his sight at once; and he arose and was baptized.

19 And when he had received food, he was strengthened. Then Saul spent some days with the disciples at Damascus.

20 Immediately he preached the Christ in the synagogues, that He is the Son of God.

21 Then all who heard were amazed, and said, "Is this not he who destroyed those who called on this name in Jerusalem, and has come here for that purpose, so that he might bring them bound to the chief priests?"

22 But Saul increased all the more in strength, and confounded the Jews who dwelt in Damascus, proving that this *Jesus* is the Christ.

23 Now after many days were past, the Jews plotted to kill him.

24 But their plot became known to Saul. And they watched the gates day and night, to kill him.

25 Then the disciples took him by night and let *him* down through the wall in a large basket.

26 And when Saul had come to Jerusalem, he tried to join the disciples; but they were all afraid of him, and did not believe that he was a disciple.

27 But Barnabas took him and brought *him* to the apostles. And he declared to them how he had seen the Lord on the road, and that He had spoken to him, and how he had preached boldly at Damascus in the name of Jesus.

28 So he was with them at Jerusalem, coming in and going out.

29 And he spoke boldly in the name of the Lord Jesus and disputed against the Hellenists, but they attempted to kill him.

30 When the brethren found out, they brought him down to Caesarea and sent him out to Tarsus.

31 Then the churches throughout all Judea, Galilee, and Samaria had peace and were edified. And walk-ing in the fear of the Lord and in the comfort of the Holy Spirit, they were multiplied.

32 Now it came to pass, as Peter went through all *parts of the country,* that he also came down to the saints who dwelt in Lydda.

33 There he found a certain man named Aeneas, who had been bed-ridden eight years and was para-lyzed.

34 And Peter said to him, "Aeneas, Jesus the Christ heals you. Arise and make your bed." Then he arose immediately.

35 So all who dwelt at Lydda and Sharon saw him and turned to the Lord.

36 At Joppa there was a certain disciple named Tabitha, which is translated Dorcas. This woman was full of good works and chari-table deeds which she did.

37 But it happened in those days that she became sick and died. When they had washed her, they laid *her* in an upper room.

38 And since Lydda was near Joppa, and the disciples had heard that Peter was there, they sent two men to him, imploring *him* not to delay in coming to them.

39 Then Peter arose and went with them. When he had come, they brought *him* to the upper room. And all the widows stood by him weeping, showing the tunics and garments which Dorcas had made while she was with them.

40 But Peter put them all out, and knelt down and prayed. And turn-ing to the body he said, "Tabitha, arise." And she opened her eyes, and when she saw Peter she sat up.

41 Then he gave her *his* hand and lifted her up; and when he had called the saints and widows, he presented her alive.

42 And it became known through-out all Joppa, and many believed on the Lord.

43 So it was that he stayed many days in Joppa with Simon, a tan-ner.

10 There was a certain man in Caesarea called Cornelius, a centurion of what was called the Italian Regiment,

2 a devout *man* and one who feared God with all his household, who gave alms generously to the people, and prayed to God always.

3 About the ninth hour of the day he saw clearly in a vision an angel of God coming in and saying to him, "Cornelius!"

4 And when he observed him, he was afraid, and said, "What is it, lord?" So he said to him, "Your prayers and your alms have come up for a memorial before God.

5 "Now send men to Joppa, and send for Simon whose surname is Peter.

6 "He is lodging with Simon, a tanner, whose house is by the sea. He will tell you what you must do."

7 And when the angel who spoke to him had departed, Cornelius called two of his household servants and a devout soldier from among those who waited on him continually.

8 So when he had explained all *these* things to them, he sent them to Joppa.

9 The next day, as they went on their journey and drew near the city, Peter went up on the housetop to pray, about the sixth hour.

10 Then he became very hungry and wanted to eat; but while they made ready, he fell into a trance

11 and saw heaven opened and an object like a great sheet bound at the four corners, descending to him and let down to the earth.

12 In it were all kinds of four-footed animals of the earth, wild beasts, creeping things, and birds of the air.

13 And a voice came to him, "Rise, Peter; kill and eat."

14 But Peter said, "Not so, Lord! For I have never eaten anything common or unclean."

15 And a voice *spoke* to him again the second time, "What God has cleansed you must not call common."

16 This was done three times. And the object was taken up into heaven again.

17 Now while Peter wondered within himself what this vision which he had seen meant, behold, the men who had been sent from Cornelius had made inquiry for Simon's house, and stood before the gate.

18 And they called and asked whether Simon, whose surname was Peter, was lodging there.

19 While Peter thought about the vision, the Spirit said to him, "Behold, three men are seeking you.

20 "Arise therefore, go down and go with them, doubting nothing; for I have sent them."

21 Then Peter went down to the men who had been sent to him from Cornelius, and said, "Yes, I am he whom you seek. For what reason have you come?"

22 And they said, "Cornelius *the* centurion, a just man, one who fears God and has a good reputation among all the nation of the Jews, was divinely instructed by a holy angel to summon you to his house, and to hear words from you."

23 Then he invited them in and lodged *them*. On the next day Peter went away with them, and some brethren from Joppa accompanied him.

24 And the following day they entered Caesarea. Now Cornelius was waiting for them, and had called together his relatives and close friends.

25 As Peter was coming in, Cornelius met him and fell down at his feet and worshiped *him*.

26 But Peter lifted him up, saying, "Stand up; I myself am also a man."

27 And as he talked with him, he

What Can a Person Who Has Never Read the Bible Know About God?

Cornelius was raised in a pagan culture. Yet in Acts 10, we find him praying, fasting, and giving alms to God. How does a person learn about God if he or she has never read the Bible?

Nature

Nature tells us many things about God. First, the natural world exists as testimony to a Creator—if there were no Creator, there would be no creation. Second, creation's complexity, majesty, and exquisite design tell us that the Creator is powerful, intelligent, and loving beyond our comprehension.

Creation, then, is a kind of billboard, proclaiming to one and all the nature of the Creator. This understanding of God is available to everyone.

Conscience

We are all familiar with the promptings of conscience, but the effect of conscience varies greatly in individuals. One person may feel his conscience burning when he keeps extra change found in a vending machine. Another may feel nothing when committing armed robbery. The conscience, then, depending on the person's previous record in responding to it, serves as an echo of the moral nature God built into us.

Revelation

The most complete source of truth about God is the Bible. Properly understood, this Book gives us enormous insights into the nature of creation, including humans, and of God Himself.

What it all adds up to

Even though truth about God is available, a person can refuse to embrace it. If someone refuses to acknowledge the most fundamental truth about God—that He exists and that He rewards those who seek Him—that person eventually will lose the ability to understand spiritual truth. The Bible calls this "the darkening of the mind." For example, scientists who do not acknowledge God can gain insight to the workings of His creation but never to its purpose.

Since Cornelius responded to what he knew about God, God sent him a much fuller explanation (in this case through a person, Peter). Cornelius shows us that anyone willing to act on the knowledge of God that he or she has been given, will be given more.

went in and found many who had come together.

28 Then he said to them, "You know how unlawful it is for a Jewish man to keep company with or go to one of another nation. But God has shown me that I should not call any man common or unclean.

29 "Therefore I came without objection as soon as I was sent for. I ask, then, for what reason have you sent for me?"

30 And Cornelius said, "Four days ago I was fasting until this hour; and at the ninth hour I prayed in my house, and behold, a man stood before me in bright clothing,

31 "and said, 'Cornelius, your prayer has been heard, and your alms are remembered in the sight of God.

32 'Send therefore to Joppa and call Simon here, whose surname is Peter. He is lodging in the house of Simon, a tanner, by the sea. When he comes, he will speak to you.'

33 "So I sent to you immediately, and you have done well to come. Now therefore, we are all present before God, to hear all the things commanded you by God."

34 Then Peter opened *his* mouth and said: "In truth I perceive that God shows no partiality.

35 "But in every nation whoever fears Him and works righteousness is accepted by Him.

36 "The word which *God* sent to the children of Israel, preaching peace through Jesus Christ—He is Lord of all—

37 "that word you know, which was proclaimed throughout all Judea, and began from Galilee after the baptism which John preached;

38 "how God anointed Jesus of Nazareth with the Holy Spirit and with power, who went about doing good and healing all who were oppressed by the devil, for God was with Him.

39 "And we are witnesses of all things which He did both in the land of the Jews and in Jerusalem, whom they killed by hanging on a tree.

40 "Him God raised up on the third day, and showed Him openly,

41 "not to all the people, but to witnesses chosen before by God, *even* to us who ate and drank with Him after He arose from the dead.

42 "And He commanded us to preach to the people, and to testify that it is He who was ordained by God *to be* Judge of the living and the dead.

43 "To Him all the prophets witness that, through His name, whoever believes in Him will receive remission of sins."

44 While Peter was still speaking these words, the Holy Spirit fell upon all those who heard the word.

45 And those of the circumcision who believed were astonished, as many as came with Peter, because the gift of the Holy Spirit had been poured out on the Gentiles also.

46 For they heard them speak with tongues and magnify God. Then Peter answered,

47 "Can anyone forbid water, that these should not be baptized who have received the Holy Spirit just as we *have*?"

48 And he commanded them to be baptized in the name of the Lord. Then they asked him to stay a few days.

11 Now the apostles and brethren who were in Judea heard that the Gentiles had also received the word of God.

2 And when Peter came up to Jerusalem, those of the circumcision contended with him,

3 saying, "You went in to uncircumcised men and ate with them!"

4 But Peter explained *it* to them in order from the beginning, saying:

5 "I was in the city of Joppa praying; and in a trance I saw a vision, an object descending like a great

sheet, let down from heaven by four corners; and it came to me.

6 "When I observed it intently and considered, I saw four-footed animals of the earth, wild beasts, creeping things, and birds of the air.

7 "And I heard a voice saying to me, 'Rise, Peter; kill and eat.'

8 "But I said, 'Not so, Lord! For nothing common or unclean has at any time entered my mouth.'

9 "But the voice answered me again from heaven, 'What God has cleansed you must not call common.'

10 "Now this was done three times, and all were drawn up again into heaven.

11 "At that very moment, three men stood before the house where I was, having been sent to me from Caesarea.

12 "Then the Spirit told me to go with them, doubting nothing. Moreover these six brethren accompanied me, and we entered the man's house.

13 "And he told us how he had seen an angel standing in his house, who said to him, 'Send men to Joppa, and call for Simon whose surname is Peter,

14 'who will tell you words by which you and all your household will be saved.'

15 "And as I began to speak, the Holy Spirit fell upon them, as upon us at the beginning.

16 "Then I remembered the word of the Lord, how He said, 'John indeed baptized with water, but you shall be baptized with the Holy Spirit.'

17 "If therefore God gave them the same gift as *He gave* us when we believed on the Lord Jesus Christ, who was I that I could withstand God?"

18 When they heard these things they became silent; and they glorified God, saying, "Then God has also granted to the Gentiles repentance to life."

19 Now those who were scattered after the persecution that arose over Stephen traveled as far as Phoenicia, Cyprus, and Antioch, preaching the word to no one but the Jews only.

20 But some of them were men from Cyprus and Cyrene, who, when they had come to Antioch, spoke to the Hellenists, preaching the Lord Jesus.

21 And the hand of the Lord was with them, and a great number believed and turned to the Lord.

22 Then news of these things came to the ears of the church in Jerusalem, and they sent out Barnabas to go as far as Antioch.

23 When he came and had seen the grace of God, he was glad, and encouraged them all that with purpose of heart they should continue with the Lord.

24 For he was a good man, full of the Holy Spirit and of faith. And a great many people were added to the Lord.

25 Then Barnabas departed for Tarsus to seek Saul.

26 And when he had found him, he brought him to Antioch. So it was that for a whole year they assembled with the church and taught a great many people. And the disciples were first called Christians in Antioch.

27 And in these days prophets came from Jerusalem to Antioch.

28 Then one of them, named Agabus, stood up and showed by the Spirit that there was going to be a great famine throughout all the world, which also happened in the days of Claudius Caesar.

29 Then the disciples, each according to his ability, determined to send relief to the brethren dwelling in Judea.

30 This they also did, and sent it to the elders by the hands of Barnabas and Saul.

12 Now about that time Herod the king stretched out *his*

hand to harass some from the church.

2 Then he killed James the brother of John with the sword.

3 And because he saw that it pleased the Jews, he proceeded further to seize Peter also. Now it was *during* the Days of Unleavened Bread.

4 So when he had apprehended him, he put *him* in prison, and delivered *him* to four squads of soldiers to keep him, intending to bring him before the people after Passover.

5 Peter was therefore kept in prison, but constant prayer was offered to God for him by the church.

6 And when Herod was about to bring him out, that night Peter was sleeping, bound with two chains between two soldiers; and the guards before the door were keeping the prison.

7 Now behold, an angel of the Lord stood by *him*, and a light shone in the prison; and he struck Peter on the side and raised him up, saying, "Arise quickly!" And his chains fell off *his* hands.

8 Then the angel said to him, "Gird yourself and tie on your sandals"; and so he did. And he said to him, "Put on your garment and follow me."

9 So he went out and followed him, and did not know that what was done by the angel was real, but thought he was seeing a vision.

10 When they were past the first and the second guard posts, they came to the iron gate that leads to the city, which opened to them of its own accord; and they went out and went down one street, and immediately the angel departed from him.

11 And when Peter had come to himself, he said, "Now I know for certain that the Lord has sent His angel, and has delivered me from the hand of Herod and *from* all the expectation of the Jewish people."

12 So, when he had considered *this*, he came to the house of Mary, the mother of John whose surname was Mark, where many were gathered together praying.

13 And as Peter knocked at the door of the gate, a girl named Rhoda came to answer.

14 When she recognized Peter's voice, because of *her* gladness she did not open the gate, but ran in and announced that Peter stood before the gate.

15 But they said to her, "You are beside yourself!" Yet she kept insisting that it was so. So they said, "It is his angel."

16 Now Peter continued knocking; and when they opened *the door* and saw him, they were astonished.

17 But motioning to them with his hand to keep silent, he declared to them how the Lord had brought him out of the prison. And he said, "Go, tell these things to James and to the brethren." And he departed and went to another place.

18 Then, as soon as it was day, there was no small stir among the soldiers about what had become of Peter.

19 But when Herod had searched for him and not found him, he examined the guards and commanded that *they* should be put to death. And he went down from Judea to Caesarea, and stayed *there*.

20 Now Herod had been very angry with the people of Tyre and Sidon; but they came to him with one accord, and having made Blastus the king's chamberlain their friend, they asked for peace, because their country was supplied with food by the king's *country*.

21 So on a set day Herod, arrayed in royal apparel, sat on his throne and gave an oration to them.

22 And the people kept shouting, "The voice of a god and not of a man!"

23 Then immediately an angel of the Lord struck him, because he did not give glory to God. And he was eaten by worms and died.

24 But the word of God grew and multiplied.

25 And Barnabas and Saul returned from Jerusalem when they had fulfilled *their* ministry, and they also took with them John whose surname was Mark.

13 Now in the church that was at Antioch there were certain prophets and teachers: Barnabas, Simeon who was called Niger, Lucius of Cyrene, Manaen who had been brought up with Herod the tetrarch, and Saul.

2 As they ministered to the Lord and fasted, the Holy Spirit said, "Now separate to Me Barnabas and Saul for the work to which I have called them."

3 Then, having fasted and prayed, and laid hands on them, they sent *them* away.

4 So, being sent out by the Holy Spirit, they went down to Seleucia, and from there they sailed to Cyprus.

5 And when they arrived in Salamis, they preached the word of God in the synagogues of the Jews. They also had John as *their* assistant.

6 Now when they had gone through the island to Paphos, they found a certain sorcerer, a false prophet, a Jew whose name *was* Bar-Jesus,

7 who was with the proconsul, Sergius Paulus, an intelligent man. This man called for Barnabas and Saul and sought to hear the word of God.

8 But Elymas the sorcerer (for so his name is translated) withstood them, seeking to turn the proconsul away from the faith.

9 Then Saul, who also *is called* Paul, filled with the Holy Spirit, looked intently at him

10 and said, "O full of all deceit and all fraud, *you* son of the devil, *you*

enemy of all righteousness, will you not cease perverting the straight ways of the Lord?

11 "And now, indeed, the hand of the Lord *is* upon you, and you shall be blind, not seeing the sun for a time." And immediately a dark mist fell on him, and he went around seeking someone to lead him by the hand.

12 Then the proconsul believed, when he saw what had been done, being astonished at the teaching of the Lord.

13 Now when Paul and his party set sail from Paphos, they came to Perga in Pamphylia; and John, departing from them, returned to Jerusalem.

14 But when they departed from Perga, they came to Antioch in Pisidia, and went into the synagogue on the Sabbath day and sat down.

15 And after the reading of the Law and the Prophets, the rulers of the synagogue sent to them, saying, "Men *and* brethren, if you have any word of exhortation for the people, say on."

16 Then Paul stood up, and motioning with *his* hand said, "Men of Israel, and you who fear God, listen:

17 "The God of this people Israel chose our fathers, and exalted the people when they dwelt as strangers in the land of Egypt, and with an uplifted arm He brought them out of it.

18 "Now for a time of about forty years He put up with their ways in the wilderness.

19 "And when He had destroyed seven nations in the land of Canaan, He distributed their land to them by allotment.

20 "After that He gave *them* judges for about four hundred and fifty years, until Samuel the prophet.

21 "And afterward they asked for a king; so God gave them Saul the

son of Kish, a man of the tribe of Benjamin, for forty years.

22 "And when He had removed him, He raised up for them David as king, to whom also He gave testimony and said, *'I have found David the son of Jesse, a man after My own heart,* who will do all My will.'

23 "From this man's seed, according to *the* promise, God raised up for Israel a Savior—Jesus—

24 "after John had first preached, before His coming, the baptism of repentance to all the people of Israel.

25 "And as John was finishing his course, he said, 'Who do you think I am? I am not *He.* But behold, there comes One after me, the sandals of whose feet I am not worthy to loose.'

26 "Men *and* brethren, sons of the family of Abraham, and those among you who fear God, to you the word of this salvation has been sent.

27 "For those who dwell in Jerusalem, and their rulers, because they did not know Him, nor even the voices of the Prophets which are read every Sabbath, have fulfilled *them* in condemning *Him.*

28 "And though they found no cause for death *in Him,* they asked Pilate that He should be put to death.

29 "Now when they had fulfilled all that was written concerning Him, they took *Him* down from the tree and laid *Him* in a tomb.

30 "But God raised Him from the dead.

31 "He was seen for many days by those who came up with Him from Galilee to Jerusalem, who are His witnesses to the people.

32 "And we declare to you glad tidings—that promise which was made to the fathers.

33 "God has fulfilled this for us their children, in that He has raised up Jesus. As it is also written in the second Psalm:

'You are My Son,
Today I have begotten You.'

34 "And that He raised Him from the dead, no more to return to corruption, He has spoken thus:

'I will give you the sure mercies of David.'

35 "Therefore He also says in another *Psalm:*

'You will not allow Your Holy One to see corruption.'

36 "For David, after he had served his own generation by the will of God, fell asleep, was buried with his fathers, and saw corruption;

37 "but He whom God raised up saw no corruption.

38 "Therefore let it be known to you, brethren, that through this Man is preached to you the forgiveness of sins;

39 "and by Him everyone who believes is justified from all things from which you could not be justified by the law of Moses.

40 "Beware therefore, lest what has been spoken in the prophets come upon you:

41 *'Behold, you despisers,*
Marvel and perish;
For I work a work in your days,
A work which you will by no means believe,
Though one were to declare it to you.'"

42 And when the Jews went out of the synagogue, the Gentiles begged that these words might be preached to them the next Sabbath.

43 Now when the congregation had broken up, many of the Jews and devout proselytes followed Paul and Barnabas, who, speaking to them, persuaded them to continue in the grace of God.

44 And the next Sabbath almost the whole city came together to hear the word of God.

45 But when the Jews saw the multitudes, they were filled with envy; and contradicting and blaspheming, they opposed the things spoken by Paul.

46 Then Paul and Barnabas grew bold and said, "It was necessary that the word of God should be spoken to you first; but since you reject it, and judge yourselves unworthy of everlasting life, behold, we turn to the Gentiles.

47 "For so the Lord has commanded us:

> 'I have set you to be a light
>   to the Gentiles,
> That you should be for
>   salvation to the ends of the
>   earth.'"

48 Now when the Gentiles heard this, they were glad and glorified the word of the Lord. And as many as had been appointed to eternal life believed.

49 And the word of the Lord was being spread throughout all the region.

50 But the Jews stirred up the devout and prominent women and the chief men of the city, raised up persecution against Paul and Barnabas, and expelled them from their region.

51 But they shook off the dust from their feet against them, and came to Iconium.

52 And the disciples were filled with joy and with the Holy Spirit.

14 Now it happened in Iconium that they went together to the synagogue of the Jews, and so spoke that a great multitude both of the Jews and of the Greeks believed.

2 But the unbelieving Jews stirred up the Gentiles and poisoned their minds against the brethren.

3 Therefore they stayed there a long time, speaking boldly in the Lord, who was bearing witness to the word of His grace, granting signs and wonders to be done by their hands.

4 But the multitude of the city was divided: part sided with the Jews, and part with the apostles.

5 And when a violent attempt was made by both the Gentiles and Jews, with their rulers, to abuse and stone them,

6 they became aware of it and fled to Lystra and Derbe, cities of Lycaonia, and to the surrounding region.

7 And they were preaching the gospel there.

8 And in Lystra a certain man without strength in his feet was sitting, a cripple from his mother's womb, who had never walked.

9 *This* man heard Paul speaking. Paul, observing him intently and seeing that he had faith to be healed,

10 said with a loud voice, "Stand up straight on your feet!" And he leaped and walked.

11 Now when the people saw what Paul had done, they raised their voices, saying in the Lycaonian *language*, "The gods have come down to us in the likeness of men!"

12 And Barnabas they called Zeus, and Paul, Hermes, because he was the chief speaker.

13 Then the priest of Zeus, whose temple was in front of their city, brought oxen and garlands to the gates, intending to sacrifice with the multitudes.

14 But when the apostles Barnabas and Paul heard this, they tore their clothes and ran in among the multitude, crying out

15 and saying, "Men, why are you doing these things? We also are men with the same nature as you, and preach to you that you should turn from these vain things to the living God, who made the heaven,

the earth, the sea, and all things that are in them,

16 "who in bygone generations allowed all nations to walk in their own ways.

17 "Nevertheless He did not leave Himself without witness, in that He did good, gave us rain from heaven and fruitful seasons, filling our hearts with food and gladness."

18 And with these sayings they could scarcely restrain the multitudes from sacrificing to them.

19 Then Jews from Antioch and Iconium came there; and having persuaded the multitudes, they stoned Paul *and* dragged *him* out of the city, supposing him to be dead.

20 However, when the disciples gathered around him, he rose up and went into the city. And the next day he departed with Barnabas to Derbe.

21 And when they had preached the gospel to that city and made many disciples, they returned to Lystra, Iconium, and Antioch,

22 strengthening the souls of the disciples, exhorting *them* to continue in the faith, and *saying,* "We must through many tribulations enter the kingdom of God."

23 So when they had appointed elders in every church, and prayed with fasting, they commended them to the Lord in whom they had believed.

24 And after they had passed through Pisidia, they came to Pamphylia.

25 Now when they had preached the word in Perga, they went down to Attalia.

26 From there they sailed to Antioch, where they had been commended to the grace of God for the work which they had completed.

27 And when they had come and gathered the church together, they reported all that God had done with them, and that He had

opened the door of faith to the Gentiles.

28 So they stayed there a long time with the disciples.

15 And certain *men* came down from Judea and taught the brethren, "Unless you are circumcised according to the custom of Moses, you cannot be saved."

2 Therefore, when Paul and Barnabas had no small dissension and dispute with them, they determined that Paul and Barnabas and certain others of them should go up to Jerusalem, to the apostles and elders, about this question.

3 So, being sent on their way by the church, they passed through Phoenicia and Samaria, describing the conversion of the Gentiles; and they caused great joy to all the brethren.

4 And when they had come to Jerusalem, they were received by the church and the apostles and the elders; and they reported all things that God had done with them.

5 But some of the sect of the Pharisees who believed rose up, saying, "It is necessary to circumcise them, and to command *them* to keep the law of Moses."

6 So the apostles and elders came together to consider this matter.

7 And when there had been much dispute, Peter rose up and said to them: "Men and brethren, you know that a good while ago God chose among us, that by my mouth the Gentiles should hear the word of the gospel and believe.

8 "So God, who knows the heart, acknowledged them, by giving them the Holy Spirit just as *He did* to us,

9 "and made no distinction between us and them, purifying their hearts by faith.

10 "Now therefore, why do you test God by putting a yoke on the neck of the disciples which neither our fathers nor we were able to bear?

11 "But we believe that through the grace of the Lord Jesus Christ we shall be saved in the same manner as they."
12 Then all the multitude kept silent and listened to Barnabas and Paul declaring how many miracles and wonders God had worked through them among the Gentiles.
13 And after they had become silent, James answered, saying, "Men *and* brethren, listen to me:
14 "Simon has declared how God at the first visited the Gentiles to take out of them a people for His name.
15 "And with this the words of the prophets agree, just as it is written:

16 '*After this I will return
    And will rebuild the tabernacle
      of David which has fallen
      down.
I will rebuild its ruins,
    And I will set it up,*
17 *So that the rest of mankind
    may seek the* LORD,
*Even all the Gentiles who are
    called by My name,
Says the* LORD *who does all
    these things.'*

18 "Known to God from eternity are all His works.
19 "Therefore I judge that we should not trouble those from among the Gentiles who are turning to God,
20 "but that we write to them to abstain from things polluted by idols, *from* sexual immorality, *from* things strangled, and *from* blood.
21 "For Moses has had throughout many generations those who preach him in every city, being read in the synagogues every Sabbath."
22 Then it pleased the apostles and elders, with the whole church, to send chosen men of their own company to Antioch with Paul and Barnabas, *namely,* Judas who was also named Barsabas, and Silas, leading men among the brethren.

23 They wrote this *letter* by them:

The apostles, the elders, and
    the brethren,
To the brethren who are of the
    Gentiles in Antioch, Syria, and
    Cilicia:
Greetings.

24 Since we have heard that some who went out from us have troubled you with words, unsettling your souls, saying, '*You must* be circumcised and keep the law'—to whom we gave no *such* commandment—
25 it seemed good to us, being assembled with one accord, to send chosen men to you with our beloved Barnabas and Paul,
26 men who have risked their lives for the name of our Lord Jesus Christ.
27 We have therefore sent Judas and Silas, who will also report the same things by word of mouth.
28 For it seemed good to the Holy Spirit, and to us, to lay upon you no greater burden than these necessary things:
29 that you abstain from things offered to idols, from blood, from things strangled, and from sexual immorality. If you keep yourselves from these, you will do well.
Farewell.

30 So when they were sent off, they came to Antioch; and when they had gathered the multitude together, they delivered the letter.
31 When they had read it, they rejoiced over its encouragement.
32 Now Judas and Silas, themselves being prophets also, exhorted the brethren with many words and strengthened *them.*
33 And after they had stayed *there* for a time, they were sent back with greetings from the brethren to the apostles.
34 However, it seemed good to Silas to remain there.

35 Paul and Barnabas also remained in Antioch, teaching and preaching the word of the Lord, with many others also.

36 Then after some days Paul said to Barnabas, "Let us now go back and visit our brethren in every city where we have preached the word of the Lord, *and see* how they are doing."

37 Now Barnabas was determined to take with them John called Mark.

38 But Paul insisted that they should not take with them the one who had departed from them in Pamphylia, and had not gone with them to the work.

39 Then the contention became so sharp that they parted from one another. And so Barnabas took Mark and sailed to Cyprus;

40 but Paul chose Silas and departed, being commended by the brethren to the grace of God.

41 And he went through Syria and Cilicia, strengthening the churches.

16 Then he came to Derbe and Lystra. And behold, a certain disciple was there, named Timothy, *the* son of a certain Jewish woman who believed, but his father *was* Greek.

2 He was well spoken of by the brethren who were at Lystra and Iconium.

3 Paul wanted to have him go on with him. And he took *him* and circumcised him because of the Jews who were in that region, for they all knew that his father was Greek.

4 And as they went through the cities, they delivered to them the decrees to keep, which were determined by the apostles and elders at Jerusalem.

5 So the churches were strengthened in the faith, and increased in number daily.

6 Now when they had gone through Phrygia and the region of Galatia, they were forbidden by the Holy Spirit to preach the word in Asia.

7 After they had come to Mysia, they tried to go into Bithynia, but the Spirit did not permit them.

8 So passing by Mysia, they came down to Troas.

9 And a vision appeared to Paul in the night. A man of Macedonia stood and pleaded with him, saying, "Come over to Macedonia and help us."

10 Now after he had seen the vision, immediately we sought to go to Macedonia, concluding that the Lord had called us to preach the gospel to them.

11 Therefore, sailing from Troas, we ran a straight course to Samothrace, and the next *day* came to Neapolis,

12 and from there to Philippi, which is the foremost city of that part of Macedonia, a colony. And we were staying in that city for some days.

13 And on the Sabbath day we went out of the city to the riverside, where prayer was customarily made; and we sat down and spoke to the women who met *there.*

14 Now a certain woman named Lydia heard *us.* She was a seller of purple from the city of Thyatira, who worshiped God. The Lord opened her heart to heed the things spoken by Paul.

15 And when she and her household were baptized, she begged *us,* saying, "If you have judged me to be faithful to the Lord, come to my house and stay." And she constrained us.

16 Now it happened, as we went to prayer, that a certain slave girl possessed with a spirit of divination met us, who brought her masters much profit by fortune-telling.

17 This girl followed Paul and us, and cried out, saying, "These men are the servants of the Most High God, who proclaim to us the way of salvation."

18 And this she did for many days. But Paul, greatly annoyed, turned and said to the spirit, "I command you in the name of Jesus Christ to come out of her." And he came out that very hour.

19 But when her masters saw that their hope of profit was gone, they seized Paul and Silas and dragged *them* into the marketplace to the authorities.

20 And they brought them to the magistrates, and said, "These men, being Jews, exceedingly trouble our city;

21 "and they teach customs which are not lawful for us, being Romans, to receive or observe."

22 Then the multitude rose up together against them; and the magistrates tore off their clothes and commanded *them* to be beaten with rods.

23 And when they had laid many stripes on them, they threw *them* into prison, commanding the jailer to keep them securely.

24 Having received such a charge, he put them into the inner prison and fastened their feet in the stocks.

25 But at midnight Paul and Silas were praying and singing hymns to God, and the prisoners were listening to them.

26 Suddenly there was a great earthquake, so that the foundations of the prison were shaken; and immediately all the doors were opened and everyone's chains were loosed.

27 And the keeper of the prison, awaking from sleep and seeing the prison doors open, supposing the prisoners had fled, drew his sword and was about to kill himself.

28 But Paul called with a loud voice, saying, "Do yourself no harm, for we are all here."

29 Then he called for a light, ran in, and fell down trembling before Paul and Silas.

30 And he brought them out and

said, "Sirs, what must I do to be saved?"

31 So they said, "Believe on the Lord Jesus Christ, and you will be saved, you and your household."

32 Then they spoke the word of the Lord to him and to all who were in his house.

33 And he took them the same hour of the night and washed *their* stripes. And immediately he and all his family were baptized.

34 Now when he had brought them into his house, he set food before them; and he rejoiced, having believed in God with all his household.

35 And when it was day, the magistrates sent the officers, saying, "Let those men go."

36 So the keeper of the prison reported these words to Paul, saying, "The magistrates have sent to let you go. Now therefore depart, and go in peace."

37 But Paul said to them, "They have beaten us openly, uncondemned Romans, *and* have thrown *us* into prison. And now do they put us out secretly? No indeed! Let them come themselves and get us out."

38 And the officers told these words to the magistrates, and they were afraid when they heard that they were Romans.

39 Then they came and pleaded with them and brought *them* out, and asked *them* to depart from the city.

40 So they went out of the prison and entered *the house of* Lydia; and when they had seen the brethren, they encouraged them and departed.

17 Now when they had passed through Amphipolis and Apollonia, they came to Thessalonica, where there was a synagogue of the Jews.

2 Then Paul, as his custom was, went in to them, and for three Sabbaths reasoned with them from the Scriptures,

3 explaining and demonstrating that the Christ had to suffer and rise again from the dead, and *saying,* "This Jesus whom I preach to you is the Christ."

4 And some of them were persuaded; and a great multitude of the devout Greeks, and not a few of the leading women, joined Paul and Silas.

5 But the Jews who were not persuaded, becoming envious, took some of the evil men from the marketplace, and gathering a mob, set all the city in an uproar and attacked the house of Jason, and sought to bring them out to the people.

6 But when they did not find them, they dragged Jason and some brethren to the rulers of the city, crying out, "These who have turned the world upside down have come here too.

7 "Jason has harbored them, and these are all acting contrary to the decrees of Caesar, saying there is another king—Jesus."

8 And they troubled the crowd and the rulers of the city when they heard these things.

9 So when they had taken security from Jason and the rest, they let them go.

10 Then the brethren immediately sent Paul and Silas away by night to Berea. When they arrived, they went into the synagogue of the Jews.

11 These were more fair-minded than those in Thessalonica, in that they received the word with all readiness, and searched the Scriptures daily *to find out* whether these things were so.

12 Therefore many of them believed, and also not a few of the Greeks, prominent women as well as men.

13 But when the Jews from Thessalonica learned that the word of God was preached by Paul at Berea, they came there also and stirred up the crowds.

14 Then immediately the brethren sent Paul away, to go to the sea; but both Silas and Timothy remained there.

15 So those who conducted Paul brought him to Athens; and receiving a command for Silas and Timothy to come to him with all speed, they departed.

16 Now while Paul waited for them at Athens, his spirit was provoked within him when he saw that the city was given over to idols.

17 Therefore he reasoned in the synagogue with the Jews and with the *Gentile* worshipers, and in the marketplace daily with those who happened to be there.

18 Then certain Epicurean and Stoic philosophers encountered him. And some said, "What does this babbler want to say?" Others said, "He seems to be a proclaimer of foreign gods," because he preached to them Jesus and the resurrection.

19 And they took him and brought him to the Areopagus, saying, "May we know what this new doctrine *is* of which you speak?

20 "For you are bringing some strange things to our ears. Therefore we want to know what these things mean."

21 For all the Athenians and the foreigners who were there spent their time in nothing else but either to tell or to hear some new thing.

22 Then Paul stood in the midst of the Areopagus and said, "Men of Athens, I perceive that in all things you are very religious;

23 "for as I was passing through and considering the objects of your worship, I even found an altar with this inscription:

TO THE UNKNOWN GOD.

Therefore, the One whom you worship without knowing, Him I proclaim to you:

24 "God, who made the world and everything in it, since He is Lord of

Can We Prove That God Is Personal and Caring?

God's existence, His personality, and His care and love for us have always been evident through the creation (Acts 17:24–29). The complexity, harmony, and beauty of nature allow for no other possibility.

Added to what we can observe in nature about God, we now have, for the first time in history, astronomers' measurements of the cosmos. With these new measurements, we can learn some of the Creator's characteristics.

Astronomers have measured twenty separate aspects of the universe. In each case, if the measured characteristic were slightly different, life couldn't exist at any time in the universe's history. In many cases, the tolerance for change in a dimension is less than a few percent. In some cases, it is far less than that. Similar exacting design also is seen in forty characteristics of the earth-sun system and still more in living creatures themselves.

To take just one example, if the universe were any more massive than it is, then nuclear fusion (the hydrogen-bomb process) would work to quickly transform all the matter in the universe into heavy elements. If

the universe were less massive, then nuclear fusion would never generate elements heavier than helium. Either way, elements such as carbon, oxygen, and nitrogen would be missing, and life would be impossible. This fact tells us that God cared so much for the human race that He built one hundred billion trillion stars and exquisitely shaped and crafted them over the entire age of the universe so that, at this brief moment in time, we human beings could exist and have a wonderful place to live.

This exquisite fine-tuning implies that the Creator must be personal, because only a person has the capacity for purposeful design. It also says that He cares for the human race.

Some atheists have tried to brush away all this evidence by saying the design is a coincidence. But is the sample size large enough to explain such a coincidence? For example, if you were to sit through about a trillion poker games, you could expect to get two consecutive royal flushes in that many deals. If you were to get two consecutive royal flushes in just two deals, your rational conclusion would be that someone chose to give you those cards. In the case of the universe, the known sample size is one.

heaven and earth, does not dwell in temples made with hands.

25 "Nor is He worshiped with men's hands, as though He needed anything, since He gives to all life, breath, and all things.

26 "And He has made from one blood every nation of men to dwell on all the face of the earth, and has determined their preappointed times and the boundaries of their habitation,

27 "so that they should seek the Lord, in the hope that they might grope for Him and find Him, though He is not far from each one of us;

28 "for in Him we live and move and have our being, as also some of your own poets have said, 'For we are also His offspring.'

29 "Therefore, since we are the offspring of God, we ought not to think that the Divine Nature is like gold or silver or stone, something shaped by art and man's devising.

30 "Truly, these times of ignorance God overlooked, but now commands all men everywhere to repent,

31 "because He has appointed a day on which He will judge the world in righteousness by the Man whom He has ordained. He has given assurance of this to all by raising Him from the dead."

32 And when they heard of the resurrection of the dead, some mocked, while others said, "We will hear you again on this *matter*."

33 So Paul departed from among them.

34 However, some men joined him and believed, among them Dionysius the Areopagite, a woman named Damaris, and others with them.

18 After these things Paul departed from Athens and went to Corinth.

2 And he found a certain Jew named Aquila, born in Pontus, who had recently come from Italy with his wife Priscilla (because Claudius had commanded all the Jews to depart from Rome); and he came to them.

3 So, because he was of the same trade, he stayed with them and worked; for by occupation they were tentmakers.

4 And he reasoned in the synagogue every Sabbath, and persuaded both Jews and Greeks.

5 When Silas and Timothy had come from Macedonia, Paul was constrained by the Spirit, and testified to the Jews *that* Jesus *is* the Christ.

6 But when they opposed him and blasphemed, he shook *his* garments and said to them, "Your blood *be* upon your *own* heads; I *am* clean. From now on I will go to the Gentiles."

7 And he departed from there and entered the house of a certain *man* named Justus, *one* who worshiped God, whose house was next door to the synagogue.

8 Then Crispus, the ruler of the synagogue, believed on the Lord with all his household. And many of the Corinthians, hearing, believed and were baptized.

9 Now the Lord spoke to Paul in the night by a vision, "Do not be afraid, but speak, and do not keep silent;

10 "for I am with you, and no one will attack you to hurt you; for I have many people in this city."

11 And he continued *there* a year and six months, teaching the word of God among them.

12 Now when Gallio was proconsul of Achaia, the Jews with one accord rose up against Paul and brought him to the judgment seat,

13 saying, "This *fellow* persuades men to worship God contrary to the law."

14 And when Paul was about to open *his* mouth, Gallio said to the Jews, "If it were a matter of

wrongdoing or wicked crimes, O Jews, there would be reason why I should bear with you.

15 "But if it is a question of words and names and your own law, look *to it* yourselves; for I do not want to be a judge of such *matters*."

16 And he drove them from the judgment seat.

17 Then all the Greeks took Sosthenes, the ruler of the synagogue, and beat *him* before the judgment seat. But Gallio took no notice of these things.

18 So Paul still remained a good while. Then he took leave of the brethren and sailed for Syria, and Priscilla and Aquila *were* with him. He had *his* hair cut off at Cenchrea, for he had taken a vow.

19 And he came to Ephesus, and left them there; but he himself entered the synagogue and reasoned with the Jews.

20 When they asked *him* to stay a longer time with them, he did not consent,

21 but took leave of them, saying, "I must by all means keep this coming feast in Jerusalem; but I will return again to you, God willing." And he sailed from Ephesus.

22 And when he had landed at Caesarea, and gone up and greeted the church, he went down to Antioch.

23 After he had spent some time *there*, he departed and went over *all* the region of Galatia and Phrygia in order, strengthening all the disciples.

24 Now a certain Jew named Apollos, born at Alexandria, an eloquent man *and* mighty in the Scriptures, came to Ephesus.

25 This man had been instructed in the way of the Lord; and being fervent in spirit, he spoke and taught accurately the things of the Lord, though he knew only the baptism of John.

26 So he began to speak boldly in the synagogue. When Aquila and Priscilla heard him, they took him aside and explained to him the way of God more accurately.

27 And when he desired to cross to Achaia, the brethren wrote, exhorting the disciples to receive him; and when he arrived, he greatly helped those who had believed through grace;

28 for he vigorously refuted the Jews publicly, showing from the Scriptures that Jesus is the Christ.

19 And it happened, while Apollos was at Corinth, that Paul, having passed through the upper regions, came to Ephesus. And finding some disciples

2 he said to them, "Did you receive the Holy Spirit when you believed?" And they said to him, "We have not so much as heard whether there is a Holy Spirit."

3 And he said to them, "Into what then were you baptized?" So they said, "Into John's baptism."

4 Then Paul said, "John indeed baptized with a baptism of repentance, saying to the people that they should believe on Him who would come after him, that is, on Christ Jesus."

5 When they heard *this*, they were baptized in the name of the Lord Jesus.

6 And when Paul had laid hands on them, the Holy Spirit came upon them, and they spoke with tongues and prophesied.

7 Now the men were about twelve in all.

8 And he went into the synagogue and spoke boldly for three months, reasoning and persuading concerning the things of the kingdom of God.

9 But when some were hardened and did not believe, but spoke evil of the Way before the multitude, he departed from them and withdrew the disciples, reasoning daily in the school of Tyrannus.

10 And this continued for two years, so that all who dwelt in Asia heard the word of the Lord Jesus, both Jews and Greeks.

11 Now God worked unusual miracles by the hands of Paul,

12 so that even handkerchiefs or aprons were brought from his body to the sick, and the diseases left them and the evil spirits went out of them.

13 Then some of the itinerant Jewish exorcists took it upon themselves to call the name of the Lord Jesus over those who had evil spirits, saying, "We adjure you by the Jesus whom Paul preaches."

14 Also there were seven sons of Sceva, a Jewish chief priest, who did so.

15 And the evil spirit answered and said, "Jesus I know, and Paul I know; but who are you?"

16 Then the man in whom the evil spirit was leaped on them, overpowered them, and prevailed against them, so that they fled out of that house naked and wounded.

17 This became known both to all Jews and Greeks dwelling in Ephesus; and fear fell on them all, and the name of the Lord Jesus was magnified.

18 And many who had believed came confessing and telling their deeds.

19 Also, many of those who had practiced magic brought their books together and burned *them* in the sight of all. And they counted up the value of them, and *it* totaled fifty thousand *pieces* of silver.

20 So the word of the Lord grew mightily and prevailed.

21 When these things were accomplished, Paul purposed in the Spirit, when he had passed through Macedonia and Achaia, to go to Jerusalem, saying, "After I have been there, I must also see Rome."

22 So he sent into Macedonia two of those who ministered to him, Timothy and Erastus, but he himself stayed in Asia for a time.

23 And about that time there arose a great commotion about the Way.

24 For a certain man named Demetrius, a silversmith, who made silver shrines of Diana, brought no small profit to the craftsmen.

25 He called them together with the workers of similar occupation, and said: "Men, you know that we have our prosperity by this trade.

26 "Moreover you see and hear that not only at Ephesus, but throughout almost all Asia, this Paul has persuaded and turned away many people, saying that they are not gods which are made with hands.

27 "So not only is this trade of ours in danger of falling into disrepute, but also the temple of the great goddess Diana may be despised and her magnificence destroyed, whom all Asia and the world worship."

28 And when they heard *this*, they were full of wrath and cried out, saying, "Great *is* Diana of the Ephesians!"

29 So the whole city was filled with confusion, and rushed into the theater with one accord, having seized Gaius and Aristarchus, Macedonians, Paul's travel companions.

30 And when Paul wanted to go in to the people, the disciples would not allow him.

31 Then some of the officials of Asia, who were his friends, sent to him pleading that he would not venture into the theater.

32 Some therefore cried one thing and some another, for the assembly was confused, and most of them did not know why they had come together.

33 And they drew Alexander out of the multitude, the Jews putting him forward. And Alexander motioned with his hand, and wanted to make his defense to the people.

34 But when they found out that he was a Jew, all with one voice cried out for about two hours, "Great *is* Diana of the Ephesians!"

35 And when the city clerk had quieted the crowd, he said: "Men of Ephesus, what man is there who does not know that the city of the Ephesians is temple guardian of the great goddess Diana, and of the *image* which fell down from Zeus?

36 "Therefore, since these things cannot be denied, you ought to be quiet and do nothing rashly.

37 "For you have brought these men here who are neither robbers of temples nor blasphemers of your goddess.

38 "Therefore, if Demetrius and his fellow craftsmen have a case against anyone, the courts are open and there are proconsuls. Let them bring charges against one another.

39 "But if you have any other inquiry to make, it shall be determined in the lawful assembly.

40 "For we are in danger of being called in question for today's uproar, there being no reason which we may give to account for this disorderly gathering."

41 And when he had said these things, he dismissed the assembly.

20 After the uproar had ceased, Paul called the disciples to *him*, embraced *them*, and departed to go to Macedonia.

2 Now when he had gone over that region and encouraged them with many words, he came to Greece

3 and stayed three months. And when the Jews plotted against him as he was about to sail to Syria, he decided to return through Macedonia.

4 And Sopater of Berea accompanied him to Asia—also Aristarchus and Secundus of the Thessalonians, and Gaius of Derbe, and Timothy, and Tychicus and Trophimus of Asia.

5 These men, going ahead, waited for us at Troas.

6 But we sailed away from Philippi after the Days of Unleavened Bread, and in five days joined them at Troas, where we stayed seven days.

7 Now on the first *day* of the week, when the disciples came together to break bread, Paul, ready to depart the next day, spoke to them and continued his message until midnight.

8 There were many lamps in the upper room where they were gathered together.

9 And in a window sat a certain young man named Eutychus, who was sinking into a deep sleep. He was overcome by sleep; and as Paul continued speaking, he fell down from the third story and was taken up dead.

10 But Paul went down, fell on him, and embracing *him* said, "Do not trouble yourselves, for his life is in him."

11 Now when he had come up, had broken bread and eaten, and talked a long while, even till daybreak, he departed.

12 And they brought the young man in alive, and they were not a little comforted.

13 Then we went ahead to the ship and sailed to Assos, there intending to take Paul on board; for so he had given orders, intending himself to go on foot.

14 And when he met us at Assos, we took him on board and came to Mitylene.

15 We sailed from there, and the next *day* came opposite Chios; the following *day* we arrived at Samos and stayed at Trogyllium; the next *day* we came to Miletus.

16 For Paul had decided to sail past Ephesus, so that he would not have to spend time in Asia; for he was hurrying to be at Jerusalem, if possible, on the Day of Pentecost.

17 From Miletus he sent to Ephesus and called for the elders of the church.

18 And when they had come to

him, he said to them: "You know, from the first day that I came to Asia, in what manner I always lived among you,

19 "serving the Lord with all humility, with many tears and trials which happened to me by the plotting of the Jews;

20 "*and* how I kept back nothing that was helpful, but proclaimed it to you, and taught you publicly and from house to house,

21 "testifying to Jews, and also to Greeks, repentance toward God and faith toward our Lord Jesus Christ.

22 "And see, now I go bound in the spirit to Jerusalem, not knowing the things that will happen to me there,

23 "except that the Holy Spirit testifies in every city, saying that chains and tribulations await me.

24 "But none of these things move me; nor do I count my life dear to myself, so that I may finish my race with joy, and the ministry which I received from the Lord Jesus, to testify to the gospel of the grace of God.

25 "And indeed, now I know that you all, among whom I have gone preaching the kingdom of God, will see my face no more.

26 "Therefore I testify to you this day that I *am* innocent of the blood of all *men*.

27 "For I have not shunned to declare to you the whole counsel of God.

28 "Therefore take heed to yourselves and to all the flock, among which the Holy Spirit has made you overseers, to shepherd the church of God which He purchased with His own blood.

29 "For I know this, that after my departure savage wolves will come in among you, not sparing the flock.

30 "Also from among yourselves men will rise up, speaking perverse things, to draw away the disciples after themselves.

31 "Therefore watch, and remember that for three years I did not cease to warn everyone night and day with tears.

32 "And now, brethren, I commend you to God and to the word of His grace, which is able to build you up and give you an inheritance among all those who are sanctified.

33 "I have coveted no one's silver or gold or apparel.

34 "Yes, you yourselves know that these hands have provided for my necessities, and for those who were with me.

35 "I have shown you in every way, by laboring like this, that you must support the weak. And remember the words of the Lord Jesus, that He said, 'It is more blessed to give than to receive.' "

36 And when he had said these things, he knelt down and prayed with them all.

37 Then they all wept freely, and fell on Paul's neck and kissed him,

38 sorrowing most of all for the words which he spoke, that they would see his face no more. And they accompanied him to the ship.

21

Now it came to pass, that when we had departed from them and set sail, running a straight course we came to Cos, the following *day* to Rhodes, and from there to Patara.

2 And finding a ship sailing over to Phoenicia, we went aboard and set sail.

3 When we had sighted Cyprus, we passed it on the left, sailed to Syria, and landed at Tyre; for there the ship was to unload its cargo.

4 And finding disciples, we stayed there seven days. They told Paul through the Spirit not to go up to Jerusalem.

5 So when we had come to the end of those days, we departed and went on our way; and they all ac-

190

companied us, with wives and children, till *we were* out of the city. And we knelt down on the shore and prayed.

6 When we had taken our leave of one another, we boarded the ship, and they returned home.

7 And when we had finished *our* voyage from Tyre, we came to Ptolemais, greeted the brethren, and stayed with them one day.

8 On the next *day* we who were Paul's companions departed and came to Caesarea, and entered the house of Philip the evangelist, who was *one* of the seven, and stayed with him.

9 Now this man had four virgin daughters who prophesied.

10 And as we stayed many days, a certain prophet named Agabus came down from Judea.

11 When he had come to us, he took Paul's belt, bound his *own* hands and feet, and said, "Thus says the Holy Spirit, 'So shall the Jews at Jerusalem bind the man who owns this belt, and deliver *him* into the hands of the Gentiles.' "

12 And when we heard these things, both we and those from that place pleaded with him not to go up to Jerusalem.

13 Then Paul answered, "What do you mean by weeping and breaking my heart? For I am ready not only to be bound, but also to die at Jerusalem for the name of the Lord Jesus."

14 So when he would not be persuaded, we ceased, saying, "The will of the Lord be done."

15 And after those days we packed and went up to Jerusalem.

16 Also some of the disciples from Caesarea went with us and brought with them one, Mnason of Cyprus, an early disciple, with whom we were to lodge.

17 And when we had come to Jerusalem, the brethren received us gladly.

18 On the following *day* Paul went in with us to James, and all the elders were present.

19 When he had greeted them, he told in detail those things which God had done among the Gentiles through his ministry.

20 And when they heard *it,* they glorified the Lord. And they said to him, "You see, brother, how many myriads of Jews there are who have believed, and they are all zealous for the law;

21 "but they have been informed about you that you teach all the Jews who are among the Gentiles to forsake Moses, saying that they ought not to circumcise *their* children nor to walk according to the customs.

22 "What then? The assembly must certainly meet, for they will hear that you have come.

23 "Therefore do what we tell you: We have four men who have taken a vow.

24 "Take them and be purified with them, and pay their expenses so that they may shave *their* heads, and that all may know that those things of which they were informed concerning you are nothing, but *that* you yourself also walk orderly and keep the law.

25 "But concerning the Gentiles who believe, we have written *and* decided that they should observe no such thing, except that they should keep themselves from *things* offered to idols, from blood, from things strangled, and from sexual immorality."

26 Then Paul took the men, and the next day, having been purified with them, entered the temple to announce the expiration of the days of purification, at which time an offering should be made for each one of them.

27 And when the seven days were almost ended, the Jews from Asia, seeing him in the temple, stirred up the whole crowd and laid hands on him,

28 crying out, "Men of Israel, help! This is the man who teaches all *men* everywhere against the people, the law, and this place; and furthermore he also brought Greeks into the temple and has defiled this holy place."

29 (For they had previously seen Trophimus the Ephesian with him in the city, whom they supposed that Paul had brought into the temple.)

30 And all the city was disturbed; and the people ran together, seized Paul, and dragged him out of the temple; and immediately the doors were shut.

31 Now as they were seeking to kill him, news came to the commander of the garrison that all Jerusalem was in an uproar.

32 He immediately took soldiers and centurions, and ran down to them. And when they saw the commander and the soldiers, they stopped beating Paul.

33 Then the commander came near and took him, and commanded *him* to be bound with two chains; and he asked who he was and what he had done.

34 And some among the multitude cried one thing and some another. And when he could not ascertain the truth because of the tumult, he commanded him to be taken into the barracks.

35 And when he reached the stairs, he had to be carried by the soldiers because of the violence of the mob.

36 For the multitude of the people followed after, crying out, "Away with him!"

37 And as Paul was about to be led into the barracks, he said to the commander, "May I speak to you?" He replied, "Can you speak Greek?

38 "Are you not the Egyptian who some time ago raised an insurrection and led the four thousand assassins out into the wilderness?"

39 But Paul said, "I am a Jew from Tarsus, in Cilicia, a citizen of no mean city; and I implore you, permit me to speak to the people."

40 So when he had given him permission, Paul stood on the stairs and motioned with his hand to the people. And when there was a great silence, he spoke to *them* in the Hebrew language, saying,

22 "Men, brethren, and fathers, hear my defense before you now."

2 And when they heard that he spoke to them in the Hebrew language, they kept all the more silent. Then he said:

3 "I am indeed a Jew, born in Tarsus of Cilicia, but brought up in this city at the feet of Gamaliel, taught according to the strictness of our fathers' law, and was zealous toward God as you all are today.

4 "I persecuted this Way to the death, binding and delivering into prisons both men and women,

5 "as also the high priest bears me witness, and all the council of the elders, from whom I also received letters to the brethren, and went to Damascus to bring in chains even those who were there to Jerusalem to be punished.

6 "Now it happened, as I journeyed and came near Damascus at about noon, suddenly a great light from heaven shone around me.

7 "And I fell to the ground and heard a voice saying to me, 'Saul, Saul, why are you persecuting Me?'

8 "So I answered, 'Who are You, Lord?' And He said to me, 'I am Jesus of Nazareth, whom you are persecuting.'

9 "Now those who were with me indeed saw the light and were afraid, but they did not hear the voice of Him who spoke to me.

10 "So I said, 'What shall I do, Lord?' And the Lord said to me, 'Arise and go into Damascus, and there you will be told all things which are appointed for you to do.'

11 "And since I could not see for

the glory of that light, being led by the hand of those who were with me, I came into Damascus.

12 "Then one, Ananias, a devout man according to the law, having a good testimony with all the Jews who dwelt *there,*

13 "came to me; and he stood and said to me, 'Brother Saul, receive your sight.' And at that same hour I looked up at him.

14 "Then he said, 'The God of our fathers has chosen you that you should know His will, and see the Just One, and hear the voice of His mouth.

15 'For you will be His witness to all men of what you have seen and heard.

16 'And now why are you waiting? Arise and be baptized, and wash away your sins, calling on the name of the Lord.'

17 "Then it happened, when I returned to Jerusalem and was praying in the temple, that I was in a trance

18 "and saw Him saying to me, 'Make haste and get out of Jerusalem quickly, for they will not receive your testimony concerning Me.'

19 "So I said, 'Lord, they know that in every synagogue I imprisoned and beat those who believe on You.

20 'And when the blood of Your martyr Stephen was shed, I also was standing by consenting to his death, and guarding the clothes of those who were killing him.'

21 "Then He said to me, 'Depart, for I will send you far from here to the Gentiles.' "

22 And they listened to him until this word, and *then* they raised their voices and said, "Away with such a *fellow* from the earth, for he is not fit to live!"

23 Then, as they cried out and tore off *their* clothes and threw dust into the air,

24 the commander ordered him to be brought into the barracks, and said that he should be examined under scourging, so that he might know why they shouted so against him.

25 And as they bound him with thongs, Paul said to the centurion who stood by, "Is it lawful for you to scourge a man who is a Roman, and uncondemned?"

26 When the centurion heard *that,* he went and told the commander, saying, "Take care what you do, for this man is a Roman."

27 Then the commander came and said to him, "Tell me, are you a Roman?" He said, "Yes."

28 And the commander answered, "With a large sum I obtained this citizenship." And Paul said, "But I was born *a citizen.*"

29 Then immediately those who were about to examine him withdrew from him; and the commander was also afraid after he found out that he was a Roman, and because he had bound him.

30 The next day, because he wanted to know for certain why he was accused by the Jews, he released him from *his* bonds, and commanded the chief priests and all their council to appear, and brought Paul down and set him before them.

23 Then Paul, looking earnestly at the council, said, "Men *and* brethren, I have lived in all good conscience before God until this day."

2 And the high priest Ananias commanded those who stood by him to strike him on the mouth.

3 Then Paul said to him, "God will strike you, *you* whitewashed wall! For you sit to judge me according to the law, and do you command me to be struck contrary to the law?"

4 And those who stood by said, "Do you revile God's high priest?"

5 Then Paul said, "I did not know, brethren, that he was the high

priest; for it is written, *'You shall not speak evil of the ruler of your people.'"*

6 But when Paul perceived that one part were Sadducees and the other Pharisees, he cried out in the council, "Men *and* brethren, I am a Pharisee, the son of a Pharisee; concerning the hope and resurrection of the dead I am being judged!"

7 And when he had said this, a dissension arose between the Pharisees and the Sadducees; and the assembly was divided.

8 For *the* Sadducees say that there is no resurrection—and no angel or spirit; but the Pharisees confess both.

9 Then there arose a loud outcry. And the scribes *who were* of the Pharisees' party arose and protested, saying, "We find no evil in this man; but if a spirit or an angel has spoken to him, let us not fight against God."

10 And when there arose a great dissension, the commander, fearing lest Paul might be pulled to pieces by them, commanded the soldiers to go down and take him by force from among them, and bring *him* into the barracks.

11 But the following night the Lord stood by him and said, "Be of good cheer, Paul; for as you have testified for Me in Jerusalem, so you must also bear witness at Rome."

12 And when it was day, some of the Jews banded together and bound themselves under an oath, saying that they would neither eat nor drink till they had killed Paul.

13 Now there were more than forty who had formed this conspiracy.

14 They came to the chief priests and elders, and said, "We have bound ourselves under a great oath that we will eat nothing until we have killed Paul.

15 "Now you, therefore, together with the council, suggest to the commander that he be brought down to you tomorrow, as though you were going to make further inquiries concerning him; but we are ready to kill him before he comes near."

16 And when Paul's sister's son heard of their ambush, he went and entered the barracks and told Paul.

17 Then Paul called one of the centurions to *him* and said, "Take this young man to the commander, for he has something to tell him."

18 So he took him and brought *him* to the commander and said, "Paul the prisoner called me to *him* and asked *me* to bring this young man to you. He has something to say to you."

19 Then the commander took him by the hand, went aside and asked *him* privately, "What is it that you have to tell me?"

20 And he said, "The Jews have agreed to ask that you bring Paul down to the council tomorrow, as though they were going to inquire more fully about him.

21 "But do not yield to them, for more than forty of them lie in wait for him, men who have bound themselves by an oath that they will neither eat nor drink till they have killed him; and now they are ready, waiting for the promise from you."

22 So the commander let the young man depart, and commanded *him,* "Tell no one that you have revealed these things to me."

23 And he called for two centurions, saying, "Prepare two hundred soldiers, seventy horsemen, and two hundred spearmen to go to Caesarea at the third hour of the night;

24 "and provide mounts to set Paul on, and bring *him* safely to Felix the governor."

25 He wrote a letter in the following manner:

26 Claudius Lysias,
To the most excellent governor
Felix:
Greetings.
27 This man was seized by the
Jews and was about to be
killed by them. Coming with
the troops I rescued him,
having learned that he was a
Roman.
28 And when I wanted to know
the reason they accused him, I
brought him before their
council.
29 I found out that he was
accused concerning questions
of their law, but had nothing
charged against him worthy of
death or chains.
30 And when it was told me that
the Jews lay in wait for the
man, I sent him immediately to
you, and also commanded his
accusers to state before you
the charges against him.
Farewell.

31 Then the soldiers, as they were
commanded, took Paul and
brought *him* by night to Antipatris.
32 The next day they left the
horsemen to go on with him, and
returned to the barracks.
33 When they came to Caesarea
and had delivered the letter to the
governor, they also presented Paul
to him.
34 And when the governor had
read *it,* he asked what province he
was from. And when he understood
that *he was* from Cilicia,
35 he said, "I will hear you when
your accusers also have come."
And he commanded him to be kept
in Herod's Praetorium.

24 Now after five days Ananias
the high priest came down
with the elders and a certain orator
named Tertullus. These gave evidence
to the governor against
Paul.
2 And when he was called upon,
Tertullus began his accusation,
saying: "Seeing that through you

we enjoy great peace, and prosperity
is being brought to this nation
by your foresight,
3 "we accept *it* always and in all
places, most noble Felix, with all
thankfulness.
4 "Nevertheless, not to be tedious
to you any further, I beg you to
hear, by your courtesy, a few
words from us.
5 "For we have found this man *a*
plague, a creator of dissension
among all the Jews throughout the
world, and a ringleader of the sect
of the Nazarenes.
6 "He even tried to profane the
temple, and we seized him, and
wanted to judge him according to
our law.
7 "But the commander Lysias
came by and with great violence
took *him* out of our hands,
8 "commanding his accusers to
come to you. By examining him
yourself you may ascertain all
these things of which we accuse
him."
9 And the Jews also assented,
maintaining that these things were
so.
10 Then Paul, after the governor
had nodded to him to speak, answered:
"Inasmuch as I know that
you have been for many years a
judge of this nation, I do the more
cheerfully answer for myself,
11 "because you may ascertain
that it is no more than twelve days
since I went up to Jerusalem to
worship.
12 "And they neither found me in
the temple disputing with anyone
nor inciting the crowd, either in
the synagogues or in the city.
13 "Nor can they prove the things
of which they now accuse me.
14 "But this I confess to you, that
according to the Way which they
call a sect, so I worship the God of
my fathers, believing all things
which are written in the Law and
in the Prophets.
15 "I have hope in God, which they
themselves also accept, that there

195

will be a resurrection of *the* dead, both of *the* just and *the* unjust.

16 "This *being* so, I myself always strive to have a conscience without offense toward God and men.

17 "Now after many years I came to bring alms and offerings to my nation,

18 "in the midst of which some Jews from Asia found me purified in the temple, neither with a multitude nor with tumult.

19 "They ought to have been here before you to object if they had anything against me.

20 "Or else let those who are *here* themselves say if they found any wrongdoing in me while I stood before the council,

21 "unless *it is* for this one statement which I cried out, standing among them, 'Concerning the resurrection of the dead I am being judged by you this day.' "

22 But when Felix heard these things, having more accurate knowledge of *the* Way, he adjourned the proceedings and said, "When Lysias the commander comes down, I will make a decision on your case."

23 So he commanded the centurion to keep Paul and to let *him* have liberty, and told him not to forbid any of his friends to provide for or visit him.

24 And after some days, when Felix came with his wife Drusilla, who was Jewish, he sent for Paul and heard him concerning the faith in Christ.

25 Now as he reasoned about righteousness, self-control, and the judgment to come, Felix was afraid and answered, "Go away for now; when I have a convenient time I will call for you."

26 Meanwhile he also hoped that money would be given him by Paul, that he might release him. Therefore he sent for him more often and conversed with him.

27 But after two years Porcius Festus succeeded Felix; and Felix,

wanting to do the Jews a favor, left Paul bound.

25 Now when Festus had come to the province, after three days he went up from Caesarea to Jerusalem.

2 Then the high priest and the chief men of the Jews informed him against Paul; and they petitioned him,

3 asking a favor against him, that he would summon him to Jerusalem—while *they* lay in ambush along the road to kill him.

4 But Festus answered that Paul should be kept at Caesarea, and that he himself was going *there* shortly.

5 "Therefore," he said, "let those who have authority among you go down with *me* and accuse this man, to see if there is any fault in him."

6 And when he had remained among them more than ten days, he went down to Caesarea. And the next day, sitting on the judgment seat, he commanded Paul to be brought.

7 When he had come, the Jews who had come down from Jerusalem stood about and laid many serious complaints against Paul, which they could not prove,

8 while he answered for himself, "Neither against the law of the Jews, nor against the temple, nor against Caesar have I offended in anything at all."

9 But Festus, wanting to do the Jews a favor, answered Paul and said, "Are you willing to go up to Jerusalem and there be judged before me concerning these things?"

10 Then Paul said, "I stand at Caesar's judgment seat, where I ought to be judged. To the Jews I have done no wrong, as you very well know.

11 "For if I am an offender, or have committed anything worthy of death, I do not object to dying; but if there is nothing in these things of which these men accuse me, no

one can deliver me to them. I appeal to Caesar."

12 Then Festus, when he had conferred with the council, answered, "You have appealed to Caesar? To Caesar you shall go!"

13 And after some days King Agrippa and Bernice came to Caesarea to greet Festus.

14 When they had been there many days, Festus laid Paul's case before the king, saying: "There is a certain man left a prisoner by Felix,

15 "about whom the chief priests and the elders of the Jews informed *me*, when I was in Jerusalem, asking for a judgment against him.

16 "To them I answered, 'It is not the custom of the Romans to deliver any man to destruction before the accused meets the accusers face to face, and has opportunity to answer for himself concerning the charge against him.'

17 "Therefore when they had come together, without any delay, the next day I sat on the judgment seat and commanded the man to be brought in.

18 "When the accusers stood up, they brought no accusation against him of such things as I supposed,

19 "but had some questions against him about their own religion and about one, Jesus, who had died, whom Paul affirmed to be alive.

20 "And because I was uncertain of such questions, I asked whether he was willing to go to Jerusalem and there be judged concerning these matters.

21 "But when Paul appealed to be reserved for the decision of Augustus, I commanded him to be kept till I could send him to Caesar."

22 Then Agrippa said to Festus, "I also would like to hear the man myself." "Tomorrow," he said, "you shall hear him."

23 So the next day, when Agrippa and Bernice had come with great pomp, and had entered the auditorium with the commanders and the prominent men of the city, at Festus' command Paul was brought in.

24 And Festus said: "King Agrippa and all the men who are here present with us, you see this man about whom the whole assembly of the Jews petitioned me, both at Jerusalem and here, crying out that he was not fit to live any longer.

25 "But when I found that he had committed nothing worthy of death, and that he himself had appealed to Augustus, I decided to send him.

26 "I have nothing certain to write to my lord concerning him. Therefore I have brought him out before you, and especially before you, King Agrippa, so that after the examination has taken place I may have something to write.

27 "For it seems to me unreasonable to send a prisoner and not to specify the charges against him."

26 Then Agrippa said to Paul, "You are permitted to speak for yourself." So Paul stretched out his hand and answered for himself:

2 "I think myself happy, King Agrippa, because today I shall answer for myself before you concerning all the things of which I am accused by the Jews,

3 "especially because you are expert in all customs and questions which have to do with the Jews. Therefore I beg you to hear me patiently.

4 "My manner of life from my youth, which was spent from the beginning among my own nation at Jerusalem, all the Jews know.

5 "They knew me from the first, if they were willing to testify, that according to the strictest sect of our religion I lived a Pharisee.

6 "And now I stand and am

judged for the hope of the promise made by God to our fathers.

7 "To this *promise* our twelve tribes, earnestly serving God night and day, hope to attain. For this hope's sake, King Agrippa, I am accused by the Jews.

8 "Why should it be thought incredible by you that God raises the dead?

9 "Indeed, I myself thought I must do many things contrary to the name of Jesus of Nazareth.

10 "This I also did in Jerusalem, and many of the saints I shut up in prison, having received authority from the chief priests; and when they were put to death, I cast my vote against *them*.

11 "And I punished them often in every synagogue and compelled *them* to blaspheme; and being exceedingly enraged against them, I persecuted *them* even to foreign cities.

12 "While thus occupied, as I journeyed to Damascus with authority and commission from the chief priests,

13 "at midday, O king, along the road I saw a light from heaven, brighter than the sun, shining around me and those who journeyed with me.

14 "And when we all had fallen to the ground, I heard a voice speaking to me and saying in the Hebrew language, 'Saul, Saul, why are you persecuting Me? *It is* hard for you to kick against the goads.'

15 "So I said, 'Who are You, Lord?' And He said, 'I am Jesus, whom you are persecuting.

16 'But rise and stand on your feet; for I have appeared to you for this purpose, to make you a minister and a witness both of the things which you have seen and of the things which I will yet reveal to you.

17 'I will deliver you from the *Jewish* people, as well as *from* the Gentiles, to whom I now send you,

18 'to open their eyes *and* to turn them from darkness to light, and *from* the power of Satan to God, that they may receive forgiveness of sins and an inheritance among those who are sanctified by faith in Me.'

19 "Therefore, King Agrippa, I was not disobedient to the heavenly vision,

20 "but declared first to those in Damascus and in Jerusalem, and throughout all the region of Judea, and *then* to the Gentiles, that they should repent, turn to God, and do works befitting repentance.

21 "For these reasons the Jews seized me in the temple and tried to kill *me*.

22 "Therefore, having obtained help from God, to this day I stand, witnessing both to small and great, saying no other things than those which the prophets and Moses said would come—

23 "that the Christ would suffer, that He would be the first to rise from the dead, and would proclaim light to the *Jewish* people and to the Gentiles."

24 Now as he thus made his defense, Festus said with a loud voice, "Paul, you are beside yourself! Much learning is driving you mad!"

25 But he said, "I am not mad, most noble Festus, but speak the words of truth and reason.

26 "For the king, before whom I also speak freely, knows these things; for I am convinced that none of these things escapes his attention, since this thing was not done in a corner.

27 "King Agrippa, do you believe the prophets? I know that you do believe."

28 Then Agrippa said to Paul, "You almost persuade me to become a Christian."

29 And Paul said, "I would to God that not only you, but also all who hear me today, might become both almost and altogether such as I am, except for these chains."

30 When he had said these things, the king stood up, as well as the governor and Bernice and those who sat with them;

31 and when they had gone aside, they talked among themselves, saying, "This man is doing nothing worthy of death or chains."

32 Then Agrippa said to Festus, "This man might have been set free if he had not appealed to Caesar."

27 And when it was decided that we should sail to Italy, they delivered Paul and some other prisoners to *one* named Julius, a centurion of the Augustan Regiment.

2 So, entering a ship of Adramyttium, we put to sea, meaning to sail along the coasts of Asia. Aristarchus, a Macedonian of Thessalonica, was with us.

3 And the next *day* we landed at Sidon. And Julius treated Paul kindly and gave *him* liberty to go to his friends and receive care.

4 When we had put to sea from there, we sailed under *the shelter of* Cyprus, because the winds were contrary.

5 And when we had sailed over the sea which is off Cilicia and Pamphylia, we came to Myra, *a city* of Lycia.

6 There the centurion found an Alexandrian ship sailing to Italy, and he put us on board.

7 And when we had sailed slowly many days, and arrived with difficulty off Cnidus, the wind not permitting us to proceed, we sailed under *the* shelter of Crete off Salmone.

8 Passing it with difficulty, we came to a place called Fair Havens, near the city *of* Lasea.

9 Now when much time had been spent, and sailing was now dangerous because the Fast was already over, Paul advised them,

10 saying, "Men, I perceive that this voyage will end with disaster and much loss, not only of the cargo and ship, but also our lives."

11 Nevertheless the centurion was more persuaded by the helmsman and the owner of the ship than by the things spoken by Paul.

12 And because the harbor was not suitable to winter in, the majority advised to set sail from there also, if by any means they could reach Phoenix, a harbor of Crete opening toward the southwest and northwest, *and* winter *there*.

13 When the south wind blew softly, supposing that they had obtained *their* purpose, putting out to sea, they sailed close by Crete.

14 But not long after, a tempestuous head wind arose, called Euroclydon.

15 So when the ship was caught, and could not head into the wind, we let *her* drive.

16 And running under *the shelter of* an island called Clauda, we secured the skiff with difficulty.

17 When they had taken it on board, they used cables to undergird the ship; and fearing lest they should run aground on the Syrtis *Sands*, they struck sail and so were driven.

18 And because we were exceedingly tempest-tossed, the next *day* they lightened the ship.

19 On the third *day* we threw the ship's tackle overboard with our own hands.

20 Now when neither sun nor stars appeared for many days, and no small tempest beat on *us*, all hope that we would be saved was finally given up.

21 But after long abstinence from food, then Paul stood in the midst of them and said, "Men, you should have listened to me, and not have sailed from Crete and incurred this disaster and loss.

22 "And now I urge you to take heart, for there will be no loss of life among you, but only of the ship.

23 "For there stood by me this night an angel of the God to whom I belong and whom I serve,

24 "saying, 'Do not be afraid, Paul; you must be brought before Caesar; and indeed God has granted you all those who sail with you.'

25 "Therefore take heart, men, for I believe God that it will be just as it was told me.

26 "However, we must run aground on a certain island."

27 But when the fourteenth night had come, as we were driven up and down in the Adriatic *Sea*, about midnight the sailors sensed that they were drawing near some land.

28 And they took soundings and found *it* to be twenty fathoms; and when they had gone a little farther, they took soundings again and found *it* to be fifteen fathoms.

29 Then, fearing lest we should run aground on the rocks, they dropped four anchors from the stern, and prayed for day to come.

30 And as the sailors were seeking to escape from the ship, when they had let down the skiff into the sea, under pretense of putting out anchors from the prow,

31 Paul said to the centurion and the soldiers, "Unless these men stay in the ship, you cannot be saved."

32 Then the soldiers cut away the ropes of the skiff and let it fall off.

33 And as day was about to dawn, Paul implored *them* all to take food, saying, "Today is the fourteenth day you have waited and continued without food, and eaten nothing.

34 "Therefore I urge you to take nourishment, for this is for your survival, since not a hair will fall from the head of any of you."

35 And when he had said these things, he took bread and gave thanks to God in the presence of them all; and when he had broken *it* he began to eat.

36 Then they were all encouraged, and also took food themselves.

37 And in all we were two hundred and seventy-six persons on the ship.

38 So when they had eaten enough, they lightened the ship and threw out the wheat into the sea.

39 Now when it was day, they did not recognize the land; but they observed a bay with a beach, onto which they planned to run the ship if possible.

40 And they let go the anchors and left *them* in the sea, meanwhile loosing the rudder ropes; and they hoisted the mainsail to the wind and made for shore.

41 But striking a place where two seas met, they ran the ship aground; and the prow stuck fast and remained immovable, but the stern was being broken up by the violence of the waves.

42 Now the soldiers' plan was to kill the prisoners, lest any of them should swim away and escape.

43 But the centurion, wanting to save Paul, kept them from *their* purpose, and commanded that those who could swim should jump *overboard* first and get to land,

44 and the rest, some on boards and some on *broken pieces* of the ship. And so it was that they all escaped safely to land.

28

Now when they had escaped, they then found out that the island was called Malta.

2 And the natives showed us unusual kindness; for they kindled a fire and made us all welcome, because of the rain that was falling and because of the cold.

3 But when Paul had gathered a bundle of sticks and laid *them* on the fire, a viper came out because of the heat, and fastened on his hand.

4 So when the natives saw the creature hanging from his hand, they said to one another, "No

doubt this man is a murderer, whom, though he has escaped the sea, yet justice does not allow to live."

5 But he shook off the creature into the fire and suffered no harm.

6 However, they were expecting that he would swell up or suddenly fall down dead; but after they had looked for a long time and saw no harm come to him, they changed their minds and said that he was a god.

7 Now in that region there was an estate of the leading citizen of the island, whose name was Publius, who received us and entertained us courteously for three days.

8 And it happened that the father of Publius lay sick of a fever and dysentery. Paul went in to him and prayed, and he laid his hands on him and healed him.

9 So when this was done, the rest of those on the island who had diseases also came and were healed.

10 They also honored us in many ways; and when we departed, they provided such things as were necessary.

11 After three months we sailed in an Alexandrian ship whose figurehead was the Twin Brothers, which had wintered at the island.

12 And landing at Syracuse, we stayed three days.

13 From there we circled round and reached Rhegium. And after one day the south wind blew; and the next day we came to Puteoli,

14 where we found brethren, and were invited to stay with them seven days. And so we went toward Rome.

15 And from there, when the brethren heard about us, they came to meet us as far as Appii Forum and Three Inns. When Paul saw them, he thanked God and took courage.

16 Now when we came to Rome, the centurion delivered the prisoners to the captain of the guard; but Paul was permitted to dwell by himself with the soldier who guarded him.

17 And it came to pass after three days that Paul called the leaders of the Jews together. So when they had come together, he said to them: "Men *and* brethren, though I have done nothing against our people or the customs of our fathers, yet I was delivered as a prisoner from Jerusalem into the hands of the Romans,

18 "who, when they had examined me, wanted to let *me* go, because there was no cause for putting me to death.

19 "But when the Jews spoke against *it*, I was compelled to appeal to Caesar, not that I had anything of which to accuse my nation.

20 "For this reason therefore I have called for you, to see *you* and speak with *you*, because for the hope of Israel I am bound with this chain."

21 And they said to him, "We neither received letters from Judea concerning you, nor have any of the brethren who came reported or spoken any evil of you.

22 "But we desire to hear from you what you think; for concerning this sect, we know that it is spoken against everywhere."

23 So when they had appointed him a day, many came to him at *his* lodging, to whom he explained and solemnly testified of the kingdom of God, persuading them concerning Jesus from both the Law of Moses and the Prophets, from morning till evening.

24 And some were persuaded by the things which were spoken, and some disbelieved.

25 So when they did not agree among themselves, they departed after Paul had said one word: "The Holy Spirit spoke rightly through Isaiah the prophet to our fathers,

26 "saying,

'Go to this people and say:
"Hearing you will hear,
    and shall not understand;
And seeing you will see,
    and not perceive;
27 For the heart of this people
    has grown dull.
Their ears are hard of hearing,
    And their eyes they have
        closed,
Lest they should see with their
    eyes and hear with their ears,
Lest they should understand
    with their heart and turn,
So that I should heal them." '

28 "Therefore let it be known to you that the salvation of God has been sent to the Gentiles, and they will hear it!"

29 And when he had said these words, the Jews departed and had a great dispute among themselves.

30 Then Paul dwelt two whole years in his own rented house, and received all who came to him,

31 preaching the kingdom of God and teaching the things which concern the Lord Jesus Christ with all confidence, no one forbidding him.

THE EPISTLE OF PAUL THE APOSTLE TO THE

ROMANS

PAUL, a servant of Jesus Christ, called *to be* an apostle, separated to the gospel of God

2 which He promised before through His prophets in the Holy Scriptures,

3 concerning His Son Jesus Christ our Lord, who was born of the seed of David according to the flesh,

4 and declared *to be* the Son of God with power, according to the Spirit of holiness, by the resurrection from the dead,

5 through whom we have received grace and apostleship for obedience to the faith among all nations for His name,

6 among whom you also are the called of Jesus Christ;

7 To all who are in Rome, beloved of God, called *to be* saints:

Grace to you and peace from God our Father and the Lord Jesus Christ.

8 First, I thank my God through Jesus Christ for you all, that your faith is spoken of throughout the whole world.

9 For God is my witness, whom I serve with my spirit in the gospel of His Son, that without ceasing I make mention of you always in my prayers,

10 making request if, by some means, now at last I may find a way in the will of God to come to you.

11 For I long to see you, that I may impart to you some spiritual gift, so that you may be established—

12 that is, that I may be encouraged together with you by the mutual faith both of you and me.

13 Now I do not want you to be unaware, brethren, that I often planned to come to you (but was hindered until now), that I might have some fruit among you also, just as among the other Gentiles.

14 I am a debtor both to Greeks and to barbarians, both to wise and to unwise.

15 So, as much as is in me, *I am* ready to preach the gospel to you who are in Rome also.

16 For I am not ashamed of the gospel of Christ, for it is the power of God to salvation for everyone

who believes, for the Jew first and also for the Greek.

17 For in it the righteousness of God is revealed from faith to faith; as it is written, *"The just shall live by faith."*

18 For the wrath of God is revealed from heaven against all ungodliness and unrighteousness of men, who suppress the truth in unrighteousness,

19 because what may be known of God is manifest in them, for God has shown *it* to them.

20 For since the creation of the world His invisible *attributes* are clearly seen, being understood by the things that are made, *even* His eternal power and Godhead, so that they are without excuse,

21 because, although they knew God, they did not glorify *Him* as God, nor were thankful, but became futile in their thoughts, and their foolish hearts were darkened.

22 Professing to be wise, they became fools,

23 and changed the glory of the incorruptible God into an image made like corruptible man—and birds and four-footed beasts and creeping things.

24 Therefore God also gave them up to uncleanness, in the lusts of their hearts, to dishonor their bodies among themselves,

25 who exchanged the truth of God for the lie, and worshiped and served the creature rather than the Creator, who is blessed forever. Amen.

26 For this reason God gave them up to vile passions. For even their women exchanged the natural use for what is against nature.

27 Likewise also the men, leaving the natural use of the woman, burned in their lust for one another, men with men committing what is shameful, and receiving in themselves the penalty of their error which was due.

28 And even as they did not like to retain God in *their* knowledge,

God gave them over to a debased mind, to do those things which are not fitting;

29 being filled with all unrighteousness, sexual immorality, wickedness, covetousness, maliciousness; full of envy, murder, strife, deceit, evil-mindedness; *they are* whisperers,

30 backbiters, haters of God, violent, proud, boasters, inventors of evil things, disobedient to parents,

31 undiscerning, untrustworthy, unloving, unforgiving, unmerciful;

32 who, knowing the righteous judgment of God, that those who practice such things are worthy of death, not only do the same but also approve of those who practice them.

2 Therefore you are inexcusable, O man, whoever you are who judge, for in whatever you judge another you condemn yourself; for you who judge practice the same things.

2 But we know that the judgment of God is according to truth against those who practice such things.

3 And do you think this, O man, you who judge those practicing such things, and doing the same, that you will escape the judgment of God?

4 Or do you despise the riches of His goodness, forbearance, and longsuffering, not knowing that the goodness of God leads you to repentance?

5 But in accordance with your hardness and your impenitent heart you are treasuring up for yourself wrath in the day of wrath and revelation of the righteous judgment of God,

6 who *"will render to each one according to his deeds"*:

7 eternal life to those who by patient continuance in doing good seek for glory, honor, and immortality;

8 but to those who are self-seeking and do not obey the truth, but

Who Needs God?

Observation #1: "I don't need God; I'm doing fine without Him. I have satisfying relationships, plenty of money, and an assortment of friends. I'm in good health and like my job."

Question: What can you give someone who thinks he has everything?

Answer: Nothing. (See Matthew 16:26.)

Observation #2: "I don't have time for God. I leave Him alone, and He leaves me alone."

Question: How much time does someone have who doesn't have time for God?

Answer: Less than he thinks. (See Luke 12:16–21.)

Observation #3: "What has God ever done for me? Everything I have I earned for myself."

Question: What does the self-made person never have?

Answer: A grateful heart.

Here's a quotation often credited to the sixteenth-century philosopher Blaise Pascal: "There is a God-shaped vacuum in the heart of every man [and woman] that cannot be filled by any created thing but only by the Creator made known through Jesus Christ."

Whoever said these words certainly picked his analogy of the vacuum well. He knew that there are no natural vacuums on earth; vacuums are always a conscious act of creation. He also knew that it is the nature of a vacuum to fill itself with something. So he concludes that, when someone creates a vacuum, He probably has something specific in mind to fill it with.

In Romans 1:21, the apostle Paul warns of the destructive path of filling that God-shaped vacuum with anything but God. The journey begins by ignoring God; is compounded by a thankless attitude toward God; and ends up trying to explain away God. And it results in a foolish, darkened mind and a hardened heart unable to see a need for God.

Question: Who needs God?
Answer: Everyone.

Question: Who is aware of their need for God?
Answer:
—Those who see there's more to life than earthly pleasures.
—Those who spend time with God.
—Those who have a realistic perspective of their standing in the universe. (See Romans 6:8–11.)
—Perhaps one more than when you began to read this article.

obey unrighteousness—indignation and wrath,

9 tribulation and anguish, on every soul of man who does evil, of the Jew first and also of the Greek;

10 but glory, honor, and peace to everyone who works what is good, to the Jew first and also to the Greek.

11 For there is no partiality with God.

12 For as many as have sinned without law will also perish without law, and as many as have sinned in the law will be judged by the law

13 (for not the hearers of the law *are* just in the sight of God, but the doers of the law will be justified;

14 for when Gentiles, who do not have the law, by nature do the things *contained* in the law, these, although not having the law, are a law to themselves,

15 who show the work of the law written in their hearts, their conscience also bearing witness, and between themselves *their* thoughts accusing or else excusing *them*)

16 in the day when God will judge the secrets of men by Jesus Christ, according to my gospel.

17 Indeed you are called a Jew, and rest on the law, and make your boast in God,

18 and know His will, and approve the things that are excellent, being instructed out of the law,

19 and are confident that you yourself are a guide to the blind, a light to those who are in darkness,

20 an instructor of the foolish, a teacher of babes, having the form of knowledge and truth in the law,

21 You, therefore, who teach another, do you not teach yourself? You who preach that a man should not steal, do you steal?

22 You who say, "Do not commit adultery," do you commit adultery? You who abhor idols, do you rob temples?

23 You who make your boast in

the law, do you dishonor God through breaking the law?

24 For *"The name of God is blasphemed among the Gentiles because of you,"* as it is written.

25 For circumcision is indeed profitable if you keep the law; but if you are a breaker of the law, your circumcision has become uncircumcision.

26 Therefore, if an uncircumcised man keeps the righteous requirements of the law, will not his uncircumcision be counted as circumcision?

27 And will not the physically uncircumcised, if he fulfills the law, judge you who, *even* with *your* written *code* and circumcision, *are* a transgressor of the law?

28 For he is not a Jew who *is one* outwardly, nor *is* that circumcision *which is* outward in the flesh;

29 but *he is* a Jew who *is one* inwardly; and circumcision *is that* of the heart, in the Spirit, *and* not in the letter; whose praise *is* not from men but from God.

3 What advantage then has the Jew, or what *is* the profit of circumcision?

2 Much in every way! Chiefly because to them were committed the oracles of God.

3 For what if some did not believe? Will their unbelief make the faithfulness of God without effect?

4 Certainly not! Indeed, let God be true but every man a liar. As it is written:

> *"That You may be justified*
> *in Your words,*
> *And may overcome when*
> *You are judged."*

5 But if our unrighteousness demonstrates the righteousness of God, what shall we say? *Is* God unjust who inflicts wrath? (I speak as a man.)

6 Certainly not! For then how will God judge the world?

7 For if the truth of God has in-

creased through my lie to His glory, why am I also still judged as a sinner?

8 And *why* not *say*, "Let us do evil that good may come"?—as we are slanderously reported and as some affirm that we say. Their condemnation is just.

9 What then? Are we better *than they*? Not at all. For we have previously charged both Jews and Greeks that they are all under sin.

10 As it is written:

"There is none righteous, no, not one;

11 There is none who understands;
There is none who seeks after God.

12 They have all gone out of the way;
They have together become unprofitable;
There is none who does good, no, not one."

13 "Their throat is an open tomb;
With their tongues they have practiced deceit";
"The poison of asps is under their lips";

14 "Whose mouth is full of cursing and bitterness."

15 "Their feet are swift to shed blood;

16 Destruction and misery are in their ways;

17 And the way of peace they have not known."

18 "There is no fear of God before their eyes."

19 Now we know that whatever the law says, it says to those who are under the law, that every mouth may be stopped, and all the world may become guilty before God.

20 Therefore by the deeds of the law no flesh will be justified in His sight, for by the law *is* the knowledge of sin.

21 But now the righteousness of God apart from the law is revealed,

being witnessed by the Law and the Prophets,

22 even the righteousness of God *which is* through faith in Jesus Christ to all and on all who believe. For there is no difference;

23 for all have sinned and fall short of the glory of God,

24 being justified freely by His grace through the redemption that is in Christ Jesus,

25 whom God set forth *to be* a propitiation by His blood, through faith, to demonstrate His righteousness, because in His forbearance God had passed over the sins that were previously committed,

26 to demonstrate at the present time His righteousness, that He might be just and the justifier of the one who has faith in Jesus.

27 Where *is* boasting then? It is excluded. By what law? Of works? No, but by the law of faith.

28 Therefore we conclude that a man is justified by faith apart from the deeds of the law.

29 Or *is* He the God of the Jews only? *Is He* not also the God of the Gentiles? Yes, of the Gentiles also,

30 since *there is* one God who will justify the circumcised by faith and the uncircumcised through faith.

31 Do we then make void the law through faith? Certainly not! On the contrary, we establish the law.

4 What then shall we say that Abraham our father has found according to the flesh?

2 For if Abraham was justified by works, he has *something of which* to boast, but not before God.

3 For what does the Scripture say? *"Abraham believed God, and it was accounted to him for righteousness."*

4 Now to him who works, the wages are not counted as grace but as debt.

5 But to him who does not work but believes on Him who justifies the ungodly, his faith is accounted for righteousness,

Isn't "Just Believing" Too Simple?

Most beliefs do not stand or fall alone. For example, if you believe the world is rounded, not flat, that belief is probably connected to a series of other beliefs. You probably also have a general confidence in the findings of science, and you bring to your conclusion an implicit trust that the pictures showing the curve of the earth are not fake. If you seriously doubted any of these facts, you might begin to wonder if the earth were not flat after all!

Christian belief also has a context. A mature and grounded faith embraces an increasingly rich complex of interwoven beliefs. In Romans, the apostle Paul connects one's commitment to certain facts with the notion of faith.

Example: In Romans 4:2–5, Paul contrasts human effort to gain salvation with faith in what God has done on our behalf. Raised and educated as a Jew, Paul had believed that by his own efforts (works) he could please God. But here Paul argues that even Abraham, the father of the Jewish nation, didn't earn God's favor with his good works. Instead, Abraham believed (trusted) God. God, in turn, treated Abraham as if he were completely good

(righteous). Abraham had not earned God's favor. Rather, God gave (accounted) to Abraham a perfect standing before God as a free gift of grace.

Read the following passages from Romans for a sampling of the facts that form a foundation for faith. For a shorter study, look up only the references with an asterisk.

*1:16, 17
3:21–26
*4:20–24
5:1–5
*6:4–9
8:22–25
*10:8–11
12:1, 2

Don't be disturbed if you can't immediately grasp all you read in Romans. It's comforting that even Peter, the head of the early church, sometimes found Paul's letters difficult (2 Peter 3:14–16). But he also considered them on a level with "the rest of the Scriptures" and well worth the effort to study and understand. (It might also help you to refer to page 363 for "What Do These Biblical Terms Mean?" to better understand some of the terms Paul uses.)

For further studies of faith, see John 1:12 and Acts 4:32.

6 just as David also describes the blessedness of the man to whom God imputes righteousness apart from works:

7 *"Blessed are those whose*
 lawless deeds are forgiven,
 And whose sins are covered;
8 *Blessed is the man to whom*
 the LORD shall not impute
 sin."

9 Does this blessedness then *come* upon the circumcised *only,* or upon the uncircumcised also? For we say that faith was accounted to Abraham for righteousness.
10 How then was it accounted? While he was circumcised, or uncircumcised? Not while circumcised, but while uncircumcised.
11 And he received the sign of circumcision, a seal of the righteousness of the faith which *he had while still* uncircumcised, that he might be the father of all those who believe, though they are uncircumcised, that righteousness might be imputed to them also,
12 and the father of circumcision to those who not only *are* of the circumcision, but who also walk in the steps of the faith which our father Abraham *had while still* uncircumcised.
13 For the promise that he would be the heir of the world *was* not to Abraham or to his seed through the law, but through the righteousness of faith.
14 For if those who are of the law *are* heirs, faith is made void and the promise made of no effect,
15 because the law brings about wrath; for where there is no law *there is* no transgression.
16 Therefore *it is* of faith that it *might be* according to grace, so that the promise might be sure to all the seed, not only to those who are of the law, but also to those who are of the faith of Abraham, who is the father of us all

17 (as it is written, *"I have made you a father of many nations"*) in the presence of Him whom he believed, *even* God, who gives life to the dead and calls those things which do not exist as though they did;
18 who, contrary to hope, in hope believed, so that he became the father of many nations, according to what was spoken, *"So shall your descendants be."*
19 And not being weak in faith, he did not consider his own body, already dead (since he was about a hundred years old), and the deadness of Sarah's womb.
20 He did not waver at the promise of God through unbelief, but was strengthened in faith, giving glory to God,
21 and being fully convinced that what He had promised He was also able to perform.
22 And therefore *"it was accounted to him for righteousness."*
23 Now it was not written for his sake alone that it was imputed to him,
24 but also for us. It shall be imputed to us who believe in Him who raised up Jesus our Lord from the dead,
25 who was delivered up because of our offenses, and was raised because of our justification.

5 Therefore, having been justified by faith, we have peace with God through our Lord Jesus Christ,
2 through whom also we have access by faith into this grace in which we stand, and rejoice in hope of the glory of God.
3 And not only *that,* but we also glory in tribulations, knowing that tribulation produces perseverance;
4 and perseverance, character; and character, hope.
5 Now hope does not disappoint, because the love of God has been poured out in our hearts by the Holy Spirit who was given to us.
6 For when we were still without

strength, in due time Christ died for the ungodly.

For scarcely for a righteous man will one die; yet perhaps for a good man someone would even dare to die.

8 But God demonstrates His own love toward us, in that while we were still sinners, Christ died for us.

9 Much more then, having now been justified by His blood, we shall be saved from wrath through Him.

10 For if when we were enemies we were reconciled to God through the death of His Son, much more, having been reconciled, we shall be saved by His life.

11 And not only *that*, but we also rejoice in God through our Lord Jesus Christ, through whom we have now received the reconciliation.

12 Therefore, just as through one man sin entered the world, and death through sin, and thus death spread to all men, because all sinned—

13 (For until the law sin was in the world, but sin is not imputed when there is no law.

14 Nevertheless death reigned from Adam to Moses, even over those who had not sinned according to the likeness of the transgression of Adam, who is a type of Him who was to come.

15 But the free gift *is* not like the offense. For if by the one man's offense many died, much more the grace of God and the gift by the grace of the one Man, Jesus Christ, abounded to many.

16 And the gift *is* not like *that which came* through the one who sinned. For the judgment *which came* from one *offense resulted in* condemnation, but the free gift *which came* from many offenses *resulted in* justification.

17 For if by the one man's offense death reigned through the one, much more those who receive abundance of grace and of the gift of righteousness will reign in life through the One, Jesus Christ.)

18 Therefore, as through one man's offense *judgment* came to all men, resulting in condemnation, even so through one Man's righteous act *the free gift came* to all men, resulting in justification of life.

19 For as by one man's disobedience many were made sinners, so also by one Man's obedience many will be made righteous.

20 Moreover the law entered that the offense might abound. But where sin abounded, grace abounded much more,

21 so that as sin reigned in death, even so grace might reign through righteousness to eternal life through Jesus Christ our Lord.

6 What shall we say then? Shall we continue in sin that grace may abound?

2 Certainly not! How shall we who died to sin live any longer in it?

3 Or do you not know that as many of us as were baptized into Christ Jesus were baptized into His death?

4 Therefore we were buried with Him through baptism into death, that just as Christ was raised from the dead by the glory of the Father, even so we also should walk in newness of life.

5 For if we have been united together in the likeness of His death, certainly we also shall be *in the likeness of His* resurrection,

6 knowing this, that our old man was crucified with *Him*, that the body of sin might be done away with, that we should no longer be slaves of sin.

7 For he who has died has been freed from sin.

8 Now if we died with Christ, we believe that we shall also live with Him,

9 knowing that Christ, having

Was There Death Before Adam Sinned?

Some people interpret Romans 5:12 as saying that death didn't exist before Adam's sin, and, thus, only a few days could have transpired between the creation of the first life and Adam's sin. But whether it was days or years from the first sin to the first death is immaterial, for many species of life can't survive even three hours without food. And the ingestion of food requires the death of at least some living things, such as plants or plant parts.

One way people try to get around this problem is to say that this "death through sin" applies only to higher creatures—birds and mammals and maybe a few advanced reptiles. But of all life on earth, only human beings have earned the title "sinners." And the test says that the death Adam introduced is visited on "all men"—

no mention of plants and animals, just human beings (Romans 5:12, 18; 1 Corinthians 15:20–22).

The key point is that Romans 5:12 addresses a spiritual death, and of all life on earth, only humans are spiritual. When Adam first sinned, he instantly "died," just as God said he would ("in the day that you eat of it you shall surely die"—Genesis 2:17). Yet he remained alive physically, mentally, and emotionally. He died spiritually. He lost face-to-face companionship with God and gained an inclination to defy God.

After Adam died (spiritually), God blocked Adam's access to the "tree of life" (Genesis 3:22–24). Apparently Adam had the potential to live forever physically, even after his sin, *if* he ate from that special tree. But eternal physical life wouldn't be good for Adam or his descendants, who inherited his inclination to sin, because evil would be unrestrained.

been raised from the dead, dies no more. Death no longer has dominion over Him.

10 For *the death* that He died, He died to sin once for all; but *the life* that He lives, He lives to God.

11 Likewise you also, reckon yourselves to be dead indeed to sin, but alive to God in Christ Jesus our Lord.

12 Therefore do not let sin reign in your mortal body, that you should obey it in its lusts.

13 And do not present your members *as* instruments of unrighteousness to sin, but present yourselves to God as being alive from the dead, and your members *as* instruments of righteousness to God.

14 For sin shall not have dominion over you, for you are not under law but under grace.

15 What then? Shall we sin because we are not under law but under grace? Certainly not!

16 Do you not know that to whom you present yourselves slaves to obey, you are that one's slaves whom you obey, whether of sin to death, or of obedience to righteousness?

17 But God be thanked that *though* you were slaves of sin, yet you obeyed from the heart that form of doctrine to which you were delivered.

18 And having been set free from sin, you became slaves of righteousness.

19 I speak in human *terms* because of the weakness of your flesh. For just as you presented your members *as* slaves of uncleanness, and of lawlessness *leading* to *more* lawlessness, so now present your members *as* slaves *of* righteousness for holiness.

20 For when you were slaves of sin, you were free in regard to righteousness.

21 What fruit did you have then in the things of which you are now

ashamed? For the end of those things *is* death.

22 But now having been set free from sin, and having become slaves of God, you have your fruit to holiness, and the end, everlasting life.

23 For the wages of sin *is* death, but the gift of God *is* eternal life in Christ Jesus our Lord.

7 Or do you not know, brethren (for I speak to those who know the law), that the law has dominion over a man as long as he lives?

2 For the woman who has a husband is bound by the law to *her* husband as long as he lives. But if the husband dies, she is released from the law of *her* husband.

3 So then if, while *her* husband lives, she marries another man, she will be called an adulteress; but if her husband dies, she is free from that law, so that she is no adulteress, though she has married another man.

4 Therefore, my brethren, you also have become dead to the law through the body of Christ, that you may be married to another, *even* to Him who was raised from the dead, that we should bear fruit to God.

5 For when we were in the flesh, the passions of sins which were aroused by the law were at work in our members to bear fruit to death.

6 But now we have been delivered from the law, having died to what we were held by, so that we should serve in the newness of the Spirit and not *in* the oldness of the letter.

7 What shall we say then? *Is* the law sin? Certainly not! On the contrary, I would not have known sin except through the law. For I would not have known covetousness unless the law had said, *"You shall not covet."*

8 But sin, taking opportunity by the commandment, produced in me all *manner of evil* desire. For apart from the law sin *was* dead.

9 I was alive once without the law, but when the commandment came, sin revived and I died.

10 And the commandment, which *was* to *bring* life, I found to *bring* death.

11 For sin, taking occasion by the commandment, deceived me, and by it killed *me*.

12 Therefore the law *is* holy, and the commandment holy and just and good.

13 Has then what is good become death to me? Certainly not! But sin, that it might appear sin, was producing death in me through what is good, so that sin through the commandment might become exceedingly sinful.

14 For we know that the law is spiritual, but I am carnal, sold under sin.

15 For what I am doing, I do not understand. For what I will to do, that I do not practice; but what I hate, that I do.

16 If, then, I do what I will not to do, I agree with the law that *it is* good.

17 But now, *it is* no longer I who do it, but sin that dwells in me.

18 For I know that in me (that is, in my flesh) nothing good dwells; for to will is present with me, but *how* to perform what is good I do not find.

19 For the good that I will *to do,* I do not do; but the evil I will not *to do,* that I practice.

20 Now if I do what I will not *to do,* it is no longer I who do it, but sin that dwells in me.

21 I find then a law, that evil is present with me, the one who wills to do good.

22 For I delight in the law of God according to the inward man.

23 But I see another law in my members, warring against the law of my mind, and bringing me into captivity to the law of sin which is in my members.

24 O wretched man that I am! Who will deliver me from this body of death?

25 I thank God—through Jesus Christ our Lord! So then, with the mind I myself serve the law of God, but with the flesh the law of sin.

8 *There is* therefore now no condemnation to those who are in Christ Jesus, who do not walk according to the flesh, but according to the Spirit.

2 For the law of the Spirit of life in Christ Jesus has made me free from the law of sin and death.

3 For what the law could not do in that it was weak through the flesh, God *did* by sending His own Son in the likeness of sinful flesh, on account of sin: He condemned sin in the flesh,

4 that the righteous requirement of the law might be fulfilled in us who do not walk according to the flesh but according to the Spirit.

5 For those who live according to the flesh set their minds on the things of the flesh, but those *who* live according to the Spirit, the things of the Spirit.

6 For to be carnally minded *is* death, but to be spiritually minded *is* life and peace.

7 Because the carnal mind *is* enmity against God; for it is not subject to the law of God, nor indeed can be.

8 So then, those who are in the flesh cannot please God.

9 But you are not in the flesh but in the Spirit, if indeed the Spirit of God dwells in you. Now if anyone does not have the Spirit of Christ, he is not His.

10 And if Christ *is* in you, the body *is* dead because of sin, but the Spirit *is* life because of righteousness.

11 But if the Spirit of Him who raised Jesus from the dead dwells in you, He who raised Christ from the dead will also give life to your

212

Why Are So Many Different "Laws" Mentioned in Romans?

In all the chaos of life, laws accomplish two things for us: They set standards, and they describe the way things (and people) work. The Book of Romans helps us make sense of complex spiritual issues by identifying and defining some basic laws.

Law of God. These are statements of God's moral values, communicated to us in various forms but especially in the Ten Commandments (Exodus 20) and Jesus' Sermon on the Mount (Matthew 5—7). God has imprinted these moral values in the conscience of every person.

Law of sin and death. The pull to obey our own desires and to set our own standards rather than God's is the law of sin and death. This tendency toward sin inevitably controls a person who has not established a relationship with Christ. Even when this individual chooses to do something in keeping with God's law, that person is still following his or her own desire—even if it temporarily is in line with God's—

and thus confirms that he or she is dominated by sin. This independence from God results in eternal separation from God, the worst kind of death.

Law of the mind. Our mind in its rational state agrees with God's moral law. Yet we can't keep it on our own. Without supernatural help, "the law of sin" holds sway in us.

Law of the Spirit of life (Romans 8:2). When we receive Christ, we are given a desire to do what God wants us to. This new desire and capacity is provided by the permanent presence of the Holy Spirit within us. It exerts a counterforce to the "law of sin and death."

Conclusion. God's law is perfect. But because the law of sin rules us, we follow our own will, breaking God's law, which leads to death. Our mind agrees that God's values should be our own. But we still don't obey Him because the law of the mind is powerless to overcome the law of sin and death. Only when we receive Christ do we experience a new law at work in our lives, the law of the Spirit of life, enabling us to obey God.

mortal bodies through His Spirit who dwells in you.

12 Therefore, brethren, we are debtors—not to the flesh, to live according to the flesh.

13 For if you live according to the flesh you will die; but if by the Spirit you put to death the deeds of the body, you will live.

14 For as many as are led by the Spirit of God, these are sons of God.

15 For you did not receive the spirit of bondage again to fear, but you received the Spirit of adoption by whom we cry out, "Abba, Father."

16 The Spirit Himself bears witness with our spirit that we are children of God,

17 and if children, then heirs—heirs of God and joint heirs with Christ, if indeed we suffer with *Him*, that we may also be glorified together.

18 For I consider that the sufferings of this present time are not worthy *to be compared* with the glory which shall be revealed in us.

19 For the earnest expectation of the creation eagerly waits for the revealing of the sons of God.

20 For the creation was subjected to futility, not willingly, but because of Him who subjected *it* in hope;

21 because the creation itself also will be delivered from the bondage of corruption into the glorious liberty of the children of God.

22 For we know that the whole creation groans and labors with birth pangs together until now.

23 And not only *they*, but we also who have the firstfruits of the Spirit, even we ourselves groan within ourselves, eagerly waiting for the adoption, the redemption of our body.

24 For we were saved in this hope, but hope that is seen is not hope; for why does one still hope for what he sees?

25 But if we hope for what we do not see, *then* we eagerly wait for *it* with perseverance.

26 Likewise the Spirit also helps in our weaknesses. For we do not know what we should pray for as we ought, but the Spirit Himself makes intercession for us with groanings which cannot be uttered.

27 Now He who searches the hearts knows what the mind of the Spirit *is*, because He makes intercession for the saints according to *the will of* God.

28 And we know that all things work together for good to those who love God, to those who are the called according to *His* purpose.

29 For whom He foreknew, He also predestined *to be* conformed to the image of His Son, that He might be the firstborn among many brethren.

30 Moreover whom He predestined, these He also called; whom He called, these He also justified; and whom He justified, these He also glorified.

31 What then shall we say to these things? If God *is* for us, who *can* be against us?

32 He who did not spare His own Son, but delivered Him up for us all, how shall He not with Him also freely give us all things?

33 Who shall bring a charge against God's elect? *It is* God who justifies.

34 Who *is* he who condemns? *It is* Christ who died, and furthermore is also risen, who is even at the right hand of God, who also makes intercession for us.

35 Who shall separate us from the love of Christ? *Shall* tribulation, or distress, or persecution, or famine, or nakedness, or peril, or sword?

36 As it is written:

> "For Your sake we are killed
>   all day long;
> We are accounted as sheep
>   for the slaughter."

Why Does the Environment Have to Suffer and Decay?

Romans 8:20–22 may seem to imply that Adam's sin ushered into the creation all physical death, suffering, and decay. Some people believe the law of entropy (the increase of disorder in the universe) didn't take effect until Adam sinned. Is this belief reasonable?

In Genesis 3:16, God explains to Eve a consequence of her sin. "I will greatly multiply your sorrow and your conception." Since God used the word *multiply,* obviously some childbirth pain existed before Eve sinned.

The key problem seems to lie in our view of decay. We see decay as bad, but it isn't. Without decay, work (in the physical universe) would be impossible. Without work, physical life would be impossible. But life did exist, according to Genesis 1, at least from the third creation day onward. Thus, Romans 8:20–22 doesn't imply that Adam's sin inaugurated the entire physical process of decay.

The text more likely refers to another kind of decay, the disorder in man's environment that has resulted from his rebellion against God. In Genesis 1:28, God commanded humans to maintain their environment. But, because of sin, we have fouled it up. Our effect on the environment is like the work of a two-year-old in tidying up a closet. Left alone, the closet will become less tidy as a result of the natural tendency toward decay. But sending the two-year-old in there will greatly speed up the disarray. Just as the closet must wait for the two-year-old to grow up before it can get a proper straightening by him or her, so, too, the creation must wait for humanity to gain total freedom from sin.

Since God's plan is to conquer evil once and for all, it seems plausible that He formed the laws of physics to accomplish His purpose as quickly and efficiently as possible. These laws necessarily involve a decay process. But as soon as God completes the conquest of evil, the need for these laws will disappear. (The victory is described in Revelation 20:11–15.) Then according to Revelation 21, our present laws of physics will be replaced by new and different laws of physics. The creation will be permanently liberated from its bondage to decay.

215

37 Yet in all these things we are more than conquerors through Him who loved us.

38 For I am persuaded that neither death nor life, nor angels nor principalities nor powers, nor things present nor things to come,

39 nor height nor depth, nor any other created thing, shall be able to separate us from the love of God which is in Christ Jesus our Lord.

9 I tell the truth in Christ, I am not lying, my conscience also bearing me witness in the Holy Spirit,

2 that I have great sorrow and continual grief in my heart.

3 For I could wish that I myself were accursed from Christ for my brethren, my kinsmen according to the flesh,

4 who are Israelites, to whom *pertain* the adoption, the glory, the covenants, the giving of the law, the service *of God*, and the promises;

5 of whom *are* the fathers and from whom, according to the flesh, Christ *came*, who is over all, *the* eternally blessed God. Amen.

6 But it is not that the word of God has taken no effect. For they *are* not all Israel who *are* of Israel,

7 nor *are they* all children because they are the seed of Abraham; but, *"In Isaac your seed shall be called."*

8 That is, those who are the children of the flesh, these *are* not the children of God; but the children of the promise are counted as the seed.

9 For this *is* the word of promise: *"At this time I will come and Sarah shall have a son."*

10 And not only *this*, but when Rebecca also had conceived by one man, *even* by our father Isaac

11 (for *the children* not yet being born, nor having done any good or evil, that the purpose of God according to election might stand, not of works but of Him who calls),

12 it was said to her, *"The older shall serve the younger."*

13 As it is written, *"Jacob I have loved, but Esau I have hated."*

14 What shall we say then? *Is there* unrighteousness with God? Certainly not!

15 For He says to Moses, *"I will have mercy on whomever I will have mercy, and I will have compassion on whomever I will have compassion."*

16 So then *it is* not of him who wills, nor of him who runs, but of God who shows mercy.

17 For the Scripture says to Pharaoh, *"Even for this same purpose I have raised you up, that I might show My power in you, and that My name might be declared in all the earth."*

18 Therefore He has mercy on whom He wills, and whom He wills He hardens.

19 You will say to me then, "Why does He still find fault? For who has resisted His will?"

20 But indeed, O man, who are you to reply against God? Will the thing formed say to him who formed *it*, "Why have you made me like this?"

21 Does not the potter have power over the clay, from the same lump to make one vessel for honor and another for dishonor?

22 *What* if God, wanting to show *His* wrath and to make His power known, endured with much longsuffering the vessels of wrath prepared for destruction,

23 and that He might make known the riches of His glory on the vessels of mercy, which He had prepared beforehand for glory,

24 *even* us whom He called, not of the Jews only, but also of the Gentiles?

25 As He says also in Hosea:

> *"I will call them My people,*
> *who were not My people,*
> *And her beloved,*
> *who was not beloved."*

Do We Have Any Choice?

Throughout Scripture verses like Romans 9:10–18, claim that God not only knows everything that will happen in the future (foreknowledge), but that He also has predetermined (elected or predestined) it. Every deed, every word, and every thought that each of us will ever experience God predetermined even before He created the world.

By contrast, many Bible verses, like Acts 2:37–41 and Romans 10:9–21, say that each one of us makes choices and is personally responsible for every deed, word, and thought. That is, we humans determine our own future course.

What's going on? The Bible claims God is in control while at the same time we are in control. Free choice and predestination operate simultaneously. Isn't this a contradiction? an impossibility?

It's both a contradiction and an impossibility—in the four dimensions of space and time to which we humans are confined. But the Bible specifically claims God can move and operate in at least two dimensions of time compared to our one (see "But Who Created God?" page 298). And Luke 24:36–43 and John 20:19, 20 tell us Jesus walked through walls with a physical body. Though impossible in three dimensions of space, such an act can be achieved easily in several more dimensions. Astrophysicists now state that extra dimensions of space and time exist. Particle physics suggests a minimum of nine dimen-

sions of space just to explain all of the known fundamental particles.

We can't visualize phenomena in dimensions we don't experience (see also 1 Corinthians 2:9). But we can establish by mathematics what is possible and not possible in extra dimensions. We can also comprehend some of the advantages gained through extra dimensions.

In "Don't Christians Actually Have Three Gods?" (page 266), we see how an extra dimension of space can transform a contradiction into a solvable paradox. In "But Who Created God?" (page 298), we see how an extra time dimension transforms an impossibility into a possibility. Here are two more examples of what extra dimensions make possible:

- The Andromeda galaxy is two million light years away. If a person traveled to Andromeda at top speed (nearly the velocity of light), the round trip would take four million years. But the theory of special relativity tells us that the person making such a trip at such a speed (or even nearly so) would age only twenty or thirty years, while friends on earth would have aged (or decayed) the full four million years. Why? Because travel at or near the velocity of light changes the way time behaves.
- If time is three dimensional, God could operate on a sphere (or ball) of time. If humanity were confined to a line segment along the sphere's equator, then God, from a single point of time at the

217

sphere's north pole, could drop perpendicular time lines to both our past and our future. Thus He could operate simultaneously on our past, present, and future.

Science suggests to us that the Creator of the universe operates in at least ten dimensions of space and time. Mathematics tells us that in ten dimensions, perhaps even in fewer than ten, it's entirely possible for God to predetermine everything about our lives *and* at the same time give us genuine freedom of choice. We can't picture this possibility, but we can embrace it—and we need no longer disregard, distort, or scratch our heads over Scriptures on one side or the other of this question of who chooses.

26 "And it shall come to pass in
   the place where it was said to
   them,
   'You are not My people,'
   There they will be called sons
   of the living God."

27 Isaiah also cries out concerning
Israel:

   "Though the number of the
   children of Israel be as the
   sand of the sea,
   The remnant will be saved.
28 For He will finish the work
   and cut it short in
   righteousness,
   Because the LORD will make a
   short work upon the earth."

29 And as Isaiah said before:

   "Unless the LORD of Sabaoth
   had left us a seed,
   We would have become like
   Sodom,
   And we would have been made
   like Gomorrah."

30 What shall we say then? That
Gentiles, who did not pursue righteousness, have attained to righteousness, even the righteousness
of faith;
31 but Israel, pursuing the law of
righteousness, has not attained to
the law of righteousness.
32 Why? Because they did not seek
it by faith, but as it were, by the
works of the law. For they stumbled at that stumbling stone.
33 As it is written:

   "Behold, I lay in Zion a
   stumbling stone and rock of
   offense,
   And whoever believes on Him
   will not be put to shame."

10 Brethren, my heart's desire
and prayer to God for Israel
is that they may be saved.
2 For I bear them witness that

they have a zeal for God, but not
according to knowledge.
3 For they being ignorant of
God's righteousness, and seeking
to establish their own righteousness, have not submitted to the
righteousness of God.
4 For Christ is the end of the law
for righteousness to everyone who
believes.
5 For Moses writes about the
righteousness which is of the law,
"The man who does those things
shall live by them."
6 But the righteousness of faith
speaks in this way, "Do not say in
your heart, 'Who will ascend into
heaven?'" (that is, to bring Christ
down from above)
7 or, "'Who will descend into the
abyss?'" (that is, to bring Christ
up from the dead.)
8 But what does it say? "The
word is near you, even in your
mouth and in your heart" (that is,
the word of faith which we
preach):
9 that if you confess with your
mouth the Lord Jesus and believe
in your heart that God has raised
Him from the dead, you will be
saved.
10 For with the heart one believes
to righteousness, and with the
mouth confession is made to salvation.
11 For the Scripture says, "Whoever believes on Him will not be
put to shame."
12 For there is no distinction between Jew and Greek, for the same
Lord over all is rich to all who call
upon Him.
13 For "whoever calls upon the
name of the LORD shall be saved."
14 How then shall they call on Him
in whom they have not believed?
And how shall they believe in Him
of whom they have not heard? And
how shall they hear without a
preacher?
15 And how shall they preach unless they are sent? As it is written:

*"How beautiful are the feet of
those who preach the gospel
of peace,
Who bring glad tidings of good
things!"*

16 But they have not all obeyed
the gospel. For Isaiah says, *"Lord,
who has believed our report?"*
17 So then faith *comes* by hearing,
and hearing by the word of God.
18 But I say, have they not heard?
Yes indeed:

*"Their sound has gone out
to all the earth,
And their words to the ends
of the world."*

19 But I say, did Israel not know?
First Moses says:

*"I will provoke you to jealousy
by those who are not a
nation,
I will anger you by a foolish
nation."*

20 But Isaiah is very bold and says:

*"I was found by those
who did not seek Me;
I was made manifest to those
who did not ask for Me."*

21 But to Israel he says:

*"All day long I have stretched
out My hands
To a disobedient and contrary
people."*

11 I say then, has God cast
away His people? Certainly
not! For I also am an Israelite, of
the seed of Abraham, *of* the tribe
of Benjamin.
2 God has not cast away His people whom He foreknew. Or do you
not know what the Scripture says
of Elijah, how he pleads with God
against Israel, saying,
3 *"Lord, they have killed Your*

*prophets and torn down Your al-
tars, and I alone am left, and they
seek my life"*?
4 But what does the divine response say to him? *"I have reserved for Myself seven thousand
men who have not bowed the knee
to Baal."*
5 Even so then, at this present
time there is a remnant according
to the election of grace.
6 And if by grace, then *it is* no
longer of works; otherwise grace is
no longer grace. But if *it is* of
works, it is no longer grace; otherwise work is no longer work.
7 What then? Israel has not obtained what it seeks; but the elect
have obtained it, and the rest were
hardened.
8 Just as it is written:

*"God has given them a spirit of
stupor,
Eyes that they should not see
And ears that they should not
hear,
To this very day."*

9 And David says:

*"Let their table become a snare
and a trap,
A stumbling block and
a recompense to them;*
10 *Let their eyes be darkened,
that they may not see,
And bow down their back
always."*

11 I say then, have they stumbled
that they should fall? Certainly
not! But through their fall, to provoke them to jealousy, salvation
has come to the Gentiles.
12 Now if their fall *is* riches for the
world, and their failure riches for
the Gentiles, how much more their
fullness!
13 For I speak to you Gentiles;
inasmuch as I am an apostle to the
Gentiles, I magnify my ministry,
14 if by any means I may provoke

to jealousy *those who are* my flesh and save some of them.

15 For if their being cast away *is* the reconciling of the world, what *will* their acceptance *be* but life from the dead?

16 For if the firstfruit *is* holy, the lump *is* also *holy;* and if the root *is* holy, so *are* the branches.

17 And if some of the branches were broken off, and you, being a wild olive tree, were grafted in among them, and with them became a partaker of the root and fatness of the olive tree,

18 do not boast against the branches. But if you boast, *remember that* you do not support the root, but the root supports you.

19 You will say then, "Branches were broken off that I might be grafted in."

20 Well *said.* Because of unbelief they were broken off, and you stand by faith. Do not be haughty, but fear.

21 For if God did not spare the natural branches, He may not spare you either.

22 Therefore consider the goodness and severity of God: on those who fell, severity; but toward you, goodness, if you continue in *His* goodness. Otherwise you also will be cut off.

23 And they also, if they do not continue in unbelief, will be grafted in, for God is able to graft them in again.

24 For if you were cut out of the olive tree which is wild by nature, and were grafted contrary to nature into a good olive tree, how much more will these, who *are the* natural *branches,* be grafted into their own olive tree?

25 For I do not desire, brethren, that you should be ignorant of this mystery, lest you should be wise in your own opinion, that hardening in part has happened to Israel until the fullness of the Gentiles has come in.

26 And so all Israel will be saved, as it is written:

"The Deliverer will come out of Zion,
    And He will turn away
        ungodliness from Jacob;
27 For this is My covenant with them,
    When I take away their sins."

28 Concerning the gospel *they are* enemies for your sake, but concerning the election *they are* beloved for the sake of the fathers.

29 For the gifts and the calling of God *are* irrevocable.

30 For as you were once disobedient to God, yet have now obtained mercy through their disobedience,

31 even so these also have now been disobedient, that through the mercy shown you they also may obtain mercy.

32 For God has committed them all to disobedience, that He might have mercy on all.

33 Oh, the depth of the riches both of the wisdom and knowledge of God! How unsearchable *are* His judgments and His ways past finding out!

34 "For who has known the mind
        of the LORD?
    Or who has become His
        counselor?"
35 "Or who has first given to Him
    And it shall be repaid to him?"

36 For of Him and through Him and to Him *are* all things, to whom *be* glory forever. Amen.

12 I beseech you therefore, brethren, by the mercies of God, that you present your bodies a living sacrifice, holy, acceptable to God, *which is* your reasonable service.

2 And do not be conformed to this world, but be transformed by the renewing of your mind, that you may prove what *is* that good and acceptable and perfect will of God.

3 For I say, through the grace given to me, to everyone who is among you, not to think *of himself* more highly than he ought to think, but to think soberly, as God has dealt to each one a measure of faith.

4 For as we have many members in one body, but all the members do not have the same function,

5 so we, *being* many, are one body in Christ, and individually members of one another.

6 Having then gifts differing according to the grace that is given to us, *let us use them*: if prophecy, *let us prophesy* in proportion to our faith;

7 or ministry, *let us use it in our* ministering; he who teaches, in teaching;

8 he who exhorts, in exhortation; he who gives, with liberality; he who leads, with diligence; he who shows mercy, with cheerfulness.

9 *Let* love *be* without hypocrisy. Abhor what is evil. Cling to what is good.

10 *Be* kindly affectionate to one another with brotherly love, in honor giving preference to one another;

11 not lagging in diligence, fervent in spirit, serving the Lord;

12 rejoicing in hope, patient in tribulation, continuing steadfastly in prayer;

13 distributing to the needs of the saints, given to hospitality.

14 Bless those who persecute you; bless and do not curse.

15 Rejoice with those who rejoice, and weep with those who weep.

16 Be of the same mind toward one another. Do not set your mind on high things, but associate with the humble. Do not be wise in your own opinion.

17 Repay no one evil for evil. Have regard for good things in the sight of all men.

18 If it is possible, as much as depends on you, live peaceably with all men.

19 Beloved, do not avenge yourselves, but *rather* give place to wrath; for it is written, *"Vengeance is Mine, I will repay,"* says the Lord.

20 *"Therefore if your enemy*
hungers, feed him;
If he thirsts, give him a drink;
For in so doing you will heap
coals of fire on his head."

21 Do not be overcome by evil, but overcome evil with good.

13 Let every soul be subject to the governing authorities. For there is no authority except from God, and the authorities that exist are appointed by God.

2 Therefore whoever resists the authority resists the ordinance of God, and those who resist will bring judgment on themselves.

3 For rulers are not a terror to good works, but to evil. Do you want to be unafraid of the authority? Do what is good, and you will have praise from the same.

4 For he is God's minister to you for good. But if you do evil, be afraid; for he does not bear the sword in vain; for he is God's minister, an avenger to *execute* wrath on him who practices evil.

5 Therefore *you* must be subject, not only because of wrath but also for conscience' sake.

6 For because of this you also pay taxes, for they are God's ministers attending continually to this very thing.

7 Render therefore to all their due: taxes to whom taxes *are due*, customs to whom customs, fear to whom fear, honor to whom honor.

8 Owe no one anything except to love one another, for he who loves another has fulfilled the law.

9 For the commandments, *"You shall not commit adultery," "You shall not murder," "You shall not steal," "You shall not bear false witness," "You shall not covet,"* and if *there is* any other command-

ment, are *all* summed up in this saying, namely, *"You shall love your neighbor as yourself."*

10 Love does no harm to a neighbor; therefore love *is* the fulfillment of the law.

11 And *do* this, knowing the time, that now *it is* high time to awake out of sleep; for now our salvation *is* nearer than when we *first* believed.

12 The night is far spent, the day is at hand. Therefore let us cast off the works of darkness, and let us put on the armor of light.

13 Let us walk properly, as in the day, not in revelry and drunkenness, not in licentiousness and lewdness, not in strife and envy.

14 But put on the Lord Jesus Christ, and make no provision for the flesh, to *fulfill its* lusts.

14 Receive one who is weak in the faith, *but* not to disputes over doubtful things.

2 For one believes he may eat all things, but he who is weak eats *only* vegetables.

3 Let not him who eats despise him who does not eat, and let not him who does not eat judge him who eats; for God has received him.

4 Who are you to judge another's servant? To his own master he stands or falls. Indeed, he will be made to stand, for God is able to make him stand.

5 One person esteems *one* day above another; another esteems every day *alike*. Let each be fully convinced in his own mind.

6 He who observes the day, observes *it* to the Lord; and he who does not observe the day, to the Lord he does not observe *it*. He who eats, eats to the Lord, for he gives God thanks; and he who does not eat, to the Lord he does not eat, and gives God thanks.

7 For none of us lives to himself, and no one dies to himself.

8 For if we live, we live to the Lord; and if we die, we die to the

Lord. Therefore, whether we live or die, we are the Lord's.

9 For to this end Christ died and rose and lived again, that He might be Lord of both the dead and the living.

10 But why do you judge your brother? Or why do you show contempt for your brother? For we shall all stand before the judgment seat of Christ.

11 For it is written:

> *"As I live, says the LORD,*
> *Every knee shall bow to Me,*
> *And every tongue shall confess*
>   *to God."*

12 So then each of us shall give account of himself to God.

13 Therefore let us not judge one another anymore, but rather resolve this, not to put a stumbling block or a cause to fall in *our* brother's way.

14 I know and am convinced by the Lord Jesus that *there is* nothing unclean of itself; but to him who considers anything to be unclean, to him *it is* unclean.

15 Yet if your brother is grieved because of *your* food, you are no longer walking in love. Do not destroy with your food the one for whom Christ died.

16 Therefore do not let your good be spoken of as evil;

17 for the kingdom of God is not food and drink, but righteousness and peace and joy in the Holy Spirit.

18 For he who serves Christ in these things *is* acceptable to God and approved by men.

19 Therefore let us pursue the things *which make* for peace and the things by which one may edify another.

20 Do not destroy the work of God for the sake of food. All things indeed *are* pure, but *it is* evil for the man who eats with offense.

21 *It is* good neither to eat meat

nor drink wine nor *do anything* by which your brother stumbles or is offended or is made weak.

22 Do you have faith? Have *it* to yourself before God. Happy *is* he who does not condemn himself in what he approves.

23 But he who doubts is condemned if he eats, because *he does* not *eat* from faith; for whatever *is* not from faith is sin.

15 We then who are strong ought to bear with the scruples of the weak, and not to please ourselves.

2 Let each of us please *his* neighbor for *his* good, leading to edification.

3 For even Christ did not please Himself; but as it is written, *"The reproaches of those who reproached You fell on Me."*

4 For whatever things were written before were written for our learning, that we through the patience and comfort of the Scriptures might have hope.

5 Now may the God of patience and comfort grant you to be like-minded toward one another, according to Christ Jesus,

6 that you may with one mind *and* one mouth glorify the God and Father of our Lord Jesus Christ.

7 Therefore receive one another, just as Christ also received us, to the glory of God.

8 Now I say that Jesus Christ has become a servant to the circumcision for the truth of God, to confirm the promises *made* to the fathers,

9 and that the Gentiles might glorify God for *His* mercy, as it is written:

> *"For this reason I will confess to You among the Gentiles,
> And sing to Your name."*

10 And again he says:

> *"Rejoice, O Gentiles, with His people!"*

11 And again:

> *"Praise the LORD, all you Gentiles!
> Laud Him, all you peoples!"*

12 And again, Isaiah says:

> *"There shall be a root of Jesse;
> And He who shall rise to reign over the Gentiles,
> In Him the Gentiles shall hope."*

13 Now may the God of hope fill you with all joy and peace in believing, that you may abound in hope by the power of the Holy Spirit.

14 Now I myself am confident concerning you, my brethren, that you also are full of goodness, filled with all knowledge, able also to admonish one another.

15 Nevertheless, brethren, I have written more boldly to you on *some* points, as reminding you, because of the grace given to me by God,

16 that I might be a minister of Jesus Christ to the Gentiles, ministering the gospel of God, that the offering of the Gentiles might be acceptable, sanctified by the Holy Spirit.

17 Therefore I have reason to glory in Christ Jesus in the things which *pertain* to God.

18 For I will not dare to speak of any of those things which Christ has not accomplished through me, in word and deed, to make the Gentiles obedient—

19 in mighty signs and wonders, by the power of the Spirit of God, so that from Jerusalem and round about to Illyricum I have fully preached the gospel of Christ.

20 And so I have made it my aim to preach the gospel, not where Christ was named, lest I should build on another man's foundation,

21 but as it is written:

> *"To whom He was not*
> *announced, they shall see;*
> *And those who have not heard*
> *shall understand."*

22 For this reason I also have been much hindered from coming to you.

23 But now no longer having a place in these parts, and having a great desire these many years to come to you,

24 whenever I journey to Spain, I shall come to you. For I hope to see you on my journey, and to be helped on my way there by you, if first I may enjoy your *company* for a while.

25 But now I am going to Jerusalem to minister to the saints.

26 For it pleased those from Macedonia and Achaia to make a certain contribution for the poor among the saints who are in Jerusalem.

27 It pleased them indeed, and they are their debtors. For if the Gentiles have been partakers of their spiritual things, their duty is also to minister to them in material things.

28 Therefore, when I have performed this and have sealed to them this fruit, I shall go by way of you to Spain.

29 But I know that when I come to you, I shall come in the fullness of the blessing of the gospel of Christ.

30 Now I beg you, brethren, through the Lord Jesus Christ, and through the love of the Spirit, that you strive together with me in *your* prayers to God for me,

31 that I may be delivered from those in Judea who do not believe, and that my service for Jerusalem may be acceptable to the saints,

32 that I may come to you with joy by the will of God, and may be refreshed together with you.

33 Now the God of peace *be* with you all. Amen.

16 I commend to you Phoebe our sister, who is a servant of the church in Cenchrea,

2 that you may receive her in the Lord in a manner worthy of the saints, and assist her in whatever business she has need of you; for indeed she has been a helper of many and of myself also.

3 Greet Priscilla and Aquila, my fellow workers in Christ Jesus,

4 who risked their own necks for my life, to whom not only I give thanks, but also all the churches of the Gentiles.

5 Likewise *greet* the church that is in their house. Greet my beloved Epaenetus, who is the firstfruits of Achaia to Christ.

6 Greet Mary, who labored much for us.

7 Greet Andronicus and Junia, my kinsmen and my fellow prisoners, who are of note among the apostles, who also were in Christ before me.

8 Greet Amplias, my beloved in the Lord.

9 Greet Urbanus, our fellow worker in Christ, and Stachys, my beloved.

10 Greet Apelles, approved in Christ. Greet those who are of the *household* of Aristobulus.

11 Greet Herodion, my kinsman. Greet those who are of the *household* of Narcissus who are in the Lord.

12 Greet Tryphena and Tryphosa, who have labored in the Lord. Greet the beloved Persis, who labored much in the Lord.

13 Greet Rufus, chosen in the Lord, and his mother and mine.

14 Greet Asyncritus, Phlegon, Hermas, Patrobas, Hermes, and the brethren who are with them.

15 Greet Philologus and Julia, Nereus and his sister, and Olympas, and all the saints who are with them.

16 Greet one another with a holy kiss. The churches of Christ greet you.

17 Now I urge you, brethren, note those who cause divisions and offenses, contrary to the doctrine which you learned, and avoid them.

18 For those who are such do not serve our Lord Jesus Christ, but their own belly, and by smooth words and flattering speech deceive the hearts of the simple.

19 For your obedience has become known to all. Therefore I am glad on your behalf; but I want you to be wise in what is good, and simple concerning evil.

20 And the God of peace will crush Satan under your feet shortly. The grace of our Lord Jesus Christ *be* with you. Amen.

21 Timothy, my fellow worker, and Lucius, Jason, and Sosipater, my kinsmen, greet you.

22 I, Tertius, who wrote *this* epistle, greet you in the Lord.

23 Gaius, my host and *the host* of the whole church, greets you. Erastus, the treasurer of the city, greets you, and Quartus, a brother.

24 The grace of our Lord Jesus Christ *be* with you all. Amen.

25 Now to Him who is able to establish you according to my gospel and the preaching of Jesus Christ, according to the revelation of the mystery *which was* kept secret since the world began

26 but now has been made manifest, and by the prophetic Scriptures has been made known to all nations, according to the commandment of the everlasting God, for obedience to the faith—

27 to God, alone wise, *be* glory through Jesus Christ forever. Amen.

THE FIRST EPISTLE OF PAUL THE APOSTLE TO THE
CORINTHIANS

PAUL, called *to be* an apostle of Jesus Christ through the will of God, and Sosthenes *our* brother,

2 To the church of God which is at Corinth, to those who are sanctified in Christ Jesus, called *to be* saints, with all who in every place call on the name of Jesus Christ our Lord, both theirs and ours:

3 Grace to you and peace from God our Father and the Lord Jesus Christ.

4 I thank my God always concerning you for the grace of God which was given to you by Christ Jesus,

5 that you were enriched in everything by Him in all utterance and all knowledge,

6 even as the testimony of Christ was confirmed in you,

7 so that you come short in no gift, eagerly waiting for the revelation of our Lord Jesus Christ,

8 who will also confirm you to the end, *that you may be* blameless in the day of our Lord Jesus Christ.

9 God *is* faithful, by whom you were called into the fellowship of His Son, Jesus Christ our Lord.

10 Now I plead with you, brethren, by the name of our Lord Jesus Christ, that you all speak the same thing, and *that* there be no divisions among you, but *that* you be perfectly joined together in the same mind and in the same judgment.

11 For it has been declared to me concerning you, my brethren, by those of Chloe's *household*, that there are contentions among you.

Why Are Some People Called Blameless When They Obviously Aren't?

"Sin? I may make mistakes, but I don't sin!" Many of the people who lived in Corinth believed they didn't sin, but they sure made plenty of "mistakes" (for example, see verse 11). Why does the Bible call people blameless when they obviously aren't?

Becoming "saved" from sin is a process that starts with accepting Jesus Christ's payment of sin's penalty for us. But that's just the beginning. Below are definitions of some complex words, forms of which appear frequently in the Bible to depict the phases in the salvation process.

Justification

"We the jury find the accused . . . *not guilty!*" With a sigh of relief, the defendant realizes he has been judged innocent. This is the basic meaning of *justification*, to be found not guilty. But when it comes to breaking God's law we are, in fact, guilty! The reason we can be pronounced innocent is because Jesus paid the penalty for our sin. Believers in Christ are not justified because of their innocence, but because of Christ's.

Sanctification

Amazingly, Paul, the writer of the letter to the Corinthians, addressed the problem-plagued group as "saints," and said they were "sanctified" in Christ (1 Corinthians 1:2). *Sanctified* means to be "set apart" or to belong to God. People who belong to Christ are intended for His sole "use"; and as a believer becomes more spiritually mature, he or she experiences more power over sin.

Glorification

What do expressions like "Glory be!" or "Old Glory" have in common? To "glory" is to see the splendor of someone or something. When we experience "glorification," God's splendor will be reflected in us. But glorification won't be complete until we reach heaven. Then we will be freed from the presence of sin as well as from sin's penalty and power over us. Until then, sin will still be present in our lives as well as in our environment.

Conclusion

Salvation is a process that begins with being declared "not guilty." We are justified because Christ was innocent and took the penalty for our sins. It continues in sanctification as God works within us to free us from sin's power. It culminates in glorification, when, in heaven, we will live sin-free lives in a perfect environment, reflecting God's splendor.

12 Now I say this, that each of you says, "I am of Paul," or "I am of Apollos," or "I am of Cephas," or "I am of Christ."

13 Is Christ divided? Was Paul crucified for you? Or were you baptized in the name of Paul?

14 I thank God that I baptized none of you except Crispus and Gaius,

15 lest anyone should say that I had baptized in my own name.

16 Yes, I also baptized the household of Stephanas. Besides, I do not know whether I baptized any other.

17 For Christ did not send me to baptize, but to preach the gospel, not with wisdom of words, lest the cross of Christ should be made of no effect.

18 For the message of the cross is foolishness to those who are perishing, but to us who are being saved it is the power of God.

19 For it is written:

> *"I will destroy the wisdom of the wise,*
> *And bring to nothing the understanding of the prudent."*

20 Where *is* the wise? Where *is* the scribe? Where *is* the disputer of this age? Has not God made foolish the wisdom of this world?

21 For since, in the wisdom of God, the world through wisdom did not know God, it pleased God through the foolishness of the message preached to save those who believe.

22 For Jews request a sign, and Greeks seek after wisdom;

23 but we preach Christ crucified, to the Jews a stumbling block and to the Greeks foolishness,

24 but to those who are called, both Jews and Greeks, Christ the power of God and the wisdom of God.

25 Because the foolishness of God is wiser than men, and the weakness of God is stronger than men.

26 For you see your calling, brethren, that not many wise according to the flesh, not many mighty, not many noble, *are* called.

27 But God has chosen the foolish things of the world to put to shame the wise, and God has chosen the weak things of the world to put to shame the things which are mighty;

28 and the base things of the world and the things which are despised God has chosen, and the things which are not, to bring to nothing the things that are,

29 that no flesh should glory in His presence.

30 But of Him you are in Christ Jesus, who became for us wisdom from God—and righteousness and sanctification and redemption—

31 that, as it is written, *"He who glories, let him glory in the LORD."*

2 And I, brethren, when I came to you, did not come with excellence of speech or of wisdom declaring to you the testimony of God.

2 For I determined not to know anything among you except Jesus Christ and Him crucified.

3 I was with you in weakness, in fear, and in much trembling.

4 And my speech and my preaching *were* not with persuasive words of human wisdom, but in demonstration of the Spirit and of power,

5 that your faith should not be in the wisdom of men but in the power of God.

6 However, we speak wisdom among those who are mature, yet not the wisdom of this age, nor of the rulers of this age, who are coming to nothing.

7 But we speak the wisdom of God in a mystery, the hidden *wisdom* which God ordained before the ages for our glory,

8 which none of the rulers of this

age knew; for had they known, they would not have crucified the Lord of glory.

9 But as it is written:

> "Eye has not seen, nor ear heard,
> Nor have entered into the heart of man
> The things which God has prepared for those who love Him."

10 But God has revealed *them* to us through His Spirit. For the Spirit searches all things, yes, the deep things of God.

11 For what man knows the things of a man except the spirit of the man which is in him? Even so no one knows the things of God except the Spirit of God.

12 Now we have received, not the spirit of the world, but the Spirit who is from God, that we might know the things that have been freely given to us by God.

13 These things we also speak, not in words which man's wisdom teaches but which the Holy Spirit teaches, comparing spiritual things with spiritual.

14 But the natural man does not receive the things of the Spirit of God, for they are foolishness to him; nor can he know *them,* because they are spiritually discerned.

15 But he who is spiritual judges all things, yet he himself is *rightly* judged by no one.

16 For *"Who has known the mind of the Lord that he may instruct Him?"* But we have the mind of Christ.

3 And I, brethren, could not speak to you as to spiritual *people* but as to carnal, as to babes in Christ.

2 I fed you with milk and not with solid food; for until now you were not able *to receive it,* and even now you are still not able;

3 for you are still carnal. For

where *there are* envy, strife, and divisions among you, are you not carnal and behaving like *mere* men?

4 For when one says, "I am of Paul," and another, "I *am* of Apollos," are you not carnal?

5 Who then is Paul, and who *is* Apollos, but ministers through whom you believed, as the Lord gave to each one?

6 I planted, Apollos watered, but God gave the increase.

7 So then neither he who plants is anything, nor he who waters, but God who gives the increase.

8 Now he who plants and he who waters are one, and each one will receive his own reward according to his own labor.

9 For we are God's fellow workers; you are God's field, *you are* God's building.

10 According to the grace of God which was given to me, as a wise master builder I have laid the foundation, and another builds on it. But let each one take heed how he builds on it.

11 For no other foundation can anyone lay than that which is laid, which is Jesus Christ.

12 Now if anyone builds on this foundation *with* gold, silver, precious stones, wood, hay, straw,

13 each one's work will become manifest; for the Day will declare it, because it will be revealed by fire; and the fire will test each one's work, of what sort it is.

14 If anyone's work which he has built on *it* endures, he will receive a reward.

15 If anyone's work is burned, he will suffer loss; but he himself will be saved, yet so as through fire.

16 Do you not know that you are the temple of God and *that* the Spirit of God dwells in you?

17 If anyone defiles the temple of God, God will destroy him. For the temple of God is holy, which *temple* you are.

18 Let no one deceive himself. If

anyone among you seems to be wise in this age, let him become a fool that he may become wise.

19 For the wisdom of this world is foolishness with God. For it is written, *"He catches the wise in their own craftiness";*

20 and again, *"The LORD knows the thoughts of the wise, that they are futile."*

21 Therefore let no one glory in men. For all things are yours:

22 whether Paul or Apollos or Cephas, or the world or life or death, or things present or things to come—all are yours;

23 And you *are* Christ's, and Christ *is* God's.

4 Let a man so consider us, as servants of Christ and stewards of the mysteries of God.

2 Moreover it is required in stewards that one be found faithful.

3 But with me it is a very small thing that I should be judged by you or by a human court. In fact, I do not even judge myself.

4 For I know nothing against myself, yet I am not justified by this; but He who judges me is the Lord.

5 Therefore judge nothing before the time, until the Lord comes, who will both bring to light the hidden things of darkness and reveal the counsels of the hearts; and then each one's praise will come from God.

6 Now these things, brethren, I have figuratively transferred to myself and Apollos for your sakes, that you may learn in us not to think beyond what is written, that none of you may be puffed up on behalf of one against the other.

7 For who makes you differ *from another?* And what do you have that you did not receive? Now if you did indeed receive *it,* why do you glory as if you had not received *it?*

8 You are already full! You are already rich! You have reigned as kings without us—and indeed I could wish you did reign, that we also might reign with you!

9 For I think that God has displayed us, the apostles, last, as men condemned to death; for we have been made a spectacle to the world, both to angels and to men.

10 We *are* fools for Christ's sake, but you *are* wise in Christ! We *are* weak, but you *are* strong! You *are* distinguished, but we *are* dishonored!

11 *Even* to the present hour we both hunger and thirst, and we are poorly clothed, and beaten, and homeless.

12 And we labor, working with our own hands. Being reviled, we bless; being persecuted, we endure *it;*

13 being defamed, we entreat. We have been made as the filth of the world, the offscouring of all things until now.

14 I do not write these things to shame you, but as my beloved children I warn *you.*

15 For though you might have ten thousand instructors in Christ, yet *you do not have* many fathers; for in Christ Jesus I have begotten you through the gospel.

16 Therefore I urge you, imitate me.

17 For this reason I have sent Timothy to you, who is my beloved and faithful son in the Lord, who will remind you of my ways in Christ, as I teach everywhere in every church.

18 Now some are puffed up, as though I were not coming to you.

19 But I will come to you shortly, if the Lord wills, and I will know, not the word of those who are puffed up, but the power.

20 For the kingdom of God *is* not in word but in power.

21 What do you want? Shall I come to you with a rod, or in love and a spirit of gentleness?

5 It is actually reported *that there is* sexual immorality among you, and such sexual im-

morality as is not even named among the Gentiles—that a man has his father's wife!

2 And you are puffed up, and have not rather mourned, that he who has done this deed might be taken away from among you.

3 For I indeed, as absent in body but present in spirit, have already judged, as though I were present, *concerning* him who has so done this deed.

4 In the name of our Lord Jesus Christ, when you are gathered together, along with my spirit, with the power of our Lord Jesus Christ,

5 deliver such a one to Satan for the destruction of the flesh, that his spirit may be saved in the day of the Lord Jesus.

6 Your glorying *is* not good. Do you not know that a little leaven leavens the whole lump?

7 Therefore purge out the old leaven, that you may be a new lump, since you truly are unleavened. For indeed Christ, our Passover, was sacrificed for us.

8 Therefore let us keep the feast, not with old leaven, nor with the leaven of malice and wickedness, but with the unleavened *bread* of sincerity and truth.

9 I wrote to you in my epistle not to keep company with sexually immoral people.

10 Yet *I* certainly *did* not *mean* with the sexually immoral people of this world, or with the covetous, or extortioners, or idolaters, since then you would need to go out of the world.

11 But now I have written to you not to keep company with anyone named a brother, who is a fornicator, or covetous, or an idolater, or a reviler, or a drunkard, or an extortioner—not even to eat with such a person.

12 For what *have* I *to do* with judging those also who are outside? Do you not judge those who are inside?

13 But those who are outside God judges. Therefore *"put away from yourselves that wicked person."*

6 Dare any of you, having a matter against another, go to law before the unrighteous, and not before the saints?

2 Do you not know that the saints will judge the world? And if the world will be judged by you, are you unworthy to judge the smallest matters?

3 Do you not know that we shall judge angels? How much more, things that pertain to this life?

4 If then you have judgments concerning things pertaining to this life, do you appoint those who are least esteemed by the church to judge?

5 I say this to your shame. Is it so, that there is not a wise man among you, not even one, who will be able to judge between his brethren?

6 But brother goes to law against brother, and that before unbelievers!

7 Now therefore, it is already an utter failure for you that you go to law against one another. Why do you not rather accept wrong? Why do you not rather *let yourselves* be defrauded?

8 No, you yourselves do wrong and defraud, and *you do* these things *to your* brethren!

9 Do you not know that the unrighteous will not inherit the kingdom of God? Do not be deceived. Neither fornicators, nor idolaters, nor adulterers, nor homosexuals, nor sodomites,

10 nor thieves, nor covetous, nor drunkards, nor revilers, nor extortioners will inherit the kingdom of God.

11 And such were some of you. But you were washed, but you were sanctified, but you were justified in the name of the Lord Jesus and by the Spirit of our God.

12 All things are lawful for me, but all things are not helpful. All things are lawful for me, but I will

Will My Sins Keep Me from God?

Corinth was a wild city. In the Roman world, if someone called you a "Corinthian," it was not a compliment to your moral character. Paul warns the Corinthian Christians against the immorality of their society.

In 1 Corinthians 6:9–11, Paul lists ten types of people who are disqualified from God's kingdom. "Fornicators" are those who have sex outside of marriage. "Idolaters" are people who place something or someone before God. The idol may be a statue or an invisible god of our own making. It may be wealth, power, a relationship or a cause to which we give more devotion than we give to God (Colossians 3:5).

Does anyone qualify?

After reading the list, most of us swallow hard and ask, "Who, then, can qualify for God's kingdom?"

Paul's answer is found in verse 11. He writes, "Such were some of you." But he doesn't identify them with their sin any longer. Instead he points out, "You were washed, . . . in the name of the Lord Jesus." (See "Why Are Some People Called Blameless When They Obviously Aren't?" page 227 for a discussion of *sanctified* and *justified*.)

All the sins Paul lists here are forgiven anyone who turns from them and accepts Christ's death and resurrection. (See "What Sin? What Judgment?" page 149.) This doesn't mean the Corinthian Christians had become perfect. In fact, Paul wrote this letter because, surrounded as the church was by immorality, it was condoning many of the sins of its members.

Like the Corinthians, Christians still fall prey to temptation. They may struggle with some of the sins on this list. But when they do, they need not fall into despair. God isn't angry with believers who want to change but fail. Rather God's promise to these imperfect Corinthians and to the rest of us is found in chapter one, verses 7 and 8: "Our Lord Jesus Christ . . . will also confirm you to the end, *that you may be* blameless."

No sin need keep us from God if we are willing to be forgiven and changed. (For more about how to gain Christ's forgiveness, see "What in the World Is God Up To?" page 343 and "How Can I Get to Heaven?" page 362.)

not be brought under the power of any.

13 Foods for the stomach and the stomach for foods, but God will destroy both it and them. Now the body is not for sexual immorality but for the Lord, and the Lord for the body.

14 And God both raised up the Lord and will also raise us up by His power.

15 Do you not know that your bodies are members of Christ? Shall I then take the members of Christ and make *them* members of a harlot? Certainly not!

16 Or do you not know that he who is joined to a harlot is one body *with her?* For *"The two,"* He says, *"shall become one flesh."*

17 But he who is joined to the Lord is one spirit *with* Him.

18 Flee sexual immorality. Every sin that a man does is outside the body, but he who commits sexual immorality sins against his own body.

19 Or do you not know that your body is the temple of the Holy Spirit *who is* in you, whom you have from God, and you are not your own?

20 For you were bought at a price; therefore glorify God in your body and in your spirit, which are God's.

7 Now concerning the things of which you wrote to me: It is good for a man not to touch a woman.

2 Nevertheless, because of sexual immorality, let each man have his own wife, and let each woman have her own husband.

3 Let the husband render to his wife the affection due her, and likewise also the wife to her husband.

4 The wife does not have authority over her own body, but the husband *does.* And likewise the husband does not have authority over his own body, but the wife *does.*

5 Do not deprive one another ex-cept with consent for a time, that you may give yourselves to fasting and prayer; and come together again so that Satan does not tempt you because of your lack of self-control.

6 But I say this as a concession, not as a commandment.

7 For I wish that all men were even as I myself. But each one has his own gift from God, one in this manner and another in that.

8 But I say to the unmarried and to the widows: It is good for them if they remain even as I am;

9 but if they cannot exercise self-control, let them marry. For it is better to marry than to burn *with* passion.

10 Now to the married I command, *yet* not I but the Lord: A wife is not to depart from *her* husband.

11 But even if she does depart, let her remain unmarried or be recon-ciled to *her* husband. And a hus-band is not to divorce *his* wife.

12 But to the rest I, not the Lord, say: If any brother has a wife who does not believe, and she is willing to live with him, let him not di-vorce her.

13 And a woman who has a hus-band who does not believe, if he is willing to live with her, let her not divorce him.

14 For the unbelieving husband is sanctified by the wife, and the un-believing wife is sanctified by the husband; otherwise your children would be unclean, but now they are holy.

15 But if the unbeliever departs, let him depart; a brother or a sister is not under bondage in such *cases.* But God has called us to peace.

16 For how do you know, O wife, whether you will save *your* hus-band? Or how do you know, O husband, whether you will save *your* wife?

17 But as God has distributed to each one, as the Lord has called each one, so let him walk. And so I ordain in all the churches.

18 Was anyone called while circumcised? Let him not become uncircumcised. Was anyone called while uncircumcised? Let him not be circumcised.

19 Circumcision is nothing and uncircumcision is nothing, but keeping the commandments of God *is what matters.*

20 Let each one remain in the same calling in which he was called.

21 Were you called *while* a slave? Do not be concerned about it; but if you can be made free, rather use *it.*

22 For he who is called in the Lord *while* a slave is the Lord's freedman. Likewise he who is called *while* free is Christ's slave.

23 You were bought at a price; do not become slaves of men.

24 Brethren, let each one remain with God in that *calling* in which he was called.

25 Now concerning virgins: I have no commandment from the Lord; yet I give judgment as one whom the Lord in His mercy *has made* trustworthy.

26 I suppose therefore that this is good because of the present distress—that *it is* good for a man to remain as he is:

27 Are you bound to a wife? Do not seek to be loosed. Are you loosed from a wife? Do not seek a wife.

28 But even if you do marry, you have not sinned; and if a virgin marries, she has not sinned. Nevertheless such will have trouble in the flesh, but I would spare you.

29 But this I say, brethren, the time *is* short, so that from now on even those who have wives should be as though they had none,

30 those who weep as though they did not weep, those who rejoice as though they did not rejoice, those who buy as though they did not possess,

31 and those who use this world as not misusing *it.* For the form of this world is passing away.

32 But I want you to be without care. He who is unmarried cares for the things *that belong* to the Lord—how he may please the Lord.

33 But he who is married cares about the things of the world—how he may please *his* wife.

34 There is a difference between a wife and a virgin. The unmarried woman cares about the things of the Lord, that she may be holy both in body and in spirit. But she who is married cares about the things of the world—how she may please *her* husband.

35 And this I say for your own profit, not that I may put a leash on you, but for what is proper, and that you may serve the Lord without distraction.

36 But if any man thinks he is behaving improperly toward his virgin, if she is past the flower of *her* youth, and thus it must be, let him do what he wishes; he does not sin; let them marry.

37 Nevertheless he who stands steadfast in his heart, having no necessity, but has power over his own will, and has so determined in his heart that he will keep his virgin, does well.

38 So then he who gives *her* in marriage does well, but he who does not give *her* in marriage does better.

39 A wife is bound by law as long as her husband lives; but if her husband dies, she is at liberty to be married to whom she wishes, only in the Lord.

40 But she is happier if she remains as she is, according to my judgment—and I think I also have the Spirit of God.

8 Now concerning things offered to idols: We know that we all have knowledge. Knowledge puffs up, but love edifies.

2 And if anyone thinks that he

knows anything, he knows nothing yet as he ought to know.

3 But if anyone loves God, this one is known by Him.

4 Therefore concerning the eating of things offered to idols, we know that an idol *is* nothing in the world, and that *there is* no other God but one.

5 For even if there are so-called gods, whether in heaven or on earth (as there are many gods and many lords),

6 yet for us *there is only* one God, the Father, of whom *are* all things, and we for Him; and one Lord Jesus Christ, through whom *are* all things, and through whom we live.

7 However, *there is* not in everyone that knowledge; for some, with consciousness of the idol, until now eat *it* as a thing offered to an idol; and their conscience, being weak, is defiled.

8 But food does not commend us to God; for neither if we eat are we the better, nor if we do not eat are we the worse.

9 But beware lest somehow this liberty of yours become a stumbling block to those who are weak.

10 For if anyone sees you who have knowledge eating in an idol's temple, will not the conscience of him who is weak be emboldened to eat those things offered to idols?

11 And because of your knowledge shall the weak brother perish, for whom Christ died?

12 But when you thus sin against the brethren, and wound their weak conscience, you sin against Christ.

13 Therefore, if food makes my brother stumble, I will never again eat meat, lest I make my brother stumble.

9 Am I not an apostle? Am I not free? Have I not seen Jesus Christ our Lord? Are you not my work in the Lord?

2 If I am not an apostle to others, yet doubtless I am to you. For you are the seal of my apostleship in the Lord.

3 My defense to those who examine me is this:

4 Do we have no right to eat and drink?

5 Do we have no right to take along a believing wife, as *do* also the other apostles, the brothers of the Lord, and Cephas?

6 Or *is it* only Barnabas and I *who* have no right to refrain from working?

7 Who ever goes to war at his own expense? Who plants a vineyard and does not eat of its fruit? Or who tends a flock and does not drink of the milk of the flock?

8 Do I say these things as a *mere* man? Or does not the law say the same also?

9 For it is written in the law of Moses, *"You shall not muzzle an ox while it treads out the grain."* Is it oxen God is concerned about?

10 Or does He say *it* altogether for our sakes? For our sakes, no doubt, *this* is written, that he who plows should plow in hope, and he who threshes in hope should be partaker of his hope.

11 If we have sown spiritual things for you, *is it* a great thing if we reap your material things?

12 If others are partakers of *this* right over you, *are* we not even more? Nevertheless we have not used this right, but endure all things lest we hinder the gospel of Christ.

13 Do you not know that those who minister the holy things eat *of the things* of the temple, and those who serve at the altar partake of *the offerings* of the altar?

14 Even so the Lord has commanded that those who preach the gospel should live from the gospel.

15 But I have used none of these things, nor have I written these things that it should be done so to me; for it *would be* better for me to die than that anyone should make my boasting void.

16 For if I preach the gospel, I have nothing to boast of, for necessity is laid upon me; yes, woe is me if I do not preach the gospel!

17 For if I do this willingly, I have a reward; but if against my will, I have been entrusted with a stewardship.

18 What is my reward then? That when I preach the gospel, I may present the gospel of Christ without charge, that I may not abuse my authority in the gospel.

19 For though I am free from all *men*, I have made myself a servant to all, that I might win the more;

20 and to the Jews I became as a Jew, that I might win Jews; to those *who are* under the law, as under the law, that I might win those *who are* under the law;

21 to those *who are* without law, as without law (not being without law toward God, but under law toward Christ), that I might win those *who are* without law;

22 to the weak I became as weak, that I might win the weak. I have become all things to all *men*, that I might by all means save some.

23 Now this I do for the gospel's sake, that I may be partaker of it with *you*.

24 Do you not know that those who run in a race all run, but one receives the prize? Run in such a way that you may obtain *it*.

25 And everyone who competes *for the prize* is temperate in all things. Now they *do it* to obtain a perishable crown, but we *for* an imperishable *crown*.

26 Therefore I run thus: not with uncertainty. Thus I fight: not as one who beats the air.

27 But I discipline my body and bring *it* into subjection, lest, when I have preached to others, I myself should become disqualified.

10 Moreover, brethren, I do not want you to be unaware that all our fathers were under the cloud, all passed through the sea,

2 all were baptized into Moses in the cloud and in the sea,

3 all ate the same spiritual food,

4 and all drank the same spiritual drink. For they drank of that spiritual Rock that followed them, and that Rock was Christ.

5 But with most of them God was not well pleased, for *their bodies* were scattered in the wilderness.

6 Now these things became our examples, to the intent that we should not lust after evil things as they also lusted.

7 And do not become idolaters as *were* some of them. As it is written, *"The people sat down to eat and drink, and rose up to play."*

8 Nor let us commit sexual immorality, as some of them did, and in one day twenty-three thousand fell;

9 nor let us tempt Christ, as some of them also tempted, and were destroyed by serpents;

10 nor murmur, as some of them also murmured, and were destroyed by the destroyer.

11 Now all these things happened to them as examples, and they were written for our admonition, on whom the ends of the ages have come.

12 Therefore let him who thinks he stands take heed lest he fall.

13 No temptation has overtaken you except such as is common to man; but God *is* faithful, who will not allow you to be tempted beyond what you are able, but with the temptation will also make the way of escape, that you may be able to bear *it*.

14 Therefore, my beloved, flee from idolatry.

15 I speak as to wise men; judge for yourselves what I say.

16 The cup of blessing which we bless, is it not the communion of the blood of Christ? The bread which we break, is it not the communion of the body of Christ?

17 For we, *being* many, are one

bread *and* one body; for we all partake of that one bread.

18 Observe Israel after the flesh: Are not those who eat of the sacrifices partakers of the altar?

19 What am I saying then? That an idol is anything, or what is offered to idols is anything?

20 But *I* say that the things which the Gentiles sacrifice they sacrifice to demons and not to God, and I do not want you to have fellowship with demons.

21 You cannot drink the cup of the Lord and the cup of demons; you cannot partake of the Lord's table and of the table of demons.

22 Or do we provoke the Lord to jealousy? Are we stronger than He?

23 All things are lawful for me, but all things are not helpful; all things are lawful for me, but all things do not edify.

24 Let no one seek his own, but each one the other's *well-being*.

25 Eat whatever is sold in the meat market, asking no questions for conscience' sake;

26 for *"The earth is the LORD's, and all its fullness."*

27 If any of those who do not believe invites you *to dinner*, and you desire to go, eat whatever is set before you, asking no question for conscience' sake.

28 But if anyone says to you, "This was offered to idols," do not eat it for the sake of the one who told you, and for conscience' sake; for *"The earth is the LORD's, and all its fullness."*

29 Conscience, I say, not your own, but that of the other. For why is my liberty judged by another *man's* conscience?

30 But if I partake with thanks, why am I evil spoken of for the *food* over which I give thanks?

31 Therefore, whether you eat or drink, or whatever you do, do all to the glory of God.

32 Give no offense, either to the Jews or to the Greeks or to the church of God,

33 just as I also please all *men* in all *things*, not seeking my own profit, but the *profit* of many, that they may be saved.

11 Imitate me, just as I also *imitate* Christ.

2 Now I praise you, brethren, that you remember me in all things and keep the traditions as I delivered *them* to you.

3 But I want you to know that the head of every man is Christ, the head of woman *is* man, and the head of Christ *is* God.

4 Every man praying or prophesying, having *his* head covered, dishonors his head.

5 But every woman who prays or prophesies with *her* head uncovered dishonors her head, for that is one and the same as if her head were shaved.

6 For if a woman is not covered, let her also be shorn. But if it is shameful for a woman to be shorn or shaved, let her be covered.

7 For a man indeed ought not to cover *his* head, since he is the image and glory of God; but woman is the glory of man.

8 For man is not from woman, but woman from man.

9 Nor was man created for the woman, but woman for the man.

10 For this reason the woman ought to have *a symbol of* authority on *her* head, because of the angels.

11 Nevertheless, neither *is* man independent of woman, nor woman independent of man, in the Lord.

12 For as the woman *was* from the man, even so the man also *is* through the woman; but all things are from God.

13 Judge among yourselves. Is it proper for a woman to pray to God with her head uncovered?

14 Does not even nature itself teach you that if a man has long hair, it is a dishonor to him?

15 But if a woman has long hair, it is a glory to her; for *her* hair is given to her for a covering.

16 But if anyone seems to be contentious, we have no such custom, nor *do* the churches of God.

17 Now in giving these instructions I do not praise you, since you come together not for the better but for the worse.

18 For first of all, when you come together as a church, I hear that there are divisions among you, and in part I believe it.

19 For there must also be factions among you, that those who are approved may be recognized among you.

20 Therefore when you come together in one place, it is not to eat the Lord's Supper.

21 For in eating, each one takes his own supper ahead of *others;* and one is hungry and another is drunk.

22 What! Do you not have houses to eat and drink in? Or do you despise the church of God and shame those who have nothing? What shall I say to you? Shall I praise you in this? I do not praise *you.*

23 For I received from the Lord that which I also delivered to you: that the Lord Jesus on the *same* night in which He was betrayed took bread;

24 and when He had given thanks, He broke *it* and said, "Take, eat; this is My body which is broken for you; do this in remembrance of Me."

25 In the same manner *He* also *took* the cup after supper, saying, "This cup is the new covenant in My blood. This do, as often as you drink *it,* in remembrance of Me."

26 For as often as you eat this bread and drink this cup, you proclaim the Lord's death till He comes.

27 Therefore whoever eats this bread or drinks *this* cup of the Lord in an unworthy manner will be guilty of the body and blood of the Lord.

28 But let a man examine himself, and so let him eat of *that* bread and drink of *that* cup.

29 For he who eats and drinks in an unworthy manner eats and drinks judgment to himself, not discerning the Lord's body.

30 For this reason many *are* weak and sick among you, and many sleep.

31 For if we would judge ourselves, we would not be judged.

32 But when we are judged, we are chastened by the Lord, that we may not be condemned with the world.

33 Therefore, my brethren, when you come together to eat, wait for one another.

34 But if anyone is hungry, let him eat at home, lest you come together for judgment. And the rest I will set in order when I come.

12 Now concerning spiritual gifts, brethren, I do not want you to be ignorant:

2 You know that you were Gentiles, carried away to these dumb idols, however you were led.

3 Therefore I make known to you that no one speaking by the Spirit of God calls Jesus accursed, and no one can say that Jesus is Lord except by the Holy Spirit.

4 Now there are diversities of gifts, but the same Spirit.

5 There are differences of ministries, but the same Lord.

6 And there are diversities of activities, but it is the same God who works all in all.

7 But the manifestation of the Spirit is given to each one for the profit *of all:*

8 for to one is given the word of wisdom through the Spirit, to another the word of knowledge through the same Spirit,

9 to another faith by the same

Spirit, to another gifts of healings by the same Spirit,

10 to another the working of miracles, to another prophecy, to another discerning of spirits, to another *different* kinds of tongues, to another the interpretation of tongues.

11 But one and the same Spirit works all these things, distributing to each one individually as He wills.

12 For as the body is one and has many members, but all the members of that one body, being many, are one body, so also *is* Christ.

13 For by one Spirit we were all baptized into one body—whether Jews or Greeks, whether slaves or free—and have all been made to drink into one Spirit.

14 For in fact the body is not one member but many.

15 If the foot should say, "Because I am not a hand, I am not of the body," is it therefore not of the body?

16 And if the ear should say, "Because I am not an eye, I am not of the body," is it therefore not of the body?

17 If the whole body *were* an eye, where *would* be the hearing? If the whole *were* hearing, where *would* be the smelling?

18 But now God has set the members, each one of them, in the body just as He pleased.

19 And if they *were* all one member, where *would* the body *be*?

20 But now indeed *there are* many members, yet one body.

21 And the eye cannot say to the hand, "I have no need of you"; nor again the head to the feet, "I have no need of you."

22 No, much rather, those members of the body which seem to be weaker are necessary.

23 And those *members* of the body which we think to be less honorable, on these we bestow greater honor; and our unpresentable *parts* have greater modesty,

24 but our presentable *parts* have no need. But God composed the body, having given greater honor to that *part* which lacks it,

25 that there should be no schism in the body, but *that* the members should have the same care for one another.

26 And if one member suffers, all the members suffer with *it;* or if one member is honored, all the members rejoice with *it.*

27 Now you are the body of Christ, and members individually.

28 And God has appointed these in the church: first apostles, second prophets, third teachers, after that miracles, then gifts of healings, helps, administrations, varieties of tongues.

29 *Are* all apostles? *Are* all prophets? *Are* all teachers? *Are* all workers of miracles?

30 Do all have gifts of healings? Do all speak with tongues? Do all interpret?

31 But earnestly desire the best gifts. And yet I show you a more excellent way.

13 Though I speak with the tongues of men and of angels, but have not love, I have become *as* sounding brass or a clanging cymbal.

2 And though I have *the gift of* prophecy, and understand all mysteries and all knowledge, and though I have all faith, so that I could remove mountains, but have not love, I am nothing.

3 And though I bestow all my goods to feed *the poor,* and though I give my body to be burned, but have not love, it profits me nothing.

4 Love suffers long *and* is kind; love does not envy; love does not parade itself, is not puffed up;

5 does not behave rudely, does not seek its own, is not provoked, thinks no evil;

6 does not rejoice in iniquity, but rejoices in the truth;

7 bears all things, believes all

things, hopes all things, endures all things.

8 Love never fails. But whether *there are* prophecies, they will fail; whether *there are* tongues, they will cease; whether *there is* knowledge, it will vanish away.

9 For we know in part and we prophesy in part.

10 But when that which is perfect has come, then that which is in part will be done away.

11 When I was a child, I spoke as a child, I understood as a child, I thought as a child; but when I became a man, I put away childish things.

12 For now we see in a mirror, dimly, but then face to face. Now I know in part, but then I shall know just as I also am known.

13 And now abide faith, hope, love, these three; but the greatest of these *is* love.

14 Pursue love, and desire spiritual *gifts*, but especially that you may prophesy.

2 For he who speaks in a tongue does not speak to men but to God, for no one understands *him;* however, in the spirit he speaks mysteries.

3 But he who prophesies speaks edification and exhortation and comfort to men.

4 He who speaks in a tongue edifies himself, but he who prophesies edifies the church.

5 I wish you all spoke with tongues, but even more that you prophesied; for he who prophesies *is* greater than he who speaks with tongues, unless indeed he interprets, that the church may receive edification.

6 But now, brethren, if I come to you speaking with tongues, what shall I profit you unless I speak to you either by revelation, by knowledge, by prophesying, or by teaching?

7 Even things without life, whether flute or harp, when they make a sound, unless they make a distinction in the sounds, how will it be known what is piped or played?

8 For if the trumpet makes an uncertain sound, who will prepare himself for battle?

9 So likewise you, unless you utter by the tongue words easy to understand, how will it be known what is spoken? For you will be speaking into the air.

10 There are, it may be, so many kinds of languages in the world, and none of them *is* without significance.

11 Therefore, if I do not know the meaning of the language, I shall be a foreigner to him who speaks, and he who speaks *will be* a foreigner to me.

12 Even so you, since you are zealous for spiritual *gifts, let it be* for the edification of the church *that* you seek to excel.

13 Therefore let him who speaks in a tongue pray that he may interpret.

14 For if I pray in a tongue, my spirit prays, but my understanding is unfruitful.

15 What is *the result* then? I will pray with the spirit, and I will also pray with the understanding. I will sing with the spirit, and I will also sing with the understanding.

16 Otherwise, if you bless with the spirit, how will he who occupies the place of the uninformed say "Amen" at your giving of thanks, since he does not understand what you say?

17 For you indeed give thanks well, but the other is not edified.

18 I thank my God I speak with tongues more than you all;

19 yet in the church I would rather speak five words with my understanding, that I may teach others also, than ten thousand words in a tongue.

20 Brethren, do not be children in understanding; however, in malice be babes, but in understanding be mature.

240

21 In the law it is written:

> "With men of other tongues
>   and other lips
> I will speak to this people;
> And yet, for all that,
>   they will not hear Me,"

says the Lord.

22 Therefore tongues are for a sign, not to those who believe but to unbelievers; but prophesying is not for unbelievers but for those who believe.

23 Therefore if the whole church comes together in one place, and all speak with tongues, and there come in *those who are* uninformed or unbelievers, will they not say that you are out of your mind?

24 But if all prophesy, and an unbeliever or an uninformed person comes in, he is convinced by all, he is judged by all.

25 And thus the secrets of his heart are revealed; and so, falling down on *his* face, he will worship God and report that God is truly among you.

26 How is it then, brethren? Whenever you come together, each of you has a psalm, has a teaching, has a tongue, has a revelation, has an interpretation. Let all things be done for edification.

27 If anyone speaks in a tongue, *let there be* two or at the most three, *each* in turn, and let one interpret.

28 But if there is no interpreter, let him keep silent in church, and let him speak to himself and to God.

29 Let two or three prophets speak, and let the others judge.

30 But if *anything* is revealed to another who sits by, let the first keep silent.

31 For you can all prophesy one by one, that all may learn and all may be encouraged.

32 And the spirits of the prophets are subject to the prophets.

33 For God is not *the author* of confusion but of peace, as in all the churches of the saints.

34 Let your women keep silent in the churches, for they are not permitted to speak; but *they are* to be submissive, as the law also says.

35 And if they want to learn something, let them ask their own husbands at home; for it is shameful for women to speak in church.

36 Or did the word of God come *originally* from you? Or *was it* you only that it reached?

37 If anyone thinks himself to be a prophet or spiritual, let him acknowledge that the things which I write to you are the commandments of the Lord.

38 But if anyone is ignorant, let him be ignorant.

39 Therefore, brethren, desire earnestly to prophesy, and do not forbid to speak with tongues.

40 Let all things be done decently and in order.

15 Moreover, brethren, I declare to you the gospel which I preached to you, which also you received and in which you stand,

2 by which also you are saved, if you hold fast that word which I preached to you—unless you believed in vain.

3 For I delivered to you first of all that which I also received: that Christ died for our sins according to the Scriptures,

4 and that He was buried, and that He rose again the third day according to the Scriptures,

5 and that He was seen by Cephas, then by the twelve.

6 After that He was seen by over five hundred brethren at once, of whom the greater part remain to the present, but some have fallen asleep.

7 After that He was seen by James, then by all the apostles.

8 Then last of all He was seen by me also, as by one born out of due time.

9 For I am the least of the apostles, who am not worthy to be called an apostle, because I persecuted the church of God.

10 But by the grace of God I am what I am, and His grace toward me was not in vain; but I labored more abundantly than they all, yet not I, but the grace of God *which was* with me.

11 Therefore, whether *it was* I or they, so we preach and so you believed.

12 Now if Christ is preached that He has been raised from the dead, how do some among you say that there is no resurrection of the dead?

13 But if there is no resurrection of the dead, then Christ is not risen.

14 And if Christ is not risen, then our preaching *is* vain and your faith *is* also vain.

15 Yes, and we are found false witnesses of God, because we have testified of God that He raised up Christ, whom He did not raise up—if in fact the dead do not rise.

16 For if *the* dead do not rise, then Christ is not risen.

17 And if Christ is not risen, your faith *is* futile; you are still in your sins!

18 Then also those who have fallen asleep in Christ have perished.

19 If in this life only we have hope in Christ, we are of all men the most pitiable.

20 But now Christ is risen from the dead, *and* has become the first-fruits of those who have fallen asleep.

21 For since by man *came* death, by Man also *came* the resurrection of the dead.

22 For as in Adam all die, even so in Christ all shall be made alive.

23 But each one in his own order: Christ the firstfruits, afterward those *who are* Christ's at His coming.

24 Then *comes* the end, when He delivers the kingdom to God the Father, when He puts an end to all rule and all authority and power.

25 For He must reign till He has put all enemies under His feet.

26 The last enemy *that* will be destroyed *is* death.

27 For "*He has put all things under His feet.*" But when He says "all things are put under *Him,*" *it* is evident that He who put all things under Him is excepted.

28 Now when all things are made subject to Him, then the Son Himself will also be subject to Him who put all things under Him, that God may be all in all.

29 Otherwise, what will they do who are baptized for the dead, if the dead do not rise at all? Why then are they baptized for the dead?

30 And why do we stand in jeopardy every hour?

31 I affirm, by the boasting in you which I have in Christ Jesus our Lord, I die daily.

32 If, in the manner of men, I have fought with beasts at Ephesus, what advantage *is it* to me? If *the* dead do not rise, "*Let us eat and drink, for tomorrow we die.*"

33 Do not be deceived: "Evil company corrupts good habits."

34 Awake to righteousness, and do not sin; for some do not have the knowledge of God. I speak *this* to your shame.

35 But someone will say, "How are the dead raised up? And with what body do they come?"

36 Foolish one, what you sow is not made alive unless it dies.

37 And what you sow, you do not sow that body that shall be, but mere grain—perhaps wheat or some other *grain.*

38 But God gives it a body as He pleases, and to each seed its own body.

39 All flesh *is* not the same flesh, but *there is* one *kind of* flesh of men, another flesh of beasts, another of fish, *and* another of birds.

40 *There are* also celestial bodies and terrestrial bodies; but the glory of the celestial *is* one, and the *glory* of the terrestrial *is* another.

41 *There is* one glory of the sun,

242

Did Jesus Rise from the Dead?

According to the apostle Paul, the Christian faith stands or falls on Jesus' bodily resurrection (1 Corinthians 15:12–32). The belief that Christians will rise from the dead must be confirmed or discarded based on the evidence that Jesus of Nazareth was resurrected. That evidence, both eyewitness and circumstantial, is weighty to behold.

Eyewitness evidence

Eyewitnesses to the resurrected Christ included the twelve apostles on several occasions, Paul, several women, James and the apostles, and in one instance, more than five hundred people (1 Corinthians 15:4–8). The apostle John testified that he and the other disciples not only saw Jesus in His resurrected state but also touched Him and ate with Him (John 20; 21; 1 John 1:1–3).

The first public proclamation of this eyewitness evidence took place in Jerusalem seven weeks after the event. Of the crowd listening to Peter's message, three thousand put their lives on the line by being baptized into the Christian community. In the next few days, that number multiplied greatly. From Jerusalem the testimonials, both written and oral, spread throughout the Roman Empire.

Though often ignored by their contemporaries, the testimony of these eyewitnesses was never refuted. Despite severe persecution for their testimony, none of the eyewitnesses ever recanted. Of Jesus' eleven apostles, tradition states all but one were executed for their faith in Jesus' resurrection. Most of the early church leaders also died as martyrs. The only explanation for men of such outstanding character steadfastly maintaining their testimony in the face of persecution and death is that their testimony was true.

When it comes to the written accounts, the quality is beyond historical comparison. More than 16,000 complete manuscripts of the New Testament exist, some from as early as the fourth century A.D. Many more thousands of fragments exist. A fragment of the Gospel of John dates to A.D. 119 (the original gospel was likely written in the A.D. 80–90s). It is hard to believe that a testimony with that wealth of manuscript support, dating that close to the original event and the original documents, could have suffered significant distortion.

Circumstantial evidence

As impressive as the eyewitness evidence is, it is buttressed by equally strong circumstantial evidence. There is no other way to explain the events that took place.

The tomb was closed with a two- to three-ton rock. Guarded by a cohort (16 to 200) of Roman soldiers, it was stamped with a Roman seal. If the seal were broken by anyone in any way, Roman law required that the entire cohort of soldiers be crucified. Again it is inconceivable that any of Jesus' disciples could have overcome so many professional soldiers who were committed to defending that seal to the death. The story that the guards fell asleep while the disciples sneaked by also is without foundation. The penalty for a Roman soldier falling asleep while guarding a Roman seal was the same—crucifixion.

The suggestion that the Romans or the Jewish enemies of Jesus stole the body likewise is incredible. If they possessed the body, they would have produced it as an effective means to crush the fledgling Christian group. Instead, they did their best to ignore the evidence of the empty tomb.

Then there is the matter of the grave clothes. Jesus' body (but not His head) was wrapped in many layers of linen strips that had pressed into them 75 to 100 pounds of resinous spices. In three days those spices would have set hard. John

reports that one look in the tomb at Jesus' grave clothes convinced both him and Peter of Jesus' resurrection.

What John and Peter probably saw was an empty, unbroken body cast. Knowing that three days earlier Jesus' body had been in that cast, they had just one explanation: Jesus had supernaturally passed through the cast.

This is but a portion of the evidence establishing that the bodily resurrection of Jesus of Nazareth is a historical fact. There is only one possible verdict—He's alive!

For further evidence, you can read: "The Evidence for the Resurrection," J.N.D. Anderson (InterVarsity Press); *Who Moved the Stone?* Frank Morison (InterVarsity Press); *The Resurrection Factor,* Josh McDowell (Thomas Nelson Publishers).

another glory of the moon, and another glory of the stars; for *one* star differs from *another* star in glory.

42 So also is the resurrection of the dead. *The body* is sown in corruption, it is raised in incorruption.

43 It is sown in dishonor, it is raised in glory. It is sown in weakness, it is raised in power.

44 It is sown a natural body, it is raised a spiritual body. There is a natural body, and there is a spiritual body.

45 And so it is written, *"The first man Adam became a living being."* The last Adam *became* a life-giving spirit.

46 However, the spiritual is not first, but the natural, and afterward the spiritual.

47 The first man *was* of the earth, *made* of dust; the second Man *is* the Lord from heaven.

48 As *was* the *man* of dust, so also *are* those *who are made* of dust; and as *is* the heavenly *Man*, so also *are* those *who are* heavenly.

49 And as we have borne the image of the *man* of dust, we shall also bear the image of the heavenly *Man.*

50 Now this I say, brethren, that flesh and blood cannot inherit the kingdom of God; nor does corruption inherit incorruption.

51 Behold, I tell you a mystery: We shall not all sleep, but we shall all be changed—

52 in a moment, in the twinkling of an eye, at the last trumpet. For the trumpet will sound, and the dead will be raised incorruptible, and we shall be changed.

53 For this corruptible must put on incorruption, and this mortal *must* put on immortality.

54 So when this corruptible has put on incorruption, and this mortal has put on immortality, then shall be brought to pass the saying that is written: *"Death is swallowed up in victory."*

55 *"O Death, where is your sting? O Hades, where is your victory?"*

56 The sting of death *is* sin, and the strength of sin *is* the law.

57 But thanks *be* to God, who gives us the victory through our Lord Jesus Christ.

58 Therefore, my beloved brethren, be steadfast, immovable, always abounding in the work of the Lord, knowing that your labor is not in vain in the Lord.

16 Now concerning the collection for the saints, as I have given orders to the churches of Galatia, so you must do also:

2 On the first *day* of the week let each one of you lay something aside, storing up as he may prosper, that there be no collections when I come.

3 And when I come, whomever you approve by *your* letters I will send to bear your gift to Jerusalem.

4 But if it is fitting that I go also, they will go with me.

5 Now I will come to you when I pass through Macedonia (for I am passing through Macedonia).

6 But it may be that I will remain, or even spend the winter with you, that you may send me on my journey, wherever I go.

7 For I do not wish to see you now on the way; but I hope to stay a while with you, if the Lord permits.

8 But I will tarry in Ephesus until Pentecost.

9 For a great and effective door has opened to me, and *there are* many adversaries.

10 Now if Timothy comes, see that he may be with you without fear; for he does the work of the Lord, as I also *do.*

11 Therefore let no one despise him. But send him on his journey in peace, that he may come to me; for I am waiting for him with the brethren.

12 Now concerning *our* brother Apollos, I strongly urged him to come to you with the brethren, but he was quite unwilling to come at this time; however, he will come when he has a convenient time.

13 Watch, stand fast in the faith, be brave, be strong.

14 Let all *that* you *do* be done with love.

15 I urge you, brethren—you know the household of Stephanas, that it is the firstfruits of Achaia, and *that* they have devoted themselves to the ministry of the saints—

16 that you also submit to such, and to everyone who works and labors with *us*.

17 I am glad about the coming of Stephanas, Fortunatus, and Achaicus, for what was lacking on your part they supplied.

18 For they refreshed my spirit and yours; therefore acknowledge such men.

19 The churches of Asia greet you. Aquila and Priscilla greet you heartily in the Lord, with the church that is in their house.

20 All the brethren greet you. Greet one another with a holy kiss.

21 The salutation with my own hand—Paul.

22 If anyone does not love the Lord Jesus Christ, let him be accursed. O Lord, come!

23 The grace of our Lord Jesus Christ *be* with you.

24 My love *be* with you all in Christ Jesus. Amen.

THE SECOND EPISTLE OF PAUL THE APOSTLE TO THE

CORINTHIANS

PAUL, an apostle of Jesus Christ by the will of God, and Timothy *our* brother,

To the church of God which is at Corinth, with all the saints who are in all Achaia:

2 Grace to you and peace from God our Father and the Lord Jesus Christ.

3 Blessed *be* the God and Father of our Lord Jesus Christ, the Father of mercies and God of all comfort,

4 who comforts us in all our tribulation, that we may be able to comfort those who are in any trouble, with the comfort with which we ourselves are comforted by God.

5 For as the sufferings of Christ abound in us, so our consolation also abounds through Christ.

6 Now if we are afflicted, *it is* for your consolation and salvation, which is effective for enduring the same sufferings which we also suffer. Or if we are comforted, *it is* for your consolation and salvation.

7 And our hope for you is steadfast, because we know that as you are partakers of the sufferings, so also *you will partake* of the consolation.

8 For we do not want you to be ignorant, brethren, of our trouble which came to us in Asia: that we were burdened beyond measure, above strength, so that we despaired even of life.

9 Yes, we had the sentence of death in ourselves, that we should not trust in ourselves but in God who raises the dead,

10 who delivered us from so great a death, and does deliver us; in

whom we trust that He will still deliver *us*,

11 you also helping together in prayer for us, that thanks may be given by many persons on our behalf for the gift *granted* to us through many.

12 For our boasting is this: the testimony of our conscience that we conducted ourselves in the world in simplicity and godly sincerity, not with fleshly wisdom but by the grace of God, and more abundantly toward you.

13 For we are not writing any other things to you than what you read or understand. Now I trust you will understand, even to the end

14 (as also you have understood us in part), that we are your boast as you also *are* ours, in the day of the Lord Jesus.

15 And in this confidence I intended to come to you before, that you might have a second benefit—

16 to pass by way of you to Macedonia, to come again from Macedonia to you, and be helped by you on my way to Judea.

17 Therefore, when I was planning this, did I do it lightly? Or the things I plan, do I plan according to the flesh, that with me there should be Yes, Yes, and No, No?

18 But *as* God *is* faithful, our word to you was not Yes and No.

19 For the Son of God, Jesus Christ, who was preached among you by us—by me, Silvanus, and Timothy—was not Yes and No, but in Him was Yes.

20 For all the promises of God in Him *are* Yes, and in Him Amen, to the glory of God through us.

21 Now He who establishes us with you in Christ and has anointed us *is* God,

22 who also has sealed us and given us the Spirit in our hearts as a deposit.

23 Moreover I call God as witness against my soul, that to spare you I came no more to Corinth.

24 Not that we have dominion over your faith, but are fellow workers for your joy; for by faith you stand.

2 But I determined this within myself, that I would not come again to you in sorrow.

2 For if I make you sorrowful, then who is he who makes me glad but the one who is made sorrowful by me?

3 And I wrote this very thing to you, lest, when I came, I should have sorrow over those from whom I ought to have joy, having confidence in you all that my joy is *the joy* of you all.

4 For out of much affliction and anguish of heart I wrote to you, with many tears, not that you should be grieved, but that you might know the love which I have so abundantly for you.

5 But if anyone has caused grief, he has not grieved me, but all of you to some extent—not to be too severe.

6 This punishment which *was inflicted* by the majority *is* sufficient for such a man,

7 so that, on the contrary, you *ought* rather to forgive and comfort *him*, lest perhaps such a one be swallowed up with too much sorrow.

8 Therefore I urge you to reaffirm *your* love to him.

9 For to this end I also wrote, that I might put you to the test, whether you are obedient in all things.

10 Now whom you forgive anything, I also *forgive*. For if indeed I have forgiven anything, I have forgiven that one for your sakes in the presence of Christ,

11 lest Satan should take advantage of us; for we are not ignorant of his devices.

12 Furthermore, when I came to Troas to *preach* Christ's gospel, and a door was opened to me by the Lord,

13 I had no rest in my spirit, because I did not find Titus my

brother; but taking my leave of them, I departed for Macedonia.

14 Now thanks *be* to God who always leads us in triumph in Christ, and through us diffuses the fragrance of His knowledge in every place.

15 For we are to God the fragrance of Christ among those who are being saved and among those who are perishing.

16 To the one *we are* the aroma of death to death, and to the other the aroma of life to life. And who *is* sufficient for these things?

17 For we are not, as so many, peddling the word of God; but as of sincerity, but as from God, we speak in the sight of God in Christ.

3 Do we begin again to commend ourselves? Or do we need, as some *others*, epistles of commendation to you or *letters* of commendation from you?

2 You are our epistle written in our hearts, known and read by all men;

3 *you are* manifestly an epistle of Christ, ministered by us, written not with ink but by the Spirit of the living God, not on tablets of stone but on tablets of flesh, *that is*, of the heart.

4 And we have such trust through Christ toward God.

5 Not that we are sufficient of ourselves to think of anything as *being* from ourselves, but our sufficiency *is* from God,

6 who also made us sufficient as ministers of the new covenant, not of the letter but of the Spirit; for the letter kills, but the Spirit gives life.

7 But if the ministry of death, written *and* engraved on stones, was glorious, so that the children of Israel could not look steadily at the face of Moses because of the glory of his countenance, which *glory* was passing away,

8 how will the ministry of the Spirit not be more glorious?

9 For if the ministry of condemnation *had* glory, the ministry of righteousness exceeds much more in glory.

10 For even what was made glorious had no glory in this respect, because of the glory that excels.

11 For if what is passing away *was* glorious, what remains *is* much more glorious.

12 Therefore, since we have such hope, we use great boldness of speech—

13 unlike Moses, *who* put a veil over his face so that the children of Israel could not look steadily at the end of what was passing away.

14 But their minds were hardened. For until this day the same veil remains unlifted in the reading of the Old Testament, because the *veil* is taken away in Christ.

15 But even to this day, when Moses is read, a veil lies on their heart.

16 Nevertheless when one turns to the Lord, the veil is taken away.

17 Now the Lord is the Spirit; and where the Spirit of the Lord *is*, there is liberty.

18 But we all, with unveiled face, beholding as in a mirror the glory of the Lord, are being transformed into the same image from glory to glory, just as by the Spirit of the Lord.

4 Therefore, since we have this ministry, as we have received mercy, we do not lose heart.

2 But we have renounced the hidden things of shame, not walking in craftiness nor handling the word of God deceitfully, but by manifestation of the truth commending ourselves to every man's conscience in the sight of God.

3 But even if our gospel is veiled, it is veiled to those who are perishing,

4 whose minds the god of this age has blinded, who do not believe, lest the light of the gospel of the glory of Christ, who is the image of God, should shine on them.

5 For we do not preach ourselves, but Christ Jesus the Lord, and ourselves your servants for Jesus' sake.

6 For it is the God who commanded light to shine out of darkness who has shone in our hearts to *give* the light of the knowledge of the glory of God in the face of Jesus Christ.

7 But we have this treasure in earthen vessels, that the excellence of the power may be of God and not of us.

8 *We are* hard pressed on every side, yet not crushed; *we are* perplexed, but not in despair;

9 persecuted, but not forsaken; struck down, but not destroyed—

10 always carrying about in the body the dying of the Lord Jesus, that the life of Jesus also may be manifested in our body.

11 For we who live are always delivered to death for Jesus' sake, that the life of Jesus also may be manifested in our mortal flesh.

12 So then death is working in us, but life in you.

13 But since we have the same spirit of faith, according to what is written, *"I believed and therefore I spoke,"* we also believe and therefore speak,

14 knowing that He who raised up the Lord Jesus will also raise us up with Jesus, and will present *us* with you.

15 For all things *are* for your sakes, that grace, having spread through the many, may cause thanksgiving to abound to the glory of God.

16 Therefore we do not lose heart. Even though our outward man is perishing, yet the inward *man* is being renewed day by day.

17 For our light affliction, which is but for a moment, is working for us a far more exceeding *and* eternal weight of glory,

18 while we do not look at the things which are seen, but at the things which are not seen. For the things which are seen *are* temporary, but the things which are not seen *are* eternal.

5 For we know that if our earthly house, *this* tent, is destroyed, we have a building from God, a house not made with hands, eternal in the heavens.

2 For in this we groan, earnestly desiring to be clothed with our habitation which is from heaven,

3 if indeed, having been clothed, we shall not be found naked.

4 For we who are in *this* tent groan, being burdened, not because we want to be unclothed, but further clothed, that mortality may be swallowed up by life.

5 Now He who has prepared us for this very thing *is* God, who also has given us the Spirit as a guarantee.

6 Therefore *we are* always confident, knowing that while we are at home in the body we are absent from the Lord.

7 For we walk by faith, not by sight.

8 We are confident, yes, well pleased rather to be absent from the body and to be present with the Lord.

9 Therefore we make it our aim, whether present or absent, to be well pleasing to Him.

10 For we must all appear before the judgment seat of Christ, that each one may receive the things *done* in the body, according to what he has done, whether good or bad.

11 Knowing, therefore, the terror of the Lord, we persuade men; but we are well known to God, and I also trust are well known in your consciences.

12 For we do not commend ourselves again to you, but give you opportunity to glory on our behalf, that you may have *something to answer* those who glory in appearance and not in heart.

13 For if we are beside ourselves, *it is* for God; or if we are of sound mind, *it is* for you.

14 For the love of Christ constrains us, because we judge thus: that if One died for all, then all died;

15 and He died for all, that those who live should live no longer for themselves, but for Him who died for them and rose again.

16 Therefore, from now on, we regard no one according to the flesh. Even though we have known Christ according to the flesh, yet now we know *Him thus* no longer.

17 Therefore, if anyone *is* in Christ, *he is* a new creation; old things have passed away; behold, all things have become new.

18 Now all things *are* of God, who has reconciled us to Himself through Jesus Christ, and has given us the ministry of reconciliation,

19 that is, that God was in Christ reconciling the world to Himself, not imputing their trespasses to them, and has committed to us the word of reconciliation.

20 Therefore we are ambassadors for Christ, as though God were pleading through us: we implore *you* on Christ's behalf, be reconciled to God.

21 For He made Him who knew no sin *to be* sin for us, that we might become the righteousness of God in Him.

6 We then, *as* workers together with Him also plead with you not to receive the grace of God in vain.

2 For He says:

> "In an acceptable time I have
>   heard you,
> And in the day of salvation I
>   have helped you."

Behold, now *is* the accepted time; behold, now *is* the day of salvation.

3 We give no offense in anything, that our ministry may not be blamed.

4 But in all *things* we commend ourselves as ministers of God: in much patience, in tribulations, in needs, in distresses,

5 in stripes, in imprisonments, in tumults, in labors, in sleeplessness, in fastings;

6 by purity, by knowledge, by longsuffering, by kindness, by the Holy Spirit, by sincere love,

7 by the word of truth, by the power of God, by the armor of righteousness on the right hand and on the left,

8 by honor and dishonor, by evil report and good report; as deceivers, and *yet* true;

9 as unknown, and *yet* well known; as dying, and behold we live; as chastened, and *yet* not killed;

10 as sorrowful, yet always rejoicing; as poor, yet making many rich; as having nothing, and *yet* possessing all things.

11 O Corinthians! We have spoken openly to you, our heart is wide open.

12 You are not restricted by us, but you are restricted by your *own* affections.

13 Now in return for the same (I speak as to children), you also be open.

14 Do not be unequally yoked together with unbelievers. For what fellowship has righteousness with lawlessness? And what communion has light with darkness?

15 And what accord has Christ with Belial? Or what part has a believer with an unbeliever?

16 And what agreement has the temple of God with idols? For you are the temple of the living God. As God has said:

> "I will dwell in them
> And walk among them.
> I will be their God,
> And they shall be My people."

17 Therefore

> "Come out from among them

*And be separate, says the Lord.
Do not touch what is unclean,
And I will receive you."*
18"*I will be a Father to you,
And you shall be My sons
and daughters,
Says the Lord Almighty."*

7 Therefore, having these promises, beloved, let us cleanse ourselves from all filthiness of the flesh and spirit, perfecting holiness in the fear of God.

2 Open *your hearts* to us. We have wronged no one, we have corrupted no one, we have defrauded no one.

3 I do not say *this* to condemn; for I have said before that you are in our hearts, to die together and to live together.

4 Great *is* my boldness of speech toward you, great *is* my boasting on your behalf. I am filled with comfort. I am exceedingly joyful in all our tribulation.

5 For indeed, when we came to Macedonia, our flesh had no rest, but we were troubled on every side. Outside *were* conflicts, inside *were* fears.

6 Nevertheless God, who comforts the downcast, comforted us by the coming of Titus,

7 and not only by his coming, but also by the consolation with which he was comforted in you, when he told us of your earnest desire, your mourning, your zeal for me, so that I rejoiced even more.

8 For even if I made you sorry with my letter, I do not regret it; though I did regret it. For I perceive that the same epistle made you sorry, though only for a while.

9 Now I rejoice, not that you were made sorry, but that your sorrow led to repentance. For you were made sorry in a godly manner, that you might suffer loss from us in nothing.

10 For godly sorrow produces repentance to salvation, not to be regretted; but the sorrow of the world produces death.

11 For observe this very thing, that you sorrowed in a godly manner: What diligence it produced in you, *what* clearing of *yourselves, what* indignation, *what* fear, *what* vehement desire, *what* zeal, *what* vindication! In all *things* you proved yourselves to be clear in this matter.

12 Therefore, although I wrote to you, *I did* not *do it* for the sake of him who had done the wrong, nor for the sake of him who suffered wrong, but that our care for you in the sight of God might appear to you.

13 Therefore we have been comforted in your comfort. And we rejoiced exceedingly more for the joy of Titus, because his spirit has been refreshed by you all.

14 For if in anything I have boasted to him about you, I am not ashamed. But as we spoke all things to you in truth, even so our boasting to Titus was found true.

15 And his affections are greater for you as he remembers the obedience of you all, how with fear and trembling you received him.

16 Therefore I rejoice that I have confidence in you in everything.

8 Moreover, brethren, we make known to you, the grace of God bestowed on the churches of Macedonia:

2 that in a great trial of affliction the abundance of their joy and their deep poverty abounded in the riches of their liberality.

3 For I bear witness that according to *their* ability, yes, and beyond *their* ability, *they were* freely willing,

4 imploring us with much urgency that we would receive the gift and the fellowship of the ministering to the saints.

5 And *this they did*, not as we had

hoped, but first gave themselves to the Lord, and *then* to us by the will of God.

6 So we urged Titus, that as he had begun, so he would also complete this grace in you as well.

7 But as you abound in everything—in faith, in speech, in knowledge, in all diligence, and in your love for us—*see* that you abound in this grace also.

8 I speak not by commandment, but I am testing the sincerity of your love by the diligence of others.

9 For you know the grace of our Lord Jesus Christ, that though He was rich, yet for your sakes He became poor, that you through His poverty might become rich.

10 And in this I give *my* advice: It is to your advantage not only to be doing what you began and were desiring to do a year ago;

11 but now you also must complete the doing *of it;* that as *there was* a readiness to desire *it,* so *there* also *may be* a completion out of what *you* have.

12 For if there is first a willing mind, *it is* accepted according to what one has, *and* not according to what he does not have.

13 For *I do* not *mean* that others should be eased and you burdened;

14 but by an equality, *that* now at this time your abundance may *supply* their lack, that their abundance also may *supply* your lack—that there may be equality.

15 As it is written, *"He who gathered much had nothing left over, and he who gathered little had no lack."*

16 But thanks *be* to God who puts the same earnest care for you into the heart of Titus.

17 For he not only accepted the exhortation, but being more diligent, he went to you of his own accord.

18 And we have sent with him the brother whose praise *is* in the gospel throughout all the churches,

19 and not only *that,* but who was also chosen by the churches to travel with us with this gift, which is administered by us to the glory of the Lord Himself and *to show* your ready mind,

20 avoiding this: that anyone should blame us in this lavish gift which is administered by us—

21 providing honorable things, not only in the sight of the Lord, but also in the sight of men.

22 And we have sent with them our brother whom we have often proved diligent in many things, but now much more diligent, because of the great confidence which *we have* in you.

23 If *anyone inquires* about Titus, *he is* my partner and fellow worker concerning you. Or if our brethren *are inquired about, they are* messengers of the churches, the glory of Christ.

24 Therefore show to them, and before the churches, the proof of your love and of our boasting on your behalf.

9 Now concerning the ministering to the saints, it is superfluous for me to write to you;

2 for I know your willingness, about which I boast of you to the Macedonians, that Achaia was ready a year ago; and your zeal has stirred up the majority.

3 Yet I have sent the brethren, lest our boasting of you should be in vain in this respect, that, as I said, you may be ready;

4 lest if *some* Macedonians come with me and find you unprepared, we (not to mention you!) should be ashamed of this confident boasting.

5 Therefore I thought it necessary to exhort the brethren to go to you ahead of time, and prepare your bountiful gift beforehand, which *you had* previously promised, that it may be ready as *a matter of* generosity and not as a grudging obligation.

6 But this *I say:* He who sows sparingly will also reap sparingly, and he who sows bountifully will also reap bountifully.

7 *So let* each one *give* as he purposes in his heart, not grudgingly or of necessity; for God loves a cheerful giver.

8 And God *is* able to make all grace abound toward you, that you, always having all sufficiency in all *things,* have an abundance for every good work.

9 As it is written:

"He has dispersed abroad,
He has given to the poor;
His righteousness remains
    forever."

10 Now may He who supplies seed to the sower, and bread for food, supply and multiply the seed you have *sown* and increase the fruits of your righteousness,

11 while *you are* enriched in everything for all liberality, which causes thanksgiving through us to God.

12 For the administration of this service not only supplies the needs of the saints, but also is abounding through many thanksgivings to God,

13 while, through the proof of this ministry, they glorify God for the obedience of your confession to the gospel of Christ, and for *your* liberal sharing with them and all *men,*

14 and by their prayer for you, who long for you because of the exceeding grace of God in you.

15 Thanks *be* to God for His indescribable gift!

10 Now I, Paul, myself am pleading with you by the meekness and gentleness of Christ—who in presence *am* lowly among you, but being absent am bold toward you.

2 But I beg *you* that when I am present I may not be bold with that confidence by which I intend to be bold against some, who think of us as if we walked according to the flesh.

3 For though we walk in the flesh, we do not war according to the flesh.

4 For the weapons of our warfare *are* not carnal but mighty in God for pulling down strongholds,

5 casting down arguments and every high thing that exalts itself against the knowledge of God, bringing every thought into captivity to the obedience of Christ,

6 and being ready to punish all disobedience when your obedience is fulfilled.

7 Do you look at things according to the outward appearance? If anyone is convinced in himself that he is Christ's, let him again consider this in himself, that just as he *is* Christ's, even so we *are* Christ's.

8 For even if I should boast somewhat more about our authority, which the Lord gave us for edification and not for your destruction, I shall not be ashamed—

9 lest I seem to terrify you by letters.

10 "For *his* letters," they say, "*are* weighty and powerful, but *his* bodily presence *is* weak, and *his* speech contemptible."

11 Let such a person consider this, that what we are in word by letters when we are absent, such *we will* also *be* in deed when we are present.

12 For we dare not class ourselves or compare ourselves with those who commend themselves. But they, measuring themselves by themselves, and comparing themselves among themselves, are not wise.

13 We, however, will not boast beyond measure, but within the limits of the sphere which God appointed us—a sphere which especially includes you.

14 For we are not extending our-

selves beyond *our sphere* (thus not reaching you), for it was to you that we came with the gospel of Christ;

15 not boasting of things beyond measure, *that is,* in other men's labors, but having hope, *that as* your faith is increased, we shall be greatly enlarged by you in our sphere,

16 to preach the gospel in the *regions* beyond you, *and* not to boast in another man's sphere of accomplishment.

17 But *"He who glories, let him glory in the LORD."*

18 For not he who commends himself is approved, but whom the Lord commends.

11 Oh, that you would bear with me in a little folly—and indeed you do bear with me.

2 For I am jealous for you with godly jealousy. For I have betrothed you to one husband, that I may present *you as* a chaste virgin to Christ.

3 But I fear, lest somehow, as the serpent deceived Eve by his craftiness, so your minds may be corrupted from the simplicity that is in Christ.

4 For if he who comes preaches another Jesus whom we have not preached, or *if* you receive a different spirit which you have not received, or a different gospel which you have not accepted, you may well put up with it!

5 For I consider that I am not at all inferior to the most eminent apostles.

6 Even though *I am* untrained in speech, yet *I am* not in knowledge. But we have been thoroughly made manifest among you in all things.

7 Did I commit sin in abasing myself that you might be exalted, because I preached the gospel of God to you free of charge?

8 I robbed other churches, taking wages *from them* to minister to you.

9 And when I was present with you, and in need, I was a burden to no one, for what was lacking to me the brethren who came from Macedonia supplied. And in everything I kept myself from being burdensome to you, and so I will keep *myself.*

10 As the truth of Christ is in me, no one shall stop me from this boasting in the regions of Achaia.

11 Why? Because I do not love you? God knows!

12 But what I do, I will also continue to do, that I may cut off the opportunity from those who desire an opportunity to be regarded just as we are in the things of which they boast.

13 For such *are* false apostles, deceitful workers, transforming themselves into apostles of Christ.

14 And no wonder! For Satan himself transforms himself into an angel of light.

15 Therefore *it is* no great thing if his ministers also transform themselves into ministers of righteousness, whose end will be according to their works.

16 I say again, let no one think me a fool. If otherwise, at least receive me as a fool, that I also may boast a little.

17 What I speak, I speak not according to the Lord, but as it were, foolishly, in this confidence of boasting.

18 Seeing that many boast according to the flesh, I also will boast.

19 For you put up with fools gladly, since you *yourselves* are wise!

20 For you put up with it if one brings you into bondage, if one devours *you,* if one takes *from you,* if one exalts himself, if one strikes you on the face.

21 To *our* shame, I say that we were too weak for that! But in whatever anyone is bold—I speak foolishly—I am bold also.

22 Are they Hebrews? So *am* I. Are

they Israelites? So *am* I. Are they the seed of Abraham? So *am* I.

23 Are they ministers of Christ?—I speak as a fool—I *am* more: in labors more abundant, in stripes above measure, in prisons more frequently, in deaths often.

24 From the Jews five times I received forty *stripes* minus one.

25 Three times I was beaten with rods; once I was stoned; three times I was shipwrecked; a night and a day I have been in the deep;

26 *in* journeys often, *in* perils of waters, *in* perils of robbers, *in* perils of *my own* countrymen, *in* perils of the Gentiles, *in* perils in the city, *in* perils in the wilderness, *in* perils in the sea, *in* perils among false brethren;

27 in weariness and toil, in sleeplessness often, in hunger and thirst, in fastings often, in cold and nakedness—

28 besides the other things, what comes upon me daily: my deep concern for all the churches.

29 Who is weak, and I am not weak? Who is made to stumble, and I do not burn with indignation?

30 If I must boast, I will boast in the things which concern my infirmity.

31 The God and Father of our Lord Jesus Christ, who is blessed forever, knows that I am not lying.

32 In Damascus the governor, under Aretas the king, was guarding the city of the Damascenes with a garrison, desiring to apprehend me;

33 but I was let down in a basket through a window in the wall, and escaped from his hands.

12 It is doubtless not profitable for me to boast. I will come to visions and revelations of the Lord:

2 I know a man in Christ who fourteen years ago—whether in the body I do not know, or whether out of the body I do not know, God knows—such a one was caught up to the third heaven.

3 And I know such a man—whether in the body or out of the body I do not know, God knows—

4 how he was caught up into Paradise and heard inexpressible words, which it is not lawful for a man to utter.

5 Of such a one I will boast; yet of myself I will not boast, except in my infirmities.

6 For though I might desire to boast, I will not be a fool; for I will speak the truth. But I forbear, lest anyone should think of me above what he sees me *to be* or hears from me.

7 And lest I should be exalted above measure by the abundance of the revelations, a thorn in the flesh was given to me, a messenger of Satan to buffet me, lest I be exalted above measure.

8 Concerning this thing I pleaded with the Lord three times that it might depart from me.

9 And He said to me, "My grace is sufficient for you, for My strength is made perfect in weakness." Therefore most gladly I will rather boast in my infirmities, that the power of Christ may rest upon me.

10 Therefore I take pleasure in infirmities, in reproaches, in needs, in persecutions, in distresses, for Christ's sake. For when I am weak, then I am strong.

11 I have become a fool in boasting; you have compelled me. For I ought to have been commended by you; for in nothing was I behind the most eminent apostles, though I am nothing.

12 Truly the signs of an apostle were accomplished among you with all perseverance, in signs and wonders and mighty deeds.

13 For what is it in which you were inferior to other churches, except that I myself was not burdensome to you? Forgive me this wrong!

14 Now *for* the third time I am

ready to come to you. And I will not be burdensome to you; for I do not seek yours, but you. For the children ought not to lay up for the parents, but the parents for the children.

15 And I will very gladly spend and be spent for your souls; though the more abundantly I love you, the less I am loved.

16 But be that *as it may*, I did not burden you. Nevertheless, being crafty, I caught you with guile!

17 Did I take advantage of you by any of those whom I sent to you?

18 I urged Titus, and sent our brother with *him*. Did Titus take advantage of you? Did we not walk in the same spirit? Did *we* not *walk* in the same steps?

19 Again, do you think that we excuse ourselves to you? We speak before God in Christ. But *we do* all things, beloved, for your edification.

20 For I fear lest, when I come, I shall not find you such as I wish, and *that* I shall be found by you such as you do not wish; lest *there* be contentions, jealousies, outbursts of wrath, selfish ambitions, backbitings, whisperings, conceits, tumults;

21 *and* lest, when I come again, my God will humble me among you, and I shall mourn for many who have sinned before and have not repented of the uncleanness, fornication, and licentiousness which they have practiced.

13 This *will be* the third *time* I am coming to you. *"By the mouth of two or three witnesses every word shall be established."*

2 I have told you before, and foretell as if I were present the second time, and now being absent I write to those who have sinned before,

and to all the rest, that if I come again I will not spare—

3 since you seek a proof of Christ speaking in me, who is not weak toward you, but mighty in you.

4 For though He was crucified in weakness, yet He lives by the power of God. For we also are weak in Him, but we shall live with Him by the power of God toward you.

5 Examine yourselves *as to* whether you are in the faith. Prove yourselves. Do you not know yourselves, that Jesus Christ is in you?—unless indeed you are disqualified.

6 But I trust that you will know that we are not disqualified.

7 Now I pray to God that you do no evil, not that we should appear approved, but that you should do what is honorable, though we may seem disqualified.

8 For we can do nothing against the truth, but for the truth.

9 For we are glad when we are weak and you are strong. And this also we pray, that you may be made complete.

10 Therefore I write these things being absent, lest being present I should use sharpness, according to the authority which the Lord has given me for edification and not for destruction.

11 Finally, brethren, farewell. Become complete. Be of good comfort, be of one mind, live in peace; and the God of love and peace will be with you.

12 Greet one another with a holy kiss.

13 All the saints greet you.

14 The grace of the Lord Jesus Christ, and the love of God, and the communion of the Holy Spirit *be* with you all. Amen.

THE EPISTLE OF PAUL THE APOSTLE TO THE
GALATIANS

PAUL, an apostle (not from men nor through man, but through Jesus Christ and God the Father who raised Him from the dead),

2 and all the brethren who are with me,

To the churches of Galatia:

3 Grace to you and peace from God the Father and our Lord Jesus Christ,

4 who gave Himself for our sins, that He might deliver us from this present evil age, according to the will of our God and Father,

5 to whom *be* glory forever and ever. Amen.

6 I marvel that you are turning away so soon from Him who called you in the grace of Christ, to a different gospel,

7 which is not another; but there are some who trouble you and want to pervert the gospel of Christ.

8 But even if we, or an angel from heaven, preach any other gospel to you than what we have preached to you, let him be accursed.

9 As we have said before, so now I say again, if anyone preaches any other gospel to you than what you have received, let him be accursed.

10 For do I now persuade men, or God? Or do I seek to please men? For if I still pleased men, I would not be a servant of Christ.

11 But I make known to you, brethren, that the gospel which was preached by me is not according to man.

12 For I neither received it from man, nor was I taught *it*, but *it came* through the revelation of Jesus Christ.

13 For you have heard of my former conduct in Judaism, how I persecuted the church of God beyond measure and *tried to* destroy it.

14 And I advanced in Judaism beyond many of my contemporaries in my own nation, being more exceedingly zealous for the traditions of my fathers.

15 But when it pleased God, who separated me from my mother's womb and called *me* through His grace,

16 to reveal His Son in me, that I might preach Him among the Gentiles, I did not immediately confer with flesh and blood,

17 nor did I go up to Jerusalem to those *who were* apostles before me; but I went to Arabia, and returned again to Damascus.

18 Then after three years I went up to Jerusalem to see Peter, and remained with him fifteen days.

19 But I saw none of the other apostles except James, the Lord's brother.

20 (Now *concerning* the things which I write to you, indeed, before God, I do not lie.)

21 Afterward I went into the regions of Syria and Cilicia.

22 and I was unknown by face to the churches of Judea which *were* in Christ.

23 But they were hearing only, "He who formerly persecuted us now preaches the faith which he once *tried to* destroy."

24 And they glorified God in me.

2 Then after fourteen years I went up again to Jerusalem with Barnabas, and also took Titus with *me*.

2 And I went up by revelation, and communicated to them that gospel which I preach among the Gentiles, but privately to those who were of reputation, lest by any means I might run, or had run, in vain.

3 Yet not even Titus who *was* with me, being a Greek, was compelled to be circumcised.

What Is a Cult?

Some very devout groups that honor Christ and the Bible are called "cults." What makes them different from all the other churches and denominations called "Christian"?

One of the key points of difference is what they teach about Jesus.

Cults will usually deny that

Jesus is God. The Bible tells us that Jesus was God in human form. He was truly God and not some created being. Many cults say Jesus never claimed to be God. They often refer to the four gospels in which Jesus called Himself the "Son of Man." But this was a title for His ministry leading up to His sacrifice on the cross. After His resurrection, Jesus was called the "Son of God" in honor of His completed work. Also, the term "Son of Man" was used in Daniel 7:13, 14 to refer to the coming Messiah, who could only be God.

Jesus is man. Jesus is not only 100 percent God, but He is also 100 percent human. Frankly, theologians are baffled by how Jesus could have been completely God and completely human. However, the Bible affirms that He was human. He experienced hunger, fatigue, pain, and temptation. Some cults teach that Jesus was

indeed God but that God wasn't fully human.

Jesus died for our sins and was raised from the dead. Some cults deny Jesus actually died or that He was raised in physical body. Some will admit that He died and was raised in spirit but believe His death simply provided a way for His followers to "save themselves." True Christianity has always maintained that Jesus' death and bodily resurrection rescues all who put their trust in Him rather than in their own efforts. Cults usually demand some additional "work" to obtain salvation.

The Bible is our best source of truth. Virtually all cults have additional book(s) or teacher(s) whose instructions are held as the highest truth. While the Bible may be honored, this other source is viewed as more reliable, and the Bible's teachings are adjusted to fit the additional book(s), teacher(s), or guru(s).

Conclusion: There is only one gospel: God became human and died in our place so we can have forgiveness of sin through faith in Him. Cults deny or distort this simple concept and thereby transform the most liberating of truths into a deadly trap for the unwary.

4 But *this occurred* because of false brethren secretly brought in (who came in by stealth to spy out our liberty which we have in Christ Jesus, that they might bring us into bondage),

5 to whom we did not yield submission even for an hour, that the truth of the gospel might continue with you.

6 But from those who seemed to be something—whatever they were, it makes no difference to me; God shows personal favoritism to no man—for those who seemed *to be something* added nothing to me.

7 But on the contrary, when they saw that the gospel for the uncircumcised had been committed to me, as *the gospel* for the circumcised *was* to Peter

8 (for He who worked effectively in Peter for the apostleship to the circumcised also worked effectively in me toward the Gentiles),

9 and when James, Cephas, and John, who seemed to be pillars, perceived the grace that had been given to me, they gave me and Barnabas the right hand of fellowship, that we *should* go to the Gentiles and they to the circumcised.

10 *They desired* only that we should remember the poor, the very thing which I also was eager to do.

11 But when Peter had come to Antioch, I withstood him to his face, because he was to be blamed;

12 for before certain men came from James, he would eat with the Gentiles; but when they came, he withdrew and separated himself, fearing those who were of the circumcision.

13 And the rest of the Jews also played the hypocrite with him, so that even Barnabas was carried away with their hypocrisy.

14 But when I saw that they were not straightforward about the truth of the gospel, I said to Peter before *them* all, "If you, being a Jew, live in the manner of Gentiles and not as the Jews, why do you compel Gentiles to live as Jews?

15 "We *who are* Jews by nature, and not sinners of the Gentiles,

16 "knowing that a man is not justified by the works of the law but by faith in Jesus Christ, even we have believed in Christ Jesus, that we might be justified by faith in Christ and not by the works of the law; for by the works of the law no flesh shall be justified.

17 "But if, while we seek to be justified by Christ, we ourselves also are found sinners, *is* Christ therefore a minister of sin? Certainly not!

18 "For if I build again those things which I destroyed, I make myself a transgressor.

19 "For I through the law died to the law that I might live to God.

20 "I have been crucified with Christ; it is no longer I who live, but Christ lives in me; and the *life* which I now live in the flesh I live by faith in the Son of God, who loved me and gave Himself for me.

21 "I do not set aside the grace of God; for if righteousness *comes* through the law, then Christ died in vain."

3 O foolish Galatians! Who has bewitched you that you should not obey the truth, before whose eyes Jesus Christ was clearly portrayed among you as crucified?

2 This only I want to learn from you: Did you receive the Spirit by the works of the law, or by the hearing of faith?

3 Are you so foolish? Having begun in the Spirit, are you now being made perfect by the flesh?

4 Have you suffered so many things in vain—if indeed *it was* in vain?

5 Therefore He who supplies the Spirit to you and works miracles among you, *does He do it* by the works of the law, or by the hearing of faith?—

6 just as Abraham *"believed God, and it was accounted to him for righteousness."*

7 Therefore know that *only* those who are of faith are sons of Abraham.

8 And the Scripture, foreseeing that God would justify the nations by faith, preached the gospel to Abraham beforehand, *saying, "In you all the nations shall be blessed."*

9 So then those who *are* of faith are blessed with believing Abraham.

10 For as many as are of the works of the law are under the curse; for it is written, *"Cursed is everyone who does not continue in all things which are written in the book of the law, to do them."*

11 But that no one is justified by the law in the sight of God is evident, for *"The just shall live by faith."*

12 Yet the law is not of faith, but *"The man who does them shall live by them."*

13 Christ has redeemed us from the curse of the law, having become a curse for us (for it is written, *"Cursed is everyone who hangs on a tree"*),

14 that the blessing of Abraham might come upon the Gentiles in Christ Jesus, that we might receive the promise of the Spirit through faith.

15 Brethren, I speak in the manner of men: Though *it is* only a man's covenant, yet *if it is* confirmed, no one annuls or adds to it.

16 Now to Abraham and his Seed were the promises made. He does not say, "And to seeds," as of many, but as of one, *"And to your Seed,"* who is Christ.

17 And this I say, *that* the law, which was four hundred and thirty years later, cannot annul the covenant that was confirmed before by God in Christ, that it should make the promise of no effect.

18 For if the inheritance *is* of the law, *it is* no longer of promise; but God gave *it* to Abraham by promise.

19 What purpose then *does* the law serve? It was added because of transgressions, till the Seed should come to whom the promise was made; *and it was* appointed through angels by the hand of a mediator.

20 Now a mediator does not *mediate* for one *only,* but God is one.

21 *Is* the law then against the promises of God? Certainly not! For if there had been a law given which could have given life, truly righteousness would have been by the law.

22 But the Scripture has confined all under sin, that the promise by faith in Jesus Christ might be given to those who believe.

23 But before faith came, we were kept under guard by the law, kept for the faith which would afterward be revealed.

24 Therefore the law was our tutor *to bring us* to Christ, that we might be justified by faith.

25 But after faith has come, we are no longer under a tutor.

26 For you are all sons of God through faith in Christ Jesus.

27 For as many of you as were baptized into Christ have put on Christ.

28 There is neither Jew nor Greek, there is neither slave nor free, there is neither male nor female; for you are all one in Christ Jesus.

29 And if you *are* Christ's, then you are Abraham's seed, and heirs according to the promise.

4 Now I say *that* the heir, as long as he is a child, does not differ at all from a slave, though he is master of all,

2 but is under guardians and stewards until the time appointed by the father.

3 Even so we, when we were children, were in bondage under the elements of the world.

4 But when the fullness of the time had come, God sent forth His Son, born of a woman, born under the law,

5 to redeem those who were under the law, that we might receive the adoption as sons.

6 And because you are sons, God has sent forth the Spirit of His Son into your hearts, crying out, "Abba, Father!"

7 Therefore you are no longer a slave but a son, and if a son, then an heir of God through Christ.

8 But then, indeed, when you did not know God, you served those which by nature are not gods.

9 But now after you have known God, or rather are known by God, how *is it that* you turn again to the weak and beggarly elements, to which you desire again to be in bondage?

10 You observe days and months and seasons and years.

11 I am afraid for you, lest I have labored for you in vain.

12 Brethren, I urge you to become as I *am*, for I *am* as you *are*. You have not injured me at all.

13 You know that because of physical infirmity I preached the gospel to you at the first.

14 And my trial which was in my flesh you did not despise or reject, but you received me as an angel of God, *even* as Christ Jesus.

15 What then was the blessing you *enjoyed?* For I bear you witness that, if possible, you would have plucked out your own eyes and given them to me.

16 Have I therefore become your enemy because I tell you the truth?

17 They zealously court you, *but* for no good; yes, they want to exclude you, that you may be zealous for them.

18 But it is good to be zealous in a good thing always, and not only when I am present with you.

19 My little children, for whom I labor in birth again until Christ is formed in you,

20 I would like to be present with you now and to change my tone; for I have doubts about you.

21 Tell me, you who desire to be under the law, do you not hear the law?

22 For it is written that Abraham had two sons: the one by a bondwoman, the other by a freewoman.

23 But he *who was* of the bondwoman was born according to the flesh, and he of the freewoman through promise,

24 which things are symbolic. For these are the two covenants: the one from Mount Sinai which gives birth to bondage, which is Hagar—

25 for this Hagar is Mount Sinai in Arabia, and corresponds to Jerusalem which now is, and is in bondage with her children—

26 but the Jerusalem above is free, which is the mother of us all.

27 For it is written:

> "Rejoice, O barren,
> You who do not bear!
> Break forth and shout,
> You who do not travail!
> For the desolate has
>   many more children
> Than she who has a husband."

28 Now we, brethren, as Isaac *was,* are children of promise.

29 But, as he who was born according to the flesh then persecuted him *who was born* according to the Spirit, even so *it is* now.

30 Nevertheless what does the Scripture say? *"Cast* out the bondwoman and her son, for the son of the bondwoman shall not be heir with the son of the freewoman."

31 So then, brethren, we are not children of the bondwoman but of the free.

5 Stand fast therefore in the liberty by which Christ has made us free, and do not be entangled again with a yoke of bondage.

2 Indeed I, Paul, say to you that if you become circumcised, Christ will profit you nothing.

3 And I testify again to every man who becomes circumcised that he is a debtor to keep the whole law.

4 You have become estranged from Christ, you who *attempt* to be justified by law; you have fallen from grace.

5 For we through the Spirit eagerly wait for the hope of righteousness by faith.

6 For in Christ Jesus neither circumcision nor uncircumcision avails anything, but faith working through love.

7 You ran well. Who hindered you from obeying the truth?

8 This persuasion does not *come* from Him who calls you.

9 A little leaven leavens the whole lump.

10 I have confidence in you, in the Lord, that you will have no other mind; but he who troubles you shall bear his judgment, whoever he is.

11 And I, brethren, if I still preach circumcision, why do I still suffer persecution? Then the offense of the cross has ceased.

12 I could wish that those who trouble you would even cut themselves off!

13 For you, brethren, have been called to liberty; only do not *use* liberty as an opportunity for the flesh, but through love serve one another.

14 For all the law is fulfilled in one word, *even* in this: *"You shall love your neighbor as yourself."*

15 But if you bite and devour one another, beware lest you be consumed by one another!

16 I say then: Walk in the Spirit, and you shall not fulfill the lust of the flesh.

17 For the flesh lusts against the Spirit, and the Spirit against the flesh; and these are contrary to one another, so that you do not do the things that you wish.

18 But if you are led by the Spirit, you are not under the law.

19 Now the works of the flesh are evident, which are: adultery, fornication, uncleanness, licentiousness,

20 idolatry, sorcery, hatred, contentions, jealousies, outbursts of wrath, selfish ambitions, dissensions, heresies,

21 envy, murders, drunkenness, revelries, and the like; of which I tell you beforehand, just as I also told *you* in time past, that those who practice such things will not inherit the kingdom of God.

22 But the fruit of the Spirit is love, joy, peace, longsuffering, kindness, goodness, faithfulness,

23 gentleness, self-control. Against such there is no law.

24 And those *who are* Christ's have crucified the flesh with its passions and desires.

25 If we live in the Spirit, let us also walk in the Spirit.

26 Let us not become conceited, provoking one another, envying one another.

6 Brethren, if a man is overtaken in any trespass, you who *are* spiritual restore such a one in a spirit of gentleness, considering yourself lest you also be tempted.

2 Bear one another's burdens, and so fulfill the law of Christ.

3 For if anyone thinks himself to be something, when he is nothing, he deceives himself.

4 But let each one examine his own work, and then he will have rejoicing in himself alone, and not in another.

5 For each one shall bear his own load.

6 Let him who is taught the word share in all good things with him who teaches.

7 Do not be deceived, God is not mocked; for whatever a man sows, that he will also reap.

8 For he who sows to his flesh will of the flesh reap corruption, but he

Am I Really Responsible for the Consequences of My Actions?

"It hardly seems fair," some people complain, "to be held accountable for every single thing I do. After all, I don't have control over all the twists and turns of fate that my decisions may lead to."

Wouldn't it be nice to know how things were going to work out before you ventured down a particular path?

The tale of two doors

Imagine yourself in an ancient arena facing two identical doors. You are told that behind one door is a hungry wolf, ready to leap out and devour you. Behind the other is one who loves you more than life itself, ready to meet your deepest need. You are free to choose either door (though you are *not* free *not* to choose). Which do you choose?

You look and listen, hoping for some clue as to which door offers death and which offers life. If only there were a window in each door, so you could look before you turned the latch.

A choice of two paths

Galatians 5:16, 17 presents you with a similar dilemma. You can walk down the path of the "Spirit" (letting God guide your steps), or you can take the path of the "flesh" (letting your natural inclinations control your actions). Which path is right for you?

Unlike the dilemma of the two doors, the choice between the Spirit and the flesh is not a blind one. The consequences are clearly spelled out. Choose the path of the Spirit and "love, joy, peace, longsuffering [patience], kindness, goodness, faithfulness, gentleness, self-control" await you (Galatians 5:22, 23). Choose the path of the flesh, and you will encounter sexual impurity, hatred, jealousy, rage, selfish ambition, and violence, just to name a few of the companions on this path (Galatians 5:19–21).

Conclusion

Are you responsible for your choices? If life really were a matter of choosing between two "blind" doors, then you might not be. But that isn't the case. God, in this passage, provides you with a "window," so you can see clearly where each of these two paths will lead.

And now, the choice is yours.

who sows to the Spirit will of the Spirit reap everlasting life.

9 And let us not grow weary while doing good, for in due season we shall reap if we do not lose heart.

10 Therefore, as we have opportunity, let us do good to all, especially to those who are of the household of faith.

11 See with what large letters I have written to you with my own hand!

12 As many as desire to make a good showing in the flesh, these *try to* compel you to be circumcised, only that they may not suffer persecution for the cross of Christ.

13 For not even those who are circumcised keep the law, but they desire to have you circumcised that they may glory in your flesh.

14 But God forbid that I should glory except in the cross of our Lord Jesus Christ, by whom the world has been crucified to me, and I to the world.

15 For in Christ Jesus neither circumcision nor uncircumcision avails anything, but a new creation.

16 And as many as walk according to this rule, peace and mercy *be* upon them, and upon the Israel of God.

17 From now on let no one trouble me, for I bear in my body the marks of the Lord Jesus.

18 Brethren, the grace of our Lord Jesus Christ *be* with your spirit. Amen.

THE EPISTLE OF PAUL THE APOSTLE TO THE

EPHESIANS

PAUL, an apostle of Jesus Christ by the will of God,

To the saints who are in Ephesus, and faithful in Christ Jesus:

2 Grace to you and peace from God our Father and the Lord Jesus Christ.

3 Blessed *be* the God and Father of our Lord Jesus Christ, who has blessed us with every spiritual blessing in the heavenly *places* in Christ,

4 just as He chose us in Him before the foundation of the world, that we should be holy and without blame before Him in love,

5 having predestined us to adoption as sons by Jesus Christ to Himself, according to the good pleasure of His will,

6 to the praise of the glory of His grace, by which He has made us accepted in the Beloved.

7 In Him we have redemption through His blood, the forgiveness of sins, according to the riches of His grace

8 which He made to abound toward us in all wisdom and prudence,

9 having made known to us the mystery of His will, according to His good pleasure which He purposed in Himself,

10 that in the dispensation of the fullness of the times He might gather together in one all things in Christ, both which are in heaven and which are on earth—in Him,

11 in whom also we have obtained an inheritance, being predestined according to the purpose of Him who works all things according to the counsel of His will,

12 that we who first trusted in Christ should be to the praise of His glory.

13 In Him you also *trusted*, after you heard the word of truth, the gospel of your salvation; in whom also, having believed, you were sealed with the Holy Spirit of promise,

14 who is the guarantee of our inheritance until the redemption of the purchased possession, to the praise of His glory.

15 Therefore I also, after I heard of your faith in the Lord Jesus and your love for all the saints,

16 do not cease to give thanks for you, making mention of you in my prayers:

17 that the God of our Lord Jesus Christ, the Father of glory, may give to you the spirit of wisdom and revelation in the knowledge of Him,

18 the eyes of your understanding being enlightened; that you may know what is the hope of His calling, what are the riches of the glory of His inheritance in the saints,

19 and what *is* the exceeding greatness of His power toward us who believe, according to the working of His mighty power

20 which He worked in Christ when He raised Him from the dead and seated *Him* at His right hand in the heavenly *places*,

21 far above all principality and power and might and dominion, and every name that is named, not only in this age but also in that which is to come.

22 And He put all *things* under His feet, and gave Him *to be* head over all *things* to the church,

23 which is His body, the fullness of Him who fills all in all.

2 And you *He made alive*, who were dead in trespasses and sins,

2 in which you once walked according to the course of this world,

according to the prince of the power of the air, the spirit who now works in the sons of disobedience,

3 among whom also we all once conducted ourselves in the lusts of our flesh, fulfilling the desires of the flesh and of the mind, and were by nature children of wrath, just as the others.

4 But God, who is rich in mercy, because of His great love with which He loved us,

5 even when we were dead in trespasses, made us alive together with Christ (by grace you have been saved),

6 and raised *us* up together, and made *us* sit together in the heavenly *places* in Christ Jesus,

7 that in the ages to come He might show the exceeding riches of His grace in *His* kindness toward us in Christ Jesus.

8 For by grace you have been saved through faith, and that not of yourselves; *it is* the gift of God,

9 not of works, lest anyone should boast.

10 For we are His workmanship, created in Christ Jesus for good works, which God prepared beforehand that we should walk in them.

11 Therefore remember that you, once Gentiles in the flesh—who are called Uncircumcision by what is called the Circumcision made in the flesh by hands—

12 that at that time you were without Christ, being aliens from the commonwealth of Israel and strangers from the covenants of promise, having no hope and without God in the world.

13 But now in Christ Jesus you who once were far off have been made near by the blood of Christ.

14 For He Himself is our peace, who has made both one, and has broken down the middle wall of division *between us*,

15 having abolished in His flesh the

Don't Christians Actually Have Three Gods?

In the space of a few verses in Ephesians, Paul mentions the Holy Spirit, the Lord Jesus, and the Father of glory. And Jesus said His followers should be baptized "in the name of the Father and of the Son and of the Holy Spirit" (Matthew 28:19). Do Christians worship three separate Gods?

Like their Jewish ancestors, the early Christians believed there was only one God (John 17:3; 1 Corinthians 8:6). In Matthew 28:19, even though the Father, Son, and Holy Spirit are all mentioned, Jesus' followers are told to baptize in the *name*, not names, of God. All these verses leave us with a paradox: How can God be three *and* one, simultaneously plural and singular?

What is impossible for us is easily achievable for God. Science helps us to understand this when we realize it operates under the assumption that at least ten dimensions exist. God could move about in any of them.

Though the ten dimensions can be demonstrated mathematically, they can't be visualized. We can't "see" dimensions we can't experience. But we can visualize the advantages of extra dimensions.

For example, in two dimensions of space, triangles aren't equal to circles. In three dimensions of space, triangles are still triangles and circles still circles, but a triangle can be rotated, forming a cone shape. And a cone is a series of concentric circles. So what is contradictory in two dimensions can be fully resolved in three. The same is true from three to four, four to five, and so on. So, too, the Trinity is incomprehensible to us in our limited dimensions, but it is quite feasible when more dimensions are added.

Because only the Bible of all the holy books teaches that God is a tri-unity of Person(s), a Trinity, this serves as a proof that it comes from a supernatural source. Since a Trinity is beyond the capacity of humans to visualize, it's not at all surprising that humanly invented religions never describe God this way.

enmity, *that is,* the law of commandments *contained* in ordinances, so as to create in Himself one new man *from* the two, *thus* making peace,

16 and that He might reconcile them both to God in one body through the cross, thereby putting to death the enmity.

17 And He came and preached peace to you who were afar off and to those who were near.

18 For through Him we both have access by one Spirit to the Father.

19 Now, therefore, you are no longer strangers and foreigners, but fellow citizens with the saints and members of the household of God,

20 having been built on the foundation of the apostles and prophets, Jesus Christ Himself being the chief cornerstone,

21 in whom the whole building, being joined together, grows into a holy temple in the Lord,

22 in whom you also are being built together for a habitation of God in the Spirit.

3 For this reason I, Paul, the prisoner of Jesus Christ for you Gentiles—

2 if indeed you have heard of the dispensation of the grace of God which was given to me for you,

3 how that by revelation He made known to me the mystery (as I wrote before in a few words,

4 by which, when you read, you may understand my knowledge in the mystery of Christ),

5 which in other ages was not made known to the sons of men, as it has now been revealed by the Spirit to His holy apostles and prophets:

6 that the Gentiles should be fellow heirs, of the same body, and partakers of His promise in Christ through the gospel,

7 of which I became a minister according to the gift of the grace of God given to me by the effective working of His power.

8 To me, who am less than the least of all the saints, this grace was given, that I should preach among the Gentiles the unsearchable riches of Christ,

9 and to make all *people* see what *is* the fellowship of the mystery, which from the beginning of the ages has been hidden in God who created all things through Jesus Christ;

10 to the intent that now the manifold wisdom of God might be made known by the church to the principalities and powers in the heavenly *places,*

11 according to the eternal purpose which He accomplished in Christ Jesus our Lord,

12 in whom we have boldness and access with confidence through faith in Him.

13 Therefore I ask that you do not lose heart at my tribulations for you, which is your glory.

14 For this reason I bow my knees to the Father of our Lord Jesus Christ,

15 from whom the whole family in heaven and earth is named,

16 that He would grant you, according to the riches of His glory, to be strengthened with might through His Spirit in the inner man,

17 that Christ may dwell in your hearts through faith; that you, being rooted and grounded in love,

18 may be able to comprehend with all the saints what *is* the width and length and depth and height—

19 to know the love of Christ which passes knowledge; that you may be filled with all the fullness of God.

20 Now to Him who is able to do exceedingly abundantly above all that we ask or think, according to the power that works in us,

21 to Him *be* glory in the church by Christ Jesus throughout all ages, world without end. Amen.

4 I, therefore, the prisoner of the Lord, beseech you to have a walk worthy of the calling with which you were called,

2 with all lowliness and gentleness, with longsuffering, bearing with one another in love,

3 endeavoring to keep the unity of the Spirit in the bond of peace.

4 *There is* one body and one Spirit, just as you were called in one hope of your calling;

5 one Lord, one faith, one baptism;

6 one God and Father of all, who *is* above all, and through all, and in you all.

7 But to each one of us grace was given according to the measure of Christ's gift.

8 Therefore He says:

> *"When He ascended on high,*
> *He led captivity captive,*
> *And gave gifts to men."*

9 (Now this, *"He ascended"*— what does it mean but that He also first descended into the lower parts of the earth?

10 He who descended is also the One who ascended far above all the heavens, that He might fill all things.)

11 And He Himself gave some *to be* apostles, some prophets, some evangelists, and some pastors and teachers,

12 for the equipping of the saints for the work of ministry, for the edifying of the body of Christ,

13 till we all come to the unity of the faith and the knowledge of the Son of God, to a perfect man, to the measure of the stature of the fullness of Christ;

14 that we should no longer be children, tossed to and fro and carried about with every wind of doctrine, by the trickery of men, in the cunning craftiness by which they lie in wait to deceive,

15 but, speaking the truth in love,

may grow up in all things into Him who is the head—Christ—

16 from whom the whole body, joined and knit together by what every joint supplies, according to the effective working by which every part does its share, causes growth of the body for the edifying of itself in love.

17 This I say, therefore, and testify in the Lord, that you should no longer walk as the rest of the Gentiles walk, in the futility of their mind,

18 having their understanding darkened, being alienated from the life of God, because of the ignorance that is in them, because of the hardening of their heart;

19 who, being past feeling, have given themselves over to licentiousness, to work all uncleanness with greediness.

20 But you have not so learned Christ,

21 if indeed you have heard Him and have been taught by Him, as the truth is in Jesus:

22 that you put off, concerning your former conduct, the old man which grows corrupt according to the deceitful lusts,

23 and be renewed in the spirit of your mind,

24 and that you put on the new man which was created according to God, in righteousness and true holiness.

25 Therefore, putting away lying, each one speak truth with his neighbor, for we are members of one another.

26 *"Be angry, and do not sin"*: do not let the sun go down on your wrath,

27 nor give place to the devil.

28 Let him who stole steal no longer, but rather let him labor, working with *his* hands what is good, that he may have something to give him who has need.

29 Let no corrupt communication proceed out of your mouth, but

what is good for necessary edification, that it may impart grace to the hearers.

30 And do not grieve the Holy Spirit of God, by whom you were sealed for the day of redemption.

31 Let all bitterness, wrath, anger, clamor, and evil speaking be put away from you, with all malice.

32 And be kind to one another, tenderhearted, forgiving one another, just as God in Christ also forgave you.

5 Therefore be followers of God as dear children.

2 And walk in love, as Christ also has loved us and given Himself for us, an offering and a sacrifice to God for a sweet-smelling aroma.

3 But fornication and all uncleanness or covetousness, let it not even be named among you, as is fitting for saints;

4 neither filthiness, nor foolish talking, nor coarse jesting, which are not fitting, but rather giving of thanks.

5 For this you know, that no fornicator, unclean person, nor covetous man, who is an idolater, has any inheritance in the kingdom of Christ and God.

6 Let no one deceive you with empty words, for because of these things the wrath of God comes upon the sons of disobedience.

7 Therefore do not be partakers with them.

8 For you were once darkness, but now *you are* light in the Lord. Walk as children of light

9 (for the fruit of the Spirit *is* in all goodness, righteousness, and truth),

10 proving what is acceptable to the Lord.

11 And have no fellowship with the unfruitful works of darkness, but rather expose *them*.

12 For it is shameful even to speak of those things which are done by them in secret.

13 But all things that are exposed

are made manifest by the light, for whatever makes manifest is light.

14 Therefore He says:

"Awake, you who sleep,
    Arise from the dead,
    And Christ will give you light."

15 See then that you walk circumspectly, not as fools but as wise,

16 redeeming the time, because the days are evil.

17 Therefore do not be unwise, but understand what the will of the Lord *is*.

18 And do not be drunk with wine, in which is dissipation; but be filled with the Spirit,

19 speaking to one another in psalms and hymns and spiritual songs, singing and making melody in your heart to the Lord,

20 giving thanks always for all things to God the Father in the name of our Lord Jesus Christ,

21 submitting to one another in the fear of God.

22 Wives, submit to your own husbands, as to the Lord.

23 For the husband is head of the wife, as also Christ is head of the church; and He is the Savior of the body.

24 Therefore, just as the church is subject to Christ, so *let* the wives *be* to their own husbands in everything.

25 Husbands, love your wives, just as Christ also loved the church and gave Himself for it,

26 that He might sanctify and cleanse it with the washing of water by the word,

27 that He might present it to Himself a glorious church, not having spot or wrinkle or any such thing, but that it should be holy and without blemish.

28 So husbands ought to love their own wives as their own bodies; he who loves his wife loves himself.

29 For no one ever hated his own flesh, but nourishes and cherishes

How Do You Get Rid of Bitterness?

It has been said that if you swallow your anger, your stomach will keep score. Actually, the results of harboring bitterness are even more serious than stomach problems. Ephesians 4:30–32 warns that bitterness and its companions "wrath, anger, . . . and evil speaking [slander]" can turn you into a walking volcano, painfully at odds with the world.

It's easy to see how bitterness (a feeling of resentment), if not healed, opens the door to wrath, an inward seething that gnaws at our stomach. Wrath, if not healed, may lead to outbursts of fury. Anger, if not healed, may express itself as slander (character assassination). Slander, if not dealt with, leads to malice or even physical violence. Is it any wonder these unchecked feelings and actions "grieve the Holy Spirit of God"? (God the Spirit experiences sorrow when we allow hurts to tear apart our lives rather than allowing His healing to flow.)

But the Bible never draws our attention to a problem without also providing a solution. The apostle Paul goes on to write, "be kind to one another." How does this apply to healing bitterness?

Look back to the start of this sequence, to the first hurt in the chain. In looking at the person who inflicted that pain, try to see past the person's hurtful words or actions to what may have given rise to them. Chances are you'll discover some problem or unmet need in that person's life. If you do, you'll also become "tenderhearted," possessing the compassion that enables you to understand, perhaps even to start caring again for that individual's needs. Thus you will break the chain of bitterness by "forgiving one another" (the process of letting go of an offense until you can release it forever).

Everyone who's been wounded (and who hasn't?) knows how hard it can be to take this suggestion. In fact, apart from God's grace (see "What's So Amazing About Grace?" page 294) it's impossible for us to completely forgive. We can't even start the healing process without admitting we can't do it apart from God's enabling. That's why Paul buttresses his advice with two prayers (Ephesians 1:15–21 and 3:14–21)—that you might know the "exceeding greatness of His power toward us who believe" (1:19) and that God would grant you "to be strengthened with might through His Spirit in the inner man [person]" (3:16).

God never asks anything of us that He doesn't provide the resources to accomplish.

it, just as the Lord *does* the church.

30 For we are members of His body, of His flesh and of His bones.

31 *"For this reason a man shall leave his father and mother and be joined to his wife, and the two shall become one flesh."*

32 This is a great mystery, but I speak concerning Christ and the church.

33 Nevertheless let each one of you in particular so love his own wife as himself, and let the wife *see* that she respects *her* husband.

6 Children, obey your parents in the Lord, for this is right.

2 *"Honor your father and mother,"* which is the first commandment with promise:

3 *"that it may be well with you and you may live long on the earth."*

4 And you, fathers, do not provoke your children to wrath, but bring them up in the training and admonition of the Lord.

5 Servants, be obedient to those who are your masters according to the flesh, with fear and trembling, in sincerity of heart, as to Christ;

6 not with eyeservice, as menpleasers, but as servants of Christ, doing the will of God from the heart,

7 with good will doing service, as to the Lord, and not to men,

8 knowing that whatever good anyone does, he will receive the same from the Lord, whether *he is* a slave or free.

9 And you, masters, do the same things to them, giving up threatening, knowing that your own Master also is in heaven, and there is no partiality with Him.

10 Finally, my brethren, be strong in the Lord and in the power of His might.

11 Put on the whole armor of God, that you may be able to stand against the wiles of the devil.

12 For we do not wrestle against flesh and blood, but against principalities, against powers, against the rulers of the darkness of this age, against spiritual *hosts* of wickedness in the heavenly *places*.

13 Therefore take up the whole armor of God, that you may be able to withstand in the evil day, and having done all, to stand.

14 Stand therefore, having girded your waist with truth, having put on the breastplate of righteousness,

15 and having shod your feet with the preparation of the gospel of peace;

16 above all, taking the shield of faith with which you will be able to quench all the fiery darts of the wicked one.

17 And take the helmet of salvation, and the sword of the Spirit, which is the word of God;

18 praying always with all prayer and supplication in the Spirit, being watchful to this end with all perseverance and supplication for all the saints—

19 and for me, that utterance may be given to me, that I may open my mouth boldly to make known the mystery of the gospel,

20 for which I am an ambassador in chains; that in it I may speak boldly, as I ought to speak.

21 But that you also may know my affairs *and* how I am doing, Tychicus, a beloved brother and faithful minister in the Lord, will make all things known to you;

22 whom I have sent to you for this very purpose, that you may know our affairs, and *that* he may comfort your hearts.

23 Peace to the brethren, and love with faith, from God the Father and the Lord Jesus Christ.

24 Grace *be* with all those who love our Lord Jesus Christ in sincerity. Amen.

THE EPISTLE OF PAUL THE APOSTLE TO THE
PHILIPPIANS

P AUL and Timothy, servants of
Jesus Christ,

To all the saints in Christ Jesus
who are in Philippi, with the bishops and deacons:

2 Grace to you and peace from
God our Father and the Lord Jesus
Christ.

3 I thank my God upon every remembrance of you,

4 always in every prayer of mine
making request for you all with
joy,

5 for your fellowship in the gospel
from the first day until now,

6 being confident of this very
thing, that He who has begun a
good work in you will complete *it*
until the day of Jesus Christ;

7 just as it is right for me to think
this of you all, because I have you
in my heart, inasmuch as both in
my chains and in the defense and
confirmation of the gospel, you all
are partakers with me of grace.

8 For God is my witness, how
greatly I long for you all with the
affection of Jesus Christ.

9 And this I pray, that your love
may abound still more and more in
knowledge and all discernment,

10 that you may approve the
things that are excellent, that you
may be sincere and without offense till the day of Christ,

11 being filled with the fruits of
righteousness which *are* by Jesus
Christ, to the glory and praise of
God.

12 But I want you to know, brethren, that the things *which happened* to me have actually turned
out for the furtherance of the gospel,

13 so that it has become evident to
the whole palace guard, and to all
the rest, that my chains are in
Christ;

14 and most of the brethren in the
Lord, having become confident by
my chains, are much more bold to
speak the word without fear.

15 Some indeed preach Christ even
from envy and strife, and some
also from good will:

16 The former preach Christ from
selfish ambition, not sincerely, supposing to add affliction to my
chains;

17 but the latter out of love, knowing that I am appointed for the
defense of the gospel.

18 What then? Only *that* in every
way, whether in pretense or in
truth, Christ is preached; and in
this I rejoice, yes, and will rejoice.

19 For I know that this will turn
out for my salvation through your
prayer and the supply of the Spirit
of Jesus Christ,

20 according to my earnest expectation and hope that in nothing I
shall be ashamed, but *that* with all
boldness, as always, so now also
Christ will be magnified in my
body, whether by life or by death.

21 For to me, to live *is* Christ, and
to die *is* gain.

22 But if *I* live on in the flesh, this
will mean fruit from *my* labor; yet
what I shall choose I cannot tell.

23 For I am hard pressed between
the two, having a desire to depart
and be with Christ, *which is* far
better.

24 Nevertheless to remain in the
flesh *is* more needful for you.

25 And being confident of this, I
know that I shall remain and continue with you all for your progress and joy of faith,

26 that your rejoicing for me may
be more abundant in Jesus Christ
by my coming to you again.

27 Only let your conduct be worthy of the gospel of Christ, so that
whether I come and see you or am
absent, I may hear of your affairs,
that you stand fast in one spirit,

vith one mind striving together for
he faith of the gospel,

8 and not in any way terrified by
our adversaries, which is to them
 proof of perdition, but to you of
alvation, and that from God.

9 For to you it has been granted
n behalf of Christ, not only to
elieve in Him, but also to suffer
or His sake,

0 having the same conflict which
ou saw in me and now hear *is* in
ne.

2 Therefore if *there is* any consolation in Christ, if any comfort
f love, if any fellowship of the
pirit, if any affection and mercy,

2 fulfill my joy by being like-
ninded, having the same love, *be-
ng* of one accord, of one mind.

Let nothing *be done* through
elfish ambition or conceit, but in
owliness of mind let each esteem
thers better than himself.

Let each of you look out not
nly for his own interests, but also
or the interests of others.

Let this mind be in you which
vas also in Christ Jesus,

who, being in the form of God,
lid not consider it robbery to be
qual with God,

but made Himself of no reputa-
ion, taking the form of a servant,
nd coming in the likeness of men.

And being found in appearance
s a man, He humbled Himself and
ecame obedient to *the point of*
leath, even the death of the cross.

Therefore God also has highly
xalted Him and given Him the
ame which is above every name,

0 that at the name of Jesus every
nee should bow, of those in
eaven, and of those on earth, and
f those under the earth,

1 and *that* every tongue should
onfess that Jesus Christ *is* Lord,
o the glory of God the Father.

2 Therefore, my beloved, as you
ave always obeyed, not as in my
resence only, but now much more
n my absence, work out your own

salvation with fear and trembling;
13 for it is God who works in you
both to will and to do for *His* good
pleasure.

14 Do all things without murmuring and disputing,

15 that you may become blameless
and harmless, children of God
without fault in the midst of a
crooked and perverse generation,
among whom you shine as lights in
the world,

16 holding fast the word of life, so
that I may rejoice in the day of
Christ that I have not run in vain
or labored in vain.

17 Yes, and if I am being poured
out *as a drink offering* on the sacrifice and service of your faith, I am
glad and rejoice with you.

18 For the same reason you also be
glad and rejoice with me.

19 But I trust in the Lord Jesus to
send Timothy to you shortly, that I
also may be encouraged when I
know your state.

20 For I have no one like-minded,
who will sincerely care for your
state.

21 For all seek their own, not the
things which are of Christ Jesus.

22 But you know his proven character, that as a son with *his* father
he served with me in the gospel.

23 Therefore I hope to send him at
once, as soon as I see how it goes
with me.

24 But I trust in the Lord that I
myself shall also come shortly.

25 Yet I considered it necessary to
send to you Epaphroditus, my
brother, fellow worker, and fellow
soldier, but your messenger and
the one who ministered to my
need;

26 since he was longing for you all,
and was distressed because you
had heard that he was sick.

27 For indeed he was sick almost
unto death; but God had mercy on
him, and not only on him but on
me also, lest I should have sorrow
upon sorrow.

28 Therefore I sent him the more eagerly, that when you see him again you may rejoice, and I may be less sorrowful.

29 Receive him therefore in the Lord with all gladness, and hold such men in esteem;

30 because for the work of Christ he came close to death, not regarding his life, to supply what was lacking in your service toward me.

3 Finally, my brethren, rejoice in the Lord. For me to write the same things to you *is* not tedious, but for you *it is* safe.

2 Beware of dogs, beware of evil workers, beware of the mutilation!

3 For we are the circumcision, who worship God in the Spirit, rejoice in Christ Jesus, and have no confidence in the flesh,

4 though I also might have confidence in the flesh. If anyone else thinks he may have confidence in the flesh, I more so:

5 circumcised the eighth day, of the stock of Israel, *of* the tribe of Benjamin, a Hebrew of the Hebrews; concerning the law, a Pharisee;

6 concerning zeal, persecuting the church; concerning the righteousness which is in the law, blameless.

7 But what things were gain to me, these I have counted loss for Christ.

8 But indeed I also count all things loss for the excellence of the knowledge of Christ Jesus my Lord, for whom I have suffered the loss of all things, and count them as rubbish, that I may gain Christ

9 and be found in Him, not having my own righteousness, which *is* from the law, but that which *is* through faith in Christ, the righteousness which is from God by faith;

10 that I may know Him and the power of His resurrection, and the fellowship of His sufferings, being conformed to His death,

11 if, by any means, I may attain to the resurrection from the dead.

12 Not that I have already attained, or am already perfected; but I press on, that I may lay hold of that for which Christ Jesus has also laid hold of me.

13 Brethren, I do not count myself to have apprehended; but one thing *I do,* forgetting those things which are behind and reaching forward to those things which are ahead,

14 I press toward the goal for the prize of the upward call of God in Christ Jesus.

15 Therefore let us, as many as are mature, have this mind; and if in anything you think otherwise, God will reveal even this to you.

16 Nevertheless, to *the degree* that we have already attained, let us walk by the same rule, let us be of the same mind.

17 Brethren, join in following my example, and note those who so walk, as you have us for a pattern.

18 For many walk, of whom I have told you often, and now tell you even weeping, *that they are* the enemies of the cross of Christ:

19 whose end *is* destruction, whose god *is their* belly, and *whose glory is* in their shame—who set their mind on earthly things.

20 For our citizenship is in heaven, from which we also eagerly wait for the Savior, the Lord Jesus Christ,

21 who will transform our lowly body that it may be conformed to His glorious body, according to the working by which He is able even to subdue all things to Himself.

4 Therefore, my beloved and longed-for brethren, my joy and crown, so stand fast in the Lord, beloved.

2 I implore Euodia and I implore Syntyche to be of the same mind in the Lord.

3 And I urge you also, true companion, help these women who la

274

bored with me in the gospel, with Clement also, and the rest of my fellow workers, whose names *are* in the Book of Life.

4 Rejoice in the Lord always. Again I will say, rejoice!

5 Let your gentleness be known to all men. The Lord *is* at hand.

6 Be anxious for nothing, but in everything by prayer and supplication, with thanksgiving, let your requests be made known to God;

7 and the peace of God, which surpasses all understanding, will guard your hearts and minds through Christ Jesus.

8 Finally, brethren, whatever things are true, whatever things *are* noble, whatever things *are* just, whatever things *are* pure, whatever things *are* lovely, whatever things *are* of good report, if *there is* any virtue and if *there is* anything praiseworthy—meditate on these things.

9 The things which you learned and received and heard and saw in me, these do, and the God of peace will be with you.

10 But I rejoiced in the Lord greatly that now at last your care for me has flourished again; though you surely did care, but you lacked opportunity.

11 Not that I speak in regard to need, for I have learned in whatever state I am, to be content:

12 I know how to be abased, and I know how to abound. Everywhere and in all things I have learned both to be full and to be hungry, both to abound and to suffer need.

13 I can do all things through Christ who strengthens me.

14 Nevertheless you have done well that you shared in my distress.

15 Now you Philippians know also that in the beginning of the gospel, when I departed from Macedonia, no church shared with me concerning giving and receiving but you only.

16 For even in Thessalonica you sent *aid* once and again for my necessities.

17 Not that I seek the gift, but I seek the fruit that abounds to your account.

18 Indeed I have all and abound. I am full, having received from Epaphroditus the things *which were* sent from you, a sweet-smelling aroma, an acceptable sacrifice, well pleasing to God.

19 And my God shall supply all your need according to His riches in glory by Christ Jesus.

20 Now to our God and Father *be* glory forever and ever. Amen.

21 Greet every saint in Christ Jesus. The brethren who are with me greet you.

22 All the saints greet you, but especially those who are of Caesar's household.

23 The grace of our Lord Jesus Christ be with you all. Amen.

PAUL, an apostle of Jesus Christ by the will of God, and Timothy our brother,

2 To the saints and faithful brethren in Christ *who are* in Colosse:

Grace to you and peace from God our Father and the Lord Jesus Christ.

3 We give thanks to the God and Father of our Lord Jesus Christ, praying always for you,

4 since we heard of your faith in Christ Jesus and of your love for all the saints;

5 because of the hope which is laid up for you in heaven, of which you heard before in the word of the truth of the gospel,

6 which has come to you, as *it has* also in all the world, and is bringing forth fruit, as *it is* also among you since the day you heard and knew the grace of God in truth;

7 as you also learned from Epaphras, our dear fellow servant, who is a faithful minister of Christ on your behalf,

8 who also declared to us your love in the Spirit.

9 For this reason we also, since the day we heard it, do not cease to pray for you, and to ask that you may be filled with the knowledge of His will in all wisdom and spiritual understanding;

10 that you may have a walk worthy of the Lord, fully pleasing *Him*, being fruitful in every good work and increasing in the knowledge of God;

11 strengthened with all might, according to His glorious power, for all patience and longsuffering with joy;

12 giving thanks to the Father who has qualified us to be partakers of the inheritance of the saints in the light.

13 He has delivered us from the power of darkness and translated *us* into the kingdom of the Son of His love,

14 in whom we have redemption through His blood, the forgiveness of sins.

15 He is the image of the invisible God, the firstborn over all creation.

16 For by Him all things were created that are in heaven and that are on earth, visible and invisible, whether thrones or dominions or principalities or powers. All things were created through Him and for Him.

17 And He is before all things, and in Him all things consist.

18 And He is the head of the body, the church, who is the beginning, the firstborn from the dead, that in all things He may have the preeminence.

19 For it pleased *the Father that* in Him all the fullness should dwell,

20 and by Him to reconcile all things to Himself, by Him, whether things on earth or things in heaven, having made peace through the blood of His cross.

21 And you, who once were alienated and enemies in your mind by wicked works, yet now He has reconciled

22 in the body of His flesh through death, to present you holy, and blameless, and irreproachable in His sight—

23 if indeed you continue in the faith, grounded and steadfast, and are not moved away from the hope of the gospel which you heard, which was preached to every creature under heaven, of which I, Paul, became a minister.

24 I now rejoice in my sufferings for you, and fill up in my flesh what is lacking in the afflictions of Christ, for the sake of His body, which is the church,

25 of which I became a minister

according to the stewardship from God which was given to me for you, to fulfill the word of God,

26 the mystery which has been hidden from ages and from generations, but now has been revealed to His saints.

27 To them God willed to make known what are the riches of the glory of this mystery among the Gentiles: which is Christ in you, the hope of glory.

28 Him we preach, warning every man and teaching every man in all wisdom, that we may present every man perfect in Christ Jesus.

29 To this *end* I also labor, striving according to His working which works in me mightily.

2 For I want you to know what a great conflict I have for you and those in Laodicea, and *for* as many as have not seen my face in the flesh,

2 that their hearts may be encouraged, being knit together in love, and *attaining* to all riches of the full assurance of understanding, to the knowledge of the mystery of God, both of the Father and of Christ,

3 in whom are hidden all the treasures of wisdom and knowledge.

4 Now this I say lest anyone should deceive you with persuasive words.

5 For though I am absent in the flesh, yet I am with you in spirit, rejoicing to see your *good* order and the steadfastness of your faith in Christ.

6 As you have therefore received Christ Jesus the Lord, so walk in Him,

7 rooted and built up in Him and established in the faith, as you have been taught, abounding in it with thanksgiving.

8 Beware lest anyone cheat you through philosophy and empty deceit, according to the tradition of men, according to the basic principles of the world, and not according to Christ.

9 For in Him dwells all the fullness of the Godhead bodily;

10 and you are complete in Him, who is the head of all principality and power.

11 In Him you were also circumcised with the circumcision made without hands, by putting off the body of the sins of the flesh, by the circumcision of Christ,

12 buried with Him in baptism, in which you also were raised with *Him* through faith in the working of God, who raised Him from the dead.

13 And you, being dead in your trespasses and the uncircumcision of your flesh, He has made alive together with Him, having forgiven you all trespasses,

14 having wiped out the handwriting of requirements that was against us, which was contrary to us. And He has taken it out of the way, having nailed it to the cross.

15 Having disarmed principalities and powers, He made a public spectacle of them, triumphing over them in it.

16 Therefore let no one judge you in food or in drink, or regarding a festival or a new moon or sabbaths,

17 which are a shadow of things to come, but the substance is of Christ.

18 Let no one defraud you of your reward, taking delight in *false* humility and worship of angels, intruding into those things which he has not seen, vainly puffed up by his fleshly mind,

19 and not holding fast to the Head, from whom all the body, nourished and knit together by joints and ligaments, grows with the increase *which is* from God.

20 Therefore, if you died with Christ from the basic principles of the world, why, as *though* living in the world, do you subject yourselves to regulations—

21 "Do not touch, do not taste, do not handle,"

Is Astrology a Reliable Way to Learn Who I Am and What the Future Holds?

In Paul's letter to the people of Colosse, he contrasts Christianity with various philosophies and says these philosophies were founded on "the basic principles of the world" (Colossians 2:8).

Astrology is not mentioned by Paul. However, its assumption that our identity and destiny are wrapped up in the planets and the stars causes one to wonder how it squares with the Bible.

In ancient times, planets like Mars and Venus were thought to *directly* influence human lives. Today's astrologers are more likely to claim that the planets' positions *reveal* the "cosmic forces" affecting our lives, much as a weather satellite forecasts next week's storm.

Three objections to astrology should be considered before you read your next horoscope:

1. Astrology is built on a faulty view of the physical universe; its claims of scientific justification aren't true.

—Most astrological calculations assume the earth is at the center of the universe and fail to take into account much of our solar system.

—Astrology assumes the influence of solar system bodies is the same regardless of their size or gravitational pull.

—Astrology ignores the wobble in the earth's rotation axis, which by now has shifted the astrological signs by one or two constellations. Thus someone who thinks of him or herself as a Leo should actually exhibit a Gemini's qualities.

2. Astrology is associated with divination, pagan religions, and spiritism, which can lead one into contact with dangerous spiritual beings.

—Astrology begins with the ancient, pagan belief that the soul enters the body at birth (thus the emphasis on one's birthday rather than conception).

—Astrology's occasional accuracy begs some kind of explanation: either self-fulfilling prophecy or evidence of the supernatural. It is no accident that the Bible lists astrology with sorcery and spells. (See Isaiah 47:12–15.)

3. The Bible forbids us from seeking to discern our future or to draw our identity from any part of creation. (See Colossians 2:8.)

—The Bible claims that our primary reference point is God, not His creation. God establishes our personalities and our days (Psalm 139:13–16).

—The heavens are a sign pointing to God, not a substitute for Him (Psalm 19:1–6).

In other words, astrology looks in the wrong place for the answers to life. Why would anyone want to consult the stars when he or she can talk directly to the One who made them?

22 which all concern things which perish with the using—according to the commandments and doctrines of men?

23 These things indeed have an appearance of wisdom in self-imposed religion, *false* humility, and neglect of the body, *but are* of no value against the indulgence of the flesh.

3 If then you were raised with Christ, seek those things which are above, where Christ is, sitting at the right hand of God.

2 Set your mind on things above, not on things on the earth.

3 For you died, and your life is hidden with Christ in God.

4 When Christ *who is* our life appears, then you also will appear with Him in glory.

5 Therefore put to death your members which are on the earth: fornication, uncleanness, passion, evil desire, and covetousness, which is idolatry.

6 Because of these things the wrath of God is coming upon the sons of disobedience,

7 in which you also once walked when you lived in them.

8 But now you must also put off all these: anger, wrath, malice, blasphemy, filthy language out of your mouth.

9 Do not lie to one another, since you have put off the old man with his deeds,

10 and have put on the new *man* who is renewed in knowledge according to the image of Him who created him,

11 where there is neither Greek nor Jew, circumcised nor uncircumcised, barbarian, Scythian, slave *nor* free, but Christ *is* all and in all.

12 Therefore, as *the* elect of God, holy and beloved, put on tender mercies, kindness, humbleness of mind, meekness, longsuffering;

13 bearing with one another, and forgiving one another, if anyone has a complaint against another; even as Christ forgave you, so you also *must* do.

14 But above all these things put on love, which is the bond of perfection.

15 And let the peace of God rule in your hearts, to which also you were called in one body; and be thankful.

16 Let the word of Christ dwell in you richly in all wisdom, teaching and admonishing one another in psalms and hymns and spiritual songs, singing with grace in your hearts to the Lord.

17 And *whatever* you do in word or deed, *do* all in the name of the Lord Jesus, giving thanks to God the Father through Him.

18 Wives, submit to your own husbands, as is fitting in the Lord.

19 Husbands, love your wives and do not be bitter toward them.

20 Children, obey your parents in all things, for this is well pleasing to the Lord.

21 Fathers, do not provoke your children, lest they become discouraged.

22 Servants, obey in all things your masters according to the flesh, not with eyeservice, as men-pleasers, but in sincerity of heart, fearing God.

23 And whatever you do, do it heartily, as to the Lord and not to men,

24 knowing that from the Lord you will receive the reward of the inheritance; for you serve the Lord Christ.

25 But he who does wrong will be repaid for *the wrong* which he has done, and there is no partiality.

4 Masters, give your servants what is just and fair, knowing that you also have a Master in heaven.

2 Continue earnestly in prayer, being vigilant in it with thanksgiving;

3 meanwhile praying also for us,

that God would open to us a door for the word, to speak the mystery of Christ, for which I am also in chains,

4 that I may make it manifest, as I ought to speak.

5 Walk in wisdom toward those *who are* outside, redeeming the time.

6 *Let* your speech always *be* with grace, seasoned with salt, that you may know how you ought to answer each one.

7 Tychicus, *who is* a beloved brother, a faithful minister, and a fellow servant in the Lord, will tell you all the news about me.

8 I am sending him to you for this very purpose, that he may know your circumstances and comfort your hearts,

9 with Onesimus, a faithful and beloved brother, who is *one* of you. They will make known to you all things which *are happening* here.

10 Aristarchus my fellow prisoner greets you, with Mark the cousin of Barnabas (about whom you received instructions: if he comes to you, welcome him),

11 and Jesus who is called Justus. These *are my* only fellow workers for the kingdom of God who are of the circumcision; they have proved to be a comfort to me.

12 Epaphras, who is *one* of you, a servant of Christ, greets you, always laboring fervently for you in prayers, that you may stand perfect and complete in all the will of God.

13 For I bear him witness that he has a great zeal for you, and those who are in Laodicea, and those in Hierapolis.

14 Luke the beloved physician and Demas greet you.

15 Greet the brethren who are in Laodicea, and Nymphas and the church that *is* in his house.

16 Now when this epistle is read among you, see that it is read also in the church of the Laodiceans, and that you likewise read the epistle from Laodicea.

17 And say to Archippus, "Take heed to the ministry which you have received in the Lord, that you may fulfill it."

18 This salutation by my own hand—Paul. Remember my chains. Grace *be* with you. Amen.

THE FIRST EPISTLE OF PAUL THE APOSTLE TO THE

THESSALONIANS

PAUL, Silvanus, and Timothy,

To the church of the Thessalonians in God the Father and the Lord Jesus Christ:

Grace to you and peace from God our Father and the Lord Jesus Christ.

2 We give thanks to God always for you all, making mention of you in our prayers,

3 remembering without ceasing your work of faith, labor of love, and patience of hope in our Lord Jesus Christ in the sight of our God and Father,

4 knowing, beloved brethren, your election by God.

5 For our gospel did not come to you in word only, but also in power, and in the Holy Spirit and in much assurance, as you know what kind of men we were among you for your sake.

6 And you became followers of us and of the Lord, having received the word in much affliction, with joy of the Holy Spirit,

7 so that you became examples to all in Macedonia and Achaia who believe.

8 For from you the word of the Lord has sounded forth, not only in Macedonia and Achaia, but also in every place. Your faith toward God has gone out, so that we do not need to say anything.

9 For they themselves declare concerning us what manner of entry we had to you, and how you turned to God from idols to serve the living and true God,

10 and to wait for His Son from heaven, whom He raised from the dead, *even* Jesus who delivers us from the wrath to come.

2 For you yourselves know, brethren, that our coming to you was not in vain.

2 But even after we had suffered before and were spitefully treated at Philippi, as you know, we were bold in our God to speak to you the gospel of God in much conflict.

3 For our exhortation *did* not *come* from deceit or uncleanness, nor *was it* in guile.

4 But as we have been approved by God to be entrusted with the gospel, even so we speak, not as pleasing men, but God who tests our hearts.

5 For neither at any time did we use flattering words, as you know, nor a cloak for covetousness—God *is* witness.

6 Nor did we seek glory from men, either from you or from others, when we might have made demands as apostles of Christ.

7 But we were gentle among you, just as a nursing *mother* cherishes her own children.

8 So, affectionately longing for you, we were well pleased to impart to you not only the gospel of God, but also our own lives, because you had become dear to us.

9 For you remember, brethren, our labor and toil; for laboring night and day, that we might not be a burden to any of you, we preached to you the gospel of God.

10 You *are* witnesses, and God *also*, how devoutly and justly and blamelessly we behaved ourselves among you who believe;

11 as you know how we exhorted, and comforted, and charged every one of you, as a father *does* his own children,

12 that you would have a walk worthy of God who calls you into His own kingdom and glory.

13 For this reason we also thank God without ceasing, because when you received the word of God which you heard from us, you welcomed *it* not *as* the word of men, but as it is in truth, the word of God, which also effectively works in you who believe.

14 For you, brethren, became imitators of the churches of God which are in Judea in Christ Jesus. For you also suffered the same things from your own countrymen, just as they *did* from the Jews,

15 who killed both the Lord Jesus and their own prophets, and have persecuted us; and they do not please God and are contrary to all men,

16 forbidding us to speak to the Gentiles that they may be saved, so as always to fill up *the measure of* their sins; but wrath has come upon them to the uttermost.

17 But we, brethren, having been taken away from you for a short time in presence, not in heart, endeavored more eagerly to see your face with great desire.

18 Therefore we wanted to come to you—even I, Paul, time and again—but Satan hindered us.

19 For what *is* our hope, or joy, or crown of rejoicing? *Is it* not even you in the presence of our Lord Jesus Christ at His coming?

20 For you are our glory and joy.

3 Therefore, when we could no longer endure it, we thought it good to be left in Athens alone,

2 and sent Timothy, our brother and minister of God, and our fellow laborer in the gospel of Christ, to establish you and encourage you concerning your faith,

3 that no one should be shaken by these afflictions; for you yourselves know that we are appointed to this.

4 For, in fact, we told you before when we were with you that we would suffer tribulation, just as it happened, and you know.

5 For this reason, when I could no longer endure it, I sent to know your faith, lest by some means the tempter had tempted you, and our labor might be in vain.

6 But now that Timothy has come to us from you, and brought us good news of your faith and love, and that you always have good remembrance of us, greatly desiring to see us, as we also *to see* you—

7 therefore, brethren, in all our affliction and distress we were comforted concerning you by your faith.

8 For now we live, if you stand fast in the Lord.

9 For what thanks can we render to God for you, for all the joy with which we rejoice for your sake before our God,

10 night and day praying exceedingly that we may see your face and perfect what is lacking in your faith?

11 Now may our God and Father Himself, and our Lord Jesus Christ, direct our way to you.

12 And may the Lord make you increase and abound in love to one another and to all, just as we *do* to you,

13 so that He may establish your hearts blameless in holiness before our God and Father at the coming of our Lord Jesus Christ with all His saints.

4 Finally then, brethren, we urge and exhort in the Lord Jesus that you should abound more and

more, just as you received from us how you ought to walk and to please God;

2 for you know what commandments we gave you through the Lord Jesus.

3 For this is the will of God, your sanctification: that you should abstain from sexual immorality;

4 that each of you should know how to possess his own vessel in sanctification and honor,

5 not in passion of lust, like the Gentiles who do not know God;

6 that no one should take advantage of and defraud his brother in this matter, because the Lord *is* the avenger of all such, as we also forewarned you and testified.

7 For God did not call us to uncleanness, but in holiness.

8 Therefore he who rejects *this* does not reject man, but God, who has also given us His Holy Spirit.

9 But concerning brotherly love you have no need that I should write to you, for you yourselves are taught by God to love one another;

10 and indeed you do so toward all the brethren who are in all Macedonia. But we urge you, brethren, that you increase more and more;

11 that you also aspire to lead a quiet life, to mind your own business, and to work with your own hands, as we commanded you,

12 that you may walk properly toward those who are outside, and *that* you may lack nothing.

13 But I do not want you to be ignorant, brethren, concerning those who have fallen asleep, lest you sorrow as others who have no hope.

14 For if we believe that Jesus died and rose again, even so God will bring with Him those who sleep in Jesus.

15 For this we say to you by the word of the Lord, that we who are alive *and* remain until the coming of the Lord will by no means precede those who are asleep.

16 For the Lord Himself will descend from heaven with a shout, with the voice of an archangel, and with the trumpet of God. And the dead in Christ will rise first.

17 Then we who are alive *and* remain shall be caught up together with them in the clouds to meet the Lord in the air. And thus we shall always be with the Lord.

18 Therefore comfort one another with these words.

5 But concerning the times and the seasons, brethren, you have no need that I should write to you.

2 For you yourselves know perfectly that the day of the Lord so comes as a thief in the night.

3 For when they say, "Peace and safety!" then sudden destruction comes upon them, as labor pains upon a pregnant woman. And they shall not escape.

4 But you, brethren, are not in darkness, so that this Day should overtake you as a thief.

5 You are all sons of light and sons of the day. We are not of the night nor of darkness.

6 Therefore let us not sleep, as others *do*, but let us watch and be sober.

7 For those who sleep, sleep at night, and those who get drunk are drunk at night.

8 But let us who are of the day be sober, putting on the breastplate of faith and love, and *as* a helmet the hope of salvation.

9 For God did not appoint us to wrath, but to obtain salvation through our Lord Jesus Christ,

10 who died for us, that whether we wake or sleep, we should live together with Him.

11 Therefore comfort each other and edify one another, just as you also are doing.

12 And we urge you, brethren, to recognize those who labor among you, and are over you in the Lord and admonish you,

13 and to esteem them very highly in love for their work's sake. Be at peace among yourselves.

14 Now we exhort you, brethren, warn those who are unruly, comfort the fainthearted, uphold the weak, be patient with all.

15 See that no one renders evil for evil to anyone, but always pursue what is good both for yourselves and for all.

16 Rejoice always,

17 pray without ceasing,

18 in everything give thanks; for this is the will of God in Christ Jesus for you.

19 Do not quench the Spirit.

20 Do not despise prophecies.

21 Test all things; hold fast what is good.

22 Abstain from every form of evil.

23 Now may the God of peace Himself sanctify you completely; and may your whole spirit, soul, and body be preserved blameless at the coming of our Lord Jesus Christ.

24 He who calls you *is* faithful, who also will do *it.*

25 Brethren, pray for us.

26 Greet all the brethren with a holy kiss.

27 I charge you by the Lord that this epistle be read to all the holy brethren.

28 The grace of our Lord Jesus Christ *be* with you. Amen.

Do I Have to Take Christianity on Blind Faith?

Faith is central to the Christian message, and the Bible says that "without faith it is impossible to please *Him* [God]" (Hebrews 11:6). The kind of faith the Bible celebrates, however, never could be called "blind."

Biblically defined faith involves firm convictions about God's existence and character *and* a transfer of dependence to God. Both knowing and trusting are essential, and both are crucially tied to facts, to reality. How firm can (or should) our convictions about God be if supported only by warm feelings or hearsay or intuitive hunches? While these things are not bad or worthless, how steadfast and secure are we likely to be in turning over our complete trust for the past, the present, and the future to God if they are the sole basis for our convictions?

Consider the analogy we see in human relationships. Would we commend—or recommend—the marriage of two people who have only just met but feel strongly attracted to each other, or whose knowledge of each other comes solely from the reports of others? Wisdom and experience say no.

Consider, also, the examples of faith we are given in Hebrews 11. If God intends our faith to be subjective, or "blind," Abraham and many other key figures who saw and spoke with God (or His "Angel") would have to be omitted from the roster. And what could we say of the "faith" of those who saw and heard and touched and walked side by side with Jesus Christ during His years here on earth?

It must be added, however, that even with all their firsthand experience, it was by the Holy Spirit's work that these men and women received their salvation. Obviously, a paradox concerning our part in believing and God's part lies at the core of this issue (see "Do We Have Any Choice?" page 217).

Perhaps the simplest and most direct statement from God about our part in the connection between facts and faith appears in 1 Thessalonians 5:21, which says, "Test all things." No other holy book, no other god, dares to say anything like that. None other than the Bible and the God of the Bible stand up under honest, objective, humble-hearted investigation and prove to be perfect, pure, and true. (For more about believing, see "What Does It Mean to 'Believe'?" page 123 and "How Does Your Life Change When You Believe?" page 163.)

THE SECOND EPISTLE OF PAUL THE APOSTLE TO THE

THESSALONIANS

PAUL, Silvanus, and Timothy,

To the church of the Thessalonians in God our Father and the Lord Jesus Christ:

2 Grace to you and peace from God our Father and the Lord Jesus Christ.

3 We are bound to thank God always for you, brethren, as it is fitting, because your faith grows exceedingly, and the love of every one of you all abounds toward each other,

4 so that we ourselves boast of you among the churches of God for your patience and faith in all your persecutions and tribulations that you endure,

5 which is manifest evidence of the righteous judgment of God, that you may be counted worthy of the kingdom of God, for which you also suffer;

6 since it is a righteous thing with God to repay with tribulation those who trouble you,

7 and to give you who are troubled rest with us when the Lord Jesus is revealed from heaven with His mighty angels,

8 in flaming fire taking vengeance on those who do not know God, and on those who do not obey the gospel of our Lord Jesus Christ.

9 These shall be punished with everlasting destruction from the presence of the Lord and from the glory of His power,

10 when He comes, in that Day, to be glorified in His saints and to be admired among all those who believe, because our testimony among you was believed.

11 Therefore we also pray always for you that our God would count you worthy of this calling, and fulfill all the good pleasure of His goodness and the work of faith with power,

12 that the name of our Lord Jesus Christ may be glorified in you, and you in Him, according to the grace of our God and the Lord Jesus Christ.

2 Now, brethren, concerning the coming of our Lord Jesus Christ and our gathering together to Him, we ask you,

2 not to be soon shaken in mind or troubled, either by spirit or by word or by letter, as if from us, as though the day of Christ had come.

3 Let no one deceive you by any means; for that Day will not come unless the falling away comes first, and the man of sin is revealed, the son of perdition,

4 who opposes and exalts himself above all that is called God or that is worshiped, so that he sits as God in the temple of God, showing himself that he is God.

5 Do you not remember that when I was still with you I told you these things?

6 And now you know what is restraining, that he may be revealed in his own time.

7 For the mystery of lawlessness is already at work; only He who now restrains will do so until He is taken out of the way.

8 And then the lawless one will be revealed, whom the Lord will consume with the breath of His mouth and destroy with the brightness of His coming.

9 The coming of the lawless one is according to the working of Satan, with all power, signs, and lying wonders,

10 and with all unrighteous deception among those who perish, because they did not receive the love of the truth, that they might be saved.

11 And for this reason God will send them strong delusion, that they should believe the lie,

12 that they all may be condemned who did not believe the truth but had pleasure in unrighteousness.

13 But we are bound to give thanks to God always for you, brethren beloved by the Lord, because God from the beginning chose you for salvation through sanctification by the Spirit and belief in the truth,

14 to which He called you by our gospel, for the obtaining of the glory of our Lord Jesus Christ.

15 Therefore, brethren, stand fast and hold the traditions which you were taught, whether by word or our epistle.

16 Now may our Lord Jesus Christ Himself, and our God and Father, who has loved us and given *us* everlasting consolation and good hope by grace,

17 comfort your hearts and establish you in every good word and work.

3 Finally, brethren, pray for us, that the word of the Lord may have *free* course and be glorified, just as *it is* with you,

2 and that we may be delivered from unreasonable and wicked men; for not all have faith.

3 But the Lord is faithful, who will establish you and guard *you* from the evil one.

4 And we have confidence in the Lord concerning you, both that you do and will do the things we command you.

5 Now may the Lord direct your hearts into the love of God and into the patience of Christ.

6 But we command you, brethren, in the name of our Lord Jesus

Christ, that you withdraw from every brother who walks disorderly and not according to the tradition which he received from us.

7 For you yourselves know how you ought to follow us, for we were not disorderly among you;

8 nor did we eat anyone's bread free of charge, but worked with labor and toil night and day, that we might not be a burden to any of you,

9 not because we do not have authority, but to make ourselves an example of how you should follow us.

10 For even when we were with you, we commanded you this: If anyone will not work, neither shall he eat.

11 For we hear that there are some who walk among you in a disorderly manner, not working at all, but are busybodies.

12 Now those who are such we command and exhort through our Lord Jesus Christ that they work in quietness and eat their own bread.

13 But *as for* you, brethren, do not grow weary *in* doing good.

14 And if anyone does not obey our word in this epistle, note that person and do not keep company with him, that he may be ashamed.

15 Yet do not count *him* as an enemy, but admonish *him* as a brother.

16 Now may the Lord of peace Himself give you peace always in every way. The Lord *be* with you all.

17 The salutation of Paul with my own hand, which is a sign in every epistle; so I write.

18 The grace of our Lord Jesus Christ *be* with you all. Amen.

THE FIRST EPISTLE OF PAUL THE APOSTLE TO

TIMOTHY

PAUL, an apostle of Jesus Christ, by the commandment of God our Savior and the Lord Jesus Christ, our hope,

2 To Timothy, *my* true son in the faith:

Grace, mercy, *and* peace from God our Father and Jesus Christ our Lord.

3 As I urged you when I went into Macedonia—remain in Ephesus that you may charge some that they teach no other doctrine, 4 nor give heed to fables and endless genealogies, which cause disputes rather than godly edification which is in faith.

5 Now the purpose of the commandment is love from a pure heart, *from* a good conscience, and *from* sincere faith,

6 from which some, having strayed, have turned aside to idle talk,

7 desiring to be teachers of the law, understanding neither what they say nor the things which they affirm.

8 But we know that the law *is* good if one uses it lawfully,

9 knowing this: that the law is not made for a righteous person, but for the lawless and insubordinate, for *the* ungodly and for sinners, for *the* unholy and profane, for murderers of fathers and murderers of mothers, for manslayers,

10 for fornicators, for sodomites, for kidnappers, for liars, for perjurers, and if there is any other thing that is contrary to sound doctrine,

11 according to the glorious gospel of the blessed God which was committed to my trust.

12 And I thank Christ Jesus our Lord who has enabled me, because He counted me faithful, putting *me* into the ministry,

13 although I was formerly a blasphemer, a persecutor, and an insolent man; but I obtained mercy because I did *it* ignorantly in unbelief.

14 And the grace of our Lord was exceedingly abundant, with faith and love which are in Christ Jesus.

15 This *is* a faithful saying and worthy of all acceptance, that Christ Jesus came into the world to save sinners, of whom I am chief.

16 However, for this reason I obtained mercy, that in me first Jesus Christ might show all longsuffering, as a pattern to those who are going to believe on Him for everlasting life.

17 Now to the King eternal, immortal, invisible, to God who alone is wise, *be* honor and glory forever and ever. Amen.

18 This charge I commit to you, son Timothy, according to the prophecies previously made concerning you, that by them you may wage the good warfare,

19 having faith and a good conscience, which some having rejected, concerning the faith have suffered shipwreck,

20 of whom are Hymenaeus and Alexander, whom I delivered to Satan that they may learn not to blaspheme.

2 Therefore I exhort first of all that supplications, prayers, intercessions, *and* giving of thanks be made for all men,

2 for kings and all who are in authority, that we may lead a quiet and peaceable life in all godliness and reverence.

3 For this *is* good and acceptable in the sight of God our Savior,

4 who desires all men to be saved and to come to the knowledge of the truth.

5 For *there is* one God and one Mediator between God and men, *the* Man Christ Jesus,

6 who gave Himself a ransom for all, to be testified in due time,

7 for which I was appointed a preacher and an apostle—I am speaking the truth in Christ *and* not lying—a teacher of the Gentiles in faith and truth.

8 Therefore I desire that the men pray everywhere, lifting up holy hands, without wrath and doubting;

9 in like manner also, that the women adorn themselves in modest apparel, with propriety and moderation, not with braided hair or gold or pearls or costly clothing,

10 but, which is proper for women professing godliness, with good works.

11 Let a woman learn in silence with all submission.

12 And I do not permit a woman to teach or to have authority over a man, but to be in silence.

13 For Adam was formed first, then Eve.

14 And Adam was not deceived, but the woman being deceived, fell into transgression.

15 Nevertheless she will be saved in childbearing if they continue in faith, love, and holiness, with self-control.

3 This *is* a faithful saying: If a man desires the position of a bishop, he desires a good work.

2 A bishop then must be blameless, the husband of one wife, temperate, sober-minded, of good behavior, hospitable, able to teach;

3 not given to wine, not violent, not greedy for money, but gentle, not quarrelsome, not covetous;

4 one who rules his own house well, having *his* children in submission with all reverence

5 (for if a man does not know how to rule his own house, how will he take care of the church of God?);

6 not a novice, lest being puffed up with pride he fall into the *same* condemnation as the devil.

7 Moreover he must have a good testimony among those who are outside, lest he fall into reproach and the snare of the devil.

8 Likewise deacons *must be* reverent, not double-tongued, not given to much wine, not greedy for money,

9 holding the mystery of the faith with a pure conscience.

10 But let these also first be proved; then let them serve as deacons, being *found* blameless.

11 Likewise *their* wives *must be* reverent, not slanderers, temperate, faithful in all things.

12 Let deacons be the husbands of one wife, ruling *their* children and their own houses well.

13 For those who have served well as deacons obtain for themselves a good standing and great boldness in the faith which is in Christ Jesus.

14 These things I write to you, though I hope to come to you shortly;

15 but if I am delayed, *I write* so that you may know how you ought to conduct yourself in the house of God, which is the church of the living God, the pillar and ground of the truth.

16 And without controversy great is the mystery of godliness:

God was manifested in the flesh,
Justified in the Spirit,
Seen by angels,
Preached among the Gentiles,
Believed on in the world,
Received up in glory.

4 Now the Spirit expressly says that in latter times some will depart from the faith, giving heed to deceiving spirits and doctrines of demons,

2 speaking lies in hypocrisy, having their own conscience seared with a hot iron,

3 forbidding to marry, *and* commanding to abstain from foods

What Does God Have Against Women?

In reading the highlighted passage in 1 Timothy (also 1 Corinthians 14:33–40), we might conclude that God (speaking through Paul) wants women to be only "plainly" seen and not heard at all. However obvious this conclusion may seem from the verses at hand, is it really reasonable in light of the rest of Scripture?

Beginning with the story of God's creating Eve to be a partner for Adam in building a family and managing the earth; then in more stories (both Old Testament and New) of God's communicating to women and through them to kings, military leaders, fellow prophets, husbands, and churches, we see a respect for women that is unique in the ancient world. While other religions taught that women were made of inferior stuff, the Bible said God made man and woman of the same flesh. Both male and female reflected His image.

In Galatians 3:26–29, Paul writes that all God's children are equal heirs of His promises. We are one in Christ, without regard to nationality, social standing, or gender. Neither do we see gender distinction in the distribution of spiritual gifts (Romans 12; 1 Corinthians 12; Ephesians 4).

Paul spoke glowingly of women colaborers in spreading the gospel, perhaps most notably of Priscilla, who with her husband, Aquila, made tents, taught the Scriptures, and led a fellowship in their home. Paul also praises the ministry of Phoebe, Euodia and Syntyche, Lois and Eunice, and other women.

So what are we to make of these words to Timothy, the pastor at Ephesus? The traditionalist view says that these verses affirm the ultimate leadership of men in the church, reflecting the chain of hierarchy from God to Christ to man to woman.

An alternate views says that the key to understanding this passage lies in the consideration of more complete and detailed information about it, especially its language and its context—compositional, historical, and cultural. This view holds that Paul's words were aimed at countering certain false teachings and pagan practices, against which Timothy was called to guard the fellowship of believers. The specific problems—women asserting superiority and women rejecting marriage and childbearing as unholy things—are still around. And God's answers—humble-hearted submission to His instruction and faith, love, and purity in family relationships—still apply.

which God created to be received with thanksgiving by those who believe and know the truth.

4 For every creature of God *is* good, and nothing is to be refused if it is received with thanksgiving;

5 for it is sanctified by the word of God and prayer.

6 If you instruct the brethren in these things, you will be a good minister of Jesus Christ, nourished in the words of faith and of the good doctrine which you have carefully followed.

7 But reject profane and old wives' fables, and exercise yourself *rather* to godliness.

8 For bodily exercise profits a little, but godliness is profitable for all things, having promise of the life that now is and of that which is to come.

9 This *is* a faithful saying and worthy of all acceptance.

10 For to this *end* we both labor and suffer reproach, because we trust in the living God, who is *the* Savior of all men, especially of those who believe.

11 These things command and teach.

12 Let no one despise your youth, but be an example to the believers in word, in conduct, in love, in spirit, in faith, in purity.

13 Till I come, give attention to reading, to exhortation, to doctrine.

14 Do not neglect the gift that is in you, which was given to you by prophecy with the laying on of the hands of the presbytery.

15 Meditate on these things; give yourself entirely to them, that your progress may be evident to all.

16 Take heed to yourself and to the doctrine. Continue in them, for in doing this you will save both yourself and those who hear you.

5 Do not rebuke an older man, but exhort *him* as a father, *the* younger men as brothers,

2 *the* older women as mothers, *the* younger as sisters, with all purity.

3 Honor widows who are really widows.

4 But if any widow has children or grandchildren, let them first learn to show piety at home and to repay their parents; for this is good and acceptable before God.

5 Now she who is really a widow, and left alone, trusts in God and continues in supplications and prayers night and day.

6 But she who lives in pleasure is dead while she lives.

7 And these things command, that they may be blameless.

8 But if anyone does not provide for his own, and especially for those of his household, he has denied the faith and is worse than an unbeliever.

9 Do not let a widow under sixty years old be taken into the number, *and not unless* she has been the wife of one man,

10 well reported for good works: if she has brought up children, if she has lodged strangers, if she has washed the saints' feet, if she has relieved the afflicted, if she has diligently followed every good work.

11 But refuse *the* younger widows; for when they have begun to grow wanton against Christ, they desire to marry,

12 having condemnation because they have cast off their first faith.

13 And besides they learn *to be* idle, wandering about from house to house, and not only idle but also gossips and busybodies, saying things which they ought not.

14 Therefore I desire that *the* younger *widows* marry, bear children, manage the house, give no opportunity to the adversary to speak reproachfully.

15 For some have already turned aside after Satan.

16 If any believing man or woman has widows, let them relieve them,

and do not let the church be burdened, that it may relieve those who are really widows.

17 Let the elders who rule well be counted worthy of double honor, especially those who labor in the word and doctrine.

18 For the Scripture says, *"You shall not muzzle an ox while it treads out the grain,"* and, "The laborer *is* worthy of his wages."

19 Do not receive an accusation against an elder except from two or three witnesses.

20 Those who are sinning rebuke in the presence of all, that the rest also may fear.

21 I charge *you* before God and the Lord Jesus Christ and the elect angels that you observe these things without prejudice, doing nothing with partiality.

22 Do not lay hands on anyone hastily, nor share in other people's sins; keep yourself pure.

23 No longer drink only water, but use a little wine for your stomach's sake and your frequent infirmities.

24 Some men's sins are clearly evident, preceding *them* to judgment, but those of some *men* follow later.

25 Likewise, the good works of *some* are clearly evident, and those that are otherwise cannot be hidden.

6 Let as many servants as are under the yoke count their own masters worthy of all honor, so that the name of God and *His* doctrine may not be blasphemed.

2 And those who have believing masters, let them not despise *them* because they are brethren, but rather serve *them* because those who are benefited are believers and beloved. Teach and exhort these things.

3 If anyone teaches otherwise and does not consent to wholesome words, *even* the words of our Lord Jesus Christ, and to the doctrine which is according to godliness,

4 he is proud, knowing nothing, but is obsessed with disputes and arguments over words, from which come envy, strife, reviling, evil suspicions,

5 useless wranglings of men of corrupt minds and destitute of the truth, who suppose that godliness is a *means of* gain. From such withdraw yourself.

6 But godliness with contentment is great gain.

7 For we brought nothing into *this* world, *and it is* certain we can carry nothing out.

8 And having food and clothing, with these we shall be content.

9 But those who desire to be rich fall into temptation and a snare, and *into* many foolish and harmful lusts which drown men in destruction and perdition.

10 For the love of money is a root of all *kinds of* evil, for which some have strayed from the faith in their greediness, and pierced themselves through with many sorrows.

11 But you, O man of God, flee these things and pursue righteousness, godliness, faith, love, patience, gentleness.

12 Fight the good fight of faith, lay hold on eternal life, to which you were also called and have confessed the good confession in the presence of many witnesses.

13 I urge you in the sight of God who gives life to all things, and *before* Christ Jesus who witnessed the good confession before Pontius Pilate,

14 that you keep *this* commandment without spot, blameless until our Lord Jesus Christ's appearing,

15 which He will manifest in His own time, *He who is* the blessed and only Potentate, the King of kings and Lord of lords,

16 who alone has immortality, dwelling in unapproachable light, whom no man has seen or can see, to whom be honor and everlasting power. Amen.

17 Command those who are rich in this present age not to be haughty, nor to trust in uncertain riches but in the living God, who gives us richly all things to enjoy.

18 *Let them* do good, that they be rich in good works, ready to give, willing to share,

19 storing up for themselves a good foundation for the time to come, that they may lay hold on eternal life.

20 O Timothy! Guard what was committed to your trust, avoiding the profane *and* vain babblings and contradictions of what is falsely called knowledge—

21 by professing it, some have strayed concerning the faith. Grace *be* with you. Amen.

THE SECOND EPISTLE OF PAUL THE APOSTLE TO

TIMOTHY

PAUL, an apostle of Jesus Christ by the will of God, according to the promise of life which is in Christ Jesus,

2 To Timothy, *my* beloved son:

Grace, mercy, *and* peace from God the Father and Christ Jesus our Lord.

3 I thank God, whom I serve with a pure conscience, as *my* forefathers *did,* as without ceasing I remember you in my prayers night and day,

4 greatly desiring to see you, being mindful of your tears, that I may be filled with joy,

5 when I call to remembrance the genuine faith that is in you, which dwelt first in your grandmother Lois and your mother Eunice, and I am persuaded is in you also.

6 Therefore I remind you to stir up the gift of God which is in you through the laying on of my hands.

7 For God has not given us a spirit of fear, but of power and of love and of a sound mind.

8 Therefore do not be ashamed of the testimony of our Lord, nor of me His prisoner, but share with me in the sufferings for the gospel according to the power of God,

9 who has saved us and called *us* with a holy calling, not according to our works, but according to His own purpose and grace which was given to us in Christ Jesus before time began,

10 but has now been revealed by the appearing of our Savior Jesus Christ, *who* has abolished death and brought life and immortality to light through the gospel,

11 to which I was appointed a preacher, an apostle, and a teacher of the Gentiles.

12 For this reason I also suffer these things; nevertheless I am not ashamed, for I know whom I have believed and am persuaded that He is able to keep what I have committed to Him until that Day.

13 Hold fast the pattern of sound words which you have heard from me, in faith and love which are in Christ Jesus.

14 That good thing which was committed to you, keep by the Holy Spirit who dwells in us.

15 This you know, that all those in Asia have turned away from me, among whom are Phygellus and Hermogenes.

16 The Lord grant mercy to the household of Onesiphorus, for he often refreshed me, and was not ashamed of my chain;

17 but when he arrived in Rome, he sought me out very diligently and found *me*.

18 The Lord grant to him that he may find mercy from the Lord in that Day—and you know very well how many ways he ministered to me at Ephesus.

2 You therefore, my son, be strong in the grace that is in Christ Jesus.

2 And the things that you have heard from me among many witnesses, commit these to faithful men who will be able to teach others also.

3 You therefore must endure hardship as a good soldier of Jesus Christ.

4 No one engaged in warfare entangles himself with the affairs of *this* life, that he may please him who enlisted him as a soldier.

5 And also if anyone competes in athletics, he is not crowned unless he competes according to the rules.

6 The hard-working farmer must be first to partake of the crops.

7 Consider what I say, and may the Lord give you understanding in all things.

8 Remember that Jesus Christ, of the seed of David, was raised from the dead according to my gospel,

9 for which I suffer trouble as an evildoer, *even* to the point of chains; but the word of God is not chained.

10 Therefore I endure all things for the sake of the elect, that they also may obtain the salvation which is in Christ Jesus with eternal glory.

11 *This is* a faithful saying:

For if we died with *Him*,
We shall also live with *Him*.

12 If we endure,
We shall also reign with *Him*.
If we deny *Him*,
He also will deny us.

13 If we are faithless,
He remains faithful;
He cannot deny Himself.

14 Remind *them* of these things, charging *them* before the Lord not to strive about words to no profit, to the ruin of the hearers.

15 Be diligent to present yourself approved to God, a worker who does not need to be ashamed, rightly dividing the word of truth.

16 But shun profane *and* vain babblings, for they will increase to more ungodliness.

17 And their message will spread like cancer. Hymenaeus and Philetus are of this sort,

18 who have strayed concerning the truth, saying that the resurrection is already past; and they overthrow the faith of some.

19 Nevertheless the solid foundation of God stands, having this seal: "The Lord knows those who are His," and, "Let everyone who names the name of Christ depart from iniquity."

20 But in a great house there are not only vessels of gold and silver, but also of wood and clay, some for honor and some for dishonor.

21 Therefore if anyone cleanses himself from the latter, he will be a vessel for honor, sanctified and useful for the Master, prepared for every good work.

22 Flee also youthful lusts; but pursue righteousness, faith, love, peace with those who call on the Lord out of a pure heart.

23 But avoid foolish and ignorant disputes, knowing that they generate strife.

24 And a servant of the Lord must not quarrel but be gentle to all, able to teach, patient,

25 in humility correcting those who are in opposition, if God perhaps will grant them repentance, so that they may know the truth,

26 and *that* they may come to their senses *and escape* the snare of the devil, having been taken captive by him to do his will.

3 But know this, that in the last days perilous times will come:

2 For men will be lovers of them-

What's So Amazing About Grace?

We often save the most important words for last: the end of a conversation or of a letter. For this reason, we pay special attention to a person's last words in life. In 2 Timothy, we read Paul's parting words to his long-time friend and "son" in the faith. And what is his theme? God's grace (2 Timothy 2:1).

What is grace?

A scared and sorrowful teenage boy enters the courtroom for sentencing. He has pleaded guilty to charges of manslaughter for killing a pedestrian in a moment's reckless driving. He approaches the bench.

"I hereby sentence you to five years in jail and payment of $100,000 to the family of the deceased," says the judge as he brings down the gavel.

Feeling the weight but also the fairness of his sentence, the boy turns in silence to leave the court.

At that moment, the judge, who is also the boy's father, steps down from the bench, takes the boy's place between the guards and says, "You're free, son. I'll take the full sentence for you."

Likewise our compassionate, heavenly Father gives us what we don't deserve— it's called "grace." Grace is not some kind of assistance to help us work our way to forgiveness—it's God's love expressed through the life and death of His Son. Through His grace, God steps down from His bench as the just judge of the universe and pays the penalty for us—a penalty that is impossibly beyond our ability to pay.

Who is eligible for God's grace?

We are given God's grace when we accept Jesus as the One who died for all our sins (past, present, and future) and invite Jesus to be our own Lord and Savior. God doesn't put us on probation; the fine is fully paid. (See "Can You *Know* What Your Eternal Destiny Will Be?" page 335.)

When we receive God's grace, we become God's children (1 John 3:1) forever loved beyond measure (Ephesians 1:4–6). We can never be separated from Christ's love (Romans 8:35–39).

No wonder Paul completes this, his last letter to Timothy, with the words: "Grace be with you."

selves, lovers of money, boasters, proud, blasphemers, disobedient to parents, unthankful, unholy,

3 unloving, unforgiving, slanderers, without self-control, brutal, despisers of good,

4 traitors, headstrong, haughty, lovers of pleasure rather than lovers of God,

5 having a form of godliness but denying its power. And from such people turn away!

6 For of this sort are those who creep into households and make captives of gullible women loaded down with sins, led away by various lusts,

7 always learning and never able to come to the knowledge of the truth.

8 Now as Jannes and Jambres resisted Moses, so do these also resist the truth: men of corrupt minds, disapproved concerning the faith;

9 but they will progress no further, for their folly will be manifest to all, as theirs also was.

10 But you have carefully followed my doctrine, manner of life, purpose, faith, longsuffering, love, perseverance,

11 persecutions, afflictions, which happened to me at Antioch, at Iconium, at Lystra—what persecutions I endured. And out of *them* all the Lord delivered me.

12 Yes, and all who desire to live godly in Christ Jesus will suffer persecution.

13 But evil men and impostors will grow worse and worse, deceiving and being deceived.

14 But *as for* you, continue in the things which you have learned and been assured of, knowing from whom you have learned *them*,

15 and that from childhood you have known the Holy Scriptures, which are able to make you wise for salvation through faith which is in Christ Jesus.

16 All Scripture *is* given by inspiration of God, and *is* profitable for doctrine, for reproof, for correc-

tion, for instruction in righteousness,

17 that the man of God may be complete, thoroughly equipped for every good work.

4 I charge *you* therefore before God and the Lord Jesus Christ, who will judge the living and the dead at His appearing and His kingdom:

2 Preach the word! Be ready in season *and* out of season. Convince, rebuke, exhort, with all longsuffering and teaching.

3 For the time will come when they will not endure sound doctrine, but according to their own desires, *because* they have itching ears, they will heap up for themselves teachers;

4 and they will turn *their* ears away from the truth, and be turned aside to fables.

5 But you be watchful in all things, endure afflictions, do the work of an evangelist, fulfill your ministry.

6 For I am already being poured out *as a drink offering*, and the time of my departure is at hand.

7 I have fought the good fight, I have finished the race, I have kept the faith.

8 Finally, there is laid up for me the crown of righteousness, which the Lord, the righteous Judge, will give to me on that Day, and not to me only but also to all who have loved His appearing.

9 Be diligent to come to me quickly;

10 for Demas has forsaken me, having loved this present world, and has departed for Thessalonica—Crescens for Galatia, Titus for Dalmatia.

11 Only Luke is with me. Get Mark and bring him with you, for he is useful to me for ministry.

12 And Tychicus I have sent to Ephesus.

13 Bring the cloak that I left with Carpus at Troas when you come—

Can't a Person Just Pick Out the Best from Each Religion?

"All religions have points of commonality; why can't we just pick out those and live accordingly?" This popular belief betrays ignorance of the deep-seated differences that underlie the world's major religions (including current movements, such as New Age, that are rooted in this kind of thinking). Rather than survey the various religions regarding their views of reality, the nature of God, and so on, let's consider one core issue: What is humanity's basic problem, and how do various religions attempt to solve it?

Hinduism. God's existence is part of our own. He's not a separate being. Instead, all reality consists of one thing, and we are wrong to imagine that you and I are separate or distinct from that tree or this grapefruit. Humanity's problem is thinking that change or separateness exist. The goal is to discard this illusion and attain a timeless unity with the cosmic "all." This can be done through ethical living, devotion to an image representing reality in some form, or meditative exercises.

Islam. Followers of the religion founded by Mohammed believe in one god, "Allah," who is pleased by having people submit to him. Humanity's problem is lack of submission to Allah. The Islamic believer demonstrates his or her submission by reciting the Islamic creed, praying five times a day, fasting, giving alms, and going on a pilgrimage to the holy city of Mecca.

Buddhism. Buddhists differ on God's nature but agree that humanity's basic problem is having desires, many of which can never be met, resulting in unhappiness. Our goal is to keep from wanting. That would ultimately result in extinguishing one's own self or ego.

Christianity. Unlike Hinduism, Christianity teaches that humankind is distinct from God, yet God values us and wants a relationship with us. Our desires were built into us by Him and are not our fundamental problem, as Buddhism teaches. Our problem is that God's moral standards are above our own. While through discipline one can obey the god of Islam, no one can possibly obey the commandments the God of the Bible has given us. Human effort always falls short. As a result, Jesus entered the world—God in human form—to live a life that would please God. When Jesus was crucified and raised from the dead, it became possible for God to transfer Jesus' moral perfection to those who put their trust in Him.

and the books, especially the parchments.

14 Alexander the coppersmith did me much harm. May the Lord repay him according to his works.

15 You also must beware of him, for he has greatly resisted our words.

16 At my first defense no one stood with me, but all forsook me. May it not be charged against them.

17 But the Lord stood with me and strengthened me, so that the message might be preached fully through me, and *that* all the Gentiles might hear. And I was delivered out of the mouth of the lion.

18 And the Lord will deliver me from every evil work and preserve *me* for His heavenly kingdom. To Him *be* glory forever and ever. Amen!

19 Greet Prisca and Aquila, and the household of Onesiphorus.

20 Erastus stayed in Corinth, but Trophimus I have left in Miletus sick.

21 Do your utmost to come before winter. Eubulus greets you, as well as Pudens, Linus, Claudia, and all the brethren.

22 The Lord Jesus Christ be with your spirit. Grace be with you. Amen.

THE EPISTLE OF PAUL THE APOSTLE TO

TITUS

PAUL, a servant of God and an apostle of Jesus Christ, according to the faith of God's elect and the acknowledgment of the truth which is according to godliness,

2 in hope of eternal life which God, who cannot lie, promised before time began,

3 but has in due time manifested His word through preaching, which was committed to me according to the commandment of God our Savior;

4 To Titus, *my* true son in *our* common faith:

Grace, mercy, *and* peace from God the Father and the Lord Jesus Christ our Savior.

5 For this reason I left you in Crete, that you should set in order the things that are lacking, and appoint elders in every city as I commanded you—

6 if a man is blameless, the husband of one wife, having faithful children not accused of dissipation or insubordination.

7 For a bishop must be blameless, as a steward of God, not self-willed, not quick-tempered, not given to wine, not violent, not greedy for money,

8 but hospitable, a lover of what is good, sober-minded, just, holy, self-controlled,

9 holding fast the faithful word as he has been taught, that he may be able, by sound doctrine, both to exhort and convict those who contradict.

10 For there are many insubordinate, both idle talkers and deceivers, especially those of the circumcision,

11 whose mouths must be stopped, who subvert whole households, teaching things which they ought not, for the sake of dishonest gain.

12 One of them, a prophet of their own, said, "Cretans *are* always liars, evil beasts, lazy gluttons."

13 This testimony is true. There-

297

But Who Created God?

This isn't just a child's question, even though it's usually a child who ventures to ask it. Even children are developing awareness of cause and effect and the single direction of time. They will later discover that the universe and everything in it is confined to a single, finite line of time that is moving forward and can't be reversed or stopped. That's why we can never undo ramming into the car in front of us on the way to work this morning, nor can we hold on to the precious moment our baby learned to walk.

Science and mathematics teach us that anything with these kinds of time limits must have a starting point or a beginning. In other words, the universe and everything in it must have been originated.

The necessity of a beginning for God, however, would apply only if He, too, were confined to a time dimension as we are. But according to Titus 1:2 and the theory of general relativity, He is not. General relativity says that the space and time dimensions of the universe must have originated at the same time as matter and energy. Time is the realm in which cause and effect rule, which brings us back to not being able to undo the auto accident but instead having to get the bumper unwrinkled. Because of cause and effect, whoever caused the universe must operate in a sort of time dimension that is independent of and existing before the time dimension of the universe. Scripture tells us that time as we know it has a beginning and that God engaged in cause and effect before that time dimension began (Titus 1:2; 2 Timothy 1:9; Ephesians 1:4; 1 Peter 1:20). So both the Bible and general relativity speak of at least one other time dimension in which God can exist.

In two or more dimensions of time, there is freedom from the necessity of a beginning. If time were two-dimensional, for example, with both a length and a width (that is, a plane), an infinite number of lines running in an infinite number of directions would be possible. If God moves and operates along an infinite number of time lines independent of the time line of our universe, He would have had no beginning and no end. He would not have been created. John 1:3 and Colossians 1:16, 17 affirm He was not.

fore rebuke them sharply, that they may be sound in the faith,

14 not giving heed to Jewish fables and commandments of men who turn from the truth.

15 To the pure all things are pure, but to those who are defiled and unbelieving nothing is pure; but even their mind and conscience are defiled.

16 They profess to know God, but in works they deny Him, being abominable, disobedient, and disqualified for every good work.

2 But as for you, speak the things which are proper for sound doctrine:

2 that the older men be sober, reverent, temperate, sound in faith, in love, in patience;

3 the older women likewise, that they be reverent in behavior, not slanderers, not given to much wine, teachers of good things—

4 that they admonish the young women to love their husbands, to love their children,

5 to be discreet, chaste, homemakers, good, obedient to their own husbands, that the word of God may not be blasphemed.

6 Likewise exhort the young men to be sober-minded,

7 in all things showing yourself *to be* a pattern of good works; in doctrine *showing* integrity, reverence, incorruptibility,

8 sound speech that cannot be condemned, that one who is an opponent may be ashamed, having nothing evil to say of you.

9 *Exhort* servants to be obedient to their own masters, to be well pleasing in all *things*, not answering back,

10 not pilfering, but showing all good fidelity, that they may adorn the doctrine of God our Savior in all things.

11 For the grace of God that brings salvation has appeared to all men,

12 teaching us that, denying un-godliness and worldly lusts, we should live soberly, righteously, and godly in the present age,

13 looking for the blessed hope and glorious appearing of our great God and Savior Jesus Christ,

14 who gave Himself for us, that He might redeem us from every lawless deed and purify for Himself *His* own special people, zealous for good works.

15 Speak these things, exhort, and rebuke with all authority. Let no one despise you.

3 Remind them to be subject to rulers and authorities, to obey, to be ready for every good work,

2 to speak evil of no one, to be peaceable, gentle, showing all humility to all men.

3 For we ourselves were also once foolish, disobedient, deceived, serving various lusts and pleasures, living in malice and envy, hateful and hating one another.

4 But when the kindness and the love of God our Savior toward man appeared,

5 not by works of righteousness which we have done, but according to His mercy He saved us, through the washing of regeneration and renewing of the Holy Spirit,

6 whom He poured out on us abundantly through Jesus Christ our Savior,

7 that having been justified by His grace we should become heirs according to the hope of eternal life.

8 This is a faithful saying, and these things I want you to affirm constantly, that those who have believed in God should be careful to maintain good works. These things are good and profitable to men.

9 But avoid foolish disputes, genealogies, contentions, and strivings about the law; for they are unprofitable and useless.

10 Reject a divisive man after the first and second admonition,

11 knowing that such a person is warped and sinning, being self-condemned.

12 When I send Artemas to you, or Tychicus, be diligent to come to me at Nicopolis, for I have decided to spend the winter there.

13 Send Zenas the lawyer and Apollos on their journey with haste, that they may lack nothing.

14 And let our *people* also learn to maintain good works, to *meet* urgent needs, that they may not be unfruitful.

15 All who *are* with me greet you. Greet those who love us in the faith. Grace *be* with you all. Amen.

THE EPISTLE OF PAUL THE APOSTLE TO

PHILEMON

PAUL, a prisoner of Christ Jesus, and Timothy *our* brother,

To Philemon our beloved *friend* and fellow laborer,

2 to the beloved Apphia, Archippus our fellow soldier, and to the church in your house:

3 Grace to you and peace from God our Father and the Lord Jesus Christ.

4 I thank my God, making mention of you always in my prayers,

5 hearing of your love and faith which you have toward the Lord Jesus and toward all the saints,

6 that the sharing of your faith may become effective by the acknowledgment of every good thing which is in you in Christ Jesus.

7 For we have great joy and consolation in your love, because the hearts of the saints have been refreshed by you, brother.

8 Therefore, though I might be very bold in Christ to command you what is fitting,

9 *yet* for love's sake I rather appeal *to you*—being such a one as Paul, the aged, and now also a prisoner of Jesus Christ—

10 I appeal to you for my son Onesimus, whom I have begotten *while* in my chains,

11 who once was unprofitable to you, but now is profitable to you and to me.

12 I am sending him back. You therefore receive him, that is, my own heart,

13 whom I wished to keep with me, that on your behalf he might minister to me in my chains for the gospel.

14 But without your consent I wanted to do nothing, that your good deed might not be by compulsion, as it were, but voluntary.

15 For perhaps he departed for a while for this *purpose*, that you might receive him forever,

16 no longer as a slave but more than a slave, *as* a beloved brother, especially to me but how much more to you, both in the flesh and in the Lord.

17 If then you count me as a partner, receive him as *you would* me.

18 But if he has wronged you or owes *you* anything, put that on my account.

19 I, Paul, am writing with my own hand. I will repay—not to mention to you that you owe me even your own self besides.

20 Yes, brother, let me have joy

from you in the Lord; refresh my heart in the Lord.

21 Having confidence in your obedience, I write to you, knowing that you will do even more than I say.

22 But, meanwhile, also prepare a guest room for me, for I trust that through your prayers I shall be granted to you.

23 Epaphras, my fellow prisoner in Christ Jesus, greets you,

24 *as do* Mark, Aristarchus, Demas, Luke, my fellow laborers.

25 The grace of our Lord Jesus Christ *be* with your spirit. Amen.

THE EPISTLE TO THE

HEBREWS

GOD, who at various times and in different ways spoke in time past to the fathers by the prophets, 2 has in these last days spoken to us by *His* Son, whom He has appointed heir of all things, through whom also He made the worlds;

3 who being the brightness of *His* glory and the express image of His person, and upholding all things by the word of His power, when He had by Himself purged our sins, sat down at the right hand of the Majesty on high,

4 having become so much better than the angels, as He has by inheritance obtained a more excellent name than they.

5 For to which of the angels did He ever say:

"You are My Son,
Today I have begotten You"?

And again:

"I will be to Him a Father,
And He shall be to Me a Son"?

6 But when He again brings the firstborn into the world, He says:

"Let all the angels of God
worship Him."

7 And of the angels He says:

"Who makes His angels spirits
And His ministers a flame of
fire."

8 But to the Son He says:

"Your throne, O God,
is forever and ever;
A scepter of righteousness is
the scepter of Your Kingdom.
9 *You have loved righteousness*
and hated lawlessness;
Therefore God, Your God,
has anointed You
With the oil of gladness more
than Your companions."

10 And:

"You, LORD, in the beginning
laid the foundation of the
earth,
And the heavens are the work
of Your hands;
11 *They will perish, but You*
remain;
And they will all grow old
like a garment;
12 *Like a cloak You will fold them*
up,
And they will be changed.
But You are the same,
And Your years will not fail."

Has God Changed His Mind About How He Relates to Us?

The Old Testament seems to be full of God's wrath and judgment, while the New Testament displays His love and forgiveness. Even the way God speaks to His people seems to have changed over time. God used to communicate through the prophets, but "in these last days" (the period from Jesus' life until His return), He has spoken through His Son (Hebrews 1:1, 2).

The writer of Hebrews goes on, for the rest of the book, to contrast God's interaction with His people under the Old Testament Covenant of Law and the New Testament Covenant of Grace. Has God changed His attitude toward us?

First, the Old Testament presents God's love just as forcefully as it does His wrath (Psalm 103:8–11). And the New Testament never shies away from expressing God's wrath (Romans 1:18). In both testaments, He rewards those who do good in His name and protects against the spread of evil. If He didn't, we couldn't call Him "good." Good doesn't wink at evil; it confronts it. But God's love and judgment have always been true.

What has changed is that God doesn't exterminate entire societies anymore. That's because Jesus'

resurrection enabled the Holy Spirit to indwell believers permanently. His presence prevents societies from becoming universally reprobate like Sodom and Gomorrah.

Second, God's standard (as seen in the Ten Commandments) may appear, at first glance, to be outwardly achievable: Don't lie, don't steal, don't murder, and so on. However, *outward compliance* has never been the standard. The law was given to wake us up—to make us realize just how bad off we are *inwardly*. Jesus says that if we entertain even one bad thought, we're guilty of breaking the whole law (Matthew 5:17–28). Who gets even close to that kind of standard? It's like requiring everyone to jump unaided to the moon.

God gave the law to show us our desperate need for His grace; and the New Covenant shows how Jesus satisfied the law's demands. This has been God's plan all along (see "What in the World Is God Up To?" page 343). During the giving of the law, God described His three-fold relationship with His people, and that hasn't changed (Exodus 29:45, 46): I will be their God; they will be My people; and I will dwell in their midst. He may have expressed Himself in different external ways, but His thoughts and intents have never changed.

13 But to which of the angels has He ever said:

> "Sit at My right hand,
> Till I make Your enemies
> Your footstool"?

14 Are they not all ministering spirits sent forth to minister for those who will inherit salvation?

2 Therefore we must give the more earnest heed to the things we have heard, lest we drift away.

2 For if the word spoken through angels proved steadfast, and every transgression and disobedience received a just reward,

3 how shall we escape if we neglect so great a salvation, which at the first began to be spoken by the Lord, and was confirmed to us by those who heard *Him*,

4 God also bearing witness both with signs and wonders, with various miracles, and gifts of the Holy Spirit, according to His own will?

5 For He has not put the world to come, of which we speak, in subjection to angels.

6 But one testified in a certain place, saying:

> "What is man that You
>   are mindful of him,
> Or the son of man that You
>   take care of him?
7 You made him a little lower
>   than the angels;
> You crowned him with glory
>   and honor,
> And set him over the works
>   of Your hands.
8 You have put all things
>   in subjection under his feet."

For in that He put all in subjection under him, He left nothing *that is* not put under him. But now we do not yet see all things put under him.

9 But we see Jesus, who was made a little lower than the angels, for the suffering of death crowned with glory and honor, that He, by the grace of God, might taste death for everyone.

10 For it was fitting for Him, for whom *are* all things and by whom *are* all things, in bringing many sons to glory, to make the author of their salvation perfect through sufferings.

11 For both He who sanctifies and those who are being sanctified *are* all of one, for which reason He is not ashamed to call them brethren,

12 saying:

> "I will declare Your name to My
>   brethren;
> In the midst of the
>   congregation I will sing
>   praise to You."

13 And again:

> "I will put My trust in Him."

And again:

> "Here am I and the children
>   whom God has given Me."

14 Inasmuch then as the children have partaken of flesh and blood, He Himself likewise shared in the same, that through death He might destroy him who had the power of death, that is, the devil,

15 and release those who through fear of death were all their lifetime subject to bondage.

16 For indeed He does not give aid to angels, but He does give aid to the seed of Abraham.

17 Therefore, in all things He had to be made like *His* brethren, that He might be a merciful and faithful High Priest in things *pertaining* to God, to make propitiation for the sins of the people.

18 For in that He Himself has suffered, being tempted, He is able to aid those who are tempted.

3 Therefore, holy brethren, partakers of the heavenly calling, consider the Apostle and High

303

Priest of our confession, Christ Jesus,

2 who was faithful to Him who appointed Him, as Moses also *was* faithful in all His house.

3 For this One has been counted worthy of more glory than Moses, inasmuch as He who built the house has more honor than the house.

4 For every house is built by someone, but He who built all things is God.

5 And Moses indeed *was* faithful in all His house as a servant, for a testimony of those things which would be spoken *afterward*,

6 but Christ as a Son over His own house, whose house we are if we hold fast the confidence and the rejoicing of the hope firm to the end.

7 Therefore, as the Holy Spirit says:

> *"Today, if you will hear His voice,*
> 8 *Do not harden your hearts as in the rebellion,*
> *In the day of trial in the wilderness,*
> 9 *Where your fathers tested Me, proved Me,*
> *And saw My works forty years.*
> 10 *Therefore I was angry with that generation,*
> *And said, 'They always go astray in their heart,*
> *And they have not known My ways.'*
> 11 *So I swore in My wrath,*
> *'They shall not enter My rest.' "*

12 Beware, brethren, lest there be in any of you an evil heart of unbelief in departing from the living God;

13 but exhort one another daily, while it is called *"Today,"* lest any of you be hardened through the deceitfulness of sin.

14 For we have become partakers of Christ if we hold the beginning of our confidence steadfast to the end,

15 while it is said:

> *"Today, if you will hear His voice,*
> *Do not harden your hearts as in the rebellion."*

16 For who, having heard, rebelled? Indeed, *was it* not all who came out of Egypt, led by Moses?

17 Now with whom was He angry forty years? *Was it* not with those who sinned, whose corpses fell in the wilderness?

18 And to whom did He swear that they would not enter His rest, but to those who did not obey?

19 So we see that they could not enter in because of unbelief.

4 Therefore, since a promise remains of entering His rest, let us fear lest any of you seem to have come short of it.

2 For indeed the gospel was preached to us as well as to them; but the word which they heard did not profit them, not being mixed with faith in those who heard *it.*

3 For we who have believed do enter that rest, as He has said:

> *"So I swore in My wrath,*
> *'They shall not enter My rest,' "*

although the works were finished from the foundation of the world.

4 For He has spoken in a certain place of the seventh *day* in this way: *"And God rested on the seventh day from all His works";*

5 and again in this *place:* *"They shall not enter My rest."*

6 Since therefore it remains that some *must* enter it, and those to whom it was first preached did not enter because of disobedience,

7 again He designates a certain day, saying in David, *"Today,"* after such a long time, as it has been said:

What Is Jesus Like?

The Book of Hebrews offers a fascinating glimpse into Jesus' identity and character. Here are forty descriptive phrases about Jesus, from just this one book, to help us understand who He is and what He has done for us.

Christ's identity and moral character:

1. Creator of the universe 1:2; 1:10
2. The Son of God the Father 1:2
3. Heir of all things 1:2
4. Exactly represents God's being 1:3
5. Superior to the angels 1:4
6. King for all eternity 1:8
7. Perfect in righteousness 1:8
8. Lover of righteousness, hater of wickedness 1:9
9. Exalted above all others by God the Father 1:9
10. Eternal and unchangeable 1:11, 12
11. Crowned with glory and honor 2:7
12. Authority over everything 2:8
13. Made a human being 2:17
14. A merciful and faithful High Priest 2:17
15. Worthy of great honor 3:3
16. All-seeing (nothing can be hidden from Him) 4:13
17. Tempted in every possible way, yet without sin 4:15
18. Truthful 6:18
19. Holy, blameless, and completely pure 7:26
20. The great Shepherd of God's sheep 13:20

Christ's accomplishments and actions:

1. Sustains all things by His word 1:3
2. Provided purification for sins 1:3
3. Radiates God's glory 1:3
4. Announced salvation of human race 2:3
5. Suffered and tasted death for everyone 2:9
6. Makes holy everyone who receives Him 2:11
7. Makes those whom He saved members of His own family 2:11
8. Destroyed the power of the devil and death 2:14
9. Helps those who are tempted 2:18
10. Saves all who obey Him 5:9
11. Intercedes for those who have trusted Him 7:25
12. Meets our every need 7:26
13. Made a sacrifice for all sins once and for all 7:27
14. Cleanses the conscience of those who trust Him 9:14
15. Died to ransom us from sins 9:15
16. Acts as our lawyer and advocate before God the Father 9:24
17. Originates and perfects our faith 12:2
18. Protects His own, removes all our fear 13:6
19. Equips us with everything needed to do God's will 13:21
20. Works in us to make us pleasing to God 13:21

> *"Today, if you will hear His voice,*
>   *Do not harden your hearts."*

8 For if Joshua had given them rest, then He would not afterward have spoken of another day.

9 There remains therefore a rest for the people of God.

10 For he who has entered His rest has himself also ceased from his works as God *did* from His.

11 Let us therefore be diligent to enter that rest, lest anyone fall after the same example of disobedience.

12 For the word of God *is* living and powerful, and sharper than any two-edged sword, piercing even to the division of soul and spirit, and of joints and marrow, and is a discerner of the thoughts and intents of the heart.

13 And there is no creature hidden from His sight, but all things *are* naked and open to the eyes of Him to whom we *must give* account.

14 Seeing then that we have a great High Priest who has passed through the heavens, Jesus the Son of God, let us hold fast *our* confession.

15 For we do not have a High Priest who cannot sympathize with our weaknesses, but was in all *points* tempted as *we are,* yet without sin.

16 Let us therefore come boldly to the throne of grace, that we may obtain mercy and find grace to help in time of need.

5 For every high priest taken from among men is appointed for men in things *pertaining* to God, that he may offer both gifts and sacrifices for sins.

2 He can have compassion on those who are ignorant and going astray, since he himself is also beset by weakness.

3 Because of this he is required as for the people, so also for himself, to offer for sins.

4 And no man takes this honor to himself, but he who is called by God, just as Aaron *was.*

5 So also Christ did not glorify Himself to become High Priest, *but it* was He who said to Him:

> *"You are My Son,*
>   *Today I have begotten You."*

6 As *He* also *says* in another place:

> *"You are a priest forever*
>   *According to the order of*
>   *Melchizedek";*

7 who, in the days of His flesh, when He had offered up prayers and supplications, with vehement cries and tears to Him who was able to save Him from death, and was heard because of His godly fear,

8 though He was a Son, *yet* He learned obedience by the things which He suffered.

9 And having been perfected, He became the author of eternal salvation to all who obey Him,

10 called by God as High Priest *"according to the order of Melchizedek,"*

11 of whom we have much to say, and hard to explain, since you have become dull of hearing.

12 For though by this time you ought to be teachers, you need *someone* to teach you again the first principles of the oracles of God; and you have come to need milk and not solid food.

13 For everyone who partakes *only* of milk *is* unskilled in the word of righteousness, for he is a babe.

14 But solid food belongs to those who are of full age, *that is,* those who by reason of use have their senses exercised to discern both good and evil.

6 Therefore, leaving the discussion of the elementary *principles* of Christ, let us go on to per-

fection, not laying again the foundation of repentance from dead works and of faith toward God,

2 of the doctrine of baptisms, of laying on of hands, of resurrection of the dead, and of eternal judgment.

3 And this we will do if God permits.

4 For *it is* impossible for those who were once enlightened, and have tasted the heavenly gift, and have become partakers of the Holy Spirit,

5 and have tasted the good word of God and the powers of the age to come,

6 if they fall away, to renew them again to repentance, since they crucify again for themselves the Son of God, and put *Him* to an open shame.

7 For the earth which drinks in the rain that often comes upon it, and bears herbs useful for those by whom it is cultivated, receives blessing from God;

8 but if it bears thorns and briars, *it is* rejected and near to being cursed, whose end *is* to be burned.

9 But, beloved, we are confident of better things concerning you, yes, things that accompany salvation, though we speak in this manner.

10 For God *is* not unjust to forget your work and labor of love which you have shown toward His name, *in that* you have ministered to the saints, and do minister.

11 And we desire that each one of you show the same diligence to the full assurance of hope until the end,

12 that you do not become sluggish, but imitate those who through faith and patience inherit the promises.

13 For when God made a promise to Abraham, because He could swear by no one greater, He swore by Himself,

14 saying, *"Surely blessing I will bless you, and multiplying I will multiply you."*

15 And so, after he had patiently endured, he obtained the promise.

16 For men indeed swear by the greater, and an oath for confirmation *is* for them an end of all dispute.

17 Thus God, determining to show more abundantly to the heirs of promise the immutability of His counsel, confirmed *it* by an oath,

18 that by two immutable things, in which it *is* impossible for God to lie, we might have strong consolation, who have fled for refuge to lay hold of the hope set before *us.*

19 This *hope* we have as an anchor of the soul, both sure and steadfast, and which enters the Presence *behind* the veil,

20 where the forerunner has entered for us, even Jesus, having become High Priest forever according to the order of Melchizedek.

7 For this Melchizedek, king of Salem, priest of the Most High God, who met Abraham returning from the slaughter of the kings and blessed him,

2 to whom also Abraham gave a tenth part of all, first being translated "king of righteousness," and then also king of Salem, meaning "king of peace,"

3 without father, without mother, without genealogy, having neither beginning of days nor end of life, but made like the Son of God, remains a priest continually.

4 Now consider how great this man *was,* to whom even the patriarch Abraham gave a tenth of the spoils.

5 And indeed those who are of the sons of Levi, who receive the priesthood, have a commandment to receive tithes from the people according to the law, that is, from their brethren, though they have come from the loins of Abraham;

6 but he whose genealogy is not

derived from them received tithes from Abraham and blessed him who had the promises.

7 Now beyond all contradiction the lesser is blessed by the better.

8 Here mortal men receive tithes, but there he *receives them,* of whom it is witnessed that he lives.

9 Even Levi, who receives tithes, paid tithes through Abraham, so to speak,

10 for he was still in the loins of his father when Melchizedek met him.

11 Therefore, if perfection were through the Levitical priesthood (for under it the people received the law), what further need *was there* that another priest should rise according to the order of Melchizedek, and not be called according to the order of Aaron?

12 For the priesthood being changed, of necessity there is also a change of the law.

13 For He of whom these things are spoken belongs to another tribe, from which no man has officiated at the altar.

14 For *it is* evident that our Lord arose from Judah, of which tribe Moses spoke nothing concerning priesthood.

15 And it is yet far more evident if, in the likeness of Melchizedek, there arises another priest

16 who has come, not according to the law of a fleshly commandment, but according to the power of an endless life.

17 For He testifies:

> "You are a priest forever
> According to the order of
> Melchizedek."

18 For on the one hand there is an annulling of the former commandment because of its weakness and unprofitableness,

19 for the law made nothing perfect; on the other hand, *there is the* bringing in of a better hope, through which we draw near to God.

20 And inasmuch as *He was* not *made priest* without an oath

21 (for they have become priests without an oath, but He with an oath by Him who said to Him:

> "The LORD has sworn
> And will not relent,
> 'You are a priest forever
> According to the order of
> Melchizedek' "),

22 by so much more Jesus has become a surety of a better covenant.

23 And there were many priests, because they were prevented by death from continuing.

24 But He, because He continues forever, has an unchangeable priesthood.

25 Therefore He is also able to save to the uttermost those who come to God through Him, since He ever lives to make intercession for them.

26 For such a High Priest was fitting for us, *who is* holy, harmless, undefiled, separate from sinners, and has become higher than the heavens;

27 who does not need daily, as those high priests, to offer up sacrifices, first for His own sins and then for the people's, for this He did once for all when He offered up Himself.

28 For the law appoints as high priests men who have weakness, but the word of the oath, which came after the law, *appoints* the Son who has been perfected forever.

8 Now *this is* the main point of the things we are saying: We have such a High Priest, who is seated at the right hand of the throne of the Majesty in the heavens,

2 a Minister of the sanctuary and of the true tabernacle which the Lord erected, and not man.

3 For every high priest is appointed to offer both gifts and sac-

rifices. Therefore *it is* necessary that this One also have something to offer.

4 For if He were on earth, He would not be a priest, since there are priests who offer the gifts according to the law;

5 who serve the copy and shadow of the heavenly things, as Moses was divinely instructed when he was about to make the tabernacle. For He said, *"See that you make all things according to the pattern shown you on the mountain."*

6 But now He has obtained a more excellent ministry, inasmuch as He is also Mediator of a better covenant, which was established on better promises.

7 For if that first *covenant* had been faultless, then no place would have been sought for a second.

8 Because finding fault with them, He says: *"Behold, the days are coming, says the LORD, when I will make a new covenant with the house of Israel and with the house of Judah—*

9 *"not according to the covenant that I made with their fathers in the day when I took them by the hand to lead them out of the land of Egypt; because they did not continue in My covenant, and I disregarded them, says the LORD.*

10 *"For this is the covenant that I will make with the house of Israel after those days, says the LORD: I will put My laws in their mind and write them on their hearts; and I will be their God, and they shall be My people.*

11 *"None of them shall teach his neighbor, and none his brother, saying, 'Know the LORD,' for all shall know Me, from the least of them to the greatest of them.*

12 *"For I will be merciful to their unrighteousness, and their sins and their lawless deeds I will remember no more."*

13 In that He says, *"A new covenant,"* He has made the first obsolete. Now what is becoming obsolete and growing old is ready to vanish away.

9 Then indeed, even the first *covenant* had ordinances of divine service and the earthly sanctuary.

2 For a tabernacle was prepared: the first *part,* in which *was* the lampstand, the table, and the showbread, which is called the sanctuary;

3 and behind the second veil, the part of the tabernacle which is called the Holiest of All,

4 which had the golden altar of incense and the ark of the covenant overlaid on all sides with gold, in which *were* the golden pot that had the manna, Aaron's rod that budded, and the tablets of the covenant;

5 and above it were the cherubim of glory overshadowing the mercy seat. Of these things we cannot now speak in detail.

6 Now when these things had been thus prepared, the priests always went into the first part of the tabernacle, performing *the ser-vices.*

7 But into the second part the high priest *went* alone once a year, not without blood, which he offered for himself and *for* the people's sins *committed* in ignorance;

8 the Holy Spirit indicating this, that the way into the Holiest of All was not yet made manifest while the first tabernacle was still standing.

9 It *was* symbolic for the present time in which both gifts and sacrifices are offered which cannot make him who performed the service perfect in regard to the conscience—

10 *concerned* only with foods and drinks, various washings, and fleshly ordinances imposed until the time of reformation.

11 But Christ came *as* High Priest of the good things to come, with the greater and more perfect tabernacle not made with hands, that is, not of this creation.

12 Not with the blood of goats and calves, but with His own blood He entered the Most Holy Place once for all, having obtained eternal redemption.

13 For if the blood of bulls and goats and the ashes of a heifer, sprinkling the unclean, sanctifies for the purifying of the flesh,

14 how much more shall the blood of Christ, who through the eternal Spirit offered Himself without spot to God, purge your conscience from dead works to serve the living God?

15 And for this reason He is the Mediator of the new covenant, by means of death, for the redemption of the transgressions under the first covenant, that those who are called may receive the promise of the eternal inheritance.

16 For where there *is* a testament, there must also of necessity be the death of the testator.

17 For a testament *is* in force after men are dead, since it has no power at all while the testator lives.

18 Therefore not even the first *covenant* was dedicated without blood.

19 For when Moses had spoken every precept to all the people according to the law, he took the blood of calves and goats, with water, scarlet wool, and hyssop, and sprinkled both the book itself and all the people,

20 saying, *"This is the blood of the covenant which God has commanded you."*

21 Then likewise he sprinkled with blood both the tabernacle and all the vessels of the ministry.

22 And according to the law almost all things are purged with blood, and without shedding of blood there is no remission.

23 Therefore *it was* necessary that the copies of the things in the heavens should be purified with these, but the heavenly things

themselves with better sacrifices than these.

24 For Christ has not entered the holy places made with hands, *which are* copies of the true, but into heaven itself, now to appear in the presence of God for us;

25 not that He should offer Himself often, as the high priest enters the Most Holy Place every year with blood of another—

26 He then would have had to suffer often since the foundation of the world; but now, once at the end of the ages, He has appeared to put away sin by the sacrifice of Himself.

27 And as it is appointed for men to die once, but after this the judgment,

28 so Christ was offered once to bear the sins of many. To those who eagerly wait for Him He will appear a second time, apart from sin, for salvation.

10 For the law, having a shadow of the good things to come, *and* not the very image of the things, can never with these same sacrifices, which they offer continually year by year, make those who approach perfect.

2 For then would they not have ceased to be offered? For the worshipers, once purged, would have had no more consciousness of sins.

3 But in those *sacrifices there is* a reminder of sins every year.

4 For *it is* not possible that the blood of bulls and goats could take away sins.

5 Therefore, when He came into the world, He said:

> *"Sacrifice and offering You did not desire,*
> *But a body You have prepared for Me.*
> 6 *In burnt offerings and sacrifices for sin*
> *You had no pleasure.*
> 7 *Then I said, 'Behold, I have come—*

> *In the volume of the book*
> *it is written of Me—*
> *To do Your will, O God.'"*

8 Previously saying, *"Sacrifice and offering, burnt offerings, and offerings for sin You did not desire, nor had pleasure in them"* (which are offered according to the law),

9 then He said, *"Behold, I have come to do Your will, O God."* He takes away the first that He may establish the second.

10 By that will we have been sanctified through the offering of the body of Jesus Christ once *for all.*

11 And every priest stands ministering daily and offering repeatedly the same sacrifices, which can never take away sins.

12 But this Man, after He had offered one sacrifice for sins forever, sat down at the right hand of God,

13 from that time waiting till His enemies are made His footstool.

14 For by one offering He has perfected forever those who are being sanctified.

15 And the Holy Spirit also witnesses to us; for after He had said before,

16 *"This is the covenant that I will make with them after those days, says the Lord: I will put My laws into their hearts, and in their minds I will write them,"*

17 then He adds, *"Their sins and their lawless deeds I will remember no more."*

18 Now where there is remission of these, *there is* no longer an offering for sin.

19 Therefore, brethren, having boldness to enter the Holiest by the blood of Jesus,

20 by a new and living way which He consecrated for us, through the veil, that is, His flesh,

21 and *having* a High Priest over the house of God,

22 let us draw near with a true heart in full assurance of faith, having our hearts sprinkled from an evil conscience and our bodies washed with pure water.

23 Let us hold fast the confession of *our* hope without wavering, for He who promised *is* faithful.

24 And let us consider one another in order to stir up love and good works,

25 not forsaking the assembling of ourselves together, as *is* the manner of some, but exhorting *one another,* and so much the more as you see the Day approaching.

26 For if we sin willfully after we have received the knowledge of the truth, there no longer remains a sacrifice for sins,

27 but a certain fearful expectation of judgment, and fiery indignation which will devour the adversaries.

28 Anyone who has rejected Moses' law dies without mercy on the testimony of two or three witnesses.

29 Of how much worse punishment, do you suppose, will he be thought worthy who has trampled the Son of God underfoot, counted the blood of the covenant by which he was sanctified a common thing, and insulted the Spirit of grace?

30 For we know Him who said, *"Vengeance is Mine, I will repay,"* says the Lord. And again, *"The Lord will judge His people."*

31 It is a fearful thing to fall into the hands of the living God.

32 But recall the former days in which, after you were illuminated, you endured a great struggle with sufferings:

33 partly while you were made a spectacle both by reproaches and tribulations, and partly while you became companions of those who were so treated;

34 for you had compassion on me in my chains, and joyfully accepted the plundering of your goods, knowing that you have a better and an enduring possession for yourselves in heaven.

35 Therefore do not cast away your confidence, which has great reward.

36 For you have need of endurance, so that after you have done the will of God, you may receive the promise:

37 *"For yet a little while,*
And He who is coming will
come and will not tarry.
38 *Now the just shall live by*
faith;
But if anyone draws back,
My soul has no pleasure in
him."

39 But we are not of those who draw back to perdition, but of those who believe to the saving of the soul.

11 Now faith is the substance of things hoped for, the evidence of things not seen.

2 For by it the elders obtained a good testimony.

3 By faith we understand that the worlds were framed by the word of God, so that the things which are seen were not made of things which are visible.

4 By faith Abel offered to God a more excellent sacrifice than Cain, through which he obtained witness that he was righteous, God testifying of his gifts; and through it he being dead still speaks.

5 By faith Enoch was translated so that he did not see death, *"and was not found because God had translated him"*; for before his translation he had this testimony, that he pleased God.

6 But without faith *it is* impossible to please *Him*, for he who comes to God must believe that He is, and *that* He is a rewarder of those who diligently seek Him.

7 By faith Noah, being divinely warned of things not yet seen, moved with godly fear, prepared an ark for the saving of his household, by which he condemned the world and became heir of the righteousness which is according to faith.

8 By faith Abraham obeyed when he was called to go out to the place which he would *afterward* receive as an inheritance. And he went out, not knowing where he was going.

9 By faith he sojourned in the land of promise as *in* a foreign country, dwelling in tents with Isaac and Jacob, the heirs with him of the same promise;

10 for he waited for the city which has foundations, whose builder and maker *is* God.

11 By faith Sarah herself also received strength to conceive seed, and she bore a child when she was past the age, because she judged Him faithful who had promised.

12 Therefore from one man, and him as good as dead, were born *as many* as the stars of the sky in multitude—innumerable as the sand which is by the seashore.

13 These all died in faith, not having received the promises, but having seen them afar off were assured of *them*, embraced *them*, and confessed that they were strangers and pilgrims on the earth.

14 For those who say such things declare plainly that they seek a homeland.

15 And truly if they had called to mind that *country* from which they had come out, they would have had opportunity to return.

16 But now they desire a better, that is, a heavenly *country*. Therefore God is not ashamed to be called their God, for He has prepared a city for them.

17 By faith Abraham, when he was tested, offered up Isaac, and he who had received the promises offered up his only begotten *son,*

18 of whom it was said, *"In Isaac your seed shall be called,"*

19 accounting that God *was* able to raise *him* up, even from the

dead, from which he also received him in a figurative sense.

20 By faith Isaac blessed Jacob and Esau concerning things to come.

21 By faith Jacob, when he was dying, blessed each of the sons of Joseph, and worshiped, *leaning* on the top of his staff.

22 By faith Joseph, when he was dying, made mention of the departure of the children of Israel, and gave instructions concerning his bones.

23 By faith Moses, when he was born, was hidden three months by his parents, because they saw *he was* a beautiful child; and they were not afraid of the king's command.

24 By faith Moses, when he became of age, refused to be called the son of Pharaoh's daughter,

25 choosing rather to suffer affliction with the people of God than to enjoy the passing pleasures of sin,

26 esteeming the reproach of Christ greater riches than the treasures in Egypt; for he looked to the reward.

27 By faith he forsook Egypt, not fearing the wrath of the king; for he endured as seeing Him who is invisible.

28 By faith he kept the Passover and the sprinkling of blood, lest he who destroyed the firstborn should touch them.

29 By faith they passed through the Red Sea as by dry *land*, *whereas* the Egyptians, attempting *to do* so, were drowned.

30 By faith the walls of Jericho fell down after they were encircled for seven days.

31 By faith the harlot Rahab did not perish with those who did not believe, when she had received the spies with peace.

32 And what more shall I say? For the time would fail me to tell of Gideon and Barak and Samson and Jephthah, also *of* David and Samuel and the prophets:

33 who through faith subdued kingdoms, worked righteousness, obtained promises, stopped the mouths of lions,

34 quenched the violence of fire, escaped the edge of the sword, out of weakness were made strong, became valiant in battle, turned to flight the armies of the aliens.

35 Women received their dead raised to life again. And others were tortured, not accepting deliverance, that they might obtain a better resurrection.

36 Still others had trial of mockings and scourgings, yes, and of chains and imprisonment.

37 They were stoned, they were sawn in two, were tempted, were slain with the sword. They wandered about in sheepskins and goatskins, being destitute, afflicted, tormented—

38 of whom the world was not worthy. They wandered in deserts and mountains, *in* dens and caves of the earth.

39 And all these, having obtained a good testimony through faith, did not receive the promise,

40 God having provided something better for us, that they should not be made perfect apart from us.

12 Therefore we also, since we are surrounded by so great a cloud of witnesses, let us lay aside every weight, and the sin which so easily ensnares *us*, and let us run with endurance the race that is set before us,

2 looking unto Jesus, the author and finisher of *our* faith, who for the joy that was set before Him endured the cross, despising the shame, and has sat down at the right hand of the throne of God.

3 For consider Him who endured such hostility from sinners against Himself, lest you become weary and discouraged in your souls.

4 You have not yet resisted to bloodshed, striving against sin.

5 And you have forgotten the ex-

hortation which speaks to you as
to sons:

> *"My son, do not despise the
> chastening of the LORD,
> Nor be discouraged when you
> are rebuked by Him;*
> 6 *For whom the LORD loves He
> chastens,
> And scourges every son whom
> He receives."*

7 If you endure chastening, God
deals with you as with sons; for
what son is there whom a father
does not chasten?
8 But if you are without chastening, of which all have become partakers, then you are illegitimate
and not sons.
9 Furthermore, we have had human fathers who corrected us, and
we paid *them* respect. Shall we not
much more readily be in subjection to the Father of spirits and
live?
10 For they indeed for a few days
chastened *us* as seemed *best* to
them, but He for *our* profit, that
we may be partakers of His holiness.
11 Now no chastening seems to be
joyful for the present, but griev-
ous; nevertheless, afterward it
yields the peaceable fruit of righteousness to those who have been
trained by it.
12 Therefore strengthen the hands
which hang down, and the feeble
knees,
13 and make straight paths for
your feet, so that what is lame may
not be *dislocated*, but rather be
healed.
14 Pursue peace with all *men*, and
holiness, without which no one
will see the Lord:
15 looking diligently lest anyone
fall short of the grace of God; lest
any root of bitterness springing up
cause trouble, and by this many
become defiled;
16 lest there *be* any fornicator or
profane person like Esau, who for
one morsel of food sold his birth-
right.
17 For you know that afterward,
when he wanted to inherit the
blessing, he was rejected, for he
found no place for repentance,
though he sought it diligently with
tears.
18 For you have not come to the
mountain that may be touched and
that burned with fire, and to blackness and darkness and tempest,
19 and the sound of a trumpet and
the voice of words, so that those
who heard *it* begged that the word
should not be spoken to them anymore.
20 (For they could not endure
what was commanded: *"And if so
much as a beast touches the
mountain, it shall be stoned or
thrust through with an arrow."*
21 And so terrifying was the sight
that Moses said, *"I am exceedingly
afraid and trembling."*)
22 But you have come to Mount
Zion and to the city of the living
God, the heavenly Jerusalem, to an
innumerable company of angels,
23 to the general assembly and
church of the firstborn *who are*
registered in heaven, to God the
Judge of all, to the spirits of just
men made perfect,
24 to Jesus the Mediator of the
new covenant, and to the blood of
sprinkling that speaks better
things than *that of* Abel.
25 See that you do not refuse Him
who speaks. For if they did not
escape who refused Him who
spoke on earth, much more *shall
we not escape* if we turn away
from Him who *speaks* from
heaven,
26 whose voice then shook the
earth; but now He has promised,
saying, *"Yet once more I shake
not only the earth, but also
heaven."*
27 Now this, *"Yet once more,"* indicates the removal of those things

Why Does God Allow Evil and Suffering?

A baby dies in a car accident. A madman opens fire in a fast-food restaurant. A crazed dictator slaughters millions of his own citizens. Wouldn't a loving, all-powerful God step in to prevent such evil and suffering?

But free will couldn't exist without our potential for evil. The Bible indicates that God created a perfect humanity. But He also gave us the ability to choose to love and obey Him or to turn from Him and disobey. We are not robots. If God had forcibly prevented us from sinning, we would not be free. And if we were not free, we could not express genuine love. Much of the pain and suffering on this planet comes from the free choices of people who fall short of God's desires.

But the Bible also teaches that

Suffering serves a purpose. Suffering teaches us about ourselves, our values, and our choices. It builds endurance, character, and hope. It also humbles us, reminding us of our weakness (2 Corinthians 12:7–10).

Death seals and protects those who have chosen God while it limits the degradation and ultimate punishment of those who reject

God. It puts boundaries on the spread of wickedness in society, for as Genesis 19 shows us, humanity, given long life spans, uses the additional time to increase wickedness rather than goodness.

God is involved in our suffering. God identifies personally with our sufferings (Matthew 25:31–46). Christ has suffered and been tempted as severely as anyone (Hebrews 4:15, 16).

He also promises that *everything* will work out for the best for those who love Him (Romans 8:28). For those who are hurting, He offers His help and comfort (Matthew 28:20; Hebrews 13:5, 6).

Suffering plays a part in God's eternal plan. This life is roughly analogous to a school course with a final examination. Our lifetime is our chance to choose or reject God's offer of love and to choose or reject His training for a better life, training that often comes through suffering. Too much time or too little time would not be good for us, but the best time frame varies for each of us. As we cooperate with Christ in opposing evil, the perfecting process progresses (Philippians 2:13; 2 Thessalonians 3:5; 2 Timothy 2:26).

Perhaps most comforting of all is knowing that our suffering is temporary. In God's eventual re-creation, sin, suffering, death, and evil will have no part (Revelation 21:4).

that are being shaken, as of things that are made, that the things which cannot be shaken may remain.

28 Therefore, since we are receiving a kingdom which cannot be shaken, let us have grace, by which we may serve God acceptably with reverence and godly fear. 29 For our God *is* a consuming fire.

13 Let brotherly love continue. 2 Do not forget to entertain strangers, for by so *doing* some have unwittingly entertained angels.

3 Remember the prisoners as if chained with them, *and* those who are mistreated, since you yourselves are in the body also.

4 Marriage *is* honorable among all, and the bed undefiled; but fornicators and adulterers God will judge.

5 *Let* your conduct *be* without covetousness, *and* be content with such things as you have. For He Himself has said, *"I will never leave you nor forsake you."*

6 So we may boldly say:

"The LORD is my helper;
I will not fear.
What can man do to me?"

7 Remember those who rule over you, who have spoken the word of God to you, whose faith follow, considering the outcome of *their* conduct.

8 Jesus Christ *is* the same yesterday, today, and forever.

9 Do not be carried about with various and strange doctrines. For *it is* good that the heart be established by grace, not with foods which have not profited those who have been occupied with them.

10 We have an altar from which those who serve the tabernacle have no right to eat.

11 For the bodies of those beasts, whose blood is brought into the sanctuary by the high priest for sin, are burned outside the camp. 12 Therefore Jesus also, that He might sanctify the people with His own blood, suffered outside the gate.

13 Therefore let us go forth to Him, outside the camp, bearing His reproach.

14 For here we have no continuing city, but we seek the one to come.

15 Therefore by Him let us continually offer the sacrifice of praise to God, that is, the fruit of *our* lips, giving thanks to His name.

16 But do not forget to do good and to share, for with such sacrifices God is well pleased.

17 Obey those who rule over you, and be submissive, for they watch out for your souls, as those who must give account. Let them do so with joy and not with grief, for that would be unprofitable for you.

18 Pray for us; for we are confident that we have a good conscience, in all things desiring to live honorably.

19 But I especially urge you to do this, that I may be restored to you the sooner.

20 Now may the God of peace who brought up our Lord Jesus from the dead, that great Shepherd of the sheep, through the blood of the everlasting covenant,

21 make you complete in every good work to do His will, working in you what is well pleasing in His sight, through Jesus Christ, to whom *be* glory forever and ever. Amen.

22 And I appeal to you, brethren, bear with the word of exhortation, for I have written to you in few words.

23 Know that *our* brother Timothy has been set free, with whom I shall see you if he comes shortly.

24 Greet all those who rule over you, and all the saints. Those from Italy greet you.

25 Grace *be* with you all. Amen.

THE EPISTLE OF

JAMES

JAMES, a servant of God and of the Lord Jesus Christ,

To the twelve tribes which are scattered abroad:

Greetings.

2 My brethren, count it all joy when you fall into various trials,

3 knowing that the testing of your faith produces patience.

4 But let patience have *its* perfect work, that you may be perfect and complete, lacking nothing.

5 If any of you lacks wisdom, let him ask of God, who gives to all liberally and without reproach, and it will be given to him.

6 But let him ask in faith, with no doubting, for he who doubts is like a wave of the sea driven and tossed by the wind.

7 For let not that man suppose that he will receive anything from the Lord;

8 *he is* a double-minded man, unstable in all his ways.

9 Let the lowly brother glory in his exaltation,

10 but the rich in his humiliation, because as a flower of the field he will pass away.

11 For no sooner has the sun risen with a burning heat than it withers the grass; its flower falls, and its beautiful appearance perishes. So the rich man also will fade away in his pursuits.

12 Blessed *is* the man who endures temptation; for when he has been proved, he will receive the crown of life which the Lord has promised to those who love Him.

13 Let no one say when he is tempted, "I am tempted by God"; for God cannot be tempted by evil, nor does He Himself tempt anyone.

14 But each one is tempted when he is drawn away by his own desires and enticed.

15 Then, when desire has conceived, it gives birth to sin; and sin, when it is full-grown, brings forth death.

16 Do not be deceived, my beloved brethren.

17 Every good gift and every perfect gift is from above, and comes down from the Father of lights, with whom there is no variation or shadow of turning.

18 Of His own will He brought us forth by the word of truth, that we might be a kind of firstfruits of His creatures.

19 Therefore, my beloved brethren, let every man be swift to hear, slow to speak, slow to wrath;

20 for the wrath of man does not produce the righteousness of God.

21 Therefore lay aside all filthiness and overflow of wickedness, and receive with meekness the implanted word, which is able to save your souls.

22 But be doers of the word, and not hearers only, deceiving yourselves.

23 For if anyone is a hearer of the word and not a doer, he is like a man observing his natural face in a mirror;

24 for he observes himself, goes away, and immediately forgets what kind of man he was.

25 But he who looks into the perfect law of liberty and continues *in it*, and is not a forgetful hearer but a doer of the work, this one will be blessed in what he does.

26 If anyone among you thinks he is religious, and does not bridle his tongue but deceives his own heart, this one's religion *is* useless.

27 Pure and undefiled religion before God and the Father is this: to visit orphans and widows in their trouble, *and* to keep oneself unspotted from the world.

2 My brethren, do not hold the faith of our Lord Jesus Christ,

the Lord of glory, with partiality.
2 For if there should come into your assembly a man with gold rings, in fine apparel, and there should also come in a poor man in filthy clothes,

3 and you pay attention to the one wearing the fine clothes and say to him, "You sit here in a good place," and say to the poor man, "You stand there," or, "Sit here at my footstool,"

4 have you not shown partiality among yourselves, and become judges with evil thoughts?

5 Listen, my beloved brethren: Has God not chosen the poor of this world *to be* rich in faith and heirs of the kingdom which He promised to those who love Him?

6 But you have dishonored the poor man. Do not the rich oppress you and drag you into the courts?

7 Do they not blaspheme that noble name by which you are called?

8 If you really fulfill *the* royal law according to the Scripture, *"You shall love your neighbor as yourself,"* you do well;

9 but if you show partiality, you commit sin, and are convicted by the law as transgressors.

10 For whoever shall keep the whole law, and yet stumble in one *point*, he is guilty of all.

11 For He who said, *"Do not commit adultery,"* also said, *"Do not murder."* Now if you do not commit adultery, but you do murder, you have become a transgressor of the law.

12 So speak and so do as those who will be judged by the law of liberty.

13 For judgment is without mercy to the one who has shown no mercy. Mercy triumphs over judgment.

14 What *does it* profit, my brethren, if someone says he has faith but does not have works? Can faith save him?

15 If a brother or sister is naked and destitute of daily food,

16 and one of you says to them, "Depart in peace, be warmed and filled," but you do not give them the things which are needed for the body, what *does it* profit?

17 Thus also faith by itself, if it does not have works, is dead.

18 But someone will say, "You have faith, and I have works." Show me your faith without your works, and I will show you my faith by my works.

19 You believe that there is one God. You do well. Even the demons believe—and tremble!

20 But do you want to know, O foolish man, that faith without works is dead?

21 Was not Abraham our father justified by works when he offered Isaac his son on the altar?

22 Do you see that faith was working together with his works, and by works faith was made perfect?

23 And the Scripture was fulfilled which says, *"Abraham believed God, and it was accounted to him for righteousness."* And he was called the friend of God.

24 You see then that a man is justified by works, and not by faith only.

25 Likewise, was not Rahab the harlot also justified by works when she received the messengers and sent *them* out another way?

26 For as the body without the spirit is dead, so faith without works is dead also.

3 My brethren, let not many of you become teachers, knowing that we shall receive a stricter judgment.

2 For we all stumble in many things. If anyone does not stumble in word, he *is* a perfect man, able also to bridle the whole body.

3 Indeed, we put bits in horses' mouths that they may obey us, and we turn their whole body.

4 Look also at ships: although

they are so large and are driven by fierce winds, they are turned by a very small rudder wherever the pilot desires.

5 Even so the tongue is a little member and boasts great things. See how great a forest a little fire kindles!

6 And the tongue *is* a fire, a world of iniquity. The tongue is so set among our members that it defiles the whole body, and sets on fire the course of nature; and it is set on fire by hell.

7 For every kind of beast and bird, of reptile and creature of the sea, is tamed and has been tamed by mankind.

8 But no man can tame the tongue.. *It is* an unruly evil, full of deadly poison.

9 With it we bless our God and Father, and with it we curse men, who have been made in the similitude of God.

10 Out of the same mouth proceed blessing and cursing. My brethren, these things ought not to be so.

11 Does a spring send forth fresh *water* and bitter from the same opening?

12 Can a fig tree, my brethren, bear olives, or a grapevine bear figs? Thus no spring *can* yield both salt water and fresh.

13 Who *is* wise and understanding among you? Let him show by good conduct *that* his works *are done* in the meekness of wisdom.

14 But if you have bitter envy and self-seeking in your hearts, do not boast and lie against the truth.

15 This wisdom does not descend from above, but *is* earthly, sensual, demonic.

16 For where envy and self-seeking *exist*, confusion and every evil thing *will be* there.

17 But the wisdom that is from above is first pure, then peaceable, gentle, willing to yield, full of mercy and good fruits, without partiality and without hypocrisy.

18 Now the fruit of righteousness is sown in peace by those who make peace.

4 Where do wars and fights *come* from among you? Do *they* not *come* from your *desires for* pleasure that war in your members?

2 You lust and do not have. You murder and covet and cannot obtain. You fight and war. Yet you do not have because you do not ask.

3 You ask and do not receive, because you ask amiss, that you may spend *it* on your pleasures.

4 Adulterers and adulteresses! Do you not know that friendship with the world is enmity with God? Whoever therefore wants to be a friend of the world makes himself an enemy of God.

5 Or do you think that the Scripture says in vain, "The Spirit who dwells in us yearns jealously"?

6 But He gives more grace. Therefore He says:

> "God resists the proud,
> But gives grace to the
> humble."

7 Therefore submit to God. Resist the devil and he will flee from you.

8 Draw near to God and He will draw near to you. Cleanse *your* hands, *you* sinners; and purify *your* hearts, *you* double-minded.

9 Lament and mourn and weep! Let your laughter be turned to mourning and *your* joy to gloom.

10 Humble yourselves in the sight of the Lord, and He will lift you up.

11 Do not speak evil of one another, brethren. He who speaks evil of a brother and judges his brother, speaks evil of the law and judges the law. But if you judge the law, you are not a doer of the law but a judge.

12 There is one Lawgiver, who is able to save and to destroy. Who are you to judge another?

13 Come now, you who say, "Today or tomorrow we will go to

What if I've Tried Religion, and It Doesn't Work for Me?

Many people have tried to pray, read the Bible, or go to church in an effort to feel close to God. But nothing seems to work. Still, James 4:8 states, "Draw near to God and He will draw near to you." Before you give up on Christianity, you might want to consider a few possibilities:

1. The answer is not to try harder. Being close to God doesn't begin with the practice of religious behaviors. It may be that you have simply "drawn near" to rituals rather than to God Himself. We're to pursue a relationship, not a religion.

The strain and distance we experience in relationships is the result of sin. The way to get close to God is through Jesus. In Ephesians 2:13 the apostle Paul explains, "You who once were far off have been made near by the blood of Christ." (See "How Can I Get to Heaven?" page 362.)

2. The answer is not to redefine the relationship on your terms. Sometimes we sidetrack our relationship with God by imposing conditions. We think: *I know Jesus died for me on the cross. Now, if He would just . . . (heal my child, bring my husband back, get me out of debt, give me a special sign, and so on) . . . I'll know He really loves me.*

This kind of bargaining attempts to redefine the basis of our relationship with God. Wanting some "miracle" in our lives takes the place of God's statement of love in Christ's death.

Sometimes the issue isn't that we *can't* draw near to God; it's that we're not sure we *want* to get too close. All we're looking for is a little warmth and comfort but not an intimate relationship with our Creator. We've transferred our patterns of relating with people to our interaction with God. We fear being hurt by Him so we keep Him at arm's length. (See "If I Give Myself to God, Won't He Make My Life Miserable?" page 100.)

What next?

Reconsider what you may have been looking for in past attempts to come to God. He may be nearer than you think. James 4:10 says, "Humble yourselves in the sight of the Lord, and He will lift you up"—not smash you down. He wants to lift you up into His arms, now and forever.

such and such a city, spend a year there, buy and sell, and make a profit";

14 whereas you do not know what *will happen* tomorrow. For what *is* your life? It is even a vapor that appears for a little time and then vanishes away.

15 Instead you *ought* to say, "If the Lord wills, we shall live and do this or that."

16 But now you boast in your arrogance. All such boasting is evil.

17 Therefore, to him who knows to do good and does not do *it*, to him it is sin.

5 Come now, *you* rich, weep and howl for your miseries that are coming upon *you!*

2 Your riches are corrupted, and your garments are moth-eaten.

3 Your gold and silver are corroded, and their corrosion will be a witness against you and will eat your flesh like fire. You have heaped up treasure in the last days.

4 Indeed the wages of the laborers who mowed your fields, which you kept back by fraud, cry out; and the cries of the reapers have reached the ears of the Lord of Sabaoth.

5 You have lived on the earth in pleasure and luxury; you have fattened your hearts as in a day of slaughter.

6 You have condemned, you have murdered the just; he does not resist you.

7 Therefore be patient, brethren, until the coming of the Lord. See *how* the farmer waits for the precious fruit of the earth, waiting patiently for it until it receives the early and latter rain.

8 You also be patient. Establish your hearts, for the coming of the Lord is at hand.

9 Do not grumble against one another, brethren, lest you be con-demned. Behold, the Judge is standing at the door!

10 My brethren, take the prophets, who spoke in the name of the Lord, as an example of suffering and patience.

11 Indeed we count them blessed who endure. You have heard of the perseverance of Job and seen the end *intended by* the Lord—that the Lord is very compassionate and merciful.

12 But above all, my brethren, do not swear, either by heaven or by earth or with any other oath. But let your "Yes" be "Yes," and *your* "No," "No," lest you fall into judgment.

13 Is anyone among you suffering? Let him pray. Is anyone cheerful? Let him sing psalms.

14 Is anyone among you sick? Let him call for the elders of the church, and let them pray over him, anointing him with oil in the name of the Lord.

15 And the prayer of faith will save the sick, and the Lord will raise him up. And if he has committed sins, he will be forgiven.

16 Confess *your* trespasses to one another, and pray for one another, that you may be healed. The effective, fervent prayer of a righteous man avails much.

17 Elijah was a man with a nature like ours, and he prayed earnestly that it would not rain; and it did not rain on the land for three years and six months.

18 And he prayed again, and the heaven gave rain, and the earth produced its fruit.

19 Brethren, if anyone among you wanders from the truth, and someone turns him back,

20 let him know that he who turns a sinner from the error of his way will save a soul from death and cover a multitude of sins.

THE FIRST EPISTLE OF

PETER

PETER, an apostle of Jesus Christ,

To the pilgrims of the Dispersion in Pontus, Galatia, Cappadocia, Asia, and Bithynia,
2 elect according to the foreknowledge of God the Father, in sanctification of the Spirit, for obedience and sprinkling of the blood of Jesus Christ:

Grace to you and peace be multiplied.
3 Blessed *be* the God and Father of our Lord Jesus Christ, who according to His abundant mercy has begotten us again to a living hope through the resurrection of Jesus Christ from the dead,
4 to an inheritance incorruptible and undefiled and that does not fade away, reserved in heaven for you,
5 who are kept by the power of God through faith for salvation ready to be revealed in the last time.
6 In this you greatly rejoice, though now for a little while, if need be, you have been grieved by various trials,
7 that the genuineness of your faith, *being* much more precious than gold that perishes, though it is tested by fire, may be found to praise, honor, and glory at the revelation of Jesus Christ,
8 whom having not seen you love. Though now you do not see *Him,* yet believing, you rejoice with joy inexpressible and full of glory,
9 receiving the end of your faith—the salvation of *your* souls.
10 Of this salvation the prophets have inquired and searched diligently, who prophesied of the grace *that would come* to you,
11 searching what, or what manner of time, the Spirit of Christ who was in them was indicating when He testified beforehand the sufferings of Christ and the glories that would follow.
12 To them it was revealed that, not to themselves, but to us they were ministering the things which now have been reported to you through those who have preached the gospel to you by the Holy Spirit sent from heaven—things which angels desire to look into.
13 Therefore gird up the loins of your mind, be sober, and rest *your* hope fully upon the grace that is to be brought to you at the revelation of Jesus Christ;
14 as obedient children, not conforming yourselves to the former lusts, *as* in your ignorance;
15 but as He who called you *is* holy, you also be holy in all *your* conduct,
16 because it is written, *"Be holy, for I am holy."*
17 And if you call on the Father, who without partiality judges according to each one's work, conduct yourselves throughout the time of your sojourning *here* in fear;
18 knowing that you were not redeemed with corruptible things, *like* silver or gold, from your aimless conduct *received* by tradition from your fathers,
19 but with the precious blood of Christ, as of a lamb without blemish and without spot.
20 He indeed was foreordained before the foundation of the world, but was manifest in these last times for you
21 who through Him believe in God, who raised Him from the dead and gave Him glory, so that your faith and hope are in God.
22 Since you have purified your souls in obeying the truth through the Spirit in sincere love of the brethren, love one another fervently with a pure heart,

23 having been born again, not of corruptible seed but incorruptible, through the word of God which lives and abides forever,
24 because

*"All flesh is as grass,
And all the glory of man
as the flower of the grass.
The grass withers,
And its flower falls away,*
25 *But the word of the LORD
endures forever."*

Now this is the word which by the gospel was preached to you.

2 Therefore, laying aside all malice, all guile, hypocrisy, envy, and all evil speaking,
2 as newborn babes, desire the pure milk of the word, that you may grow thereby,
3 if indeed you have tasted that the Lord *is* gracious.
4 Coming to Him *as* to a living stone, rejected indeed by men, but chosen by God *and* precious,
5 you also, as living stones, are being built up a spiritual house, a holy priesthood, to offer up spiritual sacrifices acceptable to God through Jesus Christ.
6 Therefore it is also contained in the Scripture,

*"Behold, I lay in Zion
A chief cornerstone, elect,
precious,
And he who believes on Him
will by no means be put to
shame."*

7 Therefore, to you who believe, He *is* precious; but to those who are disobedient,

*"The stone which the builders
rejected
Has become the chief
cornerstone,"*

8 and

*"A stone of stumbling
And a rock of offense."*

They stumble, being disobedient to the word, to which they also were appointed.
9 But you *are* a chosen generation, a royal priesthood, a holy nation, His own special people, that you may proclaim the praises of Him who called you out of darkness into His marvelous light;
10 who once *were* not a people but *are* now the people of God, who had not obtained mercy but now have obtained mercy.
11 Beloved, I beg *you* as sojourners and pilgrims, abstain from fleshly lusts which war against the soul,
12 having your conduct honorable among the Gentiles, that when they speak against you as evildoers, they may, by *your* good works which they observe, glorify God in the day of visitation.
13 Therefore submit yourselves to every ordinance of man for the Lord's sake, whether to the king as supreme,
14 or to governors, as to those who are sent by him for the punishment of evildoers and *for the* praise of those who do good.
15 For this is the will of God, that by doing good you may put to silence the ignorance of foolish men—
16 as free, yet not using *your* liberty as a cloak for vice, but as servants of God.
17 Honor all *people.* Love the brotherhood. Fear God. Honor the king.
18 Servants, *be* submissive to *your* masters with all fear, not only to the good and gentle, but also to the harsh.
19 For this *is* commendable, if because of conscience toward God one endures grief, suffering wrongfully.
20 For what credit *is it* if, when you are beaten for your faults, you take it patiently? But when you do

good and suffer *for it*, if you take it patiently, this *is* commendable before God.

21 For to this you were called, because Christ also suffered for us, leaving us an example, that you should follow His steps:

22 "Who committed no sin,
   Nor was guile found in His
      mouth";

23 who, when He was reviled, did not revile in return; when He suffered, He did not threaten, but committed *Himself* to Him who judges righteously;

24 who Himself bore our sins in His own body on the tree, that we, having died to sins, might live for righteousness—by whose stripes you were healed.

25 For you were like sheep going astray, but have now returned to the Shepherd and Overseer of your souls.

3 Likewise *you* wives, *be* submissive to your own husbands, that even if some do not obey the word, they, without a word, may be won by the conduct of their wives,

2 when they observe your chaste conduct *accompanied* by fear.

3 Do not let your beauty be that outward *adorning* of arranging the hair, of wearing gold, or of putting on *fine* apparel;

4 but *let it be* the hidden person of the heart, with the incorruptible *ornament* of a gentle and quiet spirit, which is very precious in the sight of God.

5 For in this manner, in former times, the holy women who trusted in God also adorned themselves, being submissive to their own husbands,

6 as Sarah obeyed Abraham, calling him lord, whose daughters you are if you do good and are not afraid with any terror.

7 Likewise *you* husbands, dwell with *them* with understanding,

giving honor to the wife, as to the weaker vessel, and as *being* heirs together of the grace of life, that your prayers may not be hindered.

8 Finally, all of *you be* of one mind, having compassion for one another; love as brothers, *be* tenderhearted, *be* courteous;

9 not returning evil for evil or reviling for reviling, but on the contrary blessing, knowing that you were called to this, that you may inherit a blessing.

10 For

   "He who would love life
      And see good days,
   Let him refrain his tongue
         from evil,
   And his lips from speaking
         guile;

11 Let him turn away from evil
      and do good;
   Let him seek peace and pursue
      it.

12 For the eyes of the LORD
      are on the righteous,
   And his ears are open to their
         prayers;
   But the face of the LORD is
      against those who do evil."

13 And who *is* he who will harm you if you become followers of what is good?

14 But even if you should suffer for righteousness' sake, *you are* blessed. *"And do not be afraid of their threats, nor be troubled."*

15 But sanctify the Lord God in your hearts, and always *be* ready to *give* a defense to everyone who asks you a reason for the hope that is in you, with meekness and fear;

16 having a good conscience, that when they defame you as evildoers, those who revile your good conduct in Christ may be ashamed.

17 For *it is* better, if it is the will of God, to suffer for doing good than for doing evil.

18 For Christ also suffered once for sins, the just for the unjust, that

He might bring us to God, being put to death in the flesh but made alive by the Spirit,

19 by whom also He went and preached to the spirits in prison,

20 who formerly were disobedient, when once the longsuffering of God waited in the days of Noah, while *the* ark was being prepared, in which a few, that is, eight souls, were saved through water.

21 There is also an antitype which now saves us, *namely* baptism (not the removal of the filth of the flesh, but the answer of a good conscience toward God), through the resurrection of Jesus Christ,

22 who has gone into heaven and is at the right hand of God, angels and authorities and powers having been made subject to Him.

4 Therefore, since Christ suffered for us in the flesh, arm yourselves also with the same mind, for he who has suffered in the flesh has ceased from sin,

2 that he no longer should live the rest of *his* time in the flesh for the lusts of men, but for the will of God.

3 For we *have spent* enough of our past lifetime in doing the will of the Gentiles—when we walked in licentiousness, lusts, drunkenness, revelries, drinking parties, and abominable idolatries.

4 In regard to these, they think it strange that you do not run with *them* in the same flood of dissipation, speaking evil of *you.*

5 They will give an account to Him who is ready to judge the living and the dead.

6 For this reason the gospel was preached also to those who are dead, that they might be judged according to men in the flesh, but live according to God in the spirit.

7 But the end of all things is at hand; therefore be serious and watchful in your prayers.

8 And above all things have fervent love for one another, for *"love will cover a multitude of sins."*

9 *Be* hospitable to one another without grumbling.

10 As each one has received a gift, minister it to one another, as good stewards of the manifold grace of God.

11 If anyone speaks, *let him speak* as the oracles of God. If anyone ministers, *let him do it* as with the ability which God supplies, that in all things God may be glorified through Jesus Christ, to whom belong the glory and the dominion forever and ever. Amen.

12 Beloved, do not think it strange concerning the fiery trial which is to try you, as though some strange thing happened to you;

13 but rejoice to the extent that you partake of Christ's sufferings, that when His glory is revealed, you may also be glad with exceeding joy.

14 If you are reproached for the name of Christ, blessed *are you,* for the Spirit of glory and of God rests upon you. On their part He is blasphemed, but on your part He is glorified.

15 But let none of you suffer as a murderer, a thief, an evildoer, or as a busybody in other people's matters.

16 Yet if *anyone suffers* as a Christian, let him not be ashamed, but let him glorify God in this matter.

17 For the time *has come* for judgment to begin at the house of God; and if *it begins* with us first, what will *be* the end of those who do not obey the gospel of God?

18 Now

> *"If the righteous one is scarcely saved,*
> *Where will the ungodly and the sinner appear?"*

19 Therefore let those who suffer according to the will of God commit their souls *to Him* in doing good, as to a faithful Creator.

5 The elders who are among you I exhort, I who am a fellow

elder and a witness of the sufferings of Christ, and also a partaker of the glory that will be revealed:

2 Shepherd the flock of God which is among you, serving as overseers, not by constraint but willingly, not for dishonest gain but eagerly;

3 nor as being lords over those entrusted to you, but being examples to the flock;

4 and when the Chief Shepherd appears, you will receive the crown of glory that does not fade away.

5 Likewise you younger people, submit yourselves to *your* elders. Yes, all of *you* be submissive to one another, and be clothed with humility, for

"God resists the proud,
   But gives grace to the
   humble."

6 Therefore humble yourselves under the mighty hand of God, that He may exalt you in due time,

7 casting all your care upon Him, for He cares for you.

8 Be sober, be vigilant; because your adversary the devil walks about like a roaring lion, seeking whom he may devour.

9 Resist him, steadfast in the faith, knowing that the same sufferings are experienced by your brotherhood in the world.

10 But may the God of all grace, who called us to His eternal glory by Christ Jesus, after you have suffered a while, perfect, establish, strengthen, and settle *you.*

11 To Him *be* the glory and the dominion forever and ever. Amen.

12 By Silvanus, our faithful brother as I consider him, I have written to you briefly, exhorting and testifying that this is the true grace of God in which you stand.

13 She who is in Babylon, elect together with *you*, greets you; and *so does* Mark my son.

14 Greet one another with a kiss of love. Peace to you all who are in Christ Jesus. Amen.

THE SECOND EPISTLE OF
PETER

SIMON PETER, a servant and apostle of Jesus Christ,

To those who have obtained like precious faith with us by the righteousness of our God and Savior Jesus Christ:

2 Grace and peace be multiplied to you in the knowledge of God and of Jesus our Lord,

3 as His divine power has given to us all things that *pertain* to life and godliness, through the knowledge of Him who called us by glory and virtue,

4 by which have been given to us exceedingly great and precious promises, that through these you may be partakers of the divine nature, having escaped the corruption *that is* in the world through lust.

5 But also for this very reason, giving all diligence, add to your faith virtue, to virtue knowledge,

6 to knowledge self-control, to self-control perseverance, to perseverance godliness,

7 to godliness brotherly kindness, and to brotherly kindness love.

8 For if these things are yours and abound, *you will be* neither barren

nor unfruitful in the knowledge of our Lord Jesus Christ.

9 For he who lacks these things is shortsighted, even to blindness, and has forgotten that he was purged from his old sins.

10 Therefore, brethren, be even more diligent to make your calling and election sure, for if you do these things you will never stumble;

11 for so an entrance will be supplied to you abundantly into the everlasting kingdom of our Lord and Savior Jesus Christ.

12 Therefore I will not be negligent to remind you always of these things, though you know *them*, and *are* established in the present truth.

13 Yes, I think it is right, as long as I am in this tent, to stir you up by reminding *you*,

14 knowing that shortly I *must* put off my tent, just as our Lord Jesus Christ showed me.

15 Moreover I will be careful to ensure that you always have a reminder of these things after my decease.

16 For we did not follow cunningly devised fables when we made known to you the power and coming of our Lord Jesus Christ, but were eyewitnesses of His majesty.

17 For He received from God the Father honor and glory when such a voice came to Him from the Excellent Glory: "This is My beloved Son, in whom I am well pleased."

18 And we heard this voice which came from heaven when we were with Him on the holy mountain.

19 We also have the prophetic word made more sure, which you do well to heed as a light that shines in a dark place, until the day dawns and the morning star rises in your hearts;

20 knowing this first, that no prophecy of Scripture is of any private interpretation,

21 for prophecy never came by the will of man, but holy men of God spoke *as they were* moved by the Holy Spirit.

2 But there were also false prophets among the people, even as there will be false teachers among you, who will secretly bring in destructive heresies, even denying the Lord who bought them, *and* bring on themselves swift destruction.

2 And many will follow their destructive ways, because of whom the way of truth will be blasphemed.

3 By covetousness they will exploit you with deceptive words; for a long time their judgment has not been idle, and their destruction does not slumber.

4 For if God did not spare the angels who sinned, but cast *them* down to hell and delivered *them* into chains of darkness, to be reserved for judgment;

5 and did not spare the ancient world, but saved Noah, *one of* eight *people*, a preacher of righteousness, bringing in the flood on the world of the ungodly;

6 and turning the cities of Sodom and Gomorrah into ashes, condemned *them* to destruction, making *them* an example to those who afterward would live ungodly;

7 and delivered righteous Lot, *who was* oppressed with the filthy conduct of the wicked

8 (for that righteous man, dwelling among them, tormented *his* righteous soul from day to day by seeing and hearing *their* lawless deeds)—

9 *then* the Lord knows how to deliver the godly out of temptations and to reserve the unjust under punishment for the day of judgment,

10 and especially those who walk according to the flesh in the lust of uncleanness and despise authority. *They are* presumptuous, self-willed; they are not afraid to speak evil of dignitaries,

11 whereas angels, who are greater

in power and might, do not bring a reviling accusation against them before the Lord.

12 But these, like natural brute beasts made to be caught and destroyed, speak evil of the things they do not understand, and will utterly perish in their own corruption,

13 *and* will receive the wages of unrighteousness, *as* those who count it pleasure to carouse in the daytime. *They are* spots and blemishes, carousing in their own deceptions while they feast with you,

14 having eyes full of adultery and that cannot cease from sin, beguiling unstable souls. *They have* a heart trained in covetous practices, *and are* accursed children.

15 They have forsaken the right way and gone astray, following the way of Balaam the *son* of Beor, who loved the wages of unrighteousness;

16 but he was rebuked for his iniquity: a dumb donkey speaking with a man's voice restrained the madness of the prophet.

17 These are wells without water, clouds carried by a tempest, to whom the gloom of darkness is reserved forever.

18 For when they speak great swelling *words* of emptiness, they allure through the lusts of the flesh, through licentiousness, the ones who have actually escaped from those who live in error.

19 While they promise them liberty, they themselves are slaves of corruption; for by whom a person is overcome, by him also he is brought into bondage.

20 For if, after they have escaped the pollutions of the world through the knowledge of the Lord and Savior Jesus Christ, they are again entangled in them and overcome, the latter end is worse for them than the beginning.

21 For it would have been better for them not to have known the way of righteousness, than having known *it*, to turn from the holy commandment delivered to them.

22 But it has happened to them according to the true proverb: *"A dog returns to his own vomit,"* and, "a sow, having washed, to her wallowing in the mire."

3 Beloved, I now write to you this second epistle (in *both of* which I stir up your pure minds by way of reminder),

2 that you may be mindful of the words which were spoken before by the holy prophets, and of the commandment of us the apostles of the Lord and Savior,

3 knowing this first: that scoffers will come in the last days, walking according to their own lusts,

4 and saying, "Where is the promise of His coming? For since the fathers fell asleep, all things continue as *they were* from the beginning of creation."

5 For this they willfully forget: that by the word of God the heavens were of old, and the earth standing out of water and in the water,

6 by which the world *that* then existed perished, being flooded with water.

7 But the heavens and the earth *which* now *exist* are kept in store by the same word, reserved for fire until the day of judgment and perdition of ungodly men.

8 But, beloved, do not forget this one thing, that with the Lord one day *is* as a thousand years, and a thousand years as one day.

9 The Lord is not slack concerning *His* promise, as some count slackness, but is longsuffering toward us, not willing that any should perish but that all should come to repentance.

10 But the day of the Lord will come as a thief in the night, in which the heavens will pass away with a great noise, and the elements will melt with fervent heat;

both the earth and the works that are in it will be burned up.

11 Therefore, since all these things will be dissolved, what manner *of persons* ought you to be in holy conduct and godliness,

12 looking for and hastening the coming of the day of God, because of which the heavens will be dissolved being on fire, and the elements will melt with fervent heat?

13 Nevertheless we, according to His promise, look for new heavens and a new earth in which righteousness dwells.

14 Therefore, beloved, looking forward to these things, be diligent to be found by Him in peace, without spot and blameless;

15 and account *that* the longsuffering of our Lord *is* salvation—as also our beloved brother Paul, according to the wisdom given to him, has written to you,

16 as also in all his epistles, speaking in them of these things, in which are some things hard to understand, which those *who are* untaught and unstable twist to their own destruction, as *they do* also the rest of the Scriptures.

17 You therefore, beloved, since you know *these things* beforehand, beware lest you also fall from your own steadfastness, being led away with the error of the wicked;

18 but grow in the grace and knowledge of our Lord and Savior Jesus Christ. To Him *be* the glory both now and forever. Amen.

THE FIRST EPISTLE OF
JOHN

THAT which was from the beginning, which we have heard, which we have seen with our eyes, which we have looked upon, and our hands have handled, concerning the Word of life—

2 the life was manifested, and we have seen, and bear witness, and declare to you that eternal life which was with the Father and was manifested to us—

3 that which we have seen and heard we declare to you, that you also may have fellowship with us; and truly our fellowship *is* with the Father and with His Son Jesus Christ.

4 And these things we write to you that your joy may be full.

5 This is the message which we have heard from Him and declare to you, that God is light and in Him is no darkness at all.

6 If we say that we have fellow-

ship with Him, and walk in darkness, we lie and do not practice the truth.

7 But if we walk in the light as He is in the light, we have fellowship with one another, and the blood of Jesus Christ His Son cleanses us from all sin.

8 If we say that we have no sin, we deceive ourselves, and the truth is not in us.

9 If we confess our sins, He is faithful and just to forgive us *our* sins and to cleanse us from all unrighteousness.

10 If we say that we have not sinned, we make Him a liar, and His word is not in us.

2 My little children, these things I write to you, that you may not sin. And if anyone sins, we have an Advocate with the Father, Jesus Christ the righteous.

2 And He Himself is the propitiation for our sins, and not for ours only but also for the whole world.

3 Now by this we know that we know Him, if we keep His commandments.

4 He who says, "I know Him," and does not keep His commandments, is a liar, and the truth is not in him.

5 But whoever keeps His word, truly the love of God is perfected in him. By this we know that we are in Him.

6 He who says he abides in Him ought himself also to walk just as He walked.

7 Brethren, I write no new commandment to you, but an old commandment which you have had from the beginning. The old commandment is the word which you heard from the beginning.

8 Again, a new commandment I write to you, which thing is true in Him and in you, because the darkness is passing away, and the true light is already shining.

9 He who says he is in the light, and hates his brother, is in darkness until now.

10 He who loves his brother abides in the light, and there is no cause for stumbling in him.

11 But he who hates his brother is in darkness and walks in darkness, and does not know where he is going, because the darkness has blinded his eyes.

12 I write to you, little children,
    Because your sins are
        forgiven you for His name's
        sake.

13 I write to you, fathers,
    Because you have known
        Him *who is* from the
        beginning.
    I write to you, young men,
    Because you have overcome
        the wicked one.
    I write to you, little children,
    Because you have known the
        Father.

14 I have written to you, fathers,
    Because you have known
        Him *who is* from the
        beginning.
    I have written to you, young
        men,
    Because you are strong, and
        the word of God abides in
        you,
    And you have overcome the
        wicked one.

15 Do not love the world or the things in the world. If anyone loves the world, the love of the Father is not in him.

16 For all that *is* in the world—the lust of the flesh, the lust of the eyes, and the pride of life—is not of the Father but is of the world.

17 And the world is passing away, and the lust of it; but he who does the will of God abides forever.

18 Little children, it is the last hour; and as you have heard that the Antichrist is coming, even now many antichrists have come, by which we know that it is the last hour.

19 They went out from us, but they were not of us; for if they had been of us, they would have continued with us; but *they went out* that they might be made manifest, that none of them were of us.

20 But you have an anointing from the Holy One, and you know all things.

21 I have not written to you because you do not know the truth, but because you know it, and that no lie is of the truth.

22 Who is a liar but he who denies that Jesus is the Christ? He is antichrist who denies the Father and the Son.

23 Whoever denies the Son does not have the Father either; he who acknowledges the Son has the Father also.

24 Therefore let that abide in you which you heard from the beginning. If what you heard from the beginning abides in you, you also

will abide in the Son and in the Father.

25 And this is the promise that He has promised us—eternal life.

26 These *things* I have written to you concerning those who *try to* deceive you.

27 But the anointing which you have received from Him abides in you, and you do not need that anyone teach you; but as the same anointing teaches you concerning all things, and is true, and is not a lie, and just as it has taught you, you will abide in Him.

28 And now, little children, abide in Him, that when He appears, we may have confidence and not be ashamed before Him at His coming.

29 If you know that He is righteous, you know that everyone who practices righteousness is born of Him.

3 Behold what manner of love the Father has bestowed on us, that we should be called children of God! Therefore the world does not know us, because it did not know Him.

2 Beloved, now we are children of God; and it has not yet been revealed what we shall be, but we know that when He is revealed, we shall be like Him, for we shall see Him as He is.

3 And everyone who has this hope in Him purifies himself, just as He is pure.

4 Whoever commits sin also commits lawlessness, and sin is lawlessness.

5 And you know that He was manifested to take away our sins, and in Him there is no sin.

6 Whoever abides in Him does not sin. Whoever sins has neither seen Him nor known Him.

7 Little children, let no one deceive you. He who practices righteousness is righteous, just as He is righteous.

8 He who sins is of the devil, for the devil has sinned from the be-ginning. For this purpose the Son of God was manifested, that He might destroy the works of the devil.

9 Whoever has been born of God does not sin, for His seed remains in him; and he cannot sin, because he has been born of God.

10 In this the children of God and the children of the devil are manifest: Whoever does not practice righteousness is not of God, nor *is* he who does not love his brother.

11 For this is the message that you heard from the beginning, that we should love one another,

12 not as Cain *who* was of the wicked one and murdered his brother. And why did he murder him? Because his works were evil and his brother's righteous.

13 Do not marvel, my brethren, if the world hates you.

14 We know that we have passed from death to life, because we love the brethren. He who does not love *his* brother abides in death.

15 Whoever hates his brother is a murderer, and you know that no murderer has eternal life abiding in him.

16 By this we know love, because He laid down His life for us. And we also ought to lay down *our* lives for the brethren.

17 But whoever has this world's goods, and sees his brother in need, and shuts up his heart from him, how does the love of God abide in him?

18 My little children, let us not love in word or in tongue, but in deed and in truth.

19 And by this we know that we are of the truth, and shall assure our hearts before Him.

20 For if our heart condemns us, God is greater than our heart, and knows all things.

21 Beloved, if our heart does not condemn us, we have confidence toward God.

22 And whatever we ask we re-ceive from Him, because we keep

His commandments and do those things that are pleasing in His sight.

23 And this is His commandment: that we should believe on the name of His Son Jesus Christ and love one another, as He gave us commandment.

24 Now he who keeps His commandments abides in Him, and He in him. And by this we know that He abides in us, by the Spirit whom He has given us.

4 Beloved, do not believe every spirit, but test the spirits, whether they are of God; because many false prophets have gone out into the world.

2 By this you know the Spirit of God: Every spirit that confesses that Jesus Christ has come in the flesh is of God,

3 and every spirit that does not confess that Jesus Christ has come in the flesh is not of God. And this is the *spirit* of the Antichrist, which you have heard was coming, and is now already in the world.

4 You are of God, little children, and have overcome them, because He who is in you is greater than he who is in the world.

5 They are of the world. Therefore they speak *as* of the world, and the world hears them.

6 We are of God. He who knows God hears us; he who is not of God does not hear us. By this we know the spirit of truth and the spirit of error.

7 Beloved, let us love one another, for love is of God; and everyone who loves is born of God and knows God.

8 He who does not love does not know God, for God is love.

9 In this the love of God was manifested toward us, that God has sent His only begotten Son into the world, that we might live through Him.

10 In this is love, not that we loved God, but that He loved us and sent

His Son *to be* the propitiation for our sins.

11 Beloved, if God so loved us, we also ought to love one another.

12 No one has seen God at any time. If we love one another, God abides in us, and His love has been perfected in us.

13 By this we know that we abide in Him, and He in us, because He has given us of His Spirit.

14 And we have seen and testify that the Father has sent the Son *as* Savior of the world.

15 Whoever confesses that Jesus is the Son of God, God abides in him, and he in God.

16 And we have known and believed the love that God has for us. God is love, and he who abides in love abides in God, and God in him.

17 Love has been perfected among us in this: that we may have boldness in the day of judgment; because as He is, so are we in this world.

18 There is no fear in love; but perfect love casts out fear, because fear involves torment. But he who fears has not been made perfect in love.

19 We love Him because He first loved us.

20 If someone says, "I love God," and hates his brother, he is a liar; for he who does not love his brother whom he has seen, how can he love God whom he has not seen?

21 And this commandment we have from Him: that he who loves God *must* love his brother also.

5 Whoever believes that Jesus is the Christ is born of God, and everyone who loves Him who begot also loves him who is begotten of Him.

2 By this we know that we love the children of God, when we love God and keep His commandments.

3 For this is the love of God, that we keep His commandments. And

His commandments are not burdensome.

4 For whatever is born of God overcomes the world. And this is the victory that has overcome the world—our faith.

5 Who is he who overcomes the world, but he who believes that Jesus is the Son of God?

6 This is He who came by water and blood—Jesus Christ; not only by water, but by water and blood. And it is the Spirit who bears witness, because the Spirit is truth.

7 For there are three who bear witness in heaven: the Father, the Word, and the Holy Spirit; and these three are one.

8 And there are three that bear witness on earth: the Spirit, the water, and the blood; and these three agree as one.

9 If we receive the witness of men, the witness of God is greater; for this is the witness of God which He has testified of His Son.

10 He who believes in the Son of God has the witness in himself; he who does not believe God has made Him a liar, because he has not believed the testimony that God has given of His Son.

11 And this is the testimony: that God has given us eternal life, and this life is in His Son.

12 He who has the Son has life; he who does not have the Son of God does not have life.

13 These things I have written to you who believe in the name of the Son of God, that you may know that you have eternal life, and that you may *continue to* believe in the name of the Son of God.

14 Now this is the confidence that we have in Him, that if we ask anything according to His will, He hears us.

15 And if we know that He hears us, whatever we ask, we know that we have the petitions that we have asked of Him.

16 If anyone sees his brother sinning a sin *which does* not *lead* to death, he will ask, and He will give him life for those who commit sin not *leading* to death. There is sin *leading* to death. I do not say that he should pray about that.

17 All unrighteousness is sin, and there is sin not *leading* to death.

18 We know that whoever is born of God does not sin; but he who has been born of God keeps himself, and the wicked one does not touch him.

19 We know that we are of God, and the whole world lies *under the sway of* the wicked one.

20 And we know that the Son of God has come and has given us an understanding, that we may know Him who is true; and we are in Him who is true, in His Son Jesus Christ. This is the true God and eternal life.

21 Little children, keep yourselves from idols. Amen.

Can You *Know* What Your Eternal Destiny Will Be?

Life is packed with uncertainties. Eventually we each discover the one thing or person we thought we could always count on lets us down. Nothing seems certain.

That's why the apostle John goes to great lengths to assure his readers they can count on one thing. They can know (not think, hope, or wish) that they have eternal life, and he points out two ways to be certain:

Head assurance. John roots the certainty of a person's heavenly residence in two truths that add up to a logical conclusion.
Fact 1: Whoever "has the Son" has eternal life (1 John 5:11, 12).
Fact 2: I have the Son (for I have asked Him to have me, and He said *yes*—1 John 5:14, 15).
Conclusion: Therefore, I know that I have eternal life (1 John 5:13).

Heart assurance. As we see ourselves obeying God's Word, we gain even greater confidence that we are in Him. For in our hearts, the core of our being, we know that it's only His Spirit who can produce joyful obedience in us (1 John 2:5).

When our conscience condemns us for disobeying God, the Spirit reminds that we are not condemned but forgiven. He corrects our conscience and restores our confidences (1 John 3:18–24).

A final word. The assurance of eternal life is wrapped up in God's character. He is faithful and true, even when we are not. Lack of assurance usually arises from doubting self rather than from doubting Him. We wonder if we are really His. That concern in itself suggests that we are.

But anyone who chooses to live continually disregarding God's will has cause to question whether he or she has entered into eternal life in the first place (see "How Can I Get to Heaven?" page 362).

John gives us words of comfort and hope in 1 John—or shows us we have reason to be concerned. Whatever the case, he provides us with the necessary facts to know what our eternal destiny will be.

THE SECOND EPISTLE OF
JOHN

THE ELDER,

To the elect lady and her children, whom I love in truth, and not only I, but also all those who have known the truth,

2 because of the truth which abides in us and will be with us forever:

3 Grace, mercy, *and* peace will be with you from God the Father and from the Lord Jesus Christ, the Son of the Father, in truth and love.

4 I rejoiced greatly that I have found *some* of your children walking in truth, as we received commandment from the Father.

5 And now I plead with you, lady, not as though I wrote a new commandment to you, but that which we have had from the beginning: that we love one another.

6 This is love, that we walk according to His commandments. This is the commandment, that as you have heard from the beginning, you should walk in it.

7 For many deceivers have gone out into the world who do not confess Jesus Christ *as* coming in the flesh. This is a deceiver and an antichrist.

8 Look to yourselves, that we do not lose those things we worked for, but *that* we may receive a full reward.

9 Whoever transgresses and does not abide in the doctrine of Christ does not have God. He who abides in the doctrine of Christ has both the Father and the Son.

10 If anyone comes to you and does not bring this doctrine, do not receive him into your house nor greet him;

11 for he who greets him shares in his evil deeds.

12 Having many things to write to you, I did not wish *to do so* with paper and ink; but I hope to come to you and speak face to face, that our joy may be full.

13 The children of your elect sister greet you. Amen.

THE THIRD EPISTLE OF
JOHN

THE ELDER,

To the beloved Gaius, whom I love in truth:

2 Beloved, I pray that you may prosper in all things and be in health, just as your soul prospers.

3 For I rejoiced greatly when brethren came and testified of the truth *that is* in you, just as you walk in the truth.

4 I have no greater joy than to hear that my children walk in truth.

5 Beloved, you do faithfully whatever you do for the brethren and for strangers,

6 who have borne witness of your love before the church. *If* you send them forward on their journey in a manner worthy of God, you will do well,

7 because they went forth for His name's sake, taking nothing from the Gentiles.

8 We therefore ought to receive such, that we may become fellow workers for the truth.

9 I wrote to the church, but Diotrephes, who loves to have the preeminence among them, does not receive us.

10 Therefore, if I come, I will call to mind his deeds which he does, prating against us with malicious words. And not content with that, he himself does not receive the brethren, and forbids those who wish to, putting *them* out of the church.

11 Beloved, do not imitate what is evil, but what is good. He who does good is of God, but he who does evil has not seen God.

12 Demetrius has a *good* testimony from all, and from the truth itself. And we also bear witness, and you know that our testimony is true.

13 I had many things to write, but I do not wish to write to you with pen and ink;

14 but I hope to see you shortly, and we shall speak face to face. Peace to you. Our friends greet you. Greet the friends by name.

THE EPISTLE OF
JUDE

JUDE, a servant of Jesus Christ, and brother of James,

To those who are called, sanctified by God the Father, and preserved in Jesus Christ:

2 Mercy, peace, and love be multiplied to you.

3 Beloved, while I was very diligent to write to you concerning our common salvation, I found it necessary to write to you exhorting you to contend earnestly for the faith which was once for all delivered to the saints.

4 For certain men have crept in unnoticed, who long ago were marked out for this condemnation, ungodly men, who turn the grace of our God into licentiousness and deny the only Lord God and our Lord Jesus Christ.

5 But I want to remind you, though you once knew this, that the Lord, having saved the people out of the land of Egypt, afterward destroyed those who did not believe.

6 And the angels who did not keep their proper domain, but left their own habitation, He has reserved in everlasting chains under darkness for the judgment of the great day;

7 as Sodom and Gomorrah, and the cities around them in a similar manner to these, having given themselves over to sexual immorality and gone after strange flesh, are set forth as an example, suffering the vengeance of eternal fire.

8 Likewise also these dreamers defile the flesh, reject authority, and speak evil of dignitaries.

9 Yet Michael the archangel, in contending with the devil, when he disputed about the body of Moses, dared not bring against him a reviling accusation, but said, "The Lord rebuke you!"

10 But these speak evil of whatever they do not know; and whatever they know naturally, like brute beasts, in these things they corrupt themselves.

11 Woe to them! For they have gone in the way of Cain, have run greedily in the error of Balaam for profit, and perished in the rebellion of Korah.

12 These are spots in your love feasts, while they feast with you without fear, serving *only* themselves; *they are* clouds without water, carried about by the winds; late autumn trees without fruit, twice dead, pulled up by the roots;

13 raging waves of the sea, foaming up their own shame; wandering stars for whom is reserved the blackness of darkness forever.

14 Now Enoch, the seventh from Adam, prophesied about these men also, saying, "Behold, the Lord comes with ten thousands of His saints,

15 "to execute judgment on all, to convict all who are ungodly among them of all their ungodly deeds which they have committed in an ungodly way, and of all the harsh things which ungodly sinners have spoken against Him."

16 These are murmurers, complainers, walking according to their own lusts; and they mouth great swelling *words*, flattering people to gain advantage.

17 But you, beloved, remember the words which were spoken before by the apostles of our Lord Jesus Christ:

18 how they told you that there would be mockers in the last time who would walk according to their own ungodly lusts.

19 These are sensual persons, who cause divisions, not having the Spirit.

20 But you, beloved, building yourselves up on your most holy faith, praying in the Holy Spirit,

21 keep yourselves in the love of God, looking for the mercy of our Lord Jesus Christ unto eternal life.

22 And on some have compassion, making a distinction;

23 but others save with fear, pulling *them* out of the fire, hating even the garment defiled by the flesh.

24 Now to Him who is able
    to keep you from stumbling,
    And to present *you* faultless
    Before the presence of His
        glory with exceeding joy,

25 To God our Savior,
    Who alone is wise,
    Be glory and majesty,
    Dominion and power,
    Both now and forever.
    Amen.

THE REVELATION

OF JESUS CHRIST

THE Revelation of Jesus Christ, which God gave Him to show His servants—things which must shortly take place. And He sent and signified *it* by His angel to His servant John,

2 who bore witness to the word of God, and to the testimony of Jesus Christ, and to all things that he saw.

3 Blessed *is* he who reads and those who hear the words of this prophecy, and keep those things which are written in it; for the time *is* near.

4 John, to the seven churches which are in Asia:

Grace to you and peace from Him who is and who was and who is to come, and from the seven Spirits who are before His throne,

5 and from Jesus Christ, the faith-

338

Why Doesn't Revelation Reveal?

Many people experience confusion and frustration in studying Revelation. They would be helped if they knew that Revelation is a summary and an explanation of all the Old and New Testament prophetic books. The author, the apostle John, assumes that the reader is familiar with all these Scriptures. Much of what readers presume to be symbolic is simply John saving space by referring to word pictures articulated in other Bible books. For example, the "two olive trees" of Revelation 11 are described in Zechariah 4. Because John makes such frequent use of this referral method, readers will find a concordance (a book listing all the words in the Bible and the verses in which they may be found) to be a useful tool in understanding this book.

In addition to referring to items described in other Bible books, John uses other symbols, again to save space. These symbols need not mystify the reader. Every symbol John employs is either defined in the text (for example, the lampstands of Revelation 1) or in some other Bible book (for example, the locusts of Revelation 9 and the sea of Revelation 13). In fact, a symbol definition should be accepted *only* if the symbol is defined as such elsewhere in the Bible.

Revelation makes only occasional use of figures of speech. Every passage should be taken literally unless its context clearly indicates it should be taken figuratively (for example, the 666 of Revelation 13).

Revelation will prove less confusing, too, if the reader realizes that it is more than a book of prophecy and a description of the wonder of God. Revelation also describes the splendor of the church (which consists of all believers) and contains instruction about church conduct; doctrinal teaching about heaven, hell, Christ's deity, judgment, angels, the resurrection, and the new creation; and exhortation to unbelievers to repent and to believers to persevere, to purify, and to ready themselves for the Lord's return.

According to Daniel 12:4, end-times prophecy will become clearer as we approach the time of fulfillment. Daniel said that this time would begin in a period of explosive growth in human travel and knowledge. Now may be the time. (See "Is the End Near?" page 69.) Thus the reader is encouraged to keep returning to this book for further insights into new developments.

Revelation promises a special blessing to all who read it and take its message to heart.

ful witness, the firstborn from the dead, and the ruler over the kings of the earth. To Him who loved us and washed us from our sins in His own blood,

6 and has made us kings and priests to His God and Father, to Him *be* glory and dominion forever and ever. Amen.

7 Behold, He is coming with clouds, and every eye will see Him, and they *also* who pierced Him. And all the tribes of the earth will mourn because of Him. Even so, Amen.

8 "I am the Alpha and the Omega, *the* Beginning and *the* End," says the Lord, "who is and who was and who is to come, the Almighty."

9 I, John, both your brother and companion in tribulation, and in the kingdom and patience of Jesus Christ, was on the island that is called Patmos for the word of God and for the testimony of Jesus Christ.

10 I was in the Spirit on the Lord's Day, and I heard behind me a loud voice, as of a trumpet,

11 saying, "I am the Alpha and the Omega, the First and the Last," and, "What you see, write in a book and send *it* to the seven churches which are in Asia: to Ephesus, to Smyrna, to Pergamos, to Thyatira, to Sardis, to Philadelphia, and to Laodicea."

12 Then I turned to see the voice that spoke with me. And having turned I saw seven golden lampstands,

13 and in the midst of the seven lampstands *One* like the Son of Man, clothed with a garment down to the feet and girded about the chest with a golden band.

14 His head and *His* hair *were* white like wool, as white as snow, and His eyes like a flame of fire;

15 His feet *were* like fine brass, as if refined in a furnace, and His voice as the sound of many waters;

16 He had in His right hand seven stars, out of His mouth went a

sharp two-edged sword, and His countenance *was* like the sun shining in its strength.

17 And when I saw Him, I fell at His feet as dead. But He laid His right hand on me, saying to me, "Do not be afraid; I am the First and the Last.

18 "I *am* He who lives, and was dead, and behold, I am alive forevermore. Amen. And I have the keys of Hades and of Death.

19 "Write the things which you have seen, and the things which are, and the things which will take place after this.

20 "The mystery of the seven stars which you saw in My right hand, and the seven golden lampstands: The seven stars are the angels of the seven churches, and the seven lampstands which you saw are the seven churches.

2 "To the angel of the church of Ephesus write,

'These things says He who holds the seven stars in His right hand, who walks in the midst of the seven golden lampstands:

2 "I know your works, your labor, your patience, and that you cannot bear those who are evil. And you have tested those who say they are apostles and are not, and have found them liars;

3 "and you have persevered and have patience, and have labored for My name's sake and have not become weary.

4 "Nevertheless I have *this* against you, that you have left your first love.

5 "Remember therefore from where you have fallen; repent and do the first works, or else I will come to you quickly and remove your lampstand from its place— unless you repent.

6 "But this you have, that you hate the deeds of the Nicolaitans, which I also hate.

7 "He who has an ear, let him hear what the Spirit says to the churches. To him who overcomes I

will give to eat from the tree of life, which is in the midst of the Paradise of God." '

8 "And to the angel of the church in Smyrna write,

'These things says the First and the Last, who was dead, and came to life:

9 "I know your works, tribulation, and poverty (but you are rich); and *I know* the blasphemy of those who say they are Jews and are not, but *are* a synagogue of Satan.

10 "Do not fear any of those things which you are about to suffer. Indeed, the devil is about to throw *some* of you into prison, that you may be tested, and you will have tribulation ten days. Be faithful until death, and I will give you the crown of life.

11 "He who has an ear, let him hear what the Spirit says to the churches. He who overcomes shall not be hurt by the second death." '

12 "And to the angel of the church in Pergamos write,

'These things says He who has the sharp two-edged sword:

13 "I know your works, and where you dwell, where Satan's throne *is.* And you hold fast to My name, and did not deny My faith even in the days in which Antipas *was* My faithful martyr, who was killed among you, where Satan dwells.

14 "But I have a few things against you, because you have there those who hold the doctrine of Balaam, who taught Balak to put a stumbling block before the children of Israel, to eat things sacrificed to idols, and to commit sexual immorality.

15 "Thus you also have those who hold the doctrine of the Nicolaitans, which thing I hate.

16 "Repent, or else I will come to you quickly and will fight against them with the sword of My mouth.

17 "He who has an ear, let him hear what the Spirit says to the churches. To him who overcomes I will give some of the hidden manna to eat. And I will give him a white stone, and on the stone a new name written which no one knows except him who receives *it.*" '

18 "And to the angel of the church in Thyatira write,

'These things says the Son of God, who has eyes like a flame of fire, and His feet like fine brass:

19 "I know your works, love, service, faith, and your patience; and *as* for your works, the last *are* more than the first.

20 "Nevertheless I have a few things against you, because you allow that woman Jezebel, who calls herself a prophetess, to teach and beguile My servants to commit sexual immorality and to eat things sacrificed to idols.

21 "And I gave her time to repent of her sexual immorality, and she did not repent.

22 "Indeed I will cast her into a sickbed, and those who commit adultery with her into great tribulation, unless they repent of their deeds.

23 "And I will kill her children with death. And all the churches shall know that I am He who searches the minds and hearts. And I will give to each one of you according to your works.

24 "But to you I say, and to the rest in Thyatira, as many as do not have this doctrine, and who have not known the depths of Satan, as they call *them,* I will put on you no other burden.

25 "But hold fast wnat you have till I come.

26 "And he who overcomes, and keeps My works until the end, to him I will give power over the nations—

27 'He shall rule them with a rod of iron;
  As the potter's vessels
    shall be broken to pieces'—

as I also have received from My Father;

28 "and I will give him the morning star.

29 "He who has an ear, let him hear what the Spirit says to the churches." '

3 "And to the angel of the church in Sardis write,

'These things says He who has the seven Spirits of God and the seven stars: "I know your works, that you have a name that you are alive, but you are dead.

2 "Be watchful, and strengthen the things which remain, that are ready to die, for I have not found your works perfect before God.

3 "Remember therefore how you have received and heard; hold fast and repent. Therefore if you will not watch, I will come upon you as a thief, and you will not know what hour I will come upon you.

4 "You have a few names even in Sardis who have not defiled their garments; and they shall walk with Me in white, for they are worthy.

5 "He who overcomes shall be clothed in white garments, and I will not blot out his name from the Book of Life; but I will confess his name before My Father and before His angels.

6 "He who has an ear, let him hear what the Spirit says to the churches." '

7 "And to the angel of the church in Philadelphia write,

'These things says He who is holy, He who is true, "*He who has the key of David, He who opens and no one shuts, and shuts and no one opens*":

8 "I know your works. See, I have set before you an open door, and no one can shut it; for you have a little strength, have kept My word, and have not denied My name.

9 "Indeed I will make *those* of the synagogue of Satan, who say they are Jews and are not, but lie—indeed I will make them come and worship before your feet, and to know that I have loved you.

10 "Because you have kept My command to persevere, I also will keep you from the hour of trial which shall come upon the whole world, to test those who dwell on the earth.

11 "Behold, I come quickly! Hold fast what you have, that no one may take your crown.

12 "He who overcomes, I will make him a pillar in the temple of My God, and he shall go out no more. And I will write on him the name of My God and the name of the city of My God, the New Jerusalem, which comes down out of heaven from My God. And *I will write on him* My new name.

13 "He who has an ear, let him hear what the Spirit says to the churches." '

14 "And to the angel of the church of the Laodiceans write,

'These things says the Amen, the Faithful and True Witness, the Beginning of the creation of God:

15 "I know your works, that you are neither cold nor hot. I could wish you were cold or hot.

16 "So then, because you are lukewarm, and neither cold nor hot, I will spew you out of My mouth.

17 "Because you say, 'I am rich, have become wealthy, and have need of nothing'—and do not know that you are wretched, miserable, poor, blind, and naked—

18 "I counsel you to buy from Me gold refined in the fire, that you may be rich; and white garments, that you may be clothed, *that* the shame of your nakedness may not be revealed; and anoint your eyes with eye salve, that you may see.

19 "As many as I love, I rebuke and chasten. Therefore be zealous and repent.

20 "Behold, I stand at the door and knock. If anyone hears My voice and opens the door, I will come in to him and dine with him, and he with Me.

What in the World Is God Up To?

Have you ever wondered, *What is God doing? Does He have some overall plan for the world? How do I fit in?* This final book of the Bible reveals some of God's grand design for time and eternity, but it also gives us a hint of what He desires for each of us. As you answer the following questions, you'll discover for yourself what the Bible says about God's plan for humanity and your part in it. (See page x for tips on how to find your way around the Bible.)

God and you

What sort of relationship does God desire to have with you? (See Revelation 3:20 for the answer.)

If you were to come to know God personally (as described in Revelation 3:20), how would that effect your behavior toward other people? (Look in 1 John 4:7, 8, 11.)

How does God want people to live? List several attitudes and actions from the following passages: 1 Thessalonians 5:15–18, 22; Colossians 1:9–11; 1 Thessalonians 4:1–3.

The problem

Romans 3:11–18, describes what God sees in us. List the characteristics.

According to Romans 5:12 and Romans 3:23, why do humans exhibit these characteristics? What percentage of the human race suffers from this problem?

What does Romans 1:18–20 say about the notion that "people generally do the best they know how"?

Why does the Bible call all people "sinners," even though some are much worse than others? (See James 2:10, 11. Hint: The "law" is God's perfect standard of right and wrong expressed in the Law of the Old Testament.)

The solution

What does John 3:16–18 tell us God has done about humankind's problem?

According to Romans 8:1, 2, how can we avoid being condemned (separated from God)? (Hint: "Flesh" means our human tendencies that lead us away from God. "Spirit" refers to God's own Spirit.)

How can a person be "in Christ"? (Look up John 1:12; Acts 3:19, 20.)

Based on the questions and answers listed above: what is God's plan for humanity? How can you be a part of it?

21 "To him who overcomes I will grant to sit with Me on My throne, as I also overcame and sat down with My Father on His throne.
22 "He who has an ear, let him hear what the Spirit says to the churches." ' "

4 After these things I looked, and behold, a door *standing* open in heaven. And the first voice which I heard *was* like a trumpet speaking with me, saying, "Come up here, and I will show you things which must take place after this."
2 Immediately I was in the Spirit; and behold, a throne set in heaven, and *One* sat on the throne.
3 And He who sat there was like a jasper and a sardius stone in appearance; and *there was* a rainbow around the throne, in appearance like an emerald.
4 Around the throne *were* twenty-four thrones, and on the thrones I saw twenty-four elders sitting, clothed in white robes; and they had crowns of gold on their heads.
5 And from the throne proceeded lightnings, thunderings, and voices. And *there were* seven lamps of fire burning before the throne, which are the seven Spirits of God.
6 Before the throne *there was* a sea of glass, like crystal. And in the midst of the throne, and around the throne, *were* four living creatures full of eyes in front and in back.
7 The first living creature *was* like a lion, the second living creature like a calf, the third living creature had a face like a man, and the fourth living creature *was* like a flying eagle.
8 And *the* four living creatures, each having six wings, were full of eyes around and within. And they do not rest day or night, saying:

"Holy, holy, holy,
Lord God Almighty,

Who was and is and is to come!"

9 Whenever the living creatures give glory and honor and thanks to Him who sits on the throne, who lives forever and ever,
10 the twenty-four elders fall down before Him who sits on the throne and worship Him who lives forever and ever, and cast their crowns before the throne, saying:

11 "You are worthy, O Lord,
To receive glory and honor and power;
For You created all things,
And by Your will they exist and were created."

5 And I saw in the right *hand* of Him who sat on the throne a scroll written inside and on the back, sealed with seven seals.
2 Then I saw a strong angel proclaiming with a loud voice, "Who is worthy to open the scroll and to loose its seals?"
3 And no one in heaven or on the earth or under the earth was able to open the scroll, or to look at it.
4 So I wept much, because no one was found worthy to open and read the scroll, or to look at it.
5 But one of the elders said to me, "Do not weep. Behold, the Lion of the tribe of Judah, the Root of David, has prevailed to open the scroll and to loose its seven seals."
6 And I looked, and behold, in the midst of the throne and of the four living creatures, and in the midst of the elders, stood a Lamb as though it had been slain, having seven horns and seven eyes, which are the seven Spirits of God sent out into all the earth.
7 Then He came and took the scroll out of the right hand of Him who sat on the throne.
8 Now when He had taken the scroll, the four living creatures and the twenty-four elders fell down

before the Lamb, each having a harp, and golden bowls full of incense, which are the prayers of the saints.

9 And they sang a new song, saying:

"You are worthy to take the scroll,
And to open its seals;
For You were slain,
And have redeemed us to God by Your blood
Out of every tribe and tongue and people and nation,
10 And have made us kings and priests to our God;
And we shall reign on the earth."

11 Then I looked, and I heard the voice of many angels around the throne, the living creatures, and the elders; and the number of them was ten thousand times ten thousand, and thousands of thousands, 12 saying with a loud voice:

"Worthy is the Lamb who was slain
To receive power and riches and wisdom,
And strength and honor and glory and blessing!"

13 And every creature which is in heaven and on the earth and under the earth and such as are in the sea, and all that are in them, I heard saying:

"Blessing and honor and glory and power
Be to Him who sits on the throne,
And to the Lamb, forever and ever!"

14 Then the four living creatures said, "Amen!" And the twenty-four elders fell down and worshiped Him who lives forever and ever.

6 Now I saw when the Lamb opened one of the seals; and I heard one of the four living creatures saying with a voice like thunder, "Come and see."

2 And I looked, and behold, a white horse. And he who sat on it had a bow; and a crown was given to him, and he went out conquering and to conquer.

3 When He opened the second seal, I heard the second living creature saying, "Come and see."

4 And another horse, fiery red, went out. And it was granted to the one who sat on it to take peace from the earth, and that *people* should kill one another; and there was given to him a great sword.

5 When He opened the third seal, I heard the third living creature say, "Come and see." And I looked, and behold, a black horse, and he who sat on it had a pair of scales in his hand.

6 And I heard a voice in the midst of the four living creatures saying, "A quart of wheat for a denarius, and three quarts of barley for a denarius; and do not harm the oil and the wine."

7 When He opened the fourth seal, I heard the voice of the fourth living creature saying, "Come and see."

8 And I looked, and behold, a pale horse. And the name of him who sat on it was Death, and Hades followed with him. And power was given to them over a fourth of the earth, to kill with sword, with hunger, with death, and by the beasts of the earth.

9 When He opened the fifth seal, I saw under the altar the souls of those who had been slain for the word of God and for the testimony which they held.

10 And they cried with a loud voice, saying, "How long, O Lord, holy and true, until You judge and avenge our blood on those who dwell on the earth?"

11 And a white robe was given to each of them; and it was said to

What's So Terrible About the End-Times?

Jesus' physical return to earth will be prefaced by a seven-year period often referred to as the "Great Tribulation." During these seven years, God devastates the earth through three judgment sequences with seven judgments in each sequence.

Seal judgments (Revelation 6:1—8:1). The first series flows from the breaking of seven "seals"— wax or clay fasteners that allow a tightly rolled scroll to be opened section by section.
1) The world will be conquered by the Antichrist, the half-human, half-satanic person who will mobilize the world against God in the end-times. 2) A worldwide series of wars will break out following the Antichrist's rise. 3) Terrible famines will overtake the war-torn earth. 4) Plagues will be added to the previous devastations. 5) A great number of Christians (in heaven) will cry out to God. 6) Planet-rattling earthquakes accompanied by signs in the sky will strike fear into the most hardened heart. 7) A hush will fall in heaven, followed by thunder and lightning on earth.

Trumpet judgments (Revelation 8:7—12:6). While the focus of the seal judgments was on humanity, the target of the trumpet judgments is the environment.

1) Cataclysmic fires will burn up one-third of the world's forests and grasses. 2) A meteoric object smashes into the ocean, bringing widespread oceanic death and changing the ocean's color to reddish-brown. 3) Another object from space will poison a third of the world's fresh water. 4) Much of the sky will darken, perhaps because of debris catapulted into the atmosphere from the first three trumpet judgments. 5) Evil spirits will be released from captivity and many humans will experience the awful impact of evil spiritual beings. 6) About 200 million soldiers will spread disaster. 7) The seventh trumpet will announce the third series of judgments.

Bowl judgments (Revelation 16:1—21).

1) Horrible sores will break out on those who worship the Antichrist. 2) All ocean life that had survived to this point will be destroyed. 3) All the rivers and springs will be made useless for drinking. 4) The world will become hotter, scorching those exposed to direct sunlight. 5) Darkness will envelop the world, accentuating the misery of its inhabitants. 6) The surviving armies will fight a final, climactic battle. 7) One hundred-pound hailstones will fall on the corrupt political and religious system of the Antichrist.

To end on a note of comfort, God's people will never experience His full wrath.

them that they should rest a little while longer, until both *the number of* their fellow servants and their brethren, who would be killed as they *were*, was completed.

12 I looked when He opened the sixth seal, and behold, there was a great earthquake; and the sun became black as sackcloth of hair, and the moon became like blood.

13 And the stars of heaven fell to the earth, as a fig tree drops its late figs when it is shaken by a mighty wind.

14 Then the sky receded as a scroll when it is rolled up, and every mountain and island was moved out of its place.

15 And the kings of the earth, the great men, the rich men, the commanders, the mighty men, every slave and every free man, hid themselves in the caves and in the rocks of the mountains,

16 and said to the mountains and rocks, "Fall on us and hide us from the face of Him who sits on the throne and from the wrath of the Lamb!

17 "For the great day of His wrath has come, and who is able to stand?"

7 After these things I saw four angels standing at the four corners of the earth, holding the four winds of the earth, that the wind should not blow on the earth, on the sea, or on any tree.

2 Then I saw another angel ascending from the east, having the seal of the living God. And he cried with a loud voice to the four angels to whom it was granted to harm the earth and the sea,

3 saying, "Do not harm the earth, the sea, or the trees till we have sealed the servants of our God on their foreheads."

4 And I heard the number of those who were sealed. One hundred *and* forty-four thousand of all the tribes of the children of Israel *were* sealed:

5 of the tribe of Judah
    twelve thousand *were* sealed;
of the tribe of Reuben
    twelve thousand *were* sealed;
of the tribe of Gad
    twelve thousand *were* sealed;
6 of the tribe of Asher
    twelve thousand *were* sealed;
of the tribe of Naphtali
    twelve thousand *were* sealed;
of the tribe of Manasseh
    twelve thousand *were* sealed;
7 of the tribe of Simeon
    twelve thousand *were* sealed;
of the tribe of Levi
    twelve thousand *were* sealed;
of the tribe of Issachar
    twelve thousand *were* sealed;
8 of the tribe of Zebulun
    twelve thousand *were* sealed;
of the tribe of Joseph
    twelve thousand *were* sealed;
of the tribe of Benjamin
    twelve thousand *were* sealed.

9 After these things I looked, and behold, a great multitude which no one could number, of all nations, tribes, peoples, and tongues, standing before the throne and before the Lamb, clothed with white robes, with palm branches in their hands,

10 and crying out with a loud voice, saying, "Salvation *belongs* to our God who sits on the throne, and to the Lamb!"

11 And all the angels stood around the throne and the elders and the four living creatures, and fell on their faces before the throne and worshiped God,

12 saying:

"Amen! Blessing and glory
    and wisdom,
Thanksgiving and honor and
    power and might,
Be to our God forever and
    ever.
Amen."

13 Then one of the elders answered, saying to me, "Who are

these arrayed in white robes, and where did they come from?"

14 And I said to him, "Sir, you know." So he said to me, "These are the ones who come out of the great tribulation, and washed their robes and made them white in the blood of the Lamb.

15 "Therefore they are before the throne of God, and serve Him day and night in His temple. And He who sits on the throne will dwell among them.

16 "They shall neither hunger anymore nor thirst anymore; the sun shall not strike them, nor any heat;

17 "for the Lamb who is in the midst of the throne will shepherd them and lead them to living fountains of waters. And God will wipe away every tear from their eyes."

8 When He opened the seventh seal, there was silence in heaven for about half an hour.

2 And I saw the seven angels who stand before God, and to them were given seven trumpets.

3 Then another angel, having a golden censer, came and stood at the altar. And he was given much incense, that he should offer *it* with the prayers of all the saints upon the golden altar which was before the throne.

4 And the smoke of the incense, with the prayers of the saints, ascended before God from the angel's hand.

5 Then the angel took the censer, filled it with fire from the altar, and threw *it* to the earth. And there were noises, thunderings, lightnings, and an earthquake.

6 So the seven angels who had the seven trumpets prepared themselves to sound.

7 The first angel sounded: And hail and fire followed, mingled with blood, and they were thrown to the earth; and a third of the trees were burned up, and all green grass was burned up.

8 Then the second angel sounded: And *something* like a great mountain burning with fire was thrown into the sea, and a third of the sea became blood;

9 and a third of the living creatures in the sea died, and a third of the ships were destroyed.

10 Then the third angel sounded: And a great star fell from heaven, burning like a torch, and it fell on a third of the rivers and on the springs of water;

11 and the name of the star is Wormwood; and a third of the waters became wormwood; and many men died from the water, because it was made bitter.

12 Then the fourth angel sounded: And a third of the sun was struck, a third of the moon, and a third of the stars, so that a third of them were darkened; and a third of the day did not shine, and likewise the night.

13 And I looked, and I heard an angel flying through the midst of heaven, saying with a loud voice, "Woe, woe, woe to the inhabitants of the earth, because of the remaining blasts of the trumpet of the three angels who are about to sound!"

9 Then the fifth angel sounded: And I saw a star fallen from heaven to the earth. And to him was given the key to the bottomless pit.

2 And he opened the bottomless pit, and smoke arose out of the pit like the smoke of a great furnace. And the sun and the air were darkened because of the smoke of the pit.

3 Then out of the smoke locusts came upon the earth. And to them was given power, as the scorpions of the earth have power.

4 They were commanded not to harm the grass of the earth, or any green thing, or any tree, but only those men who do not have the seal of God on their foreheads.

5 And they were not given *authority* to kill them, but to torment

them *for* five months. And their torment *was* like the torment of a scorpion when it strikes a man.

6 In those days men will seek death and will not find it; they will desire to die, and death will flee from them.

7 And the shape of the locusts was like horses prepared for battle; and on their heads *were* crowns of something like gold, and their faces *were* like the faces of men.

8 They had hair like women's hair, and their teeth were like lions' *teeth.*

9 And they had breastplates like breastplates of iron, and the sound of their wings *was* like the sound of chariots with many horses running into battle.

10 They had tails like scorpions, and there were stings in their tails. And their power *was* to hurt men five months.

11 And they had as king over them the angel of the bottomless pit, whose name in Hebrew *is* Abaddon, but in Greek he has the name Apollyon.

12 One woe is past. Behold, still two more woes are coming after these things.

13 Then the sixth angel sounded: And I heard a voice from the four horns of the golden altar which is before God,

14 saying to the sixth angel who had the trumpet, "Release the four angels who are bound at the great river Euphrates."

15 So the four angels, who had been prepared for the hour and day and month and year, were released to kill a third of mankind.

16 Now the number of the army of the horsemen *was* two hundred million, and I heard the number of them.

17 And thus I saw the horses in the vision: those who sat on them had breastplates of fiery red, hyacinth blue, and sulfur yellow; and the heads of the horses *were* like the heads of lions; and out of their mouths came fire, smoke, and brimstone.

18 By these three *plagues* a third of mankind was killed—by the fire and the smoke and the brimstone which came out of their mouths.

19 For their power is in their mouth and in their tails; for their tails *are* like serpents, having heads; and with them they do harm.

20 But the rest of mankind, who were not killed by these plagues, did not repent of the works of their hands, that they should not worship demons, and idols of gold, silver, brass, stone, and wood, which can neither see nor hear nor walk;

21 and they did not repent of their murders or their sorceries or their sexual immorality or their thefts.

10

And I saw still another mighty angel coming down from heaven, clothed with a cloud. And a rainbow *was* on his head, his face *was* like the sun, and his feet like pillars of fire.

2 And he had a little book open in his hand. And he set his right foot on the sea and *his* left *foot* on the land,

3 and cried with a loud voice, as *when* a lion roars. And when he cried out, seven thunders uttered their voices.

4 Now when the seven thunders uttered their voices, I was about to write; but I heard a voice from heaven saying to me, "Seal up the things which the seven thunders uttered, and do not write them."

5 And the angel whom I saw standing on the sea and on the land lifted up his hand to heaven

6 and swore by Him who lives forever and ever, who created heaven and the things that are in it, the earth and the things that are in it, and the sea and the things that are in it, that there should be delay no longer,

7 but in the days of the sounding

of the seventh angel, when he is about to sound, the mystery of God would be finished, as He declared to His servants the prophets.

8 Then the voice which I heard from heaven spoke to me again and said, "Go, take the little book which is open in the hand of the angel who stands on the sea and on the earth."

9 And I went to the angel and said to him, "Give me the little book." And he said to me, "Take and eat it; and it will make your stomach bitter, but it will be as sweet as honey in your mouth."

10 And I took the little book out of the angel's hand and ate it, and it was as sweet as honey in my mouth. But when I had eaten it, my stomach became bitter.

11 And he said to me, "You must prophesy again about many peoples, nations, tongues, and kings."

11 Then I was given a reed like a measuring rod. And the angel stood, saying, "Rise and measure the temple of God, the altar, and those who worship there.

2 "But leave out the court which is outside the temple, and do not measure it, for it has been given to the Gentiles. And they will tread the holy city under foot *for* forty-two months.

3 "And I will give *power* to my two witnesses, and they will prophesy one thousand two hundred and sixty days, clothed in sackcloth."

4 These are the two olive trees and the two lampstands standing before the God of the earth.

5 And if anyone wants to harm them, fire proceeds from their mouth and devours their enemies. And if anyone wants to harm them, he must be killed in this manner.

6 These have power to shut heaven, so that no rain falls in the days of their prophecy; and they

have power over waters to turn them to blood, and to strike the earth with all plagues, as often as they desire.

7 Now when they finish their testimony, the beast that ascends out of the bottomless pit will make war against them, overcome them, and kill them.

8 And their dead bodies *will lie* in the street of the great city which spiritually is called Sodom and Egypt, where also our Lord was crucified.

9 Then *those* from the peoples, tribes, tongues, and nations will see their dead bodies three and a half days, and not allow their dead bodies to be put into graves.

10 And those who dwell on the earth will rejoice over them, make merry, and send gifts to one another, because these two prophets tormented those who dwell on the earth.

11 Now after the three and a half days the breath of life from God entered them, and they stood on their feet, and great fear fell on those who saw them.

12 And they heard a loud voice from heaven saying to them, "Come up here." And they ascended to heaven in a cloud, and their enemies saw them.

13 In the same hour there was a great earthquake, and a tenth of the city fell. In the earthquake seven thousand men were killed, and the rest were afraid and gave glory to the God of heaven.

14 The second woe is past. Behold, the third woe is coming quickly.

15 Then the seventh angel sounded: And there were loud voices in heaven, saying, "The kingdoms of this world have become *the kingdoms* of our Lord and of His Christ, and He shall reign forever and ever!"

16 And the twenty-four elders who sat before God on their thrones fell on their faces and worshiped God, 17 saying:

"We give You thanks,
  O Lord God Almighty,
  The One who is and who was
    and who is to come,
  Because You have taken Your
    great power and reigned.
18 The nations were angry,
    and Your wrath has come,
  And the time of the dead,
    that they should be judged,
  And that You should reward
    Your servants the prophets
    and the saints,
  And those who fear Your
    name, small and great,
  And should destroy those
    who destroy the earth."

19 Then the temple of God was opened in heaven, and the ark of His covenant was seen in His temple. And there were lightnings, noises, thunderings, an earthquake, and great hail.

12 Now a great sign appeared in heaven: a woman clothed with the sun, with the moon under her feet, and on her head a garland of twelve stars.
2 Then being with child, she cried out in labor and in pain to give birth.
3 And another sign appeared in heaven: behold, a great, fiery red dragon having seven heads and ten horns, and seven diadems on his heads.
4 His tail drew a third of the stars of heaven and threw them to the earth. And the dragon stood before the woman who was ready to give birth, to devour her Child as soon as it was born.
5 And she bore a male Child who was to rule all nations with a rod of iron. And her Child was caught up to God and to His throne.
6 Then the woman fled into the wilderness, where she has a place prepared by God, that they should feed her there one thousand two hundred and sixty days.
7 And war broke out in heaven: Michael and his angels fought against the dragon; and the dragon and his angels fought,
8 but they did not prevail, nor was a place found for them in heaven any longer.
9 So the great dragon was cast out, that serpent of old, called the Devil and Satan, who deceives the whole world; he was cast to the earth, and his angels were cast out with him.
10 Then I heard a loud voice saying in heaven, "Now salvation, and strength, and the kingdom of our God, and the power of His Christ have come, for the accuser of our brethren, who accused them before our God day and night, has been cast down.
11 "And they overcame him by the blood of the Lamb and by the word of their testimony, and they did not love their lives to the death.
12 "Therefore rejoice, O heavens, and you who dwell in them! Woe to the inhabitants of the earth and the sea! For the devil has come down to you, having great wrath, because he knows that he has a short time."
13 Now when the dragon saw that he had been cast to the earth, he persecuted the woman who gave birth to the male *Child.*
14 But the woman was given two wings of a great eagle, that she might fly into the wilderness to her place, where she is nourished for a time and times and half a time, from the presence of the serpent.
15 So the serpent spewed water out of his mouth like a flood after the woman, that he might cause her to be carried away by the flood.
16 But the earth helped the woman, and the earth opened its mouth and swallowed up the flood which the dragon had spewed out of his mouth.
17 And the dragon was enraged with the woman, and he went to make war with the rest of her off-

351

spring, who keep the commandments of God and have the testimony of Jesus Christ.

13 Then I stood on the sand of the sea. And I saw a beast rising up out of the sea, having seven heads and ten horns, and on his horns ten crowns, and on his heads a blasphemous name.

2 Now the beast which I saw was like a leopard, his feet were like *the feet of* a bear, and his mouth like the mouth of a lion. And the dragon gave him his power, his throne, and great authority.

3 I saw one of his heads as if it had been mortally wounded, and his deadly wound was healed. And all the world marveled and followed the beast.

4 So they worshiped the dragon who gave authority to the beast; and they worshiped the beast, saying, "Who *is* like the beast? Who is able to make war with him?"

5 And he was given a mouth speaking great things and blasphemies, and he was given authority to continue for forty-two months.

6 Then he opened his mouth in blasphemy against God, to blaspheme His name, His tabernacle, and those who dwell in heaven.

7 And it was granted to him to make war with the saints and to overcome them. And authority was given him over every tribe, tongue, and nation.

8 And all who dwell on the earth will worship him, whose names have not been written in the Book of Life of the Lamb slain from the foundation of the world.

9 If anyone has an ear, let him hear.

10 He who leads into captivity shall go into captivity; he who kills with the sword must be killed with the sword. Here is the patience and the faith of the saints.

11 Then I saw another beast coming up out of the earth, and he had two horns like a lamb and spoke like a dragon.

12 And he exercises all the authority of the first beast in his presence, and causes the earth and those who dwell in it to worship the first beast, whose deadly wound was healed.

13 He performs great signs, so that he even makes fire come down from heaven on the earth in the sight of men.

14 And he deceives those who dwell on the earth by those signs which he was granted to do in the sight of the beast, telling those who dwell on the earth to make an image to the beast who was wounded by the sword and lived.

15 He was granted *power* to give breath to the image of the beast, that the image of the beast should both speak and cause as many as would not worship the image of the beast to be killed.

16 And he causes all, both small and great, rich and poor, free and slave, to receive a mark on their right hand or on their foreheads,

17 and that no one may buy or sell except one who has the mark or the name of the beast, or the number of his name.

18 Here is wisdom. Let him who has understanding calculate the number of the beast, for it is the number of a man: His number *is* 666.

14 Then I looked, and behold, a Lamb standing on Mount Zion, and with Him one hundred *and* forty-four thousand, having His Father's name written on their foreheads.

2 And I heard a voice from heaven, like the voice of many waters, and like the voice of loud thunder. And I heard the sound of harpists playing their harps.

3 And they sang as it were a new song before the throne, before the four living creatures, and the elders; and no one could learn that song except the hundred *and* forty-four thousand who were redeemed from the earth.

4 These are the ones who were not defiled with women, for they are virgins. These are the ones who follow the Lamb wherever He goes. These were redeemed from *among* men, *being* firstfruits to God and to the Lamb.

5 And in their mouth was found no guile, for they are without fault before the throne of God.

6 Then I saw another angel flying in the midst of heaven, having the everlasting gospel to preach to those who dwell on the earth—to every nation, tribe, tongue, and people—

7 saying with a loud voice, "Fear God and give glory to Him, for the hour of His judgment has come; and worship Him who made heaven and earth, the sea and springs of water."

8 And another angel followed, saying, "Babylon is fallen, is fallen, that great city, because she has made all nations drink of the wine of the wrath of her fornication."

9 Then a third angel followed them, saying with a loud voice, "If anyone worships the beast and his image, and receives *his* mark on his forehead or on his hand,

10 "he himself shall also drink of the wine of the wrath of God, which is poured out full strength into the cup of His indignation. And he shall be tormented with fire and brimstone in the presence of the holy angels and in the presence of the Lamb.

11 "And the smoke of their torment ascends forever and ever; and they have no rest day or night, who worship the beast and his image, and whoever receives the mark of his name."

12 Here is the patience of the saints; here *are* those who keep the commandments of God and the faith of Jesus.

13 And I heard a voice from heaven saying to me, "Write: 'Blessed *are* the dead who die in the Lord from now on.'" "Yes,"

says the Spirit, "that they may rest from their labors, and their works follow them."

14 And I looked, and behold, a white cloud, and on the cloud sat *One* like the Son of Man, having on His head a golden crown, and in His hand a sharp sickle.

15 And another angel came out of the temple, crying with a loud voice to Him who sat on the cloud, "Thrust in Your sickle and reap, for the time has come for You to reap, for the harvest of the earth is ripe."

16 So He who sat on the cloud thrust in His sickle on the earth, and the earth was reaped.

17 Then another angel came out of the temple which is in heaven, he also having a sharp sickle.

18 And another angel came out from the altar, who had power over fire, and he cried with a loud cry to him who had the sharp sickle, saying, "Thrust in your sharp sickle and gather the clusters of the vine of the earth, for her grapes are fully ripe."

19 So the angel thrust his sickle into the earth and gathered the vine of the earth, and threw *it* into the great winepress of the wrath of God.

20 And the winepress was trampled outside the city, and blood came out of the winepress, up to the horses' bridles, for one thousand six hundred furlongs.

15 Then I saw another sign in heaven, great and marvelous: seven angels having the seven last plagues, for in them the wrath of God is complete.

2 And I saw *something* like a sea of glass mingled with fire, and those who have the victory over the beast, over his image and over his mark *and* over the number of his name, standing on the sea of glass, having harps of God.

3 And they sing the song of Moses, the servant of God, and the song of the Lamb, saying:

"Great and marvelous *are* Your
works,
Lord God Almighty!
Just and true *are* Your ways,
O King of the saints!
4 Who shall not fear You, O
Lord, and glorify Your name?
For *You* alone *are* holy.
For all nations shall come and
worship before You,
For Your judgments have been
manifested."

5 After these things I looked, and,
behold, the temple of the tabernacle of the testimony in heaven was
opened.
6 And out of the temple came the
seven angels having the seven
plagues, clothed in pure bright
linen, and having their chests
girded with golden bands.
7 Then one of the four living creatures gave to the seven angels
seven golden bowls full of the
wrath of God who lives forever
and ever.
8 The temple was filled with
smoke from the glory of God and
from His power, and no one was
able to enter the temple till the
seven plagues of the seven angels
were completed.

16 Then I heard a loud voice
from the temple saying to the
seven angels, "Go and pour out
the bowls of the wrath of God on
the earth."
2 So the first went and poured out
his bowl upon the earth, and a foul
and loathsome sore came upon the
men who had the mark of the
beast and those who worshiped his
image.
3 Then the second angel poured
out his bowl on the sea, and it
became blood as of a dead *man;*
and every living creature in the sea
died.
4 Then the third angel poured out
his bowl on the rivers and springs
of water, and they became blood.
5 And I heard the angel of the
waters saying:

"You are righteous, O Lord,
The One who is and who was
and who is to be,
Because You have judged
these things.
6 For they have shed the blood
of saints and prophets,
And You have given them
blood to drink.
For it is their just due."

7 And I heard another from the
altar saying, "Even so, Lord God
Almighty, true and righteous *are*
Your judgments."
8 Then the fourth angel poured
out his bowl on the sun, and power
was given to him to scorch men
with fire.
9 And men were scorched with
great heat, and they blasphemed
the name of God who has power
over these plagues; and they did
not repent and give Him glory.
10 Then the fifth angel poured out
his bowl on the throne of the
beast, and his kingdom became full
of darkness; and they gnawed their
tongues because of the pain.
11 And they blasphemed the God
of heaven because of their pains
and their sores, and did not repent
of their deeds.
12 Then the sixth angel poured out
his bowl on the great river Euphrates, and its water was dried up, so
that the way of the kings from the
east might be prepared.
13 And I saw three unclean spirits
like frogs *coming* out of the mouth
of the dragon, out of the mouth of
the beast, and out of the mouth of
the false prophet.
14 For they are spirits of demons,
performing signs, *which* go out to
the kings of the earth and of the
whole world, to gather them to the
battle of that great day of God
Almighty.
15 "Behold, I am coming as a thief.
Blessed *is* he who watches, and
keeps his garments, lest he walk
naked and they see his shame."

16 And they gathered them together to the place called in Hebrew, Armageddon.

17 Then the seventh angel poured out his bowl into the air, and a loud voice came out of the temple of heaven, from the throne, saying, "It is done!"

18 And there were noises and thunderings and lightnings; and there was a great earthquake, such a mighty and great earthquake as had not occurred since men were on the earth.

19 Now the great city was divided into three parts, and the cities of the nations fell. And great Babylon was remembered before God, to give her the cup of the wine of the fierceness of His wrath.

20 Then every island fled away, and the mountains were not found.

21 And great hail from heaven fell upon men, *every hailstone* about the weight of a talent. And men blasphemed God because of the plague of the hail, since that plague was exceedingly great.

17 Then one of the seven angels who had the seven bowls came and talked with me, saying to me, "Come, I will show you the judgment of the great harlot who sits on many waters,

2 "with whom the kings of the earth committed fornication, and the inhabitants of the earth were made drunk with the wine of her fornication."

3 So he carried me away in the Spirit into the wilderness. And I saw a woman sitting on a scarlet beast *which was* full of names of blasphemy, having seven heads and ten horns.

4 The woman was arrayed in purple and scarlet, and adorned with gold and precious stones and pearls, having in her hand a golden cup full of abominations and the filthiness of her fornication.

5 And on her forehead a name *was* written:

MYSTERY,
BABYLON THE GREAT,
THE MOTHER OF HARLOTS
AND OF THE ABOMINATIONS
OF THE EARTH.

6 And I saw the woman, drunk with the blood of the saints and with the blood of the martyrs of Jesus. And when I saw her, I marveled with great amazement.

7 But the angel said to me, "Why did you marvel? I will tell you the mystery of the woman and of the beast that carries her, which has the seven heads and the ten horns.

8 "The beast that you saw was, and is not, and will ascend out of the bottomless pit and go to perdition. And those who dwell on the earth will marvel, whose names are not written in the Book of Life from the foundation of the world, when they see the beast that was, and is not, and yet is.

9 "Here *is* the mind which has wisdom: The seven heads are seven mountains on which the woman sits.

10 There are also seven kings. Five have fallen, one is, *and* the other has not yet come. And when he comes, he must continue a short time.

11 "And the beast that was, and is not, is himself also the eighth, and is of the seven, and is going to perdition.

12 "And the ten horns which you saw are ten kings who have received no kingdom as yet, but they receive authority for one hour as kings with the beast.

13 "These are of one mind, and they will give their power and authority to the beast.

14 "These will make war with the Lamb, and the Lamb will overcome them, for He is Lord of lords and King of kings; and those *who are* with Him *are* called, chosen, and faithful."

15 And he said to me, "The waters

which you saw, where the harlot sits, are peoples, multitudes, nations, and tongues.

16 "And the ten horns which you saw on the beast, these will hate the harlot, make her desolate and naked, eat her flesh and burn her with fire.

17 "For God has put it into their hearts to fulfill His purpose, to be of one mind, and to give their kingdom to the beast, until the words of God are fulfilled.

18 "And the woman whom you saw is that great city which reigns over the kings of the earth."

18 After these things I saw another angel coming down from heaven, having great authority, and the earth was illuminated with his glory.

2 And he cried mightily with a loud voice, saying, "Babylon the great is fallen, is fallen, and has become a habitation of demons, a prison for every foul spirit, and a cage for every unclean and hated bird!

3 "For all the nations have drunk of the wine of the wrath of her fornication, the kings of the earth have committed fornication with her, and the merchants of the earth have become rich through the abundance of her luxury."

4 And I heard another voice from heaven saying, "Come out of her, my people, lest you share in her sins, and lest you receive of her plagues.

5 "For her sins have reached to heaven, and God has remembered her iniquities.

6 "Render to her just as she rendered to you, and repay her double according to her works; in the cup which she has mixed, mix for her double.

7 "In the measure that she glorified herself and lived luxuriously, in the same measure give her torment and sorrow; for she says in her heart, 'I sit *as* queen, and am

no widow, and will not see sorrow.'

8 "Therefore her plagues will come in one day—death and mourning and famine. And she will be utterly burned with fire, for strong *is* the Lord God who judges her.

9 "And the kings of the earth who committed fornication and lived luxuriously with her will weep and lament for her, when they see the smoke of her burning,

10 "standing at a distance for fear of her torment, saying, 'Alas, alas, that great city Babylon, that mighty city! For in one hour your judgment has come.'

11 "And the merchants of the earth will weep and mourn over her, for no one buys their merchandise anymore:

12 "merchandise of gold and silver, precious stones and pearls, fine linen and purple, silk and scarlet, every kind of citron wood, every kind of object of ivory, every kind of object of most precious wood, bronze, iron, and marble;

13 "and cinnamon and incense, fragrant oil and frankincense, wine and oil, fine flour and wheat, cattle and sheep, horses and chariots, and bodies and souls of men.

14 "And the fruit that your soul longed for has gone from you, and all the things which are rich and splendid have gone from you, and you shall find them no more at all.

15 "The merchants of these things, who became rich by her, will stand at a distance for fear of her torment, weeping and wailing,

16 "and saying, 'Alas, alas, that great city that was clothed in fine linen, purple, and scarlet, and adorned with gold and precious stones and pearls!

17 'For in one hour such great riches came to nothing.' And every shipmaster, all who travel by ship, sailors, and as many as trade on the sea, stood at a distance

18 "and cried out when they saw

the smoke of her burning, saying, 'What *is* like this great city?'

19 "And they threw dust on their heads and cried out, weeping and wailing, and saying, 'Alas, alas, that great city, in which all who had ships on the sea became rich by her wealth! For in one hour she is made desolate.'

20 "Rejoice over her, O heaven, and *you* holy apostles and prophets, for God has avenged you on her!"

21 Then a mighty angel took up a stone like a great millstone and threw *it* into the sea, saying, "Thus with violence the great city Babylon shall be thrown down, and shall not be found anymore.

22 "The sound of harpists, musicians, flutists, and trumpeters shall not be heard in you anymore. And no craftsman of any craft shall be found in you anymore. And the sound of a millstone shall not be heard in you anymore.

23 "And the light of a lamp shall not shine in you anymore. And the voice of bridegroom and bride shall not be heard in you anymore. For your merchants were the great men of the earth, for by your sorcery all the nations were deceived.

24 "And in her was found the blood of prophets and saints, and of all who were slain on the earth."

19 After these things I heard a loud voice of a great multitude in heaven, saying, "Alleluia! Salvation and glory and honor and power to the Lord our God!

2 "For true and righteous *are* His judgments, because He has judged the great harlot who corrupted the earth with her fornication; and He has avenged on her the blood of His servants *shed* by her."

3 Again they said, "Alleluia! And her smoke rises up forever and ever!"

4 And the twenty-four elders and the four living creatures fell down and worshiped God who sat on the throne, saying, "Amen! Alleluia!"

5 Then a voice came from the throne, saying, "Praise our God, all you His servants and those who fear Him, both small and great!"

6 And I heard, as it were, the voice of a great multitude, as the sound of many waters and as the sound of mighty thunderings, saying, "Alleluia! For the Lord God Omnipotent reigns!

7 "Let us be glad and rejoice and give Him glory, for the marriage of the Lamb has come, and His wife has made herself ready."

8 And to her it was granted to be arrayed in fine linen, clean and bright, for the fine linen is the righteous acts of the saints.

9 Then he said to me, "Write: 'Blessed *are* those who are called to the marriage supper of the Lamb!' " And he said to me, "These are the true sayings of God."

10 And I fell at his feet to worship him. But he said to me, "See *that you do* not *do that!* I am your fellow servant, and of your brethren who have the testimony of Jesus. Worship God! For the testimony of Jesus is the spirit of prophecy."

11 Then I saw heaven opened, and behold, a white horse. And He who sat on him *was* called Faithful and True, and in righteousness He judges and makes war.

12 His eyes *were* like a flame of fire, and on His head *were* many crowns. He had a name written that no one knew except Himself.

13 He *was* clothed with a robe dipped in blood, and His name is called The Word of God.

14 And the armies in heaven, clothed in fine linen, white and clean, followed Him on white horses.

15 Now out of His mouth goes a sharp sword, that with it He should strike the nations. And He Himself will rule them with a rod of iron. He Himself treads the winepress of the fierceness and wrath of Almighty God.

16 And He has on *His* robe and on His thigh a name written:

KING OF KINGS
AND LORD OF LORDS.

17 Then I saw an angel standing in the sun; and he cried with a loud voice, saying to all the birds that fly in the midst of heaven, "Come and gather together for the supper of the great God,

18 "that you may eat the flesh of kings, the flesh of captains, the flesh of mighty men, the flesh of horses and of those who sit on them, and the flesh of all *people,* free and slave, both small and great."

19 And I saw the beast, the kings of the earth, and their armies, gathered together to make war against Him who sat on the horse and against His army.

20 Then the beast was captured, and with him the false prophet who worked signs in his presence, by which he deceived those who received the mark of the beast and those who worshiped his image. These two were cast alive into the lake of fire burning with brimstone.

21 And the rest were killed with the sword which proceeded from the mouth of Him who sat on the horse. And all the birds were filled with their flesh.

20 Then I saw an angel coming down from heaven, having the key to the bottomless pit and a great chain in his hand.

2 He laid hold of the dragon, that serpent of old, who is *the* Devil and Satan, and bound him for a thousand years;

3 and he cast him into the bottomless pit, and shut him up, and set a seal on him, so that he should deceive the nations no more till the thousand years were finished. But after these things he must be released for a little while.

4 And I saw thrones, and they sat on them, and judgment was committed to them. And *I saw* the souls of those who had been beheaded for their witness to Jesus and for the word of God, who had not worshiped the beast or his image, and had not received *his* mark on their foreheads or on their hands. And they lived and reigned with Christ for a thousand years.

5 But the rest of the dead did not live again until the thousand years were finished. This *is* the first resurrection.

6 Blessed and holy *is* he who has part in the first resurrection. Over such the second death has no power, but they shall be priests of God and of Christ, and shall reign with Him a thousand years.

7 Now when the thousand years have expired, Satan will be released from his prison

8 and will go out to deceive the nations which are in the four corners of the earth, Gog and Magog, to gather them together to battle, whose number *is* as the sand of the sea.

9 They went up on the breadth of the earth and surrounded the camp of the saints and the beloved city. And fire came down from God out of heaven and devoured them.

10 And the devil, who deceived them, was cast into the lake of fire and brimstone where the beast and the false prophet *are.* And they will be tormented day and night forever and ever.

11 Then I saw a great white throne and Him who sat on it, from whose face the earth and the heaven fled away. And there was found no place for them.

12 And I saw the dead, small and great, standing before God, and books were opened. And another book was opened, which *is the Book* of Life. And the dead were judged according to their works, by the things which were written in the books.

13 The sea gave up the dead who were in it, and Death and Hades delivered up the dead who were in them. And they were judged, each one according to his works.

14 Then Death and Hades were cast into the lake of fire. This is the second death.

15 And anyone not found written in the Book of Life was cast into the lake of fire.

21 And I saw a new heaven and a new earth, for the first heaven and the first earth had passed away. Also there was no more sea.

2 Then I, John, saw the holy city, New Jerusalem, coming down out of heaven from God, prepared as a bride adorned for her husband.

3 And I heard a loud voice from heaven saying, "Behold, the tabernacle of God *is* with men, and He will dwell with them, and they shall be His people, and God Himself will be with them *and be* their God.

4 "And God will wipe away every tear from their eyes; there shall be no more death, nor sorrow, nor crying; and there shall be no more pain, for the former things have passed away."

5 Then He who sat on the throne said, "Behold, I make all things new." And He said to me, "Write, for these words are true and faithful."

6 And He said to me, "It is done! I am the Alpha and the Omega, the Beginning and the End. I will give of the fountain of the water of life freely to him who thirsts.

7 "He who overcomes shall inherit all things, and I will be his God and he shall be My son.

8 "But the cowardly, unbelieving, abominable, murderers, sexually immoral, sorcerers, idolaters, and all liars shall have their part in the lake which burns with fire and brimstone, which is the second death."

9 Then one of the seven angels who had the seven bowls filled with the seven last plagues came to me and talked with me, saying, "Come, I will show you the bride, the Lamb's wife."

10 And he carried me away in the Spirit to a great and high mountain, and showed me the great city, the holy Jerusalem, descending out of heaven from God,

11 having the glory of God. And her light *was* like a most precious stone, like a jasper stone, clear as crystal.

12 Also she had a great and high wall with twelve gates, and twelve angels at the gates, and names written on them, which are *the names* of the twelve tribes of the children of Israel:

13 three gates on the east, three gates on the north, three gates on the south, and three gates on the west.

14 Now the wall of the city had twelve foundations, and on them were the names of the twelve apostles of the Lamb.

15 And he who talked with me had a gold reed to measure the city, its gates, and its wall.

16 And the city is laid out as a square, and its length is as great as its breadth. And he measured the city with the reed: twelve thousand furlongs. Its length, breadth, and height are equal.

17 Then he measured its wall: one hundred *and* forty-four cubits, *according* to the measure of a man, that is, of an angel.

18 And the construction of its wall was *of* jasper; and the city *was* pure gold, like clear glass.

19 And the foundations of the wall of the city *were* adorned with all kinds of precious stones: the first foundation *was* jasper, the second sapphire, the third chalcedony, the fourth emerald,

20 the fifth sardonyx, the sixth sardius, the seventh chrysolite, the eighth beryl, the ninth topaz, t

tenth chrysoprase, the eleventh jacinth, and the twelfth amethyst. 21 And the twelve gates *were* twelve pearls: each individual gate was of one pearl. And the street of the city *was* pure gold, like transparent glass.

22 But I saw no temple in it, for the Lord God Almighty and the Lamb are its temple.

23 And the city had no need of the sun or of the moon to shine in it, for the glory of God illuminated it, and the Lamb *is* its light.

24 And the nations of those who are saved shall walk in its light, and the kings of the earth bring their glory and honor into it.

25 Its gates shall not be shut at all by day (there shall be no night there).

26 And they shall bring the glory and the honor of the nations into it.

27 But there shall by no means enter it anything that defiles, or causes an abomination or a lie, but only those who are written in the Lamb's Book of Life.

22 And he showed me a pure river of water of life, clear as crystal, proceeding from the throne of God and of the Lamb.

2 In the middle of its street, and on either side of the river, *was* the tree of life, which bore twelve fruits, each *tree* yielding its fruit every month. And the leaves of the tree *were* for the healing of the nations.

3 And there shall be no more curse, but the throne of God and of the Lamb shall be in it, and His servants shall serve Him.

4 They shall see His face, and His name *shall be* on their foreheads.

5 And there shall be no night there: They need no lamp nor light of the sun, for the Lord God gives them light. And they shall reign forever and ever.

6 Then he said to me, "These words *are* faithful and true." And the Lord God of the holy prophets

sent His angel to show His servants the things which must shortly take place.

7 "Behold, I am coming quickly! Blessed *is* he who keeps the words of the prophecy of this book."

8 Now I, John, saw and heard these things. And when I heard and saw, I fell down to worship before the feet of the angel who showed me these things.

9 Then he said to me, "See *that you do* not *do that*. For I am your fellow servant, and of your brethren the prophets, and of those who keep the words of this book. Worship God."

10 And he said to me, "Do not seal the words of the prophecy of this book, for the time is at hand.

11 "He who is unjust, let him be unjust still; he who is filthy, let him be filthy still; he who is righteous, let him be righteous still; he who is holy, let him be holy still."

12 "And behold, I am coming quickly, and My reward is with Me, to give to every one according to his work.

13 "I am the Alpha and the Omega, *the* Beginning and *the* End, the First and the Last."

14 Blessed *are* those who do His commandments, that they may have the right to the tree of life, and may enter through the gates into the city.

15 But outside *are* dogs and sorcerers and sexually immoral and murderers and idolaters, and whoever loves and practices a lie.

16 "I, Jesus, have sent My angel to testify to you these things in the churches. I am the Root and the Offspring of David, the Bright and Morning Star."

17 And the Spirit and the bride say, "Come!" And let him who hears say, "Come!" And let him who thirsts come. And whoever desires, let him take the water of life freely.

18 For I testify to everyone who hears the words of the prophecy of

this book: If anyone adds to these things, God will add to him the plagues that are written in this book;

19 and if anyone takes away from the words of the book of this prophecy, God shall take away his part from the Book of Life, from the holy city, and *from* the things which are written in this book.

20 He who testifies to these things says, "Surely I am coming quickly." Amen. Even so, come, Lord Jesus!

21 The grace of our Lord Jesus Christ *be* with you all. Amen.

How Can I Get to Heaven?

Most of us want to go to heaven. But how can we get there?

Our idea:

We get to heaven by being good. But how good is good enough?

Most would agree that Adolf Hitler was not good enough. But what about the person who never killed anyone but sometimes felt like it? What about those who were faithful to their spouses but occasionally fantasized about someone else? In short, what about us "normal" people?

Jesus gave a clear answer: If we hold anger toward someone or call a person a fool, we have committed murder in our hearts. If we look at someone with lust, we have in essence committed adultery (Matthew 5:21–28). Obviously, we fall hopelessly short of God's standard of goodness. (See "What Sin? What Judgment?" page 149.) If we ever have any of these attitudes (and which of us hasn't?) we deserve hell, not heaven. If we want to earn heaven, we have to keep God's law *perfectly* (James 2:10, 11), something no one—except Jesus—has ever been able to do (Romans 3:20).

His idea:

Thank God, there is another way to heaven. God knew we couldn't meet His perfect standard so He came to earth to bridge the gap for us and to open the door to heaven. (See "What's So Amazing About Grace?" page 294.)

We can't earn and don't deserve the gift of heaven and eternal life. But, like any gift, we either receive or refuse it. If we accept, Christ said He would come into our lives and begin to change us into citizens of heaven. (See "What in the World Is God Up To?" page 343.)

If we choose to accept, we need to tell Him so through prayer. God already knows our hearts and doesn't care if our words are eloquent. If you'd like some help in forming your prayer, here is one:

"Dear God, I know I have not always kept Your perfect law; I have sinned against You. I want Your gift of forgiveness. Please come into my life and make me Yours. I want to learn from You and obey You. I trust You to make that possible. Thank You for Your gift of heaven through Christ's death and resurrection. Amen."

When you pray this prayer and mean it, your sins are forgiven, and you are on your way to heaven! (See "Can You *Know* What Your Eternal Destiny Will Be?" page 335.)

What Do These Biblical Terms Mean?

Part of the mystery of a specialized field of study are the terms used exclusively in that area. For example, talking to a doctor or a computer specialist can seem like a journey into a foreign country in which few words make sense. That can be true of the Bible, too. Some common words take on new shades of meaning while other words are foreign to the uninitiated. The following definitions are provided to serve as a map for you as you travel through the New Testament. Turn to it for help whenever you feel lost in a forest of new phrases. The first set of terms are words that may be familiar to you, but they take on specific meaning for Christians. The second set of terms are words translated from the original Greek the New Testament was written in. But it is difficult to use just one word to translate the full meaning of each into English, so these definitions will help you understand the passages they appear in.

Words with special meaning to Christians

BLASPHEMY AGAINST THE HOLY SPIRIT—See "Are Some Sins Unforgivable?" page 49.

CHURCH—(a) the entire company of Christian believers both alive and dead; (b) an assembly of people professing to be Christian believers gathered to worship Christ, to enjoy fellowship with God and one another, to be instructed and trained in the Christian life, and to be equipped to bring the good news of Jesus to others.

GOD THE FATHER—exists as a Spirit and has a relationship with humans that is predominantly one of loving them and giving them grace. He gave His only Son, Jesus Christ, to die for the sins of the world and raised Him bodily from the dead.

GOD THE HOLY SPIRIT—exists as a Spirit, and has a relationship with humanity that is predominantly one of revealing truth, testifying of Christ, convicting people of sin, revealing coming judgment, and urging everyone to reconcile with God. To the believer He also gives understanding of Scripture, assurance, hope, comfort, power to minister, and power to grow more and more like Jesus in character.

GOD THE SON—Jesus Christ, who possesses an eternal, glorious, and indestructible body. He is the physical demonstration of what God is like. His predominant role with respect to humankind is to bridge the gap between people and God in the only way possible—by paying the ransom that only He could pay (because He alone lived a sinless life on earth) for each one's sin of rebellion against God. He is the cocreator with God the Father and God the Holy Spirit of the universe, of all angels, of all human beings, of all power, and of all authority. At His first coming, He humbly took the form of a human being while

363

retaining the nature of God. He was both man and God, and in laying down His life at the cross, He could and did pay the ransom for everyone's sinfulness. Therefore, the Father has exalted Him, giving to Him all judgment and authority.

HEAVEN—the realm in which God is fully manifested, in which God rules, and in which God abundantly and eternally communes with and rewards His followers.

HELL—the realm to which are consigned angels and humans who rebel against God by disregarding His authority. Hell is eternally separate from God and is a place of eternal torment without respite.

HUMAN RESPONSIBILITY—the accountability everyone bears in deciding how he or she will respond to God's revelation of Himself in the creation and in the Person of Jesus Christ.

LAST JUDGMENT—See "What Sin? What Judgment?" page 149.

PROPITIATION—meeting God's demand for justice. Through His death for us, Jesus became the means to keep our sins from separating us from God.

REGENERATION—the new life, the "rebirth," experienced by a person who puts his or her faith and trust in the crucified and resurrected Christ, a process by which the believer comes to share in the

character and eternal life of Christ.

RESURRECTION—restoration of life to that which was dead. For all believers, living or dead, this term refers to the transformation of their corruptible, mortal bodies into perfect and eternal bodies when Jesus "raptures" them, that is, snatches them away from earth, prior to His second coming.

SALVATION—See "How Can I Get to Heaven?" page 362.

SATAN—See "Is the Devil Real?" page 5.

SCRIPTURE—all or part of the message sent from God to man through His chosen spokesmen. Those who passed rigorous tests for qualifications as God's messengers wrote only what was communicated to them by God. The personal writing style of each messenger was retained, but the writings communicate truth and nothing but truth, not only in spiritual matters, but in all realms of knowledge. All Scripture is inspired by God and is useful for teaching, convicting, correcting, and practical training in righteousness (submission and conformity to the moral standards and purposes of God). Scripture is meant to be taken literally unless the context clearly indicates otherwise.

SECOND COMING—Jesus' physical return to rescue the world and all people who have put their trust in Him from certain destruction, to mete out justice to those guilty of ignoring His lordship, and to establish His thousand-year kingdom on earth.

SIN AND SINS—See "What Sin? What Judgment?" page 149.

TRINITY—See "Don't Christians Actually Have Three Gods?" page 266.

VIRGIN BIRTH—Jesus was born of a virgin, Mary, whose fiancé (later husband) was Joseph. Mary was especially blessed among women, for Jesus was conceived in her by the Holy Spirit.

Difficult Greek Terms to Translate

APOSTASY—total rejection of faith in God; defection from the truth.

BAPTIZE—to place into.

BELIEVE—to trust or be convinced (see "What Does It Mean to 'Believe'?" page 123).

CARNAL—fleshly, sensual, controlled by human inclinations rather than by God's Spirit. "Flesh" sometimes refers to the actual human body but more often to the fallen nature in us that opposes God and resists His Spirit.

CHASTEN, CHASTISE—to train, discipline, or educate. God lovingly chastens His children for their benefit, not out of revenge or anger

(Hebrews 12:6–10).

COMFORT—to encourage (literally, "to come alongside"). Also to console, exhort, counsel, advocate, or defend. "Comforter" is a name for the Holy Spirit (translated "Helper") and for Jesus ("Advocate").

COVENANT—a binding promise or an undertaking made by one party to another.

COVET—to passionately desire, long for, or lust for.

DEATH— incapacitation or separation.

DOCTRINE—what is taught or believed; a tenet or set of tenets.

EDIFY, EDIFICATION—to build up, to promote spiritual strength in others.

ELECT, ELECTION—the chosen ones; picking out, choosing.

FAITH—believing and trusting. See "Do I Have to Take Christianity on Blind Faith?" page 284.

FLESH, FLESHLY—See *carnal*.

FORNICATION—sex outside marriage. See "Will My Sins Keep Me from God?" page 232.

GLORIFICATION—the ultimate effect of salvation. See "Why Are Some People Called Blameless When

They Obviously Aren't?" page 227.

GOSPEL—the good news that we can have forgiveness and new life in Christ. The true teaching about Christ and salvation (Galatians 2:14–16).

GRACE—undeserved blessings. (See "What's So Amazing About Grace?" page 294.)

HADES—the spiritual abode of all those departed spirits (people) who rejected Christ's offer of salvation. (Prior to the ascension of Christ it included a place for those who died trusting in God's salvation. Following the ascension, these individuals were taken up to heaven.) Hades and its inhabitants (except for the blessed dead) will be placed into the lake of fire following the great white throne judgment (Revelation 20:11–15).

HARLOT—prostitute. Used symbolically of a coming evil kingdom in Revelation 17.

IDOLATERS, IDOLATRY—worship(ers) of anything or anyone but God. See "Will My Sins Keep Me from God?" page 232.

IMPUTE—to reckon, take into account, or charge to a person's account. When we have received Christ, God does not reckon our sins against us (2 Corinthians 5:19) but charges them to the account established by Christ's death.

JUSTIFICATION—the initial effect of salvation. See "Why Are Some

People Called Blameless When They Obviously Aren't?" page 227.

LAKE OF FIRE—the place of eternal torment for all the demons and all humans who reject Christ's offer of salvation.

REMISSION—release, dismissal. Remission (dismissal of the debt) of our sins comes through Christ's death.

REPENT—to change one's mind and purpose for the better; to turn from evil to good, from rebellion against God and His purposes to submission to God and His purposes.

REVILE—to abuse verbally, reproach, upbraid, rail at, or speak profanely to.

RIGHTEOUS, RIGHTEOUSNESS—just, without prejudice or partiality, a right standing in a legal sense. God is righteous by character but sinful humans can be given *righteousness* (a legal position) through Christ's death.

SANCTIFICATION—the ongoing effect of salvation; set apart. See "Why Are Some People Called Blameless When They Obviously Aren't?" page 227.

WICKED, WICKEDNESS—lawless; being a law unto oneself; commitment to run from or ignore God's authority; doing what is right in one's eyes while ignoring what is right in God's eyes.

About New King James Version

Purpose

In the Preface to the 1611 edition, the translators of the Authorized King James Version state that it was not their purpose "to make a new translation . . . but to make a good one better." Indebted to the earlier work of William Tyndale and others, they saw their best contribution to consist in revising and enhancing the excellence of the English versions which had sprung from the Reformation of the sixteenth century.

After nearly four hundred years, the King James is still deeply revered among English-speaking peoples throughout the world. This is in part due to the majesty of the form of the work, but also because it has been the mainspring of the religion, language, and legal foundations of our civilization. For these reasons the publishers have followed the method of the original translators, thus unlocking for today's readers the spiritual treasures found especially in the Authorized Version of the Holy Scriptures.

The 1611 scholars understood that a genuinely worshipful form is appropriate to the expression of divine matters. They accordingly disciplined their talents to render not only well-chosen English words appropriate to their time, but also a graceful, often musical arrangement of language which has stirred the hearts of Bible readers through the years. The translators and editors of the present edition, while sensitive to the late twentieth-century English idiom, and while making precise comparisons with the Hebrew and Greek texts, have similarly exercised special care to maintain the lyrical quality which is a notable characteristic of the Authorized Version.

English usage has undergone profound change since the first publication of the King James edition. This has created a growing difficulty for readers of our time, although students of the Bible still applaud the reverence of attitude which is timeless in the Authorized Version. In 1786 the Catholic scholar, Alexander Geddes, said of the King James, "If accuracy and strictest attention to the letter of the text be supposed to constitute an excellent version, this is of all versions the most excellent." George Bernard Shaw became a literary legend in our century because of his severe and often humorous criticisms of our most cherished values. Surprisingly, however, Shaw pays the following tribute to the scholars commissioned by King James: "The translation was extraordinarily well done because to the translators what they were translating was not merely a curious collection of ancient books written by different authors in different stages of culture, but the Word of God divinely revealed through His chosen and expressly inspired scribes. In this conviction they carried out their work with boundless reverence and care and achieved a beautifully artistic result." History agrees with these estimates. Therefore, in unveiling the treasured sublimity of form in the traditional English Bible, scrupulous care has been taken in the present edition to honor and preserve the work of precision which is also the legacy of the original translators. This purpose is achieved largely by careful integration of present-day vocabulary, punctuation, and syntax wherever obscurity exists. Words representing ancient objects, such as *chariot* and *phylacteries,* have no modern substitutes and are necessarily retained.

Paraphrasing has been avoided as a common method of solution to difficulties of translation in the New King James Version. Where new translation has been appropriate, the most precise reproduction of the original has been sought by considering the history, usage, and etymology relating to each text. In these cases, to maintain the integrity of King James diction, words are employed which are already part of the general vocabulary of the 1611 version, when they are agreeable to the context under consideration.

The style

A special feature of the New King James Version is its conformity to the thought-flow of the 1611 version. The reader discovers that the sequence and identity of words, phrases, and clauses of the new edition, while much clearer, are so close to the traditional that there is remarkable ease in listening to the public reading of either edition while following with the other.

King James doctrinal and theological terms are generally familiar to English-speaking peoples.

Such terms have been retained except where the original language indicates the need for clarification.

Readers of the Authorized Version will immediately be struck by the absence of several pronouns: *thee, thou,* and *ye* are replaced by the simple *you,* while *your* and *yours* are substitued for *thy* and *thine* as applicable. *Thee, thou, thy,* and *thine* were once forms of address to express a special relationship to human as well as divine persons. These pronouns are no longer part of our language. However, reverence for God in the present work is preserved by capitalizing pronouns, including *You, Your,* and *Yours,* which refer to Him.

In addition to the pronoun usages of the seventeenth century, the *-eth* and *-est* verb endings so familiar in the earlier King James editions are now obsolete. Unless a speaker is schooled in the peculiar verb endings, there is common difficulty in selecting the correct form to be used with a given subject of the verb in vocal prayer. For example, should we use *love, loveth,* or *lovest? do, doeth, doest,* or *dost? have, hath* or *hast?* Because of such problems, contemporary English usage has been substituted for the previous verb endings.

Throughout their investigations, the publishers have observed that the real character of the Authorized Version does not reside in its archaic pronouns or verbs or other grammatical forms of the seventeenth century but rather in the care taken by its scholars to impart the letter and spirit of the original text in a stately and reverent cadence.

The format

The format of the New King James Version is designed to enhance the intrinsic characteristics of vividness and devotion in the Holy Scriptures:

—Page headings assist the reader to identify topics and transitions in the biblical content.

—Oblique typeface in the New Testament indicates a quotation from the Old Testament.

—Verse numbers in bold type indicate the beginning of a paragraph.

—Poetry is structured as contemporary verse to enhance the original poetic beauty of the passage.

—The covenant name of God was usually translated from the Hebrew as "LORD" (using capital letters as shown), in the King James Old Testament. This excellent tradition is maintained. Wherever this name is quoted in the New Testament, the name is likewise capitalized.

—Words in *italics* indicate the use of additional English words where expressions in the original language require clarification, the same method practiced throughout the history of the King James Version.

In faithfulness to our readers, it has seemed consistent with our task to cooperate with competent scholars who are governed by the first principle of divine authorship of the Holy Scriptures, as the Bible itself attests. Therefore, all participating scholars have signed a document of subscription to the plenary and verbal inspiration of the original autographs of the Bible.

New Testament

There is more manuscript support for the New Testament than for any other body of ancient literature. Over five thousand Greek, eight thousand Latin, and many more manuscripts in other languages attest to the integrity of the New Testament. There is only one basic New Testament used by Protestants, Roman Catholics, and Orthodox, by conservatives and liberals. Minor variations in hand copying have appeared through the centuries, before mechanical printing began in A.D. 1450.

Some variations exist in the spelling of Greek words, in word order, and in similar details. These ordinarily do not show up in translation and do not affect the sense of the text.

Other manuscript differences, regarding the omission or inclusion of a word or clause, and two paragraphs in the Gospels, should not overshadow the overwhelming degree of *agreement* which exists among the ancient records. Bible readers may be assured that the most important differences in the English New Testament of today are due, not to manuscript divergence, but to the way in which translators view the task of translation: How literally should the text be rendered? How does the translator view the matter of biblical inspiration? Does the translator adopt a paraphrase when a literal rendering would be quite clear and more to the point?

The New King James Version, following the historic precedent of the Authorized Version, maintains a literal approach to translation, except where the idiom of the original language is not readily understood in our tongue.

The manuscript preferences cited in many contemporary translations of the New Testament are due to recent reliance on a relatively few manuscripts discovered in the late nineteenth and early twentieth centuries. Dependence on these manuscripts, especially two, the Sinaitic and Vatican manuscripts, is due to the greater age of these documents. However, in spite of their age, some scholars have reasons to doubt their faithfulness to the autographs, since they often disagree with one another and show other signs of unreliability. The Greek text obtained by using these sources and related papyri is known as the Alexandrian text.

On the other hand, the great majority of existing manuscripts are in substantial agreement. Even though many are late, and none are earlier than the fifth century, most of their readings are verified by ancient papyri, ancient versions and quotations in the writings of the early church fathers. This large body of manuscripts is the source of the Greek text underlying the King James Bible. It is the Greek text used by Greek-speaking churches for many centuries, presently known as the Textus Receptus, or Received Text, of the New Testament.

Since the latter part of the nineteenth century the theory has been held by some scholars that this traditional text of the New Testament had been officially edited by the fourth-century church. Recent studies have caused significant changes in this view, and a growing number of scholars now regard the Received Text as far more reliable than previously thought. In light of these developments, and with the knowledge that most textual variants have no practical effect on translation, the New King James New Testament has been based on this Received Text, thus perpetuating the tradition begun by William Tyndale in 1525 and continued by the 1611 translators in rendering the Authorized Version.

Readers may be assured that textual debate does not affect one in a thousand words of the Greek New Testament. Furthermore, no established doctrine is called into question by any doubts about this or that text. The Christian can approach the New Testament with confidence.